Frommer's

France
day BY day

1st Edition

by Anna E. Brooke and Alison Culliford

WILEY

John Wiley and Sons, Inc.

> The cafes of St-Germain-de-Prés in Paris have inspired countless stories, paintings, and daydreams.

Contents

PAGE 3

PAGE 28

PAGE 34

PAGE 236

PAGE 281

PAGE 315

PAGE 370

PAGE 395

PAGE 449

PAGE 472

PAGE 504

PAGE 551

PAGE 565

PAGE 605

PAGE 624

PAGE 670

PAGE 689

> A vineyard thrives on a steep hillside in Tain-l'Hermitage, on the left bank of the Rhône River in the Drôme.

PUBLISHED BY

John Wiley & Sons, Inc.

111 River St., Hoboken, NJ 07030-5774

ISBN 978-0-470-87632-9

Frommer's®

Editorial by Frommer's

EDITOR Maureen Clarke	**PHOTO EDITOR** Cherie Cincilla
CARTOGRAPHER Andrew Murphy	**CAPTIONS** Anna Brooke
COVER PHOTO EDITOR Richard Fox	**COVER DESIGN** Paul Dinovo

Produced by Sideshow Media

PUBLISHER Dan Tucker	**MANAGING EDITOR** Megan McFarland
PROJECT EDITOR Pamela Nelson	**PHOTO EDITOR** John Martin
PHOTO RESEARCHER Tessa Perliss	**DESIGN** Kevin Smith, And Smith LLC

SPOTLIGHT FEATURE DESIGN
Em Dash Design LLC

For information on our other products and services or to obtain technical support, please contact our Customer Care Department within the U.S. at 800/762-2974, outside the U.S. at 317/572-3993 or fax 317/572-4002.

Wiley also publishes its books in a variety of electronic formats. Some content that appears in print may not be available in electronic formats.

MANUFACTURED IN CHINA

5 4 3 2 1

How to Use This Guide

The Day by Day guides present a series of itineraries that take you from place to place. The itineraries are organized by time (Paris in 1 Day), by region (The Rhône Valley), by town (Nice), and by special interest (Bordeaux for Wine Lovers). You can follow these itineraries to the letter, or customize your own based on the information we provide. Within the tours, we suggest cafes, bars, or restaurants where you can take a break. Each of these stops is marked with a coffee-cup icon ☕. In each chapter, we provide detailed hotel and restaurant reviews so you can select the places that are right for you.

The hotels, restaurants, and attractions listed in this guide have been ranked for quality, value, service, amenities, and special features using a **star-rating system.** Hotels, restaurants, attractions, shopping, and nightlife are rated on a scale of zero stars (recommended) to three stars (exceptional). In addition to the star-rating system, we also use a kids icon kids to point out the best bets for families.

The following **abbreviations** are used for credit cards:

AE American Express	**MC** MasterCard
DC Diners Club	**V** Visa
DISC Discover	

A Note on Prices

Frommer's lists exact prices in local currency. Currency conversions fluctuate, so before departing consult a currency exchange website such as **www.oanda.com/currency/converter** to check up-to-the-minute conversion rates.

How to Contact Us

In researching this book, we discovered many wonderful places—hotels, restaurants, shops, and more. We're sure you'll find others. Please tell us about them, so we can share the information with your fellow travelers in upcoming editions. If you were disappointed with a recommendation, we'd love to know that, too. Please email us at frommersfeed back@wiley.com or write to:

Frommer's France Day by Day, 1st Edition
John Wiley & Sons, Inc.
111 River Street
Hoboken, NJ 07030-5774

Travel Resources at Frommers.com

Frommer's travel resources don't end with this guide. **Frommers.com** has travel information on more than 4,000 destinations. We update features regularly, giving you access to the most current trip-planning information and the best airfare, lodging, and car-rental bargains. You can also listen to podcasts, connect with other Frommers.com members through our active reader forums, share your travel photos, read blogs from guidebook editors and fellow travelers, and much more.

Advisory & Disclaimer

Travel information can change quickly and unexpectedly, and we strongly advise you to confirm important details locally before traveling, including information on visas, health and safety, traffic and transport, accommodation, shopping, and eating out. We also encourage you to stay alert while traveling and to remain aware of your surroundings. Avoid civil disturbances, and keep a close eye on cameras, purses, wallets, and other valuables.

While we have endeavored to ensure that the information contained within this guide is accurate and up-to-date at the time of publication, we make no representations or warranties with respect to the accuracy or completeness of the contents of this work and specifically disclaim all warranties, including without limitation warranties of fitness for a particular purpose. We accept no responsibility or liability for any inaccuracy or errors or omissions, or for any inconvenience, loss, damage, costs, or expenses of any nature whatsoever incurred or suffered by anyone as a result of any advice or information contained in this guide.

The inclusion of a company, organization or website in this guide as a service provider and/or potential source of further information does not mean that we endorse them or the information they provide. Be aware that information provided through some websites may be unreliable and can change without notice. Neither the publisher or author shall be liable for any damages arising herefrom.

About the Authors

After growing up in a Francophile household and studying French at university, **Anna Brooke** (annaebrooke@yahoo.fr) moved to Paris in 2000 and hasn't looked back since. She is the author of six Frommer's guides to Paris and France, and she regularly writes for *The Sunday Times Travel Magazine, Time Out,* and *Financial Times Magazine.* When she is not writing, she is acting, in film and theater, and song-writing for her electro-pop group Monkey Anna (www.myspace.com/musicmonkeyanna). Born in England's West Country, **Alison Culliford** was a journalist in London for 12 years before buying a one-way Eurostar ticket to Paris in 2001. She worked in the Paris bureau of *Time Out* and now freelances as a travel journalist and guidebook author, taking every opportunity to discover the diverse regions of France by road, train, bicycle, and on foot. **Nathalie Jordi** is a cheesemaker, food and travel writer *(The Los Angeles Times, Bon Appetit, The New York Times),* and co-owner of People's Pops (www.peoplespops.com), in the Chelsea Market in Manhattan. New York–based historian and travel writer **Tony Perrottet** (www.tonyperrottet.com) is the author of *Napoleon's Privates: 2,500 Years of History Unzipped* and *The Sinner's Grand Tour: A Journey Through the Historical Underbelly of Europe.* Sideshow Media project editor **Kathryn Williams** is the author of *The Lost Summer, The Debutante,* and *Roomies.*

Acknowledgments

Anna Brooke extends "a *très grand merci* to the editor of this book, Maureen Clarke, and to the rest of the Frommer's team in the U.S. and U.K." Alison Culliford offers "thanks to Ramin Mazaheri for his help in researching this guide, to Bill Burroughs for sharing his patch of France, and to all the regional tourist boards for their guidance, in particular the Comités Regionaux de Tourisme for the Auvergne, Midi-Pyrénées and Languedoc-Roussillon." Maureen Clarke would like to thank Frommer's editors Kathleen Warnock and Jennifer Polland for providing additional research in the manuscript stage.

About the Photographers

Hamburg-based photographer **Anne Ackermann** (www.anneackermann.com) shoots for *GEO* and *Stern,* among other publications, and exhibits her photographs around the world. London-based French photographer **Elisabeth Blanchet** contributes to *Time Out London,* various U.K. weekend supplements, and publications in France and Belgium. Marseille-based paramotor pilot **Matthieu Colin** (www.matthieucolin.com) specializes in aerial photography in the South of France. **Alden Gewirtz,** a New York–based photographer and photo editor who has had a camera in his hand since he was 3 years old, works for publishing, corporate, and nonprofit clients. Award-winning photographer **Georgios Makkas** (www.gmakkas.com), whose work is in the permanent collection of the Greek Museum of Photography, contributes to major Greek magazines, works on private commissions for clients around the world, and has exhibited his photographs in the U.K. and Greece. Based in Galicia, Spain, **Oscar Pinal** (http://www.lightstalkers.org/oscar-pinal-rodriguez) contributes to regional and international publications specializing in sports and documentary photographs. The work of award-winning, Bilbao-based photographer **Markel Redondo** (www.markelredondo.com) has been published by *The Wall Street Journal, Le Monde, Le Figaro Magazine, The New York Times, Monocle, Greenpeace, Internatzionale, The Sunday Telegraph,* UNESCO, and The British Council. A photographer, filmmaker, and licensed pilot and PADI diver, **Kirsten Scully** (www.scullyfoto.com) uses her love of travel and extreme sports to make a living by shooting for the *Guardian, The Sunday Times,* and major international travel and sailing magazines.

The Best of France

Our Favorite Moments in France

Absorbing the beauty of Paris. No matter how many times you've seen the city, there's no exhausting the extent of its loveliness. Spend a day along the river, between the Eiffel Tower and Notre-Dame Cathedral, dipping in and out of iconic museums and contemplating the Seine's silvery, tree-lined waters. In the evening, climb the cobblestone hills of Montmartre and watch the City of Light twinkling below. See chapter 3.

Châteaux-hopping in the Loire Valley. It's impossible not to feel inspired by the stone-clad beauty of the many Renaissance castles in this verdant, vine-rich valley. Follow the footsteps of the Valois kings along the UNESCO-protected Loire River, leaving a trail of turrets, classically inspired carvings, and landscaped gardens in your wake. This region is also known as the "garden of France," so get out your knife and fork for some of the best *gastronomie* in Europe. See chapter 4.

Taking in the Côte d'Azur's heart-stopping coastline. Alternately jagged and sloping, with sandy beaches, rocky creeks, and boat-lined fishing ports, these shores can be described by one word only: *magnifique*. Travel between Marseille and Menton to watch a kaleidoscope of landscapes unfurl: from the cacti-clad slopes of Rayol's Mediterranean gardens to glittering St-Tropez, from the million-euro towers of Monaco to the jaw-dropping Roman vestiges in La Turbie. See chapter 11.

Eating and drinking along the Atlantic coast and through Bordeaux. Gluttony (*la gourmandise* in French) is not a sin around these parts—in fact, it's wholly expected in this land abundant with Bordeaux wines and remarkably fresh seafood. Build long, lazy lunches into your days; stop at as many vineyards as you can. Slurp oysters in seaside shacks around Arcachon. Tuck into pink Pauillac lamb in a chic Bordeaux restaurant. Our favorite? **Le Chapon Fin** (p. 586). See chapter 13.

Time-traveling with French architecture. Across France, more than 2 millennia of *patrimoine* (heritage) is manifest in the cityscapes, propelling pedestrians through history as they travel from one place to the next. Step back to the Roman era in **Arles** (p. 397, ❹) and **Nîmes** (p. 432), where some of Europe's best-preserved amphitheaters still wow crowds; or explore medieval châteaux-topped villages in the **Dordogne** (p. 598). Another one of our favorite hotbeds of history is **Marseille** (p. 426)—an ancient intercontinental crossroads, where you can pass from Gallo-Roman remains and medieval cobblestone hills to 19th-century apartments and starkly modern skyscrapers within a mile radius.

Viewing art in Alsace and Lorraine. The cultured cities of these two eastern *départements* have amassed more than a respectable French region's share of art, but now they can also boast one of the nation's newest art attractions, the **Centre Pompidou-Metz** (p. 275, ❿)—as exciting for its out-of-this-world architecture as for what's inside. And then there's Strasbourg, which has the astounding **modern art museum** (p. 298, ❶); the **fine art museum** in the historic Palais Rohan (p. 301, ❹); and for light relief, the political and erotic cartoons in the **Tomi Ungerer Museum** (p. 301, ❺). Nancy has all you need to know about **Art Nouveau** (p. 292), and Colmar is home to the fabulous **Isenheim Altarpiece** (p. 269, ❷). Combine this with oodles of sauerkraut and fine Alsatian wines. See chapter 7.

Sipping aperitifs on cafe terraces. Like happy hour in the U.S. and four o'clock tea in England, "the hour of the aperitif" is a national institution in France. At 6pm, it's down with tools and off to the nearest cafe, to soak up the remaining sun and to people-watch while sipping an appetizing drink. Whether they're drinking *pastis* on the quays of **Marseille** (p. 426), a muscat in **Perpignan** (p. 536), a *kir royale* in **Nice** (p. 468), or a *demi* (beer) on the Grande Place in **Lille** (p. 652), the French are happy and mellow at this time of day, which should prove to be the magic hour for visitors, too.

> PREVIOUS PAGE *Château de Villandry is best known for its 16th-century-style gardens.* THIS PAGE *The Château d'Amboise is where François I, France's great Renaissance king, spent much of his childhood.*

The Most Breathtaking Scenery

> Pilgrims on their way to Compostela used to pass through this idyllic Ariège countryside in the High Pyrenees around St-Lizier.

The cliffs of Etretat. Monet found on his palette the exact creamy-pinky-white to express the beauty of these stunning cliffs on Normandy's Alabaster Coast. Climb the coastal path above the town of Etretat to see the "needle" and the "elephant" as the waves crash down below. See p. 194, ❺.

Provence's lavender fields. In the summer, between Manosque in Haute-Provence and Salon de Provence, you'll find southwestern France at its most iconic: endless, aromatic carpets of purple lavender rolling over the hills as far as the eye can see. As you're driving by, open the window and smell the light, floral fragrance in the balmy air. See chapter 10.

Camargue. Nowhere else in France resembles the Rhône Delta—a hauntingly beautiful land of salt flats, dunes, rice paddies, and lakes frequented by ibises and pink flamingos. As you drive around, you'll cross grassy fields filled with black bulls trained for Camargian *corridas,* elegant white horses, and low-slung *gardians'* cabins with steep roofs and white-washed walls. It's a living, breathing postcard of ancient traditions and heart-stopping landscapes. See p. 413, ❷.

Corsica. Wild and mountainous, alternately forested and barren, with golden beaches that roll gently into the deep, turquoise sea, the island of Corsica is superlatively picturesque from every angle. Come in late spring, when the mountains are flecked with the rainbow blossoms of flowering flora, or try October, when the still-balmy weather accompanies the fiery hues of autumn. See p. 472.

The High Pyrenees. No mountain view can beat that from the **Pic du Midi observatory** (p. 504, ❻), an early 19th-century astronomical observatory that looks like a fortress in the sky as you approach by cable car. Be sure to take your shades, and watch the sunset or the clouds unfolding over the Cirque de Gavarnie and the other surrounding peaks as you lounge on the observation deck. See p. 500.

Auvergne volcanoes. Yes, there really are volcanoes in the center of France. Although they may not have erupted for thousands of years, their domes and craters form a peculiar and fascinating landscape in the area around Clermont-Ferrand. Ascending Puy de Dôme, you'll have an optimal view of the chain of smaller volcanoes; on a clear day, the vista stretches as far as Mont Blanc. See p. 626.

The Best of the Outdoors

Cycling in the Loire Valley. The Loire is blissfully flat, with well-traveled cycle routes between the strings of opulent Renaissance châteaux (see Loire à Vélo, p. 177). If you cover the western section, beyond Nantes, the *Estuaire Nantes St-Nazaire* route leads you toward the sea past monumental, thought-provoking pieces of modern art. See chapter 4.

Hiking in the Alps. These days the Alps are just as popular for summer as for winter sports. In addition to enjoying the stunning scenery, take the extensive system of cable cars and ski lifts to the high plateaus, where the air is clean and mountain flowers grow. Several national parks and regional natural parks cover the Alps; exploring on foot will reveal their treasures. Each park office can pair you with a knowledgeable guide, or you can follow one of the hundreds of marked routes. See chapter 9.

Walking in Corsica. France's biggest off-shore island is home to the GR20 hiking route—one of the most challenging and gratifying walking experiences for veteran ramblers. It takes you through much of Corsica's National Park (the PNRC), past a breathtaking medley of fertile and sun-parched landscapes. See p. 477.

Snowshoeing in the Pyrenees. If skiing isn't your thing, get into snowshoeing—or *raquettes,* as the French call it. Gavarnie in the Pyrenees is a center for showshoeing. The **Cirque de Gavarnie,** surrounded by high peaks and with a 420m (1,378 ft.) waterfall, provides a dramatic setting, and it's a great workout, too. See p. 503, ④.

Following the Somme battlefields circuit. The World War I battlefields are moving and educational, in beautiful outdoor settings. Start by learning about trench life at the Musée Somme 1916 in Albert, then hop memorials to reach the Historial de la Grande Guerre in Péronne, to see how soldiers survived. See p. 644.

> *Hiking in Corsica is one of the best ways to take in the island's dramatic scenery.*

The Best of Hip France

Paris. Paris's *je ne sais quoi* irradiates from its bars, restaurants, clubs, and boutiques all over the city. The only question is, which type of Parisian nightlife appeals to you? Moneyed crowds populate the 8th and 16th arrondissements, where flashy restaurant-clubs cater to designer-labeled, stiletto-heeled crews; while arty types congregate in Montmartre and the northeast of Paris around Oberkampf and Père Lachaise. See p. 128.

Nantes. Easily the hippest city in western France, Nantes is a cultural capital with artistic tendencies that reveal themselves in smart factory reconversions, such as the **Lieu Unique** multidisciplinary center (p. 179, ❸). One of the funkiest places you can visit is **Les Machines de l'Ile** (p. 181, ❽), set on the old industrial Ile de Nantes in the town center. It's a fantasy world of wooden and metal machines, where you can ride on the back of a giant elephant and climb the branches of a steel tree. See p. 178.

Lyon. As France's second city, Lyon is as hip to new trends as Paris itself, and it's a fabulous shopping destination. Most of the commerce is on the Presqu'île, where chain stores line rue de la République, heading upmarket to boutiques as you approach place de la République. Plenty of lively bars are found in the side streets around here, but rue St-Jean in Vieux Lyon is the epicenter of the city's nightlife and a must for bar-crawling. Several nightclubs on boats are moored on the Rhône. See p. 378.

Marseille. In Marseille's bohemian cours Julien, shabby-chic cafes and restaurants back onto the boutiques and workshops of clothes and jewelry designers. Marseille's nightlife is also worth sampling, in the bars and clubs of the Vieux Port and around the Belle de Mai district. See p. 426.

Montpellier. You have only to see its funkily decorated trams to realize that Montpellier is a hip and fun city. It has a huge student population that roams the Old Town in high

> *Post-fashion-show partygoers and Paris's "It" crowd flock to L'Arc restaurant and nightclub.*

spirits, drinking in its many friendly bars and pubs. There are also more sophisticated wine bars, especially as you climb to the top of the Old Town, north of rue Foch. In summer, a riverside terrace scene comes to life on the Esplanade de l'Europe, at the end of the Ricardo Bofill–designed Antigone Quarter. See p. 532.

Perpignan. Perpignan is close to Spain, and soon it will seem even closer. The high-speed rail link to Barcelona due to open in 2014 will surely draw an influx of hip urban Catalans over the border to France. In the meantime, though, you won't lack for entertainment here, as Perpignan already caters to the Latin love of late-night eating and revelry. The Old Town is where it's at; bars don't seem to close around here. St-Jacques is also happening, with an edgy, bohemian vibe. The new Théâtre de l'Archipel complex promises to be the next hip place to hang out. See p. 536.

The Most Memorable Food & Wine

> *Before selling their oysters, farmers turn each mollusk about 30 times to facilitate growth.*

Parisian brasseries. There is something plainly sophisticated about eating hearty French cuisine, such as *steak-frites* and rum babas, under the high ceilings of an iconic brasserie in Paris. The decor tends to be sumptuously vintage—either Belle Epoque or Art Deco—and the dance of the black-and-white-clad servers might seem almost choreographed. The flashiest decor is in **Le Train Bleu** (p. 113) in the Gare de Lyon train station—a jamboree of turn-of-the-century gilding and sculpture built for the 1900 World's Fair.

Champagne wine trail. Nothing beats tasting champagne alongside those who made it; and between Reims and Epernay, dozens of family-run *producteurs* welcome you to their vineyards for tastings. The drive through voluptuous hills of vines is lovely, and in autumn, many houses let visitors join in on the grape picking. See p. 253.

Foie gras ice cream in the Pyrenees. In the small town of St-Girons, the third generation of an ice cream–making family came up with the idea of making savory ice creams, a phenomenon now being explored by all the top chefs. In Philippe Faur's restaurant, you sample this new taste sensation as an accompaniment to entrées and talk to the inventor himself. See p. 509.

La Galinette's tomatoes. Perpignan is home to the largest wholesale fruit and vegetable market in Europe, but that doesn't interest chef Christophe Comes, who grows nearly 85 rare and unusual varieties of produce on his own. You'll see La Galinette's tomatoes, a humble staple of Catalan cuisine, in a new light when you dine at Comes's restaurant, where he serves various inventive vegetable concoctions with meat and fish. See p. 538.

La Rochelle & the Atlantic coast. For lovers of seafood, France's west coast is a hot spot. From Michelin-starred restaurants and pubs serving *moules-frites* (mussels with fries) in La Rochelle, to the Marennes and Arcachon basins, famous for their oysters, you'll be hard-pressed to find such a dense concentration of delicious, briny delights in the whole of France. See chapter 14.

Salers beef in Salers. Nothing beats eating a Salers beef steak in the town of Salers itself, where these deep ginger-colored cows were saved from extinction. The town's best restaurant is **Le Baillage** (p. 629).

The Best Family Adventures

> *Impressive by day, the parades at Disneyland Paris are downright magical at night.*

Disneyland Paris. For fans of Buzz Lightyear, Mickey, Pooh, and friends, few theme parks can beat Paris's Disneyland. Pack a picnic to avoid the expensive junk food. See p. 136.

Océanopolis & Arbreizh Adventure. These two great attractions are near **Brest** in Brittany, which is our overall top pick for family vacations. Océanopolis is an amazing aquarium with, most notably, an exuberant and comical polar penguin exhibition. Nearby Arbreizh Adventure outfits kids with harnesses so they can swing through the tree canopy. See p. 208, ❸.

Parc de la Préhistoire de Bretagne. Near the Tarascon caves containing prehistoric art, this museum in a theme park takes an innovative approach to teaching about our ancestors and the links between their art and ours. Best of all are the educators who demonstrate to rapt children how to light a fire, track an animal, and other prehistoric skills. See p. 208, ❹.

Futuroscope. Poitiers' technology-themed park will have your kids screaming with delight on rollercoasters and 4-D rides where the seats move along with the 3-D action on the screen. See p. 569, ❸.

Aquarium de La Rochelle. This aquarium has to be one of the best in France—a high-tech ode to oceanic creatures across the globe. Kids love descending in the submarine lift and then walking through the jellyfish tunnel to get to the pools and tanks of creatures, including ferocious-looking sharks. See p. 591, ❹.

Vulcania. In the heart of the Auvergne's volcano-studded landscape, Vulcania is a 21st-century science park with an awe-inspiring re-creation of an active volcano and a 4-D cinematic simulator of an eruption, among other attractions. Your kids will be having so much fun they won't even realize they're learning. See p. 627, ❷.

The Best of France by Rail

> *France's streamlined TGVs (high-speed trains) have been whizzing through the countryside since 1981.*

Reims. History, architecture, and champagne are on the cards in Reims, capital of the Champagne region, just 45 minutes from Paris by train. Around its flamboyant Notre-Dame Cathedral, where every king of France was crowned from Louis the Pious in 815 to Charles X in 1825, you'll find hidden **Art Deco** treasures (see "Art Deco Reims," p. 258) and enough champagne cellars to sink a ship. When the tastings are over, sober up at the **Salle de la Reddition** (p. 256, ❽), where the Germans surrendered in World War II. See p. 254.

Strasbourg. Two hours and 20 minutes from Paris by train, Strasbourg is the glistening capital of eastern France. Displaying a fascinating mixture of French and German influences and a strong identity all its own, Strasbourg is the home of the European Union government institutions and two prestigious art museums. For intellectual stimulation, watch a Court of Human Rights debate; for sustenance, try one of the cozy *winstub* restaurants. See p. 298.

Lyon. In the time it takes to read a magazine, France's highest-speed rail line will transport you from Paris to the heart of the Rhône-Alps—that's 2 hours to cover 467km (290 miles). Take the cable car up to Fourvière Hill for a spellbinding overview of France's second city, with its red rooftops; explore the *traboule* passageways in the Old Town; visit the nation's most important art collection after the Louvre; and take your pick from a competitive cluster of award-winning restaurants. See p. 378.

Avignon. Just 2½ hours from Paris by TGV, Avignon, in Provence, woos you with two of Europe's finest medieval legacies: the gargantuan **Palais des Papes** (p. 403, ❸), center of Christendom during a period known as the Babylonian Captivity, and the **Pont d'Avignon** (p. 422, ❷), sung about by students of French around the world (*"Sur le pont d'Avignon on y danse . . ."*). The city is also a cultural capital, with a world-famous theater festival, numerous top-notch museums, and a multitude of shaded cafe terraces for blissful people-watching. See p. 422.

Montpellier. This ebullient city has a newfound pace and luster since it found itself better connected. Train travel speeds you from Paris to Montpellier and the Mediterranean coast in just 3½ hours. The recently enlarged Fabre art museum, a vibrant performing arts scene, and plentiful and affordable restaurants and bars breathe new life into the city's medieval and 17th-century architecture and its 100 fountains. See p. 532.

The Best of Budget France

> St-Malo is one of the best towns in Brittany for a savory pancake—try Crêperie Margaux.

Taking advantage of free museums. France's national museums charge an admission fee, but they waive it nationwide on the first Sunday of the month. As long as you're prepared to wait in line, you can save a considerable sum. Municipal museums often have free permanent collections and charge only for temporary exhibitions. One of our favorite freebies is the **Musée Carnavalet** in Paris (p. 84, ❻); set across two dazzling mansions in the Marais, it takes you through the history of Paris via themed rooms, including a

replica of Proust's bedroom. A mention must go, too, to Dijon's **Musée des Beaux-Arts** (p. 334, ❷), which is entirely free.

Choosing fine dining at lunchtime. If you're hankering for a meal in an expensive restaurant but can't afford the splurge, remember that the best restaurants serve their top-notch cuisine at lower prices at lunchtime. One such place is wonderful **Yoshi** in the Hôtel Métropole in Monte Carlo (p. 467), where lip-smacking, Michelin-starred Japanese menus climb to around 200€ at night but start at just 32€ at lunchtime.

Making a picnic. In France a picnic is one of life's great pleasures—and not just for travelers on a shoestring budget. Save on restaurant bills by purchasing a warm baguette at the bakery, adding some cheese from the local *fromagerie* and fresh figs from the fruit seller, and picking up a bottle of wine and a cheap corkscrew. Then find the perfect outdoor spot for lunch.

Sampling Breton *crêperies.* Forget those Parisian *crêpe* stands selling soggy excuses for a pancake. A true Breton *crêpe* is a meal in itself, and for no more than a few euros. Strictly speaking, we are talking about the *galette,* the savory *crêpe* made from buckwheat flour and filled with egg, cheese, and ham, or any number of more extravagant fillings (scallops with Armorican sauce is our favorite). You probably won't have room for the sweet pancake that can follow as dessert. Great *crêperies* abound throughout Brittany, but **Quimper** (p. 202, ❺) is particularly famous for this local pauper's dish.

Visiting a Pyrenean spa. You've seen the Royal Evian and Caudalie spas in luxury travel magazines, but there are far less expensive ways to experience spas in France. The Pyrenees have recently sprouted several leisure spa complexes with stunning facilities and affordable prices, geared to the people who live in the region year-round. Imagine a world of water jets, Roman mosaics, authentic Moroccan hammams, Finnish saunas, and outdoor Jacuzzis, all yours for only 22€. See p. 528.

The Best French Markets

Les Puces de St-Ouen. If you're into precious knickknacks and old furniture, nothing beats this Parisian antiques market—a place so big it has street names, restaurants, and cafes. Come here to find everything from Napoleonic fittings to period dresses and 1950s tableware. See p. 99.

Alsatian Christmas markets. This long tradition, going back more than 4 centuries, has generated its own tourist industry drawing people from all over the globe. Strasbourg's is the oldest, with a dramatic setting on the Cathedral square, but the towns along the wine route also get very festive. Shopping for gifts—wooden toys, knitted hats, and all sorts of novelties—is made all the more joyful by live band music and abundant amounts of *glühwein* (gingerbread). See p. 277, ❷.

Avignon. Avignon's covered market, Les Halles (on place Pie), caresses your senses with more than 40 bright stands of aromatic fruit, vegetables, fish, and meats. Listen to the jovial workers plying their wares—and on Saturday mornings, watch the cooking demonstrations when local chefs whip up sizzling dishes for hungry onlookers. See p. 424.

Nice. The best spot to witness the south of France's theatrical tradition for selling local produce is Nice's cours Saleya morning market, where singsongy voices hawk fresh lemons and olives, silvery fish, and multihued fruits and vegetables piled high on canapé-shaded tables. Try the fresh *socca*, a delicious pizzalike *niçois* specialty doused in fragrant olive oil. See p. 468, ❶.

Toulouse. The covered Marché Victor Hugo is a Sunday institution, not only for its amazing stalls displaying game with feather and fur, Toulouse sausages, *raie* and lobster, cheeses, and artisan ice cream, but for the popping corks of its wine bars, lively with rugby chat. After shopping in the market, everyone piles upstairs to the restaurant floor for a noisy, convivial Sunday lunch. See p. 541, ❹.

> Between May and July, Nice's cours Saleya market is the place to go on the Côte d'Azur for cherries.

Périgueux. The capital of Dordogne is renowned for its sophisticated but earthy food traditions, featuring geese, ducks, truffles, and prunes. There are two distinct types of market: the regular produce market and the *gras*, with all the preserved food that traditionally kept the peasants going through the winter. Stocking up on some of these delicacies in their tins or jars will give you an excuse to prolong your experience of the region, with a Périgord feast back home. See p. 618, ❼.

Our Favorite Works of Art

La Fée Electricité. Paris's Musée d'Art Moderne contains Raoul Dufy's gargantuan oil painting—the biggest in the world at 624 sq. m (6,717 sq. ft.). *The Electricity Fairy* was painted between 1936 and 1937 for the Paris World's Fair. It wows today with its oversize proportions, which spread a rainbow of color and scenes of daily life across the museum walls. See p. 60, ➊.

La Portes de l'Enfer. In the peaceful gardens of Paris's Musée Rodin, the sculptor's spectacular *Gates of Hell* depicts scenes from *The Inferno,* the first section of Danté's *Divine Comedy.* As you stand in front of it, admire some 180 figures, including miniature versions of Rodin's most famous works, *The Kiss* and *The Thinker.* See p. 52, ➍.

Les Braves. One of the most haunting pieces of land art you will ever see, Anilore Banon's *The Brave Ones* features 17 sails of steel, each up to 9m (30 ft.) high, clustered on the beach where the Allied D-Day landings took place. Sometimes marooned on the beach, sometimes submerged by the waves, it is a permanent but ever-changing reminder of the bravery of those who fought for freedom. See "The Longest Day," p. 216.

The Apocalypse Tapestry. Angers's castle is home to this major medieval artwork—an early 14th-century depiction of the Apocalypse—as described in the last book of the New Testament—made from 76 intricately woven panels. Its beauty is arresting, as are its sheer length (100m/328 ft.) and the mythological elements of its design—dragons and beasts with 10 horns and seven heads rising out of the sea. See p. 159, ➎.

Christ Leaving the Praetorium. Though it is neither modern nor contemporary, Gustav Doré's gargantuan masterwork *Christ Leaving the Praetorium* is the star exhibit at Strasbourg's MAMAC modern art museum, and it looks all the more impressive in this stark white setting. Emotional turmoil reigns on the sidelines of the painting, where Roman soldiers, beggars, Moors, and supplicants jockey for a view of Christ serenely cutting a path through the center of the chaos. See p. 298, ➊.

La Cathédrale. Less is more, indeed. The power of that concept resonates from Nicolas de Staël's ghostly white cathedral on its inky background, reducing all the intricacy of a Gothic edifice to a simple monolith. You'll find yourself spellbound if you stare at the painting long enough, at the Musée des Beaux-Arts de Lyon. See p. 381, ➎.

> Les Braves *monument on Omaha Beach in St-Laurent-sur-Mer was erected for the 60th anniversary of the 1944 D-Day landings.*

The Best Architecture

> Behind these walls at Versailles, about 100 assistants attended to Louis XIV each morning.

Paris. The French capital's astonishing architectural treasures date from Roman times until today. Everything is here, from Roman baths and medieval mansions, visible side by side in the **Thermes de Cluny** (p. 55, ⑪); to 17th-century townhouses in **Le Marais** (p. 82); 19th-century Haussmann apartments along the **Grands Boulevards** (p. 665); 1970s high-rises in **Montparnasse** (p. 92); and spanking-new, high-tech builds such as the **Musée du Quai Branly** (p. 53, ⑥), designed by the great French architect Jean Nouvel. See chapter 3.

Versailles. Absolute rulers have to build palaces, and for pure magnificence, Louis XIV's Versailles has yet to be superseded, however many have tried. It is a town in itself, with royal apartments, government offices, homes for thousands of courtiers and the royal mistress, and Marie-Antoinette's play farm. See p. 135, ①.

Loire Valley châteaux. The Renaissance architecture of the Loire Valley châteaux is unrivaled in the world. Admire the symmetry of **Azay-le-Rideau** (p. 160), with its delicate proportions reflected in the Indre River. Take in the turrets of **Chenonceau** (p. 149, ④) from Catherine de Medici's gardens, and walk through the castle's graceful gallery, which spans the Cher River over a series of handsome arches. See chapter 5.

Centre Pompidou-Metz. Museum design is a creative field for architects these days, and the Pompidou-Metz, by Demathieu & Bard, is our favorite new construction in France. Mushroom, honeycomb, flattened Eiffel Tower, or Dali-esque cafe chair? You decide. See p. 275, ⑩.

Provence & the Riviera. The Riviera and Provence abound in legacies from the Roman era. Admire age-old amphitheaters in **Arles** (p. 397, ④) and **Nîmes** (p. 432), meander through vestiges of a Roman town in **Vaison-la-Romaine** (p. 402, ①), and climb La Turbie's triumphant **Trophée des Alpes** (p. 462, ⑦) for sweeping panoramas over Monaco. See chapters 10 and 11.

Bordeaux. The most impressive neoclassical architecture in France is in Bordeaux, where the riverfront is bejeweled by elegant 18th-century merchants' houses—throwbacks from the days when the city was a major wine port. Jovial masks of Bacchus and river gods decorate the facades of place de la Bourse in the Chartrons Quarter. See chapter 13.

Our Favorite Museums

> *The Musée d'Orsay's glass walkway is a relic of the museum's first life as a train station.*

The Louvre. A triumph of royal and imperial French architecture on the outside, the world's most famous museum shelters on the inside some of humanity's greatest art treasures, including Leonardo's *Mona Lisa* and the *Venus de Milo.* See p. 50, ❶.

Musée d'Orsay. The elegant glass-and-iron canopies of this former Paris railway station frame one of Europe's most awe-inspiring museums, devoted to 19th-century art. Its Impressionist section, with Monets, Renoirs, and Pissaros galore, is unrivaled. See p. 51, ❷.

Centre Pompidou. This Parisian citadel of 20th-century art wows you with its quirky exoskeletal structure of blue, red, green, and yellow pipes. Inside, exhibitions draw from more than 40,000 works from 1900 to today, including Jackson Pollack's priceless eruption of *Silver over Black, White, Yellow and Red.* See p. 61, ❹.

Fondation Maeght. Established as a showcase for the collections of art dealers Aimé and Marguerite Maeght, this avant-garde museum in St-Paul-de-Vence features splendors by Giacometti, Chagall, and Matisse. Plus, the glass-walled structure offers fine views over the Provençal landscape. See p. 450, ❸.

Fondation Bemberg. An incredible gift to Toulouse by an Argentinean collector, Fondation Bemberg has a surprisingly broad art collection ranging from Dutch master works to Impressionist paintings (most notably, some luminous Bonnards). Of particular interest, besides the stunning, historic building itself, is the ground floor, where the art is displayed in room sets along with period furniture, knick-knacks, and ceramics. See p. 28, ❹.

LaM. Lille's new Museum of Modern and Contemporary Art and Art Brut, showcases 20th- and 21st-century art in a collection of 4,500 works. Art Brut, or "Raw Art," is a term coined by French painter Jean Dubuffet to describe works created outside the established art world, such as paintings by the mentally ill. See p. 654, ❾.

Our Favorite Churches & Cathedrals

Notre-Dame de Paris. Thanks to Victor Hugo's novel *The Hunchback of Notre-Dame,* this stunning symbol of medieval faith and power is famed throughout the world. It dazzles in the morning and at sunset, when its reflection shimmers in the Seine. For the best views, climb Quasimodo's bell towers and watch the city unfurl beneath the watchful gaze of monstrous gargoyle chimeras. See p. 41, ❼.

Notre-Dame de Chartres. Our Lady of Chartres was declared a High Gothic "French Acropolis" by none other than Auguste Rodin. It was the first cathedral to use flying buttresses, and its stained glass, which projects mystical patterns of light onto the stone floors, is so intense that its dominant color came to be known as "Chartres Blue." See p. 138.

Notre-Dame de Reims. After Clovis's baptism here in A.D. 496, the cathedral was expanded as a sanctuary for the coronation of French monarchs—a function it would fulfill until 1825, despite a fire that led to its reconstruction in the 13th century. Its majestic proportions are humbling, as are the intense blue stained-glass windows by Marc Chagall. See p. 254, ❶.

Notre-Dame de Rouen. Richard the Lionheart's tomb is in this awe-inspiring Gothic cathedral, which displays exquisite 16th-century stained glass and intricate sculptures of the Tree of Jesse around its monumental entrance. The cathedral is most famous for the fascination it inspired in Monet, who painted it 28 times. See p. 249, ❶.

Eglise Monolithe de St-Jean, Aubeterre-sur-Drônne. An anomaly not just in name, this 5th-century church, carved directly into rock, is Europe's largest subterranean church. Soaring a full 20m (66 ft.) from floor to ceiling, it has an atmospheric austerity enhanced today by colored backlighting. Climb to the high cloisters for the best view. See p. 608, ❽.

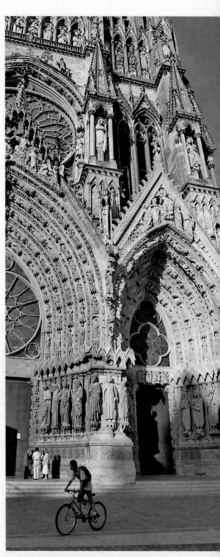

> *In 1429 Charles VII was crowned in the Cathédrale Notre-Dame de Reims in the company of Joan of Arc.*

The Best Luxury Hotels

Château de Verrières. You'll feel like a 19th-century noble when you stay in this town house in Saumur. Antique furniture litters the rooms; an open fireplace in the lounge warms toes in winter; the gardens cry out to nature lovers; and some rooms afford dreamy views onto Saumur's fairy-tale château. See p. 183.

La Bastide de Moustiers. You have to drive down a narrow lane, past potters' workshops and villas, to reach this slice of rural heaven—chef Alain Ducasse's former country home, now a Michelin-starred hotel-restaurant. The food is exemplary, drawing heavily on the on-site organic vegetable garden, and the rooms are rustically regal. See p. 459.

Grand Hotel du Cap-Ferrat. Welcome to the lap of luxury—a sumptuous mansion, coveted by celebrities and the Riviera's most wealthy denizens. The white lobby, strewn with precious paintings and chandeliers, is a piece of art in itself; the gardens exude Mediterranean charm; and the swimming pool lies next to a path that leads to the peninsula's lighthouse. See p. 463.

Grand Hôtel Loreamar Thalasso Spa. What we love most about this hotel on the Basque coast is that it's luxurious but doesn't feel at all cut off from the convivial pleasures of the seaside. Its restaurant terrace is beside the boardwalk, and you can step out of the rarified world of its candle-lit, vaulted spa right onto the beach, where children are playing with buckets and spades. Built as a golfing hotel for the English, it still has a 1920s air, with its cocktail bar and floral fabrics. The restaurant, run by a team of young cooks, serves creative French cuisine prepared in a Japanese-style open kitchen. See p. 529.

Château de la Treyne. This fairy-tale château, overlooking the Dordogne River where swans glide by, is a dream come true. The feeling when you stay here is that you are the guests of fortunate friends. Butlers wait on you with discreet but friendly service, and the owners insist on first-name terms. The dinner, served in a high-ceilinged room draped with tapestries, is simply divine. See p. 625.

> *Parts of the Château de la Treyne date from the 14th and 17th centuries.*

The Best Affordable Sleeps

Solar Hôtel. Paris's Solar doesn't look like anything special from the outside, but inside it's comfortable as well as environmentally friendly, recycling its water, serving organic breakfasts, and using solar panels to light up its facade. There are bikes for guests, too, stocked in the hotel's peaceful courtyard garden. All of this goes for around 60€ per night, whatever time of year you visit. See p. 121.

Villa Hamster. This Nantes B&B wins a prize for being the most hilarious place to stay in France—a mock hamster cage fit with a giant wheel. What's more, the bed is comfy—with a normal mattress, not wood shavings. See p. 182.

Hôtel la Couleuvrine. More tourists visit Sarlat than anyplace else in the Dordogne, but the owners of this cozy hotel make everyone feel special. In a historic building that includes part of the old city wall, it's full of twists and turns and corridors, and the rooms are attractively lined in toile de Jouy. Better yet, there's no need to hunt any further for your evening meal than the hotel's reasonably priced, excellent restaurant. See p. 610.

Hôtel Saint Paul. Vieux Lyon has become so chic that reasonably priced hotels are few and far between. But the Saint Paul has kept its prices down, and guests are often surprised that it hasn't received a higher star classification. In a 13th-century building, it is decorated with some style, and the owner loves nothing more than to recommend places to sightsee and dine in the city. See p. 384.

La Fontaine du Grand Fussy. This 19th-century home in Burgundy exemplifies why some visitors prefer the personal touches of a B&B over a big hotel. If each room looks as though it has been decorated professionally, that's because it has been: The hostess, Dominique Bron, is an interior decorator and talented painter who has made this *chambres d'hôtes* a labor of love. She also bakes her own bread for your breakfast and dinner. See p. 333.

> *Hôtel La Couleuvrine in Sarlat lies inside the city's last medieval defensive corner tower.*

La Jabotte. Tommy the fluffy Westie welcomes you to this small and charming hotel in Antibes. Rooms are cozy with a rustic, Provençal theme, and breakfast and aperitifs are served in the flowery garden, beyond which you can make out the sound of the waves crashing in the distance. See p. 463.

2
The Best
All-France
Itineraries

France in 1 Week

For a memorable trip to Paris, 1 week provides barely enough time. If you budget your time, however, you can spend a few days in the French capital, venture to Versailles and Chartres on day trips, head to the Loire to explore some châteaux, and round out the week with a day on the coast in Bordeaux. We recommend staying in Paris for the first 3 nights; then either hop on a high-speed TGV train or drive the rest of the route. Be prepared to rise early, and wear comfortable shoes.

> PREVIOUS PAGE Les tournesols (sunflowers) came from the Americas in the 16th century, but the paintings of Vincent Van Gogh forever associate the yellow blooms with sunny Provence. THIS PAGE The Trocadéro is the best place in Paris for admiring the Iron Lady's filigree girders.

START Fly into Paris's Charles de Gaulle international airport. TRIP LENGTH 1 week; 660km (410 miles) by car on fast roads; 300km (190 miles) by train.

1 **Paris.** The Paris chapter of this book suggests good 1- and 2-day walking tours of the city (p. 38). Here we'll provide one more option: this walk along the Seine River, which allows you to take in the beauty of the city outdoors before visiting museums on Day 2.

Start at Métro St-Paul and take the narrow rue du Prévot to rue de Charlemagne (named after the first king of the Franks), which leads leftward, to the vestiges of Paris's **old city wall,** built under King Philippe Auguste in the early 13th century. From here rue des Jardins St-Paul, whose doorways join the **Village St-Paul antiques quarter** (p. 101), takes you to the Seine. Follow the waterway toward the right and cross the first bridge (Pont Marie) to **Ile St-Louis,** lined with 17th-century mansions and, on rue St-Louis en l'Ile, tempting boutiques. Then it's on to **Ile de la Cité** (p. 46, **1**), where you can climb the lofty towers of **Notre-Dame Cathedral** (p. 41, **7**) for sweeping panoramas over the city. From here, cross the Seine to the Left Bank, where the tumbledown English-language bookshop **Shakespeare & Company** (p. 71, **5**), on quai Montebello, stands as a beacon to old literary Paris.

1 Paris
2 Château de Versailles
3 Chartres
4 Blois
5 Tours
6 La Rochelle

After lunch, follow the river westward. From now on, as you walk along the striking tree-lined quays, it's one grand monument after the other: The neoclassical walls of the colossal **Louvre** (p. 50, 1) on your right give way to the **Musée d'Orsay** (p. 51, 2), a former railway station now filled with Impressionist paintings and other 19th-century treasures, on your left. Next up, **place de la Concorde**'s gold-tipped Egyptian column twinkles opposite the French government's **Assemblée Nationale** (p. 38, 1). Then the Belle Epoque **Grand Palais** and **Petit Palais** art museums (p. 49) compete for your attention opposite the Sun King's gold-domed military hospital, **L'Hôtel**

des Invalides (p. 47, 4), now a military museum. After walking past the rows of iron cannons, take rue de Grenelle westward toward the grande dame of ironwork, the **Eiffel Tower** (p. 48, 5).

By now, you're probably desperate for a drink, so walk beneath the tower's four pillars and cross the bridge to the 1930s **Palais de Chaillot** (p. 49) at Trocadéro. From here the views are sublime, and inside the east wing, the **Café de l'Homme,** 17 place du Trocadéro, Musée de l'Homme (☎ 01-44-05-30-15; www.restaurant-cafedelhomme.com), serves restorative coffees and cocktails with uninterrupted views of the Eiffel Tower.

> *The exoskeletal pipes of Paris's Centre Pompidou never fail to impress as you exit Rambuteau Métro.*

Finish your day by jumping onto the Métro (line 6, Métro Trocadéro) to Charles de Gaulle–Etoile (or by walking) to the **Arc de Triomphe** (p. 48, ⑥) and descending the most famous avenue in the world, **Les Champs-Elysées** (p. 45, ⑩).

On Day 2, explore in greater depth whatever interested you most on Day 1. The **Louvre** museum is a requisite stop for famous art treasures, including the *Mona Lisa;* while the **Musée d'Orsay,** opposite, houses one of the world's best collections of Impressionist art. The **Centre Pompidou** (p. 61, ④) is a temple to modern art housed in a hip, multicolored exoskeletal structure. If you'd rather lose yourself in a more intimate museum, head to **Le Marais** (p. 82), where free museums such as the **Musée Carnavalet** (p. 84, ⑥) and the **Maison de Victor Hugo** (p. 84, ⑧), where the great author once lived, sit amid age-old surroundings. In the late afternoon, either stay in the Marais for an aperitif, or head to the bohemian bars around

Bastille. Or why not jump on the Métro to Abbesses in Montmartre and watch the sun go down beneath the white, domed **Sacré-Coeur** basilica (p. 90, ⑩), where you'll learn indelibly why Paris is nicknamed the City of Light? ⏱ 2 days.

On Day 3, catch the RER line C1 (see "Paris Fast Facts," p. 141) at the Gare d'Austerlitz, St-Michel, Musée d'Orsay, Invalides, Ponte de l'Alma, Champ de Mars, or Javel stop. Take it to the Versailles Rive Gauche station (35–40 min.; do not get off at Versailles Chantier, which will leave you on the other end of town, a long walk from the château). The round-trip fare is 5.60€.

❷ **Château de Versailles.** In 1661, Louis XIV set out to build a palace that would be the envy of Europe and created a symbol of opulence copied, yet never duplicated, the world over. The king used his new playground to amuse the nobles of France with constant entertainment and lavish banquets. While the aristocrats played, however, the peasants on the estates sowed the seeds of the Revolution. When Louis XIV died in 1715, his great-grandson Louis XV succeeded him and continued the outrageous pomp even as he predicted the outcome: *"Après moi le déluge"* ("After me, the deluge"). The next monarch, Louis XVI, found his forebear's behavior scandalous, but the frivolity and spending of his queen, Marie Antoinette, indeed led to their downfall: Louis and Marie Antoinette were at Versailles on October 6, 1789, when they learned that mobs were marching on the palace. As predicted, *le déluge* had arrived, and the rest is history.

Napoleon stayed at Versailles but never seemed fond of it. Louis-Philippe (who reigned from 1830 to 1848) prevented the destruction of the palace by converting it into a museum dedicated to the glory of France. Decades later, John D. Rockefeller contributed toward the restoration of Versailles, and work continues today. ⏲ 1 day. See p. 135.

Head back to Paris for the night. Rise early on Day 4 and take the train from Paris Montparnasse to Chartres (1 hr.). Or drive along A10/A11 southwest from the Périphérique (Paris's ring road) and follow signs to Le Mans and Chartres (1½ hr.; 91km/57miles).

❸ **Chartres.** Chartres is home to France's greatest Gothic cathedral, famed for its glorious 13th-century stained-glass windows, which recount Bible stories in sumptuous colors, and a medieval stone labyrinth on the nave floor. Around the cathedral, you'll discover other wonders: half-timbered houses that line the cobblestone streets; steep *tertres* (staircases) leading to the Eure River, dotted with picturesque mills and bridges; and the **Musée des Beaux-Arts,** 29 cloître Notre-Dame (☎ 02-37-90-45-80; www.ville-chartres.fr; admission 3.10€; Wed–Sat 10am–noon and 2–5pm, Sun 2–5pm), in the former Episcopal palace, with an excellent collection of 17th- and 18th-century furniture and paintings. Also worthy of your attention is the Benedictine **St-Pierre** abbey church, famed for yet more stained glass, and the Romanesque **Eglise St-André** near the river, used for temporary art exhibitions. ⏲ 1 day. See p. 138.

> *A segment of the vivid stained glass windows in Chartres Cathedral.*

Return to Paris for the night, and on Day 5 catch the train from the Gare d'Austerlitz (1½ hr.–2 hr.) to Blois. Or, spend the night in Chartres and on Day 5 leave via N154 to A10 (toward Orleans), exit at junction 17, and follow signs to Blois, via N252 and D200 (129km/80 miles total).

A Free Concert

If you visit Chartres on a Sunday afternoon in July or August, you'll be able to catch free organ concerts at 4:45pm, when the filtered light brings the cathedral's western windows to life.

> Tours's pretty cobbled streets are a plum spot for alfresco dining.

> *A picture of peace today, La Rochelle's harbors were once the backdrop for a bloody siege led by Cardinal Richelieu in the early 17th century.*

④ Blois. With its tree-lined quays and elegant **Cathédrale St-Louis,** Blois looks particularly lovely when seen from across the Loire River. Its pedestrianized streets in the old town delight architecture lovers with a myriad of noble 16th- and 17th-century mansions, romantic courtyards, and half-timbered houses. But the highlight of your fifth day *en tour* will be the **Château de Blois** (p. 146, **①**), the main royal residence until Henri IV took the court to Paris in the 16th century, and home of François I's Renaissance masterpiece: a monumental spiral staircase in an octagonal tower with a gallery from where the king could watch jousting tournaments. ⊕ 1 day. See p. 157, **②**.

On Day 6, either drive via A10 from Blois to Tours (65km/40 miles), or hop on a train from the Gare de Blois to Tours-Centre (30–40 min.).

⑤ Tours. The traditional gateway to the Loire Valley châteaux, Tours is an ideal town in which to acquaint yourself with French life. Sit on a cafe terrace at bustling **place Plumereau,** the main square, and watch the locals go about their daily business. Then meander through the medieval streets around **rue Briçonnet** and take in the flamboyant Gothic facade of the **Cathédrale St-Gatien** farther east. If you're into fine art, step in and view the wonderful collection at the **Musée des Beaux-Arts,** including Mantegna's 1459 *The Resurrection.* ⊕ 1 day. For detailed information on Tours, see p. 150, **①**.

On your last day, catch a direct train to La Rochelle from Tours-Centre (2 hr. 45 min.). Or, drive west along A10 (toward Poitiers), exiting at junction 33 and following signs to La Rochelle (236km/146 miles).

⑥ La Rochelle. This charming historical port—where the locals have a penchant for preparing fine seafood and the boutiques are hidden below stone archways—counterbalances your whirlwind inland tour with a slice of life on the Atlantic coast. ⊕ 1 day. For detailed information on La Rochelle, see p. 588.

Where to Stay & Dine in Blois

Try a room at **16 place St-Louis**—an 18th-century town house in a peaceful, central area within walking distance of the château (16 place St-Louis; ☎ 02-54-74-13-61; www.16placesaintlouis.fr; 3 units; doubles 90€–140€; MC, V). One of Blois's best restaurants is the **Orangerie du Château,** 1 av. Jean Laigret (☎ 02-54-78-05-36; www.orangerie-du-chateau.fr; fixed menus from 34€; MC, V; lunch Thurs-Tues, dinner Thurs-Sat and Mon-Tues; closed Feb 15–Mar 15), set in a huge, late-15th-century house and serving gourmet French menus.

France in 2 Weeks

This itinerary takes in six of France's finest cities and allows for excursions into the surrounding countryside and smaller towns. While each city is richly endowed with culture and monuments, you'll be amazed by the contrast in atmosphere, from wine-rich Bordeaux to proudly southwestern Toulouse; the Mediterranean cities of Montpellier and Marseille; Provençal Aix; and the large metropolis of Lyon, France's second city. Because of the distances involved, we highly recommend you follow this tour by train, which is twice as fast as car travel and allows you more time and energy for sightseeing.

> *In 1792 the first guillotine of the French Revolution was used here on place de Grève (today's place de l'Hôtel de Ville).*

START Fly into Paris's Charles de Gaulle International Airport. **TRIP LENGTH** 1,700km (1,056 miles) by train.

1 Paris. If this is your first visit to the City of Light, you'll probably want to see the most important sights first, so follow our "Paris in 1 Day" itinerary from the Paris chapter (p. 38), which takes in place de la Concorde, the Tuileries, Musée d'Orsay, Notre-Dame Cathedral, and St-Germain. If you're jetlagged, you'll have walked your way through the afternoon slump, and by evening you'll probably be feeling

energetic enough to squeeze in one last stop for the day: the **Eiffel Tower** (p. 48, **5**). Open until 11:45pm September through June and 12:45am July and August, the tower is at its most scintillating at night, as you'll be right inside the glittering structure with all of Paris spread out below. Don't worry—tomorrow we'll take it a bit easier. Repeat visitors might prefer to follow the walking tour based around the Seine in "France in 1 Week" (p. 20), or take your pick from the themes in the Paris chapter (p. 32).

1 Paris
2 Giverny
3 Bordeaux
4 Toulouse
5 Montpellier
6 Marseille
7 Aix-en-Provence
8 Lyon

On Day 2, be sure to spend at least some time on a cafe terrace, as this is an essential part of reveling in the ambience of Paris. Choose one cultural exhibit, one shopping destination, and one fine meal to make the most of your day. We suggest the **Centre Pompidou** (p. 61, **4**) or the **Louvre** (p. 50, **1**) for the first (they are closed on alternate days at the beginning of the week); the **Marais** (p. 82) for the second; and **Le Train Bleu** (p. 113) or **Chartier** (p. 110) for the third—both are bustling Art Nouveau brasseries, but Chartier is affordable to all. And then to bed: You've got a lot ahead of you. ☺ **2 days.**

On Day 3, take the train from Paris's Gare St-Lazare to Vernon (40–50 min.), then choose your mode of transport to Giverny: Walk 5km (3 miles), catch bus no. 240, cycle (you can hire a bike in front of the station), or take a taxi.

2 **Giverny.** Monet's garden is so much more than just a garden. A quintessence of the image of France that many of us have from the Impressionists, it's like walking into a painting. If you've already seen Giverny, however, consider visiting **Versailles** (p. 135), **Chartres** (p. 138), **Fontainebleau** (p. 134), or,

> *Bordeaux's center encompasses an eclectic mix of Renaissance and late-medieval architecture.*

> *The frescoes under place du Capitole's arcades recount Toulouse's history.*

if you're traveling with kids, **Disneyland Paris** (p. 136). Alternatively, there's the rest of Paris to explore. ⊕ 1 day. See p. 137.

Rise early on Day 4 to catch a train to Bordeaux from Paris Montparnasse (3 hr. 20 min.).

❸ **Bordeaux.** Before you start calling on the wine cellars of Bordeaux, spend a day in the city, exploring the riches that wine built. The Bordeaux city tour highlights the capital's most important sights. Make sure to linger long enough near place de la Bourse to see J. M. Llorca's *miroir d'eau* rise as a mist and then flood the square with a thin film of water that evokes an ephemeral Venice. You'll then get to take in **Cathédrale St-André** and the

Musée des Beaux-Arts in the **Palais Rohan,** as well as many beautiful streets and squares. Finish your day at one of the many restaurants on the quays of the Garonne, such as **L'Estacade** (p. 587).

For your second day in Bordeaux, either hire a car to explore the *vignoble* and the town of **St-Emilion** (40km/24 miles), or savor the wines on one of the tourist office's excellent all-inclusive excursions. For 135€ per person, including wine and food, take the tour *Une journée à St-Emilion* (reservations ☎ 05-57-30-04-27; www.bordeaux-tourisme.com), which leads you through a tasting in a vineyard, lunch in St-Emilion, a guided visit of the medieval fortified town, and a visit to the subterranean wine cellars of one of St-Emilion's finest *Grands Crus Classés.* ⊕ 2 days. For detailed information on Bordeaux, see p. 582.

On Day 6, take the train from Bordeaux to Toulouse (2½ hr.).

❹ **Toulouse.** Take our tip, and choose the Métro over taxis in Toulouse, as cab prices are high and Métro service is excellent. The **Hôtel des Beaux-Arts** (p. 543) makes an ideal base for exploring the Pink City. Once you've dumped your bags, sit down in the hotel's Art Nouveau **brasserie** to enjoy a leisurely lunch. It is only a short walk from here to the **Fondation Bemberg,** Hôtel d'Assézat, place d'Assézat (☎ 05-61-12-06-89; www.fondation-bemberg. fr; admission 5€ adults, 3€ ages 8–18, free for children 7 and under; Tues–Wed and Fri–Sun 10am–12:30pm and 1:30–6pm; Thurs 10am–12:30pm and 1:30–9pm), an art foundation with a panoply of masterpieces from the Renaissance to the Impressionist eras. A wander around the neighborhood south of here, between Métro Carmes and the river, reveals antiques shops and enticing *bistrots à vin* where you may decide to take your evening meal.

Start Day 7 with a visit to the historic covered market, **Marché Victor Hugo,** possibly the best market in France—and not just for its amazing array of food products. Here you'll get a strong taste of the city and its inhabitants, especially if you lunch amid the vivacious crowd on the restaurant floor above. In the afternoon take in the sights: **place du Capitole,** with its Roman forum feeling; the **Musée des Augustins;** and the architecturally impressive **Basilique St-Sernin.** Those interested in art or technology might visit **Les Abattoirs** contemporary art space or, slightly out of town, the **Cité de l'Espace,** which celebrates Toulouse's preeminence in aerospace innovation.

🕐 2 days. For detailed information on Toulouse, see p. 540.

On Day 8, take the train from Toulouse to Montpellier (2 hr.).

⑤ **Montpellier.** Get your bearings in Montpellier by sitting on a cafe terrace on place de la Comédie, which really is the center of this two-part city. Northwest of here is the beautifully preserved old town, and east is the new neighborhood of Antigone, extending down to the river. Spend your afternoon at the **Musée Fabre,** one of the city's main attractions, which has become a major player since an inspired renovation and the addition of a wing devoted to abstract expressionist Pierre Soulages. Dine at the **Jardin des Sens** or at the simpler but attractively placed **Le Grillardin.**

A second day in Montpellier gives you plenty of time to explore the historic old town. We highly recommend the tourist office's guided tours, to access the architectural treasures hidden behind the facades here. These excursions are also the only means of ascending the Arc de Triomphe for a view of the city (Montpellier does not have many high buildings). In the afternoon, visit the **Jardin des Plantes** (Botanical Gardens) or the surprising Serre Amazonienne at the **Montpellier Zoo.** 🕐 2 days. For detailed information on Montpellier, see p. 532.

> *One of chef Mickaël Diore's fetish dishes at Le Grillardin in Montpellier is pan-fried foie gras with bread pudding and caramelized strawberries.*

> *Ragged and wild, Marseille's Frioul Islands have an unspoiled charm.*

Trains from Montpellier to Marseille can range from 90 minutes to 4 hours, so be sure to get a direct fare for your trip on Day 10. You'll enjoy some attractive landscapes on the way.

6 Marseille. You've been to bourgeois Bordeaux and rugby-loving Toulouse; now prepare for another contrast. Marseille is a magnificent city whose energy emanates from its ancient port. **Vieux Port** is the home of the city's fishing industry and the arrival point for the wave upon wave of immigrants who have made this the colorful and vibrant place it is today, after more than 2,500 years as an international crossroads. If you've arrived before 1pm, you'll be able to catch the fishmongers hawking their wares on the quai des Belges. Then go and eat. If you want the finest bouillabaisse, you'll have to book 2 days in advance at **Le Miramar** (p. 431), but there are plenty of other fishy delights to be had in the portside restaurants—just look for those places that are filling up fast with locals.

Before you embark on the climb to the **Basilique de Notre-Dame-de-la-Garde** that crowns the city, visit the **Musée de Histoire de Marseille** and the Greek remains just behind the Vieux Port. It's a 1-hour walk from the Vieux Port to the basilica, or you can take bus no. 60 from cours Ballard at the corner of quai des Belges. The most impressive approach, however, is from the east side, with its 251 steps—just don't attempt it without stopping frequently to catch your breath and admire the view. Return to the Vieux Port for a stroll and some people-watching, perhaps from the balcony of **La Caravelle.**

On your second day in Marseille, visit a museum, go shopping, or wander around admiring architecture, such as Le Corbusier's

> *Blend in with the residents of Aix-en-Provence by lunching outdoors in the balmy shade of a parasol.*

Cité Radieuse. We also recommend a walking tour of the **Le Panier** neighborhood; **L'Estaque,** which was painted by the Impressionists; or the spectacular limestone cliffs called the **Calanques** (p. 415, ⑨). There's always the beach as well. ☉ 2 days. For detailed information on Marseille, see p. 426.

On Day 12, take the train from Marseille to Aix-en-Provence (12 min.).

⑦ **Aix-en-Provence.** As it's so near, you can visit Aix-en-Provence as a day trip from Marseille, but you won't want to rush back to the big city after a relaxing evening meal here, so we recommend booking accommodation in Aix. A graceful and artistic Provençal spa town, Aix is a delight to wander around in, either on your own or with a guided tour. Setting off early in the morning will enable you to take in a quintessential **Provençal market** before lunch (p. 420), then **Cézanne's house,** and then the **Musée Granet.** Dine at **Le Formal** or on one of the restaurant terraces on atmospheric cours Mirabeau. ☉ 1 day. For detailed information on Aix-en-Provence, see p. 418.

On Day 13, take the train from Aix-en-Provence to Lyon (1 hr. 25 min.).

⑧ **Lyon.** You'll spend your last 2 days in France's second city, where several great eras of prosperity have left behind an impressive body of architecture that runs the gamut from Roman ruins to medieval and Renaissance buildings to contemporary monuments. **Vieux Lyon** and **Lugdunum,** with its basilica and magnificent Roman theater, will occupy you for the better part of a day. Stay in the Renaissance part of Lyon for an evening meal at **Les Terrasses de Lyon,** which has a great view of the old city's red rooftops.

On your final day, explore the *traboules* (covered passages connecting buildings) along the steep streets of the 19th-century silk workers' neighborhood, **La Croix-Rousse,** shop on the Presqu'île, and visit the **Musée des Beaux-Arts**—perhaps the best fine-arts museum in France outside Paris. ☉ 2 days. For detailed information on Lyon, see p. 378.

On Day 14, fly out of Lyon St-Exupéry airport, or return to Paris via TGV train (2 hr.).

3
Paris & Ile de France

Favorite Moments in Paris

Rolling elegantly outward from the banks of the Seine River, this "moveable feast" (as Ernest Hemingway so aptly called Paris) has more remnants of history, exquisite cuisine, breathtaking museums, chichi boutiques, idyllic cafes, and beautiful architecture squeezed into one little *rue* (street) than most cities have in their entire square mileage. No matter how many times you visit the French capital, nothing can beat the excitement of seeing the Eiffel Tower sparkle at night, or the thrill of strolling along the Seine on a warm summer evening. The list of wonderful experiences to be had here is endless, but these are our most dependable favorites.

> PREVIOUS PAGE *A pensive gargoyle at Cathédrale Notre-Dame watches over the city.* THIS PAGE *The quays around the pont des Arts make for a romantic stroll along the Seine.*

❶ Rubbing shoulders with Notre-Dame's gargoyles. Climb the uneven stone steps to the top of Notre-Dame's towers, and you're in the precipitous realm of Quasimodo, where hideous stone sculptures stick out their tongues at the city below. The views from here are mesmerizing, especially on a cloudy day, when the sky looks moody. See p. 41, ❼.

❷ Ambling along the Seine toward the islands. Countless painters have fallen under its spell, and so will you as you watch lovers walking hand in hand, *bateaux mouches* (tour boats) cruising slowly by, *bouquinistes* (secondhand-book dealers; see p. 76) peddling postcards and 100-year-old pornography, and rollerbladers dodging passersby.

❸ Walking through the Musée du Louvre courtyard early in the morning. Hurry to be among the first in line, and catch the morning sun glinting off the glass pyramids in the courtyard—it only heightens the excitement of waiting to see the masterpieces inside. See p. 50, ❶.

❹ Sitting in the center sculpture court of the Musée d'Orsay. Through the frosted glass that surrounds the huge ornate clock above the entrance, you can see the shadows of people passing by on invisible walkways. The sheer scale of this museum is astounding, and then there are the sculptures by some of history's finest artists. See p. 51, ❷.

> *Old bookstores and cafes line Paris's atmospheric covered shopping passages.*

⑤ Getting lost in the Château de Versailles gardens. This opulent château of Sun King Louis XIV was the *bijou* (jewel) in the royal crown. Nothing can beat a day spent ambling through the terraced gardens, admiring the fountains and Marie Antoinette's hamlet. Classical music extravaganzas take place here during the warmer months. See p. 135.

⑥ Contemplating the latest contemporary art installation at the Palais de Tokyo. It's priceless—that moment when everything you know about art flies out the window and you are confronted with something entirely new and unconventional. When you're ready for a break, ponder these revelations over a plate of delicious noodles in the gallery's Japanese restaurant, Tokyo Eat. See p. 60, ②.

⑦ Treating yourself in the Bristol's Michelin-starred restaurant. Just across the street from the French royal residence, politicians, stars, and socialites frequent Hôtel le Bristol's wood-paneled oval restaurant. Chef Eric Fréchon's legendary Bresse chicken is probably the most delicious *poulet* you'll ever taste. If you can't afford the evening menu, come for the less expensive lunch fare. See p. 118.

⑧ Attending a ballet at the Opéra Garnier. Charles Garnier's grande dame of performance spaces provides a breathtaking backdrop for ballet. Climb the majestic central staircase, order champagne for the *entr'acte* (intermission), and sink into your red velvet chair to admire Chagall's famous ceiling fresco before the lights go down. See p. 44, ⑧.

⑨ Shopping 'til you drop. Are you a designer junkie? A department store lover? A scavenger rooting out the world's most unique boutique? No matter. Paris provides a myriad of spending opportunities. And not just for clothes and accessories—family-run food shops, artisan outlets, and flea markets round out the shopping spectrum. See "Paris Shopping A to Z," p. 99.

⑩ Sipping tea in the Musée de la Vie Romantique's summer rose garden. The pink, ivy-clad house once frequented by George

Favorite Moments in Paris

1 Rubbing shoulders with Notre-Dame's gargoyles

2 Ambling along the Seine toward the islands

3 Walking through the Musée du Louvre courtyard early in the morning

4 Sitting in the center sculpture court of the Musée d'Orsay

5 Getting lost in the Château de Versailles gardens

6 Contemplating the latest contemporary art installation at the Palais de Tokyo

7 Treating yourself in the Bristol's Michelin-starred restaurant

8 Attending a ballet at the Opéra Garnier

9 Shopping 'til you drop

10 Sipping tea in the Musée de la Vie Romantique's summer rose garden

11 Climbing the streets of Montmartre

12 Tucking into steak frites at Chartier

13 Discovering Paris's covered passages

14 Marveling at the inventions in the Musée des Arts et Métiers

15 Strolling along Canal St-Martin

16 Enjoying a picnic in the Parc des Buttes Chaumont

17 Observing the "it" crowd at Mama Shelter

> *George Sand and Chopin once wandered this pretty rose garden—today's outdoor tearoom at the Musée de la Vie Romantique.*

Sand and Chopin feels like Paris's best-kept secret. Visit the museum, and then wind down in the garden over a Darjeeling tea and a *tarte du jour* (pie of the day), with just the buzzing of bees and the clinking of teacups for company. See p. 53.

⑪ Climbing the streets of Montmartre. In this hilly, hopelessly romantic neighborhood, a sweeping view of the city spreads out before you from almost every street corner. Every twist reveals yet another evocative stone staircase, which leads to yet another old pastel-painted building and down another cobblestone street. See p. 88.

⑫ Tucking into *steak frites* at Chartier. Waiters at this inexpensive yet classically Parisian restaurant, set in a huge 19th-century dining room, manage to be at once brusque and friendly, approving of all efforts to speak French. At the end of your meal, they add up the bill on the white paper that covers your table. See p. 110.

⑬ Discovering Paris's covered passages. These 18th- and 19th-century shelters for shopping and meeting are like living scenes from an old French detective novel. Each has its own personality and wood-paneled boutiques selling secondhand books, vintage accessories, handmade toys, gourmet treats, and more. See p. 105.

⑭ Marveling at the inventions in the Musée des Arts et Métiers. This museum contains some of the world's greatest inventions: Blaise Pascal's 17th-century calculator, the first plane to cross the English Channel, steam-powered carriages, and Henry Ford's Model T car and automated toys. See p. 55, ⑩.

⑮ Strolling along Canal St-Martin. Pass by the delicate iron bridges, the locks, and the occasional fisherman; lose yourself in bohemian boutiques; stop for a *café* before arriving at the Bassin de la Villette. Then continue to Parc de la Villette for a picnic or a trip around the Cité des Sciences museum. See p. 96, ❶.

⑯ Enjoying a picnic in the Parc des Buttes Chaumont. This man-made park in the northeast part of the city lends an edge to the city's green scene, with a glorious array of meandering paths, vertical cliffs, waterfalls, a lake, and hilltop views over Paris. Nowhere else in town will you see Buddhist monks meditating as children play football, chic Parisians take tai chi lessons, and joggers run by.

⑰ Observing the "it" crowd at Mama Shelter. We challenge you to find a trendier spot than this Philippe Starck–designed hotel-restaurant, where fashionistas flock for cocktails and excellent brasserie fare. People-watching has never been more fun. See p. 119.

Paris in 1 Day

From the fountain-strewn expanses of place de la Concorde, a mosaic of elegant squares, palaces, and parks unfurls. Once you've spent some time with the Musée d'Orsay's 19th-century masterpieces, the narrow cobblestone streets of Paris's islands beckon, before pointing you toward a cafe terrace in St-Germain for pre-dinner drinks. For this whirlwind, 1-day tour, we aim to show you everything we would want to see if we had only 24 hours in the City of Light. It's an ambitious itinerary, so start early and wear comfortable shoes.

> *The turreted Conciergerie is the oldest remaining part of the city's first royal palace, the Palais de la Cité.*

START Take the Métro to the Concorde stop.

① ★★ **Place de la Concorde.** The city's largest square is your own instant Paris postcard at any time of day or night. First admire the view of the **Eiffel Tower** (p. 48, **⑤**); then position yourself so you can see down the long, straight line of the avenue des **Champs-Elysées** (p. 45, **⑩**) to the formidable **Arc de Triomphe** (p. 48, **⑥**), a monument to Napoleon's conquests. Now turn 180 degrees, and find the **Tuileries gardens** (**②**, below) and, beyond that, the

Palais du Louvre, home to the world-class **Louvre Museum** (p. 50, **①**). To your left is the massive 19th-century, neoclassical **Madeleine Church**—a mirror image of the **Assemblée Nationale** across the Seine, which is home to the lower house of the French Parliament. Amid the fountains, tourists, and traffic stands the sleek, 3,300-year-old **Luxor Obelisk** (a gift from Egypt in 1829), near the spot where, in 1792, thousands of victims of the Revolution were guillotined, including Louis XVI and Marie Antoinette. Métro: Concorde.

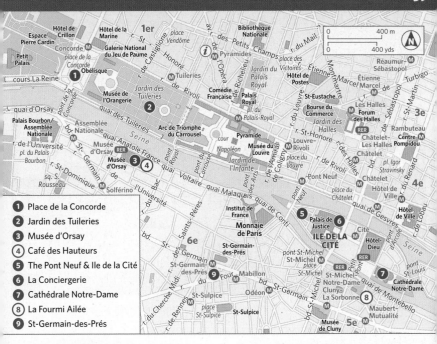

Map legend:

1. Place de la Concorde
2. Jardin des Tuileries
3. Musée d'Orsay
4. Café des Hauteurs
5. The Pont Neuf & Ile de la Cité
6. La Conciergerie
7. Cathédrale Notre-Dame
8. La Fourmi Ailée
9. St-Germain-des-Prés

2 ★★ kids **Jardin des Tuileries.** Place de la Concorde ends where the Palais du Louvre's stately gardens begin. On a space about the size of two football fields, lacy chestnut trees shade sculpted paths that stretch off the dusty main *allée* (path) leading to the Louvre Museum. ⏲ **20 min.** Jardin des Tuileries, 1st (bordering place de la Concorde). Métro: Tuileries, Palais Royal–Musée du Louvre, or Concorde.

3 ★★★ **Musée d'Orsay.** Architects created one of the world's great art museums from an old railway station, the neoclassical Gare d'Orsay, across the Seine from the Louvre. Devoted to the watershed years of painting, from 1848 to 1914, the collection contains treasures by the big-name Impressionists and post-Impressionists, plus the lesser-known groups (symbolists, pointillists, Nabis, realists, and late Romantics). ⏲ **2 hr.** See p. 51, **2**.

4 🍴 **Café des Hauteurs.** Have sandwiches and onion soup in the Musée d'Orsay's bustling top-floor cafe, and then indulge in a slice of rich chocolate cake. In summer, you can eat outside on the balcony while taking in views of the Seine. ☎ 01-45-49-47-03. Sandwich and cake 15€.

5 ★★★ **The Pont Neuf & Ile de la Cité.** When the weather's fine, one of the most Parisian things you can do is stroll along the Seine to the Ile de la Cité, the birthplace of Paris. Cross onto the island at the pont Neuf (New Bridge), which, despite its name, is the oldest bridge in the city, commissioned by Henri IV in 1578 (his statue still watches over the *pont*). Only one 16th-century square remains on the island—the pretty place Dauphine, recognizable by its pink brickwork, a reflection of Henri's taste for Italian classicism. Métro: Pont Neuf.

6 ★★ kids **La Conciergerie.** The fairy-tale towers that soar above the north end of the Ile de la Cité near the pont Neuf lead you to the fortress where Marie Antoinette was imprisoned before her execution. Its intimidating look is largely courtesy of a makeover from the 1850s, but most of the building is much older—several parts date to the 12th and 13th centuries, when it was a royal palace. During the French Revolution (p. 664), torture and execution were commonplace here, and the place became a symbol of terror. You can visit cells where prisoners were held, as well as former banquet halls and guard rooms; next door is the medieval

> Sun seekers lounge in the Square du Vert Gallant, an oasis of greenery at the foot of pont Neuf.

Ste-Chapelle (buy a dual ticket upon arrival), one of the most breathtaking chapels you'll ever see; the "light show" cast on the interior when the sun shines through the stained-glass windows is famed for its beauty. ⏱ 1 hr. 2 bd. du Palais, 1st. ☎ 01-53-40-60-97. http://conciergerie.monuments-nationaux.fr. Admission 7€ adults, 4.50€ ages 18–25, free for ages 17 and under. Mar–Oct daily 9:30am–6pm; Nov–Feb daily 9am–5pm. Métro: Cité.

SITE GUIDE PAGE 41

⑦ ★★★ Cathédrale Notre-Dame. Founded in 1160 by Maurice de Sully, bishop of Paris, Notre-Dame endured the passing of several wars of religion and centuries of kings before losing its riches to plunderers during the Revolution. Napoleon crowned himself Emperor here in 1804. But as the 19th century wore on, the cathedral fell into disrepair; it was scheduled for demolition until Victor Hugo, author of *The Hunchback of Notre-Dame,* led a successful campaign for its restoration.

⑧ 🍴 ★ **La Fourmi Ailée.** Escape the crowds by crossing pont du Double to the Left Bank, where the "Flying Ant" tearoom serves sticky cakes and excellent hot

dishes, such as veal blanquette (15€), in a lovely, shabby dining room reminiscent of a library. 8 rue du Fouarre, 5th. ☎ 01-43-29-40-99. Métro: Maubert Mutualité, Cluny-La Sorbonne.

⑨ ★★ St-Germain-des-Prés. This area was the incubator for artistic creativity in the 1920s and for student revolution in 1968. These days, you can get a great cup of coffee, drop a wad of money on high-fashion clothes, or spend a night on the town. The best way to experience the neighborhood is to wander along glittering, tree-lined boulevard St-Germain and its adjacent streets, taking in the street life and stopping at shops that spark your interest. The district is also the realm of Paris's historic literary cafes: the **Café de Flore,** 172 bd. St-Germain (☎ 01-45-48-55-26; www.cafedeflore.fr), a favorite of philosopher Jean-Paul Sartre, and **Les Deux Magots** (p. 125), a regular haunt of both Sartre and Hemingway. Both serve good food but at expensive prices. Keep in mind, though, that for the cost of your drink or meal, you can stay at your table and people-watch as long as you like. For a guided walk around St-Germain-des-Prés, see p. 78.

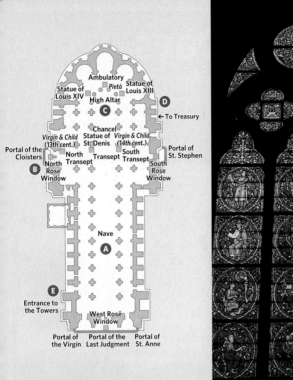

7 Cathédrale Notre-Dame

At the far end of the **A** **nave** are three elaborately sculpted 13th-century portals: on the left, the Portal of the Virgin; in the center, the Portal of the Last Judgment; and on the right, the Portal of St. Anne. Above them all glow the ruby hues of the West Rose Window, its beauty surpassed only by the **B** **North Rose Window.** The colors are especially vivid in the late afternoon. Near the altar is the 14th-century **C** **Virgin and Child.** In the **D** **treasury** is a collection of crosses and ancient reliquaries, including the Crown of Thorns (brought from Ste-Chapelle). Free guided visits in English take place most afternoons (usually 2–3pm, but check the website for details: http://notre-dame-de-paris.monuments-nationaux.fr). For a close look at the cathedral's famous gargoyles, you must climb 67m (220 ft.) up the **E** **tower** on an old stone staircase—a strenuous workout rewarded by views over Paris and the fanciful *Galerie des Chimères,* where you'll find yourself surrounded by hobgoblins, horned devils, and birds of prey.
🕐 1 hr. Parvis Notre-Dame/Place Jean Paul II, 4th. ☎ 01-42-34-56-10. www.cathedraledeparis.com. Free admission to cathedral, 8€ to towers, 3€ to treasury. Cathedral: daily 8am–6:45pm. Crypt: Apr–Sept daily 10am–6:30pm. Towers: Apr–Sept Mon–Fri 10am–6:30pm, Sat–Sun 10am–11pm; Jun–Aug daily 10am–11pm; Oct–Mar daily 10am–5:30pm. Treasury: Mon–Sat 9:30am–6pm, Sun 2–6pm. Métro: Cité.

Paris in 2 Days

If you followed the 1-day tour of Paris, you've already had a good introduction to the city. This Day 2 itinerary covers major sights on the Right Bank and will suit just about everybody, from lovers of art and architecture to those who like to wander the streets and let providence guide them to hidden treasures.

> *Napoleon's 50m-tall (164-ft.) Arc de Triomphe is a triumphant symbol of the French nation.*

START Take the Métro to the Louvre stop.

1 ★★★ **Musée du Louvre.** Arrive early, or after 6pm on Wednesdays and Fridays, to catch the shortest lines at what is arguably the world's greatest art museum. ⊙ 2 hr. See p. 50, **1**.

2 ★★ **Musée des Arts Décoratifs.** If lines into the Louvre are too long or you love interior design, don't miss this excellent museum, which contains one of the world's primary collections of design and decorative art. Set inside the palace but separate from the Louvre Museum, and sharing space with the Musée de la Mode and the Musée de la Publicité (fashion and advertising museums; both open for temporary exhibitions only), the museum covers a breathtaking anthology of pieces: medieval liturgical items, Art Nouveau and Art Deco furniture, Gothic paneling, Renaissance porcelain, psychedelic carpets from the 1970s, furniture by Philippe Starck, furnishings from France's high-speed TGV trains. Ten period rooms show how the museum's collections would have looked in a real house; the most memorable are couturier Jeanne Lanvin's early Art Deco purple boudoir and a grandiose Louis-Philippe bedchamber. ⊙ 1½ hr. 107 rue de Rivoli, 1st. ☎ 01-44-55-57-50. www. lesartsdecoratifs.fr. Admission 9€ adults, 7.50€ ages 18–25, free for ages 17 and under. Tues–Wed and Fri–Sun 11am–6pm; Thurs 11am–9pm. Métro: Palais Royal–Musée du Louvre.

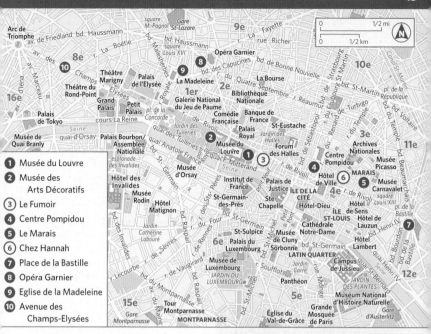

1. Musée du Louvre
2. Musée des Arts Décoratifs
3. Le Fumoir
4. Centre Pompidou
5. Le Marais
6. Chez Hannah
7. Place de la Bastille
8. Opéra Garnier
9. Eglise de la Madeleine
10. Avenue des Champs-Elysées

③ 🍷 ★ **Le Fumoir.** This handy spot near the Louvre and Arts Décoratifs museums has a faithful following from Paris's literary and media crowd. Sink into a Chesterfield armchair and order a refreshing fruit cocktail; or fill up on salads, steak, or vegetarian risotto. **6 rue de l'amiral Coligny, 1st. ☎ 01-42-92-00-24. Main courses 17€. Métro: Louvre-Rivoli.**

④ ★★ **Centre Pompidou.** This is the world's leading modern and contemporary art museum after MoMA in New York. The museum's bold, exoskeletal architecture, with brightly painted pipes, ducts, and escalator tubes crisscrossing on the outside, looks eccentric even by today's standards. ⏱ 1½ hr. See p. 61, ④.

⑤ ★★ **Le Marais.** Walk off your cultural overload on the winding medieval streets of the Marais district—traditionally the city's Jewish quarter. The neighborhood is home to magnificent 17th- and 18th-century mansions (called

> *La Belle Hortense in Le Marais (p. 127) nourishes minds with literature and souls with wine.*

hôtels), charming boutiques, tiny Jewish bakeries, and absorbing museums. One of its most picturesque squares is the pink-brick **place des Vosges,** formed by 36 arcades with sharply pitched roofs. In 1615, a 3-day party was held here to celebrate Louis XIII's marriage to Anne of Austria. Victor Hugo, author of *Les Misérables* and *The Hunchback of Notre-Dame,* lived here at

Paris in 3 Days

If you have 72 hours in the City of Light, spend your last day in Montmartre and follow the neighborhood walk on p. 88.

> *A palace? No, just the Opéra Garnier's sumptuous ceiling.*

no. 6. Today, his former apartments are a small museum displaying his first editions, more than 500 drawings, and his homemade furniture (6 place des Vosges, 4th; ☎ 01-42-72-10-16; www.musee-hugo.paris.fr; free admission; Tues–Sun 10am–6pm). Contemporary art lovers should flock to the northernmost part of the Marais, around rues Charlot, Turenne, and St-Onge, to take in Paris's most exciting commercial art galleries (p. 82). ⏱ 2 hr. Jewish shops and restaurants close on Sat. Many boutiques open on Sun. Métro: St-Paul or Rambuteau.

---

⑥   🍽 ★ **Chez Hannah.** Be prepared to queue at this buzzy cafe, which, along with the As du Falafel down the same street (no. 34) makes the best falafel sandwiches in the city (4€). 54 rue des Rosiers, 4th. ☎ 01-42-74-74-99. Sandwiches 6€–9€. Métro: St-Paul.

⑦ ★ **Place de la Bastille.** This square is the site of one of the most famous moments in French revolutionary history: the storming of the Bastille prison on July 14, 1789 (a few remnants of the prison can be seen on the nearby Métro platform). Today, the site is not so threatening—it's home to the modern **Opéra Bastille** (p. 133), whose resident Opéra National de Paris plays to the highest of standards. In the center of the busy traffic circle is the **Colonne de Juillet,** a column raised to honor the victims of the 1830 revolution, which, ironically, put Louis-Philippe on the throne after the upheaval of the Napoleonic Wars. Métro: Bastille.

⑧ ★★ **Opéra Garnier.** Now go see what opera used to look like in Paris, at Charles Garnier's architectural explosion, which goes beyond baroque and well into rococo. This was the city's main opera house until Opéra Bastille came along; now it also hosts ballet performances beneath an elaborate ceiling painted by Marc Chagall in 1964. The facade is all marble and flowing sculpture, with gilded busts, multihued pillars, and vivid mosaics. This is where the Phantom did his haunting (a lake below the opera house inspired novelist Gaston Leroux to create his tragic hero). Even if you don't want to see a ballet, buy a visitor's ticket (9€; 5€ for ages 24 and under) to admire the flamboyant, gilded interior, including the grand staircase and the main theater (daily 10am–5pm, until 1pm on matinee performance days). ⏱ 1 hr. Place de l'Opéra, 9th. ☎ 08-92-89-90-90 (0.34€/min.). www.operadeparis.fr. Tickets 23€–150€. Métro: Opéra.

⑨ ★★ **Eglise de la Madeleine.** Tear yourself away from the Art Nouveau–style department stores behind the opera house, on boulevard Haussmann (**Galeries Lafayette** and **Au Printemps,** p. 102), and head to this neoclassical church. It was designed by Barthélémy Vignon in 1806 as a "temple of glory" for Napoleon

Bonaparte, but after Napoleon's fall, construction slowed down and it wasn't consecrated until 1845. The exterior, which mirrors the **Assemblée Nationale** on the other side of place de la Concorde (p. 38, **❶**), is marked by fluted Corinthian columns. Inside highlights include a wonderful frieze of the Last Judgment and a painting of the history of Christianity by Jules-Claude Ziegler. The square around the church, **place de la Madeleine,** is a foodie paradise with top-end restaurants and luxury food shops such as **Fauchon** (p. 103). ⏱1 hr. Place de la Madeleine, 8th. ☎01-44-51-69-00. www.eglise-lamadeleine.com. Free admission. Daily 9:30am–7pm. Métro: Opéra.

❿ ★★ **Avenue des Champs-Elysées.** Although it's not as beautiful as most of us imagine, this 2km (1¼-mile) avenue—the symbolic gathering place for national parades and sports victory celebrations, thanks to Napoleon's early-19th-century **Arc de Triomphe** (p. 48, **❻**)—is inseparable from Paris in the minds of most people. It is part of Paris's **Golden Triangle** (along with avs. Georges V and Montaigne), where Chanel, Louis Vuitton, and other designer boutiques stand alongside lavish palace hotels such as the Hôtel Georges V. You'll find plenty for tighter budgets, too: high-street shops such as Virgin Megastore, FNAC, and Zara line the sidewalk, along with cinemas, bars, the **Lido** cabaret (p. 129), and the famous **Queen** nightclub (p. 132).

> *Couturier Jeanne Lanvin's Art Deco bedchamber is on display at the Musée des Arts Décoratifs.*

Monumental Paris

As you wander around Paris, every new turn seems to bring a different architectural icon into view—from the neoclassical splendor of the Palais de Justice on Ile de la Cité to the pointed, filigree heights of the Eiffel Tower. If you start this tour early and keep moving, you'll see many of the city's most glorious edifices all in one go, leaving enough time to make it to the Arc de Triomphe for sunset.

START Take the Métro to the Cité stop.

1 ★★★ **Palais de Justice, La Conciergerie & Ste-Chapelle.** This triple set of buildings comprises the **Palais de Justice** (law courts), the **kids Conciergerie** (formerly a prison, now a museum), and the exquisite **Ste-Chapelle.** The Palais is still the center of the French judicial system, and it's worth a peek inside at the grand lobby. Once a palace, the Conciergerie was converted to a prison during the Revolution and became a symbol of terror. Inside, you can visit the old cells, including a reconstruction of the jail where, in 1793, Marie Antoinette

stayed before being guillotined on place de la Concorde (p. 38, **1**). The Ste-Chapelle was built in the 13th century to hold a crown of thorns (now in Notre-Dame) that King Louis IX believed Christ wore during his crucifixion. World-renowned for its biblical stained glass, the chapel is stunning in afternoon light. ⏱1 hr. 2–6 bd. du Palais, 1st. ☎ 01-53-40-60-80. http://conciergerie.monuments-nationaux. fr. Palais de Justice: free admission. Combined Conciergerie and Ste-Chapelle: 11€ adults, 7.50€ ages 18–25, free for ages 17 and under. Mar–Oct daily 9:30am–6pm; Nov–Feb 9:30am–5pm. Métro: Cité.

> The Tour Eiffel is repainted brown by hand every 7 years.

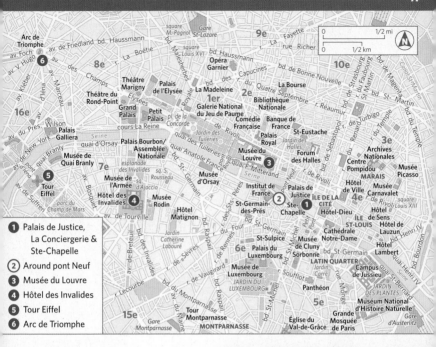

② 🍴 ★ **Around pont Neuf.** Place Dauphine, where the pont Neuf crosses the island, has several decent restaurants. Or, if you've brought a picnic lunch, go to the Square du Vert Galant opposite, at the tip of the Ile de la Cité, and spread out on the grass or at the water's edge. **Metro: Pont Neuf, Cité.**

❸ ★★★ **Musée du Louvre.** In 1527, François replaced most of the old Palais du Louvre (built by Philippe Auguste in 1190 as a fortress to protect Paris from the Vikings) with a Renaissance château. For the next 400 years, every king and queen made adjustments. The museum's newest addition is the sleek, modern renovation of the Visconti wing, which houses the Islamic art collection, slated to open in 2012. ⏱ 45 min. See p. 50, ❶.

❹ ★★★ **Hôtel des Invalides.** This imposing complex, with its beautiful Dôme des Invalides church (home to Napoleon's tomb), was built in 1670 by Louis XIV as a military hospital. Inside, the excellent **Musée de l'Armée** has enough historic weaponry to mount another revolution. *The Historical Charles de Gaulle* is a high-tech audiovisual monument covering

> *Elegant fountains were erected in 1840 to embellish place de la Concorde—home of the infamous guillotine during the Revolution.*

General de Gaulle's role in World War II. The **Musée des Plans Reliefs** houses the collection of scale-model cities used by Sébastien Vauban, a 17th-century military engineer, for

> *The Arc de Triomphe's arches are engraved with the names of those who died for the glory of France.*

planning attacks. ⏱ 1½ hr. 129 rue de Grenelle, 7th. ☎ 08-10-11-33-99. Admission 8.50€ adults, 6.50€ ages 18–26, free for ages 17 and under. Oct–Mar daily 10am–5pm; Apr–May and Sept daily 10am–6pm. Closed 1st Mon of the month. Métro: Invalides.

❺ ★★★ Tour Eiffel. The world's most famous iron tower, built by Gustave Eiffel in 1889 as a temporary exhibition for the World's Fair, was saved from demolition only by the advent of radio, when the tower, as the tallest structure in Europe at the time, seemed purpose-made for an antenna. The tower is 324m (1,063 ft.) high, and from the top you can see for 65km (40 miles). It's entirely worth the trip up. Visible from most parts of the city, it is best admired at night, when more than 3,000 bulbs sparkle for 10 minutes, on the hour. ⏱ 2 hr. Champ de Mars, 7th. ☎ 01-44-11-23-23. www.tour-eiffel.fr. Admission: Elevator to 1st floor 4.50€ adults, 2.30€ ages 3–11; elevator to 2nd floor 8€ adults, 6.40€ ages 12–24; top floor 13€ adults, 9.90€ ages 12–24; stairs to 1st and 2nd floors 4.50€ adults, 3.50€ ages 12–24, 3€

ages 4–11. Free for children 2 and under. Sept to mid-June 9:30am–11:45pm (last elevator to top floor 10:30pm, to 2nd floor 11pm, stairs 6pm); mid-June to Aug 9:30am–12:45am (last elevator to top 11pm, to 2nd floor and stairs midnight). Métro: Trocadéro, Ecole Militaire, or Bir-Hakeim. RER: Champ de Mars–Tour Eiffel.

❻ ★★★ Arc de Triomphe. The world's largest triumphal arch was commissioned by Napoleon in 1806 to commemorate the victories of his Grand Armée, but it wasn't finished until 1836, after his death. His remains, brought from Ste-Helena in 1840, passed under the arch on their journey to his final resting place at the Hôtel des Invalides. These days the arch is the focal point of state funerals and the site of the tomb of the Unknown Soldier, in whose honor an eternal flame burns. ⏱ 45 min. Place Charles de Gaulle-Etoile, 8th. ☎ 01-55-37-73-77. http://arc-de-triomphe.monuments-nationaux.fr. Admission 9€ adults, 5.50€ ages 18–25, free for ages 17 and under. Apr–Sept daily 10am–11pm; Oct–Mar daily 10am–10:30pm. Métro: Charles de Gaulle-Etoile.

Paris of the World Fairs

World Fairs (*Expositions Universelles*) in the 19th and early 20th centuries changed Paris's skyline forever, bestowing on the city wildly innovative constructions such as the ★★★ **Eiffel Tower** and Belle Epoque splendors such as the ★★★ **Grand Palais,** 3 av. du Général Eisenhower, 8th (☎ 01-44-13-17-17; www.rmn.fr; prices vary per exhibition; exhibitions only: Wed 10am–10pm, Thurs–Mon 10am–8pm; Métro: Champs-Elysées-Clémenceau or Franklin D. Roosevelt; RER: Invalides). The Grand Palais, a festival of Art Nouveau ironwork with a humongous glass roof, was built for the 1900 World's Fair. Inside you'll find the **Galeries Nationales,** one of France's most important exhibition centers, assembling world-class retrospectives of historically important artists. Also inside is the Palais de la Découverte science museum, av. Franklin D. Roosevelt (☎ 01-56-43-20-20; www.palais-decouverte.fr; admission 7€ adults, 4.50€ ages 24 and under; Tues–Sat 9:30am–6pm; Sun and some public holidays 10am–7pm). ★★★ Le Petit Palais, opposite the Grand Palais, was also built for the 1900

World's Fair, to stage French art. It's daintier in style, with Ionic columns, a dome, and a grand porch that echo those of the Hôtel des Invalides military museum across the river. A vast, angular, neoclassical structure, the ★★ **Palais de Chaillot** was built by Azéma, Boileau, and Carlu in 1937 as part of the International Exposition, replacing the Trocadéro Palace built for the 1878 World's Fair. Decorated with inscriptions by Paul Valéry and sculptures of Apollo by Henri Bouchard, it contains three museums—the kids **Cité de l'Architecture et du Patrimoine** architecture museum (p. 53, **7**); the kids **Musée National de la Marine,** 17 place du Trocadéro, 16th (☎ 01-53-65-69-69; www.musee-marine.fr); and the **Musée de l'Homme** (closed for renovations until further notice)—as well as the avant-garde dance **Théâtre National de Chaillot** (p. 133). If you want to eat in a dining room that's nearly unchanged since the 1900 World's Fair, head to the **Train Bleu** (p. 113)—a sumptuous example of Belle Epoque architecture, with gilded moldings and fresco-clad ceilings inside the Gare de Lyon (12th).

Best Museums

You'd need a lifetime to fully explore the hundreds of museums in Paris. Our selection includes behemoths such as the Louvre and the Centre Pompidou but also more intimate addresses dedicated to sculpture, inventions, and architecture. This section is not a tour per se, but a list to be dipped into as you please. All of Paris's municipal museums are free (see www.paris.fr for a full list).

> The Louvre's Winged Victory of Samothrace (c. 200 B.C.) would once have stood on the prow of a ship.

START Take the Métro to the Palais-Royal Musée du Louvre stop.

1 ★★★ **Musée du Louvre.** Now housing the most famous museum in France, if not the world, the Palais du Louvre was originally built in the 12th century as a royal fortress and palace for Philip II. (Remnants of the original structure can still be seen in the museum's basement.) This grand building contains paintings, sculptures, *objets d'art,* and graphic art from the Middle Ages to the late 19th century, as well as Greek, Etruscan, Roman, Oriental, and Egyptian antiquities. The vast collection just keeps getting bigger; a brand new Islamic art section is set to open in 2012

in the Visconti wing. Crowds flock to glimpse the Louvre's most famous ladies: the beguiling **Mona Lisa** (called *La Joconde* in French), the armless **Venus de Milo,** and the headless **Winged Victory** (c. 200 B.C.), discovered at Samothrace. But 30,000 additional works

Discount Admissions

If you plan to visit several nonmunicipal museums over 2, 4, or 6 days, you'll save money with the **Paris Museum Pass** (www. parismuseumpass.com; 2 days 32€, 4 days 48€, 6 days 64€), available for purchase at more than 60 participating museums.

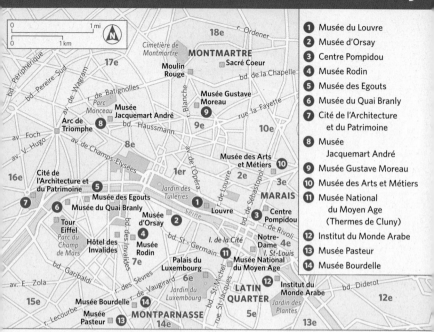

1. Musée du Louvre
2. Musée d'Orsay
3. Centre Pompidou
4. Musée Rodin
5. Musée des Egouts
6. Musée du Quai Branly
7. Cité de l'Architecture et du Patrimoine
8. Musée Jacquemart André
9. Musée Gustave Moreau
10. Musée des Arts et Métiers
11. Musée National du Moyen Age (Thermes de Cluny)
12. Institut du Monde Arabe
13. Musée Pasteur
14. Musée Bourdelle

await your discovery, in eight different departments: Egyptian Antiquities; Oriental Antiquities; Greek, Etruscan, and Roman Antiquities; Sculpture; Painting; Islamic Arts; Decorative Arts; and Graphic Arts. *Tip:* To avoid the lines, buy tickets from the automatic machines and enter the museum inside the Carousel du Louvre, 99 rue de Rivoli. Avoid the crowds by visiting either first thing in the morning or after 6pm Wednesday or Friday. ⏱ 2 hr. Louvre, 1st (entrance via glass pyramid in the main courtyard or at 99 rue de Rivoli). ☎ 01-40-20-50-50. www.louvre.fr. Admission 9€ adults, free for ages 17 and under, free for everyone 1st Sun of the month. Thurs and Sat-Mon 9am–6pm; Wed and Fri 9am–10pm. Métro: Palais Royal–Musée du Louvre or Louvre Rivoli.

2 ★★★ **Musée d'Orsay.** This old Belle Epoque train station, built for the 1900 World's Fair, picks up where the Louvre leaves off, with works from 1848 to 1914. Fans of Impressionism will be in paradise amid masterpieces such as Manet's *Le déjeuner sur l'herbe (The Picnic on the Grass)* and Degas's ballerinas, who still twirl for the crowds' cameras as if they were painted yesterday. Numerous works by Cézanne, Sisley, and Monet complete the set. The post-Impressionist collection includes world-renowned pieces by van Gogh, Cross, Seurat, Rousseau, and Gauguin and others from the School of Pont-Aven.

Be sure to spend some time in the light-filled central hall, dominated by a huge, ornate clock. Statues of robust maidens and eager men by Rude, Barye, and Carrier-Belleuse (all 19th-century sculptors) stand where the train tracks once lay. Those by Carpeaux, including *La Danse* (once controversial for its frolicking nude figures), are extraordinary. Check the schedule for the museum's excellent lunchtime and evening classical music concerts, often held in conjunction with temporary exhibitions in the downstairs auditorium. ⏱ 2–3 hr. 1 rue de la Légion d'Honneur, 7th. ☎ 01-40-49-48-14. www.musee-orsay.fr. Admission 9.50€ adults, 8€ ages 18–25, free for ages 17 and under (you can buy tickets in advance online or from FNAC). Tues–Wed and Fri–Sun 9:30am–6pm; Thurs 9:30am–9:45pm. Métro: Solférino and Assemblée Nationale. RER: Musée d'Orsay.

3 ★★★ **Centre Pompidou.** This flashy, multicolored construction—dreamed up by former French president George Pompidou and constructed in 1977 by architects Richard Roger

> *Trains once stood where some of the world's best 19th-century art hangs today in the Musée d'Orsay.*

> *Pondering away in the Musée Rodin's garden, Le Penseur (The Thinker) embodies the best of Rodin's technique.*

and Renzo Piano—is a requisite stop for lovers of modern art. Be sure to take the panoramic escalators to the top for breathtaking views over Paris's gray rooftops. ⏱ 2 hr. See p. 61, ④.

④ ★★★ **Musée Rodin.** This museum, housed in the glorious 18th-century mansion that was once Rodin's studio, inspires thoughts of romance. Rodin's most famous statue, *Le Penseur (The Thinker),* entertains his thoughts in the sublime gardens, while inside the lovers in *Le Baiser* are locked in a permanent embrace. The "father of modern sculpture" willed to the French state many of the works on display, in exchange for his free lodgings here. The shaded alleys and gardens can be visited separately from the museum and provide plenty of opportunities for canoodling. ⏱ 1 hr. Hôtel Biron, 79 rue de Varenne, 7th. ☎ 01-44-18-61-10. www.musee-rodin.fr. Museum admission 6€ adults, 5€ ages 18–25, free for ages 17 and under; gardens only 1€. Tues–Sun 10am–5:45pm. Métro: Varenne or Invalides. RER: Invalides.

> *Street signs guide visitors through the bowels of the city in the Musée des Egouts.*

⑤ ★ kids Musée des Egouts. Deep below the streets of Paris lies a vast network of limestone tunnels, sewers, and Métro lines that are as much a part of daily life as the streets above (see "What Lies Beneath," p. 58). Paris's smelliest museum retraces the history of all 2,100km (1,305 miles) of the city's sewers, in a fascinating series of films, exhibitions, and tours through the tunnels. Closed in bad weather. ⏱ 45 min. Pont de l'Alma (Left Bank, opposite 53 quai d'Orsay), 7th. ☎ 01-53-68-27-81. www.paris.fr. Admission 4.30€ adults, 3.50€ ages 6–16 and students with valid card,

free for children 5 and under. May–Sept Sat–Wed 11am–5pm; Oct–Apr Sat–Wed 11am–4pm. Métro: Alma-Marceau. RER: Pont de l'Alma.

⑥ ★★ Musée du Quai Branly. This museum, in a quirky building designed by Jean Nouvel, explores the treasures, arts, and civilizations of Africa, Oceania, and the Americas. ⏱ 1 hr. 37–55 Quai Branly, 7th. ☎ 01-56-61-70-00. www.quaibranly.fr. Admission 8.50€ adults, 6€ ages 18–25. Thurs–Sat 11am–9pm, Sun and Tues–Wed 11am–7pm. RER: Pont de l'Alma.

⑦ ★★ Cité de l'Architecture et du Patrimoine. Comprising 8 sq. km (3 sq. miles) of space in the east wing of the Palais de Chaillot, the City of Architecture and Heritage is dedicated to French architectural heritage and its development through the ages. More than 850 copies of architectural treasures are on display; these include molded portions of churches, châteaux, and great French cathedrals and also reconstructions of modern architecture, the centerpiece of which is an apartment by Le Corbusier. Don't miss the wall painting gallery downstairs, with its stunning reconstructed church vaults, domed ceilings, and a collection of frescoes copied from medieval murals. ⏱ 2 hr. Palais de Chaillot, 1 place du Trocadéro, 16th. ☎ 01-58-51-52-00. www.citechaillot.org. Admission 8€

A Cultural Tea Break: Musée de la Vie Romantique

Hidden from the rest of the world, the rose garden at the ★★★ **Musée de la Vie Romantique**—a charming, green-shuttered, 18th-century mansion that once hosted Rossini, Chopin, George Sand, and Delacroix—doubles as an outdoor tearoom. Decadence is yours for the price of your *café* and *tarte au citron* (lemon tart). *16 rue Chaptal, 9th. ☎ 01-55-31-95-67. www.paris.fr. Tues–Sun 10am–6pm. Free admission. Métro: Pigalle, St-Georges, or Blanche.*

> *Painter Gustave Moreau's ornate staircase leads to his third-floor artist's atelier.*

adults, 5€ ages 19–25, free for ages 18 and under, free 1st Sun of the month. Wed and Fri–Mon 11am–7pm; Thurs 11am–9pm. Métro: Trocadéro.

⑧ ★★ Musée Jacquemart André. This collection of rare 18th-century French paintings and furnishings, 17th-century Dutch and Flemish paintings, and Italian Renaissance works is fit for a king. The salons drip with gilt and the ultimate in *fin de siècle* style. Works by Bellini, Carpaccio, Uccelo, Van Dyck, Rembrandt, Tiepolo, Rubens, Watteau, Boucher, Fragonard, and Mantegna hang on the walls. If you fancy a decadent *pause gourmand* (gourmet snack), Mme. Jacquemart's high-ceilinged tearoom complies, with sticky cakes and piping hot tea (11:45am–5:30pm). ⏱ 1 hr. 158 bd. Haussmann, 8th. ☎ 01-45-62-11-59. www.musee-jacquemart-andre.com. Admission 10€ adults, 7.50€ ages 7–17, free for children 6 and under. Daily 10am–6pm. Métro: Miromesnil or St-Philippe du Roule.

⑨ ★★ Musée Gustave Moreau. Moreau was around at the same time as the Impressionists, but he worked against the prevailing mood, drawing inspiration from the Bible, Greek mythology, Leonardo da Vinci, and Indian miniatures. This atmospheric museum, where he lived and worked, reveals Moreau's obsession for knickknacks and furniture, which are displayed alongside his fabulous mythical beasts and fantasy worlds. Don't miss his masterpiece, *Jupiter & Sémélé,* the lovers Zeus struck down with lightning after saving their child Dionysus, god of wine, agriculture, and theater. **Tip:** The museum closes at lunchtime, but if you start your visit in the morning, you can reenter in the afternoon using the same ticket. ⏱ 1 hr. 14 rue de la Rochefoucauld, 9th. ☎ 01-48-74-38-50. www.musee-moreau.fr. Admission 5€ adults, 3€ ages 18–25, free for ages 17 and under, free for everyone 1st Sun of the month. Wed–Mon 10am–12:45pm and 2–5:15pm. Métro: Trinité.

Museum Curiosities

Parisians have a taste for the weird and wonderful—a fact reflected in three surprising museums. The **Musée de l'Erotisme,** 72 bd. de Clichy, 18th (☎ 01-42-58-28-73; www.musee-erotisme.com; admission 8€; daily 10am–2am), in Pigalle's red-light district, presents a tasteful but risqué collection of erotic art and artifacts, including an informative section on Paris's 19th-century brothels. The **Musée de la Préfecture de Police,** set inside a working police station at 4 rue de la Montagne St-Geneviève, 5th (☎ 01-44-41-52-50; www.prefecturedepolice.interieur.gouv.fr; admission free; Mon–Fri 9am–5pm, Sat 10am–5pm), covers a different aspect of Paris's underbelly: Crime is the focus here, brought to life through VIP arrest warrants and an array of gruesome-looking weapons. The **Musée Dupuytren,** 15 rue de l'Ecole-de-Medecine, Centre des Cordeliers, 6th (☎ 01-42-34-68-60; www.upmc.fr; admission 5€; Mon–Fri 2–5pm), part of a Paris medical school, features jars from the 18th to the 20th centuries containing intriguing body parts gone wrong—namely tumors, cysts, and even a Cyclops foetus.

> *Napoleon III once welcomed guests inside this monumental winter garden at the Musée Jacquemart André.*

10 ★★★ **Musée des Arts et Métiers.** This museum, founded in the 18th century by Abbot Grégoire as "a store for useful, new inventions," is an absolute gem. Housed in the former Benedictine church and priory of St-Martin-des-Champs, it exhibits some of the world's greatest inventions, from Pascal's calculating devices and celestial spheres to the first computers, steam-powered vehicles, and even airplanes (including the monoplane Louis Blériot flew across the English Channel in 1909). ⏲ 2 hr. 60 rue Réamur, 3rd. ☎ 01-53-01-82-00. www.arts-et-metiers.net. Admission 6.50€ adults, 4.50€ ages 18–25, free for ages 17 and under. Tues, Wed, Fri–Sun 10am–6pm; Thurs 10am–9:30pm. Métro: Arts et Métiers.

11 ★★ **Musée National du Moyen Age (Thermes de Cluny).** Along with the Hôtel de Sens in the Marais, the Hôtel de Cluny is all that remains of domestic medieval architecture in Paris. Enter through the cobblestoned **Cour d'Honneur** (Court of Honor), where you can admire the flamboyant Gothic building with

> *L'Avion 3, in the Musée des Arts et Métiers, hangs with its original wings of silk and bamboo.*

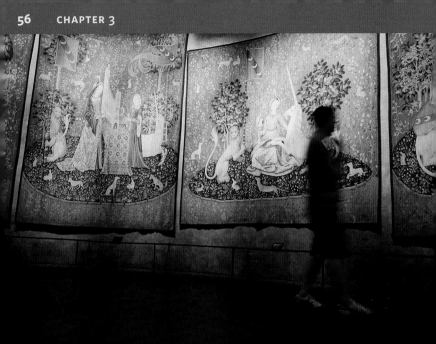

> *At the Musée National du Moyen Age, five of the six* Lady and the Unicorn *tapestries symbolize the senses: taste, smell, hearing, touch, and sight.*

its vines, turreted walls, gargoyles, and dormers with seashell motifs. Most people come to see the *La dame à la licorne (The Lady and the Unicorn)* series of tapestries, the most acclaimed of their kind, in which all the romance of the age of chivalry—a beautiful princess, her handmaiden, beasts of prey, and house pets—lives on. Downstairs are the ruins of the **Roman baths** (c. A.D. 200), including a column dedicated to Jupiter called the *Column of the Boatmen,* believed to be the oldest sculpture created in Paris. ⏱ 1½ hr. 6 place Paul Painlevé, 5th. ☎ 01-53-73-78-00. www.musee-moyenage. fr. Admission 8.50€ adults, 6.50€ ages 18–25, free for ages 17 and under, free for everyone 1st Sun of the month. Wed–Mon 9:15am–5:45pm. Métro: Cluny–La Sorbonne, St-Michel, or Odéon.

⓬ ★★ **Institut du Monde Arabe.** Designed in 1987 by architect Jean Nouvel, this museum explores Arab religion, philosophy, and politics through calligraphy, decorative arts, architecture, and photography. ⏱ 1 hr. 1 rue des Fossés St-Bernard, place Mohammed V, 5th. ☎ 01-40-51-38-38. www.imarabe.org. Admission 5€ adults, 4€ students, free for children 11 and under. Temporary exhibits vary. Roof terrace and cafe: free admission. Tues–Sun 10am–6pm. Métro: Jussieu or Cardinal Le Moine.

⓭ ★★ **Musée Pasteur.** Louis Pasteur revolutionized the modern diet, with his namesake process of "pasteurization"; the fascinating Musée Pasteur is where he lived and worked. Learn about his discoveries in the former lab, and visit his apartments, still adorned with family portraits and *objets d'art.* The basement crypt, where Pasteur's body was laid to rest, is a breathtaking neo-Byzantine–style mausoleum covered with intricate mosaics, several of which refer to his scientific discoveries. ⏱ 1 hr. 25 rue du Docteur-Roux, 15th. ☎ 01-45-68-82-83. www.pasteur.fr. Admission 3€ adults, 1.50€ students. Mon–Fri 2–5:30pm. Métro: Pasteur.

⓮ ★★ **Musée Bourdelle.** Hidden away from the hustle and bustle of Montparnasse is the workshop where Rodin's star pupil, Antoine Bourdelle (1861–1929), lived and worked. The sumptuous array of statues, many inspired

> *The geometric motifs on the Institut du Monde Arabe's facade are moving apertures designed to regulate sunlight.*

by Greek mythology, includes the *Centaure Mourant (Dying Centaur)*, writhing in agony; *Penelope*, Ulysses' wife, who waited 20 years for her husband to return; and, in the gorgeous walled garden, the colossal *General Alvear* horse statue (part of an allegorical monument that was never finished). ⊕ 1½ hr. 16–18 rue Antoine-Bourdelle, 15th. ☎ 01-49-54-73-73. www.bourdelle.paris.fr. Free admission. Tues–Sun 10am–6pm. Closed public holidays. Métro: Montparnasse-Bienvenue.

> *Sculptor Antoine Bourdelle was greatly influenced by Greek and Medieval sculpture.*

WHAT LIES BENEATH
The City of Light's Dark Underbelly

BY ANNA BROOKE

SINCE BEFORE ROMAN TIMES, settlers quarried the limestone bedrock of Paris in order to build the streetscape above. As the city expanded, so too did the man-made cavern system below it, chiseled out, stone by stone, creating a mysterious underground labyrinth of tunnels, crypts, transport lines, canals, reservoirs, sewers, quarries, and cemeteries.

LES CARRIERES (THE QUARRIES)

The scope of Paris's underground remained unknown until 1774, when a building collapsed into a quarry *(un carrière)*, prompting Louis XVI to create the IGC (Inspection Général des Carrières), to map out every passageway. The IGC still monitors the *carrières* today, ensuring that structures remain stable and that people don't roam where they shouldn't.

Initially created to provide building materials, *les carrières* have functioned as cemeteries, mushroom farms, wine storage areas, Nazi bunkers, and hiding places for the Resistance in World War II. Some Parisians had doorways in their basements that led to the quarries, but in 1955, passage was made illegal.

That hasn't stopped trespassers, known as *cataphiles* (pictured above), who descend, sometimes for days at a time, for clandestine parties or to paint art on the walls. Some *cataphiles* go deeper, bringing oxygen tanks and diving gear in case they come across water chambers. Since the 1980s, a special police force (nicknamed the *cataflics*) works to see they don't end up like Philibert Aspairt, a Parisian who descended into the *carrières* in 1793 and didn't reappear until his skeleton was found in 1804.

PLASTER OF PARIS

Limestone covers most of the Left Bank, but to the north, especially around Montmartre, the quarries yielded gypsum, used to make Plaster of Paris. Just below the Butte, the Métro Blanche ("white") takes its name from the white rock and dust resulting from gypsum extraction.

THE CATACOMBS

In the late 18th century, the Cimetière des Innocents (Innocents Cemetery) in Les Halles was bursting at the seams and spreading disease, so the city rehoused the rotting bodies in the tunnels below Denfert-Rochereau. Workers respectfully piled millions of bones along the tunnel walls, fashioning skulls, tibias, and femurs into facades. Open to visitors (see p. 94, **7**), the eerie sight has intrigued thousands of people over the centuries, including Napoleon III, who visited in 1860.

THE MUSHROOMS

In the early 19th century, Parisians disposed of horse droppings in the *carrières*. In 1814, a vegetable grower named Monsieur Chambry investigated the disused quarry tunnels below his gardens and discovered edible mushrooms growing on piles of manure. Thus was born *le*

champignon de Paris. Nowadays, Scandinavia, China, and the U.S. dominate the market for the fungus, but for years, France was the world's largest *champignon de Paris* producer.

UNDERGROUND LAKES

The Opéra Garnier (p. 44, **8**) sits above an underground lake. When architect Charles Garnier was building the structure in 1861, water from an ancient, buried branch of the Seine kept infiltrating the foundations. Garnier's solution was to pump the water away into a man-made underground lagoon 55m (180 ft.) long and 3.7m (12 ft.) deep. In 1910 the lake below the Opéra Garnier inspired Gaston Laroux to write *The Phantom of the Opera*. Today the lake is home to some fish and to *pompiers* (firefighters), practicing underwater rescue.

THE SEWERS

Paris has one of the world's oldest sewer systems—*les égouts* (p. 53, **5**)—created in the 1850s by Baron Haussmann. Some 2,500km (1,305 miles) of sewer pipes and tunnels—equivalent to the distance between Paris and Istanbul—run under the city. When Paris was at war, the armed forces used the sewers to hide weapons and soldiers. In the 1980s, when it became fashionable to keep exotic pets, it wasn't uncommon to find abandoned animals in the sewers.

Best Modern & Contemporary Art

You have only to look at the Louvre's glass pyramid or the Centre Pompidou's madcap building to recognize that Parisians can be unconventional when they put their minds to it—a fact that is reflected in the city's art scene. This guide shows you where to find Paris's biggest contemporary art venues as well as a selection of interesting smaller galleries.

> *Palais de Tokyo is famed for its weird and wild art installations that please both young and old.*

START Take the Métro to the Rambuteau stop.

1 ★★ **Musée d'Art Moderne de la Ville de Paris.** Take yourself on a journey through 20th-century "isms" as expressed in works by Braque, Dufy, Picasso, Léger, Matisse, and others, presented chronologically. ⏱ 2 hr. 11 av. du Président Wilson, 16th. ☎ 01-53-67-40-00. www.mam.paris.fr. Free admission. Tues–Sun 10am–6pm (until 10pm Thurs for temporary exhibitions). Métro: Alma-Marceau or Iéna. RER: Pont de l'Alma.

2 ★★ **Palais de Tokyo.** This *site de création contemporaine* is a showcase for experimental art on a big scale. Selected artists are invited to temporarily fill the space with whatever eccentricities they can muster. It is hard to leave this cutting-edge gallery without feeling as though you've challenged your perception of art. ⏱ 2 hr. 13 av. du Président Wilson, 16th. ☎ 01-47-23-38-86. www.palaisdetokyo.com. Admission 6€ adults, 4.50€ ages 19–26, free for ages 18 and under. Open Tues–Sun noon–midnight. Métro: Alma-Marceau or Iéna. RER: Pont de l'Alma.

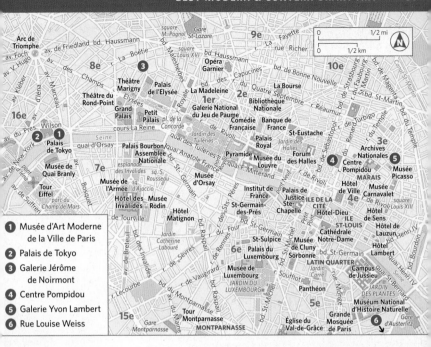

1. Musée d'Art Moderne de la Ville de Paris
2. Palais de Tokyo
3. Galerie Jérôme de Noirmont
4. Centre Pompidou
5. Galerie Yvon Lambert
6. Rue Louise Weiss

③ Galerie Jérôme de Noirmont. French and international artists of worldwide renown, plus a few newcomers, are on display here. Exhibitions are consistently eye-catching, including work by the iconoclastic American Jeff Koons and kitschy double-act Pierre et Gilles. ⏱ 45 min. 36–38 av. Matignon, 8th. ☎ 01-42-89-89-00. www.denoirmont.com. Free admission. Mon–Sat 11am–7pm. Métro: Miromesnil.

④ ★★★ Centre Pompidou. This benchmark art venue, designed by Richard Rogers and Renzo Piano, is one of the best-known sites in Paris, holding the largest collection of modern art in Europe. The permanent collections cover 20th- and 21st-century art, with some 40,000 rotating works. The fifth floor is dedicated to modern art from 1905 to 1960, covering fauvism, cubism, interwar art, surrealism, abstract expressionism, and neorealism. The fourth floor covers 1960 to the modern day, with themed rooms that focus on movements such as anti-form art (arte povera) and video installations. Don't miss the viewing point on the sixth floor, where Paris itself becomes a masterpiece. In a nearby annex, the Atelier Brancusi displays sculptor Constantin

Brancusi's fragile wood and plaster works in a re-creation of his workshop. ⏱ 2 hr. Place Georges Pompidou, 4th. ☎ 01-44-78-12-33. www.centre-pompidou.fr. Admission 10€ adults, 8€ students and ages 18–25, free for ages 17 and under. Wed–Mon 11am–10pm (until 11pm Thurs). Métro: Rambuteau or Hôtel de Ville. RER: Châtelet–Les Halles.

⑤ ★ Galerie Yvon Lambert. This multidisciplinary Paris gallery, with branches in New York and Avignon (p. 424, ⑦), includes a showroom exhibiting work by leading international artists such as Sol LeWitt and Jenny Holzer and an art bookshop–cum–basement gallery where younger artists are given precious exhibition space. ⏱ 45 min. 108 rue Vieille du Temple, 3rd. ☎ 01-42-71-09-33. www.yvon-lambert.com. Free admission. Tues–Fri 2:30–7pm; Sat 10am–7pm. Métro: République.

⑥ ★★ Rue Louise Weiss. This street in the 13th arrondissement is one of the hippest places to exhibit work. Try **Air de Paris** (no. 32) for extreme neoconceptualism; **GB Agency** (no. 20) for emerging artists; and **Jousse Enterprise** (nos. 24–34) for avant-garde furniture. ⏱ 1 hr. Métro: Chevaleret.

Paris with Kids

Let's face it: Most kid-approved attractions are outdoors, which means you're dangerously reliant on good weather. But this selection has been designed to keep them smiling come rain or shine. Of course, even the best-laid plans fail—in which case you can rush them off for a day at Disneyland Paris (p. 136).

> *Horseback or carriage? Kids love a ride on the carousel at the foot of the Eiffel Tower.*

START Take the Métro to the Odéon stop.

1 ★★★ **Jardin du Luxembourg.** Kids can run amok in these elegant gardens. Statues peek out everywhere as children sail toy boats on the ponds, ride the ponies, or catch a puppet show. Kids can also watch the locals play *boules* and chess, though it's unlikely they'll be invited to join in. Don't miss the ornate, evocative **fontaine Médicis,** in the northeast corner of the park. ⏲ 1 hr. See p. 78, **1**.

2 **Musée National d'Histoire Naturelle.** A giant whale skeleton greets kids just inside the front door of this natural history museum. Beyond those bones are more skeletons of dinosaurs and mastodons, and galleries filled with sparkling minerals and rare plants. In the surrounding gardens (the Jardin des Plantes, p. 72, **11**), there's even a menagerie with small animals in simulated natural habitats. ⏲ 1½ hr. See p. 73, **12**.

3 ★★★ **Parc de la Villette.** Take the Métro to Jaurès or Stalingrad in the 19th arrondissement, to stroll or bike along the redeveloped Canal de l'Ourcq to Parc de la Villette, a retro-futurist succession of gardens for kids to run around in. There's also an **IMAX cimema,** 26 av. Corentin-Cariou (☎ 01-40-05-79-99; www.lageode.fr), and a children's science museum, **Cité des Sciences.** The **Parc des Buttes Chaumont** is also nearby. ⏲ 3 hr. See p. 97, **8**.

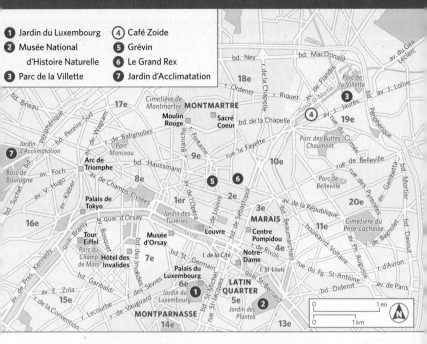

1. Jardin du Luxembourg
2. Musée National d'Histoire Naturelle
3. Parc de la Villette
4. Café Zoide
5. Grévin
6. Le Grand Rex
7. Jardin d'Acclimatation

④ 🍴 ★ **Café Zoide.** If your family needs refreshments along the canal, try Café Zoide. It's a children-friendly cafe with dozens of games, for babies to kids up to 16 years old. 92bis quai de la Loire, 19th. ☎ 01-42-38-26-37. www.cafezoide.asso. fr. Drinks from 2€. Métro: Jaurès.

⑤ **Grévin.** At this waxworks museum, kids can wander among celebrities—both international, from Madonna to Gandhi, and French, including soccer star Zinédine Zidane. Among the 300 wax figures, you'll find heads of state, artists, writers, and historical figures. 🕐 1 hr. 10 bd. Montmartre, 9th. ☎ 01-47-70-85-05. www.grevin.com. Admission 20€ adults, 12€ ages 6-14, 10€ ages 5 and under. Mon-Fri 10am-6:30pm; Sat-Sun 10am-7pm. Métro: Grands Boulevards.

⑥ ★★★ **Le Grand Rex.** The Grand Rex Cinema is one of Europe's last remaining Art Deco movie palaces. It is a hit with families; tours lead them into the heart of cinema projection, backstage into the projection room, behind the giant screen, into the film director's office, and into a special effects room where visitors become Hollywood actors and remake scenes from famous movies, such as *King Kong*. 🕐 1 hr. Le Grand Rex, 1 bd. Poissonière. ☎ 01-45-08-93-58. www.legrandrex.com. Admission 15.50€ adults, 13.50€ ages 15 and under. Wed-Sun (and public holidays) 10am-7pm. Métro: Bonne-Nouvelle.

⑦ ★★ **Jardin d'Acclimatation.** Let the kids while away the rest of a sunny afternoon here. You can start with a ride on a narrow-gauge train from Porte Maillot to the entrance (every 30 min., Wed and Sat-Sun). In the park, there's a house of mirrors, an archery range, miniature golf, a small zoo, a bowling alley, a puppet theater, playgrounds, kid-size rides, shooting galleries, and food stalls. Kids can ride ponies, paddle about in boats, and even drive little cars. Bear in mind that it's only for little ones; teenagers will likely hate it. 🕐 2-3 hr. Bois de Boulogne, 16th. ☎ 01-40-67-90-82. www.jardindacclimatation.fr. Admission: 2.90€ to enter (then prices vary for each attraction), free for children 3 and under. June-Sept daily 10am-7pm; Oct-May daily 10am-6pm. Métro: Sablons or Porte Maillot.

Free & Dirt-Cheap Paris

Paris is without doubt one of the world's most expensive cities, with something on every street corner tempting you to forfeit your precious euros. Even so, it's possible to spend a day in the city without spending more than 20€. Paris's majestic streets themselves provide unlimited, free eye candy, and it takes just a bit of planning to experience even more on a shoestring. We recommend packing a picnic for lunch and a bottle of water.

START Take the Métro to the Champs-Elysées–Clémenceau stop.

1 ★★★ **Le Petit Palais.** Built in 1900 for the World's Fair, and lit entirely by natural light, the "Little Palace" is one of Paris's loveliest fine arts museums, with paintings and sculptures from the Renaissance to 1900 and an extensive collection of works by Ingrès, Delacroix, Courbet, and the Impressionists. Art Nouveau fans get more than an eyeful in the downstairs galleries; sections are devoted to Belle Epoque luminaries such as Hector Guimard (designer of Paris's iconic Métro entrances), whose entire dining room is reproduced here, and ceramicist Jean Carriès, whose grotesque masks and imaginary creatures add an element of fairy-tale fantasy. ⊕ 1 hr. Av. Winston Churchill, 8th. ☎ 01-53-43-40-00. www.petitpalais.paris.fr. Free admission. Tues–Sun 10am–6pm. Closed public holidays. Métro: Champs-Elysées–Clémenceau.

> *An Art Nouveau-era plate in Le Petit Palais.*

2 ★★ **Musée Cernuschi.** Besides being one of Paris's oldest museums, inaugurated in 1898, the fabulous Cernuschi contains France's second-largest collection of Chinese art. More than 900 pieces are on display, assembled by Italian banker Henri Cernuschi on his travels to the Far East in the 1870s. The collection covers a complete range of Chinese dynasties, from Neolithic terracottas and Wei dynasty funeral statues (A.D. 386–534) to Sung porcelain, jade amulets, and a rare assortment of Liao dynasty gold *objets d'art* (A.D. 907–1125). ⊕ 1 hr. 7 av. Vélasquez, 8th. ☎ 01-53-96-21-50. www.cernuschi.paris.fr. Free admission. Tues–Sun 10am–6pm. Closed public holidays. Métro: Villiers or Monceau.

③ 🍃 **Parc Monceau.** Welcome to your picnic spot. Ringed with stunning 18th- and 19th-century mansions, this elegant park was designed by Carmontelle in 1778

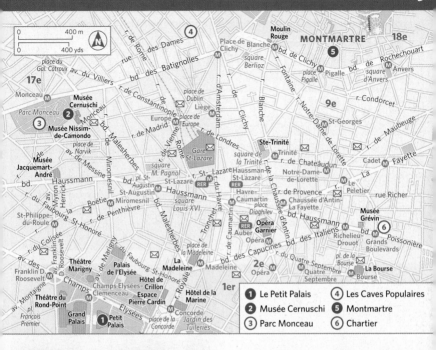

❶ Le Petit Palais	❹ Les Caves Populaires
❷ Musée Cernuschi	❺ Montmartre
❸ Parc Monceau	❻ Chartier

> Food platters and wine are served with a smile at Les Caves Populaires.

as a hideaway for the Duke of Orleans. Admire the Roman columns and a small Egyptian pyramid as you tuck into your baguette. If you haven't bought your food yet, we recommend the street market on rue de Lévis by the Villiers Métro stop. Métro: Monceau or Villiers.

④ 🍷 **Les Caves Populaires.** This rustic local haunt on one of Paris's most bohemian streets is the perfect spot for a coffee or a glass of wine after lunch. Starting at just 2.50€, it's a steal. **22 rue des Dames, 17th. ☎ 01-53-04-08-32. Mon–Sat 8am–2am, Sun 11am–2am. Métro: place de Clichy.**

❺ ★★★ **Montmartre.** You could spend a day wandering the arty streets of this village within the city and taking in some of Paris's finest views along the way. ⏱ **2 hr. See p. 88.**

⑥ 🍷 **Chartier.** This classic French brasserie serves some of the best no-frills French cuisine in town, with starters from 1.80€ (think carrot salad with vinaigrette) and main courses from 8.70€ (such as chicken and fries). **7 rue du Faubourg, Montmartre, 9th. See p. 110.**

Deals on Wheels

This itinerary is designed for walkers, but for 1€ you could also hire a **Vélib** (www.velib.paris.fr), one of Paris's self-service bikes.

Hip Paris: The 20th Arrondissement

Hip urbanites flock to this underdeveloped area north of Père-Lachaise Cemetery, in the 20th arrondissement—basically two former villages, Charonne and Ménilmontant, annexed to Paris in 1860. Here, semiproletariat buildings are being gentrified by some of city's most creative thinkers. On this tour you'll find the atmospheric streets and historical buildings that attracted the cool crowds in the first place, as well as some of the latest bars and clubs to see and be seen in.

> Bands battle it out on La Flêche d'Or's coveted stage.

START Take the Métro to the Alexandre Dumas stop.

1 Rue de Bagnolet. The route up rue de Bagnolet from Alexandre Dumas is, at first sight, far from trendy: Chinese and kebab takeaways, supermarkets, and cheap shops plaster both sidewalks. But look at the locals and you'll notice a distinctly arty vein; walk on and you'll soon find a sprinkling of hip bars. By the time you've had a coffee at the **Piston Pélican** (no. 15), you'll be ready for the bucolic, unkempt charm of adjacent streets such as rue de Lesseps, which harbors the pocket-size **Jardin Naturel,** where wildflowers and boisterous frogs have free reign; and **Villa Godin,** a narrow, flower-clad alley of highly sought-after old workers' cottages—a gorgeous throwback to a time when the village of Charonne was rural. (Both streets are on the left.) Métro: Alexandre Dumas.

2 ★★ Mama Shelter Hotel & Restaurant. You'll be hard-pressed to find anywhere quite as pioneering and trendy as Mama Shelter, farther up rue de Bagnolet (no. 109). This beacon of design by Philippe Starck—with its steely gray-and-black dining room, pizza bar,

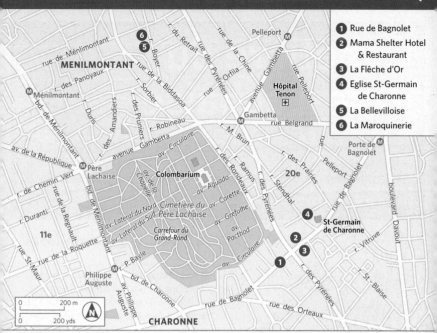

1. Rue de Bagnolet
2. Mama Shelter Hotel & Restaurant
3. La Flèche d'Or
4. Eglise St-Germain de Charonne
5. La Bellevilloise
6. La Maroquinerie

cocktail bar, and bedrooms with quirky Hulk and Batman light fittings—is a den for both international "it" crowds fresh off the plane and homegrown fashionistas. See p. 119. Métro: Alexandre Dumas or Porte de Bagnolet.

3 ★★ La Flèche d'Or. Set in the old Charonne railway station just opposite Mama Shelter, this hotbed of musical creation is Paris's ultimate indie-rock and electro club. See p. 132. Métro: Alexandre Dumas or Porte de Bagnolet.

4 ★ Eglise St-Germain de Charonne. Next door to Mama, the St-Germain de Charonne church is a gem. It was around this building that the former village of Charonne first sprawled; if you walk up the cobblestones of rue St-Blaise opposite (the former main street), it's a cinch to imagine how the church would have looked in its heyday, surrounded by vines. It was built in honor of St. Germain, bishop of Auxerre, who supposedly passed through the area in the 5th century. Some sections date back to the 12th century (mainly the tower pillars), but the majority is from the 15th and 16th centuries. The church indisputably contributes to the area's quaintness today, making the surrounding real estate prize pickings for those who can afford

it. ⏱ 15 min. 4 place St-Blaise. ☎ 01-43-71-42-04. Métro: Alexandre Dumas or Porte de Bagnolet.

5 ★★ La Bellevilloise. This multidisciplinary attraction (in the former village of Ménilmontant and set inside France's first cooperative building—a vast Art Deco brick building with a rooftop terrace and large, warehouse-like spaces) was converted into several bars, two restaurants, a club, exhibition space, and a concert hall with an exciting program of arts and summer festivals. Some of Paris's most exciting bands have been launched on its stages. 19 rue Boyer, 20th. ☎ 01-46-36-07-07. www.labellevilloise.com. Admission prices vary (sometimes free). Wed–Fri 5:30pm–2am; Sat–Sun 11am–2am. Métro: Gambetta or Ménilmontant.

6 ★★ La Maroquinerie. Just next door to the Bellevilloise, the Maroquinerie is yet another urban conversion—a former factory turned into a happening locale for literary discussions, excellent food, and, in the downstairs theater, rock concerts. 23 rue Boyer, 20th. ☎ 01-40-33-35-05. www.myspace.com/lamaroquinerie. Admission prices vary. Restaurant daily 7–10pm; concerts 8pm. Métro: Gambetta or Ménilmontant.

Cimetière du Père-Lachaise

Père-Lachaise Cemetery became one of the world's most famous cemeteries when Jim Morrison died (or didn't die, as some fans believed) and was buried here in 1971. Almost immediately, his grave became a site of pilgrimage, and the place filled with tourists—most of whom you can avoid if you stay away from Morrison's grave.

> The composer Frédéric Chopin's grave.

START Take the Métro to the Père-Lachaise stop.

❶ Main Entrance. Pick up a map from the newsstand in front of the Métro (bd. de Ménilmontant) and enter via the steps at av. Gambetta. **Free admission. Daily 8am–6pm.**

❷ Colette (1873–1954). French writer Sidonie-Gabrielle Colette published 50 novels, including *Gigi*. When she died in 1954, she was given a state funeral but was refused Roman Catholic rites because of her naughty lifestyle. **Section 4.**

❸ Gioachino Antonio Rossini (1792–1868). The Italian musical composer is best known for his operas *The Barber of Seville* and *William Tell*. His dramatic style led other composers to nickname him "Monsieur Crescendo." **Section 4.**

❹ Héloïse & Abelard (1101–1164 and 1079–1142, respectively). The earliest inhabitants of the cemetery were kept apart their entire lives by Héloïse's family, but their passionate love letters to one another were published and survived the ages. **Section 7.**

❺ Jim Morrison (1943–1971). If you must visit Morrison's grave, simply follow the crowds. The bust that once stood at the head of the tomb was stolen years ago by one of his "fans." The cigarette butts stubbed out in the grave are also courtesy of his so-called fans, as are the graffiti and the stench of old beer. What a mess. **Section 6.**

❻ Frédéric Chopin (1810–1849). Retrace your steps across avenue Casimir-Perier to section

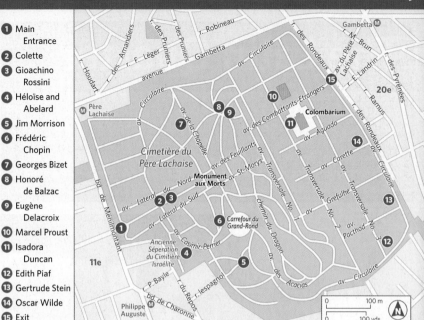

1. Main Entrance
2. Colette
3. Gioachino Rossini
4. Héloïse and Abelard
5. Jim Morrison
6. Frédéric Chopin
7. Georges Bizet
8. Honoré de Balzac
9. Eugène Delacroix
10. Marcel Proust
11. Isadora Duncan
12. Edith Piaf
13. Gertrude Stein
14. Oscar Wilde
15. Exit

11, where you'll find Chopin's appropriately elaborate grave, marked with a statue of Erato, the muse of music. **Section 11.**

7 Georges Bizet (1838–1875). The bespectacled 19th-century composer of *Carmen* was a child prodigy who entered the prestigious Conservatoire de Paris at age 9. **Section 68.**

8 Honoré de Balzac (1799–1850). The passionate French novelist wrote for up to 15 hours a day, drinking prodigious quantities of coffee to keep him going. His writing was often sloppy and uninspired, but it makes an excellent record of 19th-century Parisian life. **Section 48.**

9 Eugène Delacroix (1798–1863). This dramatic and intensely romantic painter's *La Liberté Guidant le Peuple* (*Liberty Leading the People*) is a lesson in topless inspiration. His bizarre phallic tomb puzzles (and vaguely horrifies) every time. **Section 49.**

10 Marcel Proust (1871–1922). The wistful 19th-century novelist died before he could finish editing his famous series of books, *A la Recherche du Temps Perdu* (*Remembrance of Things Past*), yet he's still considered one of the world's great writers. **Section 85.**

11 Isadora Duncan (1877–1927). The tragic death of this marvelous modern dancer is legendary: She favored long, dramatic scarves and convertibles, and one day one of those wrapped around the other, and that was the end of Isadora. **Section 87.**

12 Edith Piaf (1915–1963). This is the resting place of famed French songbird Edith Piaf, beloved by brokenhearted lovers and gay men everywhere. **Section 97.**

13 Gertrude Stein (1874–1946). The early-20th-century writer and unlikely muse shares a simple, double-sided tomb with her longtime companion, Alice B. Toklas. **Section 94.**

14 Oscar Wilde (1854–1900). The avenue des Etrangers Morts pour la France (Avenue of Dead Foreigners) leads you to the fantastical tomb of this gay 19th-century wit and writer. The size of the member with which the artist equipped the statue was quite the buzz in Paris until a vengeful woman knocked it off. **Section 89.**

15 Exit. Leave the cemetery at rue de la Réunion, and from there head to the Alexandre Dumas Métro station (or the nearest wine bar—there are plenty to choose from).

The Latin Quarter

In the 1920s, this district was the heart of Parisian cafe society; and you'll still find plenty of cafes, plus universities and shops, constantly buzzing with activity. This traditionally arty, intellectual, and bohemian district also has a history of political unrest. In 1871, place St-Michel was the center of the Paris Commune; almost a century later, in 1968, student riots took place around the Sorbonne. Today, however, it is one of Paris's most interesting and picturesque quarters to walk around.

> Table space is rare when it's aperitif time at place St-Michel.

START Take the RER or Métro to the St-Michel stop.

1 Place St-Michel. An elaborate 1860 fountain depicting St. Michael slaying a dragon presides over this bustling cafe- and shop-lined square, where skirmishes between occupying Germans and French Resistance fighters once took place. This is the beginning of busy boulevard St-Michel, trendy long ago but now a disappointing line of fast-food chains and down-market stores. It is, however, the main student quarter, and a young, lively atmosphere prevails. **Métro: St-Michel. RER: St-Michel Notre Dame.**

2 Rue du Chat-qui-Pêche. Bypass the endless kebab and pizza joints to reach what is reputed to be the narrowest lane in Paris. Its name—"Street of the Cat Who Fishes"—has given rise to plenty of local tales about the history behind it, but nobody knows for sure. Still, the sign makes a great photo. **Métro: St-Michel. RER: St-Michel Notre Dame.**

3 **Eglise St-Séverin.** This charming medieval church was built in the early 13th century and reconstructed in the 15th. Don't miss the whimsical gargoyles and monsters projecting from the roof. Inside, linger over the rare Rouault etchings from the 1920s. ⏲ 30 min. 1 rue des Prêtres St-Séverin, 5th. ☎ 01-42-34-93-50. Mon–Sat 11am–7:30pm; Sun 9am–10:30pm. Métro: St-Michel. RER: St-Michel Notre Dame.

4 **Eglise St-Julien-le-Pauvre.** After snapping a picture of the quaint old houses along rue Galande, seek out this medieval church, which dates (in part) to 1170. Note the unusual capitals covered in carved vines and leaves. The garden contains one of the oldest trees in Paris and one of the best views of Notre-Dame Cathedral. ⏲ 20 min. Rue St-Julien-le-Pauvre, 5th. ☎ 01-43-54-52-16. Mon–Sat 9:30am–noon and 3–6:30pm. Métro: La Sorbonne.

5 ★★ **Shakespeare & Company.** This famous bookstore on the Left Bank was once frequented by Ernest Hemingway, F. Scott Fitzgerald, and Gertrude Stein. Under Sylvia Whitman (daughter of famous 90-something owner George Whitman), the shop has gone from flagship secondhand bookstore to literary institution, with regular readings and signings, and even an

> *Floor to ceiling shelves gratify book lovers at Shakespeare & Company.*

> Voltaire's lifelike statue watches over his tomb in Le Panthéon, also the home of Foucault's pendulum.

annual literature festival that attracts more than 5,000 visitors. Despite the attention, the shop's modus operandi remains: secondhand American and European literature at competitive prices. 37 rue de la Bûcherie, 5th. ☎ 01-43-25-40-93. www.shakespeareandcompany.com. Daily 10am–11pm. Métro: St-Michel.

⑥ ★★ **Musée National du Moyen Age (Thermes de Cluny).** With one of the world's best collections of medieval art, this small and manageable museum is not to be missed. This is where you'll find the world famous *The Lady and the Unicorn* tapestry as well as numerous collections relating to daily life, especially from the late Middle Ages. ⏱ 1 hr. See p. 55, **⑪**.

⑦ ★ **La Sorbonne.** France's most famous university, dating back some 700 years, has all the venerable buildings and confident, scraggly-haired students you might imagine. Teachers here have included Thomas Aquinas, and the alumni association counts Dante, Calvin, and Longfellow among its past members. This is a sprawling place, and only the

courtyard and galleries are open to the public when school is in session—follow the crowds and the scarce signs to get a peek. ⏱ 30 min. 12 rue de la Sorbonne, 5th. ☎ 01-40-46-22-11. www.sorbonne.fr. Métro: Cluny–La Sorbonne.

⑧ ★ **Eglise de la Sorbonne.** On the grounds of the Sorbonne, this 17th-century church holds the elaborate tomb of Cardinal Richelieu (1585–1642). Richelieu was a staunch defender of the monarchy's power and did much to unify the French state. The tomb's extraordinary statue of a figure mourning at the cardinal's feet represents science, and the one supporting him represents religion. ⏱ 30 min. Rue de la Sorbonne, 5th. Métro: Cluny–La Sorbonne.

⑨ ★★ **Le Panthéon.** Louis XV began building this magnificent monument in 1758 as a tribute to Ste-Geneviève. Since the Revolution, however, more earthly heroes have been honored here. Here are France's great dead, including Voltaire, Rousseau, Emile Zola, and Victor Hugo. Recent additions include Marie Curie, whose remains were moved here in 1995, and Alexandre Dumas, who arrived in 2002. Appropriately, there's a Foucault's pendulum here. The famous device, which proved that the Earth rotates on an axis, was said to hang from "the eye of God"; although the pendulum appears to swing, it's not moving—the Earth is. ⏱ 1 hr. Place du Panthéon, 5th. ☎ 01-44-32-18-00. http://pantheon.monuments-nationaux.fr. Admission 8€ adults; 5€ non-EU citizens ages 18–25; free for ages 17 and under and for EU citizens ages 24 and under. Apr–Sept daily 10am–6:30pm; Oct–May daily 10am–6pm. Métro: Cardinal Lemoine. RER: Luxembourg.

⑩ 🍽 **Les Papilles.** This sweet, Provençal-style cafe is dedicated to southern French food and adventurous wine. The menu changes with the seasons, and the wines change with the owners' moods. Try the excellent stewed chicken or the hearty cassoulet, if they're available. 30 rue Gay-Lussac, 5th. ☎ 01-43-25-20-79. Main courses from 16€; fixed-price menus 22€–31€. RER: Luxembourg.

⑪ ★★ 🧒 **Jardin des Plantes.** Paris's botanical gardens started life in 1626 as the medicinal garden of Louis XIII's doctor. The grounds now encompass more than 10,000 species of flora, including a false acacia planted in 1636 and a cedar from 1734; a tropical greenhouse (in the Faculté de Pharmacie, 4 rue de l'Observatoire); formal gardens; rose, winter, and alpine gardens (in the Ecole Botanique); and a little zoo, the **Ménagerie** (see ⓲, below). Plant lovers can educate themselves by downloading themed guides (general, trees, and Oriental plants) from the website. ⏱1 hr. Rue Cuvier, rue Buffon, rue Geoffroy-St-Hilaire, place Valhubert, 5th. ☎ 01-40-79-56-01. www. mnhn.fr. Free admission. Main park 7:30am–7:30pm. Métro: Gare d'Austerlitz, Censier Daubenton, or Jussieu.

⓬ kids **Musée National d'Histoire Naturelle.** Inside the Jardin des Plantes, this natural history museum was founded in 1635 by Guy de la Brosse, physician to Louis XIII, as a center for research on science and nature. It looks a little tired around the edges, but it's still worth seeing, with displays on dinosaurs and endangered and vanished species, and galleries that specialize in paleontology and anatomy (Galerie de Paléontologie et Anatomie Comparée), evolution (Grande Galerie de l'Evolution), and mineralogy (Galerie de Minéralogie). *Tip:* The **Pass 2 Jours** saves you money on all the museum's sites, including the **Menagerie** and **Jardin,** over a 2-day period (25€ adults, 20€ ages 4–13). Upon presentation of a full-price ticket (valid within a 3-month period), visitors gain reduced entry to any other part of the museum. ⏱1 hr. 56 rue Cuvier, 5th. ☎ 01-40-79-54-79. www.mnhn.fr. Admission: Galerie de Minéralogie 8€ adults, 5€ ages 4–13; Galerie de Paléontologie 7€ adults, 5€ ages 4–13; Galerie de l'Evolution 7€ adults, 5€ ages 4–13. Wed–Mon 10am–6pm. Métro: Jussieu or Gare d'Austerlitz.

⓭ kids **Menagerie de Jardin des Plantes.** As heads rolled in the aftermath of the Revolution, the exotic fauna collected by the defunct aristocrats needed a new home. This 5.3-hectare (13-acre) menagerie—the world's oldest zoo—was the unlikely solution. Today small animals take pride of place: more than 190 species in total, including kangaroos, antelopes, wallabies, black pigs, camels, llamas, the famous Przewalski horse (so rare that it disappeared from the wild 40 years ago),

> *A mammoth welcome awaits you at the Musée National d'Histoire Naturelle.*

and a couple of panthers in the Fauverie. The animals seem happy and well tended. 3 quai St-Bernard or 57 rue Cuvier, 5th. ☎ 01-40-79-37-94. www.mnhn.fr. Apr–Oct daily 9am–6pm; Nov–Mar daily 9am–5pm. Admission 8€ adults, 6€ ages 4–13, free for children 3 and under. See Musée National d'Histoire Naturelle, above, for info on combined tickets. Métro: Gare d'Austerlitz or Jussieu.

The Islands

The Ile de la Cité is where it all began, long before the Romans came in 53 B.C., when Paris was a small settlement populated by the Celtic Parisii tribe. Over the next 2,000 years, Paris was expanded by the Romans, the Franks, the Merovingians, and the Capetian kings, but the city's soul rests here, around Notre-Dame Cathedral. Across the bridge, Ile St-Louis is a coveted residential area filled with glorious 17th-century mansions built on what were once marsh-lands. This tour takes you through both islands and along some of the loveliest stretches of the Seine. Stops 1 through 6 are on Ile de la Cité; stops 7 through 12 are on Ile St-Louis.

> *Pont des Arts, overlooking the Islands, was built in the 1980s as a copy of the original 19th-century bridge, which collapsed in 1979.*

START Take the Métro to the Cité stop.

1 ★ **kids La Conciergerie.** This intimidating building, originally a royal medieval palace, was converted into a prison during the Revolution and became an object of terror to the public at a time when idle accusations could result in spontaneous executions. Marie Antoinette, Danton, and Robespierre all were held here before their executions by guillotine. Today you can see the cells where they were held and the rooms where they were tried and condemned. ⏲ 1 hr. See p. 39, **6**.

2 ★ **Ste-Chapelle.** Tucked away among the huge Conciergerie and the vast law courts of the Palais de Justice, this tiny church is hard to find, but those who persevere will discover a precious jewel box of a chapel, made almost entirely of dazzling stained-glass windows. Unfortunately, it's not undiscovered, and there is often a long line waiting to get in. ⏲ 40 min. See p. 46, **1**.

3 **Marché aux Fleurs.** This vivid flower market just opposite the Palais de Justice is a photo opportunity simply crying out for your

① La Conciergerie
② Ste-Chapelle
③ Marché aux Fleurs
④ Cathédrale Notre-Dame
⑤ Crypte Archéologique du Parvis Notre-Dame
⑥ Mémorial de la Déportation
⑦ Rue St-Louis-en-l'Ile
⑧ Berthillon
⑨ Eglise St-Louis-en-l'Ile
⑩ Hôtel de Lauzun

camera's attention. It must be one of the most photographed places on Earth—and for good reason. On Sundays it's transformed into a bird market, though the treatment of the birds leaves something to be desired. ⏱ 30 min. Place Louis Lépine, quai de la Corse, quai des Fleurs, 4th. Mon–Sat 8am–7:30pm; Sun 8am–7pm. Métro: Cité.

④ ★★★ **Cathédrale Notre-Dame.** This world-famous cathedral is more beautiful in person than on film. Climb its towers to see malicious gargoyles and sweeping panoramas over the city. ⏱ 40 min. See p. 41, **⑦**.

⑤ **Crypte Archéologique du Parvis Notre-Dame.** Paris has more layers than a giant club sandwich (especially on Ile de la Cité, where its history began), and this archaeological crypt in the square in front of Notre-Dame offers a rare opportunity to discern those layers. Roman ramparts, quaysides, medieval shops, pavements, portions of an 18th-century hospital, and part of a 19th-century sewer—each section reveals snippets about the lives of those who lived here during the last 2,000 years. You'll need a good imagination for some segments, but on the whole it's fascinating. ⏱ 1 hr. 7 place du Parvis Notre-Dame–Place

Ile de la Cité

By medieval times, Paris's central section was a thriving island town with huddles of houses and narrow streets. All, however, were swept away in the 19th century, when Baron Haussmann evicted some 25,000 people and destroyed around 20 churches to make way for the large administrative buildings we see today. Few have written more movingly about the island's heyday than Victor Hugo, who invited the reader "to observe the fantastic display of lights against the darkness of that gloomy labyrinth of buildings; cast upon it a ray of moonlight, showing the city in glimmering vagueness, with its towers lifting their great heads from that foggy sea." You have only to climb Notre-Dame's towers to see what he's talking about: On a cloudy day, the skies cast an eerie light over the island. A beautiful way to reach Ile de la Cité is via the bridge known as pont Neuf (Métro: Pont Neuf), beneath a statue of Henri IV. The name means "new bridge"—ironic, considering that it's Paris's oldest bridge, dating back to the time of Catherine de Medici in the 16th century.

> *Below this sculpted sign lies Paris's Crypte Archéologique, which shows how the city developed over the centuries.*

Jean-Paul II, 4th. ☎ 01-55-42-50-10. www. carnavalet.paris.fr. Admission 4€ adults, 3€ students, 2€ ages 13–18, free for ages 12 and under. Tues–Sun 10am–6pm. Closed public holidays. Métro: Cité. RER: St-Michel–Notre-Dame.

⑥ **Mémorial de la Déportation.** Approached through a garden behind Notre-Dame on the tip of Ile de la Cité, this poignant underground memorial commemorates the French Jews,

Ile St-Louis

Despite its central location, Ile St-Louis feels like a tranquil backwater—removed, somehow, from the rest of the buzzing city. The 17th-century buildings lining the narrow streets are some of the city's most expensive properties; many have hosted, at one point or another, French literary stars from Racine to Molière. A bourgeois, arty crowd still frequents the many art galleries that dot these neighborhoods. It's a lovely place to wander—so tiny, it's almost impossible to get lost.

homosexuals, Communists, and Resistance fighters who were deported to concentration camps and exterminated during World War II. ⏱ 20 min. Free admission. Mon–Fri 8:30am–nightfall; Sat–Sun 9am–nightfall. Métro: Cité.

⑦ **Rue St-Louis-en-l'Ile.** Ile St-Louis's central artery is gorgeous, narrow, and lined with restaurants and boutiques selling art, food, clothes, hats, precious stones and minerals, and jewelry. Hôtel Chenizot, at no. 51, has fantastic carved dragons and bearded fauns on

Bouquinistes

Paris's literary history makes it a book hunter's paradise. Wander around the 5th, and you'll find plenty of dusty bookshops filled with Hemingway wannabes and local *intellectuels.* Perhaps the most iconic and pleasurable of all bookshops aren't really bookshops per se—they are the *bouquinistes:* those green metal containers that line the riverbanks (mainly in the 4th and 5th, opposite Notre-Dame), peddling more than 300,000 old and new books. This is where the educated eye can find real treasures, from first-edition Jules Verne novels to rare illustrated Bibles and fairy tales.

> *In 1846 the Archbishop of Paris rented rooms behind the dragon-clad facade of the Hôtel Chenizot.*

its facade. If you can, go through the door and admire the sculpted facade in the courtyard beyond. A second courtyard also contains craft shops and galleries. **Métro: Pont Marie.**

⑧ 🍦 kids **Berthillon.** On Ile St-Louis, even the ice cream stores are sophisticated. This place proves it, with polite crowds queuing outside for cones to go, and others perched at the tables inside to try flavors like lemon, hazelnut, mango, and good old chocolate. **31 rue St-Louis-en-l'Ile, 4th.** ☎ **01-43-54-31-61.** www. berthillon.fr. Ice cream around 3€ a scoop. **Métro: Pont Marie.**

⑨ **Eglise St-Louis-en-l'Ile.** This 17th-century church, vastly overshadowed by its famous neighbor, has wonderful rococo (late baroque) architecture, including a lovely sunburst above the altar. It is not as dramatic as Notre-Dame, but it's more intimate and enchanting. ⏱ 20 min. **19 rue St-Louis-en-l'Ile, 4th.**

☎ **01-46-34-11-60.** Tues–Sun 9am–noon and 3–7pm. **Métro: Pont Marie.**

⑩ ★★ **Hôtel de Lauzun.** This astonishing place, with fantastic drains in the shapes of sea serpents, was the scene of famously long, hazy hashish parties thrown by Baudelaire and Théophile Gautier. Baudelaire wrote *Les Fleurs Du Mal (The Flowers of Evil)* while living here, although it's hard to see how he could have been so depressed living somewhere so pretty. The building takes its name from a former occupant, the Duc de Lauzun—a favorite of Louis XIV until he asked for the hand of the king's cousin, the Duchess de Montpensier. Louis refused and had Lauzun tossed into the Bastille. Eventually the *duchesse* convinced Louis to release him, and they married secretly and moved here in 1682. Racine, Molière, and La Fontaine also stayed here intermittently. **17 quai d'Anjou.** Generally closed to the public (except for art exhibits—check with the tourist office). **Métro: Pont Marie.**

Floating Down the Seine

The Seine cries out to be sailed upon, so while you're at pont Neuf, catch one of the long, low boats run by **Vedettes du Pont Neuf,** Square du Vert Galant, 4th (☎ 01-46-33-98-38; www. vedettesdupontneuf.com; rates 12€ adults, 6€ ages 4–12; Mar–Oct daily 10:30am–10:30pm, about every 30 min.; Nov–Feb daily 10:30am–10pm, about every 45 min.). By night, they glow with lights as they navigate the river, offering magical views of Paris. Other boat companies include **Bateaux Parisians** (☎ 08-25-01-01-01; www.bateauxparisiens.com), which leaves from in front of Notre-Dame and the Eiffel Tower and offers lunch and dinner cruises; and **Bateaux Mouches** (☎ 01-42-25-96-10; www.bateaux-mouches.fr), which also provides lunch and dinner cruises as well as an hour-long sightseeing ride from pont de l'Alma.

St-Germain-des-Prés

This was the place to be in the 1920s. Here the literati met the glitterati, and all of Paris marveled at the ensuing explosion of creativity and alcoholism. On these streets, Sartre fumed while Hemingway and Fitzgerald drank and quarreled. Today many of the bookshops have been replaced by designer boutiques, but it's still the place to go for a night on the town.

> In the 1930s, the Café de Flore was the favorite haunt of Jean-Paul Sartre and Simone de Beauvoir.

START Take the RER to the Luxembourg stop.

① ★★ kids **Jardin & Palais du Luxembourg.** There's a certain justice in the fact that this former palace, built between 1615 and 1627 for the widow of Henri IV, is now home to the democratically elected French Senate. The lovely Italianate building in the 6th arrondissement also houses the **Musée du Luxembourg,** 19 rue de Vaugirard (☎ 01-42-34-25-95; www.museeduluxembourg.fr; admission and hours vary), famed for its world-class temporary art exhibitions. Most people, however, come for the gardens. The picturesque paths of the **Jardin du Luxembourg** have always been a favorite of artists, although children, students from the nearby Sorbonne, and tourists are more common than painters nowadays. Hemingway claimed to have survived a winter by poaching pigeons here for his supper, and Gertrude Stein used to cross the gardens on her way to sit for Picasso. There are statues everywhere—more than 80 of them vie for your attention: a longhaired French queen, a tiny Statue of Liberty, a huge Cyclops. It's fanciful and delightful; you could spend hours here and fail to uncover all of the park's secrets. ⏱ 1 hr. 6th. ☎ 01-42-34-23-62 (garden). Métro: Odéon. RER: Luxembourg.

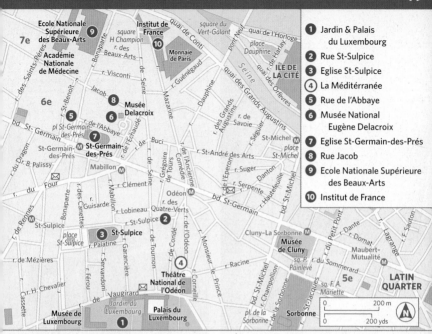

1 Jardin & Palais
   du Luxembourg
2 Rue St-Sulpice
3 Eglise St-Sulpice
4 La Méditérranée
5 Rue de l'Abbaye
6 Musée National
   Eugène Delacroix
7 Eglise St-Germain-des-Prés
8 Rue Jacob
9 Ecole Nationale Supérieure
   des Beaux-Arts
10 Institut de France

> Autumnal fun in the Jardin du Luxembourg.

2 **Rue St-Sulpice.** Welcome to shopping heaven (or window-shopping purgatory, depending on your cash flow). This is Paris's answer to New York's Fifth Avenue or London's Bond Street. All the usual designer suspects are here for your inspection—agnès b., Christian Lacroix, YSL, perfumer Annick Goutal, and friends. If you want to stock up for a picnic, pop down to **Poilâne** bakery, 8 rue du Cherche-Midi, for some of the city's best breads and sandwiches to go. Métro: Odéon.

3 ★★ **Eglise St-Sulpice.** It took 120 years (from 1646) and six architects to get St-Sulpice standing as proudly as it does today, with its ostentatious Italianate facade and paintings by Delacroix, including *La Lutte de Jacob avec l'Ange* (Jacob's Fight with the Angel). Take time to meditate and view the gorgeous frescoes. The church has one of the world's largest organs, comprising 6,700 pipes—a national treasure, especially when it's played. ⏱ 30 min. Rue St-Sulpice, 6th. ☎ 01-46-33-21-78. Daily 7:30am–7:30pm. Métro: St-Sulpice.

4 🍽 **La Méditérranée.** A short walk away stands this restaurant filled with murals by 20th-century stage designers Christian Bérard and Marcel Vertés, and paintings by Picasso and Chagall. It was once a haunt of Jackie Kennedy, Picasso, and Cocteau, whose work enlivens the plates and menus. The chef delivers creative interpretations of traditional dishes, including gorgeous fried fish with fresh spinach salad, and an incredible bouillabaisse, thick with seafood. 2 place de l'Odéon, 6th. ☎ 01-43-26-02-30. Prix-fixe menu 28€–35€. Métro: Odéon.

> *Watching over his works, Delacroix's bust sits in the Musée National Eugène Delacroix.*

⑤ Rue de l'Abbaye. St-Germain was built around an old abbey that once towered over this street, although there's virtually nothing left of it today. With houses and churches built of red brick, the area is charming, particularly rue de Furstenberg—once the abbot's stables, it's now filled with upmarket interior-design shops. **Métro: St-Germain-des-Prés.**

⑥ ★ Musée National Eugène Delacroix. Romantic painter Eugène Delacroix lived and worked in this lovely house on rue de Furstenberg from 1857 until his death in 1863. The museum sits on a charming square, with a romantic garden. Most of Delacroix's major works are in the Louvre, but the collection here is unusually personal, including an early self-portrait and letters and notes to friends such as Baudelaire and George Sand. You can also see his work in the Chapelle des Anges in Eglise St-Sulpice (stop ③, above). ⏱ 1 hr. 6 rue de Furstenberg, 6th. ☎ 01-44-41-86-50.

Hemingway's Cafes

For fans of Papa Hemingway, a trip to Paris is a pilgrimage. This is where the author honed his craft, married more than once, had countless mistresses, and whiled away endless hours in Paris's Left Bank cafes. One of his haunts was **Café Pré aux Clercs,** 30 rue Bonaparte, 6th (☎ 01-43-29-74-34), a short walk from the Hôtel d'Angleterre, where he slept in room no. 14 on his first night in Paris. Hemingway also frequented **Les Deux Magots,** 6 place St-Germain-des-Prés, 6th (☎ 01-45-48-55-25; www.lesdeuxmagots.fr), the preeminent hangout of the arty expat crowd, where he charmed the girls, picked fights with the critics, and hassled the tourists. It's touristy today, but it's still a good place to have a coffee and wonder what he'd think of it all now.

www.musee-delacroix.fr. Admission 5€ adults, free for ages 17 and under. Sept–May Wed–Mon 9:30am–5pm; Jun–Aug Wed–Mon 9:30am–5:30pm). Métro: St-Germain-des-Prés.

7 ★ **Eglise St-Germain-des-Prés.** This exquisite little church is the oldest in Paris and a rarity in France—only a few buildings this old exist in such complete form. It dates to the 6th century, when a Benedictine abbey was founded here, though little remains from that time. Its aged columns still bear their medieval paint in breathtaking detail. You can visit the tomb of French philosopher René Descartes (1596–1650) in the second chapel. At one time, the abbey was a pantheon for Merovingian kings. During the restoration of the site of their tombs, Chapelle de St-Symphorien, previously unknown Romanesque paintings were discovered. ◷ 30 min. 3 place St-Germain-des-Prés, 6th. ☎ 01-55-42-81-33. www.eglise-sgp.org. Mon–Sat 8am–7:45pm; Sun 9am–8pm. Métro: St-Germain-des-Prés.

8 **Rue Jacob.** This elegant street, with clean lines and classic 19th-century architecture, was once home to such illustrious residents as the writer Colette and composer Richard Wagner. Today it's very posh-bohemian, with charming bookstores and antiques shops. Métro: St-Germain-des-Prés.

9 **Ecole Nationale Supérieure des Beaux-Arts.** The main attraction at this fine arts school is the architecture. The school occupies a 17th-century convent and the 18th-century Hôtel de Chimay. Attending an exhibition (these are held frequently) will grant you a peek inside. If nothing is scheduled, just wander down rue Bonaparte, which is lined with lovely little art galleries. ◷ 30 min. 14 rue Bonaparte, 6th. ☎ 01-47-03-50-00. www.ensba.fr. Courtyard: Mon–Fri 9am–5pm (Tues–Sun 1–7pm during exhibitions). Métro: St-Germain-des-Prés.

10 **Institut de France.** Turn right along the river and it's hard to miss this elegant domed baroque building, home to five subgovernmental agencies all lumped together as the rather ominously named l'Institut. Here the Académie Française, where Jacques Cousteau was once a member, zealously guards the purity of the French language from "Franglais" encroachment. Other, lesser-known agencies

here—such as the Academies des Sciences, des Inscriptions et Belles Lettres, des Beaux-Arts, and des Sciences Morales et Politiques—do, well, whatever it is they do. The brave can arrange for a guided tour (available in English) as most buildings are closed to the public—perhaps not surprisingly, considering that academy members are known as "the Immortals." 23 quai de Conti, 6th. ☎ 01-44-41-44-41. Guided tours by appointment only; prices upon request. Métro: St-Germain-des-Prés.

The 1920s: Americans in Paris

The so-called Lost Generation, led by American expats Gertrude Stein and Alice B. Toklas, topped the list of celebrities who "occupied" Paris after World War I (mostly around St-Germain). Paris attracted the *littérateur,* the *bon viveur,* the drifter—notables like composer Cole Porter and writers Ernest Hemingway and F. Scott Fitzgerald (above). With the collapse of Wall Street, many returned home. The stalwart artists stayed a bit longer—such as Henry Miller, who, when he wasn't writing *Tropic of Cancer,* wandered around smoking Gauloises—but even they eventually realized 1930s Paris was collapsing as war clouds loomed. Gertrude and Alice remained in France; they are buried together in the Cimetière du Père-Lachaise (p. 68).

Le Marais

When Ile de la Cité became overcrowded, it was here, to what had been swampland, that the Parisians moved, filling the streets with fashionable mansions called hôtels. Over the years it became the center of the city's Jewish residents. Today the gay and lesbian community has adopted the area. Its many boutiques and diverse buildings make for excellent shopping and exploring.

> The Musée Carnavalet and its beautiful, arcaded gardens are free to the public.

START Take the Métro to the St-Paul stop. Outside the Métro, turn right on rue St-Antoine.

1 Hôtel de Béthune-Sully. The relief-studded facade of this gracious mansion was restored not long ago, and the building dazzles once again, as it was meant to when first designed in 1634. Once a private home, it now holds offices, part of the Jeu de Paume film and photography exhibition center, and a bookstore. The charming garden is always open and has a secret door that leads to place des Vosges (stop **7**, below). ⏱ 30 min. 62 rue St-Antoine, 4th. ☎ 01-42-74-47-75. www.jeudepaume.org.

Admission 8€. Tues–Fri noon–7pm; Sat–Sun 10am–7pm. Métro: St-Paul.

2 Hôtel de Sens. Given the leaded windows and fairy-tale turrets, you might not be surprised to find that this 15th-century mansion has a gloriously ornate courtyard in which you can wander at will most afternoons. Once a private home for archbishops and, later, queens, it now holds a library, the Bibliothèque Forney. ⏱ 20 min. 1 rue du Figurier, 4th. ☎ 01-42-78-14-60. Free admission. Courtyard: Tues–Fri 1:30–8:15pm; Sat 10am–8:15pm. Métro: St-Paul.

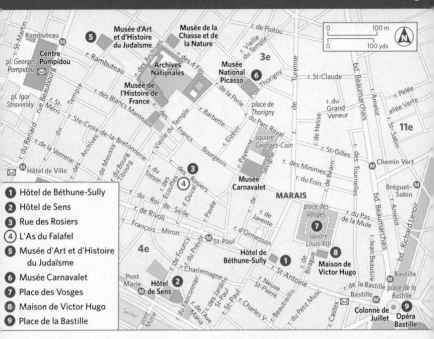

1. Hôtel de Béthune-Sully
2. Hôtel de Sens
3. Rue des Rosiers
4. L'As du Falafel
5. Musée d'Art et d'Histoire du Judaïsme
6. Musée Carnavalet
7. Place des Vosges
8. Maison de Victor Hugo
9. Place de la Bastille

3 Rue des Rosiers. Perhaps the most colorful and typical street of the city's Jewish quarter, rue des Rosiers (Street of the Rosebushes) meanders amid the old buildings. The Star of David shines here, Hebrew letters flash in neon, shops run by Moroccan or Algerian Jews sell couscous and falafel, bearded men sit in doorways, restaurants serve kosher meals, and signs appeal for Jewish liberation. It makes a plum spot for a cheap lunch on Sundays. Métro: St-Paul.

4 ★ **L'As du Falafel.** This tiny cafe serves some of the best falafel sandwiches in the city. 34 rue des Rosiers, 4th. ☎ 01-48-87-63-60. Falafel 5€. Métro: St-Paul.

5 ★ Musée d'Art et d'Histoire du Judaïsme. This museum was created in 1948 to protect the city's Jewish history after the Holocaust. It's a moving place, with historical documents and excellent Jewish decorative arts from around Europe, such as German Hanukkah lamps and a wooden sukkah cabin from Austria. There's also a memorial to the Jews who lived in the building in 1939, 13 of whom died in concentration camps. ⏱ 45 min. Hôtel de St-Aignan, 71 rue du Temple, 3rd.

> Jewish falafel vendors line rue des Rosiers in Le Marais.

> *All that remains of the formidable Bastille prison sits on this platform at Bastille Métro.*

☎ 01-53-01-86-53. www.mahj.org. Admission 6.80€ adults, free for ages 25 and under. Mon–Fri 11am–6pm, Sun 10am–6pm. Métro: Rambuteau or Hôtel de Ville.

⑥ Musée Carnavalet. Paris's past comes alive in this fascinating museum, through details such as the chessmen Louis XVI used to distract himself while awaiting his execution. Several salons cover the Revolution; others display furniture from the Louis XIV period to the early 20th century, including a replica of Marcel Proust's cork-lined bedroom. ⏱ 1 hr. 23 rue de Sévigné, 3rd. ☎ 01-44-59-58-58. www.carnavalet.paris.fr. Free admission. Tues–Sun 10am–6pm. Closed some public holidays. Métro: St-Paul or Chemin Vert.

⑦ Place des Vosges. Once the dueling ground where Henri II was killed while jousting, in 1559, place des Vosges is Paris's oldest square. Today its perfect red-brick and white-stone pavilions still rise above covered arcades, allowing pedestrians to shop even in the rain. Its perfect symmetry might be why so many writers and artists (Descartes, Pascal, Gautier, Hugo) chose to live here. Métro: St-Paul or Bastille.

⑧ Maison de Victor Hugo. The writer of *Les Misérables* lived here from 1832 to 1848, and his home has been turned into a shrine of sorts. In general, it's the usual tribute museum, with a few of the author's possessions on display, including his inkwell and some furniture. ⏱ 15 min. 6 place des Vosges, 4th. ☎ 01-42-72-10-16. Free admission. Tues–Sun 10am–6pm. Métro: St-Paul or Bastille.

⑨ ★ Place de la Bastille. Little remains of the towered 14th-century fortress that once stood here and held such prisoners as the "Man in the Iron Mask" and the Marquis de Sade. But it's worth a stop to commemorate the place where the Revolution began on July 14, 1789, when French citizens overthrew authority by storming the prison and raiding the ammunition stored there. See p. 44, ⑦.

> The cafes under place des Vosges's arcades bustle throughout the day.

JE PROTESTE!

The French Spirit of Resistance BY ANNA BROOKE

POLITICAL PROTEST has been an integral part of French life since a mob stormed the Bastille on July 14, 1789, kickstarting the Revolution and inspiring the Declaration of the Rights of Man—a blueprint for citizen-led government around the world. Hardly a year goes by in France without a demonstration making headlines, from student rebellions and union marches to *grèves générales* (general strikes) that last for several weeks. Between 2005 and 2010, strikes cost 100 lost workdays a year per every 1,000 employees. In 2009 that amounted to 1.4 million lost days of work. It's enough to rile the French into—what else?—taking to the streets in counterprotest.

THE FRENCH RESISTANCE DURING WWII

During WWII, the French *Résistance* helped secure a Nazi defeat. After Paris fell to the Germans in 1940 and France's Vichy government began collaborating with the Nazis, small groups of French men and women formed cells and risked their lives to spy, sabotage Nazi military action, publish underground newspapers, and maintain escape networks for the Allies. Many *résistants* fled cities and hid in mountains and forests, attacking Germans and helping stranded British airmen return home.

MAY 1968 These protests against the de Gaulle government remain France's largest postwar upheaval. Police brutality turned student protests over funding and class discrimination into a more violent national movement, backed by artists, celebrities, blue-collar workers, and intellectuals. For 2 weeks, two-thirds of French workers (11 million employees) went on strike. De Gaulle, fearing civil war, fled to Germany and scheduled emergency elections. His party won, but a shift occurred from old-school conservative standards to the more liberal ideals prevalent in France today.

THE TRANSPORT STRIKE In 1995 millions of strikers protested Prime Minister Alain Juppé's plan to reduce retirement benefits. After 6 million workdays were lost and public transportation and other services ground to a halt, Chirac's government made heavy concessions. During the strike, so many Parisians took to rollerblades to get around that the police set up special routes. Today 10,000 Parisians still take part in organized public skates in summer: Pari Roller on Friday nights and Rollers & Coquillages on Sunday afternoons (see photo, below).

THE PENSION PROTESTS In 2010, when President Nicolas Sarkozy announced plans to raise the national retirement age from 60 to 62, 3.5 million citizens protested, disrupting transport, blocking oil refineries, closing

schools, and picketing with bawdy signs ("Carla, we're like you, we're being screwed by the chief of state!"). Demonstrations have quieted, but with the retirement age set to rise in 2018, there's plenty of time for the protests to start up again.

Montmartre

Artsy, graceful, undulating Montmartre does something to your heart. From the moment you see its narrow, tilting houses, still windmills, and steep streets, you're in love. This part of town—known as La Butte, or "The Hill," in the 18th arrondissement—was a rural village separate from Paris until 1860, when it was absorbed into the city. Then, in the 1880s, Renoir and Toulouse-Lautrec helped to make it an artists' lair—a legacy that lives on today.

> Montmartre used to be covered in windmills like this one, which now houses the Moulin de la Galette restaurant.

START Take the Métro to the Abbesses stop.

❶ **Place des Abbesses.** Emerge from the deepest Métro station in the city—35m (115 ft.) below street level—one of the two remaining Art Nouveau stations designed by Hector Guimard at the beginning of the 20th century. Opposite the exit, another turn-of-the-century treasure awaits you—the red-brick **Eglise St-Jean-l'Evangéliste.** Erected in 1904, it was the first church built of reinforced concrete, with beautiful, slender pillars and graceful modern arches. Inside, it is imposingly beautiful, with Art Nouveau floral designs and stained-glass windows, inspired by 16th-century German paintings. ⏱ 20 min. Métro: Abbesses.

❷ **Georges Seurat's house.** The three-story white house at no. 39 rue André-Antoine is where neo-Impressionist painter Georges Seurat died suddenly from diphtheria in 1891, at age 31. Here he painted *Le Chahut,* which depicts a lively dance from a Montmartre music hall (on display in the Kröller-Müller Museum in Otterlo, Netherlands). **39 rue André-Antoine, 18th.** Métro: Abbesses.

❸ **Rue Tholozé.** Halfway up this steep, narrow street, with the adorable Blute-Fin windmill (see ❼, below) at the top, is **Studio 28,** at no. 10 (☎ 01-46-06-36-07; www.cinemastudio28.com). The city's first proper art-house cinema, it's named after the year it opened. It premiered Luis Buñuel's *L'Age d'Or* in 1930, and outraged locals ripped the screen from the wall. Today it still shows arty flicks and has a tiny bar. Métro: Abbesses.

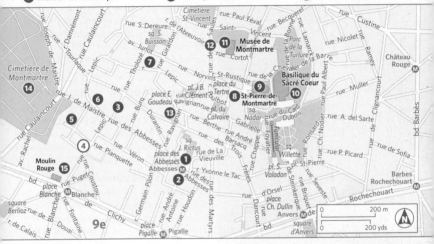

1 Place des Abbesses
2 Georges Seurat's house
3 Rue Tholozé
4 Café des Deux Moulins
5 Maison de l'Escalopier
6 Vincent van Gogh's House
7 The Windmills
8 Place du Tertre
9 St-Pierre-de-Montmartre
10 Basilique du Sacré-Coeur
11 Musée de Montmartre
12 Rue des Saules
13 Le Bateau-Lavoir
14 Cimetière de Montmartre
15 Moulin Rouge

④ 🍴 **Café des Deux Moulins.** Just past rue Tholozé, rue des Abbesses branches off into rue Lepic. It's a cliché, but if you're a fan of Jean-Pierre Jeunet's film *Amélie* (the quirky 2001 international hit that saw Audrey Tautou gallivanting around Montmartre, falling for love), bear left and follow rue Lepic south. The cafe on the corner of rue Cauchois is where Amélie worked as a waitress. If you're hungry, this is as good a spot as any for lunch. 15 rue Lepic, 18th. ☎ 01-42-54-90-50. Lunch menu 14.90€.

⑤ ★★ **Maison de l'Escalopier.** Here you'll find a hidden 19th-century folly—the sumptuous Maison de l'Escalopier, built in a heavy, Gothic style by the Comte de l'Escalopier. It's open to the public in July and August, and during the Journées du Patrimoine, but the rest of the year its wooden carvings, intricate window frames, and heavy paneling can be admired only from the outside. Impasse Marie Blanche, 18th. No phone. www.journeesdupatrimoine. culture.fr. Free admission. Jul–Aug and 1st weekend in Sept. Métro: Abbesses or Blanche.

> Utrillo once painted the pink Lapin Agile cabaret on Rue des Saules.

> Lip-locked lovers below the Basilique du Sacré-Coeur.

6 Vincent van Gogh's House. Vincent van Gogh and his brother, Théo, lived from 1886 to 1888 on the third floor. The house is closed to the public. **54 rue Lepic.**

The Man Who Walked Through Walls

To the left of the Moulin de la Galette restaurant is place Marcel-Aymé, named after the writer who lived here until his death in 1967. Here, you'll see a surreal sculpture of a man emerging from the wall. The statue was inspired by Aymé's short story *"Le Passe-Muraille"* ("The Man Who Could Walk Through Walls"). As the story goes, the man in question was a petty bureaucrat who used his superhero talent to make mischief—until one night he got trapped inside a wall, where he has remained ever since.

7 The Windmills. Farther along rue Lepic are the two remaining windmills of Montmartre: the **Blute-Fin,** hidden at the top of a slope behind some trees, and the **Moulin du Radet,** now a restaurant confusingly called the Moulin de la Galette, after the famous *bal populaire* (dance hall) once formed by both windmills. (The dance hall was immortalized by Toulouse-Lautrec, van Gogh, Utrillo, and Renoir, whose version is in the Musée d'Orsay, p. 51, **2**.)

8 Place du Tertre. This old square would be lovely were it not for the tourists—and the artists chasing you around, threatening to draw your caricature. You can buy some very good original paintings here, but you'll have to barter to get a reasonable price.

9 St-Pierre-de-Montmartre. Follow the winding streets ever upward to this old Benedictine abbey, now a small, early Gothic church. This is one of the city's most elderly churches (1133), as evidenced by its gradually bending columns. Its simplicity, in the shadow of the architectural giant below, is refreshing. ⏱ 15 min. Rue du Mont-Cenis.

10 ★★ Basilique du Sacré-Coeur. The creamy white domes of this Romano-Byzantine basilica soar high above Paris like a ready-made postcard. Inside is an artistic and archaeological explosion of color and form; out front are sweeping views of the gorgeous city in soft pastels. Construction began in 1876, and the basilica was consecrated in 1919. It's a self-whitening church, made from white stone that secretes calcium when it rains. The dome rises 78m (256 ft.) and has one of the world's heaviest bells, weighing in at nearly 19,000 kilograms (21 tons). ⏱ 1 hr. 35 rue du Chevalier-de-la-Barre, 18th. ☎ 01-53-41-89-00. www.sacre-coeur-montmartre.com. Free admission. Daily 6am–10:30pm. Métro: Abbesses.

11 Musée de Montmartre. This 17th-century building, converted into artists' studios in 1875, is an oasis of calm and will give you a good perspective on Montmartre's past. There are pictures of 19th-century Montmartre, rural and lined with windmills, along with a few Toulouse-Lautrec posters and the like. Renoir rented a studio in one wing in 1886 (where he put the finishing touches on his painting *Le*

> Built in 1889, the Moulin Rouge is the only cabaret in Paris that still stages performances of traditional cancan.

Moulin de la Galette), and in 1896 the artist Suzanne Valadon moved into the first floor with her painter son, Maurice Utrillo. ⏱ 45 min. 12 rue Cortot, 18th. ☎ 01-49-25-89-37. www.museedemontmartre.fr. Admission 8€ adults, 4€ ages 12–26, free for children 11 and under. Wed–Sun 11am–6pm. Métro: Abbesses.

⑫ **Rue des Saules.** Pause to admire the oft-photographed nightclub Au Lapin Agile, which was a favorite hangout of Picasso's back when it was called Cabaret des Assassins. It's still usually crowded with tourists, fans of old French music, and those seeking Picasso's muse. Opposite, notice the small patch of vines, a throwback from the days when Montmartre was a winegrowing village separate from Paris. The Clos Montmartre harvest (red wine) is celebrated annually in October over a very boozy weekend.

⑬ **Le Bateau-Lavoir.** This building is called the "cradle of cubism." While living here (1904–12), Picasso painted *Les Demoiselles d'Avignon* (known as the *Brothel of Avignon*). Today it's filled with art studios, some occasionally open for viewing. ⏱ 10 min. 13 place Emile Goudeau. Métro: Abbesses.

⑭ ★★ **Cimetière de Montmartre.** Pick up a map of this quiet resting place from the gate-house (there's a stack on the desk)—it will help you find the graves of Truffaut, Stendhal, Degas, and many others who rest here. ⏱ 1 hr. Access on rue Rachel by stairs from rue Caulaincourt, 18th. Mar 16–Nov 5, Mon–Sat 8am–5:30pm, Sun 9am–5:30pm; Nov 6–Mar 15, Mon–Sat 8am–6pm, Sun 9am–6pm. Métro: Blanche.

⑮ **Moulin Rouge.** Here you'll find the bright red windmill immortalized by Toulouse-Lautrec (and more recently, Nicole Kidman). It's all just as tawdry and tacky as it was when the artist downed one absinthe after another to endure it, but it's the only place in Paris where dancers still perform the real cancan. See p. 129.

Satie's Closet

While on rue Cortot, spare a thought for composer Erik Satie (nicknamed "Esoteric Satie" because of his enthusiasm for matters supernatural), who lived at no. 6, in a tiny room he called his "closet."

Montparnasse

When Montmartre artists did their jobs so well that the neighborhood became popular and rents finally went up, they all moved to Montparnasse. Before long, Picasso, Léger, and Chagall had joined Man Ray, Henry Miller, and Gertrude Stein on its somewhat forbidding streets. In terms of beauty, the two areas don't compare—concrete is abundant in Montparnasse, but it offers plenty of sights to keep you busy.

> The best view in Paris is from the 56th floor of the Tour Montparnasse.

START Take the Métro to the Montparnasse-Bienvenue stop.

1 ★ kids **Tour Montparnasse.** Completed in 1973 and rising 210m (689 ft.) above the skyline, Paris's only inner-city skyscraper was denounced by some as "bringing Manhattan to Paris." The city soon outlawed any additional structures of this size in the heart of town. Today the tower is frequented for its panoramic viewing platform on the 56th floor. Feel your ears pop as you ascend in the elevator, before splurging on a cocktail or dinner in the touristy **Ciel de Paris Restaurant** (☎ 01-40-64-77-64; 3-course menu 80€; MC, V), famed for its views over the whole city. Today, the tower houses a mammoth underground shopping mall and a train station. 33 av. du Maine, 15th. ☎ 01-45-38-52-56. www.tourmont parnasse56.com. Admission 11€ adults, 8€ students 16–20, 4.40€ ages 7–14, free for children 6 and under. Apr–Sept daily 9:30am–11:30pm; Oct–Mar Sun–Thurs 9:30am–10:30pm, Fri–Sat and day before public holidays 9:30am–11pm. Last elevator 30 min. before closing. Métro: Montparnasse-Bienvenue.

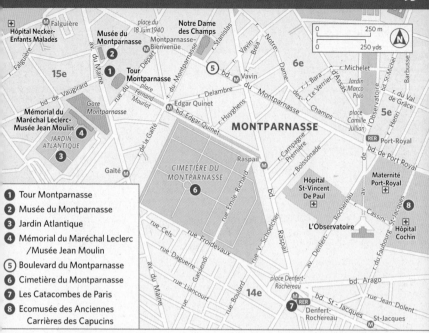

Key to map:

1. Tour Montparnasse
2. Musée du Montparnasse
3. Jardin Atlantique
4. Mémorial du Maréchal Leclerc /Musée Jean Moulin
5. Boulevard du Montparnasse
6. Cimetière du Montparnasse
7. Les Catacombes de Paris
8. Ecomusée des Anciennes Carrières des Capucins

2 Musée du Montparnasse. This small gallery, located down a cobbled lane, feels like a secret. It used to be an atelier-cum-canteen frequented by Picasso, Modigliani, and other artists. Nowadays it hosts temporary art exhibitions. 21 av. du Maine, 15th. ☎ 01-42-22-91-96. www.museedumontparnasse.net. Admission 6€ adults, 5€ students, free for children 11 and under. Tues–Sun 12:30–7pm during exhibitions only. Métro: Montparnasse-Bienvenue or Edgar Quinet.

3 Jardin Atlantique. Built in 1995, this peaceful green retreat rises above the modern concrete, 6m (20 ft.) above the tracks where trains head out toward Brittany. ☉ 30 min. Enter from Gare Montparnasse or place des Cinq Martyrs du Lycée Buffon, 15th. Daily dawn–dusk. Métro: Montparnasse-Bienvenue.

4 Mémorial du Maréchal Leclerc/Musée Jean Moulin. In the same building as the Jardin Atlantique, this rather austere-looking rooftop museum will fill you in on World War II France and the French Resistance. The absorbing and educational film archives and the art—which includes posters exhorting residents of occupied France to work in Germany—show

what the French endured. ☉ 1 hr. 23 allée de la 2e DB Jardin Atlantique (above Grandes Lignes of Gare Montparnasse), 15th. ☎ 01-40-64-39-44. www.ml-leclerc-moulin.paris.fr. Free admission. Tues–Sun 10am–6pm. Métro: Montparnasse-Bienvenue.

5 ⚲ Boulevard du Montparnasse. Just a block from the train station, this well-traveled street gets busiest at night, when its cafes, brasseries, *crêperies*, and cinemas are aglow, but at any time of day the enticing aromas may lure you to one of its many good options. Succumb to a full meal at no. 108, **Le Dôme,** now a seafood restaurant; or at no. 102, **La Coupole,** a fabulous Art Deco brasserie; or a bit farther along, at no. 171, **La Closerie des Lilas,** which includes among its former fans Picasso, Trotsky, Lenin, and Hemingway.

6 ★ Cimetière du Montparnasse. A short walk down boulevard Edgar Quinet, past its many attractive cafes, takes you to this well-known burial ground. Of the big three Parisian cemeteries (the other two being the

> *Music legend Serge Gainsbourg's tombstone is always covered in offerings from his fans.*

Cafes from the Crazy Years

Between the World Wars, the Lost Generation artists turned their backs on touristy Montmartre and centered their wild social lives on the cafes of the Left Bank. Montparnasse hangouts such as the Dôme, Coupole, Rotonde, and Sélect—still in business today—became legendary with patrons such as Picasso, Modigliani, Hemingway, and Man Ray. Fitzgerald was there when he was poor (when he was in the chips, he hung out at Le Ritz). Faulkner, Isadora Duncan, Miró, Joyce, Ford Madox Ford, and Trotsky were all in the neighborhood, too.

The life of Montparnasse still centers on its cafes and nightclubs, although many are but a shadow of what they used to be. Its heart is at the crossroads of bds. Raspail and de Montparnasse, one of the settings in Hemingway's *The Sun Also Rises*. Rodin's controversial statue of Balzac swathed in a cape stands guard over the prostitutes who cluster around the pedestal. Balzac seems to be the only one in Montparnasse who doesn't feel the impact of time and change.

Montmartre, p. 91, **14**, and the Père-Lachaise, p. 68), this is arguably at the bottom of the hierarchy, but for literary types and philosophical sorts, it's still a must-see. On its vast grounds are the graves of Samuel Beckett, Charles Baudelaire, and photographer Man Ray, as well as the shared grave of Simone de Beauvoir and Jean-Paul Sartre, usually covered in tiny notes of intellectual affection from fans. France's legendary singer-songwriter Serge Gainsbourg rests here, too; his grave is decorated in wine bottles, cigarette packets, and notes from fans of all ages—some too young to have remembered him alive. ◷ 45 min. 3 bd. Edgar-Quinet, 14th. There's a map posted to the left of the main gate. Free admission. Mon–Fri 8am–6pm; Sat 8:30am–6pm; Sun 9am–6pm. Métro: Edgar Quinet.

7 ★★ **Les Catacombes de Paris.** In the 18th century, Paris's communal graves were so full, they posed a health hazard. So in 1785, to prevent the spread of disease, more than six million graves were moved to a series of unused limestone quarries. Thus was born Paris's spookiest museum—the Catacombs—a long system of corridors, ghoulishly adorned

> *Because visitors frequently steal bones from the Catacombes, the most fragile are cemented in place.*

with anonymous bones, skulls, and altars. *Tip:* Bring a flashlight to get a good look at the bones, and wear footwear that you don't mind getting dirty. ⏲ 1 hr. 1 place Denfert-Rochereau, 14th. ☎ 01-43-22-47-63. Admission 7€ adults, 3.50€ ages 14–25, free for ages 13 and under. Tues–Sun 10am–5pm (tickets sold until 4pm). Métro/RER: Denfert Rochereau.

⑧ ★★ Ecomusée des Anciennes Carrières des Capucins. Twenty meters (66 ft.) below the Hôpital Cochin lies a maze of tunnels created in the 12th century, when Capucin monks decided to mine the limestone. About 30% of Notre-Dame's stones came from here, but more famously, the site is where the world's first *champignons de Paris* (mushrooms) appeared in the early 1800s, after cart drivers flushed their horses' dung into the holes. ⏲ 1 hr. Hôpital Cochin, rue du Faubourg St-Jacques, 14th. ☎ 01-43-89-78-03. By appointment only: Apply for a visit by emailing the SEADACC: association@seadacc.com. Free admission. RER: Port Royal.

> *A winding path at the Jardin Atlantique.*

The New Face of Paris: The Canals

In the northeast, along Canal St-Martin (10th) and Canal de l'Ourcq (19th), you will find legacies of early 20th-century industrialized Paris. The tree-lined quays, iron footbridges, and old factories are relics of the days when Edith Piaf lifted the spirits of the nation with her soulful "La Vie en Rose" (1946). Today, a bohemian vibe makes the canals' galleries, cafes, and shops a fun place to stroll. In summer, Parc de la Villette, with its museums, IMAX cinema, and open-air film festival, is an ideal place to spend a balmy day.

> *The spherical Géode cinema at Parc de la Villette gets its futuristic shine from 6,433 steel triangles.*

START Take the Métro to the République stop.

1 ★ **Canal St-Martin.** Walk up rue Faubourg du Temple, past ethnic grocers and discount stores, and turn left onto quai Valmy. Canal St-Martin, built between 1805 and 1825, begins at place de la Bastille but hides underground until boulevard Richard Lenoir nearby. This is the prettiest stretch, lined with chestnut trees and iron footbridges. If you saw the film *Amélie,* you may recognize it as the place where Audrey Tautou skimmed stones.

2 **Hôpital St-Louis.** Enter the St-Louis hospital, at the end of the avenue, founded by Henri IV to house plague victims away from the city center. It is built in the same brick-and-stone style as place des Vosges (p. 84, **7**).

3 **L'Hôtel du Nord.** The original facade from the Hôtel du Nord was made famous in director Marcel Carné's 1938 film of the same name. Today it's a bistro serving hearty French cuisine with a typical 1930s interior, and a fine address for a spot of

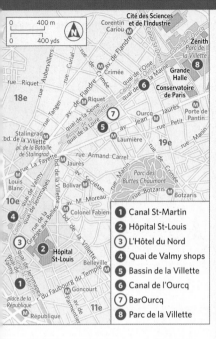

> Canal St-Martin and its locks were built in the early 19th century.

lunch. 102 quai de Jemmapes, 10th. ☎ 01-40-40-78-78. www.hoteldunord.org. Main courses from 16€. Daily lunch and dinner.

④ ★ Quai de Valmy shops. For funky women's clothes, **Dupleks,** at no. 83 (☎ 01-42-06-15-08), is a shop with a conscience, selling unusual, feminine garments made only from environmentally friendly and fair-trade materials. **Artazart,** also at no. 83 (☎ 01-40-40-24-00), is a cutting-edge bookshop that stocks glossy publications on fashion, art, and design.

⑤ Bassin de la Villette. At the top of Canal St-Martin, you reach the circular Barrière de la Villette, one of the few remaining 18th-century tollhouses designed by Nicolas Ledoux. The modernist fountains in front channel your view up the Bassin de la Villette, into Canal de l'Ourcq and past the twin MK2 art-house cinema complex, linked by a small boat. If you are a film buff, spend a few moments in the MK2's specialized bookshop (on quai de la Loire, 19th).

⑥ kids Canal de l'Ourcq. Created in 1813 by Napoleon to provide drinking water and haulage, this stretch is characterized by the retro hue of 1960s and 1970s tower blocks. It is separated from the Bassin de la Villette by an unusual hydraulic lifting bridge built in 1885.

⑦ 🍺 BarOurcq. Cheap drinks make this a popular bar, especially on a hot day when *boules* can be rented for a game of *pétanque* on the sand in front of the door. Be daring—challenge a local to a game. 68 quai de la Loire, 19th. ☎ 01-42-40-12-26. Drinks from 3€. Métro: Laumière.

⑧ ★★★ kids Parc de la Villette. A former slaughterhouse district is now a vast, retro-futurist park with lawns and playgrounds. On-site is the excellent **Cité des Sciences** (☎ 01-40-05-70-00; www.cite-sciences.fr), with a section dedicated to kids; the **Cité de la Musique** (☎ 01-44-84-44-84; www.cite-musique.fr), a museum and concert hall; **Le Zénith** concert hall (www.zenith-paris.com); and the silver-domed **Géode IMAX movie theater.** In August during the Cinéma en Plein Air festival, the park becomes an outdoor cinema with Europe's biggest inflatable screen. Av. Corentin-Cariou/av. Jean-Jaurès, 19th. ☎ 01-40-03-75-75. www.villette.com. Métro: Porte de la Villette or Porte de Pantin.

Paris Shopping Best Bets

Best Department Store
Galeries Lafayette, 40 bd. Haussmann, 9th (p. 102)

Best Place to Get That Parisian Look
Zadig & Voltaire, 42 rue des Francs Bourgeois, 3rd (p. 99)

Best Antiques
Les Puces de St-Ouen, av. de la Porte de Clignancourt, 18th (p. 99)

Best Guilt-Free Shopping
Merci, 111 bd. Beaumarchais, 3rd (p. 101)

Best Toys for Kids
Au Nain Bleu, 5 bd. Maleherbes, 8th (p. 104)

Best Bookshop
Shakespeare & Company, 37 rue de la Bûcherie, 5th (p. 71, **5**)

Best Wine
Lavinia, 3 bd. de la Madeleine, 1st (p. 104)

Best Gourmet Food
Hédiard, 21 place de la Madeleine, 8th (p. 103)

Best Sunday Shopping
Le Marais, Métro St-Paul, 3rd, 4th (p. 82)

Best Vintage Designer Clothing
Didier Ludot, 20-24 Galerie de Montpensier, Palais Royal, 1st (p. 105)

Best Environmentally Friendly Women's Clothes
Dupleks, 83 quai de Valmy, 10th (p. 103)

Best 19th-Century Shopping Malls
Passage Jouffroy, 10-12 bd. Montmartre; 9 rue de la Grange Batelière, 9th (p. 105)

Passage Verdeau, 6 rue de la Grange Batelière and 31bis rue du Faubourg Montmartre, 9th (p. 105)

Best Cheap Market
Marché Beauvau/Place Aligre, place Aligre, 12th (p. 104)

Best Organic Takeout Fare
Marché Biologique, bd. Raspail (btw. rues du Cherche-Midi and de Rennes), 6th (p. 104)

> *Shopping for old-world treasures in the Passage Jouffroy.*

Paris Shopping A to Z

Accessories, Clothing & Shoes
Gaspard Yurkievich MARAIS
End-of-season, ready-to-wear native Parisian design for men and women, plus a hot range of shoes. *38 rue Charlot, 3rd.* ☎ 01-42-77-42-48. MC, V. Métro: Filles du Calvaire.

Madelios MADELEINE
This two-floor men's megastore stocks more than 100 different labels, covering well-cut suits (both designer and high-street), shoes, and men's accessories. *23 bd. de la Madeleine, 1st.* ☎ 01-53-45-00-00. MC, V. Métro: Madeleine.

Pierre Hardy ASSEMBLEE NATIONALE
The inventive footwear for men and women is fabulously conceived—with a price tag to match. *9–11 place du Palais Bourbon, 7th.* ☎ 01-45-55-00-67. MC, V. Métro: Assemblé Nationale.

Zadig & Voltaire MARAIS
Wonder how the *parisiennes* get that cool, urban-but-chic look with faded jeans and cotton tops? Now you know. Texture is king here, with plenty of simple but wonderfully crafted tops, skirts, and bottoms. *42 rue des Francs Bourgeois, 3rd.* ☎ 01-44-54-00-60. MC, V. Métro: St-Paul or Hôtel de Ville.

Antiques & Curiosities
★★ **Les Puces de St-Ouen** ST-OUEN
Paris's most famous flea market is actually a grouping of more than a dozen flea markets—a complex of 2,500 to 3,000 open stalls and shops on the northern fringe of the city, selling everything from antiques to junk, from new to vintage clothing. Beware of pickpockets and teenage troublemakers as you make your way from the Métro. Open Sat-Mon 9am-7pm. Av.

> Organic vegetables and fresh shellfish make food shopping in Marché Beauvau a pleasure for the senses.

Dressing to the Nines
If designer clothes are your passion, you'll be happy to find exclusive *prêt-à-porter* brands on avenue Montaigne (8th; Métro: Champs-Elysées–Clémenceau) and rue du Faubourg St-Honoré (8th; Métro: Concorde). Jean Paul Gaultier stands out on his own at 2 rue Vivienne, 2nd (☎ 01-42-86-05-05; Métro: Bourse), and for luxury jewelry, try rue de la Paix and place Vendôme (1st; Métro: Opéra and Tuileries).

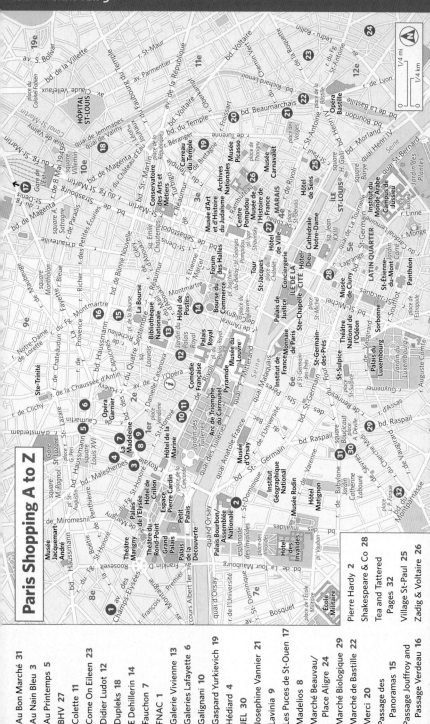

Paris Shopping A to Z

> *You'll find a mix of prices and merchandise at the Merci concept store.*

de la Porte de Clignancourt, 18th. MC, V (some stalls cash only). Métro: Porte de Clignancourt (turn left and cross bd. Ney, then walk north on av. de la Porte Montmartre and turn left onto rue des Rosiers).

Village St-Paul MARAIS
Boutiques in this minivillage of antiques, housed in small, linking courtyards, sell everything from retro furniture to clocks, kitchenware, and knickknacks. Always try to haggle down the prices. Rue St-Paul, rue Charlemagne, and quai des Célestins, 4th. MC, V. Métro: St-Paul.

Books & Music
FNAC CHAMPS-ELYSEES
This large chain of music and bookstores is known for its wide selection and good prices. Paris has several branches, the handiest of which is on the Champs-Elysées (open daily noon–midnight). You can also buy tickets to concerts and theater productions here. 74 av. des Champs-Elysées, 8th. ☎ 01-53-53-64-64. AE, MC, V. Métro: Franklin D. Roosevelt.

★ Galignani TUILERIES
Paris's first English bookstore—a venerable wood-paneled venue that has thrived since 1810—puts the emphasis on French classics, modern fiction, sociology, and fine arts. 224 rue de Rivoli, 1st. ☎ 01-42-60-76-07. MC, V. Métro: Tuileries.

Shakespeare & Company LATIN QUARTER
A beacon for secondhand American and European literature sold at competitive prices. See p. 71, ⑤.

★★ Tea and Tattered Pages ST-GERMAIN
If you fancy a cup of tea while you read, this homely English-language bookshop fits the bill nicely. 24 rue Mayet, 6th. ☎ 01-40-65-94-35. MC, V. Métro: Duroc.

Concept Stores
★ Colette TUILERIES/OPERA
This cutting-edge store is still a swank citadel for a la mode fashion. Even if you don't buy the zany accessories, designer clothes, makeup, or underground music, you can patronize the water bar with its three dozen brands of bottled water. 213 rue St-Honoré, 1st. ☎ 01-55-35-33-90. AE, MC, V. Métro: Tuileries.

★★★ Merci MARAIS/BASTILLE
This is Paris's first ever charity concept store. Items aren't always secondhand (some clothes, furniture lines, and other things have been created especially for the shop), and prices aren't always low, but there are

> Le Bon Marché is Paris's oldest department store, founded in 1863.

bargains to be had. The money raised goes to humanitarian organizations in Madagascar. There's also a funky cafe, a florist, and an Annick Goutal perfume section. 111 bd. Beaumarchais, 3rd. ☎ 01-42-77-01-90. MC, V. Métro: St-Sébastien–Froissart.

Bargain Hunting Seasons

The French government mandates three sales periods a year: 6 weeks in winter (usually in January); 6 weeks in summer (usually in June); and a third, 2-week sale, scheduled at the shopkeeper's discretion—provided it starts more than 4 weeks before the routine summer or winter sales. The best online source for current sales is www.shoppingbyparis.com.

Department Stores

★★ Au Printemps OPERA

Six floors of men and women's fashion include high-street and designer labels. Check out the magnificent stained-glass dome, through which turquoise light cascades into the sixth-floor cafe. 64 bd. Haussmann, 9th. ☎ 01-42-82-50-00. AE, MC, V. Métro: Havre-Caumartin. RER: Auber.

★ BHV MARAIS

The capital's best and most chic bazaar sells everything from DIY products to household appliances to books to men and women's clothes. 52–64 rue de Rivoli, 4th. ☎ 01-42-74-90-00. MC, V. Métro: Hôtel de Ville.

★★ Galeries Lafayette OPERA

Beneath its early-1900s stained-glass cupola, this store could provision a small city with everything from perfume to fashion. Also in the complex is **Lafayette Gourmet,** one of the

> Arrive at opening time to avoid the crowds at Au Printemps.

> *Shopping feels grand under Galeries Lafayette's Art Nouveau cupola.*

> *Window shoppers admire Josephine Vannier's chocolate sculptures.*

fanciest grocery stores in Paris. If you feel like splurging, hire a stylist for the day to help you spend your money on clothes (call for details). 40 bd. Haussmann, 9th. ☎ 01-42-82-34-56. AE, MC, V. Métro: Chaussée d'Antin. RER: Auber.

★★ Le Bon Marché ST-GERMAIN

This two-part Left Bank department store is overtly luxurious, selling fashion for men, women, and children; furniture; upscale gifts; and housewares. Also check out the next-door food court, **La Grande Epicerie de Paris**—a haven for gourmands everywhere. 22–24 rue de Sèvres, 7th. ☎ 01-44-39-80-00. AE, MC, V. Métro: Sèvres-Babylone.

Environmentally Friendly Shopping
Dupleks CANAL ST-MARTIN
Fun and ethical commerce brands, organic lingerie, and recycled leather bags for women with an eccentric edge. 83 quai de Valmy, 10th. ☎ 01-42-06-15-08. MC, V. Métro: Jacques Bonsergent.

★★★ JEL ST-GERMAIN & PASSY
Designer store **Le Bon Marché** (see above) and über-cool **Franck & Fils,** 80 rue de Passy, 16th (☎ 01-44-14-38-00; Métro: La Muette) stock JEL's highly wearable minimalist jewelry—made from Columbian gold extracted without chemicals or from recycled metals from the French clock and jewelry industry.

Food & Wine
★★ Fauchon MADELEINE
This upscale delicatessen plies gourmands with top-notch jams, crackers, pastas, breads, pastries, cheese, and chocolates. Prices are steep, but the inventory is fascinating. 26 place de la Madeleine, 8th. ☎ 01-70-39-38-10. MC, V. Métro: Madeleine.

★★ Hédiard MADELEINE
This temple of haute cuisine, which looks like a 19th-century spice emporium, is rich in coffees, teas, jams, and spices. An upstairs restaurant keeps foodies happy at lunchtime. 21 place de la Madeleine, 8th. ☎ 01-43-12-88-88. MC, V. Métro: Madeleine.

★ Josephine Vannier BASTILLE
This shop is a place in which to meditate, salivate, and overindulge in gloriously sculpted chocolates (think hearts, horses, shoes, and guitars). 4 rue du Pas de Mule, 4th. ☎ 01-44-54-03-09. MC, V. Métro: Bastille.

> *Choose which wine to taste at Lavinia.*

★★★ **Lavinia** MADELEINE

This wine paradise stocks everything from expensive rare French vintages to recent New World wines for under 10€ a bottle. Automatic wine-tasting machines on the ground floor add fun to your visit. **3 bd. de la Madeleine, 1st. ☎ 01-42-97-20-20. AE, MC, V. Métro: Madeleine.**

Kitchenware

★★ **E Dehillerin** CHÂTELET-LES-HALLES

Paris's top chefs come to this family-run business (open since 1820) for heavy copper pans, pastry tools, and clever kitchen accessories. It is heaven for anyone who has ever loved cooking. **18–20 rue Coquillière, 1st. ☎ 01-42-36-53-13. www.e-dehillerin.fr. MC, V. Mon 9am–noon and 2–6pm; Tues–Sat 9am–6pm. Métro/RER: Châtelet-Les Halles.**

Markets

Marché Beauvau/Place Aligre LEDRU-ROLLIN

The prolatariats' market (Tues–Sun 7am–2pm) is one of the cheapest in Paris—and one of the best. The covered Marché Beauvau offers uncompromisingly good meat, fish, cheese, and greens but costs more than the outside stalls. **Place Aligre, 12th. Cash only. Métro: Ledru-Rollin.**

> *E Dehillerin's interior drips in kitchen accessories.*

Marché Biologique ST-GERMAIN

Along boulevard Raspail, a tree-lined stretch between rue de Rennes and rue du Cherche-Midi, this organic market (Sun 9am–3pm) is where wealthy patrons indulge in top-notch produce, often locally sourced. You can also pick up hot soups, crêpes, and oysters to go. **Bd. Raspail (btw. rue du Cherche-Midi and rue de Rennes), 6th. Cash only. Métro: Rennes.**

★★ **Marché de Bastille** BASTILLE

This huge market (Thurs 7:30am–2:30pm; Sun 7am–3pm) is an excellent source for local cheese, meats, and fresh fish. Street performers usually liven up the shopping experience. **Bd. Richard Lenoir, 11th. Cash only. Métro: Bastille.**

Toys

★ **Au Nain Bleu** MADELEINE

Dressed up like a circus tent, the "Bleu Dwarf" has been selling children's toys since 1836. You'll find cuddly teddies, dolls, pirate ships, and wooden puppets. **5 bd. Malesherbes, 8th. ☎ 01-42-65-20-00. http://boutique.aunainbleu. com. MC, V. Métro: Madeleine.**

Sunday Shopping

Most shops close on Sundays, except in Le Marais (Métro: St-Paul), at Bercy Village (Métro: Cour St-Emilion), and in the Carousel du Louvre underneath the Louvre Museum (99 rue de Rivoli; Métro: Palais Royal–Musée du Louvre).

> *Wooden toys at Au Nain Bleu.*

The Shopping Malls of Yesteryear: Paris's Covered Passages

For charm and tantric browsing, Paris's covered passageways from the 18th and 19th centuries (www.passagesetgaleries. org) are old-world equivalents of modern shopping malls but with 10 times more atmosphere. These are some of the best:

Galerie Vivienne. Ochre paintwork, mythology-themed mosaics, and a glass roof under which shops sell everything from antiques and books to wine and silk flowers. *4 rue des Petits Champs, 5 rue de la Banque, 6 rue Vivienne, 2nd. www.galerie-vivienne.com. Métro: Bourse.*

Passage des Panoramas. Built in 1800, this was the first public area lit by gas lighting, in 1817. In one branch (Galerie St-Marc), you'll find **Stern** (no. 47), the oldest printer in town, dating from 1840. *11–13 bd. Montmartre, 151 rue Montmartre, 2nd. Métro: Richelieu Drouot or Grands Boulevards.*

★★ Passage Jouffroy & Passage Verdeau. These are the most atmospheric of the passageways (built in 1847), with the waxwork **Musée Grévin,** the **Hôtel Chopin,** where Sherlock and Watson wouldn't look out of place, and antique shops that sell everything from musical instruments to stamps, cameras, jewels, and furniture. *Passage Jouffroy is at 10–12 bd. Montmartre and 9 rue de la Grange Batelière, 9th. Passage Verdeau is at 6 rue de la Grange Batelière and 31bis rue du Faubourg Montmartre, 9th. Métro: Grands Boulevards.*

Vintage

★ Come On Eileen BASTILLE

Head downstairs to find a vast area, packed to the gunnels, with everything from 1960s shift dresses to 1970s suits to 1980s rock and punk gear. There's also a good designer section. *6–18 rue des Taillandiers, 11th.* ☎ 01-43-38-12-11. MC, V. Métro: Bastille.

★★★ Didier Ludot PALAIS-ROYAL

Recent and rare vintage haute couture and buyers with an eye for young talent (i.e., sussing out the vintage clothes of the future) make Didier Ludot an exceptional address for ordinary women with money to spend on an Audrey Hepburn wardrobe (Chanel, Hermès, and Dior). *20–24 Galerie de Montpensier, Palais Royal, 1st.* ☎ 01-42-96-06-56. MC, V. Métro: Palais Royal–Musée du Louvre.

Paris Restaurant Best Bets

Best Cheap Lunch
La Fresque, 100 rue Rambuteau, 1st (p. 111)

Coolest Low-Key Insider Spot
Frenchie, 5 rue du Nil, 2nd (p. 111)

Best Seafood
Antoine, 10 av. de New York, 16th (p. 107)

Best 1900s Parisian Brasserie
Le Train Bleu, 20 bd. Diderot, 12th (p. 113)

Best Bistro Fare
Bistrot Paul Bert, 18 rue Paul Bert, 11th (p. 107)

Best for Serious Gourmands
Le Grand Véfour, 17 rue de Beaujolais, 1st (p. 112)

Most Inventive Cuisine
La Gazetta, 29 rue de Cotte, 12th (p. 112)

Best Gluten-Free
Des Si et des Mets, 63 rue Lepic, 18th (p. 110)

Best Place for Veggies
Le Potager du Marais, 22 rue Rambuteau, 3rd (p. 112)

Best Timeless Classics on a Budget
Chartier, 7 rue du Faubourg Montmartre, 9th (p. 110)

Most Beautiful Dining Room
Bouillon Racine, 3 rue Racine, 6th (p. 107)

Best Pancakes Outside Brittany
Breizh Café, 109 rue Vieille du Temple, 3rd (p. 107)

> *Bouillon Racine has been feeding Parisians in beautiful Art Nouveau surroundings since 1906.*

Paris Restaurants A to Z

★★ **Antoine** CHAILLOT *SEAFOOD*
Seafood fans go wild for chef Mickaël Féval's perfect-every-time fish and innovative shell-fish dishes. The bouillabaisse is as good as any in Marseille, and the oysters come with shallot vinegar and creamy salted butter for your bread. It's a handy address to have up your sleeve when you're exploring the Chaillot quarters, the Champs-Elysées, and the Eiffel Tower. 10 av. de New York, 16th. ☎ 01-40-70-19-28. www.antoine-paris.fr. Main courses 35€–50€. 3-course menu 80€–100€. MC, V. Lunch and dinner daily. Métro: Alma Marceau.

★★★ **kids** **Bistrot Paul Bert** FAIDHERBE *FRENCH*
This locals' haunt has old tiled floors and a real zinc bar—just as a Parisian bistro should. The food is just as authentic and delicious: crispy duck confit with garlicky potatoes, home-made pâtés, and possibly the best *île flottante* (whisked egg whites in a vanilla sauce) in town. 11 rue Paul Bert, 12th. ☎ 01-43-72-24-01. Main courses 20€. 3-course menu 35€–40€. MC, V. Lunch and dinner Tues–Sat. Métro: Faidherbe-Chaligny.

★★★ **Bouillon Racine** ST-MICHEL *FRENCH*
The jewel-box dining room here is the best example of baroque Art Nouveau in Paris—a magnificent affair of swirling iron and wood-work, with twinkling stained glass, mirrors, and tiles. The brasserie fare is excellent, including carpaccio of beef with basil, lemon, and Parme-san; scallop risotto; and chicken blanquette. The two-course lunch menu is a steal at 15.50€. 3 rue Racine, 6th. ☎ 01-44-32-15-60. www. bouillon-racine.com. Main courses 18€. 3-course menu 35€. MC, V. Lunch and dinner daily. Métro: Odéon.

kids **Breizh Café** MARAIS *CREPERIE*
You could be in Brittany at this upbeat, mod-ern *crêperie,* which uses top-notch, mostly organic produce in its unusual and delicious fillings: think potato and smoked herring, or 70% cocoa solids in the chocolate dessert *crêpes.* You can wash it all down with one of 15 artisanal ciders. 109 rue Vieille-du-Temple, 3rd. ☎ 01-42-72-13-77. www.breizhcafe.com. Crepes 6€–14€. MC, V. Lunch and dinner Wed–Sun. Métro: Filles du Calvaire.

> *Start light at Bistrot Paul Bert, where main courses and desserts are exceptionally hearty.*

Paris Restaurants A to Z

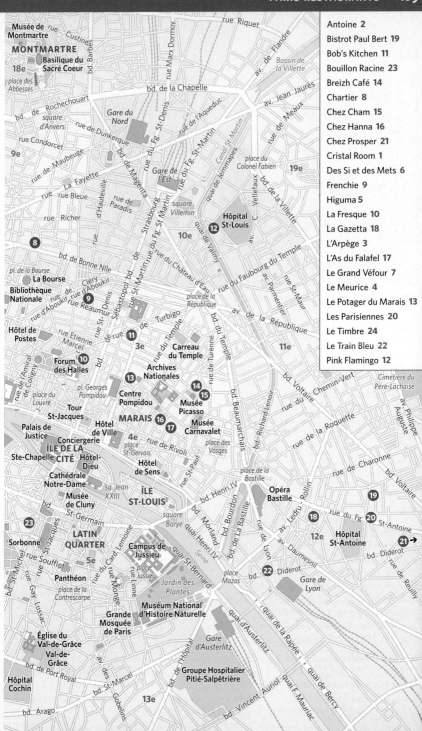

> *The Philippe Starck–designed interior of the Cristal Room.*

kids **Chartier** GRANDS BOULEVARDS *FRENCH*
This is one of the oldest and cheapest worker canteens in the whole city—a veritable institution for French staples such as *steak frites* (steak with fries), *oeuf mayonnaise* (eggs with mayonnaise), pâté, and onion soup. The impressive dining room is almost unchanged since the 19th century. **7 rue du Faubourg Montmartre, 9th. ☎ 01-47-70-86-29. www.restaurant-chartier.com. Main courses 9€. 3-course menu 18€. MC, V. Lunch and dinner daily. Métro: Grand Boulevards.**

★★ **Chez Cham** MARAIS *FRENCH FUSION*
Whether you're looking for excellent value or organic, vegetarian, or gluten-free food, Cham accommodates without forfeiting flavor in any of its healthful dishes, such as caviar of eggplant salad, roasted salmon with curry rice, and orange cake drizzled in caramel. The wine list is top of the line, too. **3 rue du Roi Doré, 3rd. ☎ 01-42-74-31-22. www.chezcham.com. Main courses 20€. Fixed-price dinner 22€; lunch 13€; 3-course menu 35€. MC, V. Lunch and dinner Mon–Sat. Métro: St-Sébastien-Froissart.**

kids **Chez Prosper** NATION *FRENCH BISTRO*
The swarm of hopefuls hankering for a table at this hip corner bistro is a sign not to be ignored. The atmosphere is buzzing, the service quick, the food lip-smacking—think *steak frites*

(13€) and humongous salads (12€)—and the bill is never a rude awakening. **7 av. du Trône, 11th. ☎ 01-43-73-08-51. Main courses from 12€. MC, V. Breakfast, lunch, and dinner daily. Métro/RER: Nation.**

Cristal Room CHAMPS-ELYSEES *HAUTE CUISINE*
You have to climb a red carpet encrusted with crystals to get to Baccarat's chic dining room. Once you're inside, chef Thomas L'Hérisson's cuisine lives up to the grand entrance with fillets of red mullet in a chickpea and coriander crust, or perfect pan-fried veal cutlet with tandoori gnocchi. A meal here includes a trip around the tiny but stunningly beautiful Baccarat museum. **11 place des Etats-Unis, 16th. ☎ 01-40-22-11-10. www.baccarat.fr. Lunch menu 38€–58€. 3-course menu 100€. MC, V. Lunch and dinner Mon–Sat. Métro: Boissière or Iéna.**

Des Si et des Mets MONTMARTRE *GLUTEN-FREE FRENCH* Traditional seafood blanquette, lemon and ginger lamb, and boeuf bourguignon with macaroni gratin are just some of the mouth-watering, gluten-free dishes prepared for you in this smart Montmartrois restaurant. **63 rue Lepic, 18th. ☎ 01-42-55-19-61. www.dessietdesmets.com. Main courses 16€. 3-course menu 26€; brunch 22€. MC, V. Lunch Sat–Sun; dinner Tues–Sun. Métro: Abbesses or Blanche.**

Frenchie SENTIER *FRENCH FUSION*
Frenchie's chef, Grégory Lemarchand, trained with Jamie Oliver in London. The result? Bold French cuisine quite unlike any other in the city. Start with calamari gazpacho, then try the braised beef with spiced spinach, and finish things off with coconut-and-strawberry tapioca. 2 rue du Nil, 2nd. ☎ 01-40-39-96-19. www.frenchie-restaurant.com. Main courses 12€–20€. 3-course menu 19€–35€. MC, V. Lunch Wed–Sat; dinner Tues–Sat. Métro: Sentier.

Higuma OPERA *JAPANESE*
This no-frills Japanese canteen is always full, so get here early if you don't want to queue in the street at mealtimes. The reasons behind its popularity are the quirky open kitchen, which fills the air with delicious-smelling steam, and the low prices—around 8€ for a giant bowl of soup, rice, or noodles, piled high with meat, seafood, or stir-fried vegetables. 32bis rue St-Anne, 1st. ☎ 01-47-03-38-59. Fixed-price menu from 13€. Main courses 9€. MC, V. Lunch and dinner daily. Métro: Pyramides.

★★ kids **La Fresque** LES HALLES *SOUTHWEST FRENCH* This cozy, atmospheric, centrally located hometown favorite is named for its frescoed walls. The southwest French cuisine is served with a smile (and usually a cheeky jibe) at unbeatable prices. 100 rue Rambuteau, 1st. ☎ 01-40-26-35-51. Main courses 17€. Lunch menu 14.50€. A la carte 25€. MC, V. Lunch Mon–Sat; dinner daily. Métro: Les Halles. RER: Châtelet–Les Halles.

Eco Eating—Where to Eat Green

Several Parisian restaurants—from Michelin-starred temples to snack joints—have made it their *raison d'être* to serve healthy dishes with traceable, organic ingredients. Here are three of the best:

Bob's Kitchen. This low-key American-run juice bar uses only organic ingredients in its soups and juices. *74 rue des Gravilliers, 3rd. ☎ 09-52-55-11-66. www.bobsjuicebar. com. Main courses from 9€. Mon–Fri 7:30am–3pm. Métro: Arts et Métiers.*

L'Arpège. Supplies for this exclusive eaterie come from chef Alain Passard's own farms in the Sarthe, Eure, and Mont-St-Michel regions, where horses replace polluting machinery, and pesticides (when necessary) are vegetable-based. *84 rue de Varenne, 7th. ☎ 01-47-05-09-06. www. alain-passard.com. Main courses 60€–140€. Mon–Fri noon–2:30pm and 7:30–10:30pm. Métro: Varenne.*

Le Meurice. This 3-star Michelin gem serves locavore menus at lunchtime; everything is sourced from Ile de France—the honey is from the Opéra Garnier (see "Fun Fact: Bees at the Opera," p. 44). *228 rue de Rivoli, 1st. ☎ 01-44-58-10-10. www.meuricehotel.fr. Main courses 60€–140€. Mon–Fri noon–2:30pm and 7:30–10pm. Métro: Tuileries.*

Falafel in Le Marais

For a scrumptious snack on the go, Le Marais's Jewish takeouts on rue des Rosiers can't be beat. **L'As du Falafel** is the most famous (no. 34). You'll find sizzling shwarmas and lip-smacking falafels wrapped in doughy bread, with salad, fried eggplant, hummus, and chili sauce at **Chez Hanna** (no. 54). Be sure you're not wearing garlic sauce when you're finished noshing. *Rue des Rosiers, 4th. Métro: St-Paul.*

★ **La Gazetta** FAIDHERBE *NOUVELLE CUISINE*
Scandinavian influences such as seaweed butter, borage leaves, and sweet-salty marinades work their way into an otherwise French menu here. It's a fabulous mix that makes the Gazetta one of the most exciting albeit low-key eateries in Paris right now. If you fancy trying a bit of everything on the menu, come in the evening for the all-inclusive seven-course menu (50€). 29 rue de Cotte, 12th. ☎ 01-43-47-47-05. www.lagazzetta.fr. Fixed-price lunch 16€–25€. Fixed-price dinner 38€–50€. MC, V. Lunch and dinner Tues–Sat. Métro: Ledru-Rollin.

★★★ **Le Grand Véfour** PALAIS ROYAL *HAUTE CUISINE* One of Paris's oldest and most historic restaurants (since 1784) is also one of the best. Watch the black-and-white-clad waiters perform a choreographed dance as they serve you blue lobster, foie gras, lamb with a pea and tomato *compressé,* and strawberry and lemon pie—with a glass of fine vintage wine to match each course. 17 rue de Beaujolais, 1st. ☎ 01-42-96-56-27. www.grand-vefour.com. Main courses 60€. 3-course menu 130€. Fixed-price lunch 88€. MC, V. Lunch Mon–Fri; dinner Mon–Thurs. Métro: Palais Royal–Musée du Louvre.

Le Potager du Marais MARAIS *VEGETARIAN* This tiny, narrow restaurant serves vegetarian dishes so tasty—think vegetable *croustillant* in mushroom sauce on a bed of rice and lentils—that meat eaters won't complain. Several equally delicious gluten-free options are also available. 22 rue Rambuteau, 3rd. ☎ 01-42-74-24-66. www.lepotagerdumarais.com. 3 courses 30€. MC, V. Lunch and dinner daily. Métro: Rambuteau.

★★ **Les Parisiennes** FAIDHERBE *PROVENCAL* French actor Edouard Baer opened this den of coolness with a group of friends from Marseille. The result is a menu that ranges from spicy Moroccan tagines to sardine tapenade, and a Thursday pastis night with a DJ from 7pm to 10pm. 243 rue du Faubourg St-Antoine,

> *Le Grand Véfour is Paris's oldest restaurant.*

> *Dining rooms don't get more opulent than this one at Le Train Bleu.*

> *Pink Flamingo's pizzas have wacky names like "Obama" and "Bjork."*

11th. ☎ 01-43-73-37-58. 3 courses 40€. MC, V. Dinner Tues–Sun. Métro: Faidherbe-Chaligny.

★★ Le Timbre LUXEMBOURG *FRENCH*
"The Stamp" is, as its name implies, a tiny restaurant. But what it lacks in space, it makes up for in the kitchen, where English chef Chris Wright creates simple dishes such as asparagus and crumbled Parmesan, pork with red onions, and *moelleux au chocolat* (squishy chocolate cake) to die for. There's an appetizing wine list, too. **3 rue Ste-Beuve, 6th.** ☎ 01-45-49-10-40. www.restaurantletimbre.com. Lunch menu 26€. 3-course menu 40€. MC, V. Lunch and dinner Tues–Sat. Métro: Vavin.

★★ Le Train Bleu GARE DE LYON *FRENCH BRASSERIE* This has to be one of the most dramatic settings for a meal in Paris—a listed dining room from the 1900 World's Fair, dressed to the nines in gold, dark wood, and painted ceilings, inside the Gare de Lyon train station. Expect fine, classic French brasserie cooking: roasted lobster, Lyon sausage peppered with pistachios, steamed cod with sea-urchin coral, and rum baba. The wine list is long and varied. **Gare de Lyon, place Louis Armand, 12th.** ☎ 01-43-43-09-06. www.le-train-bleu.com. Fixed-price menu 52€–96€. 3 courses 100€–120€. MC, V. Lunch and dinner daily. Métro/RER: Gare de Lyon.

kids Pink Flamingo CANAL ST-MARTIN *PIZZA*
Not only are the Pink's pizzas quirky (try the Poulidor: goat cheese and sliced duck breast), they're also put together with the best, freshest ingredients, and the crusts are made with organic flour. If you picnic by the canal, take a pink helium balloon, find your spot, and wait for the pizza delivery boy to cycle to you. There is a second location at 105 rue Vieille du Temple, 3rd. **67 rue Bichat, 10th.** ☎ 01-42-02-31-70. www.pinkflamingopizza.com. Pizzas from 10.50€. MC, V. Lunch and dinner Tues–Sun. Métro: Jacques Bonsergent.

Paris Hotel Best Bets

Best "Only in Paris" Hideaway
Pension les Marronniers, 78 rue d'Assas, 6th (p. 120)

Best Stylish Retreat
Hôtel Particulier, 28 av. Junot, 18th (p. 118)

Best Cheap & Centrally Located
Hôtel Henri IV, 25 place Dauphine, 1st (p. 117)

Most Hip Hotel
Mama Shelter, 107 rue de Bagnolet, 20th (p. 119)

Best for Families
Hôtel Lion d'Or, 5 rue la Sourdière, 1st (p. 118)

Best Quirky Hotel
Paris Yacht, quai de la Tournelle, 5th (p. 121)

Best B&B
Bonne Nuit Paris, 63 rue Charlot, 3rd (p. 115)

Best Authentic Neighborhood Hotel
Hôtel du Jeu de Paume, 54 rue St-Louis-en-l'Ile, 4th (p. 117)

Best Flat to Rent
Martinn, 69 rue d'Argout, 2nd (p. 119)

Best Cheap Ecologically Friendly Hotel
Solar Hôtel, 22 rue Boulard, 14th (p. 121)

Best Youth Accommodations
St-Christopher's Inn, 159 rue de Crimée, 19th (p. 121)

Best Detox Hotel
Hôtel Gabriel, 25 rue du Grand Prieuré, 11th (p. 117)

Best Value
Aviatic Hotel, 105 rue de Vaugirard, 6th (p. 115)

> *The Aviatic hotel was where World War I aviators used to hang out.*

Paris Hotels A to Z

★★★ **Aviatic Hotel** MONTPARNASSE/ST-GER-MAIN Rooms in this gem of a family-run hotel are lushly decorated in thick, patterned fabrics and parquet floors. The hearty breakfasts are served in a bistro-style room that feels like a Left Bank institution. 105 rue de Vaugirard, 6th. ☎ 01-53-63-25-50. www.aviatichotel.com. 42 units. Doubles 95€–260€. AE, MC, V. Métro: Montparnasse or St-Placide.

★★★ **Best Western Premier Regent's Garden** CHAMPS-ELYSEES A good, guilt-free night's sleep is guaranteed in this environmentally friendly hotel, whose efforts to reduce carbon emissions have earned it the difficult-to-obtain European Ecolabel. Rooms are elegant, in bold stripes and patterns; there's a relaxing spa and a flower-filled courtyard—perfect for breakfast alfresco. 6 rue Pierre Demours, 8th. ☎ 01-45-74-07-30. www.hotel-regents-paris.com. 40 units. Doubles 160€–320€. AE, MC, V. Métro: Ternes or Charles de Gaulle–Etoile.

★ **Bonne Nuit Paris** MARAIS Wooden beams and period furniture abound in this fabulous B&B, where three individually decorated rooms make you feel as if you're living in Paris rather than visiting it. It's in a great spot for delving into contemporary art galleries, locals' restaurants and cafes, and trendy one-off boutiques. 63 rue Charlot, 3rd. ☎ 01-42-71-83-56. www.bonne-nuit-paris.com. 3 units. Doubles 120€–175€. MC, V. Métro: Filles du Calvaire.

The Five Hôtel LATIN QUARTER The ultra-modern rooms are small but impressive, with Chinese lacquer, velvet fabrics, fiber-optic lighting that makes you feel as though you're sleeping under a starry sky, and your own room fragrance. In all, it's a fine design hotel and convenient base for exploring the Left Bank. 3 rue Flatters, 5th. ☎ 01-43-31-74-21. www.thefivehotel.com. 24 units. Doubles 200€–350€. MC, V. Métro: Les Gobelins. RER: Port Royal.

> *You can gaze at the Eiffel Tower from the top floor suite at the Renaissance Paris Arc de Triomphe hotel.*

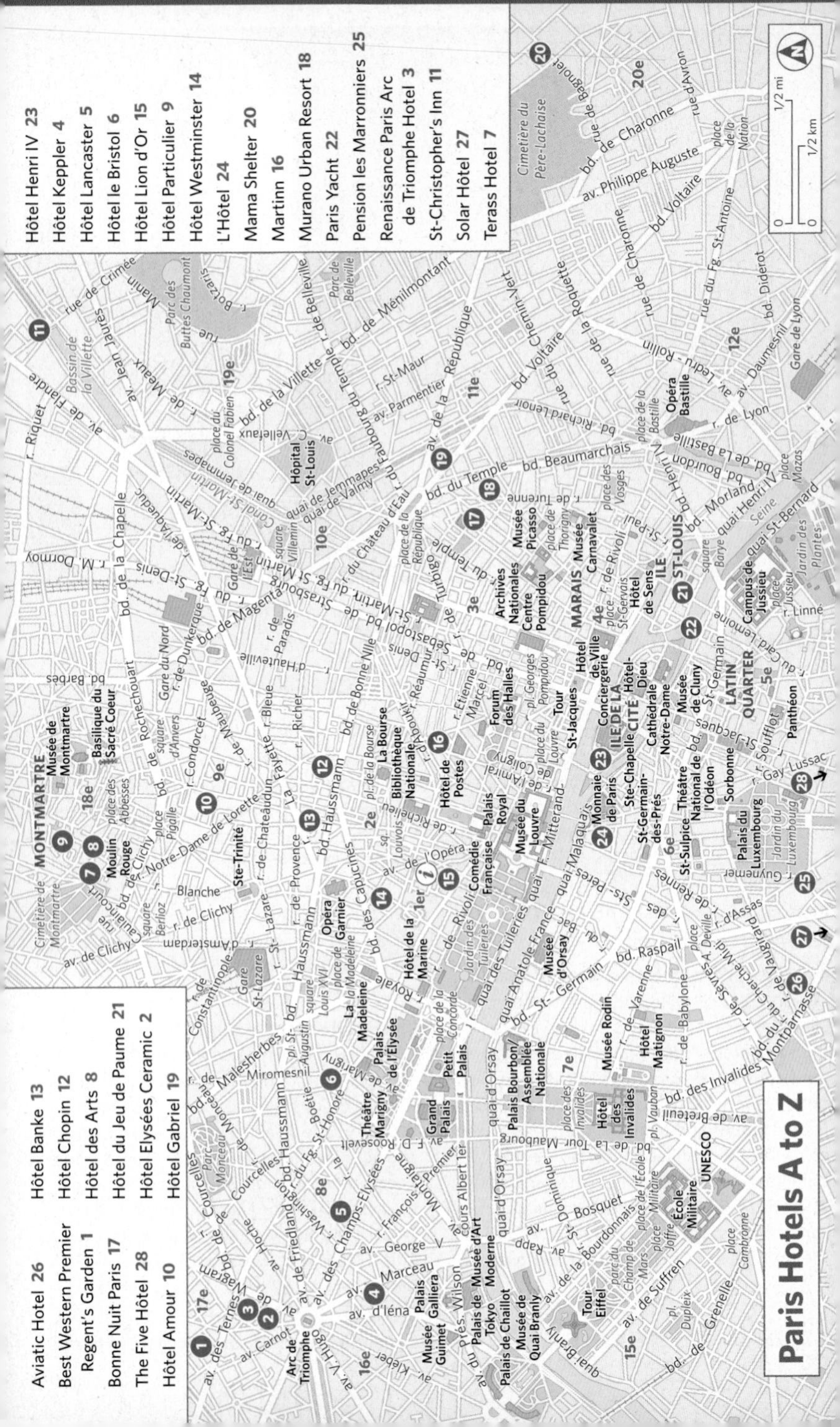

Paris Hotels A to Z

Hôtel Henri IV 23
Hôtel Keppler 4
Hôtel Lancaster 5
Hôtel le Bristol 6
Hôtel Lion d'Or 15
Hôtel Particulier 9
Hôtel Westminster 14
L'Hôtel 24
Mama Shelter 20
Martinn 16
Murano Urban Resort 18
Paris Yacht 22
Pension les Marronniers 25
Renaissance Paris Arc
de Triomphe Hotel 3
St-Christopher's Inn 11
Solar Hôtel 27
Terass Hotel 7

Aviatic Hotel 26
Best Western Premier
Regent's Garden 1
Bonne Nuit Paris 17
The Five Hôtel 28
Hôtel Amour 10

Hôtel Banke 13
Hôtel Chopin 12
Hôtel des Arts 8
Hôtel du Jeu de Paume 21
Hôtel Elysées Ceramic 2
Hôtel Gabriel 19

> *The grand lobby at the Hôtel Banke.*

★ Hôtel Amour PIGALLE

Rooms in this boutique hotel are individually decorated by progressive artists such as Sophie Calle, M&M, and Pierre Le Tan. The result in some is risqué (photos of bare bottoms), but if you mind, what are you doing in Pigalle? The brasserie-bar with a hidden garden is a hit among Paris's trendy crowds. 8 rue Navarin, 9th. ☎ 01-48-78-31-80. www.hotelamourparis. fr. 20 units. Doubles 140€–275€. AE, MC, V. Métro: Pigalle or St Georges.

★ Hôtel Banke OPERA

This smart hotel has a breathtaking neo–Belle Epoque lobby, left over from a time when the building was a bank (hence the name). Rooms are stylish in browns and reds, and beds have ultra-comfy mattresses. The restaurant offers a menu with a Spanish twist. 20 rue Lafayette, 9th. ☎ 01-55-33-22-22. www.derbyhotels.com. 94 units. Doubles 200€–350€. AE, MC, V. Métro: Le Peletier.

Hôtel Chopin GRANDS BOULEVARDS

This intimate, eccentric hotel is hidden inside a curious 19th-century covered passage. The Victorian lobby has elegant woodwork, rooms are comfortably furnished, and staff members are friendly. 10 bd. Montmartre, 9th. ☎ 01-47-70-58-10. www.hotelbretonnerie.com. 36 units. Doubles 88€–102€. Métro: Grands Boulevards.

Hôtel des Arts MONTMARTRE

A friendly black Labrador welcomes you to this old-fashioned but utterly charming hotel. Rooms are simple, but some look out over Montmartre's rooftops. You couldn't ask for a better spot for exploring *La Butte*. 5 rue Tholozé, 18th. ☎ 01-46-06-30-52. www.arts-hotel-paris.com. 50 units. Doubles 95€–165€. MC, V. Métro: Abbesses or Blanche.

★ kids Hôtel du Jeu de Paume THE ISLANDS

Seventeenth-century beams, a private garden, a games room, and a mix of period and modern furniture distinguish this hotel, set in what was formerly a tennis court for Louis XIII. It's utterly romantic, but two self-catering apartments make it a smart choice for families, too. 54 rue St-Louis-en-L'Ile, 4th. ☎ 01-43-26-14-18. www.jeudepaumehotel.com. 30 units. Doubles 285€–560€. Apartments 620€–900€. AE, MC, V. Métro: Pont Marie.

Hôtel Elysées Ceramic ETOILE

An ornate ceramic facade helps make this celebrated Art Nouveau building easy to find. Inside, the clean, modern, attractive rooms are less over-the-top, and the shaded patio is a godsend in summer. 34 av. de Wagram, 8th. ☎ 01-42-27-20-30. www.elysees-ceramic.com. 57 units. Doubles 220€. AE, DC, MC, V. Métro: Charles de Gaulle–Etoile.

★ Hôtel Gabriel REPUBLIQUE

Relaxing massages, healthy food, Zen decor, and sanctuary is what you get for your money at Paris's first-ever detox hotel. Come here to wind down from the city life outside. 25 rue du Grand Prieuré, 11th. ☎ 01-47-00-13-38. www.gabrielparismarais.com. 40 units. Doubles 160€–280€. Métro: République.

★★★ Hôtel Henri IV THE ISLANDS

This is possibly Paris's best budget hotel, at the heart of the Ile de la Cité, near Notre-Dame and pont Neuf. Rooms are very basic but clean, and the top-floor rooms have balconies. Book

> You'll be feeling "Paris'zen" after an hour at Hôtel Gabriel's detox massage room.

way in advance. Only 11 rooms have en suite bathrooms. 25 place Dauphine, 1st. ☎ 01-43-54-44-53. www.henri4hotel.fr. 15 units. Doubles 45€–75€. MC, V. Métro: Pont Neuf.

★ Hôtel Keppler CHAMPS-ELYSEES
This family-run boutique hotel has small but perfectly designed rooms decorated in stripes and block colors. The top floor's jet-setters' suites afford splendid balcony views across the city. 10 rue Keppler, 16th. ☎ 01-47-20-65-05. www.hotelkeppler.com. 39 units. Doubles 300€–850€. AE, MC, V. Métro: George V.

★★ Hôtel Lancaster CHAMPS-ELYSEES
Mick Jagger, David Lynch, and Pedro Almodóvar all love the Lancaster, with its Empire-style furniture and decor throughout. The Marlene Dietrich Suite—named after the Berlin-born actress who lived in the hotel in the 1930s—is particularly stunning. The restaurant is a fashionable address, too. 7 rue de Bérri, 8th. ☎ 01-40-76-40-76. www.hotel-lancaster.fr. 57 units. Doubles 520€–670€. AE, MC, V. Métro: Georges V.

Hôtel le Bristol FAUBOURG ST-HONORE
Set amid luxury boutiques such as Givenchy and Dolce & Gabbana, the Bristol is supremely luxurious yet discreet, with a clientele to match. Chef Eric Fréchon's Michelin-starred restaurant is possibly the best in town. 112 rue du Faubourg St-Honoré, 8th. ☎ 01-53-43-43-00. www.lebristolparis.com. 187 units. Doubles 600€–900€. AE, MC, V. Métro: Champs-Elysées–Clémenceau.

★★ kids Hôtel Lion d'Or TUILERIES
The "Golden Lion" has bright, simple rooms plus fully furnished apartments that sleep up to five people. It's well located, too, right near the Louvre. 5 rue de la Sourdière, 1st. ☎ 01-42-60-79-04. www.hotel-louvre-paris.com. 27 units. Doubles 120€–195€. Apartments: 280€–490€. MC, V. Métro: Tuileries.

★★★ Hôtel Particulier MONTMARTRE
You'll be hard-pressed to find somewhere more romantic or stylish than this hidden gem, nestled down a leafy passage by a rock called *Rocher de la Sorcière* (Witch's Rock).

> *The Bristol's swimming pool makes you feel like you're on a cruise ship.*

Avant-garde artists have given each room a special touch. 23 av. Junot, 18th. ☎ 01-53-41-81-40. http://hotel-particulier-montmartre.com. 5 units. Doubles 290€–590€. MV, V. Métro: Lamarck-Caulincourt.

★★★ Hôtel Westminster OPERA

This gorgeous hotel is favored by shoppers who prowl place Vendôme, rue du Faubourg St-Honoré, and the department stores around Opéra Garnier for chic attire. Decor is resolutely stylish: classic marbles, deep woods, and plush fabrics. The Michelin-starred restaurant is known for its fine contemporary French cuisine. 13 rue de la Paix, 2nd. ☎ 01-42-61-57-46. http://warwickwestminsteropera.com. 102 units. Doubles 350€–650€. AE, MC, V. Métro: Opéra. RER: Auber.

★★ L'Hôtel ST-GERMAIN-DES-PRES

Oscar Wilde died a pauper here, but don't just come for a pilgrimage: The Michelin-starred restaurant is a baroque affair both on the plate and in the dining room; rooms are luxuriously decorated in period styles; and Johnny Depp

has been known to frequent the bar. A *bijou* pool and spa finish off the experience. 13 rue des Beaux-Arts, 6th. ☎ 01-44-41-99-00. www.l-hotel.com. 20 units. Doubles 255€–700€. AE, MC, V. Métro: St-Germain-des-Prés or Mabillon.

★★ Mama Shelter PERE-LACHAISE

Rooms in this starkly modern designer hotel, set in a converted parking lot, are simple with fun touches, such as superhero-mask light shades and working Apple computers on the walls. Downstairs, a bar, pizza parlor, and restaurant draw a stylized crowd of international trendies. It's *the* place to see and be seen. 107 rue de Bagnolet, 20th. ☎ 01-43-48-48-48. www.mamashelter.com. 170 units. Doubles 89€–400€. MC, V. Métro: Alexandre Dumas or Porte de Bagnolet.

★★ Martinn SENTIER

This self-catering, one-bedroom apartment is the sort of place you wished you owned: Heavy doors open onto a lovely taffeta-clad bedroom, an airy living area, and a kitchen that cries out to be cooked in. Cooking classes

> *Hidden away from view, the Hôtel Particulier feels like a well-guarded secret.*

and wine-tasting are available on request. 62 rue d'Argout, 2nd. ☎ 06-23-55-34-82. www. key2paris.com. 1 unit. 680€ per week. MC, V. Métro: Sentier.

Bed & Breakast in Paris

For a special, cozy Parisian experience, consider booking a B&B. More intimate than a hotel, B&Bs can offer an insider's view of the city. Hosts range from bohemian artists and housewives to supergrannies and business folk who are away a lot. Here are some reliable places: **Alcove & Agapes** (☎ 01-44-85-06-05; www.bed-and-breakfast-in-paris.com), with more than 100 regularly inspected addresses in central Paris, and **Hôtes Qualité Paris** (www.hqp.fr), which has an excellent selection verified by City Hall. For an eccentric stay in the heart of St-Ouen's flea markets, try **Le Loft** (www.chezbertrand.com)—a ground-floor apartment with a Citroën 2CV that snugly sleeps two lovers.

★ **Murano Urban Resort** REPUBLIQUE/MARAIS With its furry elevators and wild, angular decor, this trend-setting, minimalist hotel is not everyone's cup of tea, but those who are into cutting-edge design will likely find it fun, well conceived, and possibly the most memorable place they've stayed in. The restaurant serves excellent cuisine appreciated by the locals. 13 bd. du Temple, 3rd. ☎ 01-42-71-20-00. www. muranoresort.com. 52 units. Doubles 400€–600€. AE, MC, V. Métro: Filles du Calvaire or Temple.

★★★ **Pension les Marronniers** LUXEMBOURG This is one of the city's very last *pensions de famille* (boarding houses)—perfect for nostalgic travelers looking for a slice of Paris from days gone by. It has been in the owner's family since the 1930s and offers great views over the Luxembourg Gardens. Rooms are cluttered—just as they should be. Half-board is available. 78 rue d'Assas, 6th. ☎ 01-43-26-37-71. www.pension-marronniers.com. 7 units. Doubles 40€–70€. No credit cards. Weekly and monthly rentals. Métro: Vavin.

> *Patrons of Paris Yacht can slumber on the Seine in a handsomely restored barge from 1930.*

★★ Renaissance Paris Arc de Triomphe Hotel

CHAMPS-ELYSEES   Order a Paris Sky View room and watch the Eiffel Tower twinkle from your balcony in this trendy, 5-star hotel. Expect elegantly modern architecture and, in the Macassar restaurant, scrumptious, Indonesian-inspired dishes such as *ikan dabu dabu* (marinated, roasted swordfish with basmati rice and sauce *vierge*). 39 av. de Wagram, 17th. ☎ 01-55-37-55-37. www.marriott.co.uk. 118 units. Doubles from 300€. MC, V. Métro: Ternes.

St-Christopher's Inn CANAL DE L'OURCQ

This English youth hostel chain, set inside an old boat hangar, has funky decor and unbeatable prices. Private rooms and dormers are marine-themed. Dorms are single-sex and mixed, so check when you book. 159 rue de Crimée, 19th. ☎ 01-40-34-34-40. www.st-christophers.co.uk. 350 beds. Dorm 12€ (occasional special offers)–28€. Doubles 37.50€–50€. Métro: Crimée.

★★★ Solar Hôtel DENFERT-ROCHEREAU

Paris's first low-budget, environmentally friendly hotel is a fabulous concept: Modern rooms without frills but with A/C, TV, and phones; a pretty garden where you can picnic and hire bikes; static prices year-round; and a *genuine* low-carbon charter. 22 rue Boulard, 14th. ☎ 01-43-21-08-20. www.solarhotel.fr. 34 units. Doubles 59€. MC, V. Métro/RER: Denfert-Rochereau.

Terass Hotel MONTMARTRE

This hotel is a find, with a marble-floored lobby, blond-oak paneling, antiques, and paintings. Guest rooms have high ceilings and sophisticated decor. The *terrasse* bar-restaurant affords panoramic views over the whole city. 12 rue Joseph de Maistre, 18th. ☎ 01-46-06-72-85. www.terrass-hotel.com. 98 units. Doubles 180€–345€. Métro: place de Clichy or Blanche.

Paris Yacht

Fancy your very own houseboat at the foot of Notre-Dame? This 1930s barge, which sleeps up to four guests, has to be one of the most original places you can sleep in the city—as long as you don't suffer from seasickness. In fine weather, the upper deck provides a panoramic, Seine-side setting for a drink or dinner. *Quai de la Tournelle, 5th.* ☎ 06-88-70-26-36. *www. paris-yacht.com. From 300€ /night. No credit cards. Métro: Maubert-Mutualité.*

Paris Bar & Cafe Best Bets

Best Hot Chocolate
Angelina, 226 rue de Rivoli, 1st **(p. 126)**

Best Place to Try a Wine from Each Region
Le Baron Rouge, 1 rue Théophile Roussel, 12th **(p. 127)**

Best Place to Share Space with Paris's "It" Crowds
Le Secret, 16 av. de Friedland, 8th **(p. 127)**

Best Place to Read over a Glass of Chardonnay
La Belle Hortense, 31 rue Vieille-du-Temple, 4th **(p. 127)**

Best Place to Learn to Make Cocktails
Le Forum, 4 bd. Maleherbes, 8th **(p. 125)**

Best Place to Recharge near the Eiffel Tower
La Café du Marché, 38 rue Cler, 7th **(p. 123)**

Best Expat Hangout
Harry's New York Bar, 5 rue Daunou, 2nd **(p. 125)**

Best Place to Channel Man Ray & Cocteau
Le Select, 99 bd. de Montparnasse, 6th **(p. 125)**

Most Chic Cocktail on the Rocks
Le Forum, 4 bd. Malesherbes, 8th **(p. 125)**

Best Place to Steal a Kiss over Coffee
La Palette, 36 rue de Seine, 6th **(p. 123)**

Best Place to Relax over Fries & Beer
Dédé La Frite, 135 rue de Montmartre, 2nd **(p. 127)**

> *The Belle Epoque Angelina tearoom is famous for its melted hot chocolate drink, served with whipped cream.*

Paris Bars & Cafes A to Z

Cafes

Chez Prune CANAL ST-MARTIN
This bobo magnet serves excellent, well-priced food, including some vegetarian dishes (from 13€), coffee, beer, and wine to local arty types and cool do-littlers taking in the canal-side view. 71 quai de Valmy, 10th ☎ 01-42-41-30-47. Métro: République.

kids **La Café du Marché** EIFFEL TOWER
A 10-minute walk from old Eiffel's iron edifice, this cozy cafe, on a street laden with food shops and stalls, feels off the beaten tourist track. That's good news if you're hankering for a food fix away from the baseball caps, rucksacks, cameras, and sneakers of thousands of tourists at the tower. The salads are copious, often served with fried potatoes, and the house carafes of wine are eminently drinkable. 38 rue Cler, 7th. ☎ 01-47-05-51-27. Métro: Ecole Militaire.

★ **La Palette** ST-GERMAIN-DES-PRES
This is a favorite rendezvous for students from the nearby fine arts school. It's also rather romantic (especially the fresco-painted back room). A drink here means following in the steps of Hemingway and Jim Morrison; and if you can find a seat on the leafy terrace, you may well want to sit there long enough to watch their ghosts go by. Also makes a handy base for exploring St-Germain's art galleries. 43 rue de Seine, 6th. ☎ 01-43-26-68-15. Métro: Odéon.

★ **Le Fumoir** LOUVRE
An intriguing mix of hip Parisians and Euro-loungers comes to linger over coffee or eat good food in a setting of book-lined walls that recalls the great cafes of French colonial Indochina in the 1930s. You'll also find new-generation "cafe workers"—freelancers who have convinced themselves they'll get more work done by sitting in a cafe, pumping the free Wi-Fi. 6 rue de l'Amiral-Coligny, 1st. ☎ 01-42-92-00-24. www.lefumoir.com. Métro: Louvre-Rivoli.

★ kids **Le Rostand** LUXEMBOURG
A classy, 19th-century interior, a shaded terrace, and views onto the Luxembourg garden

> *A waiter balances steak and potatoes at La Palette, one of Paris's most romantic cafes.*

Paris Bars & Cafes A to Z

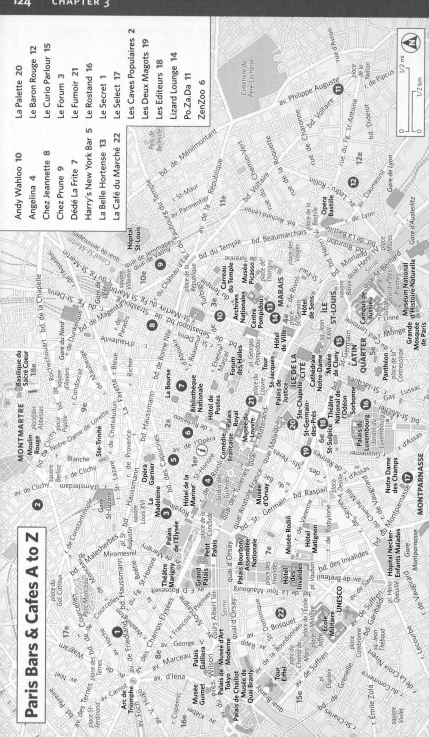

Andy Wahloo 10
Angelina 4
Chez Jeannette 8
Chez Prune 9
Dédé La Frite 7
Harry's New York Bar 5
La Belle Hortense 13
La Café du Marché 22
La Palette 20
Le Baron Rouge 12
Le Curio Parlour 15
Le Forum 3
Le Fumoir 21
Le Rostand 16
Le Secret 1
Le Select 17
Les Caves Populaires 2
Les Deux Magots 19
Les Editeurs 18
Lizard Lounge 14
Po.Za.Da 11
ZenZoo 6

> *Les Deux Magots and other literary cafes in St-Germain made the neighborhood a magnet for writers and artists in the 1920s.*

railings make this chic cafe a hot spot for locals and tourists alike. The coffee here isn't cheap, but it will give you the chance to sit at your table for hours. The brasserie menu is a delight, with hearty meat and fish dishes, while the cheaper bar menu includes omelettes and salads. 6 place Edmond Rostand, 6th. ☎ 01-43-54-61-58. RER: Luxembourg.

Les Deux Magots ST-GERMAIN-DES-PRES
Everyman and his dog seems to want a piece of Jean-Paul Sartre and Simone de Beauvoir's old hangout. If you want to avoid the crowds, come by on a weekday afternoon; Paris's literary legacy still lives on in the occasional author and editor who pop in here for a chat. The food is overpriced, and the waiters are nonchalant, but if you've never been before, it's worth tipping your hat at this legendary address. 6 place St-Germain-des-Prés, 6th. ☎ 01-45-48-55-25. www.lesdeuxmagots.fr. Métro: St-Germain-des-Prés.

★★ Les Editeurs ODEON/LUXEMBOURG
Les Editeurs quite fittingly looks like a library, covered from floor to ceiling in books and author memorabilia. This is a fine spot to relax over coffee, wine, or a meal—plus you can read the books on the shelves. Brunch is a good value at 25.50€ for juice, coffee, pastries, eggs, smoked salmon, *frommage frais* (fresh cheese), and fruit salad. 4 carrefour de l'Odéon, 6th. ☎ 01-43-26-67-76. www.lesediteurs.fr. Métro: Odéon.

Le Select MONTPARNASSE
The Lost Generation of Americans, along with Man Ray and Picasso, all used to hang out in the Select, and today the bar still does a roaring trade on their legacy. Nevertheless, you won't be disappointed; with its kitsch moldings and wooden tables, it still looks the part. On some nights (usually the first and third Thursdays of the month), you can listen in on philosophy meetings. 99 bd. du Montparnasse, 6th. ☎ 01-45-48-38-24. Métro: Vavin.

Cocktails

★★ Harry's New York Bar OPERA
At "sank roo doe noo," as the ads tell you to instruct your cabdriver, is the most famous bar in Paris. Opened on Thanksgiving Day 1911 by an expatriate named MacElhone, it's where members of the World War I ambulance corps drank themselves silly. In addition to being Hemingway's favorite haunt, Harry's is where the White Lady and Sidecar cocktails were invented; it's also the reputed birthplace of the Bloody Mary. 5 rue Daunou, 2nd. ☎ 01-42-61-71-14. www.harrys-bar.fr. Métro: Opéra.

Le Curio Parlour ST-GERMAIN-DES-PRES
This is one of the only Nikka bars outside Japan. Tequila and whiskey cocktails are also house specialities, as are a myriad of other concoctions that you won't find anywhere else in town. 16 rue des Bernardins, 5th. ☎ 01-47-07-12-47. Métro: St-Germain-des-Prés.

★★ Le Forum MADELEINE
Tout Paris flocks to this 1930s Art Deco bar for its choice of 125 cocktails. The house favorite is the Forum: Noilly Prat dry vermouth and Grand Marnier. The Caramel Manhattan (supposedly a mix of American power and British stiff upper lip)—made from Maker's Mark,

> Chez Jeannette's bar, unchanged since the 1940s.

> Cocktails are served with style at Le Forum.

vermouth, pineapple juice, caramel topping, and Peychaud bitters—is also worth the detour. On Saturdays (1–3pm) you can learn how to make (and drink) your own cocktails at the Bar School (91€). 4 bd. Malesherbes, 8th. ☎ 01-42-65-37-86. www.bar-le-forum.com. Métro: Madeleine.

Tearooms

★ **Angelina** LOUVRE

This gorgeous Belle Epoque tearoom provides an atmospheric setting for classic pick-me-ups such as Darjeeling, Orange Pekoe, and Earl Grey. The hot chocolate is one of the best in Paris—made with real chocolate, all gooey and warm, and ready to pour. Don't miss the legendary Mont Blanc cake (meringue with whipped cream and chestnut purée). 226 rue de Rivoli, 1st. ☎ 01-42-60-82-00. www.groupe-bertrand.com. Daily 9am–7pm. Métro: Tuileries.

kids **ZenZoo** OPERA

This tiny Taiwanese restaurant doubles as a tearoom (2:30–7pm) serving traditional Chinese flower teas. It is also the only place in Paris that serves China's famous tapioca tea cocktails (made with mango, kumquat, and coconut), which require an extra-wide straw, to suck up the tapioca balls (a strange sensation, but quickly addictive). 13 rue Chabanais, 2nd. ☎ 01-42-96-27-28. www.zen-zoo.com. Mon–Sat 11am–11pm. Métro: Quatre-Septembre.

Trendy Spots

★ **Andy Wahloo** MARAIS

What this tiny bar lacks in space, it makes up for in style. Created by the same folks as Momo and Sketch in London, it is a wonderfully bombastic take on a Moroccan hippy parlor, with patterned rugs thrown over the banquettes, retro North African food packaging stocked in the bookcase (just for show, man), and stools made from overturned paint barrels. Get there early if you want a seat—the place fills up with a trendy crowd after 9pm. 69 rue des Gravilliers, 3rd. ☎ 01-42-71-20-38. Métro: Arts et Métiers.

Chez Jeannette STRASBOURG-ST-DENIS

The decor in this bar hasn't changed since the 1940s—part of the bargain, when a young team bought it from former owner Jeannette. In terms of hip bars, it is a lone rider in this part of town, which makes it all the more attractive. Crowds of trendy 30-somethings lap up the cheap wine and concentrate on being cool, while the occasional old regular sweeps in, Jack Russell in tow, oblivious to the change of clientele. 47 rue du Faubourg St-Denis, 10th. ☎ 01-47-70-30-89. Métro: Strasbourg-St-Denis or Château Eau.

Dédé La Frite BOURSE

In the shadow of the stock exchange, Dédé serves beers and cocktails to a smart after-work crowd. No one intends to eat here, but many inevitably do when the wafting aroma of fries and burgers hits their noses. Later on, the music is cranked up a notch. 135 rue Montmartre, 2nd. ☎ 01-40-41-99-90. Métro: Bourse.

★★ Le Secret CHAMPS-ELYSEES

Discretion is the name of the game at "The Secret," where jet-setters flock for a night away from the spotlights. Come, therefore, to check out the clientele, but if you get lucky and spot a star, don't ask for an autograph. Instead, order Le French Love—a cocktail made from raspberry purée, apricot, vodka, and champagne—and watch the show from over your straw. 16 av. de Friedland, 8th. ☎ 01-53-53-02-02. Métro/RER: Charles de Gaulle–Etoile.

★ Lizard Lounge MARAIS

Within its bare-brick walls and vaulted cellar, the Lizard has been plying an international expat crowd with mojitos and sex on the beach for years. Happy hour here starts at 5pm. On weekends, come for the popular brunch of bacon, sausages, and eggs Benedict. 18 rue du Bourg-Tibourg, 4th. ☎ 01-42-72-81-34. www.cheapblonde.com. Métro: Hôtel de Ville.

Wine Bars

★★ La Belle Hortense MARAIS

There are dozens of other bars and cafes near this one, but none maintains a bookstore in the back, and few seem so self-consciously aware of their role as ersatz literary salon. Come for a glass of wine or a kiss in the corner, but be ready to talk literature. The place is named after a pulpy 19th-century romance set within the neighborhood. Wine costs 3€ to 7€ a glass. 31 rue Vieille-du-Temple, 4th ☎ 01-48-04-71-60. Métro: Hôtel de Ville.

★★ Le Baron Rouge LEDRU-ROLLIN

The Red Baron looks out over the **Aligre market** (p. 104), making it a prime spot for a glass of wine after a hard day's work at the stalls. Nowadays, a young, professional crowd joins in, too, chatting loudly around the giant wine barrels used as tables. There are dozens of wines to choose from, from Bourgogne Aligoté and chardonnay to leggy bordeaux. 1 rue Théophile Roussel, 12th. ☎ 01-43-43-14-32. Métro: Ledru-Rollin.

★ Les Caves Populaires PLACE DE CLICHY

You'll work hard to find a cheaper glass of decent wine (from 2.50€) and platter of cheese (7€). This popular bar, with the air of a Swiss chalet, is a place to rub shoulders with old locals and their dogs, students, and arty types from nearby Montmartre. The coffee's good, too. 22 rue des Dames, 17th. ☎ 01-53-04-08-32. Métro: place de Clichy.

★★ Po.Za.Da NATION

Come here for the selection of more than 70 wines and the tasty cuisine to accompany them (think tuna rillettes, *steak frites,* and tiramisu). If the long list of reds, whites, and rosés leaves you stumped, just say what sort of flavor you fancy, and Bidou (the young, friendly owner) will suggest something delightful. 2 rue Guénot, 11th. ☎ 01-43-70-63-24. Métro: Nation.

> You get cheap wine, food, and smiles at Les Caves Populaires.

Paris Nightlife & Entertainment Best Bets

Best Place to Get Past the Bouncers
Le Montana, 28 rue St-Benoît, 6th **(p. 131)**

Best All-Round Jazz Club
Le Sunset/Sunside, 60 rue des Lombards, 1st **(p. 131)**

Best Place for a Wild Boogie—Whatever Your Tendency
Queen, 102 av. des Champs-Elysées, 8th **(p. 132)**

Best Theater for Broadway and West-End Musicals
Théâtre du Châtelet, 1 place du Châtelet, 1st **(p. 133)**

Most Cutting-Edge Dance
Théâtre National de Chaillot, 1 place du Trocadéro, 16th **(p. 133)**

Coolest Venue for Rising Rock and Pop Stars
La Flèche d'Or, 102bis rue de Bagnolet, 20th **(p. 132)**

Best Restaurant-Bar-Club
L'Arc, 12 rue de Presbourg, 16th **(p. 131)**

Best Hall for French *Chanson*
Les Trois Baudets, 64 bd. de Clichy, 18th **(p. 132)**

Best Ballet
Opéra Garnier, place de l'Opéra, 9th **(p. 133)**

Most Beautiful Cinema
La Pagode, 57bis rue de Babylone, 7th **(p. 129)**

Best High-Tech Cabaret
Lido, 116 av. des Champs-Elysées, 8th **(p. 129)**

> *Yes it's kitsch, but the Lido cabaret is also quite classy—worth booking a table up front.*

Paris Nightlife & Entertainment A to Z

Cabaret

★★ kids Lido CHAMPS-ELYSEES

This glossy club puts on multimillion-euro performances in a dramatic reworking of the classic Parisian cabaret shows, with special effects including aerial and aquatic ballets—and even an occasional ice rink. **116bis av. des Champs-Elysées, 8th. ☎ 01-40-76-56-10. www. lido.fr. Prices 90€–280€. Métro: George-V.**

★ kids Moulin Rouge MONTMARTRE

Toulouse-Lautrec immortalized this windmill-topped building and its scantily clad dancers, who invented and still perform the cancan. Today it's true to its original theme and very cheesy, but the dancing is perfectly synchronized, and the girls are all very beautiful. **82 bd. de Clichy, 18th. ☎ 01-53-09-82-82. www. moulinrouge.fr. Prices 90€–180€. Métro: Blanche.**

Cinema

★★★ La Pagode INVALIDES/EIFFEL TOWER

This glorious 19th-century replica of a Japanese pagoda, with a ballroom clad in Oriental-themed silk tapestries, has been turned into one of the world's most beautiful movie theaters. Films tend to be art-house, but the occasional blockbuster inches its way in, too, frequently in English with French subtitles. **57bis rue de Babylone, 7th. ☎ 01-46-34-82-54. www.etoile-cinema. com. Métro: St-François-Xavier.**

kids Le Grand Rex GRANDS BOULEVARDS

From the outside, this place looks like an Art Deco wedding cake. On the inside, however, it is a fairy-tale theater with three tiers and a starlit ceiling. The blockbuster programming usually includes big French films and Hollywood action movies that let rip on the very big screen, often in 3-D. **1 bd. Poissonnière, 2nd. ☎ 08-92-68-05-96. www.legrandrex.com. Métro: Bonne Nouvelle.**

> *Will you or won't you get into Le Montana? The doorwoman gets the last word in Paris's hippest nightclub.*

Paris Nightlife & Entertainment A to Z

Au Duc des Lombards 14
Autour de Midi 5
Batofar 18
Bouffes du Nord 7
Café Cox 15
La Flèche d'Or 17
La Pagode 22
L'Arc 1

Le Grand Rex 9
Le Montana 21
Le Pulp 10
Le Sunset/Sunside 13
Les Trois Baudets 6
Le Tropic Café 12
Lido 2
Moulin Rouge 4
New Morning 8

Nouveau Casino 16
Opéra Bastille 19
Opéra Garnier 11
Théâtre du Châtelet 20
Théâtre National de Chaillot 23
Queen 3

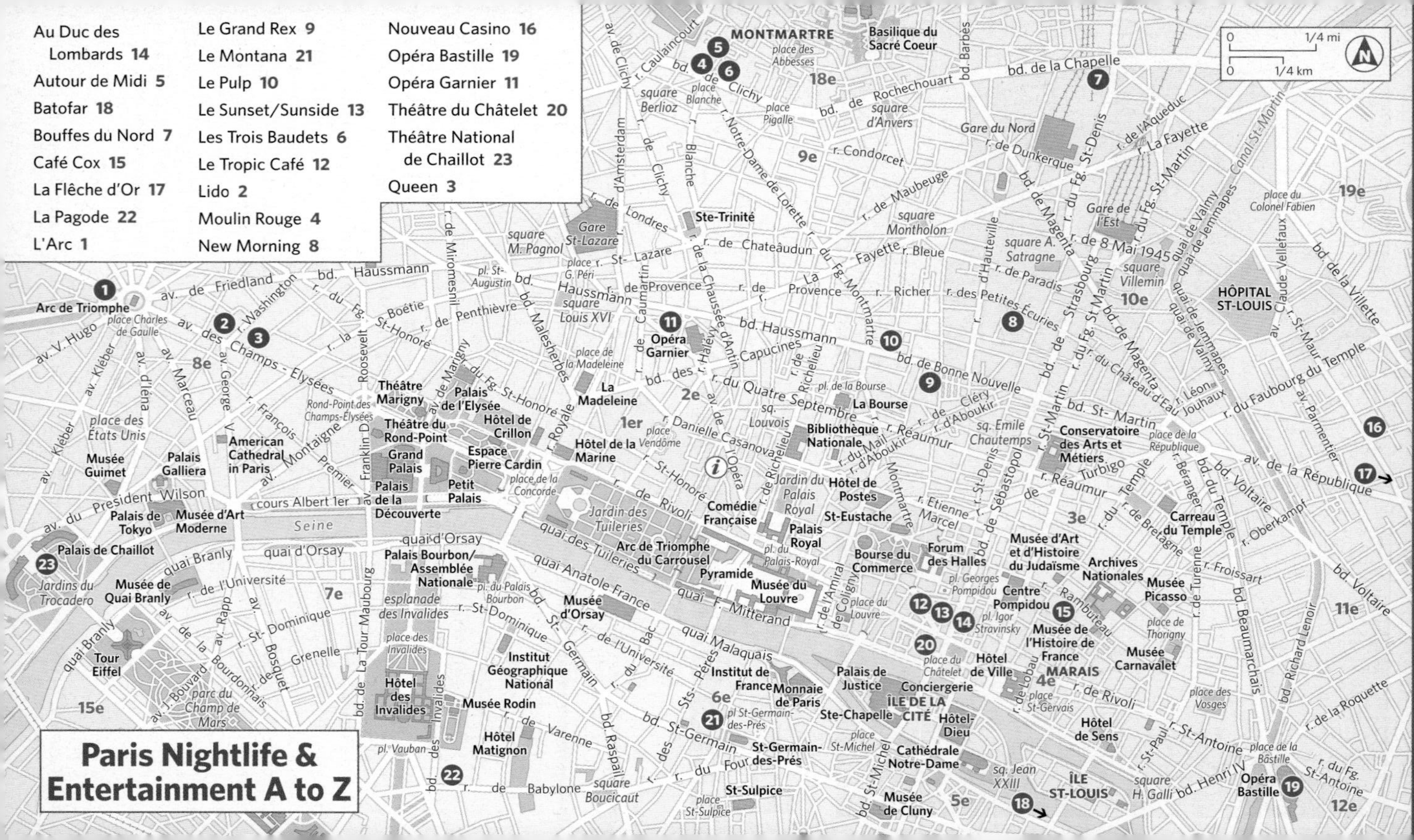

Jazz

Au Duc des Lombards LES HALLES

All the great performers of Paris's jazz era passed through the doors of this still-thriving club. Nightly performances range from free-style jazz to hard bop. Tables can be reserved, and meals are served. 42 rue des Lombards, 1st. ☎ 01-42-33-22-88. www.ducdeslombards.com. Cover 10€–25€. Métro: Châtelet.

Autour de Midi MONTMARTRE

This jazz club is free on Tuesday nights for Le Boeuf du Mardi jamming session at 9:30pm. You can expect big names, such as Laurent Epstein, Yoni Zelnik, and Bruno Casties, to attend. If hunger bites beforehand, calm the pangs in the upstairs restaurant. 11 rue Lepic, 18th. ☎ 01-55-79-16-48. www.autourdemidi.fr. Cover free–20€. Métro: Blanche.

★ Le Sunset/Sunside LES HALLES

This staple of the Parisian jazz circuit is two bars in one, with separate shows going on simultaneously. The look is minimalist, and artists are both European and U.S.-based, including many big-name performers. Le Sunside favors classic jazz, and Le Sunset goes for electric jazz and world music. Take your pick. 60 rue des Lombards, 1st. ☎ 01-40-26-84-41. www.sunset-sunside.com. Cover 15€–25€. Métro: Châtelet.

★★ New Morning STRASBOURG ST DENIS

Jazz maniacs come to drink, talk, and dance at this high-ceilinged, loft-style club. The venue might be low-key, but serious stuff takes place on the stage, from jamming sessions to swinging orchestras to jazz from Central and South Africa. 7–9 rue des Petites-Ecuries, 10th. ☎ 01-45-23-51-41. www.newmorning.com. Cover free–15€. Métro: Château-d'Eau.

Nightclubs

★★ Batofar BIBLIOTHEQUE

Virtually everybody views this club, which sits on a converted barge that floats on the Seine, as hip; Batofar attracts hundreds of 20- and 30-something followers of the invited DJs. Come here for insight into late-night Paris at its most raffish, and don't even try to categorize the patrons. In summer, the quayside turns into an extension of the boat, with food, a bar, and deck chairs. 11 quai François Mauriac, 13th. ☎ 09-71-25-50-61. www.batofar.org. Cover free–15€. Métro: Quai de la Gare.

> *Fight locals for a spot at Nouveau Casino in Oberkampf.*

★★ L'Arc CHAMPS-ELYSEES

With views onto the Arc de Triomphe, the "Arch" is one of Paris's most sought-after spots. Two levels separate the areas: the bar-cum-restaurant first floor—a luxurious vintage affair where folks eat a gourmet meal without the *boom-boom* of the discothèque—and the 1960s-style club in the basement, kitted out in black leather sofas and pink and blue lighting. Music tends to be an international mix of dance and pop. 12 rue de Presbourg, 16th. ☎ 01-45-00-78-70. http://larc-paris.com. Cover free–25€. Métro/RER: Charles de Gaulle-Etoile.

★ Le Montana ST-GERMAIN-DES-PRES

This VIP magnet, all dressed up like a boudoir, has drawn Kate Moss, Lenny Kravitz, and Vanessa Bruno in its time, and it continues to reel in the stars today—hence the vicious bouncers at the door. Smile sweetly enough, however, and you'll be boogying on down to the best sounds amid a crowd you can write home about. 28 rue St-Benoît, 6th. ☎ 01-44-39-71-70. Cover free. Métro: St-Germain-des-Prés.

> *The Flêche d'Or's bar overlooks old train tracks.*

> *Taking a breather on Nouveau Casino's upper deck.*

music theater, offering a jam-packed program of rock, electro, folk, *chanson,* and slam. Two bars and a restaurant overlooking Pigalle also draw the crowds. 64 bd. de Clichy, 18th. ☎ 01-42-62-33-33. www.lestroisbaudets.com. Cover 5€–20€. Métro: Pigalle.

★★ **Nouveau Casino** OBERKAMPF

This den of coolness is part of Paris's hyperhip countercultural scene—a drafty space (adjacent to the Café Charbon) crafted around an

★★★ **Queen** CHAMPS-ELYSEES

Even after all these years, Queen still reels in joyous throngs of gays and straights, 7 nights a week, with the promise of everything from 1970s-style disco and hardcore electro to foam parties and drag nights. 102 av. des Champs-Elysées, 8th. ☎ 01-53-89-08-90. http://queen.fr. Cover free–25€. Métro: Franklin D. Roosevelt or George V.

Rock, Pop & *Chanson*
★★★ **La Flêche d'Or** PERE-LACHAISE

The Golden Arrow—a former train station that is now one of Paris's hippest concert halls—hits the bull's-eye every time, with dirt-cheap concerts by both up-and-coming French bands and confirmed internationals. Drinks from the gigantic bar can be downed in a room overlooking the disused railway lines. 102bis rue de Bagnolet, 20th. ☎ 01-44-64-01-02. www.flechedor.fr. Cover free–15€. Métro: Alexandre Dumas, Porte de Bagnolet, or Gambetta.

Les Trois Baudets PIGALLE

Between 1947 and 1966, this small theater launched more musical careers than anywhere else—those of Serge Gainsbourg, Jacques Brel, Hénri Salvador, and Brigitte Fontaine, to name a few. Today it is still Paris's flagship francophone

Gay & Lesbian Nightlife

Gay life in Paris is centered around Les Halles and Le Marais, around the Hôtel de Ville and Rambuteau Métro stops and RER Châtelet–Les Halles. **Café Cox,** 15 rue des Archives, 4th (☎ 01-42-72-08-00), gets so busy in the early evening that the crowd stands on the sidewalk. Here you'll find the most mixed gay crowd in Paris—from hunky American tourists to sexy Parisian men. A hot, fun place in Les Halles is **Le Tropic Café,** 66 rue des Lombards, 1st (☎ 01-40-13-92-62; www.tropic-cafe.com), where the trendy, good-looking crowd parties until dawn. **Le Pulp,** 25 bd. Poissonière, 2nd (☎ 01-40-26-01-93; www.myspace.com/lepulp; Métro: Grands Boulevards), is one of the most popular lesbian dance clubs; it looks like a burgundy-colored 19th-century French music hall. The venue, as the French like to say, is *très cool,* with cutting-edge music that draws in some heteros, too.

enormous industrial bar that is always heaving. Live concerts take place nightly between 8pm and 1am; on Friday and Saturday, the party continues from midnight 'til dawn with a DJ who spins some of the most avant-garde dance music in Paris. 109 rue Oberkampf, 11th. ☎ 01-43-57-57-40. www.nouveaucasino.net. Cover free–15€. Métro: St-Maur, Parmentier, or Ménilmontant.

Theater, Opera & Dance

★★ Bouffes du Nord LA CHAPELLE

Peter Brook's Bouffes du Nord is the stronghold of English theater in Paris—and we're not just talking Shakespeare. Many plays are Brook's own adaptations, and whatever is shown, it's consistently excellent and often at the forefront. 37bis bd. de la Chapelle, 10th. ☎ 01-46-07-34-50. www.bouffesdunord.com. Ticket prices vary. Métro: La Chapelle.

★★★ Opéra Bastille BASTILLE

This huge, contemporary building hosts outstanding opera performances, such as Mozart's *Marriage of Figaro* and Tchaikovsky's *Queen of Spades,* in its three concert halls. Symphony and dance performances are held here occasionally as well. 2 place de la Bastille, 4th. ☎ 08-92-89-90-90. www.operadeparis.fr. Tickets 5€–130€. Métro: Bastille.

★★★ Opéra Garnier OPERA

The phantom did his haunting here in Charles Garnier's 1875 rococo wonder, the setting for Gaston Leroux's novel. Now it's home to the Ballet de l'Opéra National de Paris, which succeeds in producing world-class traditional and contemporary ballets, often with startling stage sets. Place de l'Opéra. ☎ 08-92-89-90-90. www.operadeparis.fr. Tickets 5€–130€. Métro: Opera. RER: Auber.

★★★ Théâtre du Châtelet CHATELET

This is the only place in Paris where you can see musicals fresh off the boat from Broadway and the West End (English with French subtitles). It also happens to be one of the most beautiful theaters in town—a velvet-and-gold ode to the Belle Epoque. 1 place du Châtelet, 1st. ☎ 01-40-28-28-00. www.chatelet-theatre.com. Tickets 10€–120€. Métro: Châtelet.

Théâtre National de Chaillot CHAMPS ELYSEES

Few other stages in Paris show such radical modern dance performances, making the Chaillot an absolute must for fans *du movement.* The setting is fabulous, too—inside the 1930s Chaillot palace with a panoramic view onto the Eiffel Tower from the bar. 1 place du Trocadéro, 16th. ☎ 01-53-65-30-00. www.theatre-chaillot.fr. Tickets 10€–120€. Métro: Trocadéro.

> The *place to see world-class ballet in Paris is the majestic Opéra Garnier.*

Day Trips from Paris

Five of France's most iconic sites make easy day trips from Paris. Just 20km (13 miles) southwest is **Versailles**—"Sun King" Louis XIV's gilded palace, where French royalty lived so extravagantly in a time of widespread poverty that their excesses spurred the nation's 1789 Revolution. An hour southwest, 13th-century **Notre-Dame de Chartres** represents the highest architectural and theological aspirations of the Middle Ages in France. Northwest, between Normandy and the Ile de France, Claude Monet lived and died at **Giverny,** where the great Impressionist painter's estate and iconic waterlily ponds are faithfully preserved. Due east of the capital, **Disneyland® Paris** is a blessing for travelers with kids. And to the southwest, **Fontainebleau** is the woodsy wildlife retreat where French kings from the Renaissance on retreated to hunt and escape city living.

> Designed by André Le Nôtre, Versailles's gardens once contained 1,400 fountains.

★★★ kids **Château de Fontainebleau.** Looking at this magnificent yet understated hunting lodge, within the vestiges of a forest that bears its name (Forêt de Fontainebleau), it is not hard to understand why little old Napoleon loved it so much. He followed the pattern of a succession of French kings in the pre-Versailles days who used Fontainebleau as a resort and hunted in its forests. François I tried to turn the hunting lodge into a royal palace in the Italian Renaissance style, bringing artists, including Benvenuto Cellini, there to work for him. Under his patronage, the School of Fontainebleau gained prestige, led by painters Rosso Fiorentino and Francesco Primaticcio; the artists adorned the 63m-long (207-ft.) stucco-framed panels of the **Gallery of François I.** One of the prettiest Renaissance rooms is the **Ballroom** (or, Gallery of Henri II), which displays the interlaced initials *H&D*, referring

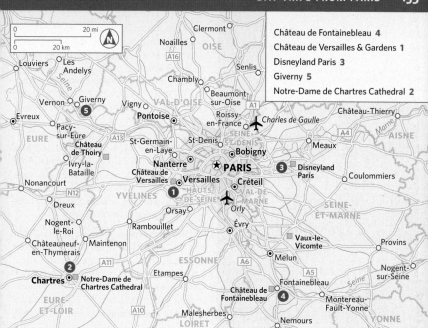

Château de Fontainebleau 4
Château de Versailles & Gardens 1
Disneyland Paris 3
Giverny 5
Notre-Dame de Chartres Cathedral 2

to Henri and his beautiful mistress, Diane de Poitiers. Competing with this illicit tandem are the initials *H&C*, symbolizing Henri and his ho-hum wife, Catherine de Medici. In the Louis XV wing, the **Musée de Napoléon** evokes imperial life via a series of period rooms. The **Petits Appartements** on the ground floor are where Napoleon and Joséphine (and later, Marie-Louise) resided; also visit the **Hunting Gallery** (*Appartement de Chasse*), which is filled with breathtaking royal furniture. **Les Jardins de Fontainebleau**—Fontainebleau's 130-hectare (321-acre) park, filled with lakes, bridges, and meandering paths—is wholly charming. Some of the prettiest parts are the **Jardin Anglais** (English Garden), with its man-made river, tall trees, and little bridge, and nearby **Pavillon de l'Etang,** which stands on the edge of a lake. ⏱ 1 day. Château de Fontainbleau is 70km (43 miles) from Paris along A6 (from Porte d'Italie or Porte d'Orléans), then follow signs for Fontainebleau and then Château. Or take the train from Gare de Lyon (dir. Montargis, Sens, or Montereau) to Fontainebleau-Avon, then take bus line A to Château. Place du Général-de-Gaulle. ☎ 01-60-71-50-70. www. musee-chateau-fontainebleau.fr. Musée de Napoléon 6.50€ (5€ reduction with guided tour ticket for main château); Petits Appartements 6.50€ (5€ reduction with guided tour ticket for main château); hunting gallery 6.50€ (5€ reduction with guided tour ticket for main château); main château 10€ adults, 8€ students. Apr–Sept Wed–Mon 9:30am–6pm; Oct–Mar Wed–Mon 9:30am–5pm.

★★★ **kids** **Château de Versailles & Gardens.** The word "sumptuous" takes on a whole new meaning inside the palace of the Sun King, Louis XIV. This masterpiece of gilding and sculpture was the seat of power between 1682 and 1789. The ★★ **King and Queen's bedchambers,** where courtiers watched the royals' every move, are exquisite; the six ★★ **Grand Appartements,** where Louis XIV held court, are overwhelmingly opulent—particularly the Hercules Salon, the ceiling of which is painted with *L'Apothéose d'Hercule (The Apotheosis of Hercules).* Versailles's highlight, however, has to be the 71m (233-ft.), glimmering ★★★ **Hall of Mirrors,** designed to reflect sunlight back into the garden and remind people that the "Sun King" lived here. In 1919, the treaty ending World War I was signed in this hall.

★★★ **Les Jardins de Versailles**—a 100-hectare (247-acre) Eden of ornamental lakes,

> The color Chartres blue derives from Chartres Cathedral's magnificent stained glass.

canals, flowerbeds, and statuary—was geometrically designed by André Le Nôtre. At the peak of the gardens' glory, 1,400 fountains spewed forth water. The fountain depicting Apollo in his chariot pulled by four horses, surrounded by Tritons rising from the water, is the centerpiece of *Les Grandes Eaux Musicales,* a water and music spectacle extravaganza, performed from April to October. On the mile-long **Grand Canal,** Louis XV used to take gondola rides with his favorite squeeze of the moment. While you're there, don't miss the pink-and-white-marble **Grand Trianon,** designed by Jules Hardouin-Mansart for Louis XIV in 1687. Nixon slept here, in the room where royal mistress Mme. de Pompadour died. Gabriel, the designer of place de la Concorde in Paris, built the **Petit Trianon** (a fanciful faux farmhouse) in 1768 for Louis XV. In time, Marie Antoinette adopted it as her favorite residence—a place to escape the rigid life at the main palace.

Once you've had enough of French royal excess, stop for a bite of simple French country cuisine in Versailles's oldest restaurant, **Le Chapeau Gris,** 7 rue Hoche (☎ 01-39-50-10-81; www.auchapeaugris.com; menus 20€

and 25€). The building has paneled walls and beamed ceilings and dates back to the construction of the château. The prix-fixe menus are an excellent value. ⏱ 1 day. Versailles is 20km (12 miles) from Paris via A13 or D10. Or take the RER C to Versailles Rive Gauche; or take a Transilien SNCF train from Paris's Gare St-Lazare to Versailles Rive-Droite, then walk to the château (10 min.). ☎ 01-30-83-78-00. www.chateauversailles.fr. Palace 14€ adults, or 12€ after 3pm; free for ages 26 and under. Both Trianons 10€ adults; free for ages 26 and under. Palace: Apr–Oct Tues–Sun 9am–6pm; Nov–Mar Tues–Sun 9am–5pm. Trianons Tues–Sun noon–6pm. Grounds daily dawn to dusk.

kids **Disneyland Paris.** The main park is split into five lands. **Main Street USA,** an idealized American town, is a plum spot for catching parades that feature Mickey, Winnie the Pooh, and the next generation of Disney stars such as *Ratatouille*'s Rémy and *Toy Story*'s Buzz Lightyear. **Frontierland** is an ode to the American Wild West, with the hair-raising Big Thunder Mountain ride and Pocahontas Indian Village—good for getting young kids away from the crowds. **Adventureland** is the realm of swashbuckling pirates and Indiana Jones and the Temple of Peril, which travels backward at breakneck speed. Little kiddies love **Fantasyland,** where Sleeping Beauty's Castle hides a fire-breathing dragon in its dungeon. **Discoveryland** explores the visions of the future, with designs drawn from the works of Leonardo da Vinci, Jules Verne, and H. G. Wells, as well as from more modern fictional creations such as *Star Wars.* This is the park's most popular area and includes Space Mountain, which emulates Jules Verne's version of what a trip from Earth to the moon would be like.

The emphasis in the second park, **Walt Disney Studio Park** (split into four lots), is on film production and special effects. It's also where most of the new rides are being installed. Feel the flames as you play an extra in the disaster movie *Armageddon;* plunge 13 floors down an elevator shaft in the **Twilight Tower of Terror;** or get your kids to talk live with the mischievous alien Stitch in his interactive stage show. Accessible without a ticket, the **Disney Village** features endless entertainment options—dance clubs, snack bars, restaurants, shops, cinemas, and bars. ⏱ 1 day. Disneyland Paris is

> *The best part of your kids' trip to Disneyland Paris could well be the colorful parades.*

32km (20 miles) along A4 east from Paris to exit 14. Or take the RER A to the Marne-la-Vallée-Chessy stop (about 40 min.) Marne-la-Vallée, Paris. ☎ 08-25-30-02-22. www.disneylandparis. com. Parking 15€ per day. Admission 1-day (one park) 53€ adults, 45€ ages 3-11, free for children 2 and under; 1-day hopper (both parks) 67€ adults, 57€ ages 3-11. Disneyland Park: Sept to mid-July Mon–Fri 10am–8pm, Sat–Sun 10am–9pm; mid-July to Aug daily 10am–11pm. Walt Disney Studios Park: winter daily 10am–6pm; summer daily 10am–7pm.

★★★ **Giverny.** Born in 1840, Claude Monet, leader of the Impressionist movement, was a brilliant innovator who excelled in presenting the effects of light at different times of day. His most famous paintings are his waterlilies, painted here in this quaint, pink country house and gardens, preserved by the **Fondation Claude Monet,** 84 rue Claude-Monet Giverny (☎ 02-32-51-28-21; www.fondation-monet. com; admission 6€ adults, 3.30€ ages 7–12, free for children 6 and under; Apr–Oct daily 9:30am–6pm, closed Nov–Mar). Monet moved to Giverny with his mistress and eight children in 1883, and he lived here until his death in 1926. The house is dotted with touching family mementos and the 32 Japanese wood-block prints collected by the artist, but no original Monet paintings hang here. The star of the show is the gardens: living tableaux of Monet's paintings, where thousands of flow-ers—including *nymphéas* (waterlilies), wisteria hanging from the Japanese bridge, weeping willows, and rhododendrons—flourish as if immortalized only yesterday. Just up the road is the **Musée des Impressionnismes Giverny,** 99 rue Claude-Monet (☎ 02-32-51-94-65; www. museedesimpressionnismesgiverny.com; admission 6.50€ adults, 3€ ages 7–12, free for children 6 and under; free 1st Sun of the month; Apr–Oct daily 10am–6pm; closed Nov–Mar). The mu-seum showcases the history of Impressionism and its influence on the 20th century—notably among U.S.-born artists, who followed in Monet's footsteps by living in Giverny. Among the more famous painters were John Singer Sargent and William Metcalf, who summered here, writing home to other artists about Giverny's glories. ⏱ 1 day. Giverny is 80km (50 miles) west of Paris along A14 (dir. Rouen), and then take A13 (dir. Vernon) to Bonnières. Exit at junction 14 and join D201 to Giverny. Or take a train from Paris's Gare St-Lazare to the Vernon

> Marie-Antoinette died before she could use this bed in the Chambre de l'Impératrice at Fontainebleau.

station, where a taxi can take you the 5km (3 miles) to Giverny.

Notre-Dame de Chartres Cathedral. Rodin described Chartres Cathedral—one of the largest Gothic edifices to be dedicated to the Virgin Mary, completed in 1260—as the French Acropolis; once you've seen it, you'll be inclined to agree. No cathedral in the world can match it for its 12th-century glass—saved from damage during World War I and World War II by parishioners who removed it, piece by piece, and stored it safely. It gave the world a new color—Chartres blue—and it is absolutely exceptional. All of the building's windows are glorious, but the three ★★★ **rose**

Giverny Museum Tip

Save money with a combined ticket for the Foundation Claude Monet and the Musée des Impressionnismes Giverny: 6€–12€.

Where to Stay in Chartres

Le Grand Monarque, in the town center, has grand rooms in period fabrics and two gourmet restaurants (22 rue des Epars; ☎ 02-37-18-15-15; www.bw-grand-monarque. com; 55 units; doubles 107€–245€; MC, V). If you're driving, you could indulge at the **Château d'Esclimont**—a charming Renaissance castle and restaurant 30 minutes from Chartres. With its moat, forest walks, and 60 hectares (148 acres) of gardens, it is a fairy-tale place in which to stay and dine (St-Symphorien-le-Château; ☎ 02-37-31-15-15; www.grandesetapes.fr; doubles from 185€; 3 courses 90€; lunch menu from 38€). The gourmet restaurant (think French classics like beef tournedos and lobster) overlooks the gardens, and in good weather, you can even eat in a hot-air balloon while sailing over the forested countryside (from 1,200€ for in-flight dinner). Rooms are stately, with marble bathrooms and thick drapes.

windows are known as the best. The sculpted bodies around the cathedral's **royal entrance** are elongated and garbed in long, flowing robes, but their faces are almost disturbingly lifelike—frowning, winking, smiling. Christis

shown at the Second Coming—his descent to Earth on the right, his ascent back to Heaven on the left. Both the **north and south portals** are carved with biblical images, including the apostles and Adam and Eve as they are expelled from the Garden of Eden. Many Gothic cathedrals once had mazes like that of the rare **Floor Labyrinth** in the nave, but virtually all were destroyed over time. The meaning of labyrinths has been lost; one theory claims they represent the passage of the soul to heaven. The underground **crypts** trace the entire history of the cathedral. Worship of the Virgin is thought to have begun here, hundreds of years ago, inside a cave. ⏱ 1 day. From Paris's Gare Montparnasse, trains run direct to Chartres (1 hr.); or you can drive along A10/A11 southwest from the Périphérique, and follow signs to Le Mans and Chartres (about 1½ hr.). The cathedral is open daily 8:30am–9:30pm. Guided tours are available in English (Apr–Oct Mon–Sat noon and 2:45pm; 5€; meet at the gift shop), as are crypt visits (Apr–Oct Mon–Sat 11am, 2:15pm, 3:30pm, and 4:30pm; June–Sept also 5:15pm; Nov–Mar 11:15am and 4:15pm only). Call ☎ 02-37-21-75-02 for more information, including prices.

> Waterlilies still bloom at Giverny, as they did when they inspired Monet.

Fast Facts

Arriving

BY PLANE Paris has two international airports—**Orly** (☎ 39-50) and **Charles de Gaulle** (☎ 39-50). **From Charles de Gaulle: RER** trains leave every 15 minutes (5am to approximately midnight), serving several of the major downtown Métro stations (trip time: 35 min.). Air France also operates two **shuttle-bus** services into Paris: one departing every 12 minutes (5:35am–11pm) for place d'Etoile and porte Maillot, and the other every 30 minutes (7am–9:30pm) for Gare Montparnasse and Gare de Lyon. A **taxi** to the city costs about 55€; the fare is higher at night (8pm–7am). The trip takes 40 to 50 minutes by bus or taxi. **From Orly:** There are no direct trains to central Paris, but the airport is served by **monorail** (Orly Val) that takes you to RER station Antony, where you can catch line B into the city (trip time: about 30 min.). **Air France buses** leave from Orly Ouest and Orly Sud every 12 minutes (5:45am–11pm) for the Gare des Invalides, where you can catch a taxi or the Métro. A **taxi** from the airport into Paris costs about 40€ (more at night). It takes 25 minutes to an hour, depending on traffic, to get to Paris by bus or taxi. BY TRAIN Paris has six major stations: **Gare d'Austerlitz,** 55 quai d'Austerlitz, 13e (serving the southwest, with trains to and from the Loire Valley, Bordeaux, the Pyrénées, and Spain); **Gare de l'Est,** place du 11-Novembre-1918, 10e (serving the east, with trains to and from Strasbourg, Reims, and beyond, to Zurich and Austria); **Gare de Lyon,** 20 bd. Diderot, 12e (serving the southeast, with trains to and from the Côte d'Azur Nice, Cannes, St-Tropez, Provence, and beyond, to Geneva and Italy); **Gare Montparnasse,** 17 bd. Vaugirard, 15e (serving the west, with trains to and from Brittany); **Gare du Nord,** 18 rue de Dunkerque, 15e (serving the north, with trains to and from London, Holland, Denmark, and northern Germany); and **Gare St-Lazare,** 13 rue d'Amsterdam, 8e (serving the northwest, with trains to and from Normandy). Buses operate between the stations, and each station has a Métro stop. For train information and to make reservations, call ☎ 08-92-35-35-35 from abroad, 36-35 from France between 8am and 8pm daily. From Paris, one-way rail passage to Tours costs 30€ to 51€; one-way to Strasbourg costs 55€ or 80€, depending on the routing. *Warning:* The stations and surrounding areas are usually seedy and frequented by pickpockets, hustlers, hookers, and addicts. Be alert, especially at night. BY BUS Most buses arrive at the Eurolines France station, 28 av. du Général-de-Gaulle, Bagnolet (☎ 08-92-89-90-91; www.eurolines.fr; Métro: Gallieni). BY CAR Driving in Paris is not recommended. Parking is difficult and traffic dense. If you drive, remember that Paris is encircled by a ring road, the *périphérique*. Always obtain detailed directions to your destination, including the name of the exit on the *périphérique* (exits aren't numbered). Avoid rush hours. The major highways into Paris are A1 from the north; A13 from Rouen, Normandy, and other points northwest; A10 from Spain and the southwest; A6 and A7 from the French Alps, the Riviera, and Italy; and A4 from eastern France.

Banks

Open Monday to Friday from 9am to 4:30pm. A few are open on Saturday morning.

Business Hours

Most shops are open Monday to Saturday 9:30am to 7pm, with some open late on Thursday (until 8pm). Some businesses close for lunch (1–3pm). Museums close Monday or Tuesday and on some national holidays.

Consulates & Embassies

UNITED STATES EMBASSY 2 av. Gabriel, 8th (☎ 01-43-12-22-22). CANADIAN EMBASSY 35 av. Montaigne, 8th (☎ 01-44-43-29-00). UNITED KINGDOM EMBASSY 35 rue du Faubourg St-Honoré, 8th (☎ 01-44-51-31-00). UNITED KINGDOM CONSULATE 16 rue d'Anjou, 8th (☎ 01-44-51-31-02). IRISH EMBASSY 12 av. Foch, 16th (☎ 01-44-17-67-50). AUSTRALIAN EMBASSY 4 rue Jean-Ray, 15th (☎ 01-40-59-33-00). NEW ZEALAND EMBASSY 7ter rue Léonard-de-Vinci, 16th (☎ 01-45-01-43-43).

Drugstores

Pharmacie Les Champs, 84 av. des Champs-Elysées, 8th (☎ 01-45-62-02-41). Open daily 24 hours.

> *Navigating the French capital can seem daunting, but there are many ways to do it.*

Emergencies

Police ☎ 17. Fire department and emergency ambulance ☎ 18. Ambulance ☎ 15. For any emergency, dial ☎ 112 from a cell phone.

English-Speaking Hospitals

Hôpital Americain, 63 bd. Victor Hugo, Neuilly-sur-Seine (☎ 01-46-41-25-25); **Institut Hospitalier Franco-Britannique,** 3 rue Barbes, Levallois Perret (☎ 01-46-39-22-22).

Getting Around

The **Métro** network is vast, reliable, and cheap, and within Paris you can transfer between the subway and the **RER** (Réseau Express Régional) regional trains at no extra cost. The Métro runs from 5:30am to 12:30pm or 1:15am daily (and an hour later on Fri and Sat). **Buses** are reliable, too; most run from 7am to 8:30pm, after which a nighttime service covers key areas until 5:30am. Services are limited on Sunday and public holidays. Detailed information is at www. ratp.fr.

Paris does have **cycle** paths, even if you have to compete with heavy traffic, and it's a fine way to sightsee. The best deal for short journeys is the **Vélib,** Paris' excellent self-service bike scheme, available 7 days a week; for just 1€, you can take a bike from any stand and use it for 24 hours. (Or hire a bike for just 30 min., free of charge.) When you're finished using the bike, return it to any bike stand; if a rack is full, check the map on the service point for the nearest stand. Tickets can be bought with your credit card at any service point. You'll have to authorize a 150€ deposit, which will be taken from your card only if the bike is not returned, and type in a pin number of your choice. The machine will give you a card, with a code that you can use to unlock the bikes.

Internet

Milk, 13 rue Soufflot, 5th (☎ 01-43-54-55-55). To find other branches in Paris, visit www. milkclub.com.

Lost Property

Service des Objets Trouvés, 36 rue des Morillons, 15th (☎ 08-21-00-25-25).

Post Office

52 rue du Louvre (☎ 36-31) is open daily 24 hours. Stamps can also be purchased from your hotel reception desk and at *tabacs.*

Tourist Office

Paris's main office is **Office du Tourisme,** 25 rue des Pyramides, 1st (www.parisinfo.com; Métro: Pyramides). Other useful websites include www.parisinfo.com and www.nouveau-paris-ile-de-france.fr. Online maps and journey planners, covering Paris and the whole of France, are available from www.mappy.fr and www. viamichelin.com. An online phone directory for businesses and services is www.pagesjaunes.fr.

4
The Loire
Valley

Favorite Moments in the Loire Valley

The regal valley of the Loire River—the longest waterway in France—is at the heart of French life. This vast, UNESCO-protected region stretches eastward from the outskirts of Greater Paris through luscious, green countryside known as the Garden of France, past fairy-tale Renaissance châteaux, troglodyte dwellings, and rolling vineyards, to the Atlantic coast around Nantes. Lip-smacking regional dishes such as perch in butter, and dozens of wine appellations—from Anjou rosés to Saumur-Champigny reds—make the valley a paradise for foodies. It would take a lifetime to list every special moment in this majestic region, but here are our favorites.

> PREVIOUS PAGE *The fairy-tale Châteaux de Saumur has been watching over the town and the Loire River since the 13th century.* THIS PAGE *In summer, the perfume of thousands of roses fills the air at Château du Rivau in Le Coudray.*

1 Riding a giant wooden elephant at Les Machines de l'Ile. You'll feel as though you've stepped into a Jules Verne novel as you explore this madcap laboratory, where a menagerie of automated creatures wait for you to climb aboard. See p. 181, **8**.

2 Hot-air ballooning from the Château de Brissac. A ride on a *montgolfière* (hot-air balloon) is the best way to take in the region's hunting forests, fish-rich rivers, rolling vineyards, and towered châteaux. The owners of Brissac, France's tallest castle, are ballooning fans and frequently hold European championships on their vast estate. See p. 176.

3 Waking up in a working vineyard in Le Puy-Notre-Dame. You may feel drunk with power as well as pleasure when you bed down like a noble in the 17th-century **Manoir de la Tête Rouge** (Red Head Manor) at the foot of a hillside of cabernet franc grapes, part of a working vineyard near Saumur. See p. 171.

4 Discovering troglodyte dwellings in the Château de Brézé. A subterranean village is hidden in the moat of this astonishing estate, with the largest underground castle complex in Europe. You can even admire an eerie projected sound-and-light show in a cave called the **Cathédrale d'Images.** See p. 161.

1. Riding a giant wooden elephant at Les Machines de l'Île
2. Hot-air ballooning from the Château de Brissac
3. Waking up in a working vineyard in Le Puy-Notre-Dame
4. Discovering troglodyte dwellings in the Château de Brézé
5. Dining alfresco at Les Menestrels
6. Visiting a mushroom farm in Montsoreau's caves
7. Stepping back in time at the Abbaye de Fontevraud
8. Meandering through the rose garden at Château du Rivau
9. Watching your kids light up at "Sleeping Beauty's castle"
10. Admiring the perfect symmetry of Azay-le-Rideau
11. Wandering through Villandry's gardens
12. Tracking down Leonardo da Vinci in Amboise

5 Dining alfresco at Les Menestrels. Les Menestrels, a restaurant in Saumur, offers one of the best eating experiences in the Loire Valley—especially on a warm day, when you can sit on the lawn and dine on iced lobster bisque, pigeon, and ginger sole. See p. 184.

6 Visiting a mushroom farm in Montsoreau's caves. The dank tufa-and-limestone caves, inside which lies the Saut aux Loups mushroom farm, date back to prehistoric times. This *champignonnière* traces the history of mushroom growing from the Middle Ages to today. Even the kids will get into this history lesson. See p. 154, 7.

7 Stepping back in time at the Abbaye de Fontevraud. You can still sense the majesty on the grounds where Richard the Lionheart lies buried alongside his parents, King Henry II of England and Eleanor of Aquitaine. See p. 154, 6.

8 Meandering through the rose garden at Château du Rivau. It's a thrill to smell the flowers, discover pieces of modern art hidden amid the blooms, and in spring and summer sample dishes made from organic produce harvested fresh from the garden. See p. 174.

9 Watching your kids light up at "Sleeping Beauty's Castle." A far cry from Disneyland, **Château d'Ussé** was the inspiration behind Charles Perrault's original *Sleeping Beauty* story. Today the castle keeps the legacy alive with a kitschy but fun waxwork display—spinning wheel and all. See p. 174, 3.

10 Admiring the perfect symmetry of Azay-le-Rideau. Balzac called this castle "a multifaceted diamond," and it is without doubt one of the most beguiling early-16th-century châteaux you can visit. Its reflection in the Indre River is especially lovely. See p. 160.

11 Wandering through Villandry's gardens. Restored to their Renaissance splendor in the early 20th century by Dr. Joachim Carvallo, the ornamental cabbages and boxed gardens at Villandry are a wonderful place to while away an afternoon. See p. 151, 2.

12 Tracking down Leonardo da Vinci in Amboise. The genius lived here for 3 years before his death in 1519. His legacy is everywhere, from the château gardens, where you'll find his tomb, to the **Clos Lucé** mansion, where models of his inventions smarten up the gardens. See p. 148, 3.

The Loire Valley in 3 Days

For more than 250 years, the Loire Valley was the seat of power for the Valois kings, who left behind world-renowned châteaux every few miles or so. This tour concentrates on the eastern end of the Loire, around the historical towns of Blois and Amboise. After only 3 days, you will have barely scratched the surface of the region's heritage and culinary pleasures; to discover more, continue your trip with "The Loire Valley in 5 Days" tour (p. 150).

> The Château de Chenonceau's arched gallery, a feat of Renaissance ingenuity, was inaugurated by Catherine de Medici in 1577.

START Blois is 184km (114 miles) southwest of Paris, and 65km (40 miles) east of Tours.
TRIP LENGTH 130km (81 miles), on both fast highways and country roads.

1 **Château de Blois.** The former fief of the counts of Blois (pronounced "Blwah") receives more than half a million visitors each year—the majority of whom flock to this pink-and-white château. Standing in the castle courtyard is like being in an architecture textbook: The **Hall of the Estates-General** is a beautiful 13th-century work; Louis XII built the **Charles d'Orléans gallery** and the **Louis XII wing** (1498–1501); and Jules Hardouin-Mansart constructed the **Gaston d'Orléans wing** (1635–37). Most remarkable, however, is the **François I wing,** a French Renaissance masterpiece, containing a spiral staircase with ornamented balustrades and the king's symbol, a salamander. In 1588, the château was the scene of a bloody episode when the Duc de Guise left a warm bed and the arms of one of Catherine de Medici's ladies-in-waiting. His archrival, King Henri III, had summoned him, but when the duke arrived, the king's guards stabbed him to death. The murder of the Duc de Guise is only one of the grisly events associated with the Château de Blois. Louis XIII banished his poor mother, Marie de Medici, here; her study—decked in 237 glorious, wooden wall panels—is supposed to contain four secret cabinets where she kept her poisons.

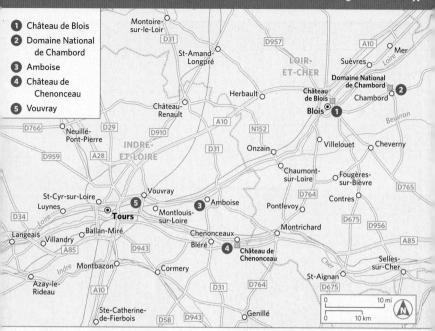

1 Château de Blois
2 Domaine National de Chambord
3 Amboise
4 Château de Chenonceau
5 Vouvray

Beyond the castle, the town of **Blois** (p. 157, 2) is a living museum of cobblestone streets, alleyways originally laid out in the Middle Ages, and restored white houses with slate roofs and red-brick chimneys. ⏱ 3 hr. Château de Blois. ☎ 02-54-90-33-33. www.chateaudeblois.fr. Admission 8€ adults, 6.50€ reduced, 4€ ages 6–17, free for children 5 and under. Apr–Jun and Sept daily 9am–6:30pm; July–Aug daily 9am–7pm; Oct to early Nov daily 9am–6pm; early Nov to late Mar daily 9am–12:30pm and 1:30–5:30pm.

From Blois, take D951 to Montlivault, join D84 to Chambord, and follow signs to the château, in Bracieux (20km/12 miles).

2 ★★★ Domaine National de Chambord.

What began as a hunting lodge in the Fôret de Boulogne later became the pinnacle of French Renaissance architecture and the largest château in the Loire Valley, thanks to François I. The estate was readied in 1519 for the visit of Charles V of Germany, who was

> *Sun King Louis XIV once slept in this opulent bed-chamber at the Château de Chambord.*

welcomed by nymphets in transparent veils tossing wildflowers in his path. Such monarchs as Henri II of France and Catherine de Medici and Louis XIII came and went from Chambord, but none loved it as much as François I did. Set within more than 5,260 hectares (about 13,000 acres) of parkland, enclosed by a wall stretching some 32km (20 miles), Chambord has a stunning facade dominated by four

Where to Stay & Dine

For hotels and restaurants in the Loire Valley, see p. 183.

> *Your kids will love Leonardo da Vinci's machines strewn around the Clos Lucé gardens in Amboise.*

monumental towers. The three-story keep has a spectacular terrace from which the ladies of the court used to watch their men returning from the hunt. There is also a rare **double-helix staircase,** superimposed upon itself so that one person may descend and another ascend without ever meeting (handy for illicit rendezvous with the king). The grandest part of the castle is Louis XIV's sumptuous red-and-gold bedchamber inside the **Sun King's state apartments.** Perhaps the most touching of all, however, is **François I's bedchamber;** disappointed by a failed love affair, he scratched a sad maxim in a pane of glass: "Every woman is fickle; he who trusts one is a fool." The castle also houses an interesting hunting museum, the **Musée de la Chasse et de la Nature** (www. chassenature.org). ⏱ 3 hr. Bracieux. ☎ 02-54-50-40-00. www.chambord.org. Admission 9.50€ adults, 8€ reduced. Parking 3€. Apr–June and Sept daily 9am–6:15pm; July–Aug 9am–7pm; Oct–Mar 9am–5:15pm.

From Chambord, follow D33 and D174 (just 2 km/1¼ miles) to the island, join D951

through Blois, and then follow N152 (toward Tours) and D952 to Amboise (total distance 54km/34 miles). Spend your first and second nights in Amboise.

❸ ★★★ **Amboise.** On a rocky spur in the center of town, the 15th-century **Château d'Amboise** was the first castle in France to reflect the Italian Renaissance, combining both Gothic and Renaissance styles. It is also one of France's most historically important buildings: Louis XI resided here, Charles VIII was born and died here, François I grew up here (as did Catherine de Medici's 10 children), and Leonardo da Vinci's tomb lies in the gardens. Amboise's second must-see sight is **Le Clos Lucé.** The quaint brick-and-stone house was constructed in the 1400s as a retreat for Queen Anne de Bretagne, wife of Charles VIII of France and Europe's richest woman in her day; but François I gave it instead to the man he reportedly dubbed "the great master in all forms of art and science": Leonardo da Vinci. Today the site is a museum, offering insights into da Vinci's life and inventions as well as the decorative arts of the era. ⏱ 1 day. Amboise Tourist Office, Quai du Général de Gaulle. ☎ 02-47-57-09-28. www.amboise-valdeloire.com. For more information on the Château d'Amboise, see p. 161; on Le Clos Lucé, see p. 172, **1**.

Leave Amboise on D431, and at the first island join D31, which veers left to become D31F. After La Croix en Touraine, join D40 to Chenonceaux (14km/8⅔ miles total).

❹ ★★★ **Château de Chenonceau.** The Château de Chenonceau is evidence that love triangles rarely work out. In 1547, Henri II gave this pleasure palace to his beautiful mistress, Diane de Poitiers, who was virtually queen of France for a time, infuriating Henri's wife, Catherine de Medici. When Henri died, Catherine became regent (her eldest son was still a child) and took pleasurable revenge by forcing Diane to return the jewelry Henri had given her and to abandon her beloved home.

Today Chenonceau is one of the most remarkable castles in France, spanning an entire river—the Cher—whose waters surge and foam beneath the château's vaulted foundations. It's also noteworthy for the fact that it was forged by women. Catherine de Medici built the two-story gallery across the bridge, inspired by her native Florence. Catherine Briçonnet, the wife of the château's first owner, built the turreted pavilion and one of France's first straight staircases. Diane de Poitiers, who introduced the artichoke to France, created the formal gardens. And in 1590, following the death of Henri III, Louise de Lorraine, his bereaved wife, painted her bedchamber in the colors of royal mourning: black and white. The castle's other interior walls are covered in an extraordinary array of Gobelin tapestries. The chapel contains a portrait of St. Antoine de Padoue by Murillo, as well as portraits of Catherine de Medici in black and white. ⏱ 3 hr. Chenonceaux. ☎ 02-47-23-90-07. www.chenonceau.com. Admission 10.50€ adults, 8€ reduced. Mid-Mar to Sept 15 daily 9am–7pm; Sept 16–Sept 30 daily 9am–6:30pm; Oct–Feb 9am–5pm.

Backtrack to Amboise (via D40, D31F, and D31), then join D431 and D952 to Vouvray (23km/14 miles).

> This tower houses a polygonal spiral staircase built by François I in the Château de Blois.

❺ ★ **Vouvray.** On your last afternoon, wind down with some wine tasting in the village of Vouvray. Made exclusively from chenin blanc and Loire pineau varietals, Vouvray wines typically mature in chestnut barrels, lending the wine a crisp flavor likened to taffeta by Renaissance author François Rabelais. **Domaine Huet l'Echansonne,** 11/13 rue de la Croix Buisée (☎ 02-47-52-78-87; www.huet-echansonne.com; Mon–Sat 9am–noon and 2–6pm), is by far the best-known vineyard here. Its vines are grown biodynamically, without chemicals, and weeded by hand. Call in advance to visit the *domaine* (estate) for a *dégustation* (tasting). Also worth a detour is the **Château de Montcontour,** rte. de Rochecorbon (☎ 02-47-52-60-77; www.moncontour.com; *dégustations* Mon–Sat 10am–noon and 2–6pm); monks first planted vines here in the 4th century. Visit the small wine museum, set in 10th-century cellars, before you taste some of Bacchus's finest. ⏱ 4 hr. Vouvray Tourist Office, 12 rue Rabelais. ☎ 02-47-52-68-73. www.tourismevouvray-valdeloire.com.

The Loire Valley in 5 Days

Historic buildings are the highlights of this tour, which starts in Tours and follows the Loire westward to beautiful, bourgeois Saumur. Besides the head-spinning châteaux, prepare yourself for France's biggest medieval abbey at Fontevraud—the resting place of Richard the Lionheart—and a trip deep into the heart of a cave in Montsoreau, where specialty mushrooms grow. To fit everything in, be prepared to rise early. For a more leisurely rhythm, follow this route over the course of 7 days. This tour also can be easily tagged onto "The Loire Valley in 3 Days" tour (p. 146), to make for a weeklong stay.

> Place Plumereau, with its half-timbered houses and cafes, is the life and soul of Tours.

START Tours is 240km (149 miles) southwest of Paris, and 212km (132 miles) west of Nantes. **TRIP LENGTH** 150km (93 miles), on both fast highways and country roads.

❶ ★★ **Tours.** At the junction of the Loire and Cher rivers, Tours is the traditional center for exploring the Loire Valley. The pedestrianized **place Plumereau** is the city's atmospheric epicenter: Set in the medieval part of Tours— an area of hidden courtyards and twisted towers—it brims with life, cafes, shops, and galleries. Nearby are pretty streets such as rue Briçonnet, with its half-timbered houses, and the place du Châteauneuf, where the Romanesque **Tour Charlemagne** stands proud— the only remaining part of a church erected for St. Martin, the first bishop of Tours, in the 4th century.

Today Tours's beacon of Christianity is the **Cathédrale St-Gatien,** place de la Cathédrale (☎ 02-47-70-21-00; daily 9am–7pm), which has a flamboyant Gothic facade flanked by

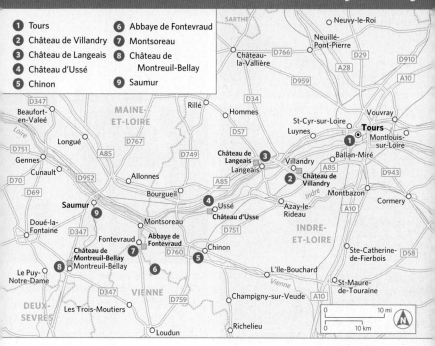

❶ Tours	❻ Abbaye de Fontevraud
❷ Château de Villandry	❼ Montsoreau
❸ Château de Langeais	❽ Château de
❹ Château d'Ussé	Montreuil-Bellay
❺ Chinon	❾ Saumur

towers with bases from the 12th century and tops from the Renaissance era. The choir and some of the glorious stained-glass windows are mostly from the 13th century. Sheltered inside, too, is the handsome 16th-century tomb of the two children of Charles VIII and Anne de Bretagne.

Art lovers shouldn't miss the **Musée des Beaux-Arts,** in the Palais des Archevêques, 18 place François-Sicard (☎ 02-47-05-68-73; admission 4€ adults, 2€ reduced, free for children 12 and under, free for everyone 1st Sun of the month; Wed–Mon 9am–6pm; closed public holidays). Its lovely rooms harbor works by masters such as Degas, Delacroix, Rembrandt, and Boucher. The classical gardens are home to an age-old giant Lebanon cedar, which provides welcome shade on a hot day.

Should you need some time out from city life, explore the kids **Jardin Botanique,** boulevard Tonnellé (☎ 02-47-21-62-68; www.parcsetjardins.fr; daily 11am–7pm); created in 1843, it's the oldest public garden in Tours. The city's university students tend to and study the many medicinal plants here. There's also a small menagerie where cute wallabies rub shoulders with peacocks. ⏲ 1 day. Tours

Tourist Office, 78/82 rue Bernard Palissy. ☎ 02-47-70-37-37. www.ligeris.com.

Early on Day 2, leave Tours on D88, join D37 (toward A10, Poitiers) to Joué-lès-Tours, and follow directions to A85. Exit A85 at junction 8, and follow D7 to Villandry (28km/17 miles total).

❷ ★★★ **Château de Villandry.** Plan to arrive early at Villandry, when the rustle of the trees and the twittering of the birds overhead are music to the ears: Villandry is one of the rare Loire parks that is more famous than its château. The magnificent 16th-century-style gardens contain miles of boxwood sculpture, and every square is like a geometric mosaic. In the area nearest the castle, the borders symbolize the faces of love: tender (with soft flowerbeds), tragic (represented by daggers), and crazy (with a labyrinth that doesn't get you anywhere). In the middle, you'll find intriguing ornamental vegetable plots, where

Where to Stay & Dine

For hotels and restaurants in the Loire Valley, see p. 183.

> The Château de Villandry's gardens are some of the country's most beautiful, famed for their ornamental vegetables.

> Lovers of fairy tales love to climb the Château d'Ussé's towers, where Sleeping Beauty awaits a restorative kiss.

the cabbages are as colorful as any flowers. The new **Jardin du Soleil** (Sun Garden) at the back of the estate contains decorative apple trees and games for children, a fountain in the shape of the sun, and little alleys of rose bushes. Above the gardens is a terrace from which you can see the small village and its 12th-century church. ⏱ 3 hr. Villandry. ☎ 02-47-50-02-09. www.chateauvillandry.com. Admission 9€ adults, 5€ ages 8–18 and students 25 and under. Gardens 6€ adults, 3.50€ ages 8–18 and students 25 and under. Château open winter daily 9am–5pm, summer daily 9am–7pm (gardens stay open 30 min. later than the château). For more on Château de Villandry, see p. 165.

The Touraine Table

Touraine cuisine (from the Tours area) is among the best regional fare in France. Delights include *rillettes* (goose or pork pâté), *andouillette* (offal sausage), *coq au vin* made with Chinon wine, delicious goat cheese, and macaroons, to list but a few.

In the early afternoon, take D7 and A85 toward Saumur/Angers, exit A85 at junction 7, and follow D952 to Langeais (11km/6¾ miles).

❸ ★ kids **Château de Langeais.** Originally built as a fortress in the 9th century, this formidable gray medieval château, with its narrow drawbridge and austere facade, dominates the town of Langeais. It was here in 1491 that Anne de Bretagne married Charles VIII, and certain rooms inside the castle reenact this golden hour with waxwork scenes. Other rooms display richly decorated apartments, dripping in historically important tapestries. ⏱ 2 hr. See p. 164.

Return to Villandry or Tours for the night. On Day 3, retrace your route to Langeais (from Tours take D952); after Langeais, at the island take D57 to La-Chapelle-aux-Naux, then join D7 to Rigny-Ussé (24km/15 miles total from Villandry; 40km/25 miles from Tours).

❹ ★★ kids **Château d'Ussé.** This castle was the inspiration for Perrault's legend of Sleeping Beauty (*La belle au bois dormant*). Whether or not you're into fairy tales, there's no denying that the château—conceived as a fortress with a complex of steeples, turrets, towers, and dormers overlooking the Indre River—is as beautiful as the girl who fell asleep in it. If you're traveling with little princes and princesses, show them the spiral stairway leading to a tower where Sleeping Beauty is still waiting for her prince to come. ◷ 2–3 hr. See p. 174, ❸.

Leave Rigny-Ussé on the route des Perres, cross Huismes, take a left down rue des Ecoles, and join D16 to Chinon (13km/8 miles). Chinon is a good spot for lunch.

❺ ★★ **Chinon.** Chinon feels like a medieval film set; it's lined with quaint cobblestone streets that rise upward, amid 15th- and 16th-century houses, toward a cliffside castle. The **Forteresse Royale de Chinon** (☎ 02-47-93-13-45; www.forteressechinon.fr; admission 7€ adults, 4.50€ reduced; Apr–Sept daily 9am–7pm; Oct–Mar daily 9:30am–7pm) is one of the oldest fortress-châteaux in France. It was here, in 1429, that Joan of Arc prevailed upon the dauphin (later Charles VII) to give her an army to fight the English, who were besieging Orléans. The rest is history, and the seat of French power stayed at Chinon until the end of the Hundred Years' War. Today, after extensive renovations, the fortress stands as a refreshingly rugged alternative to the plushly furnished châteaux you see elsewhere in the region. The **Château du Milieu** (central castle) dates from the 11th to the 15th centuries and contains the keep and the clock tower; the **Château du Coudray** contains the Tour du Coudray, where Joan of Arc once stayed. If you think that graffiti is a modern phenomenon, think again: In the 14th century, the Knights Templar were imprisoned here, and their marks still line the walls. The newest addition to the fortress is **Fort St-Georges**—a clever, contemporary take on medieval architecture—where you'll find the ticket office, an exhibition area, and the castle shop.

Chinon's other claim to fame is its scrumptious red wines. The town itself has several winetasting boutiques, but to get a real feel for Chinon's vines, head out to one of the nearby vineyards (see "The Loire Valley for Wine Lovers," p. 168). ◷ 2–3 hr. (or 1 day if combined with a wine tour). Chinon Tourist Office, place Hofheim. ☎ 02-47-93-17-85. www.chinon.com.

Leave Chinon on D749, cross St-Lazare and, at the island, turn onto D751E (past La Roche-Clermault), which joins D751. Drive through Thizay, and at Montsoreau, join D947 to L'Abbaye de Fontevraud (22km/14 miles total). Stay your next 2 nights in Fontevraud.

> *Chinon's vines, around the town castle, are renowned for creating full-bodied wines.*

6 ★★★ **Abbaye de Fontevraud.** This is the most intact medieval abbey in France—a miracle, considering its turbulent past: It was desecrated by Huguenots in 1561, attacked during the Revolution, and turned into a prison in 1804 by Napoleon III. There were prisoners held in the 12th-century Romanesque church until as recently as 1963. Today's inmates are rather more peaceful: Inside the church are the **tombs** of Henry II of England, the first Plantagenet king; Eleanor of Aquitaine, the most famous woman of the Middle Ages; their crusading son, Richard the Lionheart; and Isabelle d'Angoulême, widow of Richard's ill-famed brother, King John. Just off the church, you'll find the **Renaissance cloisters** of what used to be one of the largest nunneries in France. The garden beyond hides a rare Romanesque kitchen—the octagonal **Tour d'Evraud.** Dating from the 12th century, it is crowned with a conically roofed turret and capped by an open-air lantern tower pierced with lancets. The acoustics here are fabulous; if you decide to sing, you may well attract a crowd, as the sound will spill out all around the gardens. ⏱ 2 hr. Abbaye de Fontevraud. ☎ 02-41-51-73-52. www.abbayedefontevraud. com. Admission 7€–8.40€ adults, 5.50€–6.90€ reduced. Apr–Jun and Sept–Oct daily 9:30am–6:30pm; July–Aug daily 9:30am–7:30pm; Nov–Mar daily 10am–5:30pm.

Follow D947 from Fontevraud to Montsoreau (4.5km/2¾ miles).

7 **kids** **Montsoreau.** At the confluence of the Vienne and Loire rivers, the tiny village of Montsoreau and its white château were strategic points for rulers of Renaissance France. Today the **Château de Montsoreau** (☎ 02-41-67-12-60; www.chateau-montsoreau.com; admission 8.30€ adults, 6.80€ students, 5.20€ ages 5–14, free for children 4 and under; Apr daily 2–6pm; May–Sept daily 10am–7pm; Oct to mid-Nov daily 2–6pm; closed mid-Nov to Mar) pays tribute to this history with an exhibition on the Loire's defensive role in the region. The château has seasonal activities for children, such as treasure hunts through the castle's rooms. Montsoreau's other attraction (just outside the village center) is its *champignonnière* in a cave, the ★★ **kids** **Saut aux Loups,** rte. de Saumur (☎ 02-41-51-70-30; www.troglo-sautauxloups.com; admission 5.90€ adults, 4.50€ reduced; Mar 1–Nov 15

> On request, you can taste some wines in these perfectly preserved medieval kitchens at Château de Montreuil-Bellay.

> The bridges, tufa stone houses, and castle turrets of Saumur.

daily 10am–6pm; closed mid-Nov to Feb). This part of the Val de Loire is famous for its edible fungi, and the Saut aux Loups galleries carved into the tufa cliffside here house a fascinating mushroom museum, a century-old mushroom farm, and a restaurant that serves—what else?—mushroom-based dishes (restaurant open July to mid-Sept Wed–Mon for lunch, Fri–Sat for dinner; Mar–Jun and mid-Sept to mid-Nov Sat–Sun and public holidays for lunch only; closed mid-Nov to Feb). The museum presents cultivating techniques and infor-mation on the different types of fungi, from *champignons de Paris* to shiitakes and oyster mushrooms. Come for lunch and sample the *galipettes* (stuffed mushrooms baked with top-pings such as goat cheese, smoked salmon, or snails). ⏱ 4 hr. Montsoreau Town Hall, 24 place des Diligences. ☎ 02-41-51-70-15. www.ville-montsoreau.fr.

Head back to Fontevraud for the night. Early on Day 5, retrace your route to Montsoreau, take D947, D952, and D347 to Saumur, and follow signs to Montreuil-Bellay (31km/19 miles).

8 ★★ **Château de Montreuil-Bellay.** South of Saumur, on the Thouet River, Montreuil-Bellay is a gem of a castle, with architecture that dates from the Middle Ages to the Re-naissance. It is also a winemaking center for Saumur reds and cabernet d'Anjou rosés. Two levels of the castle can be visited: the lushly decorated ground floor, with beamed ceilings, fresco-clad walls, and furniture that spans 4 centuries; and the medieval-period kitchens downstairs. ⏱ 2–3 hr. See p. 164.

Retrace your route to Saumur, joining D960 just before you enter the center (16km/10 miles).

9 ★★★ **Saumur.** Famed for its cavalry school, its mushrooms, its turreted castle, and its elegant sparkling wines, Saumur is a majestic city with a lot to offer. You could easily make this your base during your week in the Loire. ⏱ 1 day. See p. 158, **4**.

The Loire Valley for History Buffs

This tour takes you through the valley's main historical towns, from Joan of Arc's Orléans to postcard-perfect Blois and Saumur; then onto Angers, the former capital of Anjou; and finally to arty Nantes, whose industrial heritage and maritime history set it blissfully apart from anyplace else in the Loire Valley.

START Orléans is 137km (85 miles) southwest of Paris and 116km (72 miles) northeast of Tours. **TRIP LENGTH** About 1 week; 380km (236 miles), on both fast highways and country roads.

❶ ★★ **Orléans.** Orléans is a paradoxical city: On the one hand, it is forward-thinking, with a low unemployment rate and highly competitive business clusters. This modernity is embodied in its ultra-contemporary **Pont de l'Europe,** a bridge built in 2000. On the other hand, it is deeply attached to its history—particularly the Joan of Arc years, for it was here in 1429 that the feisty little martyr fought the English. Ever since then, in April and May, the

city reenacts the events in period costume and holds blessings in the Gothic-style **Cathédrale Ste-Croix** (begun in the 13th century and rebuilt between the 17th and 19th centuries), where a stained-glass window depicts Joan being burned at the stake in Rouen in 1431. You can even visit her house, the half-timbered **Maison de Jeanne d'Arc,** at 3 place du général de Gaulle (☎ 02-38-52-99-89; www.jeannedarc.com.fr; admission 2€ adults, free for children 15 and under; May–Oct Tues–Sun 10:30am–12:30pm and 1:30–6:30pm; Nov–Apr 1:30–6:30pm). It was rebuilt in 1961, using period materials, on the site of her former digs. Joan of Arc statues surface around town, on **place du Martroi** and in front of the

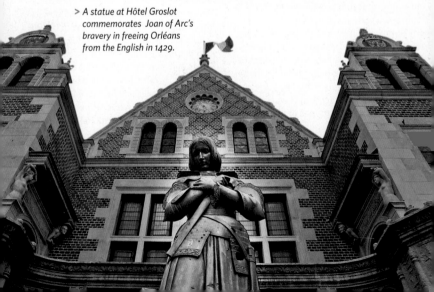

> *A statue at Hôtel Groslot commemorates Joan of Arc's bravery in freeing Orléans from the English in 1429.*

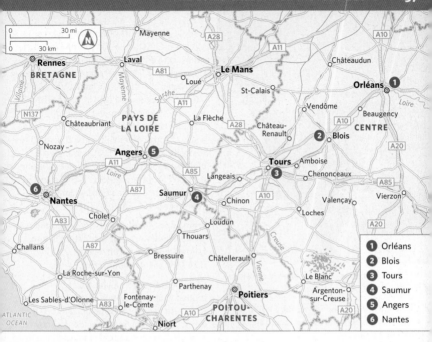

16th-century **Hôtel Groslot** (place de l'Etape). The latter is a stunning brick mansion where a long line of kings and queens—from Charles IX to Henris II and IV—all stayed. It also served as the city hall from the 18th century to 1882. Nearby, the **Musée des Beaux Arts,** 1 rue Fernand Rabier, place Ste-Croix (☎ 02-38-79-21-55; Tues–Sun 10am–6pm; closed public holidays), is well worth a detour. It contains an outstanding series of French paintings and sculptures from the 17th to the 19th centuries; a room devoted to pastels; works by Flemish, Dutch, and Italian painters; and a modern and contemporary art section. ⏱1 day. Orléans Tourist Office, 2 place de l'Etape. ☎ 02-38-24-05-05. www.tourisme-orleans.com.

From Orléans, take N152 toward Paris/Blois and join A71 and then A10, exiting at junction 17 and following signs for Blois (62km/39 miles total).

Where to Stay & Dine

For hotels and restaurants in Nantes, see p. 182; elsewhere in the Loire Valley, see p. 183.

2 ★★★ **Blois.** Elegant Blois is like a living postcard—especially around the semipedestrian area near the château, the cathedral, and the river, where quaint buildings, hidden courtyards, and stately mansions rub shoulders with boutiques and cafes. You could easily spend a whole day here, inside the **castle** (see p. 146, **1**), which was the royal court until Henri IV moved to Paris in 1598, and in the town's atmospheric streets. The **Cathédrale St-Louis** is particularly splendid—a 17th-century reconstruction of a Gothic church that was destroyed by a storm in 1678. The gardens around the **Hôtel de Ville,** or City Hall (the former bishop's palace), are also worthy of exploration, affording sweeping views over the town and river. Other highlights to look for are the **Maison des Acrobates,** opposite the cathedral, with a facade carved with acrobats and jugglers; the half-timbered **place Vauvert;** rue des Juifs, which marks the limits of the medieval Jewish ghetto; and the magnificent **Hôtel de Condé,** 3 rue des Juifs, with its stunning Renaissance galleries. ⏱1 day. Blois Tourist Office, 23 place du Château. ☎ 02-54-90-41-41. www.bloispaysdechambord.com/en.

> *Gothic alleys and stepped passages abound in the city of Blois.*

Head to Tours for the night: Take A10 from Blois and follow signs to Tours, exiting at junction 21 (65km/40 miles).

❸ ★★ **Tours.** On your 3rd day, explore Tours's elegant streets, eye-catching architecture, excellent restaurants, and rich history. The first mention of the city—as Caesarodonum, "the hill of Caesar"—dates from the 1st century A.D., when the settlement was inhabited by Romanized Gauls called the "Turones." You can still see a part of the Gallo-Roman castrum wall near rue du Petit Cupidon by the cathedral and vestiges of fortifications in the Musée des Beaux Arts' courtyard. Later, in the

Middle Ages, Tours became a major center for Western Christianity and for the French monarchy, who either reigned from the city or visited regularly. The chief ministers and advisors of Charles VII, Louis XI, Charles VIII, Louis XII, and François I all lived in Tours. Thanks to Louis XI, who set up the first group of silk manufacturers in the city, Tours flourished as a silk-making center with more than 800 resident silk masters and 6,000 journeymen. The cloth was sold during two, 2-week-long annual fairs on Place Foire le Roi (literally translated as King's Fair Square). ⏱ 1 day. For more on Tours, see p. 150, ❶.

From Tours, head west along D952 and A85 (toward Saumur). Exit at junction 3, and follow signs to Saumur, via D767, D347, and D947 (76km/47 miles total).

❹ ★★★ **Saumur.** Sophisticated Saumur, topped with its fairy-tale castle, bustles year-round. Its decent shops (especially around rue St-Jean) are a refreshing dose of normality after visiting so many châteaux, and the town woos wine lovers by the barrel with its delicious reds, rosés, and sparkling whites, many of which you can try in the **Maison des Vins,** quai Lucien Gauthier (☎ 02-41-38-45-83; www.vinsdeloire.fr). For more on Saumur wines, see "The Loire Valley for Wine Lovers," p. 168; you may wish to add a wine-tasting day trip from Saumur to a nearby vineyard. Saumur is also home to the ★★ **Cadre Noir** (Black Squad), at Terrefort (☎ 02-41-53-50-60; www.cadrenoir.fr), one of the grandest and oldest riding schools in Europe (founded in 1768), which holds public equestrian galas in May, July, and October. What lends the town its charm, however, are the stately boulevards and winding streets that harbor more than 62 listed historic monuments. The old town leads up to the turreted **Château de Saumur** (☎ 02-41-40-24-40; admission 3€; Apr–June and Sept to early Nov daily 10am–1pm and 2–5:30pm; July–Aug daily 10am–6pm), which emanates a strange mixture of vibes: both romantic (it looks like something Charles Perrault would have used in a fairy tale) and austere (a stark and foreboding fortress, it became a prison under Napoleon, then eventually a barracks and a munitions depot). Although it's undergoing extensive

Cavemen Quarters

All around Saumur, you can find some of the world's best troglodyte settlements in the soft tufa rock and natural caves that have provided ideal shelters for millennia. Old quarries at **Doué la Fontaine** contain a zoo for endangered species (p. 175, ❺); you can visit a troglodyte castle at nearby **Brézé** (p. 161); and the **Parc Pierre et Lumière,** rte. de Gennes (☎ 02-41-50-70-04; www.pierre-et-lumiere.com), in Saumur's St-Hilaire St-Florent district, contains breathtaking sculptures in the cave walls of local buildings and cathedrals.

restoration work, you can still visit two halls. Abbey Hall exhibits the evolution of the château and the historic personalities who lived there, plus there's a display by the Cadre Noir on the horse through the ages. Baille Hall houses the city's decorative arts collection, known for its 16th- to 18th-century ceramics. ⏱1–2 days. Saumur Tourist Office, Allée Ste-Catherine/place St-Michel. ☎ 02-41-51-79-45. www.saumur-tourisme.com.

Leave Saumur following signs to A85 and Angers; after about 48km (30 miles), join A11 and follow signs to Angers (67km/42 miles total).

⑤ ★ **Angers.** Dominating Angers (the historic capital of Anjou) is the striped gray-and-white slate and tufa **Château d'Angers,** 2 promenade du Bout-du-Monde (☎ 02-41-86-48-77; http://angers.monuments-nationaux.fr; admission 8€ adults, free–5€ reduced; May to early Sept daily 9:30am–6:30pm; early Sept to Apr daily 10am–5:30pm). An austere military construction with 17 defense towers, built by Louis IX, it's quite unlike the valley's other châteaux. In the 14th and 15th centuries, it was the court for the dukes of Anjou; then Good King Réné introduced Renaissance elements inside the *appartements royaux* (royal apartments) in the 15th century. After Réné, the château was used mainly as a prison and an arms warehouse. Today it houses the world's longest and oldest medieval tapestry, the ★★★ *Tapisserie de l'Apocalypse* (Apocalypse Tapestry)—76 intricately woven scenes of the Apocalypse, as described in the last book of the New Testament. You can also see a modern replica, the *Chant du Monde (Song of the World),* inside ★ **Musée Jean Lurçat,** 4 bd. Arago (☎ 02-41-24-18-48; www.musees.angers.fr; admission 4€; June–Sept daily 10am–6:30pm; Oct–May Tues–Sun 10am–noon and 2–6pm), in the medieval **Hôpital St-Jean** (a hospital for the poor from 1174 to 1854). The museum pays tribute to Lurçat, renowned for having rekindled the flame of tapestry-making in Angers in the early 20th century. The city itself is prettiest in the old town around the château and near the **Cathédrale St-Maurice,** noted for its vivid 13th-century stained-glass windows and splendid organ. ⏱1 day. Anders Tourist Office, 7 place Kennedy. ☎ 02-41-23-50-00. www.angersloiretourisme.com.

> The Château d'Angers is immediately recognizable from its unique tufa and slate striped towers.

From Angers, follow A11 and A811 to Nantes, which is well signposted (88km/55 miles).

⑥ ★★★ **Nantes.** Quite unlike any other city on the Loire, Nantes reels in the crowds with the promise of avant-garde art, bustling streets, decent shopping, and an important maritime history. History lovers will have their fill at Nantes's **Château des Ducs de Bretagne.** The last Loire château before the Altantic Ocean, it houses the **Musée d'Histoire de Nantes,** which explores major moments in European and world history, from the Edict of Nantes to the slave trade, and into the 20th century. Nantes is also the city that fed Jules Verne's imagination; his legacy lives on in the old-world **Musée Jules Verne** and at the fabulous KIDS **Les Machines de l'Ile,** where kids can ride weird and wonderful creatures carved from wood and metal. ⏱1 day. For detailed information on Nantes, see p. 178.

Saumur's Two Claims to Fame

French author Honoré de Balzac found inspiration for his classic novel, *Eugénie Grandet,* in Saumur. Coco Chanel, inventor of those little black dresses, was born here.

The Loire Valley's Best Châteaux

The legacy of the Valois kings lives on in the towns, villages, abbeys, and castles all along the Loire waterway. As you drive, signposts will draw you into a host of beautiful châteaux, resplendent amid slated rooftops, vineyards, and hunting forests—making it very hard to choose which castle to visit. This alphabetized list of the top sites is designed to help you make the right decision, whether you're looking for Renaissance architecture, flower-laden gardens, or hidden troglodyte treasures.

> *The gorgeous Château du Rivau's castle and gardens feature in Renaissance writer François Rabelais' tales of Gargantua the giant.*

★★★ **Azay-le-Rideau.** This castle's turreted towers and blue-slate roof pierced with dormers shimmer in the moat like a Monet painting. Its Renaissance structure is so beautiful that when François I saw it, he accused the builder, his finance minister Gilles Berthelot, of misappropriating funds. Berthelot was forced to flee, and the château reverted to the king, although he never lived here—he just granted it to "friends of the Crown." Enter the castle via the ticket office on rue Pinceau, then admire the building from its beautiful gardens. Inside you'll find sumptuous rooms laden with Renaissance furniture, portraits, and tapestries from Brussels, Antwerp, and Paris. ⏱ 2 hr. Azay-le-Rideau 37190, 21km (13 miles) southwest of Tours. ☎ 02-47-45-42-04. www.azay-le-rideau.monuments-nationaux. fr. Admission 8€ adults, 5€ reduced. Apr–Jun and Sept daily 9:30am–6pm; July–Aug daily 9:30am–7pm; Oct–Mar daily 10am–12:30pm and 2–5:30pm.

> *In high season at Amboise, you can access the curious Renaissance Tour des Minimes tower, built especially for horsemen.*

> *A masterpiece of 16th-century architecture, Azay-le-Rideau embodies all the elegance, panache, and beauty of the Renaissance.*

★★ **Château d'Amboise.** This is where Louis XI and Charles VIII grew up, away from the squalor of the town below. At one time, several buildings surrounded the panoramic terrace, which affords fine views over the Loire River. Alas, many of them were demolished in the 19th century by the owner, Roger Ducos, who couldn't afford their upkeep. Today only about a quarter of the once-sprawling edifice remains, but it is still very impressive. You first come to the flamboyant, Gothic Chapelle de St-Hubert, distinguished by its lacelike tracery and the tomb of Leonardo da Vinci. The rest of the château spans styles ranging from Gothic to Renaissance to Empire, periods reflected in

the stately interior. Perhaps most interesting of all are the underground tunnels, which lead to the ★★ **Tour des Minimes** (Apr–Sept only), a helter-skelter tower with a slope designed for horsemen and carts; it looks like a medieval version of New York's Guggenheim Museum. ⏱ 2 hr. Amboise, 35km (22 miles) east of Tours. ☎ 02-47-57-00-98. www.chateau-amboise.com. Admission 9.50€ adults, free–8€ reduced. Feb–Mar 15 daily 9am–noon and 1:30–5:30pm; Mar 16–31 daily 9am–5pm; Apr–Jun daily 9am–6:30pm; July–Aug daily 9am–7pm; Sept–Oct daily 9am–6pm; Nov 1–15 daily 9am–5pm; Nov 16–Jan daily 9am–12.30pm and 2–4:45pm.

★★★ **Château de Brézé.** This Renaissance and 19th-century structure is surrounded by the oldest vineyards in the Loire and has several period rooms you can visit. The main attraction is its wholly unique troglodyte village, dug out in 1448 when the castle was built by the Grand Condé, Gilles Maillé-Brézé, to serve as a fortress. Five huge chambers originally inhabited by soldiers were later used as wine cellars and a press room. But the cherry on the *gâteau* (cake) is the dry moat. At 18m (59 ft.) deep and 13m (43 ft.) wide, it is the deepest in Europe and contains living quarters, a silkworm farm, and a bakery that was last used by invading German soldiers during World War II. Your visit ends with the **Cathédrale d'Images**—a spooky, multimedia sound-and-light experience presented in three gigantic tufa cellars. The present owners are

Where to Stay & Dine

For hotels and restaurants in Nantes, see p. 182; elsewhere in the Loire Valley, see p. 183.

The Loire Valley's Best Châteaux

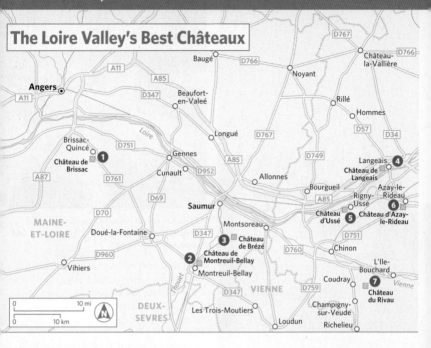

> In medieval times, a whole village was contained in this troglodyte moat at the Château de Brézé.

descendants of the Brézé nobles and, like their ancestors, enthusiastic winegrowers, winning prizes for their fantastic Saumur wines. Ask for a *dégustation* (tasting) during your visit. ⏱ 3 hr. Brézé, 74km (46 miles) west of Tours, 10km (6¼ miles) south of Saumur, 60km (37 miles) southeast of Angers. ☎ 02-41-51-60-15, www.chateaudebreze.com. Admission 11€ adults, 9€ students; 6€ other concessions. Apr–Sept daily 10am–6:30pm; Oct–Dec and Feb–Mar Tues–Sun 10am–6pm. Closed Jan.

★★ **Château de Brissac.** Known as the *Géant du Val de Loire* (Loire Giant), Brissac is the tallest château in France, with seven floors and 204 rooms. It is also very much a family home, owned by the 13th duc de Brissac, a descendant of René de Cossé, who acquired the château in 1502. Personal touches lend the castle a wonderful, lived-in feel: Family memorabilia adorns the Golden Drawing Room; there are portrait galleries of ancestors; and the dining room is dressed, ready for a meal. The rest of the interior is just as beautiful, with its gold-leaf ceilings, precious period furniture, and a sumptuous Belle Epoque theater. Within the grounds are ancient tree-lined

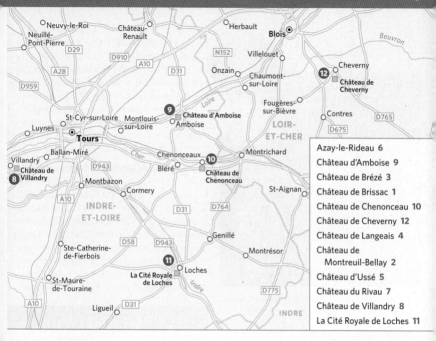

alleys, a boating area, and lovely, flower-clad paths. Brissac is also a working, 28-hectare (69-acre) vineyard. You can taste its Anjou Villages Brissac and Rosé d'Anjou wines at the end of your visit, in the château cellars. In fine weather, at dawn, hot-air balloon flights can be organized from the park (see "The Loire Valley Outdoors" tour, p. 176). You can also book a night in one of the château's lavishly decorated rooms (p. 183). ⏱ 3 hr. Brissac, 20km (12 miles) south of Angers, 113km (70 miles) east of Nantes, 40km (25 miles) west of Saumur. ☎ 02-41-91-22-21. www.brissac.net. Admission 9€ adults, 4.45€ reduced. Apr–Jun and Sept–Oct Wed–Mon 10am–12:30pm and 2–6pm; July–Aug daily 10am–6pm.

★★★ **Château de Chenonceau.** This romantic Renaissance pleasure palace, 35km (22 miles) east of Tours, is grand in every way. ⏱ 2 hr. See p. 149, ④.

★★★ **Château de Cheverny.** Just 16km (10 miles) south of Blois (along D765), the Château de Cheverny is one of the rare non-Renaissance castles in the Loire Valley. It was built in the purest Louis XIII classical style in the first part of the 17th century, lending it

> *Romance is in the air as a hot-air balloon takes off over the Château de Brissac at sunrise.*

> *During the Revolution, the Château de Montreuil-Bellay served as a prison for female royalists.*

In the park, France's oldest dungeon ruin awaits your discovery. Game areas and tree-houses provide kids with plenty of opportunities to run around. ⊙ 2 hr. Langeais, 26km (16 miles) west of Tours. ☎ 02-47-96-72-60. Admission 8.50€ adults, 7.20€ ages 18–25, 5€ ages 10–17, free for children 9 and under. Feb–Mar daily 9:30am–5:30pm; Apr–Jun and Sept–Nov 12 daily 9:30am–6:30pm; July–Aug daily 9:30am–7pm; Nov 13–Jan daily 10am–5pm.

★★★ **Château de Montreuil-Bellay.** In one of the Loire's most gracious towns, the Château de Montreuil-Bellay took 400 years to build, which is not surprising when you see the sheer scale and intricacy of its 13 interlocking towers and ramparts. It flaunts architecture from the feudal era to the Renaissance, the main part of which is the palace, the central point for guided tours (the only way to visit). Inside the palace, the dining room has beams carved with symbolic

symmetrical allure quite unlike anything else on the circuit. The facade is exactly the same as it was the day it was finished. Inside, every room is sumptuous, with 34 painted wood panels around the walls of the dining room depicting the story of Don Quixote (the hero of the Cervantes novel); the King's Chamber has a coffered ceiling that shows scenes from the myth of Perseus and Andromeda, and one chamber contains a canopied bed, with Persian embroidery, in which Henri IV slept. ⊙ 3 hr. ☎ 02-54-79-96-29. www.chateau-cheverny.fr. Admission 7.50€ adults, free for children 5 and under. Apr–July daily 9:15am–6:15pm; Aug–May daily 9:45am–5pm.

★★ kids **Château de Langeais.** This medieval, fiercely feudal fortress, constructed by Louis XI between 1465 and 1469, dominates the town of Langeais with its austere facade. But don't be fooled: Beyond the drawbridge you'll find some of the most furnished *appartements royaux* in the Val de Loire—royal apartments laden with Flemish and Aubusson tapestries. Anne de Bretagne (a mere child at the time) and Charles VIII married here in 1491, and a waxwork depiction is visible in one of the chambers. Their symbols—scallop shells, fleurs-de-lis, and ermine—still set the motif for the Salle des Gardes (Guard Room).

Loches's Torture

Loches's *donjon* (dungeon) was the site of many an unpleasant moment when King Louis XI was in town. Cardinal Jean Balue, Louis's favorite advisor, invented a suspended prison for the space, known as *le Cage.* If you entered *le Cage,* you usually died there—as Balue himself discovered, ironically, when he plotted against the king. He was imprisoned there in 1469 and swung his last in 1480.

> *It's easy to see why Perrault set* Sleeping Beauty *at the Château d'Ussé, with its magical turrets and surrounding woods.*

figures. You can also admire the Duchess of Longueville's bedroom, a large drawing room furnished with antiques, a music room, and a stupendous monumental staircase. The frescoes in the oratory were painted by a pupil of Leonardo da Vinci. On the lower floor, the medieval kitchen and foyer are astoundingly well preserved and reminiscent of those at Fontevraud Abbey (p. 154, ⑥), with 15th-century lateral chimneys and large ovens with flamboyant brass fittings. ⏱ 2–3 hr. Montreuil-Bellay, 82km (51 miles) southeast of Angers, 16km (10 miles) southwest of Saumur. ☎ 02-41-52-33-06. www. chateau-de-montreuil-bellay.fr. Admission 8€ adults, 6€ ages 15–25, 4€ ages 6–14. Apr–June and Sept–Nov 5 Wed–Mon 10am–noon and 2–6pm; July–Aug daily 10am–12:30pm and 1:30–6:30pm; closed early Nov to Mar.

★★ kids **Château d'Ussé.** Charles Perrault took his inspiration from this castle when he wrote the children's classic, *La belle au bois dormant (Sleeping Beauty)*. ⏱ 2 hr. See p. 174, ③.

★★★ kids **Château du Rivau.** Erected in the 13th century and fortified in the 15th, Rivau is simultaneously a family home, a medieval castle, a showcase for cutting-edge modern art, and one of Europe's biggest rose gardens, with more than 400 varieties. ⏱ 3 hr. See p. 174, ④.

★★★ **Château de Villandry.** A feudal castle once stood at Villandry. In 1536, Jean Lebreton, François I's chancellor, built the present Renaissance château, whose buildings form a U and are surrounded by a fish-filled moat. You'll notice that, unlike other sites, Villandry

has Empire-style appointments inside, having been decorated by the owners, the de Carvallos. Madame de Carvallo's bedroom commands a particularly pretty view over the gardens, onto the church and village. In one wing, don't miss the well-furnished picture gallery displaying Spanish religious art and a gruesome severed head by Goya. Villandry's *pièce de résistance* is the gardens. ⏱ 2–3 hr. Villandry, 32km (20 miles) northeast of Chinon, 18km (11 miles) west of Tours. For more information, see p. 151, ②.

★★ **La Cité Royale de Loches.** Agnès Sorel, the beautiful mistress of Charles VII, and Anne de Bretagne are forever linked to Loches, in the hills on the banks of the Indre River. This is also where Joan of Arc pleaded with Charles to go to Reims (p. 254) to be crowned. A real acropolis of the Loire, the château, built in the early 11th century by Foulques Nerra, stands 36m (118 ft.) high and is one of France's best examples of Norman military architecture. Inside the keep, you'll find the governor's lodge, the torture chamber, dungeons, and tunnels. The Renaissance-era royal apartments are richly furnished in Flemish tapestries, suits of armor, and paintings such as the triptych of the passion of Christ, attributed to Jean Fouquet (a great French Renaissance painter, born in Tours in the early 15th century). Agnès Sorel's effigy stands inside Anne de Bretagne's chapel. ⏱ 3 hr. Loches, 40km (25 miles) southeast of Tours. ☎ 02-47-59-01-32. www.monuments-touraine.fr. Admission 7€ adults, 4.50€ reduced. Apr–Sept daily 9:30am–7pm; Oct–Mar daily 9:30am–5pm.

RENAISSANCE KINGS

Lifestyles of the Loire's Rich & Famous BY ANNA BROOKE

WHEN FRANCE INVADED ITALY IN 1494, the greatest spoils of war were the ideals and aesthetics of the Italian Renaissance, which flourished in France for more than 150 years, most fruitfully under François I. A patron of the arts, letters, and architecture, François ruled from the Loire Valley rather than Paris and incited the region's châteaux fever, taking his courtiers from palace to palace to hunt, dine, make love, and listen to music and poetry.

François I
(1494–1547)

François I, who reigned from 1515 to 1547, loved Italian paintings—especially by Michelangelo and Leonardo, who finished his *St. John the Baptist* in Amboise at the Clos Lucé (p. 172). Although François ruled from Amboise (p. 148, **3**), he embellished the Louvre (p. 50, **1**), Fontainebleau, Chambord (p. 147, **2**), and the Château de Blois, his first Renaissance construction. He helped design many of his projects—marked with his personal emblem, a salamander—including the double staircase at Chambord, which two people can use without meeting. His downfall was his ambition to oust Charles V as Holy Roman emperor. François failed to take Italy; but he sent Giovanni da Verrazzano to the Americas, and in 1524 Verrazzano founded New Angoulême (today's NYC).

Henri II of France
(1519–1559)

The son of François I and Claude of France, Henri II married Catherine de Medici when they were both 14. She gave him heirs (François II, Charles IX, and Henri III), but for more than a quarter century, Diane de Poitiers governed Henri's affections (see below). The love triangle had a considerable effect on French politics during Henri's reign (1547–1559); his rule, like his father's, was dominated by war, waged against Italy, his wife's homeland. Yet he died not in battle but in a jousting competition, with Diane's ribbons tied to his lance.

Henri IV
(1553–1610)

Just a few months after Catherine de Medici's death, her reigning son, Henri III, was stabbed to death, leaving the throne to Henri IV, Bourbon King of Navarre. A Protestant king, Henri IV was tolerant and abated the Wars of Religon with the Edict of Nantes in 1598. Known for good looks and humor, he helped urbanize Paris, constructing the Pont Neuf (p. 39, **5**). His bonhomie didn't prevent his murder at

the hands of a Catholic extremist, but it ensured his legacy as one of history's best-loved kings.

Louis XIII
(1601–1643)

Henri IV's son, Louis XIII, was 9 when his father died, so his mother, Marie de

Medici (Henri's IV's second wife, and second cousin to Catherine), acted as regent until 1617. The young king, who was afflicted with a speech impediment and double teeth, founded the Academie Française and participated in the 30 Years' War against the Habsburgs, with his infamous first minister Cardinal Richelieu. The reign of his son, the Sun King Louis XIV, marked the end of the Renaissance and the start of the Grand Siècle.

Henri II's Love Triangle

Henri II's Italian wife, Catherine de Medici (1519–1589), had no authority during his reign, as Henri was busy doting on his mistress, Diane de Poitiers (1499–1566). Widow of Louis de Brézé and 20 years Henri's elder, Diane was the king's bit on the side for more than 25 years. She held his heart but encouraged him to sleep with his wife to produce legitimate heirs. Wrong move. When Henri died Catherine avenged the infidelity, becoming the most powerful woman around—first as advisor to her sickly son King François II; and, after his death, as regent to her sons Charles IX and, later, Henri III,

whom she counseled until her death. She banished Diane from court and confiscated the Château de Chenonceau (p. 149, **4**), a gift to Diane from Henri. Although Diane spent the rest of her life in obscurity, François Clouet and other painters immortalized her beauty. Catherine's life, meanwhile, was marked by the Wars of Religion, and some blame her for the St. Bartholomew's Day Massacre (1572), in which thousands of Protestants were slaughtered.

The Loire Valley for Wine Lovers

The Loire Valley is the country's most diverse wine region, producing dry and sweet white wines, fruity reds, elegant rosés, and sparkling whites that rival many champagnes in all but name. This tour highlights the excellent wine areas of Saumur and Chinon; you may also wish to consider Vouvray (p. 149). You can follow the tour in a long day, or stay overnight at either Saumur or Le Puy Notre-Dame and visit Chinon on the second day.

> The village of Le Puy-Notre-Dame is surrounded by vineyards that produce around 12 million bottles of wine a year.

START Saumur is 322km (200 miles) southwest of Paris and 76km (47 miles) west of Tours. **TRIP LENGTH** 1 or 2 days; 45–90km (28–56 miles), on mostly country roads.

1 ★★ **Saumur.** The rolling vineyards around castle-topped Saumur are the center for sparkling wine production in the Loire, but they also produce still wines, chiefly made from chenin blanc or chenin blanc–chardonnay blends. Saumur and Saumur-Champigny reds tend to be made from cabernet franc grapes, whereas cabernet de Saumur is a dry, light rosé made from cabernet franc and cabernet sauvignon varieties. You may also come

Where to Stay & Dine

For hotels and restaurants in the Loire Valley, see p. 183.

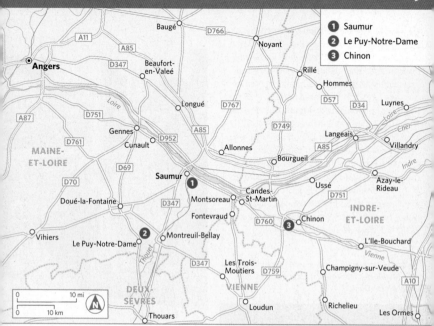

Saumur
Le Puy-Notre-Dame
Chinon

across the small, semisweet chenin blanc appellation of Coteaux de Saumur. All this becomes clear inside the **Maison des Vins** in Saumur, quai Lucien Gautier Saumur (☎ 02-41-38-45-83; www.vinsdeloire.fr; free admission; Apr–Sept Tues–Sat 9:30am–1pm and 2–7pm, Sun 10:30am–1pm, Mon 2–7pm; Oct–Mar Tues–Fri 10:30am–12:30pm and 3–6pm, Sat 10:30am–12:30pm and 2:30–6:30pm), where you can go for a list of producers and information on Loire wines, and even taste a few. If you fancy visiting a sparkling wine cellar deep in Saumur's bedrock, don't miss ★★ **Bouvet-Ladubay,** St-Hilaire St-Florent, Saumur (☎ 02-41-83-83-83; www.bouvet-ladubay.fr; June–Sept daily 9am–7pm; Oct–May daily 9am–12:30pm and 2–6pm). Vineyard staff run wine-tasting courses and offer trips around the 8km-long (5-mile) wine *caves* (cellars). Also keep your eyes peeled along the D947 road into Saumur, which is littered with *caves*. ⏱ 2 hr. to 1 day. Saumur Tourist Office, Place de la Bilange. ☎ 02-41-40-20-60. www.ot-saumur.fr.

From Saumur, take D960 and D347 to Les Faubourgs, then take D88 and D77 to Le Puy Notre-Dame (22km/14 miles).

Champignons of Saumur

A small but thriving town, Saumur produces some 100,000 tons per year of the mushrooms the French adore. Balzac left us this advice: "Taste a mushroom and delight in the essential strangeness of the place." The cool tunnels for Saumur's *champignons* also provide the ideal resting place for the celebrated sparkling wines of the region. Enjoy both of these local favorites at a neighborhood cafe.

② ★★★ **Le Puy-Notre-Dame.** In the heart of Saumur's wine country, Le Puy-Notre-Dame is a postcard-perfect village with breathtaking Romanesque religious monuments and an obvious devotion to winemaking. Numerous vineyards can be visited here. One of the friendliest is **Domaine du Moulin de l'Horizon,** 11bis rue St-Vincent Sanziers (☎ 02-41-52-25-52; www.moulindelhorizon.com; Mon–Fri 8am–noon and 2–6pm; Sat 8am–noon; reservations recommended), which organizes cellar and vineyard tours, as well as tastings of its chardonnays, sparkling Crémant blancs, and Coteaux de Saumur. ⊙ 2 hr. Le Puy-Notre-Dame Tourist Office, Sophie Sassier. ☎ 02-41-38-87-30. www.ville-lepuynotredame.fr.

> Maison des Vins in Saumur organizes wine-tastings—a fine way to sample the region's wines if you're short on time.

> Wine is matured in wooden barrels in the Domaine du Moulin de l'Horizon's limestone cellars at Le Puy-Notre-Dame.

Leave Le Puy on D77, turn left onto D88, then right onto D347; after Les Trois Moutiers (23km/14 miles), pick up D168 and follow signs to Chinon (54km/34 miles total).

❸ ★★ **Chinon.** In the film *Joan of Arc* (1948) Ingrid Bergman sought out the dauphin as he tried to conceal himself among his courtiers. This took place in real life at the **Château de Chinon,** one of the oldest fortress-châteaux in France. Charles VII centered his government at Chinon from 1429 to 1450. In 1429, with the English besieging Orléans, the Maid of Orléans prevailed upon the dauphin to give her an army. The rest is history. The seat of French power stayed at Chinon until the end of the Hundred Years' War.

Today, Chinon remains a tranquil village known mainly for its delightful wines, which crop up on prestigious lists around the world. Made from the cabernet franc grape, Chinon's wines are mostly reds, characterized by depth, suppleness, and fruity aromas. Supermarkets and wine shops throughout the region sell them; families that have been in the business longer than anyone can remember maintain the two most interesting stores. **Château de la Grille,** rte. de Huismes (☎ 02-47-93-01-95; www.chateau-de-la-grille.com; Tues–Sat 9am–noon and 2–6pm), just outside the town center, has a *cave de dégustation* (tasting cellar) where you can sample delicious reds such as its Chinon 2003—a fabulous vintage, thanks to optimum weather conditions (a cold winter followed by a hot summer). Its 2002 vintages are also delectable, with notes of cherry and rounded tannins. If you're looking for some bottles to keep, head to the ★ **Domaine P&B Couly,** 4 rue de St-Louands (☎ 02-47-93-43-97; www.pb-couly.com; call before you visit), whose complex and velvety Le V range can be kept in a cellar for between 5 and 12 years. At the **Domaine de Noiré,** also just outside Chinon's center at 160 rue de l'Olive (☎ 06-76-81-91-29; www.domainedenoire.com; call before you visit), wines are made with cabernet franc grapes (the variety loved by Renaissance author François Rabelais). Particularly tasty are its rosés, whose raspberry pinkness is created by "bleeding" (or crushing) the red grape skin. The result is an aromatic wine with hints of red fruits, which suits salads or smoked fish. At **Caves Plouzeau,** 94 rue Haute-St-Maurice (☎ 02-47-93-32-11; www.plouzeau.com; Apr–Sept Tues–Sat 11am–1pm and 3–7pm), the 12th-century cellars were dug to provide building blocks for the foundations of the château. The present management dates from 1929; bottles of red or white wine cost from 6€ to 11€. You're welcome to climb down to the cellars. The cellars at **Couly-Dutheil,** 12 rue Diderot (☎ 02-47-97-20-20; www.coulydutheil-chinon.com; tour and tasting 4€–6€, call in advance; Apr–Sept Mon–Fri 8am–noon and 1:45–5:45pm), are suitably medieval; many were carved from rock. This company produces largely Chinon wines

> *Swirl and sniff: Wine-tasting opportunities abound around Chinon.*

(mostly reds), and it's proud of the Bourgueil and St-Nicolas de Bourgueil, whose popularity in North America has grown in recent years. ⊕ 3 hr.–1 day. The Wine Syndicate of Chinon, Impasse des Caves Painctes. ☎ 02-47-93-30-44. www.chinon.com.

Loire Valley Grape Varietals

The Loire's main wine areas are Bourgueil, Chinon, Muscadet, Saumur, and Vouvray. The grape varieties range from chenin blanc, pinot noir, gamay, and cabernet franc to Malbec and Melon de Bourgogne, used in muscadets.

Staying at a Working Winery

Nothing beats the feeling of waking up to the sight of ripening vines, as you can at the **Manoir de la Tête Rouge** in Le Puy-Notre-Dame (☎ 02-41-38-76-43; www.manoirdelateterouge.com; 3 units; doubles 67€–77€; MC, V). That feeling is amplified by the estate's gorgeous 17th-century architecture and the generosity of the owners. All three bedrooms are cozy, and the *table d'hôte* serves scrumptious, home-cooked local cuisine, accompanied by the "Red Head Estate's" organic wines (30€).

The Loire Valley with Kids

The Loire is a fine destination if you have children in tow.

For a start, the fairy-tale castles look as if they're straight out of a Disney movie, and all of them have grounds the kids can explore. It is unlikely that you'll plan your entire trip around children's attractions, but if you do decide to follow this tour to the letter, you can easily cover it in 4 days, leaving adults plenty of time for satisfying moments along the way.

> *Your whole family will feel like Gulliver in a Lilliputian world when you visit the Parc des Mini-Châteaux.*

START Amboise is 226km (140 miles) southwest of Paris and 26km (17 miles) east of Tours. **TRIP LENGTH** About 350km (218 miles) on both fast and country roads.

① ★★ **Le Clos Lucé, Amboise.** If you've parked in the center of Amboise, it's just a short walk to this Renaissance, red-brick and white-tufa château. Older children will find the history interesting: It first served as a retreat for Anne de Bretagne, and then in 1516, François I invited Leonardo da Vinci to be "free to think,

dream, and work" here, until his death in 1519. Nowadays, aside from the chapel, whose frescoes were painted by da Vinci's pupils, and the Renaissance period rooms, kids love the gardens, where they can discover life-size versions of da Vinci's inventions. There are 20

Where to Stay & Dine

For hotels and restaurants in the Loire Valley, see p. 183.

interactive machines, including a helicopter, a tank, a machine gun, and a bridge. They can also sail on the lake inside a da Vinci–style boat. ⏱ 2 hr. 2 rue de Clos-Lucé. ☎ 02-47-57-00-73. www.vinci-closluce.com. Admission Mar–Nov 15 12.50€ adults, 7€ ages 6–15; Nov 16–Feb 9.50€ adults, 6€ ages 6–15 (family tickets available). Jan 10am–6pm; Feb–Jun and Sept–Oct 9am–7pm; July–Aug 9am–8pm; Nov–Dec 9am–6pm. Closed Dec 25 and Jan 1.

Take D31 from Amboise to the Parc des Mini-Château.

2 Parc des Mini-Châteaux. On the outskirts of Amboise, this park lets kids explore pint-size replicas of the Loire's most famous castles (built at 1/30th the size of the originals). It's a fun way to see the region's gems in one sweep, plus children get to dress up as knights, find their way through a labyrinth, and meet costumed princes and princesses en route. ⏱ 2 hr. La Menaudière. ☎ 02-47-23-44-57. www.aquariumduvaldeloire.com. Admission 13.50€ adults, 4.50€ ages 4–14, free for children 3 and under. Apr–May daily 10:30am–7pm; Jun–July 30 and Aug 23–31 daily 10am–7pm; July 31–Aug 22 daily 10am–8pm; Sept–Nov 14 daily 10:30am–6pm. Closed Nov 15–Mar.

> One of the many machines designed by Leonardo da Vinci in Le Clos Lucé's gardens.

> *Maleficent, the magical villain of* Sleeping Beauty, *awaits your brood at Château d'Ussé.*

Leave Amboise on D431, then join D952 and follow signs to Saumur. After Langeais join D57 and follow signs to Rigny-Ussé, via D7 (64km/40 miles total).

❸ ★★ **Château d'Ussé.** This privately owned, 15th-century castle inspired Charles Perrault's *La belle au bois dormant (Sleeping Beauty).* Today you can visit many of the private rooms, including 15th-century kitchens; the former guard room; the king's bedchamber, decorated in 18th-century silks; and the Renaissance chapel, with its sculptured portal and handsome stalls. Scenes from *Sleeping Beauty* are reenacted in one of the towers. It's kitschy, but young children will find it exciting. Adults are usually more taken by the lovely gardens, the terraces of which were designed by André Le Nôtre, landscape architect of Versailles. Botanists will also appreciate the citrus tree collection; the oldest specimens date from before the Revolution. ⏱ 2 hr. Rigny-Ussé. ☎ 02-47-95-54-05. www.chateaudusse.fr. Admission

> *More than 70 species of endangered animals live in Doué la Fontaine's zoo, including this regal African lioness.*

13€ adults, 4€ ages 8–16, free for children 7 and under. Mid-Feb to May and Sept to mid-Nov daily 10am–6pm; Apr–Aug 10am–7pm; closed mid-Nov to mid-Feb.

From Rigny-Ussé take the route des Perres to join D16. At the island, join D751, which passes through Chinon and La Roche-Clermault and then becomes D751E; continue through St-Lazare, and then join D749 to Le Coudray; the château is signposted (30km/19 miles total).

❹ ★★★ **Château du Rivau.** Joan of Arc gathered horses for her crusade against the English in the vaulted Renaissance-era stables here; and Renaissance author Rabelais used Rivau as the prize that Gargantua the Giant granted to one of his knights after the Picrocholine War, in his 16th-century novel *The Life of Gargantua and of Pantagruel.* In the garden, you'll find nods to Rabelais and his fairy-tale world in themed sections strewn with gargantuan contemporary art: giant Wellington boots by Liliane Bourgeat and mammoth running legs by Jérôme Basserode (representing the forest running away from human destruction). Come between June and September to

> *Hard hats are required for descending deep into the old Mine Bleue at Noyant-la-Gravoyère.*

sample Rivau's humongous organic vegetables in the castle cafe (menus from 15€, Sun brunch 17€). ⏱ 3 hr. Le Coudray. ☎ 02-47-95-77-47. www.chateaudurivau.com. Admission 8€ adults, 6.50€ students 24 and under, 6€ ages 5–16. Apr and mid-Oct to mid-Nov Wed–Sun 10am–12:30pm and 2–6pm; May to mid-Oct Wed–Sun 10am–7pm; closed mid-Nov to Easter.

Backtrack to La Roche-Clermault and pick up D751. Near Candes-St-Martin, turn left onto D7, then join D947 via Montsoreau. At the island join D952A, then D952 through Varennes-sur-Loire. At La Croix-Verte turn left onto D947 to Saumur. Leave Saumur via the St-Hilaire-St-Florent district and join D960. After Igné, join D69 to Doué-la-Fontaine (59km/37 miles total).

⑤ ★★ Bioparc Zoo de Doué la Fontaine. Just outside Saumur, your kids can spend a leisurely day admiring around 70 species of endangered animals at this wonderful troglodyte zoo, where well-tended giraffes, rhinoceroses, penguins, tigers, and red pandas live in habitats very similar to their natural environments. It also houses Europe's largest aviary (installed in a former tufa quarry), where children can see more than 300 South American birds including macaws, ibises, spoonbills, vultures, flamingos, terns, and stilts. When hunger strikes, the **Camp des Girafes** restaurant is a fun spot for a meal on the outdoor terraces overlooking the giraffe canyon (menus from 15€ adults, 9€ kids 11 and under). ⏱ 1 day. 103 rte. de Cholet, Doué la Fontaine. ☎ 02-41-59-18-58. www.zoodoue.fr. Admission 16.50€ adults,

11€ ages 3–10, free for children 2 and under. Feb–Mar and Oct daily 10am–6:30pm; Apr–Jun and Sept daily 9am–6pm; July–Aug daily 9am–7:30pm. Closed Nov–Jan.

Backtrack to La Croix-Verte to join D347. After 2.5km (1½ miles), take D767 toward Angers and join A85 and A11 (toward Angers), exiting on junction 17. Follow D775 (toward Rennes Laval) to Noyant-la-Gravoyère (111km/69 miles total).

⑥ ★★ La Mine Bleue. Plunge your brood 130m (427 ft.) underground in this fascinating former slate mine, which teaches families about life as a pit worker in France. Take a funicular underground to where a little train awaits to transport you into the main gallery for a light-and-sound show. Back above ground, you can learn about slate splitting and see how it is used to make roofs (rather like those on the Loire's many châteaux); follow an enigma trail; pet some cute sheep at the miniature farm; and meet Pepito, the gray donkey. There's even a wine-tasting stand, the **Cave aux Parageots,** where moms and dads can sample a beverage called *Postillonne*. The commentated tours are in French unless you request an English speaker in advance. The temperature underground is a constant 13°C (55°F), so bring warm clothing. ⏱ 5 hr. Noyant-la-Gravoyère, 50km (31 miles) northwest of Angers. ☎ 02-41-94-39-69. www.laminebleue.com. Admission 12.70€ adults, 6.90€ ages 5–11, free for children 4 and under. Apr 4–June and Sept Tues–Sun 10am–7pm; July–Aug daily 10am–7pm; Oct Sat 2–7pm, Sun 10am–7pm. Closed Nov–Apr 3.

The Loire Valley Outdoors

With UNESCO-protected waterways, a wealth of wildlife and forests, and vineyards and château gardens at every turn, the Loire Valley is a treat for lovers of the great outdoors. This section (not a tour per se) will point you in the right direction if you wish to cycle between the châteaux or command a birds-eye view of the valley from the basket of a hot-air balloon. Whether you're traveling by bicycle or by car, you can also discover the Loire's lesser-known estuary along the Estuaire Nantes–St-Nazaire—a vast trail of contemporary art between Nantes and the ocean.

> *Awash in wildflowers, woods, waterways, and flat roads, the Loire Valley is a cyclist's heaven.*

START Amboise is 226km (140 miles) southwest of Paris and 26km (17 miles) east of Tours.

★★ Blois, Chambord & Cheverny for Cyclists.

Between Blois, Chambord, and Cheverny, 300km (186 miles) of secure, well-marked cycle routes (part of a circuit known as Châteaux à Vélo) await visitors with strong legs. The tracks take you past well-known sights, but also lesser-known monuments, meandering rivers, quiet villages, and lush vineyards. Helpful information panels are installed along the way. Go to the Château à Vélo website (www.chateauxavelo.com), to download itinerary maps free of charge and also find information on accommodations, restaurants, bicycle rental, and repair shops. Alternatively, ask for information at any of the tourist offices in the area. Although distances between sites are rarely too great, it is important to be prepared with sufficient water, food, and sunscreen.

★★★ Château de Brissac via Hot-air Balloon.

Picture yourself floating on the wind over

Where to Stay & Dine

For hotels and restaurants in Nantes, see p. 182; elsewhere in the Loire Valley, see p. 183.

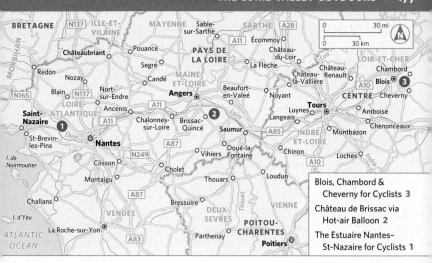

Blois, Chambord &
Cheverny for Cyclists 3

Château de Brissac via
Hot-air Balloon 2

The Estuaire Nantes–
St-Nazaire for Cyclists 1

the Loire Valley's pointy-towered castles, with endless views over landscape gardens, patchwork quilts of forest, and silvery rivers. **Montgolfières d'Anjou** lets you experience just this, between Easter and October, when six hot-air balloons take to the skies to offer some of the best panoramas in France. Four sites are covered, the main one being the lovely **Château de Brissac** (p. 162). Brissac's gardens are also frequently used for the European Hot-Air Ballooning championships. A second site is the little-known **Château de Pignerolle** (east of Angers; www.musee-communication.com), home to a small communications museum. A third is the **Ile de Gennes**—a sandy island in the middle of the Loire River, west of Saumur (www.cc-gennois.fr). And finally the **Gratien & Meyer vineyard** outside of Saumur (www.gratienmeyer.com). Flying is not permitted for children 7 and under or pregnant women. Montgolfières d'Anjou, Z.I. Les Sabotiers, Gennes. ☎ 02-41-40-48-04. www.montgolfieres.com. 190€–320€.

★★ The Estuaire Nantes–St-Nazaire for Cyclists. Along a 60km (37-mile) stretch of the Loire's estuary, between Nantes and St-Nazaire on the coast, the waterway brims with rare wildlife and is an integral part of the region's history and identity. For years, however, it was used by heavy-duty industry, and locals had stopped frequenting it. Since 2007, in a bid to breathe new life into the area

and simultaneously protect the Loire Estuary's fragile ecosystem, international artists have created humongous pieces of contemporary art all along the estuary, along a cycling trail that appeals to the art-curious and others looking for an alternative vision of the Loire Valley. Works include *Misconceivable* by Erwin Wurm (at the village of Le Pellerin), a life-size fishing boat that bends over the water's edge as if frightened to jump in; *La Villa Chiminée* by Japanese artist Tatzu Nishi (in Bouée/Cordemais), a house built atop a giant chimney, which looks as though it was blown there by Dorothy's tornado; and *L'Observatoire (Observatory)* at Lavau-sur-Loire, created by Japanese artist Tadashi Kawamata, where a wooden boardwalk with a 6m (20-ft.) lookout tower and picnic tables stretches over the mud plains to the river's edge. **For more information**, go to www.estuaire.info or contact the Lieu Unique in Nantes (☎ 02-51-82-15-00. www.lelieuunique.com).

Renting a Bike in the Loire

If you need to hire a bike, **Détours de Loire** in Nantes, Gare Routière Baco/allée de la Maison Rouge (☎ 02-40-48-75-37; www.locationdevelos.com; 14€ 1 day, 9€ half-day), has agencies all along the Loire and can organize custom excursions. You can also find information at **La Loire à Vélo** (☎ 02-40-48-24-20; www.loire-a-velo.fr).

Nantes

As the gateway to the Atlantic coast, the Vendée, the Loire Valley, and Brittany, Nantes is an important river port. It might not look as pretty as other cities in the region (World War II bombing and heavy industry left their scars), but it is one seriously cutting-edge metropolis: Jules Verne and André Breton found inspiration in Nantes, and the city continues to nourish a hip art scene today. Nantes is also one of France's greenest cities, with many hotels holding eco-certification. This whirlwind tour covers Nantes through the ages, from its 15th-century châteaux to the ultra-modern Ile de Nantes (Nantes Island). You can visit much of the city in a day; but we recommend 2 or 3 if you want to get a feel for the place.

> Behind the striking Renaissance facade of the Château des Ducs de Bretagne, you'll find a museum retracing Nantes's history.

START Nantes is 383km (238 miles) south-west of Paris and 88km (55 miles) southwest of Angers.

❶ ★★ Château des Ducs de Bretagne. Sandwiched between the cathedral and the river, in the mostly pedestrian **Quartier Bouffay** (Bouffay Quarter), the austere fortress of the dukes of Brittany, with a 500m (1,640-ft.) sentry walk punctuated by seven towers, is the last of the Loire châteaux before the Atlantic Ocean. The castle was constructed in the 9th or 10th century, enlarged in the 13th century, destroyed, and rebuilt in its present shape by François II in 1466. The inner courtyard reveals a 15th-century ducal palace built of tufa stone in the Renaissance style; inside you'll find the renovated **Musée d'Histoire de Nantes**—32 rooms displaying more than 850 historic objects, covering the history of Nantes from medieval times to the present. If you don't want to visit the museum, you can still walk around the castle grounds for free. ⏱ 2 hr. 4 place Marc Elder. ☎ 08-11-46-46-44. www.chateau-nantes.fr. Admission 5€ adults, 3€ ages 18–26, free for ages 17 and under. July–Aug daily 10am–7pm; Sept–Jun Tues–Sun 10am–6pm.

❷ ★★ Cathédrale St-Pierre et St-Paul. Begun in 1434, the cathedral wasn't finished until the end of the 19th century; still, an admirable Gothic architectural harmony reigns throughout. Inside lie two Renaissance masterpieces: the ornamented tombs of François II, duc de Bretagne, and his second wife, Marguerite de

① Château des Ducs
   de Bretagne

② Cathédrale St-Pierre
   et St-Paul

③ Lieu Unique

④ Quartier Feydeau

⑤ Rue Crébillon

⑥ Théâtre Graslin

⑦ Ile de Nantes

⑧ Les Machines de l'Ile

⑨ Musée Jules Verne

⑩ Trentemoult

Where to Stay & Dine

La Cigale **12**

La Perouse **13**

L'Atlantide **11**

Villa Hamster **14**

Foix (Anne de Bretagne's parents). ⏱ 30 min.
Place St-Pierre. Free admission. Apr–Sept daily
8:30am–7pm; Oct–Mar daily 8:30am–6pm.

③ ★★ **Lieu Unique.** Just opposite the château,
back toward the river, is this "unique place"
set in the former LU biscuit factory. Today it is
a flagship center for the arts, with a national
theater, a trendy bar (with resident DJ), a restaurant, a sauna, and an art exhibition center.
You can climb the LU tower (☎ 02-51-82-15-06;
admission 2€ adults, free for children 11 and under; Tues–Sat 1–7pm, Sun 3–7pm; closed Mon)
for a panoramic view over Nantes. ⏱ 1 hr. Quai
Ferdinand-Favre (canal St-Félix). ☎ 02-51-82-15-
00. www.lelieuunique.com. Bar: Mon 11am–8pm;

Getting Around

You can walk around much of Nantes, but
the city's environmentally friendly tram network is easy to use and covers all the most
popular attractions. You can also use the
Navibus shuttle boats between Port Maritime
and the old Trentemoult fishermen's area; or
cycle on a self-service **Bicloo bike** (www.bicloo.
nantesmetropole.fr), available at dozens of
points across the city center. If you're planning
to cover a lot of ground during your stay, you'll
save considerably with the **Pass Nantes** (www.
nantes-tourisme.com; 18€ for 24 hr., 28€ for 48
hr., 36€ for 72 hr.), which secures free transportation and admission to all the main tourist sites.

> *The most original ride in France is aboard Les Machines de l'Ile's giant, mechanical wooden elephant.*

Tues–Thurs 11am–midnight; Fri–Sat 11am–3am; Sun 3–8pm. Restaurant ☎ 02-51-72-05-55. Fixed-price lunch 13€, fixed-price dinner 17€–28€, main courses from 12€. MC, V. Mon noon–4pm; Tues–Sat noon–2:30pm and 7pm–midnight.

④ ★ Quartier Feydeau. In the 18th century, when Nantes was a seafaring and slave-trading center, the city had so many islands, it was known as the "Venice of the West." The former Ile Feydeau and Ile Gloriette islands (now known as the Feydeau Quarter) are still home to the glorious merchants' houses that overlooked the water in their heyday. Their facades are characterized by 18th-century *mascarons*—ornamental, often hideous faces designed to frighten evil spirits away. The Feydeau's *mascarons* were particularly inspired by mythology. Some of the best can be viewed along allée Turenne at nos. 3, 8, 9, 10, 11, and 13. The intricate wrought-iron balconies are another *nantais* architectural trademark.

⑤ Rue Crébillon. Leaning toward designer wear, Crébillon is so synonymous with shopping that locals replace the term for "going shopping" (*faire du shopping*) with *crébilloner* (pronounced cre-bee-yon-nay).

⑥ Théâtre Graslin. At the end of rue Crébillon, this 18th-century, neoclassical theater has eight beautiful Corinthian columns and beehives on the roof. It is home to the Angers Nantes Opera, which performs excellent contemporary takes on classics by Mozart and Verdi. For a guided tour, call the Nantes tourist office (☎ 08-92-46-40-44). Place Graslin. ☎ 02-40-69-77-18. www.angers-nantes-opera.com. 5€. Show times vary.

⑦ ★★★ Ile de Nantes. This 5km x 1km (3-mile x ⅔-mile) island sits in the very heart of the city, surrounded by stretches of the Loire River. Once used for cattle grazing, then as an industrial center for soap factories and shipyards, it is a beacon for urban renewal, showcasing innovative new architecture built by internationally renowned architects such as Jean Nouvel, Daniel Buren, Christian de Portzamparc, and Jean Prouvé. The island's working-class roots, however, are still apparent in its converted warehouses and old hangars. The **banana warehouses** on the western tip (where

A Beautiful 19th-Century Mall

Just off rue Crébillon is a sumptuous shopping arcade built in 1843: **Passage Pommeraye.** Set on a steep incline, it has three floors' worth of shops and a beautiful, monumental staircase. Over the years, the passage has attracted filmmakers, such as Nouvelle Vague director Jacques Demy, known for his 1960 movie *Lola*.

Nantes & the Sea

Set at the convergence of four rivers—the Chézine, the Cens, the Erdre, and the Sèvre Nantaise—which meet the mighty Loire in the city center, Nantes has always had an enviable maritime capacity. In the 18th century, prior to the abolition of slavery, the city's location turned it into the biggest port in France and a French capital of the slave trade. With the colonies came wealth, further stimulated by the Industrial Revolution in the 19th century. Before long, the region was an affluent shipbuilding and industrial center with factories all along the Loire and shipyards in the heart of the city, on Ile de Nantes.

❾ **Musée Jules Verne.** This museum devoted to Nantes's most famous resident, Jules Verne, is filled with memorabilia and objects inspired by Verne's stories, from ink spots to a magic lantern with glass slides. ⏱ 45 min. 3 rue de l'Hermitage. ☎ 02-40-69-72-52. www. nantes.fr/julesverne. Admission 3€ adults, 1.50€ ages 18–25 after 5pm. Mon and Wed–Sat 10am–noon and 2–6pm; Sun 2–6pm.

❿ ★ **Trentemoult.** Back toward the main town along quai de la Fosse, catch the Navibus shuttle boat from the Gare Maritime to Trentemoult. This riverside village, where fishermen once departed in barges to sail down to La Rochelle, presents a multicolored collection of quaint houses. It's a fine place for a stroll, in and out of the narrow maze of streets and riverside cafes.

imported bananas were left to ripen) now contain exhibition spaces, bars, and restaurants. The former shipbuilding hangars in the center of the island house the wacky 🅺🅸🅳🆂 **Les Machines de l'Ile** (stop ❽, below). Architecture enthusiasts should call the tourist office (☎ 08-92-46-40-44) to arrange a visit to ★ **Le Palais de Justice** (Law Courts), designed by Jean Nouvel (www. jeannouvel.com). Its Salle des Pas Perdus (Lost Footsteps Room) is a vast rectangle of light, meant to represent the transparency of justice.

❽ ★★★ 🅺🅸🅳🆂 **Les Machines de l'Ile.** Ride on the back of a 12m (40-ft.) mechanical wooden elephant, and then visit other fantastical creatures at this former boat warehouse, including the Tortoise-Giraffe, the Grouper Fish, and a giant nutshell just big enough to seat a small child. You can even walk along the prototype branch of the future Heron Tree—a vast metal tree topped by herons holding basket seats that will whizz passengers around like a fairground ride. ⏱ 2 hr. Bd. Léon Bureau. ☎ 08-10-12-12-25. www.lesmachines-nantes.fr. Admission 7€ adults, 5.50€ ages 4–17, free for children 3 and under. July–Aug daily 10am–8pm; Sept–Oct 22 Tues–Fri 10am–6pm, Sat–Sun 10am–7pm; Oct 23–Nov 3 Tues–Sun 10am–7pm; Nov 4–Dec 17 Wed–Fri 2–6pm, Sat–Sun 2–7pm; Dec 18–24 and Dec 26–31 Tues–Sun 2–7pm; mid-Feb to mid Mar Tues–Sun 2–7pm; mid-Mar to Apr 8 Wed–Fri 2–6pm, Sat–Sun 2–7pm; Apr 9–22 Tues–Fri 2–6pm, Sat–Sun 2–7pm; late Apr to July Tues–Sun 10am–7pm; closed Jan–mid Feb.

Jules Verne

The founder of modern science fiction, Jules Verne was born in Nantes in 1828 and lived here until the age of 14, in a house overlooking the Erdre and Loire rivers. He spent much of his time on Ile Feydeau (❹), where the "river winding over two or three leagues" and "so many passing ships" awakened the imagination that later fired stories such as *Twenty Thousand Leagues Under the Sea*, illustrated here in a tableau from the Musée Jules Verne (❾).

Where to Stay & Dine in Nantes

> If the walls at La Cigale could talk, they'd tell the secrets of André Breton, Jacques Demy, and other artists who spent time in this Belle Epoque treasure.

★ **La Cigale** GRASLIN *FRENCH BRASSERIE*
You can't get more Belle Epoque than this gorgeous brasserie, which has hardly changed since it opened in 1895 across from the landmark Théâtre Graslin. Treat yourself to French classics such as platters of fresh shellfish, *confit des cuisses de canard* (duckling), and rum babas. 4 place Graslin. ☎ 02-51-84-94-94. www.lacigale.com. Reservations recommended. Fixed-price menu 17€–26€. MC, V. Daily 7:30am–12:30am.

★★★ **La Perouse** CENTER
This friendly, contemporary hotel promises comfort, a great location between the cathedral and the Graslin opera theater, cutting-edge design by architects Barto & Barto, and a commitment to making your stay as environmentally friendly as possible. 3 allée Duquesne. ☎ 02-40-89-75-00. www.hotel-laperouse.fr. 46 units. Doubles 69€–150€. MC, V

★★★ **L'Atlantide** RIVERFRONT *MODERN FRENCH*
On the fourth floor of the complex that houses the city's chamber of commerce, expect a panoramic view over the river and menus steeped in the traditions of both the Loire Valley and the Breton coast. Both the lobster salad with yellow-wine sauce and the potato and herb tart capped with foie gras are delicious. The cellar stores fine vintages, with an emphasis on Anjous and muscadets. 16 quai Ernest-Renaud. ☎ 02-40-73-23-23. www.restaurant-atlantide.net. Reservations required. Fixed-price menus 30€–95€; a la carte 70€–120€. MC, V. Lunch Mon–Fri, dinner Mon–Sat. Closed first 3 weeks of Aug and Dec 23–27.

★★ kids **Villa Hamster** CENTER/CHÂTEAU
Ever wondered what it feels like to be a hamster in a cage? This wacky B&B in the heart of Nantes offers you the chance to find out, in a hamster-themed apartment equipped with a cereal dispenser and a giant hamster wheel. It's a scream. 2 rue Malherbe. ☎ 06-64-20-31-09. Email falquerho.yann@wanadoo.fr, or check www.uncoinchezsoi.net. 1 unit. Room 99€. MC, V.

Where to Stay & Dine in the Loire Valley

★★★ kids Château de Brissac BRISSAC

Here's your chance to experience life in a real Renaissance château. Brissac has been in the same family for more than 500 years, and each room is trussed up with charming period details, from four-poster beds to ancient tapestries hanging on the walls. You can dine here, too. ☎ 02-41-91-22-21. www.brissac.net. 4 units. Doubles 390€ (includes a château visit). Dinner 80€. MC, V.

★★★ Château de Verrières SAUMUR

Uno the dog welcomes you to this sumptuous Belle Epoque hideaway with no shortage of antique furniture and sculpted wood paneling. Most rooms have stunning views of Saumur's castle. 53 rue d'Alsace. ☎ 02-41-38-05-15. www.chateau-verrieres.com. 5 units. Doubles 140€–290€. MC, V.

★ Hostellerie St-Jean MONTREUIL-BELLAY

FRENCH Hearty cuisine—along the lines of venison pâté with prunes, smoked salmon with spiced-bread sauce, Val de Loire veal, regional cheeses, and caramelized apple crumble with Cointreau—is served at reasonable prices in this rustic dining room. 432 Rue Nationale. ☎ 02-41-52-30-41. www.hostellerie-saint-jean.com. Menus 18€–33€. MC, V.

★ Hôtel d'Anjou ANGERS *FRENCH*

Bedrooms here are individually decorated in plush, enveloping fabrics. A François I–style restaurant, La Salamandre, serves good traditional French cuisine. 1 bd. Foch. ☎ 02-41-21-12-11. www.hoteldanjou.fr. 53 units. Doubles from 119€. MC, V.

★ Hôtel de l'Abbeille ORLEANS

A cozy hotel has rooms with Toile de Jouy fabrics, good bathrooms, and comfy beds. A lovely rooftop garden overlooks 19th-century buildings. 64 rue Alsace Lorraine. ☎ 02-38-53-54-87. www.hoteldelabeille.com. 27 units. Doubles 79€–98€. MC, V.

★★ Hotel La Marine de Loire MONTSOREAU

Delightfully furnished rooms decorated in fresh pastels, beiges, and blues; a peaceful

> The chef at La Croix Blanche in Fontevraud uses flowers for both flavor and decoration; the result is heavenly.

garden; and a small spa make La Marine a good choice. For a special treat, the Sous la Lune suite for four people recreates the night sky with encased lights and has an in-room telescope. 9 quai de la Loire. ☎ 02-41-50-18-21. www.hotel-lamarinedeloire.com. 11 units. Doubles from 140€. MC, V.

★★ La Croix Blanche FONTEVRAUD *FRENCH*

This friendly inn, in a plum spot right by the abbey entrance, offers simple rooms, a cafe, a brasserie, and the gourmet Le Plantagenêt restaurant—one of the best in the Saumur area. Fontevraud l'Abbaye. ☎ 02-41-51-71-11. www.hotel-croixblanche.com. 12 units. Doubles 65€–125€. Main courses 12–50€. MC, V.

★ La Parenthèse ORLEANS *FRENCH*

This small restaurant was made popular by delicious dishes such as crab Chartreuse with smoked salmon and chocolate *moelleux*. Reserve in advance. 26 place du Châtelet. ☎ 02-38-62-07-50. Lunch menu from 9€, dinner menu from 21€. MC, V. Lunch and dinner Tues–Sat.

★★ Le Favre d'Anne ANGERS *CONTEMPORARY FRENCH*

Overlooking the Maine River and Château d'Amboise, this restaurant transforms local produce into Michelin-starred dishes such as fennel *tatin* (tart) with giant

> *Troglododo's rooms, below this medieval tower in Azay-le-Rideau, are set in the white tufa cliff face.*

langoustines and strawberry *vacherin* (nougat ice cream). 18 quai des Carmes. ☎ 02-41-36-12-12. www.lefavredanne.fr. Menus 40€–90€. MC, V. Lunch and dinner Tues–Sat.

★ Le Prieuré SAUMUR *FRENCH GOURMET*
Set on a rocky spur, the old priory affords breathtaking views over the Loire River. Meals are served in a 19th-century dining room and may include salad of *rillauds* (local marinated pork), cod with lobster cream, and chocolate soufflé. Rooms here are large and comfortable. Chênhutte-les-Tuffeaux, 3km (1¾ miles) west of Saumur on D947. ☎ 02-41-67-90-14. www.grandesetapes.fr. 36 units. Doubles from 170€. Fixed-price lunch 24€–31€, fixed-price dinner 33€–75€, main courses 20€. MC, V.

★★★ Les Menestrels SAUMUR *FRENCH*
Chef Christophe Hosselet conjures some of the most flavorful dishes in the region—think ravioli filled with rabbit and chorizo and a creamy caramel *religieuse* profiterole stack—at the foot of Saumur's château. 11 rue Raspail. ☎ 02-41-67-71-10. www.restaurant-les-menestrels.com. Main courses 24€; fixed-price menus 32€–68€. MC, V. Lunch Tues–Sat, dinner Mon–Sat.

★★★ kids L'Etape Gourmande VILLANDRY
REGIONAL FRENCH Think quaint farm with animals to pet; home-cooked delicacies such as homemade foie gras and chutney; and a *gîte* (holiday home) that sleeps seven, overlooking a lake. This is one of the best places to stay and dine on the castle circuit. La Giraudière, Villandry. ☎ 02-47-50-08-60. www.letapegourmande.com. Menu 15.50€–34€. *Gîte:* 590€ weekend; 1,025€–1,180€ week. MC, V.

L'Hôtel de l'Univers TOURS *FRENCH*
Throughout the last century, the Univers has welcomed the likes of Franklin Delano Roosevelt and Ernest Hemingway. Today its rooms are on the old-fashioned side but wholly comfortable, and the restaurant serves tasty regional French fare. 5 bd. de Heurteloup. ☎ 02-47-05-37-12. www.oceaniahotels.com. 85 units. Doubles 99€–300€. 3 courses 30€–40€. MC, V.

★★★ Pavillon de Lys AMBOISE *CONTEMPORARY FRENCH*
This smart guesthouse has luxuriously decorated rooms in a classy, neo-Art Deco style. In the restaurant, choose between two lip-smacking menus (one vegetarian) that feature such dishes as duck confit in spiced bread crust and mushroom ravioli in *cèpes* (porcini mushrooms) cappuccino. 9 rue d'Orange. ☎ 02-47-30-01-01. www.pavillondeslys.com. 7 units. Doubles 98€–230€. Menus 29€–39€. MC, V.

★★ kids Troglododo AZAY-LE-RIDEAU
Troglododo (*dodo* means "sleep") is your chance to spend the night in a real troglodyte dwelling. Cut into the tufa cliffside, self-contained grottos have a fridge, a cooking area, and beautifully decorated bedrooms. 9 chemin des Caves. ☎ 02-47-45-31-25. www.troglododo.fr. 5 units. Doubles 58€–70€. No credit cards.

Fast Facts

> *The Loire Valley is peppered with stone vineyard huts like this one, used by the vintners who own the land.*

Arriving & Getting Around

BY TRAIN Getting to Nantes from Paris (and other parts of the country) is quick and easy. For example, Tours and Orléans are just an hour away from the French capital (Nantes takes 2 hr. 15 min.), and you can easily hop between the main historical towns, like Saumur, Angers, and Nantes, by rail. **BY CAR** The best way to get around is by car. The region is well serviced with highways from across the whole of France, and you can hire cars at all main train stations and the historical sites. Try www.avis.com, www.hertz.com, www.citer.fr, or www.sixt.fr; indeed, a set of wheels is vital if you want to see certain châteaux. If you want to visit the region by bike, see p. 179. **BY AIR** If you want to fly to the region from the U.K., **Eastern Airways** flies three times a week from Southampton to the Angers airport (www.easternairways.com).

Doctors & Dentists

SOS medecin (☎ 3634) is a nationwide hotline for non-emergency medical referrals. Some (but not all) doctors speak English and are available day and night, including Sundays and public holidays. The doctor travels to your address for the consultation, but you may have to wait for several hours if your condition is not urgent.

Emergency

Police ☎ 17. Fire department and paramedic ☎ 18. Ambulance ☎ 15. For any emergency, dial ☎ 112 from a cell phone.

Internet

Most hotels listed in this chapter have Wi-Fi. If not, try **Cyber Espace** in Angers, 25 rue de la Roë (☎ 02-41-24-92-71; www.angersweb.com). The **Lieu Unique** in Nantes (p. 179, ❸) has Wi-Fi in its public spaces, including the cafe.

Post Office

A handy address in Tours is **La Poste,** 67 rue de la Victoire (Mon–Fri 9am–6pm, Sat 9am–noon).

Tourist Offices

Municipal tourist offices are listed at the end of the town tour stops throughout the chapter. **NANTES** 2 place St-Pierre (☎ 08-92-46-40-44; www.nantes-tourisme.com). **LOIRE VALLEY** Regional Tourist Center, 37 av. de Paris, Orléans (www.loirevalleytourism.com).

5
Normandy & Brittany

Favorite Moments in Normandy & Brittany

The dramatic coastlines and uncrowded beaches of

Normandy and Brittany draw lovers of the sea and seafood. The farther west you go, the wilder the landscape becomes, as the chalky cliffs of Normandy turn into the wave-bashed rocks of Brittany, ending in a smattering of islands. With their distinctive architecture, culinary traditions, and customs, these two northwestern regions will also take you on a history tour that spans 6,000 years: from the prehistoric standing stones of Carnac to the world's most famous medieval tapestry, Gothic cathedrals, Renaissance châteaux, and remnants of the Allied victory on these shores during World War II.

> PREVIOUS PAGE *The lighthouse on Ile d'Ouessant has saved many a sailor from the rugged rocks.*
> THIS PAGE *At dusk, lights in Etretat's 19th-century center look like lava running into the sea.*

❶ Feasting on lobster at Le Tréport. Lobster may be a dish fit for royalty, but you won't pay a ransom for the king of crustaceans at **Le Homard Bleu,** on the Alabaster Coast at Le Tréport. See "Fruits of the Sea," p. 194.

❷ Wandering through a rhapsody of rhodo-dendrons. Varengeville-sur-Mer, near Dieppe, is a garden lover's paradise. There's not a French-manicured tree in sight at **Le Parc du Bois des Moutiers,** designed by Gertrude Jekyll in lush English style—one of three beautiful gardens here. See p. 193, ❸.

❸ Standing on the cliffs of Etretat. Marvel at the "elephant" and the "needle"—strange rock formations chiseled out of Etretat's limestone cliffs by the waves, surely one of the Alabaster Coast's most stunning landmarks. See p. 194, ❺.

❹ Cheering on a winner at Deauville. Don a *costume* (suit) and *cravate* (tie) and join the smart set on race day at Deauville, Normandy's answer to Churchill Downs or Ascot. August is the height of the racing season at this well-known track. See p. 195, ❻.

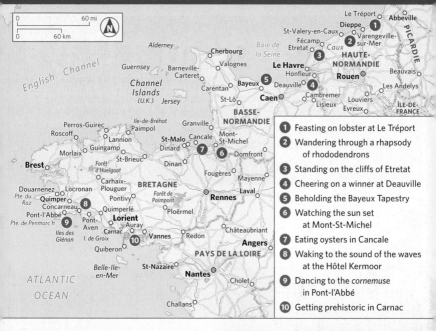

1. Feasting on lobster at Le Tréport
2. Wandering through a rhapsody of rhododendrons
3. Standing on the cliffs of Etretat
4. Cheering on a winner at Deauville
5. Beholding the Bayeux Tapestry
6. Watching the sun set at Mont-St-Michel
7. Eating oysters in Cancale
8. Waking to the sound of the waves at the Hôtel Kermoor
9. Dancing to the *cornemuse* in Pont-l'Abbé
10. Getting prehistoric in Carnac

5 Beholding the Bayeux Tapestry. No photographs can prepare you for the real thing—almost a millennium old, with vivid comic-strip depictions of William the Conqueror's invasion of England. See p. 213, **3**.

6 Watching the sun set at Mont-St-Michel. Rising like a mirage from the water, the monastic mount reveals its sublime beauty at dusk and is best seen from the coast, away from the hordes of spectators. See p. 213, **5**.

7 Eating oysters in Cancale. The king of France used to have his oysters shipped to Paris from here. There's nothing like tasting them fresh from the sea at a weather-beaten oyster shack. See p. 200, **2**.

8 Waking to the sound of the waves at the Hôtel Kermoor. In this shipshape hotel at Concarneau, you're steps from the beach, with a private deck on which to while away the hours. See p. 230.

9 Dancing to the *cornemuse* in Pont-l'Abbé. Get to the heart of Breton culture at a *fest-noz* (musical celebration) in Pont-l'Abbé, with crepes, dances, and ladies in *coiffes* (traditional lace headdresses) celebrating to the tune of Breton bagpipes. See p. 204, **9**.

> *Seafood platters don't come bigger than this one at Le Treport, near Dieppe.*

10 Getting prehistoric in Carnac. One of northern France's most awe-inspiring sights, the 4,000 standing stones of Carnac stretch as far as the eye can see and even farther back in time—some 4,000 to 7,000 years. Try to penetrate the mystery of their existence as you pace the hypnotic rows. See p. 215, **7**.

Normandy in 3 Days

Despite its idyllic appearance, with half-timbered houses and cattle grazing in the fields, Normandy has been a battleground throughout history, from the Viking raids through the Norman conquest of England to the D-Day landings in the 20th century. This short tour of the region's historic landmarks can be combined with the 3-day (p. 196) or 1-week (p. 200) Brittany tour.

> Bayeux has a haunting beauty, making it a romantic spot for a stroll.

START Rouen is 135km (84 miles) north of Paris. **TRIP LENGTH** 323km (201 miles).

❶ ★★ Rouen. The capital of the Norman duchy since A.D. 911, Rouen is dominated by its Gothic **★★★ Cathédral Notre-Dame de Rouen,** made famous by Claude Monet, who painted it 28 times in an effort to master the changing effects of light on the facade. Several of these paintings are in the Musée d'Orsay in Paris (p. 51, ❷), but you can see one of them in Rouen's own fine art museum, the **★★★ Musée des Beaux-Arts,** which also features Caravaggio, Velázquez, Géricault, and Dufy. For lunch, take your pick

from the many restaurants on ★ **place du Vieux Marché,** where the modern **Eglise Ste-Jeanne d'Arc** commemorates the martyrdom of the French warrior saint in 1431. ⏱ 5 hr. For detailed information on Rouen, see p. 224.

Leave Rouen in the late afternoon, driving west on A13 (toll road) to the coast. After 70km (43 miles), take A29 and follow signs to Honfleur (91km/57 miles total).

❷ ★ Honfleur. A pretty fishing town beloved by painter Claude Monet, poet Charles Baudelaire, and composer Eric Satie, Honfleur is perfect for a 1-night stopover. Take a walk

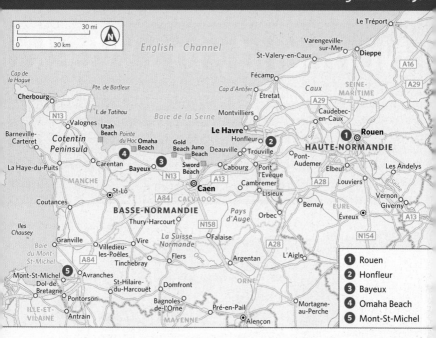

around the **Vieux Bassin** (Old Port), with its tall houses, and enjoy a fish dish in a local restaurant such as ★★ **L'Endroit** (p. 229). ⏱ 1 evening. Honfleur Tourist Office, quai Lep-aulmier. ☎ 02-31-89-23-30. www.ot-honfleur.fr.

On your second day, continue west on A13, bypassing Caen, and pick up N13 to Bayeux (92km/57 miles).

③ ★★ **kids Bayeux.** Bayeux, of course, is syn-onymous with its famous tapestry, which is displayed in a renovated seminary, the **Centre Guillaume-le-Conquérant.** A film, shown in English at midday, explains the history leading up to the Battle of Hastings, and the audio-guide points out fascinating details in the weave. You'll want to spend about an hour and a half here. If you began your day early, you'll also have time to visit the excellent **Musée Mémorial de la Bataille de Normandie** before lunch. ⏱ 4 hr. See p. 213, ③.

In the afternoon, take D6 north and then the coast road (D514) to St-Laurent-sur-Mer (18km/11 miles).

④ ★★ **Omaha Beach.** Standing on Omaha Beach is a powerful reminder of the thousands of Allied soldiers who perished here in the short space between sea and land during the 1944 landings. Their graves stand in serried rows at the **Normandy American Cemetery and Memorial** on the left flank of the beach. The memorial **museum** has many poignant personal objects and photographs. ⏱ 3 hr. See p. 213, ④.

Return to Bayeaux for the night. On your last day, follow D6 south from Bayeaux to Villers-Bocage, join A84 (toll road), and follow signs for Mont-St-Michel (122km/76 miles).

⑤ ★★★ **Mont-St-Michel.** Northern France's most spectacular monument rises out of a silk-smooth sea like a mystical castle. Still housing a small Benedictine community, its abbey was a major site of Christian pilgrimage in the 12th and 13th centuries. Today, it at-tracts even more visitors intrigued by its iconic beauty. You can visit the **abbey** and the streets of the village below, where the **Grande Rue** is filled with restaurants and gift shops. ⏱ 1 day. See p. 213, ⑤.

Where to Stay & Dine

For hotels and restaurants in Rouen, see p. 227; elsewhere in Normandy, see p. 228.

Normandy in 1 Week

A week in Normandy will allow you time to take in the Impressionist landscapes of the Alabaster Coast and the chic beach resorts of the Côte Fleuri before retracing our 3-day itinerary through the Bayeux Tapestry, the D-Day beaches, and Mont-St-Michel. This is Normandy as you dreamed of it, with whitewashed cliffs, pastel waters, and huge platters of freshly harvested seafood. As a bonus, English gardens, a medicinal liqueur, and the trail of a fictional gentleman thief are surprise treats.

> Etretat's "needle" is allegedly filled with the treasures of Arsène Lupin, the "gentleman thief" created by writer Maurice Leblanc.

START Rouen is 135km (84 miles) north of Paris. TRIP LENGTH 412km (256 miles).

1 ★ **Rouen.** A full day and night in Rouen will enable you to explore the ★★ **cathedral,** the city's undisputed star attraction; the **Musée de Beaux-Arts,** one of the most important provincial art museums in France; and the **Joan of Arc "trail."** Be sure also to leave time for shopping along Rouen's lovely streets. The centuries'-old city holds many treasures for antiques collectors, with more than 80 vendors; the area between the cathedral and the Abbatiale St-Ouen (in particular, place Barthélémy, rue Damiette, and rue Eau-de-Robec) has the greatest concentration. You'll also find many shops selling Rouen faïence, both antique and new. **Fayence-rie Augy,** 26 rue St-Romain (☎ 02-35-88-77-47; www.fayencerie-augy.com), is the last remaining producer in town. ⏱ 1 day. For detailed information on Rouen, see p. 224.

From Rouen, drive north on N15 and A151, following signs to Dieppe (63km/39 miles).

2 **Dieppe.** If you arrive in Dieppe early, take in the scene over coffee at the famous **Café des Tribunaux** (1 place des Puits Sale), a gabled house popular with artists in the 19th century and painted by Walter Richard Sickert. Be sure, however, to arrive in time for lunch, to sample the fresh catch at the port. Restaurants line the bustling **Quai Henri IV,** named after the "wise and thirsty monarch," Henri of Navarre. Local resident Peter Avis, who writes *Taste of Dieppe,* available for free in establishments around town, recommends the ★ **New Haven,** 53 quai Henri IV (☎ 02-35-84-89-72; fixed-price menus 15€–19€; MC, V; May–Sept lunch daily, dinner Wed–Mon; Oct–Apr lunch Thurs–Tues, dinner Thurs–Mon), or the more upmarket **Restaurant du Port,** 99 quai Henri IV (☎ 02-35-84-36-64; fixed-price menus 17€–38€; MC, V; Feb–Dec

1	Rouen
2	Dieppe
3	Varengeville-sur-Mer
4	Fécamp
5	Etretat
6	Deauville
7	Bayeux
8	Mont-St-Michel

lunch and dinner Mon, Tues, and Fri–Sun; lunch only Wed).

Though its fashionable heyday has long since passed, Dieppe still has the fresh-air-and-ice-cream appeal of the northern seaside where Winston Churchill used to sport his all-in-one swimsuit (before he acquired the paunch). If the pull of the beach is not too strong to resist, visit the Dieppe castle, home of the **Château Musée de Chastes,** on rue de Chastes (☎ 02-35-06-61-99; www.musees-haute-normandie. fr; admission 3.60€ adults, 2€ ages 12–17, free for children 11 and under; June–Sept daily 10am–noon and 2–6pm; Oct–May Wed–Mon 10am–noon and 2–5pm). The collection is devoted to maritime history (it includes ivories carved here from West African tusks) and art, including paintings by Courbet, Pissarro, Delacroix, Renoir, Sickert, and Braque. For supper, try the signature dish, a northern version of *bouillabaisse,* at ★ **La Marmite Dieppoise,** 8 rue St Jean (☎ 02-35-84-24-26; fixed-price menus 17€–38€; MC, V; May–Sept lunch Tues–Sun, dinner Tues–Sat; Oct–Apr lunch Tues and Thurs–Sun, dinner Tues and Thurs–Sat). ⏱ 1 day. Dieppe Tourist Office, 56 quai Duquesne. ☎ 02-32-14-40-60. www.dieppetourisme.com.

On your third day, make a day trip to **Varengeville-sur-Mer, following the coastal route (D75) west from Dieppe through Pourville (11km/6¾ miles).**

3 ★ **Varengeville-sur-Mer.** Beloved of Monet, who painted his *Cabane du Douanier (Customs Officer's Cabin)* here, Varengeville is a clifftop village connected to the sea via steep and narrow paths called *valleuses.* The Gorge des Moutiers, starting just beneath the church, is a popular route down. It's not just the French Impressionists who left their mark on the village; English garden designers endowed it with some splendid artificial landscapes. There are no fewer than three marvelous gardens to visit. If you choose just one, make it ★ **Le Parc du Bois des Moutiers,** rte. de l'Eglise (☎ 06-85-66-64-68; guided tours 6€ and 7€; Mar 15–Nov 15 10am–noon and 2–6pm). Garden designer Gertrude Jekyll's garden rooms open up into a lush domain of rhododendrons, hydrangeas, camellias, and hortensias flowing

Where to Stay & Dine

For hotels and restaurants in Rouen, see p. 227; elsewhere in Normandy, see p. 228.

> *Dieppe's Café des Tribunaux was immortalized by English painter Walter Richard Sickert in 1890.*

down to the sea, around a house by Sir Edwin Lutyens. Follow signposts from the village to **La Buissonnière** (☎ 02-35-83-17-13; fixed-price menus 35€–65€; MC, V; Mar–Dec lunch Tues–Sun, dinner Tues–Sat), a delightful restaurant in a garden. ☺ 1 day.

On Day 4, drive west to Fécamp. For the scenic route, stay on the coast road (D75 at its start) all the way, or take the more direct D925; both cover about the same distance (60km/37 miles), but the coast road is slower.

❹ **Fécamp.** Designated a "town of art and history," the port of Fécamp is architecturally rich, with fine examples of buildings from the 12th to the 18th centuries (the tourist office offers guided tours); note, in particular, two 16th-century buildings (no. 21 and no. 73 rue Arquaise) in the Hallettes neighborhood. Fécamp means "field of the fig tree," and legend has it that the trunk of a fig tree containing the blood of Christ washed up here in the 1st century, creating a fountain of gushing blood. This gory tale gave birth to a pilgrimage center and Bénédictine abbey that produced many illuminated manuscripts and, more famously, the medicinal alcoholic drink Bénédictine. All that remains of the original abbey is the 12th-century abbey church ★ **Abbatiale de la Trinité,** an enchanting place with colored shafts of light spilling in from its stained-glass windows. The present **Palais Bénédictine,** 110 rue Alexandre Le Grand (☎ 02-35-10-26-10; www.benedictine.fr; admission 7€ adults, 3€ ages 12–18, free for children 11 and under; July 10 to late Aug daily 10am–7pm; see website for off-season hours), houses the distillery, built in Gothic style in 1900 following a fire. ☺ Half-day. Fécamp Tourist Office, quai Sadi Carnot. ☎ 02-35-28-51-01. www.fecamptourisme.com.

In the afternoon head toward Etretat, 15km (9⅓ miles) west of Fécamp. Take the coast route via Yport for breathtaking cliff views.

❺ ★★ **Etretat.** The Alabaster Coast runs from Le Tréport to Le Havre. The cliffs of Etretat are

Fruits of the Sea

Normandy and Brittany are France's capitals of seafood. September to April is the best time to savor lobster, langoustines, oysters, scallops, crab, and whelk fresh from relatively cold waters. When the Dieppois feel like a special seafood feast, they head 30km (19 miles) east up the coast to Le Tréport, where ★★ **Le Homard Bleu,** 45 quai François 1er (☎ 02-35-86-15-89; www.le-homard-bleu.fr; fixed-price menus 26€–48€; AE, DC, MC, V; lunch and dinner daily), has a stellar reputation and sea views from a terrace or upstairs dining room. In Dieppe itself, the chic, Parisian-style **Comptoir à Huitres,** 12 cours de Dakar (☎ 02-35-84-19-37; main courses 14€–17€; MC, V; lunch and dinner Tues–Sat; closed 2 weeks in Mar and 3 weeks in Aug), behind the station, serves fresh oysters and an array of hot dishes imaginatively cooked with oysters and other seafood. If you are traveling on to Brittany, don't miss **Cancale,** famous for its oyster beds, which yield 25,000 tons of bivalves a year.

Bénédictine

A bittersweet concoction of 27 herbs and spices, with 40% alcohol content, Bénédictine went commercial in 1863, when Alexandre Le Grand hired a chemist to reproduce the monks' secret recipe. Though it is now a brand owned by Bacardi, Bénédictine is still distilled at the abbey, and you can visit the distillation rooms. Oddly, the biggest single consumer of Bénédictine in the world is the Burnley Miners' Club in England; some of its members retained a taste for it after a Lancashire regiment was stationed here during World War I.

its highlight, in particular the **Falaise d'Aval;** here the sea has eroded a hole into the limestone, forming what looks like an elephant dipping its trunk into the water, with the tip (or "needle," as it's known in the Arsène Lupin crime novel) rising up out of the waves nearby. Of the three natural arches, two are visible from the town itself; to see the dramatic **Manneport,** painted by Monet, you have to brave the cliff path or beach (the beach only at low tide). The GR21 hiking path runs right through town, and you can follow it onto the cliffs. ☉ Half-day. Etretat Tourist Office, place Maurice Guillard. ☎ 02-35-27-05-21. www.etretat.net.

Return to Fécamp for the night (or stay in Etretat). The next morning, take D925 and D910 south from Fécamp to join A29, just before Bolbec. Take exit 3 for Honfleur and stop there for lunch before following the coast road (D513) to Trouville and Deauville (65km/40 miles total).

6 Deauville. The St-Tropez of the north, this beach resort was a hit in the Roaring Twenties, when Chanel opened her first boutique here and wowed the promenade crowd with her slacks and striped fisherman tops. The town is still hugely fashionable with Parisians, to the point that it's known as the "21st *arrondissement.*" Strolling on the boardwalk is all about *frime* (showing off), and these days there's plenty of Versace on display. In September, the **Festival du Cinéma Américain de Deauville** (Deauville Festival of American Film; www.festival-deauville.com) even draws A-list Hollywood stars. The racecourse, golf course,

and casino also offer opportunities to spend money flamboyantly. Deauville's more low-key neighbor, **Trouville,** with its splendid sands, is slightly less expensive. ☉ 1 day. Deauville Tourist Office, place de la Mairie. ☎ 02-31-14-40-00. www.deauville.org.

From Deauville, follow the coast road to Arromanches-les-bains and turn off on D516 to Bayeux (76km/47 miles).

7 ★★ Bayeux. Spend your morning at the **Centre Guillaume-le-Conquérant** (William the Conqueror Center), where the Bayeux Tapestry is on display, depicting the 11th-century Battle of Hastings. In the afternoon, visit the sites of the D-Day landings on **★★ Omaha Beach** and the **Normandy American Cemetery and Memorial.** ☉ 1 day. See p. 213, **3**, and 213, **4**.

On your last day, take D6 south out of Bayeux, join A84 (toll road) at Villers-Bocage, and follow signs for Mont-St-Michel (122km/76 miles).

8 ★★★ Mont-St-Michel. The splendid sight of Mont-St-Michel, rising up from the shallow water of its bay, is a fitting end to your Normandy tour—or just the beginning of your trip west into Brittany, if you choose to add on a Brittany tour (p. 196 or p. 200). Visit the **abbey** and enjoy the setting sun on this not-to-be-missed Norman monument. ☉ 1 day. See p. 213, **5**.

Arsène Lupin

The cliffs of Etretat are the setting for France's most famous crime novel, featuring the "gentleman thief" Arsène Lupin. In Maurice Leblanc's *L'Aiguille Creuse* (*The Hollow Needle*), published in 1905, Lupin hides his loot in the needle at the Falaise d'Aval. Nearly a hundred years after its publication, in 2004, the book was the subject of the box-office hit *Arsène Lupin,* starring Kristen Scott Thomas and French heartthrob Romain Duris. You can buy both book and film at **★★ Le Clos Arsène Lupin,** Leblanc's house, which his granddaughter has opened to the public with an amusing and intriguing audio-guide tour about the world of the novel and its author.

Brittany in 3 Days

Visitors to Brittany will soon find that this far-western region of France, jutting into the Atlantic, has a Celtic identity all its own. If you have Irish ancestry, you'll be greeted with open arms. With its intricate coastline, Brittany is a huge area to cover in 3 days, so we've stuck to major inland attractions here. You can discover the windswept, wilder west in the weeklong tour (p. 200).

> Off-season, you can have St-Malo's beaches almost all to yourself.

START St-Malo is 70km (43 miles) north of Rennes and 47km (29 miles) east of Mont-St-Michel. **TRIP LENGTH** 226km (140 miles).

1 kids **St-Malo.** This fortified seaport, surrounded by beaches, is the ideal place to plunge into Brittany's swashbuckling maritime history. An independent republic for 4 years in the 16th century, St-Malo has always looked seaward in the pursuit of adventure and riches. It was a Breton explorer, Jacques Cartier, who discovered the mouth of the St. Lawrence River in Canada in 1534, and Malouin

sailors discovered the Falkland Islands as well (hence the islands' Spanish name, Las Malvinas). In the 17th century, the town was famous for its pirates, known as *corsairs,* who were licensed by the king to create havoc on the high seas. They included René Duguay-Trouin, who captured Rio de Janeiro from the Portuguese in 1711, and Robert Surcouf, who hounded the trade ships of the British East India Company. With their stolen wealth, these pirates built great mansions, such as the ★★ **Maison de Corsaire,** 5 rue d'Asfeld

St-Malo
1 St-Malo
2 Rennes
3 Carnac
4 Presqu'île de Quiberon

(☎ 02-99-56-09-40; www.demeure-de-corsaire.com; admission 5.50€ adults, 4.50€ children; school holidays Mon–Sat 10–11:30am and 2–5:30pm, Sun 2–5:30pm; other times Tues–Sun 3–5:30pm for 1-hr. guided visit). In the castle, the ★ **Musée d'Histoire** (☎ 02-99-40-71-57; admission 5.50€ adults, 2.80€ ages 8–18, free for children 7 and under; Apr–Sept daily 10am–12:30pm and 2–6pm; Oct–May Tues–Sat 10am–noon and 2–6pm) and the ★ **Tour Solidor** tower (☎ 012-99-40-71-58; same opening hours as the museum) contain a huge collection of nautical memorabilia from this era. Both also offer great views from their turrets. A walk around the town ramparts is essential. *Intra muros* you'll find everything from chic boutiques to tourist souvenirs. ⏱ 1 day. For more on St-Malo, see p. 206, 1.

From St-Malo, take N137 south to Rennes (70km/43 miles).

2 ★ **Rennes.** Spend your second morning discovering Rennes's historic **Old Town** (Vieux Rennes), and expect to be surprised by this future-oriented regional capital and university town, where students zip around on the city-owned white bikes by day and throng in

> A chocolate pancake from Crêperie Margaux in St-Malo.

Where to Stay & Dine

For hotels and restaurants in Brittany, see p. 230.

> *Carnac is home to the world's largest set of megaliths.*

front of bars in the narrow medieval streets by night. Rennes's intricate, half-timbered houses are quintessentially Breton, while a new museum complex gives the city a modern edge. Designed by Christian de Portzamparc, the ★★ **Musée de Bretagne,** 46 bd. Magenta (☎ 02-23-40-66-70; www.musee-bretagne. fr; admission 4€ adults, 3€ ages 25 and under, free for children 7 and under; exhibitions 7€ adults, 5€ ages 25 and under; Tues noon–9pm; Wed–Fri noon–7pm; Sat–Sun 2–7pm), has a refreshingly global outlook, with temporary exhibitions on indigenous peoples around the world: In one visit, you can go, for instance, from Celtic dolmens to the Dreyfus affair to women in Mali. The **place des Lices** also springs to life on a Saturday morning, when fresh fish, pungent cheeses, and brightly colored produce draw townsfolk in droves. In 1720 a 6-day fire destroyed much of Rennes,

but this small historic center that survived, with its colorful houses and narrow streets, offers a vivid glimpse of what the city must have been like; tiny rue de la Psalette has some of the best-preserved examples of these 400-year-old buildings. The tourist office runs a 90-minute guided tour (6.80€ adults, 4€ reduced, free for children 6 and under), starting in the plaza, of the 15th-century **Portes Mordelaises** fortifications and the cathedral, whose complicated history resulted in the neoclassical edifice seen today. The ★ **Parlement de Bretagne**'s regional law courts are also worth visiting for their Renaissance interiors, painstakingly restored after a fire in 1994. Stay on the square for lunch at **Cours des Lices,** 18 place des Lices (☎ 02-99-30-25-25; www.lecoursdeslices.fr; fixed-price menu 19€–39€; MC, V; lunch Tues–Sat, dinner Sat), or try the highly recommended modern bistro

> *Beautiful, bourgeois Rennes prides itself on its stately architecture—especially the half-timbered buildings on place des Lices.*

Le Bocal, 6 rue d'Argentré (☎ 02-99-78-34-10; main courses 14€–15€; MC, V; lunch and dinner Mon–Sat), on the other side of the river. You can also pick up some amazing handmade chocolates at **Chocolaterie Durand,** 5 quai Châteaubriand (☎ 02-99-78-10-00; www.durandchocolaterie.fr; MC, V; Mon 3–7pm, Tues–Sat 10am–7pm). ◷ Half-day. Rennes Tourist Office, 11 rue Saint-Yves. ☎ 02-99-67-11-11. www.tourisme-rennes.com.

In the afternoon, take N24 and N166 southwest to Vannes and pick up N165 west. Turn off at Auray and follow signs to Carnac (142km/88 miles total).

❸ ★★★ kids Carnac. You're in for a treat. The world's largest grouping of megaliths—4,000 of them, standing in serried ranks over 4km (2½ miles)—makes the ★★★ **Alignements de Carnac** the prehistoric equivalent of China's Terracotta Army. In July and August, the site is open until 8pm (May–June until 7pm), allowing you to see the stones in the atmospheric evening light, which casts long shadows. The following morning, visit the **Musée de Préhistoire,** the **Locmariaquer tombs,** and the **Grand Menhir Brisé.** ◷ Afternoon and the following morning. See p. 208, ❹, and 215, ❼.

On the afternoon of your last day, drive 3.5km (2¼ miles) west on D781 to the next-door village of Plouharnel, then south on D768 onto the Presqu'île de Quiberon (14km/8⅔ miles total).

❹ Presqu'île de Quiberon. For a relaxing end to this short trip, take in the golden strands and wild landscape of the Quiberon Peninsula. Beside the narrow causeway, stop off at the wide, flat sands of **Penthièvre,** backed by dunes, or continue on to the **Côte Sauvage** (Wild Coast) with its rocks, creeks, and heather-topped cliffs. The village of **Quiberon** has several eating options. ◷ Half-day. Quiberon Tourist Office, 14 rue de Verdun. ☎ 08-25-13-56-00. www.quiberon.com.

Brittany in 1 Week

This tour takes in a section of both the north and the south coasts, and you'll certainly feel you've made it somewhere far, far away when you stare out across the Atlantic Ocean from the midway point—the dramatic cliffs of the Pointe du Raz. Before and after, you'll encounter everything from working ports to prehistoric monuments, and modern art to Breton traditions, all the while enjoying fine dining, colorful beaches, and relaxing walks. This itinerary is designed to continue from the Normandy tours, which end at Mont-St-Michel, only 48km (30 miles) east of St-Malo (stop ❷, below) on N176 and N137.

> *Quimper's medieval Breton streets are watched over by St-Corentin Cathedral, a Gothic beauty begun in the 13th century.*

START Rennes is 70km (43 miles) south of St-Malo and 60km (37 miles) south of Mont-St-Michel. **TRIP LENGTH** 500km (311 miles).

❶ **Rennes.** The capital of Brittany makes a convenient starting place for your exploration of Brittany. ⊙ 1 day. See p. 197, ❷.

From Rennes, take N137 north to St-Malo (70km/43 miles).

❷ kids **St-Malo.** The birthplace of explorers who discovered the St. Lawrence River and the Falkland Islands, and home of the king's official 17th-century pirates, the *corsairs*, St-Malo has a rich maritime history. Spend a day walking the ramparts and visiting the ★ **Musée d'Histoire** in the castle, then relax on any of the beaches that lap the fortified town. In the evening, oyster aficionados can take the 15km (9⅓-mile) trip to **Cancale** (on D355) to

Where to Stay & Dine

For hotels and restaurants in Brittany, see p. 230.

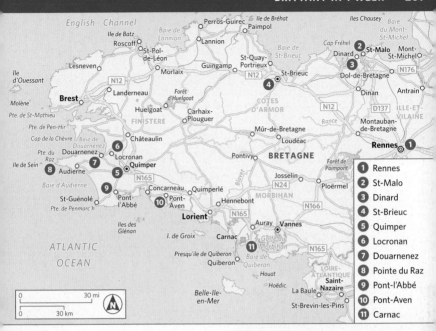

1	Rennes
2	St-Malo
3	Dinard
4	St-Brieuc
5	Quimper
6	Locronan
7	Douarnenez
8	Pointe du Raz
9	Pont-l'Abbé
10	Pont-Aven
11	Carnac

eat bivalves fresh from the sea at Port de la Houle, where they are unloaded at high tide. ⏱ 1 day. See p. 196 1.

From St-Malo, follow D168, which crosses the Rance barrage to Dinard (10km/6¼ miles).

3 ★★ kids **Dinard.** Dinard is Brittany's most fashionable resort, with its own film festival devoted to British cinema (in October) and a completely different feel from its neighbor across the river. It was the English, adept at cold-water bathing, who turned Dinard from sleepy fishing village to holiday town, and French aristocrats and the *crème de la crème* of European high society followed closely. Striped beach tents and the fantasy villas that dot the cliffs recall the elegance of the Belle

Seaside Roadster Cruise

One of the most fun things to do in Dinard is to take a *promenade romantique* in a vintage car straight out of *The Great Gatsby*. A costumed chauffeur will lead you on a tour of the villas and the coastline in a 1929 Citroen C4, or you can rent the car yourself. ☎ 02-99-46-49-22. Rates 35€ per half-hour, 50€ per hour, up to 160€ for 4 hours.

> *Fresher than fresh: Just before lunch, these juicy oysters, in Cancale, were in the sea.*

Epoque. In the 1920s, artists appropriated the town; Picasso, Lacombe, and Foujita had exhibitions here, and 21 art galleries perpetuate the tradition. Various walks traverse the cliff-top villas and gardens—at the tourist office,

> *The St-Maurice chapel is on the Pointe de Longue Roche between St-Brieuc and Val André.*

pick up the leaflet describing the **Pointe de la Malouie** option, which points out architectural highlights. The ★ kids **Usine Marémotrice de la Rance,** the world's first tidal power station, on the Rance barrage, also has a visitor center (☎ 02-99-16-37-14; temporarily closed for renovation). ⏱ 1 day. Dinard Tourist Office, 2 bd. Féart. ☎ 02-99-46-94-12. www.ot-dinard.com.

Follow the coast road (D786) west from Dinard to take in the Emerald Coast (make a detour to Cap Fréhel for a view from the cliffs), and continue to St-Brieuc (90km/56 miles).

❹ **St-Brieuc.** In this maritime town, tourism revolves around the bay, a protected nature reserve with gorgeous beaches. We've arrived in time for lunch, and it's no accident: St-Brieuc, a world center for scallops (Oct–Apr), has no fewer than three Michelin-starred restaurants: La Vieille Tour, Aux Pesked, and Youpala Bistro. ★★ **La Vieille Tour** (p. 233) has the edge, if only for its relaxed and color-ful setting by the sea. ⏱ 2 hr. St-Brieuc Tourist Office, 7 rue Saint-Gouéno. ☎ 08-25-00-22-22. www.baiedesaintbrieuc.com.

From St-Brieuc, take D700 and D790 southwest to Rostrenen, then take D3 and D15, following signs for Quimper (127km/79 miles).

❺ **Quimper.** After traveling cross-country for 2 hours through the Black Mountains, you'll be happy to finally arrive at the ancient capital of the Cornouaille region, where you'll spend your third night and the following day. A cathedral city, Quimper is the proud home of the Breton language and traditions. You'll find Celtic music CDs, teach-yourself-Breton courses, and even a full Breton costume in the shops of the **Old Town** (Vieux Quimper). Most of all, you'll find *faïence,* the glazed pottery painted with bucolic pictures of flow-ers, animals, and peasants that has been produced here since the 17th century. To go to the source, visit the 320-year-old factory **Faïencerie HB-Henriot,** 2 rue Haute (☎ 02-98-90-09-36; www.hb-henriot.com; admission 5€ adults, 2.50€ ages 8–18, free for children 7 and under; Mar–Nov Mon–Fri 1-hr. guided vis-its at 10:30am and 3pm; closed Dec–Feb and

July 1–18). More *faïence* (along with costumes and carved furniture) can be seen at the **Musée de la Faïence** and the **Musée Départemental Breton.** Unless you are a dedicated collector of the stuff, however, it's far more rewarding to spend time at the ★★ **Musée des Beaux-Arts,** 40 place St-Corentin (☎ 02-98-95-45-20; www.musee-beauxarts.quimper.fr; admission 4.50€ adults, 2.50€ ages 12–26, free for children 11 and under; July–Aug daily 10am–7pm; Sept–June Wed–Mon 10am–noon and 2–6pm), which specializes in Breton art, including work by the painters of Pont-Aven (see stop ➒, below). Do peer into the **cathedral,** too, a Gothic construction with a restored painted interior and 15th-century stained glass. With the Breton language and music come the *crêpes* and cider. Pubs, the likes of which you won't see in the rest of France, are very plentiful here, serving both Guinness and local Celtic brews. ⏱ 1½ days. Quimper Tourist Office, 7 rue Déesse. ☎ 02-98-53-04-05. www.quimper-tourisme.com.

On Day 5, take a day trip (stops ➏, ➐, and ➑) to the west, starting with Locronan, 17km (11 miles) northwest of Quimper on D39.

➏ ★ **Locronan.** A day spent exploring the area west of Quimper—the bottom jaw of the dragon's open mouth, if you look at a map of Brittany—can start at Locronan. Classed as one of France's Most Beautiful Villages, Locronan was used as a location for the films *Tess* and *A Very Long Engagement.* Why does this little town of only 1,000 inhabitants have so many grand Renaissance buildings? Well, it grew rich from the manufacture of sailcloth out of local hemp in the 15th to the 17th centuries; it even equipped the Spanish Armada, before Louis XIV spoiled it all by ending the Breton monopoly on this trade. The 15th-century church in the main cobbled square, devoted to the Irish missionary St. Ronan, is the beginning of the **Grand Troménie,** a dramatic pilgrimage in traditional costume that takes place every 6 years. In between, the **Petite Troménie** occurs annually, every second Sunday of July. ⏱ 1 hr. Locronan Tourist Office, place de la Mairie. ☎ 02-98-91-70-14. www.locronan.org/home-2.

Drive west from Locronan to Douarnenez on D7 (10km/6¼ miles).

> On a rainy day, take the kids to Douarnenez's Port Musée to see boats from all over the world.

➐ kids **Douarnenez.** A working fishing port and attractive town surrounded by beaches, Douarnenez used to be France's main sardine supplier. At the **Port du Rosmeur,** you can feast on fresh fish and watch the boats come in. The *criée,* or fish auction, takes place in the early mornings at the **New Port.** A third port, **Port Rhu,** has been turned into a living maritime museum, the ★★ **Port Musée,** place de l'Enfer (☎ 02-98-92-65-20; www.port-musee.org; admission 5.50€ adults, 3.50€ ages 6–16, 15€ families; July–Aug daily 10am–7pm; Sept–June Tues–Sun 10am–12:30pm and 2–6pm). The collection features life-size models of 30 vessels (four that you can climb), shipyards where you can see traditional boat-building techniques at work, and exhibitions on seafaring all over the world. ⏱ 4 hr. Douarnenez Tourist Office, 1 rue du Docteur Mével. ☎ 02-98-92-13-35. www.douarnenez-tourisme.com.

> *Lace and coiffes fill the streets during Pont-l'Abbé's Fête des Brodeuses, a celebration of traditional Breton culture.*

Breton Festivals

A crowd of Breton women dressed in their tall white *coiffes* is a sight to behold. Until the middle of the 19th century, local women wore them every day, as a sign of modesty and a tightly defined social order. Today the headpieces come out for weddings, pilgrimages, and festival days. At Pont-l'Abbé, an opportunity par excellence for seeing *coiffes* in the street is the **Fête des Brodeuses** (second weekend of July)—a festival celebrating the guild of embroiderers who worked here embellishing rich clothes for aristocrats and bishops. Also look out for advertisements for a *fest-noz*, the Breton version of a *ceilidh*, with music, dancing, and food; Pont-l'Abbé hosts a big one on August 15, Ascension Day. The huge **Festival InterCeltique** at **Lorient,** 70km (43 miles) east of Quimper, is in early August. The **Festi-Bigoud** traditional music festival in Pont-l'Abbé is at the end of August.

Continue west on D7 along the north coast of the peninsula to Pointe du Van (look across the bay for a view of the dramatic Pointe du Raz). Then drop down to the Baie des Trépassés and up again to the Pointe du Raz (36km/22 miles total).

8 ★★★ **Pointe du Raz.** One of Brittany's most spectacular clifftop viewpoints, Pointe du Raz during the off-season feels like the very end of the earth. Visit the small chapel (there's also one in Pointe du Van), where wives in times past prayed for the lives of their husbands out at sea. Park at the Maison de la Pointe de Raz (6€) or stop at Lescoff and follow a marked path out to the top of the cliffs. It's a perfect place to watch the sunset, which turns the rocks golden and silhouettes the lighthouse. ⏱ 1 hr. Pointe du Raz Tourist Office, Maison de la Pointe du Raz (at the end of the road to Pointe du Raz, 800m/½ mile from the cliffs). ☎ 02-98-70-67-18. www.pointeduraz.com.

Return to Quimper via D784 (57km/35 miles). On Day 6, take D785 south from Quimper to Pont-L'Abbé (21km/13 miles).

9 **Pont-l'Abbé.** The small town of Pont-l'Abbé is the capital of the Pays Bigouden, where Celtic traditions flourish. Breton is spoken as an everyday language here, and you'll see women dressed in the traditional tall lace *coiffes* for special occasions (see "Breton Festivals"). The **Musée Bigouden** (☎ 02-98-66-09-03; www.museebigouden.fr; admission 3.50€ adults, 2.50€ ages 12–26; free for children 11 and under; June–Sept daily 10am–12:30pm and 2–6pm; Oct–May Tues–Sun 2–6pm), in the baronial château overlooking the river, exhibits collections of costumes and lace and conducts lace-making demonstrations. It also doubles as the town hall. The **Eglise Notre-Dame des Carmes,** the 15th-century chapel of a Carmelite convent, displays beautiful embroidered cloths and has an exceptional organ; free concerts take place throughout the summer (Thurs 10:30am). The countryside around Pont-l'Abbé is dotted with menhirs. A few kilometers to the west is the oldest calvary in France, **Notre-Dame de Tronoën.** ⏱ Half-day. Pont-l'Abbé Tourist Office, 11 place Gambetta. ☎ 02-98-82-37-99. www.ot-pontlabbe29.fr.

Drive east from Pont-l'Abbé on D44 and D783 to Pont-Aven (45km/28 miles).

⑩ ★★ Pont-Aven. Pont-Aven used to be known as "the town of 14 mills and 15 houses." Paul Gauguin, won over by its beauty and simplicity, moved here in 1886 to paint the local people and landscapes, finding a primitive power in the Breton Catholic faith, a theme echoed in paintings of indigenous people and totems in his later Tahiti work. With Emile Bernard and Paul Sérusier, Gauguin formed the School of Pont-Aven, painting simplistically in bright, hot colors. The **Musée des Beaux-Arts de Pont-Aven,** place de l'Hôtel de Ville (☎ 02-98-06-14-43; www.museepontaven.fr; admission 4.50€ adults, free for ages 17 and under; Feb–June and Sept–Dec daily 10am–12:30pm and 2–6pm; July–Aug 10am–7pm; closed Jan), is devoted to the Pont-Aven School and exhibits works by the three founders as well as five other artists and many prestigious paintings on loan. Walks through the surrounding woods include one to the **Chapelle de Trémalo,** which houses the wooden carving of Christ portrayed in Gauguin's *Le Christ jaune (Yellow Christ)*. ☉ Half-day. Pont-Aven Tourist Office, 5 place de l'hôtel de ville. ☎ 02-98-06-04-70. www.pontaven.com.

On your last day, follow D4 out of Pont-Aven to join N165, continue on N165 until Auray, and then follow signs to Carnac on D768 (80km/50 miles).

⑪ ★★★ kids Carnac. Our prehistoric ancestors left awe-inspiring evidence of their presence in Brittany in the form of the **★★★ Alignements de Carnac,** the largest collection of standing stones in the world. Around 4,000 in total, they stretch over 4km (2½ miles) in three main groups and are characterized by their precise mathematical alignment into 10, 11, or 13 rows stretching out into the distance. To this day archaeologists can only conjecture about their purpose, which could be connected to seismic fault lines. After visiting the stones, find out more about these theories and see the collection of prehistoric artifacts at the **Musée de Préhistoire** in Carnac. The collection is dedicated to local boy Zacharie le Rouzic, who became an international expert on the megaliths after Scottish archaeologist James Miln took him on as an assistant. ☉ 1 day. See p. 208, ④, and 215, ⑦.

> *The town that stole Gauguin's heart, Pont-Aven, is as picturesque today as when the 19th-century artist first painted it.*

Brittany with Kids

Brittany has long been a favorite place to take the kids, both for French families and for the British who hop across the Channel on the ferries. And no wonder: It has beautiful, uncrowded beaches and plenty of activities, both for burning off energy outdoors and for that occasional rainy day. Brittany's inexpensive, simple cusine, including *crêpes* and *moules-frites,* served relatively early, also makes it one of the easiest regions of France in which to travel with children. Basing yourself in any of the hot spots we've chosen will give you enough to do in a week—and hopefully will ensure that you don't hear that ubiquitous phrase, "Are we there yet?" for the duration of your trip.

> *Beachcombers could spend hours analyzing the marine creatures in rock pools along the shores of Brittany.*

START St-Malo is 400km (250 miles) west of Paris, 70km (43 miles) north of Rennes, and 47km (29 miles) east of Mont-St-Michel. **TRIP LENGTH** About 1 week; 471km (292 miles).

1 St-Malo. A pirate citadel surrounded by beaches, St-Malo has everything required to fire children's imaginations. You can walk around the 1,754m-long (5,755-ft.) **ramparts** (entrance at Porte St-Vincent), check out the cannons at the **Bastion Hollandais,** and admire the view from **La Tour Bidouane.** Built on the rocks, the ramparts have endured 9 centuries and were undamaged by the World War II bombing that affected the city inside, though only the weight of the stones holds them in place. To learn more about the French king's official pirates, visit the **Maison de Corsaire,** 5 rue d'Asfeld (p. 196, **1**), with its treasure

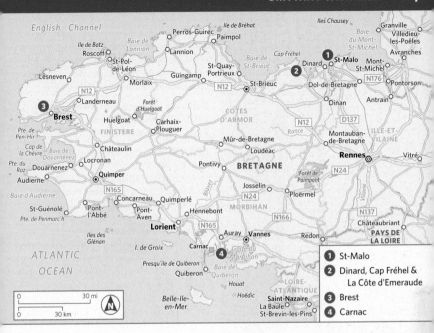

❶	St-Malo
❷	Dinard, Cap Fréhel & La Côte d'Emeraude
❸	Brest
❹	Carnac

chests, secret staircases, and weapons. Or for big adventure, take to the seas on the **côtre corsaire Renard** (☎ 02-99-40-48-72; www.etoile-marine.com), a replica of an 1812 pirate ship complete with cannons. During the vessel's longer trips (half-day, 1-day, or even longer); children 9 and older can help to sail. On dry land, little ones will enjoy the pirate maze **Labyrinthe du Corsaire,** 20 rue de la Goëletterie, rte. de Quelmer-La Passagère (☎ 02-99-81-17-23; www.labyrintheducorsaire.com; admission 7.50€ adults, free for children 2 and under; July and Aug daily 10:30am–7pm), a real maze with a bouncy castle and a life-size chess game.

The beaches start just outside the ramparts: sheltered **Mole Beach,** which gets crowded with sun worshippers; **Bon Secours Beach,** with its seawater swimming pool, from which you can walk to the island of Grand Bé at low tide; **Evantail Beach,** in front of **Fort National** (☎ 06-72-46-66-26; www.fortnational.com; guided visit 5€ adults, 3€ children; June–Sept, times according to tides); and the long strand of **Sillon Beach,** stretching out to the east. In spring and autumn, the famous *grandes mareés* (big waves) crashing

against the ramparts are a spectacular sight. In the bay below the Tour Solidor, **Balade Kayak 35** (☎ 06-62-53-18-05; www.baladekayak35.com) leads guided kayak trips. Kids 11 and under who can swim 25m (82 ft.) can go with a parent. Local fishing coach **Berry Ollivier** (☎ 06-62-79-19-67; www.guidepechesaintmalo.com) runs a fishing school on Wednesday afternoons for children ages 6 to 14; he can also take you out on a family fishing trip or a beach-combing nature walk. ⏱ 2–3 days. St-Malo Tourist Office, esplanade St-Vincent. ☎ 08-25-13-52-00. www.saint-malo-tourisme.com.

Dinard is just over the Rance River from St-Malo (10km/6¼ miles from town center to town center), via the barrage. From Dinard, follow the coast westward via D786, D34i, and D34e to reach Cap Fréhel (37km/23 miles). Val-André is 15km (9 miles) west of Fréhel. 56km (35 miles).

Where to Stay & Dine

For hotels and restaurants in Brittany, see p. 230. See also "Kid-Friendly Digs," p. 209.

> *Despite its Victorian castle–like appearance, the lighthouse at Cap Fréhel was built between 1946 and 1950.*

② **Dinard, Cap Fréhel & La Côte d'Eméraude. Dinard** (p. 201, **③**) is a relatively smart resort with old-fashioned charm, where children in Petit Bateau play beside striped beach tents. The visitor center at the **Usine Marémotrice de Rance,** the Rance River barrage tidal power station, will interest young science buffs. The exotic-sounding Côte d'Eméraude (Emerald Coast) may yet hold buried treasure, but its name derives from the color of its water and the pinewoods that run down to its sandy beaches. Espadrilles and *boules* are still in fashion here, and the region's lazy seaside villages are the perfect place to spend a relaxing beach holiday; your kids will undoubtedly learn to skip rope French-style with the locals and speak a few words of the *lingua franca.* **Cap Fréhel,** with its lighthouse and cliffs descending 70m (230 ft.) to the sea, is the dramatic highlight of the region, but the beaches of **Sables-d'Or-les-Pins, Erquy,** and **Val-André** are where the kids will jump the breakers, kayak,

or windsurf, depending on their age. There are no major tourist attractions on this stretch of coast, but look out for local summer festivities. ⏰ 1 day. For more information, see www.cotesdarmor.com or www.ot-dinard.com.

Backtrack to Dinard and take N137 south, E401/N176 west, and then N12/E50 north to Brest (182km/113 miles).

③ **Brest.** Brest may not be the most attractive city visually, but it's the casting-off point for the island of **Ouessant** (p. 221) as well as the beaches of the **Crozon Peninsula.** ★★★ **Océanopolis** (www.oceanopolis.com; admission 16.50€ adults, 11€ ages 4–17, free for children 3 and under; July–Aug daily 9am–7pm; Sept–June daily 9am–6pm) leaves other aquariums in the dust. You can easily spend a day here exploring the facility's three climate zones. In temperate waters, observe species of fish most likely to end up on a human's dinner plate; the tropical zone is an amazingly colorful world with sharks, a mangrove swamp, and a coral reef; in polar waters, the highlight is penguins in their Antarctic habitat. For some outdoor excitement, **Arbreizh Adventure** (☎ 06-64-24-06-41; www.arbreizh.com; admission 15€ adults, 10€ ages 7–10, 7€ ages 5–7; Mar–Nov Sat–Sun and national holidays 1–6pm; closed Dec–Feb), just outside Brest, offers the chance to swing from tree to tree in harnesses in Kéroual Forest. Three separate courses mean children 5 and over can take part. Five minutes from Brest, **La Recré des 3 Cures** (☎ 02-98-07-95-59; www.larecredes3cures.fr; admission 14€ adults, 12€ children 11 and under; June–Aug daily 11am–7pm; May and Sept Wed and Sat–Sun 11am–6:30pm) is an amusement park on 15 hectares (37 acres) of grounds, with water slides, toboggans, and a Ferris wheel. ⏰ 2–3 days. Brest Tourist Office, place de la Liberté. ☎ 02-98-44-24-96. www.brest-metropole.tourisme.fr.

From Brest, follow N165, D768, and D119 southeast to Carnac (180km/112 miles).

④ ★★★ **Carnac.** Most famously the home of Europe's largest collection of prehistoric **megaliths,** Carnac is also surrounded by beautiful beaches with fine, white sand and limpid, shallow water ideal for small children. The Grande Plage and St-Colomban Beach have lifeguards in high season and also offer children's activities. After visiting the ★★★ **Alignements de Carnac,** explore prehistory further with a day at the **Parc de Préhistoire de Bretagne,** La Croix Neuve, Malansac (☎ 02-97-43-34-17; www.prehistoire.com; admission 11€ adults, 7€ ages 4–11, free for children 3 and under; April to mid-Oct daily 11am–7pm; mid-Oct to Mar Sun 1–6:30pm). In this Jurassic Park–style adventure, you'll encounter life-size models of dinosaurs stalking through the undergrowth and discover a nest of dinosaur eggs. Next up are the strange animals that existed in the 60 million years *between* the dinosaurs and humans. Finally you'll reach the exhibit devoted to human evolution: Neanderthals, Cro-Magnons, and the people who built the menhirs, in scenes from daily life back then. Carnac also has a treetop adventure park, **Forêt Adrénaline,** near

Kid-Friendly Digs

Many hotels in Brittany cater to travelers with kids by offering family rooms, buffet meals with flexible hours, and children's activities. Some will prepare special deals for guests staying a week or more. See p. 223 for one of the best, Le Cardinal, on the island of Belle-Ile-En-Mer.

For traveling around, *chambres d'hôtes* (French bed-and-breakfasts) make for convenient 1-night stays, and they often will provide cots and high chairs. Tourist office websites list them.

Gîtes (self-catering homes) are a great option for weeklong stays, but be aware that they may include only the very basic provisions. Some *gîtes* will rent linens, but French families often bring their own sheets, pots, and pans when they set off for *gîte* holidays. *Gîtes d'étape,* in areas of natural beauty, allow several families to stay together. See **www.gites-de-france.com** for a large selection of *gîtes, gîtes d'étape,* and chalets. British site www.ownersdirect. co.uk also lists many well-equipped and attractive *gîtes* in Brittany.

Many campsites also rent chalets, mobile homes, and ready-erected family tents. For more information, try www. campingfrance.com.

> *The penguin area at Océanopolis in Brest is a technological feat, re-creating sub-Antarctic conditions.*

the village of Le Hanon (☎ 02-90-84-00-20; www.foretadrenaline.com; admission 16€ adults, 12.80€ ages 10–15, 8€ ages 5–9, 5€ ages 2–4; Apr 9–June and Sept Wed and Sat–Sun 2–7pm; Apr–June, Sept–Oct, and holidays daily 2–7pm; July–Aug daily 10am–7pm); while the teens and adults are swinging through the trees, there are alternative activities available for kids 2 and older. ⏱ 1 day. Carnac Tourist Office, 74 av. des Druides, Carnac Plage. ☎ 02-97-52-13-52. www.ot-carnac.fr. For more on Carnac, see p. 215, **7**.

Normandy & Brittany for History Buffs

Six thousand years of history can be relived in Normandy and Brittany, carrying you from one of the world's greatest concentrations of prehistoric standing stones right up to the thrilling and tragic stories of World War II combat. Historical A-listers William the Conqueror, Richard the Lionheart, and Joan of Arc make their appearances in this epic journey through time. Our tour only gets as far as the eastern end of Brittany; for the folk and maritime history of the far west, see the "Brittany in 1 Week" tour (p. 200).

> High on a hill in Les Andelys, the mysterious, 800-year-old fortress ruin of Château Gaillard dominates the landscape.

START Rouen is 135km (84 miles) north of Paris. **TRIP LENGTH** 1 week; 746km (464 miles).

1 ★★ **Rouen.** Remains of a Gallo-Roman settlement uncovered during Metro excavations, on display in the **Musée des Antiquités,** show that Rouen existed by at least the 3rd century A.D. It was the Viking Rollon (also known as Robert I, an ancestor of William the

Conqueror) who made the city important, establishing it as the capital of his dukedom of Normandy in the 10th century. A reproduction of his tomb (the original was destroyed in World War II) is in the ★★★ **Cathédrale Notre-Dame de Rouen.** During the Hundred Years' War, the English took Rouen after a siege in 1418, and they imprisoned and tortured Joan of Arc in 1430 in the Château de Rouen,

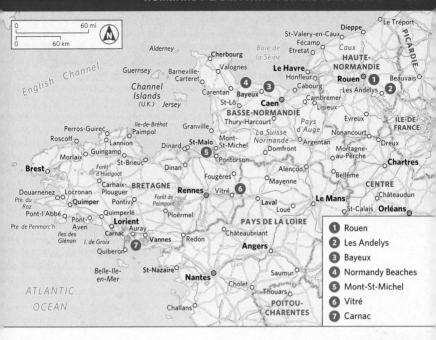

Legend	
1	Rouen
2	Les Andelys
3	Bayeux
4	Normandy Beaches
5	Mont-St-Michel
6	Vitré
7	Carnac

of which only one tower remains, the **Tour Jeanne d'Arc.** The site conveys a sense of the austere conditions in which Joan languished, though it's not the actual tower in which she was held. In 1431 Joan was taken from the **Abbatiale de St-Ouen** to its cemetery, where she was to be burned at the stake unless she recanted her claim to have seen visions of God. She signed an abjuration (later declared invalid) and was granted life imprisonment, but the English went back on the deal, burning her on the site of the cross in ★ **place du Vieux Marché** on May 30, 1431. The **Musée Jeanne d'Arc** in the square is designed for children. Lovers of history and French literature will find the **Musée Flaubert et d'Histoire de la Médecine** interesting. Author Gustave Flaubert, son of the hospital's surgeon, was born here; you can tour the Flaubert family's not-so-private rooms, an apothecary room, and medical paraphernalia from antiquity to the 20th century. ☺ 1 day. For detailed information on Rouen, see p. 224.

From Rouen, make a day trip to Les Andelys: Take N14 southeast out of Rouen and turn off at Ecouis (39km/24 miles).

> *A statue of Joan of Arc in place de Vieux Marché, Rouen.*

Where to Stay & Dine

For hotels and restaurants in Brittany, see p. 230; in Rouen, see p. 227; elsewhere in Normandy, see p. 228.

> *A section of the Bayeaux Tapestry, depicting the Battle of Hastings.*

2 ★ **Les Andelys.** Richard the Lionheart's castle, **Château Gaillard,** looms on its rocky spur 90m (295 ft.) above the town of Les Andelys. Its name means "a strapping lad"— reputedly what Richard exclaimed when he saw the castle built in just one year, in 1198; the fortifications are even more mystical and splendorous now that they're in ruins. The original defenses included a bridge, a small castle on an island, three stakes in the Seine, and lookout towers. The plan was to defend the river and never again to be caught off guard, as before when Richard's French rival Philippe-Auguste abandoned a Crusade in the Holy Land to ransack the Plantagenet king's territory. Today you can still see the complexity of its multilayered construction, including the impressive keep and jelly mold–shaped outer wall. The castle did fall again to the French, however, in 1203—5 years after Richard's death—when Philippe-Auguste's troops crawled in through the latrines. To drive up, follow the signs from rue Louis Pasteur. If you're on foot, allow a 30-minute climb from rue Richard-Coeur-de-lion, near the tourist office. The restaurant **La Chaîne d'Or,** 25 rue Grande, Petit Andely (☎ 02-43-54-00-31; lunch Tues–Sun, dinner Mon–Sat; closed Mon–Tues in winter), is a good place to have lunch. After lunch, simply wander around the town, or visit the **Musée Nicolas Poussin,** rue Ste-Clotilde (☎ 02-32-54-31-78; www.musees-haute-normandie.fr; admission 2.50€; Mon and Wed–Sun 2–6pm), or the **Mémorial Normandie-Niémen,** rue Raymond Phélip (☎ 02-32-54-49-76; admission by donation; Wed–Mon 10am–noon and 4–6pm; closed mornings in winter), a small museum devoted to the legendary air squadron that fought out of Russia in World War II. ⊙ 1 day. Andelys Tourist Office, rue Philippe Auguste. ☎ 02-32-54-41-93. http://office-tourisme.ville-andelys.fr.

Return to Rouen for the night; on your third day, take A13 (toll road) west from Rouen, bypass Caen, and pick up N13 to Bayeux (156km/97 miles).

3 ★★ **Bayeux.** Listed on UNESCO's Memory of the World register, the Bayeux Tapestry is a 70m-long (230-ft.) embroidered cloth recounting in comic-strip style the life of William the Conqueror and events leading up to the Battle of Hastings. The tapestry is thought to have been commissioned by William's half-brother, Bishop Odo, in the 1070s for the Bayeux cathedral, and embroidered in England. It is displayed at the **Centre Guillaume-le-Conquérant,** on rue de Nesmond (☎ 02-31-51-25-50; www.tapestry-bayeux.com; admission 7.80€ adults, 3.80€ ages 10–18, free for children 9 and under; Mar 15–Nov 15 daily 9am–6:30pm; Nov 16–Mar 14 daily 9:30am–12:30pm and 2–6pm; closed Dec 24–26, Dec 31–Jan 2, and 2nd week of Jan); a 16-minute film in French or English and an exhibition present the background, while audio-guides help you "read" the 58 scenes depicted. After lunch, fast-forward 9 centuries into the events of World War II at the **Musée Mémorial de la Bataille de Normandie,** on boulevard Fabian Ware (☎ 02-31-51-46-90; www.normandiememoire.com; admission 6.50€ adults, 3.80€ ages 10–18, free for children 9 and under and veterans; May–Sept daily 9:30am–6.30pm; Oct–Apr daily 10am–12:30pm and 2–6pm; closed Dec 25, Jan 1, and Jan 15–31). An informative and evocative museum, it exhibits a range of artifacts related to the war, from tanks to the personal letters of servicemen who fought on the Normandy beaches. ⏱ 1 day. Bayeux Tourist Office, pont Saint-Jean. ☎ 02-31-51-28-28. www.bayeux-tourism.com/web/index.php.

From Bayeux, take D6 north, and then the coast road (D514) to St-Laurent-sur-Mer to visit the Normandy Beaches (18km/11 miles).

4 **Normandy Beaches.** The D-Day Normandy trail runs from Merville-Franceville, 50km (31 miles) east of Bayeux, to Quineville, 70km (43 miles) to the west, taking in the sites of the British, Canadian, and American landings. Several small museums commemorate the various battles. A day spent visiting the D-Day sites could allow for visits to ★★ **Omaha Beach,** its museum, the American war cemetery, and **Pointe du Hoc** (2nd Rangers Battalion Monument and battery blockhouses, 12km/7½ miles west); the village of

> The Omaha Beach memorial bursts through the sand in memory of American soldiers who lost their lives there in 1944.

Ste-Marie du Mont and **Utah Beach** (Musée du Débarquement, 34km/21 miles west); and **Ste-Mère-Eglise** (Airborne Troops Museum, 9km/5⅔ miles west). ⏱ 1 day. For full details of the sites and museums, in English, see www.normandie44lamemoire.com. See "The Longest Day: The Allied Invasion of Normandy," p. 216, for more on the events of 1944.

Return to Bayeux for the night. The following day, take D6 south, join A84 (toll road) at Villers-Bocage, and follow signs for Mont-St-Michel (122km/76 miles).

5 ★★★ **Mont-St-Michel.** A historical tour of Normandy and Brittany would not be complete without visiting one of Europe's great attractions, the island of Mont-St-Michel. This

Travel Tip

Buy the Normandie Pass (1€) at any of the D-Day museums, and get 1€ off entry for all of them. The similar Megaliths Pass operates for the Carnac monuments and museum (see p. 215, **7**).

> *French-style gardens await you behind the Château des Rochers-Sévigné, the former residence of letter writer extraordinaire, Madame de Sévigné.*

Benedictine abbey crowns a rocky islet 78m (256 ft.) high, at the border of Normandy and Brittany. The island is connected to the mainland by a causeway; massive walls measuring more than half a mile in circumference surround the abbey. It's a steep climb up the Grande Rue, lined with 15th- and 16th-century houses, to reach the **Abbaye du Mont-St-Michel** (☎ 02-33-89-80-00; www.monuments-nationaux. fr). In the 8th century, St. Aubert, the bishop of Avranches, founded an oratory on this spot. A Benedictine monastery, founded in 966 by Richard I, replaced it. This burned in 1203, and Philippe-Auguste financed the building of an abbey later in the 13th century.

Ramparts encircle the abbey church and a three-tiered ensemble of 13th-century buildings called **La Merveille** that rise to the pointed church spire. This terraced complex is one of Europe's most important Gothic monuments, a citadel in which the concept of an independent France was nurtured during the darkest years of the English occupation of Aquitaine. On the second terrace of La Merveille is one of Mont-St-Michel's largest and most beautiful rooms, a 13th-century hall known as the **Salle des Chevaliers.** Crowning the mountain's summit is the **Eglise Abbatiale** (not to be confused with the parish church, Eglise St-Pierre, lower on the mountain). Begun in the 11th century, the abbey church consists of a Romanesque nave and transept, plus a choir in flamboyant Gothic style. The rectangular refectory dates from 1212,

and the cloisters with their pink granite columns are from 1225. **Kids Archeoscope,** chemin de la Ronde (☎ 02-33-89-01-85), is a small theater that presents *L'Eau et La Lumière (Water and Light),* celebrating the legend and lore of Mont-St-Michel and its role as a preserver of French medieval nationalism. The 30-minute show begins every 30 to 60 minutes between 9:30am and 5:30pm. The adjacent **Musée de la Mer,**

Visiting La Merveille

The **Abbaye du Mont-St-Michel** is open May through September daily from 9am to 7pm, and October to April daily from 9:30am to 6pm; from June to September, it's also open Monday through Saturday from 9pm to 1am (last entrance at midnight). Everything is closed January 1, May 1, and December 25. Mass begins at 12:15pm Tuesday through Sunday. Entrance includes a guided group tour—tours in French depart at intervals of 30 to 45 minutes, depending on the season, and there are usually two to four English-language tours per day—but you can also wander around on your own. Admission is 8.50€ for adults, 5€ for students and ages 18 to 25, and free for ages 17 and under. A combined ticket to all four attractions costs 16€ adults, 13€ students, 9€ ages 10-18, free for children 9 and under. All museums are open daily 9am to 5pm, except the Archeoscope.

Grande Rue (☎ 02-33-89-02-02) showcases marine crafts throughout history; the ecology of the local tidal flats; and illustrations of the French government's ongoing project intended to reactivate the tidal cleansing of the nearby marshes. **Musée Grévin (Musée Historique de Mont-St-Michel),** chemin de la Ronde (☎ 02-33-89-02-02), traces the history of the abbey. Another museum that's worth a visit is the **Logis Tiphaine,** Grande Rue (☎ 02-33-89-02-02), a 15th-century home originally under the control of the Duguesclin family, noted defenders of the fortress against English intrigue. In the building, next to the Eglise St-Pierre, you'll find furniture and accessories from that era, and an ostensible sense of pride in the fortress's durability as a bastion of all things French. ☼ 1 day. Mont-St-Michel Tourist Office, Corps de Garde des Bourgeois (Guard Room, left of the town gate). ☎ 02-33-60-14-30. www.ot-montsaintmichel.com/index.htm.

From Mont-St-Michel, take A84 south (toll road), exit at junction 29, and then take N12 to Fougères and D798 to Vitré (71km/44 miles).

⑥ Vitré. On the border of Normandy and Brittany, you are back in the land of castles, with the fortified towns of Fougères and Vitré only 30km (19 miles) apart. The medieval kids **Château de Vitré** (☎ 02-99-75-04-54; Apr–June 10am–noon and 2–5:30pm; July–Sept daily 10am–6pm; Oct–Mar Sun–Mon 2–5:30pm, Wed–Fri 10am–noon, closed Tues and mornings Sat–Mon), largely built by Guy XV de Laval, is one of Brittany's most impressive fortresses, with its pencil-point turrets and fortified gatehouse. A few kilometers southeast of Vitré on D88 is the **Château des Rochers-Sévigné** (☎ 02-99-96-76-51; Apr–Sept daily 10:30am–12:30pm and 2–6:30pm; Oct–Mar Fri–Sun 2–5:30pm), the former home of Mme. de Sévigné, the voracious letter writer and chronicler of life at the court of Louis XIV. The park, the chapel, and some of her rooms are open to the public. Combined ticket for both châteaux is 4€ adults, 2.50€ children. ☼ 1 day. Vitré Tourist Office, Place Général De Gaule. ☎ 02-99-75-04-46. www.ot-vitre.fr.

Continue to Carnac to spend the night. You can travel all the way to Vannes on D777, a total of 173km (107 miles); alternatively, take N157, N24, and N166 to Vannes, a total of 187km (116

> *Standing at attention, Carnac's megaliths haven't budged in more than 5,000 years.*

miles). In Vannes, pick up N165; after 22km (14 miles), at Auray, follow signs to Carnac.

⑦ ★★★ kids Carnac. The menhirs and tumuli that pepper the landscape here in amazing density are from the Megalithic era, between 5000 and 2000 B.C. The largest grouping of such megaliths in the world, the ★★ **Alignements de Carnac** (☎ 02-97-52-60-03; www.carnac.monuments-nationaux.fr; admission 4.50€, free for ages 17 and under; May–Jun daily 9am–7pm, July–Aug daily 9am–8pm, Sept–Apr daily 10am–5pm), encompass 4,000 standing stones along a 4km (2½-mile) site. Twelve kilometers (7½ miles) to the east, the **Locmariaquer** site (☎ 02-97-57-37-59; www.locmariaquer.monuments-nationaux.fr; admission 5€ adults, free for ages 17 and under; May–June daily 10am–6pm; July–Aug daily 10am–7pm; Sept–Apr daily 10am–12.30pm and 2–5:15pm) includes three prehistoric monuments: the **Table du Marchard tomb;** the **Grand Menhir Brisé,** thought to be the largest stone ever worked by prehistoric man; and the **Er Grah** funerary structure, 140m (459 ft.) long. Carnac's **Musée de Préhistoire,** 10 place de la Chapelle (☎ 02-97-52-22-04; www.museedecarnac.com; Apr–June and Sept Wed–Mon 10am–12:30pm and 2–6pm; July–Aug daily 10am–6pm; Oct–Mar Wed–Mon 10am–12:30pm and 2–5:30pm; closed bank holidays and Jan 5–31), exhibits a particularly rich collection of objects found in local excavations. ☼ 1 day. For more on Carnac, see p. 208, ④.

THE LONGEST DAY

The Allied Invasion of Normandy BY KATHRYN WILLIAMS

IN THE EARLY MORNING HOURS OF JUNE 6, 1944, Allied forces crossed the English Channel to storm the beaches of Normandy in the historic operation that would mark the turning point of World War II. Around 156,000 American, British, Canadian, and other Allied troops, supported by more than 5,000 naval vessels and 11,000 aircraft, faced German machine-gun nests, pillboxes, concrete fortifications, and seawalls. Initially hampered by disorganization and confusion, the forces fought past Nazi defenses to rendezvous with paratroops dropped behind enemy lines and with members of the French Resistance. Before their departure from England, General Dwight D. Eisenhower told the Allied Expeditionary Force, "You are about to embark upon the Great Crusade. . . . We will accept nothing less than full Victory!" The push that began on the beaches of Normandy eventually liberated occupied France and paved the way for an invasion of Germany. Less than a year after D-Day, Nazi forces surrendered unconditionally.

The Heroes

While there are no official figures for the casualties on D-Day, it is estimated that around 10,000 American, British, and Canadian troops and their allies were wounded, and more than 4,000 gave their life in the invasion. (German casualties are estimated at between 4,000 and 9,000.) Many of these soldiers are buried in the Normandy American Cemetery and Memorial overlooking Omaha Beach. The solemn white crosses marking the graves of 9,387 military dead cover 70 hectares (173 acres). The cemetery is open to the public daily, except December 25 and January 1.

Blood on the Sand

OMAHA

The amphibious assault by 43,250 troops of the American 1st and 29th Infantry Divisions began on this beach at 6:30am. Omaha was the most heavily defended beach, and German resistance was fierce. Most of the estimated 2,000 to 4,000 casualties occurred in the first few hours, and fighting continued through the night.

UTAH

The westernmost landing zone, Utah was less fortified than Omaha. The biggest obstacle the 4th Infantry Division faced here was flooding and rough terrain. By the end of the day, the Allied hold on the beach was secure, and troops were pressing inland to hook up with the 82nd Airborne Division near Ste-Mère-Eglise.

GOLD

With the help of naval and aerial bombardment, around 25,000 troops of the British 50th Infantry Division were able to take Gold Beach and obtain their objectives with relatively light casualties. They met up with Canadian forces from Juno Beach.

JUNO

It's estimated that the first wave of landing forces from the Canadian 3rd Infantry Division suffered 50% casualties. Still, the troops were able to press inland through beach exits secured by airborne forces and link up with the British who had landed at Gold Beach. They went on to advance toward Caen with the British 50th and 3rd Infantry Divisions.

SWORD

The 28,845-soldier-strong British 3rd Infantry Division faced a counterattack by a German tank division that halted movement toward the unit's ultimate objective—the city of Caen, 12km (7½ miles) south—but that was neutralized with only light casualties.

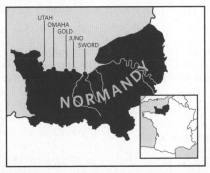

UTAH
OMAHA
GOLD
JUNO
SWORD

NORMANDY

Brittany's Wild Islands

Ranging from the desolate landscape of Sein to the smart holiday resorts of Belle-Ile-en-Mer, Brittany's islands are a chance to escape from business as usual. These precious, beautifully preserved scenes are a haven, sometimes traffic-free, for walkers and cyclists. They also provide the opportunity to learn about the extreme life of their past inhabitants, and to spot lighthouses. Each is easy to visit on a day trip, but it's more rewarding to stay a little longer. In this part of the region, some hotels insist on half-board during high season.

> *There's always time to drop a lazy line: The laid-back pace on Brittany's islands inspires relaxation.*

START Pointe de l'Arcouest, for ferries to Ile de Bréhat (10 minutes), is 142km (88 miles) northwest of Rennes and 6km (3¾ miles) from Paimpol.

❶ Ile de Bréhat. Just 2km (1¼ miles) off the north coast of Brittany, near Paimpol, Ile de Bréhat is in fact an archipelago composed of two main islands, each about a kilometer in

length and joined by a small bridge (except at high tide, when the bridge is inundated), and several tiny islets. Despite its small surface area, Bréhat has an amazingly varied landscape, with windswept meadows of hemlock and yarrow sloping down to pink rocks on the north side, and a Gulf Stream–influenced environment of palm trees, eucalyptus, and mimosa on the south. A car-free paradise that

1	Ile de Bréhat
2	Ile de Batz
3	Ile de Ouessant
4	Ile de Sein
5	Belle-Ile-en-Mer

is home to many rare plants and birds, Bréhat is easy to explore on bike or on foot, as it takes only an hour to cross the two islands. On the way you'll see colorful, well-kept cottages that are mainly holiday homes for Parisians. Bréhat's village, **Le Bourg,** is 500m (1,640 ft.) up from the harbor, **Le Port Clos;** there you'll find a few shops, a post office, a bank, and an ATM. A market takes place most days in the main square. A handful of hotels and bed-and-breakfasts can be found here. **La Vieille Auberge,** at the entrance to the village (☎ 02-96-20-00-24; www.brehat-vieilleauberge.eu; 15 units; doubles half-board 140€–156€, MC, V), is an old pirate's house built in 1711, with simply furnished rooms and a garden restaurant. For a sea view, choose the **Hôtel Bellevue** at Le Port Clos (☎ 02-96-20-00-05; www.hotel-bellevue-brehat.fr; 17 units; doubles half-board 168€–210€; room only 87€–110€ in low season; MC, V). The Bellevue has bikes for rent, as does the bike shop **Dalibot** (☎ 02-96-20-03-51; 5€ an hour, 13€ a day; open Apr–Sept). Le Bourg gets busy in summer, but it's easy to escape the crowds on the north island with a wonderfully rugged walk—don't forget your binoculars. The best beaches are in the south; there's a sailing and dive center

> *One of the best ways to get around the islands is by pedal power.*

at **Plage du Guerzido,** Les Albatros (☎ 02-96-20-07-24; www.les-albatros.com). Among various handcrafts on Bréhat is the glassmaking studio **Les Verreries de Bréhat** (☎ 02-96-20-09-09; www.verreriesdebrehat.com;

admission 2€ June 15–Sept 15, free for children 9 and under, free for everyone in off-season; Easter–Sept daily 10am–6pm; Oct–Easter Mon–Fri 10am–6pm). Housed in the old citadel between the port and Le Bourg, the studio sells strikingly contemporary handmade door handles, banister finials, and lights.

Les Vedettes de Bréhat (☎ 02-96-55-79-50; www.vedettesdebrehat.com) sails from Arcouest to Bréhat year-round: half-hourly in July and August, hourly April–June and September, and twice-hourly October–March. In summer, the first ferry leaves at 8:15am and the last return boat leaves at 7:45pm. The crossing takes 10 minutes. The round trip is 9€ adults, 7.50€ ages 3–11, and free for children 2 and under. Leave your car in Pointe de l'Arcouest. The same company runs excursions along the coast and around the island. Bréhat Tourist Office. ☎ 02-96-20-04-15. www.brehat-infos.fr.

❷ **Ile de Batz.** The 3.5km-long (2¼-mile) Ile de Batz is a working island, crisscrossed by a patchwork of 25 market-gardening farms with serried rows of potatoes, cauliflower, shallots, parsley, fennel, and lettuces. This small farm is 50% organic, and growers use cart horses to plough and fertilize the fields with seaweed. Fishing, too, is a viable industry, and seaweed is harvested for the pharmaceutical, cosmetic, and food industries. There is plenty to do, with beaches, coastal paths, landmarks such as the "serpent hole" (scene of a local legend), and the ruins of **Chapelle Ste-Anne;** an annual pilgrimage to the chapel, with participants in traditional costumes, is held the last weekend of July. On the island's eastern tip is the **Jardin Exotique Georges Delaselle** (☎ 02-98-61-75-65; www.jardin-georgesdelaselle.fr; admission 4.60€ adults, 4€ seniors and students, 2€ ages 10–16; April–June and Sept–Oct Mon and Wed–Sun 2–6pm; July–Aug daily 1–6:30pm; closed Nov–Mar). This former garden of a 19th-century plant collector was recently restored to its former glory; 2,000 species from around the world include a magnificent collection of palms. There is a guided tour on Sunday at 3pm (7€) and in July and August also on Tuesday at 10am (8€). The island has two hotels, the **Grand Hôtel Morvan,** in Pors Kernoc (☎ 02-98-61-78-06; 38 units, 12 with en suite bathrooms; doubles 60€; V), and the **Hôtel Roch'Armor** (☎ 02-98-61-78-28; www.rocharmor.net; 10 units; doubles 75€; V) near the jetty.

> *Winds gust over the granite-strewn Ile d'Ouessant year-round, earning it the nickname "Garden of Tempests."*

> Ile de Sein is famed for its rocky waters, shipwrecks, and fishermen's houses.

It is easy to visit the island as a day trip. Sailings to Batz with **CFTM** (www.vedettes-ile-de-batz.com), **Armein** (www.armein.fr), and **Armor Excursions** (www.vedettes.armor.ile.de.batz.fr) depart from Roscoff's port roughly every half-hour in July and August, every hour April to June and September, and every 2 hours October to March. In summer, the first ferry leaves at 8am, and the last returns at 7:30pm. Round trip is 9€ adults, 7.50€ ages 3–11, and free for children 2 and under. One way is 7.50€ adults, 3.75€ ages 4 to 10. **Tourist information:** www.iledebatz.com. Roscoff, 212km (132 miles) northwest of Rennes, is the sailing point for Ile de Batz, a 15-minute ferry ride away.

❸ **Ile d'Ouessant.** If you like extremities, don't miss out on a trip to Ile d'Ouessant (Ushant Island)—the westernmost point in France. The 8km-long (5-mile) island, shaped like a crab's claw, sticks out in the Atlantic after a series of other, smaller islands, mostly unpopulated (except for Molène). A wild and blustery land, it resembles Ireland's Aran Islands, with its low-lying vegetation, cliffs, and little thatched crofts. In getting here, you may encounter rough seas even in summer. If you have only a day, organize a tour of the island by taxi.

We recommend staying longer, however, in one of the hotels in Lampoul, such as the family-run **Le Fromveur** (☎ 02-98-48-81-30; 15 units; doubles 48€; V) or **Le Roc'h Ar Mor** (☎ 02-98-48-80-19; 15 units; doubles 87€; V), which also runs the most buzzing pub on the main street. Both have good restaurants, so half-board is not a bad idea, but there are also several good *crêperies* on the island. Hiring a mountain bike will give you the freedom to fully explore Ile d'Ouessant, which is something of an open-air lighthouse museum: There are six lighthouses, ranging from one built by Vauban in 1700 to the Tour Radar built in 1982 (following the Amoco-Cadiz disaster) to the Créac'h, which is one of the most powerful lighthouses in the world. Créac'h houses a lighthouse museum, the **Musée de Phares et Balises** (☎ 02-98-48-80-70; May–June daily 11am–5pm; July–Aug daily 10:30am–6pm; July 9–Aug 20 also Tues–Fri 9–11pm).

Known as the "Island of Women," Ouessant is a place where men were men, and the women were, too; they tended the land, mended the roofs and roads, and sustained themselves while their husbands were out at sea—sometimes never to return. This difficult way of life becomes easier to understand after visiting

> *Postcard-perfect Belle-Ile-en-Mer was occupied by the English between 1761 and 1763.*

the **Ecomusée des Traditions Ouessantines** (☎ 02-98-48-86-37), housed in two traditional dwellings, 1km (⅔ mile) and 2km (1¼ miles) west of Lampoul, on the upper of the two crab's pincers. A sheltered beach is found just south of Lampoul.

Penn Ar Bed (☎ 02-98-80-80-80; www.pennarbed.fr) runs ferries to Ouessant. The most regular ferry from Brest leaves at 8am or 8:30am and returns at around 5pm. Round-trip fare to visit the three islands (Ouessant, Molène, and Sein) is 30.20€ adults, 24.20€ ages 12 to 16, and 18.25€ ages 4 to 11. **Finistair**

Getting Around Belle-Ile

Crossing with your car is expensive; depending on how many are in your party and the length of your stay, it may be more economical to rent a car there. Try **Locatourisle** (☎ 02-97-31-83-56; www.locatourisle.com) or **Belle-Ile Auto** (☎ 02-97-31-30-93; www.belle-ile-auto.fr) at the port. The island's bus service, **Taol Mor**, runs only from April to September; timetables are at www.cars-verts.com/taolmor.html.

(☎ 02-98-84-64-87; www.finistair.fr; round trip 93€ adults, 57€ ages 2–12) runs flights to Ouessant daily from Brest. **Ouessant Tourist Office**. ☎ 02-98-48-85-83. www.ot-ouessant.fr. Ouessant is reached by ferry from Brest (2 hr.), 243km (151 miles) west of Rennes; from Le Conquet (1 hr.), 23km (14 miles) west of Brest; or, on certain days in high season, from Camaret (1 hr.) on the Crozon Peninsula.

❹ **Ile de Sein.** "Who sees Ouessant sees his blood/Who sees Molène sees his sorrow/Who sees Sein sees his end/Who sees Groix sees his cross." So goes an old sea shanty in Brittany, reminding people of the tempestuous weather conditions of Sein, which nevertheless recalls in its name the softest and most comforting of things: a breast. A flat island, often shrouded in fog, Sein is famed for the bravery of its islanders, who rescued several hundred sailors from shipwrecks in the 17th and 18th centuries, and who, to a man, responded to General de Gaulle's 1940 call for forces to come to London and become part of his liberating army. A monument at Men Neï commemorates this sacrifice, and the story is recounted in the **Musée Jardin de** l'Espérance, quai des Paimpolais (☎ 02-98-70-90-35; June–Sept daily 2–6pm), while the Musée de la SNSM, quai des Paimpolais (☎ 02-98-70-91-37; June–Sept daily 2–6pm), is about Sein's shipwreck history. Admission (to both museums and lighthouse) is 4€ adults, 2€ ages 7 to 14, and free for children 6 and under. There are also some ancient Celtic standing stones known as "the talkers." There are no hotels on the island, but there are bed-and-breakfasts and several crêperies. For ferry information, contact Ferries Penn Ar Bed (☎ 02-98-80-80-80; www.pennarbed.fr). Tourist information: www.mairie-iledesein.com. Ile de Sein is 8km (5 miles) off Pointe de Raz in the far west of Brittany. Ferries (1 hr.) go from Audierne, 36km (22 miles) west of Quimper, and less regularly from Brest and from Camaret on the Crozon Peninsula.

5 Belle-Ile-en-Mer. Brittany's largest island, at almost 20km x 9km (12 miles x 5½ miles), with 100km (62 miles) of coast, is also its most commercial, open to traffic and with plenty of accommodations and restaurants. Belle-Ile's full name, "beautiful island in the sea," rings true: Its beaches and coastline are exceptional. The island was appreciated in the 19th century by author Gustave Flaubert, actress Sarah Bernhardt, and artist Claude Monet, but its history goes deeper, with prehistoric megaliths, a mention by Ptolemy, and fortifications by Henri II and Louis XIV. There are four areas, each centered around a town. In **Sauzon,** you can visit the "Jean and Jeanne" menhirs and **Sarah Bernhardt's fort,** Pointe des Poulains (☎ 02-97-31-61-29; admission 4€ adults, 2€ children; Apr–Sept daily 10:30am–5:30pm). **Le Palais** is the capital, home of the **Vauban Citadel** (☎ 02-97-31-84-17; www.citadellevauban.com; admission 8€ adults, 3.50€ ages 12–16, free for children 11 and under; Apr–June and Sept–Oct 9am–6pm, July–Aug daily 9am–7pm, Nov–Mar 9am–5pm). **Bangor** has a rocky coastline punctuated by sandy beaches. **Locmaria** is distinguished by cliffs, wide beaches, and watersport facilities. Car and passenger ferries from Quiberon to Belle-Ile—between 5 and 13 a day, according to season—are run by **La Compagnie Océane** (☎ 02-97-35-02-00; www.compagnie-oceane.fr) and **SMN** (☎ 08-20-05-60-00; www.smn-navigation.fr). Return fare in high

Where to Stay on Belle-Ile

Belle-Ile has a wealth of attractive accommodations. Here are four of our top picks:

In Le Palais, stay inside the citadel itself at the ★★ **Citadelle Vauban Hôtel-Musée** (☎ 02-97-31-84-17; www.citadellevauban.com; 60 units; doubles 125€–600€; AE, DC, MC, V; closed mid-Oct to March). Sixty sumptuous rooms and suites have been decorated with antiques, brocade curtains, and gilded mirrors. Choose between a courtyard or a breathtaking sea view. The citadel also has a restaurant and a lovely terrace with a fountain.

Three kilometers (1¾ miles) outside Le Palais and 500m (1,640 ft.) from the sea, **Château Bordeneo** (☎ 02-97-31-80-77; www.chateau-bordeneo.fr; 5 units; doubles 154€–214€; MC, V) is a luxury guesthouse with its own heated swimming pool (April–Oct); massages or biokinergie sessions can be booked in your room. Its five spacious and beautifully decorated rooms include two with private terrace.

In Sauzon, kids **Le Cardinal**, Port Bellec (☎ 02-97-31-61-60; www.hotel-cardinal.fr; 65 units; 95€–170€; AE, DC, MC, V), is a modern hotel next to a pretty cove, with an attractive decked swimming pool. It features family rooms, buffet meals, and imaginative activities for children. In high season, it's bookable only by the week.

In Bangor, on the island's wild coast, ★ **Le Grand Large,** Goulphar (☎ 02-97-31-80-92; www.hotelgrandlarge.com; 35 units; doubles 119€–239€; MC, V), has glorious ocean views from its promontory, which are best appreciated from one of the hotel's private terraces. With its own gastronomic restaurant, it makes a very romantic getaway.

season is 30.15€ adults, 19€ ages 4 to 17; car rentals range from 148.30€ to 328.30€. Ferries from Vannes are run by **Navix** (www.navix.fr). Belle-Ile-en-Mer Tourist Office, quai Bonnelle, Le Palais (☎ 02-97-31-81-93. www.belle-ile.com). Belle-Ile is 45 minutes by ferry from Quiberon, which is 186km (116 miles) south of Carnac and 156km (97 miles) southwest of Rennes.

Rouen

Over the course of its history, the capital of Normandy has taken a battering from the English: They burned Joan of Arc at the stake here in 1431; and they bombed the city while it was under German occupation during World War II. But Rouen's pride was restored when its magnificent spires and medieval streets were painstakingly rebuilt using traditional techniques. Today the city betrays no clues of its past suffering. Vieux Rouen, on the right bank of the Seine River, is a joy to explore on foot.

> In 1431 Joan of Arc was burned at the stake here on Rouen's Place du Vieux Marché.

START Rouen is 135km (84 miles) northwest of Paris.

❶ ★★★ Cathédrale Notre-Dame de Rouen. The sense of déjà vu from Monet's paintings doesn't detract from the wonder of seeing this Gothic masterpiece up close. Its main door is garnished with sculptures depicting the Tree of Jesse. Consecrated in 1063, the cathedral, a symphony of lacy stonework, was reconstructed after suffering damage during World War II. Two towers distinguish it: **Tour de Beurre** (Butter Tower) was financed by the faithful who were willing to pay for the privilege of eating butter during Lent. Containing a carillon of 56 bells, **Tour Lanterne** (Lantern Tower)—built in 1877 from 740 tons of iron and bronze—rises to almost 150m (492 ft.). While the cathedral's interior is generally uniform, the choir is a masterpiece, with 14 soaring pillars. The Escalier de la Librairie (Booksellers' Stairway), in the north wing of the transept, is adorned with a stained-glass rose window that dates, in part, from the 1500s. The 13th-century chancel is beautiful. Tombs

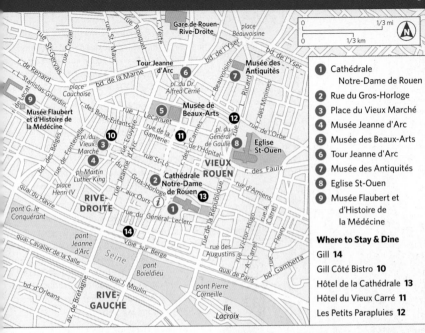

The map legend:

1. Cathédrale Notre-Dame de Rouen
2. Rue du Gros-Horloge
3. Place du Vieux Marché
4. Musée Jeanne d'Arc
5. Musée des Beaux-Arts
6. Tour Jeanne d'Arc
7. Musée des Antiquités
8. Eglise St-Ouen
9. Musée Flaubert et d'Histoire de la Médécine

Where to Stay & Dine

Gill **14**

Gill Côté Bistro **10**

Hôtel de la Cathédrale **13**

Hôtel du Vieux Carré **11**

Les Petits Parapluies **12**

include that of Richard the Lionheart—containing only his heart (see p. 154, **6**). ⏱ 1 hr. Place de la Cathédrale. ☎ 02-35-71-85-65. www. cathedrale-rouen.net. Free admission. Summer Mon 2–6pm, Tues–Sat 7:30am–7pm, Sun 8am–6pm; winter Tues–Sat 7:30am–noon and 2–6pm.

2 ★★ Rue du Gros-Horloge. One of Vieux Rouen's prettiest streets is closed to traffic, making it easy for pedestrians to browse in its small boutiques. It is named for the large Renaissance timepiece mounted on a bridge that spans the street.

3 ★ Place du Vieux Marché. It was here, at the Old Marketplace, that Joan of Arc was executed for heresy; on May 30, 1431, she was burned at a stake, and her ashes were tossed into the Seine. Today, the bustling square is filled with restaurants and hosts a morning food market every day but Monday. The medieval facades stand in stark contrast to the audaciously modern Eglise Ste-Jeanne d'Arc.

4 kids Musée Jeanne d'Arc. This small waxworks museum, in a vaulted cellar that dates back to the time of Joan of Arc herself, tells the story of the French heroine via scenes from her life, engravings, and a reproduction of her armor. ⏱ 40 min. 33 place

> Though most associated with Claude Monet, Rouen's Gothic cathedral was also immortalized by Pop artist Roy Fox Lichtenstein.

> *Joan of Arc was sentenced to life imprisonment in the beautiful, high-Gothic Eglise St-Ouen.*

du Vieux-Marché. ☎ 02-35-88-02-70. www.jeanne-darc.com. Admission 4€ adults, 2.50€ students and ages 17 and under. Apr–Sept daily 9:30am–7pm; Oct–Mar daily 10am–noon and 2–6:30pm.

⑤ ★★★ Musée des Beaux-Arts. This is one of France's most important provincial museums, with more than 65 rooms of art ranging from medieval primitives to contemporary paintings. You'll find portraits by Gérard David and works by Delacroix and Jean Auguste Ingres (seek out his *La Belle Zélie*—a portrait of Madame Aymon); a David retable (altarpiece), *La Vierge et les saints (The Virgin and the Saints)*, is a masterpiece. One salon is devoted to Géricault, including his portrait of Delacroix. Other works here are by Veronese, Velázquez, Caravaggio, Rubens, Poussin, Fragonard, and Corot, and by Impressionists such as Monet,

including several paintings of the Rouen cathedral. ⏱ 2 hr. Esplanade de Marcel Duchamp. ☎ 02-35-71-28-40. www.rouen-musees.com. Admission 5€ adults, 3€ reduced, free for ages 25 and under. Daily 10am–6pm.

⑥ Tour Jeanne d'Arc. The last remaining tower of the château where Joan of Arc was tried and imprisoned gives an idea of the misery she must have suffered. ⏱ 20 min. 61 rue du Bouvreuil. ☎ 02-35-98-16-21. Admission 1.50€ adults; free for ages 18 and under. Wed–Sat and Mon 10am–12:30pm and 2–6:30pm; Sun 2–6:30pm.

⑦ Musée des Antiquités. A Medieval cloister provides an attractive setting for Greek and Gallo-Roman archaeological finds as well as Merovingian, medieval, and Renaissance *objets d'art*. ⏱ 1 hr. 198 rue Beauvoisine. ☎ 02-35-98-55-10. Admission 3€ adults, 2€ reduced; free for ages 17 and under. Tues–Sat 10am–12:15pm and 1:30–5:30pm, Sun 2–6pm.

⑧ ★★ Eglise St-Ouen. This church is the outgrowth of a 7th-century Benedictine abbey. Flanked by four turrets, its 115m (377-ft.) octagonal lantern tower is called "the ducal crown of Normandy." The nave is from the 15th century, its choir is from the 14th (with 18th-century railings), and its stained glass is from the 14th to the 16th. On May 23, 1431, Joan of Arc was taken to the cemetery here, and officials sentenced her to be burned at the stake unless she renounced her visions. She signed a retraction, but a week later they burned her at the stake anyway. ⏱ 40 min. Place du Général-de-Gaulle. ☎ 02-32-08-31-01. Free admission. Mar–Oct Tues–Sun 10am–noon and 2–6pm; Nov–Feb Tues–Sun 10am–noon and 2–5:30pm.

⑨ Musée Flaubert et d'Histoire de la Médecine. Gustave Flaubert, author of *Madame Bovary,* was born in the director's quarters of Rouen's public hospital, where his father was the director, in 1821. The room in which he was born is intact. You'll see the glass door that separated the Flauberts from the patients. Family furniture and medical paraphernalia are also displayed. ⏱ 1 hr. Ancien Hôtel-Dieu, 51 rue de Lecat. ☎ 02-35-15-59-95. Admission 3€ adults, 1.50€ ages 18–25, free for ages 17 and under. Tues–Sat 10am–noon and 2–6pm.

Where to Stay & Dine in Rouen

> *Life's simple pleasures: On a sunny day, enjoy breakfast in the Hôtel de la Cathédrale's flower-filled courtyard.*

★★★ Gill RIVE-DROITE *MODERN FRENCH*
The minimalist decor and high-tech lighting of Rouen's best restaurant is an appropriate backdrop for the Michelin-starred cuisine of Gilles Tournadre. The best dishes are pan-fried foie gras of duckling, with caramelized turnips and a turnip-green salad; crayfish tails with tomato-and-black-pepper chutney; and Rouen-style pigeon with vegetables in rich consommé. 9 quai de la Bourse. ☎ 02-35-71-16-14. www.gill.fr. Reservations required far in advance. Main courses 30€–57€; fixed-price dinner 92€. AE, DC, MC, V. Lunch and dinner Tues–Sat. Closed Aug and 2 weeks in Apr.

Gill Côté Bistro OLD TOWN *FRENCH*
The affordable offshoot of Gill, this bistro serves elegantly presented bistro classics on its fixed-price lunch and dinner menus. The setting is contemporary, with puce chairs on the terrace. 14 place du Vieux Marché. ☎ 02-35-89-88-72. Fixed-price menu 22€. AE, DC, MC, V. Lunch and dinner daily.

Hôtel de la Cathédrale OLD TOWN
This modest but charming hotel, on a pedestrianized street beside the cathedral, has clean, traditional rooms (some with exposed timbers) and a patio flower garden. 12 rue St-Romain. ☎ 02-35-71-57-95. www.hotel-de-la-cathedrale.fr. 26 units. Doubles 69€–96€. AE, MC, V.

★ Hôtel du Vieux Carré CENTER
In a restored, half-timbered 18th-century house, this is one of the most charming and tranquil lodgings in Rouen, with rustic yet comfortable and tastefully decorated midsize guest rooms. Unusual for central Rouen, its restaurant opens onto a flower-filled courtyard. 34 rue Ganterie. ☎ 02-35-71-67-70. www.vieux-carre.fr. 13 units. Doubles 58€–65€. AE, MC, V.

Les Petits Parapluies OLD TOWN *FRENCH*
This lovely restaurant run by a husband-and-wife team inhabits a former umbrella factory with beamed ceilings. Hand-sourced luxury ingredients feature on the more expensive fixed-price menus. 46 rue Bourg l'Abbé. ☎ 02-35-88-55-26. www.lesptits-parapluies.com. Fixed-price menu 30€–62€. AE, MC, V. Lunch Tues–Fri and Sun, dinner Tues–Sat.

Where to Stay in Normandy

> *Hôtel Monet in Honfleur has 10 rooms like this one, all set around a flowery courtyard.*

Château de Bouceel MONT-ST-MICHEL
Nine kilometers (5⅔ miles) southeast of
Mont-St-Michel, this castle has been home to
the owner's family for centuries. Rooms are
exquisite, and the grounds are enchanting,
with geese and donkeys. Three former workers' cottages on the estate can be booked
by the week. Vergoncey. ☎ 02-33-48-34-61.
www.chateaudebouceel.com. 5 units. Doubles
120€–175€. AE, DC, MC, V.

Hôtel d'Argouges BAYEUX
This 18th-century hotel, set back from the
street in the heart of Bayeux, is a favorite
among tourists visiting the tapestry and the
Normandy beaches. The elegant, paneled dining room and checker-floored reception room
are grand, and the garden is relaxing. Guest

rooms are old-fashioned but comfortable.
21 rue Saint Patrice. ☎ 02-31-92-88-86. www.
hotel-dargouges.com. 28 units. Doubles 77€–
121€. AE, DC, MC, V.

★ **Hôtel de la Terrasse** VARENGEVILLE-
SUR-MER With its drawing-room piano and
English decor, this hotel feels like a private
home. Rooms have garden or sea views, and
guests can play tennis on the grounds. Half-
board is mandatory but an excellent value.
Guests dine on the terrace or in a glassed-in
room with sea views. Rte. de Vasterival. ☎ 02-
35-85-12-54. www.hotel-restaurant-la-terrasse.
com. 22 units. Doubles 104€–116€ with half-
board. AE, MC, V.

★ kids **Hôtel La Résidence** ETRETAT
In 1912, a local architect dismantled this
wooden 14th-century manor with gargoyles
and mysterious carvings and reassembled it
here. The exterior could give you nightmares,
but inside each room feels like an intimate

Travel Tip
For hotels in Rouen, see p. 227.

cocoon. Look at the website to choose your room, as each one is different. 4 bd. René Coty. ☎ 02-35-27-02-87. www.hotelsetretat.com. 15 units. Doubles 39€–120€. AE, MC, V.

Hôtel Mercure La Présidence DIEPPE
La Présidence is by far the smartest hotel on Dieppe's seafront boulevard, convenient to town and the quayside restaurants, with its own sleek restaurant. The attractive, contemporary decor combines nautical duckboarding, wooden laminate floors, toile de Jouy bedcovers, and well-considered lighting. 1 bd. de Verdun. ☎ 02-35-84-31-31. www.hotel-la-presidence.com. 85 units. Doubles 125€–140€. AE, DC, MC, V.

★ Hôtel Monet HONFLEUR
Clients rave about the owners of this modest hotel, prettily decorated in colors reminiscent of Monet's Normandy palette. Five minutes from the town center and the port, it is up a steep hill with a view of Honfleur. Reserve well in advance. Rue Carrière des Puits.

☎ 02-31-89-00-90. www.hotel-monet-honfleur. com. 10 units. Doubles 62€–88€. MC, V.

La Ferme de la Chapelle FECAMP
In an old priory farm on the cliffs overlooking Fécamp's bay and lighthouse, the "Chapel Farm" has old stones and warm, modern interiors. Rooms face an interior courtyard with a swimming pool. Three apartments sleep four or five. The restaurant serves menus for 25€ and 35€. Rte. du Phare. ☎ 02-35-10-12-12. www.fermedelachapelle.fr. 22 units. Doubles 85€–95€. AE, MC, V.

★★ Villa Josephine DEAUVILLE
A couple of minutes from the beach, this boutique hotel is in the villa originally built for the mayor of Deauville. Rooms are lusciously decorated in the rich fabrics, rare colors, and antiques of the Second Empire. Breakfast is a delight in the tea-green dining room that opens onto the garden. 23 rue des Villas. ☎ 02-31-14-18-00. www.villajosephine.fr. 7 units. Doubles 110€–380€. AE, MC, V.

Where to Dine in Normandy

Augusto DEAUVILLE SEAFOOD
Just off place Morny, Augusto is Deauville's oldest restaurant—the best place in the region to eat lobster. Classic French steaks, duck, snails, and John Dory help cater to all tastes. 27 rue Désiré le Hoc. ☎ 02-31-88-34-49. www. restaurant-augusto.com. Main courses 20€–25€; menu 35€. AE, MC, V.

La Rapière BAYEUX FRENCH
In one of Bayeux's narrow old streets, this little gem of a restaurant serves cuisine with a Norman slant. Herbs and floral aromas are used inventively in dishes such as turbot flavored with lavender and crème brûlée with jasmine. 53 rue St Jean. ☎ 02-31-21-05-45. www. larapiere.net. Lunch menu 16€, dinner menus 27.50€–33.50€, main courses 17€–25€. AE, MC, V. Lunch and dinner Fri–Tues.

★★ L'Endroit HONFLEUR BISTRO
Hidden away from the port-side restaurants, L'Endroit is the place to eat in Honfleur. The local chef specializes in slow-cooked meat

dishes and, of course, fresh fish. The setting is hip—a refurbished architect's workshop with an open kitchen and a kitsch 1950s theme. 3 rue Charles-et-Paul Bréard. ☎ 02-31-88-08-43. Menus 18€–22€; main courses 15€–20€. MC, V. Lunch and dinner Wed–Sun.

★ Le Tripot AVRANCHES (MONT-ST-MICHEL)
CREATIVE FRENCH If you're visiting Mont-St-Michel and value good food, drive to Le Tripot, 20km (12 miles) away in Avranches. You can see the mount across the bay as you feast, under a glass skylight, on dishes such as salmon mousse with citrus fruits, chaud-froid of red tuna, and veal with tarragon. 11 rue du Tripot. ☎ 02-33-60-59-25. www.letripot.fr. Menus 17€–25€; main courses 15€–20€. DC, MC, V. Lunch and dinner Tues–Sun.

Dining Tip
Note that many of the lodgings in the "Where to Stay" section house fine restaurants. For restaurants in Rouen, see p. 227.

Where to Stay in Brittany

> *Although its restored 16th-century rooms have graced the pages of design magazines, Hôtel de la Vinotière is affordable and kid-friendly.*

kids Hôtel de la Vinotière LE CONQUET

On the Atlantic, this 16th-century ship-owner's house, with stone walls and a spiral staircase, has been beautifully decorated with stone-colored linens and actual pebbles. It has appeared in several design magazines, but it's comfortable. It's also kid-friendly: Several rooms are designed for families, and it's convenient if you're visiting Océanopolis. 1 rue du Lieutenant Jourden. ☎ 02-98-89-17-79. www.lavinotiere.fr. 10 units. Doubles 60€–125€. AE, MC, V.

Hôtel Emeraude Plage DINARD

A good value, this hotel has a superb hammam (Turkish bath), with a plunge pool bathed in colored lights and a fitness suite. Mahogany, colonial-style furniture and luxury thread counts are part of the decor inspired by the grand age of travel. Accommodations range from neat little rooms to spacious suites with terraces overlooking the sea, only 30m

(98 ft.) away. 1 bd Albert 1er. ☎ 02-99-46-15-79. www.hotelemeraudeplage.com. 47 units. Doubles 107€–243€. AE, MC, V.

★ Hôtel Gradlon QUIMPER

One of the most delightful places to stay in Quimper is this converted townhouse in a calm neighborhood, 5 minutes from the Old Town. Decor is flowery but carefully considered. Guests take continental breakfast (11€) in an interior garden with roses. 30 rue de Brest. ☎ 02-98-95-04-39. www.hotel-gradlon. fr. 20 units. Doubles 80€–160€. AE, DC, MC, V. Closed Nov–Mar.

★ Hôtel Kermoor CONCARNEAU (QUIMPER)

The best place to get away from it all is on the beach at Concarneau, a historic walled town 25km (16 miles) southeast of Quimper. You can actually hear the waves from the rooms with sea views, and many have private terraces. The hotel is decorated with furniture

> *Several of La Chaumière Roz-Aven's comfortable rooms overlook the river.*

and objects salvaged from American and European freighters dating from 1910 to the present. Off-season, waves bash the windows of the cozy hotel bar. **37 rue des Sables Blancs.** ☎ 02-98-97-02-96. www.hotel-kermor.com. 11 units. Doubles 105€–155€. MC, V.

Hôtel Quic en Groigne ST-MALO
This popular hotel sits on a quiet street in the very heart of the corsairs' walled town, only minutes from the beach. It's spanking clean and nicely decorated with modern bathrooms. The friendly and flexible owners make everyone's stay a delight. **8 rue d'Estrées.** ☎ 02-99-20-22-20. www.quic-en-groigne.com. 15 units. Doubles 63€–85€. MC, V. Closed Jan.

La Chaumière Roz-Aven PONT-AVEN
This lovely thatched inn is on the banks of the Aven River, with boats going by and parasols out front for the tearoom part of the establishment. Freshly redecorated in a simple style, each guest room is unique, with either river or garden views. **11 quai Théodore Botrel.** ☎ 02-98-06-13-06. www.hotelpontaven.online.fr. 15 units. Doubles 69€–98€. AE, MC, V.

La Villefromoy ST-MALO
This 19th-century seaside hotel has a nice sense of style, with wooden floors and contemporary furniture in the communal areas and more traditional hotel decor in the rooms, many of which have balconies. You can walk straight onto the beach from the hotel, and along it to the walled Cité des Corsaires. **7 bd. Hémert.** ☎ 02-99-40-92-20. www.villefromoy.fr. 21 units. Doubles 89€–179€. AE, MC, V.

kids L'Hippocampe CARNAC
This good-value family hotel is convenient both to the beaches and prehistoric menhirs. The friendly owners are also oyster farmers; every Thursday they take visitors out to the oyster beds and follow up with a tasting. It would be hard to grow bored here, with a snooker room, a heated pool, a fitness room and sauna, and massages. **Kerhueno, rte. de Carnac, Plouharnel.** ☎ 02-97-52-39-51. www.hotel-hippocampe.fr. 20 units. Doubles 60€–100€. AE, MC, V.

Manoir Saint-Michel FREHEL (EMERALD COAST)
This lovely manor house in the heart of the countryside overlooks the beach of Sables-d'Or-les-Pins, 35km (22 miles) west of Dinard. It has attractive rooms, a lake with ducks, a garden, vast grounds, and a convivial bar/library. Next door is a golf club, and the beach is only 300m (984 ft.) below. **38 rue de la Carquois, Fréhel.** ☎ 02-96-41-48-87. www.fournel.de. 20 units. Doubles 47€–118€. MC, V. Closed Nov–Mar.

Where to Dine in Brittany

> *Seafood takes pride of place on most menus in Brittany.*

Au Pied d'Cheval CANCALE & ST-MALO
SEAFOOD This traditional oyster place has
two outlets, in St-Malo and in Cancale. Both
display oysters of different sizes in baskets out
front. Also available are fish soup, mussels,
whelks, pink prawns, winkles, langoustines,
and lobster. **In Cancale: 10 quai Gambetta;**
☎ 02-99-89-76-96. **In St-Malo: 6 rue Jacques
Cartier;** ☎ 02-99-40-98-18; www.au-pied-de-
cheval.com. Main courses 10€–15€.

★ **Bouche en Folie** ST-MALO *FRENCH*
Bouche en Folie is loved by locals. On a street
just behind Bon Secours Beach (p. 207, ❶),
mouthwatering seasonal dishes are made with
local produce, and the short menu changes
every 2 weeks. Reservations are advised.
14 rue du Boyer. ☎ 06-72-49-08-89. http://
boucheenfolie.eresto.net. Menus 22€–28€. MC,
V. Lunch and dinner Wed–Sun.

Chez Erwan QUIMPER *BRETON*
Locals swear by this place for its authentic
Breton ambiance and specialties such as *feuil-
leté à l'andouille* (flaky pastry with a spicy offal
sausage) and *kig a farz,* perhaps the nearest
thing in Brittany to an Irish stew. **3 rue Aristide
Briand.** ☎ 02-98-90-14-14. www.erwan-
restaurant.com. Main courses 16€–20€. MC, V.
Lunch Tues–Fri, dinner Tues–Sat.

Chez Ma Pomme DINARD *BISTRO*
This local favorite is just behind the Grande
Plage. Everyone raves about the *brochettes*
(skewers) of monkfish or scallops. The red
mullet *à la plancha* with chorizo and the homemade *rillettes* (fish pâtés) are great, too. **6 rue
Yves Verney.** ☎ 02-99-46-81-90. Main courses
17€–20€; menus 20€–26€. AE, MC, V. Lunch
Tues–Sun, dinner Tues–Wed and Fri–Sat.

★★ La Gonelle DINARD *SEAFOOD*
This is the place to enjoy some of the freshest seafood in Brittany. All 20 tables are on the terrace right by the Rance estuary. Bass, bream, and turbot swim in a giant tank and await their fate. Promenade du Clair de Lune. ☎ 02-99-16-40-47. www.lagonelle.com. Main courses 30€–50€. AE, DC, MC, V. Mid-Apr to June and Sept lunch and dinner Thurs–Mon; July–Aug lunch and dinner daily; closed Oct to mid-Apr.

La Krampouzerie QUIMPER *CREPERIE*
The savory *crêpes* here are made of organic buckwheat, and fillings are adventurous. How about "seaweed from the Ouessant Isles" or "beef tongue from Douarnenez"? Delicious ciders, brut or sweet, wash the pancakes down. 9 rue du Sallé. ☎ 02-98-95-13-08. Main courses 6€–9€. AE, MC, V. July–Aug lunch Mon–Sat, dinner daily; Sept–June lunch and dinner Mon–Sat.

La Taverne de la Marine RENNES *SEAFOOD*
Bridging the gap between Brittany and Paris, this smartened-up brasserie serves classic seafood platters from the day's catch. The lunchtime menu at 11€ or 13€ is a particularly good value. 2 place de Bretagne. ☎ 02-99-31-53-84. www.tavernedelamarine.com. Main courses 13€–22.50€. AE, DC, MC, V. Lunch and dinner daily.

★★ La Vieille Tour ST-BRIEUC *GASTRONOMIC*
A wonderful Breton welcome and playful works of art accompany the lively taste combinations that chef Nicolas Adam has plucked from sea, field, and kitchen garden. Menu prices range from the 18€ midweek lunch to the tasting menu at 67€. 75 rue de la Tour, Port du Lègue, Plérin. ☎ 02-96-33-10-30. www.la-vieille-tour.com. Menus 18€–67€. AE, DC, MC, V. Lunch Tues–Fri and Sun, dinner Tues–Sat.

Le Moulin de Rosmadec PONT-AVEN *SEAFOOD*
Two brothers prepare seafood-based cuisine in this old mill converted into a riverside hotel. The grilled lobster with two butters is the signature dish. A fine wine list accompanies it. The owners have also opened a younger, hipper establishment nearby, called **Sur Le Pont.**
Venelle de Rosmadec. ☎ 02-98-06-18-00. www.moulinderosmadec.com. Menus 28€–76€. AE, DC, MC, V. Lunch Tues–Wed and Fri–Sun, dinner Mon–Wed and Fri–Sat.

★ Restaurant La Côte CARNAC *FRENCH*
In the heart of the megaliths, this converted farmhouse with stone walls and a Japanese garden offers a hearty welcome and refined cuisine. The food is succulent and seasonal, featuring dishes such as rabbit risotto, wild hake, and beef cheek with chestnuts. Lieu dit Kermario. ☎ 02-97-52-02-80. www.restaurant-la-cote.com. Menus 35€, 45€, 55€. DC, MC, V. July–Aug lunch Tues–Sun, dinner Wed–Sun; Sept–June lunch Tues–Fri and Sun, dinner Tues–Sat.

★ Ty Gwelig CARNAC *BRETON*
This *crêperie* also serves mussels in cider, seafood *choucroute,* and oysters. With a long bar running the length of the room, it's bright and airy, eschewing the quaint, lacy decor of so many *crêperies*. Breton beers and ciders are on tap. 8 rue Colary. ☎ 02-97-52-92-05. Main courses 9€–12€. V. Mar–Oct lunch and dinner Tues–Sat; closed Nov–Mar.

Getting Around & Tourist Information

For information about **rail transit** in Normandy and Brittany, call ☎ 08-92-35-35-35. For bus service in Normandy, call **Bus Verts du Calvados** (☎ 08-10-21-42-14). For bus service in Brittany, call **Tibus** (☎ 08-10-22-22-22).

Municipal tourist offices are listed at the end of the town tour stops throughout the chapter. **Brittany's regional tourist office** is at 1 rue Raoul Ponchon, Rennes (☎ 02-99-36-15-15; www.brittanytourism.com). **Normandy's regional tourist office** is at 14 rue Charles Corbeau, Evreux (☎ 02-32-33-79-00; www2.normandie-tourisme.fr). **Rouen's tourist office** is at 25 place de la Cathédrale (☎ 02-32-08-32-40; www.rouenvalleedeseine.com).

For more practical information, see "France Fast Facts," p. 703.

6
Champagne

Favorite Moments in Champagne

East of Paris, the region of Champagne (pronounced Sham-*pan*-yuh) is inseparable from the decadent, sparkling elixir that bears its name. The region's low-slung, gently trestled vineyards of pinot noir, pinot meunier, and chardonnay grape varietals hug the rolling, chalky fields as living testimonies to the drink's success. But the Champagne region is also infused with history; as you travel around, you are just as likely to fall in love with deserted Romanesque churches and half-timbered medieval towns as you are with the world's greatest champagne houses. Here are some of our favorite moments in the region.

> PREVIOUS PAGE *Between Reims and Epernay, fields of vines roll on as far as the eye can see.*
THIS PAGE *For the fearless champagne drinker, sabrage—opening a champagne bottle with a sword—is easier than it looks.*

1 Entering the Salle de la Reddition in Reims. In this former schoolhouse near the railway, the Germans surrendered to General Eisenhower on May 7, 1945; the room remains exactly as it was that day. See p. 256, **8**.

2 Tucking into a rum baba at the Café du Palais in Reims. All the hearty desserts in this 1930s-style, art-filled cafe are humongous, but none more so than the liquor-infused, cream-laden rum baba, which could easily feed four. See p. 260.

3 Admiring the stained glass at Reims's Notre-Dame Cathedral. All the windows are beautiful in this cathedral where every French monarch from the 11th century on was crowned, but later installations by Chagall—biblical scenes of intense blue—are particularly stunning. See p. 254, **1**.

4 Discovering modern art in Pommery's champagne cellars. A spooky, 116-step stairway at Pommery leads to an 18km (11-mile) labyrinth of Gallo-Roman tunnels, now filled with weird and wonderful art installations. Each year, M. Vranken, Pommery's owner, invites new artists to display their creations, and the results are memorable. See p. 253.

5 Splurging on a meal at Les Crayères in Reims. Chef Philippe Mille's superlatively delicious haute French cuisine—think king crab citrus fruit confit and avocado purée, or perfect breast of Bresse chicken with black truffles and *jus de truffe*—will quite possibly be the culinary highlight of your visit. See p. 260.

6 Basking in vineyards as far as the eye can see. In the so-called Sacred Triangle—the area bordered by Reims, Epernay, and

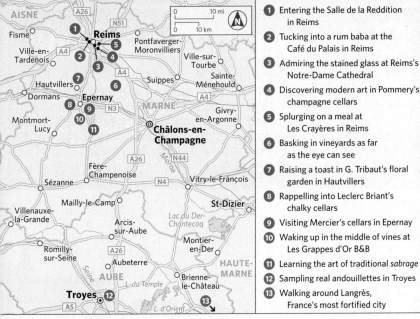

Châlons-en-Champagne—the vines of family-run champagne houses hug the earth like an emerald carpet. The best bottles usually come from the Montagne de Reims (south of Reims) and the Côte des Blancs (south of Epernay). See "The Best Champagne Houses," p. 250.

7 Raising a toast in G. Tribaut's floral garden in Hautvillers. Listening to the buzzing of bees and the clinking of glasses as you sample Tribaut's fine Grande Cuvée Spéciale, you'll be hard-pressed to imagine a more relaxing spot for tasting bubbly. See p. 251.

8 Rappelling into Leclerc Briant's chalky cellars. It takes some courage to dangle in midair on a rope and harness, but it's fabulous fun. The estate's organic and biodynamic champagnes await inside the main house afterward, to calm your nerves. See p. 252.

9 Visiting Mercier's cellars in Epernay. You'll learn about Mercier's fascinating World Fair activities, hot-air balloons, the first filmed advertisement, and the biggest champagne barrel on Earth. The champagne is mighty delicious, too. See p. 252.

10 Waking up in the middle of vines at Les Grappes d'Or B&B. This small, working champagne house, owned by Carole and Eric Isselée, is all about hearty breakfasts, vines as far as the eye can see, and fizz on your tongue during the cellar tour. See p. 261.

11 Learning the art of traditional *sabrage*. Slicing off champagne corks with a sword at Champagne Jean Milan is tremendous fun and easier than it sounds: Just hit the bottle lip three times with the blade (hard the third time), then turn the bottle the right way up as fast as possible to stop the liquid from flowing out. See p. 250.

12 Sampling real *andouillettes* in Troyes. Renowned for their odorous, pungent flavor, *andouillettes* (offal sausages) are not for everyone; but if you like tripe, trying a link will be a memorably delicious experience. See p. 244, 3.

13 Walking around Langres, France's most fortified city. With 12 towers, 7 gates, and 4.8km (3 miles) of fortified walls, Langres will take you back in time as you wander its ramparts, appreciating the lovely views of the surrounding countryside. See p. 247, 6.

Champagne in 3 Days

Champagne makes a fabulous short-break destination, especially from Paris; trains depart frequently for the 45-minute journey to the cathedral city of Reims (pronounced *Rhams*). This gastronomic hub rich in fine architecture and champagne houses makes an ideal base for visiting Epernay's avenue de Champagne (a sunset boulevard of bubbly production) and the chocolate-box village of Hautvillers, where 17th-century friar Dom Pérignon first invented sparkling wine.

> *This statue near the Montigny Sous Châtillon champagne house honors Pope Urbain II, who was born to a local knightly family and led the First Crusade in 1095.*

START Reims is 145km (90 miles) east of Paris and 125km (78 miles) north of Troyes. **TRIP LENGTH** 45km (30 miles), along both fast and country roads.

❶ ★★★ Reims. This chic cathedral city attracts foodies with excellent *champenois* cuisine and fine champagne from the internationally acclaimed champagne houses in town, such as **Pommery** (p. 253) and **Mumm** (p. 253). It also attracts history buffs, with its 13th-century Gothic **cathedral,** where

every French king since the 11th century has been crowned, and the **Salle de la Reddition,** where World War II officially ended in 1945. Fans of architecture should come here for the city's remarkable collection of buildings from the 1920s and 1930s (see p. 256, ❽); heavy

Where to Stay & Dine

For hotels and restaurants in Reims, see p. 260; elsewhere in the region, see p. 261.

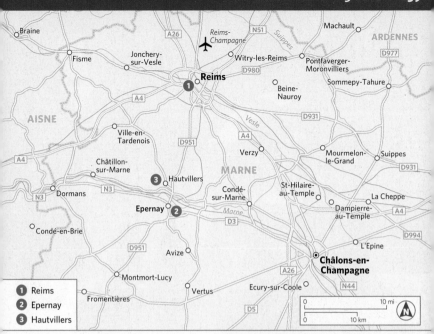

1 Reims
2 Epernay
3 Hautvillers

bombing during World War I destroyed 80% of Reims, and a vast regeneration program during the interwar period left it with an Art Deco legacy unrivaled anywhere else in France. The tourist office can provide you with audio-guides for a themed walking tour across town. ⏱ 1 day. For detailed information on Reims, see p. 254.

From Reims, take A4 and N51, following directions to Epernay (30km/19 miles).

2 ★ Epernay. On the left bank of the Marne River, Epernay has stood in the path of every French war since the 6th century, yet it miraculously stands proud as the center of France's champagne production. Heavy bombing during World War II left scars, filled in during the 1960s by unsightly apartment blocks and factories, but the city's former beauty endures on the **avenue de Champagne,** a graceful boulevard of neo-Renaissance mansions and extravagant champagne headquarters that sits atop 300km (200 miles) of serpentine chalk tunnels filled with fermenting champagne. Epernay has only one-sixth of Reims's population, but it produces almost as much champagne, as the headquarters of famous brands such as ★ **Moët et Chandon** (p. 252); ★★ **De**

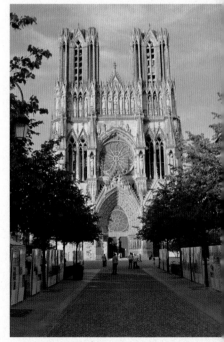

> *More than 2,300 pieces of decorative stonework ornament the facade of Reims's Gothic cathedral.*

> *A glass of champagne is included in the ticket price at Moët et Chandon in Epernay.*

Castellane (p. 251), with its beautiful, giant clock tower (a replica of the one at Gare de Lyon train station in Paris); and ★★ **Mercier** (p. 252). These houses all offer cellar tours and tastings. If you would like an introduction to dozens of the region's best *petits producteurs de champagne* (small, family-run champagne producers), don't miss ★ **C. Comme Champagne,** 8 rue Gambetta (☎ 03-26-32-09-55; www.c-comme.fr; MC, V; Sun–Thurs 10am–8pm, Fri–Sat 10am–midnight). This champagne bar-cum–informative wine cellar in Epernay is a mandatory stop. Either search the downstairs cellar and order the bottle of your choice to be brought to your table (from 31€ a bottle), or stay at your table and choose a champagne of the week—a selection of five champagnes by local viticulturists, served with tapas (from just 18€). Individual bottles to take away cost just 1€ more than they do if you buy directly from their producers (from around 13€ a bottle). ⏱ 1 day. Epernay Tourist Office, 7 av. de Champagne. ☎ 03-26-53-33-00. www.ot-epernay.fr.

Return to Reims for the night or stay in Epernay. On Day 3 from Epernay, take D40 to N2051, and follow N2051 through three islands to pick up D301 (toward A26 Reims). Join N51, cross the village of Dizy, and pick up D1 to Hautvillers (8km/5 miles total).

❸ ★★ **Hautvillers.** Champagne was born in this hilly village—a bucolic medley of narrow, picturesque alleys and houses decorated with dainty, wrought-iron signs (a tradition dating

Wine Tasting by Train

We recommend traveling by train the first 2 days of this itinerary, so you don't have to miss out on swallowing because you're driving. Reims and Epernay are well served by train: Paris to Reims takes just 45 minutes; Paris to Epernay takes 1 hour and 20 minutes; and Reims to Epernay takes about 20 to 30 minutes. This way, you'll only need a car for Day 3 in the Champagne countryside. In any case, we've provided driving directions throughout this tour.

back to medieval times). In the 17th century, the enlightened Benedictine monk Dom Pérignon (1639–1715) initiated the bubbly-making technique (see "Dom Pérignon: The Monk & His Bubbly," p. 248) while a resident in the village abbey. The monastery is closed to the public, but you can visit the monk's resting place in the abbey church; his sepulcher lies alongside that of Dom Ruinart, whose nephew founded in 1729 what would become the oldest champagne house in the world, Ruinart. In Hautvillers nowadays, Pérignon's legacy lives on, within and around 33 family-run champagne houses. Almost all of them offer tastings, usually by appointment. For sessions in English, try **Champagne J.M. Gobillard et Fils,** 38 rue de l'Eglise (☎ 03-26-59-44-20; www.champagne-gobillard.com), and **Champagne Locret-Lachaud,** 40 rue St-Vincent (☎ 03-26-59-40-20; http://pagesperso-orange.fr/champagnelocret). Or, on a sunny day, head to **G. Tribaut** (p. 251), which turns

> *This abbey in Hautvillers is where the father of champagne, monk Dom Pérignon, perfected his techniques.*

its flower-filled, panoramic garden overlooking the vines into a *dégustation* area. For all of these addresses, call ahead for a reservation.

Hautvillers itself is a walker's paradise, situated at an altitude of 288m (945 ft.) in the middle of a protected natural park and forest known as the **Montagne de Reims** (Reims Mountain). In nearby Pourcy, the **Maison du Parc,** chemin de Nanteuil (☎ 03-26-59-44-44; www.parc-montagnedereims.fr), can provide maps of rambling routes that take you past picturesque vineyards and points of geological interest and through forests packed with flora and fauna. The tourist office is another good source of information. ⏱ 1 day. Hautvillers Tourist Office, place de la République. ☎ 03-26-57-06-35. www.tourisme-hautvillers.com.

Fizzy Facts

- Romans began planting vines in Champagne in 57 B.C.

- Before the invention of champagne, the region's wine was red and mediocre, produced by peasants for local use, and bubbles were considered a major defect.

- The Champagne territory covers around 86,000 acres of French countryside, but the best grapes grow in the bottomlands south of Reims: the Côte des Blancs, Montagne de Reims, and Vallée de la Marne areas.

- Red grapes (sans skins) are still used in champagne.

- By law, only sparkling wines made in France's Champagne region can be called champagne; makers of bubbly in any other area must categorize their product as sparkling wine produced by the *méthode champenoise*, or they can face lengthy litigation.

- After naming a perfume Champagne, the late Yves St-Laurent was forced to rebrand his scent *Yvresse* (drunkenness).

Champagne in 1 Week

This weeklong tour of Champagne takes you through culturally interesting towns such as Troyes (famed for its stained glass and sausages) and Chaumont (former residence of the counts of Champagne); past plains of vines, cornfields, and lakes; and toward the fortified *cité* of Langres. If you'd like to slacken the pace, you could spend an extra few days in Le Parc Naturel Regional de la Fôret d'Orient, a national oasis of forests and lakes near Troyes (see the box on p. 246), and an extra day in Langres, your final stop on this tour.

> These medieval cloisters in the Musée du Cloitre de Notre-Dame-en-Vaux, in Châlons-en-Champagne, once stood in the nearby Notre-Dame-en-Vaux church.

START Reims is 145km (90 miles) east of Paris and 125km (78 miles) north of Troyes. **TRIP LENGTH** 1 week; 350km (217 miles).

1 ★★★ **Reims.** This beautiful, Art Deco cathedral city is inseparable from the *grandes marques* of champagne, whose smart headquarters are clustered around the **Basilique St-Rémi.** ⊙ 2 days. For detailed information on Reims, see p. 254.

From Reims, join A4 and follow signs to Châlons-en-Champagne (50km/ 30 miles).

2 ★ **Châlons-en-Champagne.** Surrounded by blanc de blanc vineyards, sleepy, bourgeois Châlons-en-Champagne looks pretty amid ancient bridges and Venice-like watercourses, including the Marne River and several canals. It is also a town of half-timbered houses, 17th- and 18th-century mansions made of chalk and red brick, and abundant religious edifices representing 7 centuries of architecture. From quai de Notre-Dame, you can take in the Romanesque towers of the UNESCO-protected **Notre-Dame-en-Vaux** church. Begun in the

1	Reims
2	Châlons-en-Champagne
3	Troyes
4	Chaumont
5	Colombey-les-Deux-Eglises
6	Langres

12th century and finished in the 13th, it is a jamboree of delicate, alternately pointy and rounded ornamentation from both the Romanesque and the Gothic eras. Just behind the church, in the town's medieval quarter, the **Musée du Cloître de Notre-Dame-en-Vaux,** rue Nicolas Durand (☎ 03-26-64-03-87; Apr–Sept daily 10am–noon and 2–6pm; Oct–Mar Mon–Fri 10am–noon and 2–5pm, Sat–Sun 10am–noon; closed public holidays), contains Notre-Dame-en-Vaux's former medieval cloisters, which were partially demolished in the 18th century and unearthed in 1963. The other jewel in Châlons's crown is the **Cathédrale St-Etienne,** which stands tall in both Gothic and baroque finery. Its interior is awash in the light that pours through the huge stained-glass windows, dappling the church in rainbows. The most impressive stained glass, inside the *trésor* (treasury), dates from the 12th century.

If you have the chance, pack a picnic and go to **Les Jards** riverside park, a vast expanse of lawns, paths, and trees frequented by locals

Where to Stay & Dine

For hotels and restaurants in Reims, see p. 260; elsewhere in the region, see p. 261.

> *Reims's oldest church, the 11th-century Basilique St-Rémi, is a UNESCO World Heritage site housing a city history museum.*

> *Rue des Chats (Cat Street) in Troyes is lined with typical half-timbered champenois houses.*

since medieval times. Lovely flowers bloom in the **Petit Jard** section, while the **Jard Anglais,** just below the canal bridge, has cycle paths. If you'd rather eat in a restaurant, head to nearby **place de la République,** which is full of bars and places to eat. ⏱ 1 day. Châlons-en-Champagne Tourist Office, 3 quai des Arts. ☎ 03-26-65-17-89. www.chalons-tourisme.com.

From Châlons, take A26 (toward Troyes), exit at junction 22, and follow signs for Troyes-centre, then Troyes (93km/57 miles).

❸ ★★ **Troyes.** Somewhat overshadowed by Reims, Troyes is a cultural wallflower that wins you over slowly with its small museums, quaint streets, Gothic churches (known for their stained glass from the famous School of Troyes), traditional half-timbered *champenois* architecture, and offal sausages known as *andouillettes.* It is probably the least champagne-oriented of the region's cities, yet it compensates with its cork-shaped borders—a

quirk of medieval urban planning that reminds you where you are every time you look at the street map. The city has been the capital of the French textile and hosiery industry since the Middle Ages; that legacy lives on in a mini-metropolis of designer and high-street factory outlet stores (at McArthur Glen and Marques Av.), both a short bus or car ride away in the suburbs (see www.troyesmagusine.com or the tourist office for details).

Back in the city center, the single-towered **Cathédrale St-Pierre-et-St-Paul,** place St-Pierre (open to the public Mon–Sat 10am–1pm and 2–6pm; Sun 10am–noon and 2–5pm; closed Mon Nov–Feb), is bathed in the mauv-ish reds and blues emanating from its spectac-ular stained-glass, School of Troyes windows. Construction began in the 13th century and continued through the 17th, so each section of windows dates from a different period. The

Champagne's Timber Churches

Between Châlons and Troyes, the **Lac du Der-Chantecoq** is a pretty lake surrounded by woods and meadows. Amid this bucolic landscape, you will find numerous Roman-esque and Renaissance *églises à pan de bois* (half-timbered churches) with gables like pointy witch hats and wooden porches called *caquetoirs.* Many contain stained-glass windows from the School of Troyes and wonderful wooden sculptures. The churches of **Bailly-le-Franc** (☎ 03-25-27-65-38), **Outine** (☎ 03-26-72-57-60; www.mairie-outines.fr), **Châtillon-sur-Broué** (☎ 03-26-72-13-48), and **Lentilles** (☎ 03-25-92-14-19) are particularly lovely and are linked by country roads. For more infor-mation, see www.tourisme-champagne-ardenne.com.

choir area is from the 13th century and depicts popes, emperors, and virgins with intense, warm colors. The nave's windows date from the 16th century and look more like paintings than pieces of glass; bold and colorful, they look brand-new, even abstract, and way ahead of their time. Look out for the 1625 "Mystical Wine Press" in one of the chapels, gruesomely depicting Jesus' blood being squeezed out by a press and turned into wine. Other churches worth visiting are the **Basilique St-Urbain,** place Vernier (open to the public Tues–Sat 10am–noon and 2–5pm; Sun 2–5pm), which has more of Troyes's famous stained glass; the **Eglise Ste-Madeleine,** rue de la Madeleine (open to the public Tues–Sat 10am–noon and 2–5pm; Sun 2–5pm), famous for its flamboyant choir screen (1508–17), carved by Jean Gailde using Troyen techniques; and the **Eglise St-Pantaléon,** rue de Vauluisant (open to the public Tues–Sat 10am–12:30pm, Sun 2–5pm), with a wooden vaulted ceiling and a collection of statues from convents destroyed during the Revolution.

Art lovers shouldn't miss the **Musée d'Art Moderne,** 14 place St-Pierre (☎ 03-25-76-26-80; admission 5€; May–Sept Tues–Fri 10am–1pm and 2–7pm, Sat–Sun 11am–7pm; Oct–Apr Tues–Fri 10am–noon and 2–5pm, Sat–Sun 11am–6pm). Set in an Episcopal palace next door to the cathedral, it contains hundreds of paintings by big-name trailblazers such as Matisse, Modigliani, Courbet, Degas, Derain, Soutine, and Seurat. It's one of the best outside Paris. ⏱ 1 day. Troyes Tourist Office has two locations: 16 bd. Carnot (☎ 03-25-82-62-70) and Rue Mignard opposite the Eglise Saint Jean (church) in the pedestrian quarters (☎ 03-25-73-36-88). www.tourisme-troyes.com.

From Troyes, take D671 to A5 (toward Lyon-Metz-Reims), exit at junction 24, and follow signs to Chaumont via N67 and D65 (100km/62 miles).

❹ kids **Chaumont.** This sleepy, bourgeois town was the residence of the powerful counts of Champagne in the 13th century. Their legacy lives on in the **Donjon des Comptes de Champagne,** the only remaining part of the old castle, presiding in feudal glory over the Old Town. Its 11th- and 12th-century square keep was used as a prison until 1866.

> Chaumont is famed for its Renaissance townhouses with turreted staircases like this one.

Andouillettes—Historical Tripe That Saved the City

In 828, Louis II was crowned king in Troyes, and he celebrated his new title with a banquet of *andouillettes* (pungent-smelling offal sausage), a Troyes specialty. Several hundred years later, in 1560, the French royal army breached the city walls to take Troyes from the governor of Champagne, the Duke de Guise. All was going well until the soldiers caught wind of a delicious smell wafting from behind the cathedral. Rushing to its source, they discovered *andouillette* sellers and threw themselves onto the food. The greedy men were caught red-handed by de Guise's army and driven out of town. *Andouillettes* are still eaten today; the best ones bear the label AAAAA (Association Amicale des Amateurs d'Andouillette Authentique). You'll find them in butcher shops and restaurants all over town. Or you can sample them at Au Jardin Gourmand (p. 262).

Today it holds the **Musée d'Art et d'Histoire de Chaumont,** place du Palais (☎ 03-25-03-01-99; www.ville-chaumont.fr; admission 1.50€ adults, free for ages 17 and under, free for everyone 1st Sun of the month; Sept–June Wed–Mon 2–6pm; July–Aug until 6:30pm), a museum filled with local archaeological finds and paintings from the French, Flemish, Dutch, and Italian schools. In the town below, look out for the city's 16th- and 17th-century *tourelles* (turreted staircases), which link together the old bourgeois townhouses, and the **St-Jean Baptiste** basilica, 1 rue Decrès, built in Chaumont's typical gray stone. The basilica's interior is particularly fetching with its intricate, vaulted ceiling and the curious Tree of Jesse—a family tree that sprouts from a sleeping Jesus. Chaumont is also famous

> *This Lorraine Cross in Colombey-les-Deux-Eglises pays tribute to ex-president Charles de Gaulle.*

for its three-story, 52-arch **viaduct.** Built in 1857 (thanks to 2,500 men and around 300 horses), it is one of Europe's most spectacular mid-19th-century constructions, crossing the Valley de la Suize like a giant, filigree wall. ⏱ 1 day. Chaumont Tourist Office, place du Général de Gaulle. ☎ 03-25-03-80-80. www.tourisme-chaumont-champagne.com.

After an afternoon in Chaumont, or after getting a fresh start the next morning, drive from Chaumont to Colombey-les-Deux-Eglises (23km/14 miles) via D65, D65C, D65B, and D619 (toward St-Dizier).

❺ Colombey-les-Deux-Eglises. This village is forever associated with former French president Charles de Gaulle (1890–1970). It was here in his family home, now the museum **La Boisserie** (☎ 03-25-01-52-52; admission 3€; Apr–Sept daily 10am–6:30pm; Oct–Mar Wed–Mon 10am–1pm and 2–5:30pm), that the war hero died. Today a huge Lorraine Cross, erected in 1972 in his honor, dominates the landscape, poking out from the trees like a golden fork. ⏱ 1 hr. For more information, call or visit the Town Hall, 68 rue Général de Gaulle

---

Le Parc Naturel Régional de la Fôret d'Orient

Just 25km (15 miles) east of Troyes lies a natural park—the **Parc Naturel Régional de la Fôret d'Orient**—encompassing a trio of artificial lakes created in the 1960s to regulate the flow of the Seine River. The **Lac d'Orient,** to the south, has a large beach, sailboat rentals, and a bird-watching park; the **Lac du Temple** attracts fishermen; while the **Lac Amance** reels in the crowds with boating and water-skiing opportunities. The park sprawls across acres of low rolling hills, lush meadows, and dozens of villages dotted with traditional *champenois* buildings and plenty of hiking paths. *For more information (including on bird-watching, botany, and geology trails), contact the tourist office, Maison du Parc, Piney. ☎ 03-25-43-38-88. www.lacs-champagne.fr or www.pnr-foret-orient.fr. July–Aug daily 10am–6pm; Apr–Oct daily 10am–noon and 2–6pm; Nov–Mar daily 1–5pm.*

> *Statue of Liberty sculptor Frédéric Auguste Bartholdi created this monument to 18th-century Enlightenment thinker Denis Diderot in Langres, the philosopher's birthplace.*

(☎ 03-25-01-50-79) or call the Tourist Office of Chaumont and Champagne (☎ 03-25-01-52-33; www.colombey-les-deux-eglises.com).

From Colombey-les-Deux-Eglises, backtrack to Chaumont, pick up D619, and follow signs to Langres, via N19 (61km/38 miles).

⑥ ★★ **Langres.** At the gateway to Burgundy, in the southernmost part of Champagne, beautiful Langres sits on a rocky spur enclosed by ramparts made up of seven gates and 12 towers built over the course of 20 centuries. One section was created from a Roman triumphal arch, built around 20 B.C.—the town's only visible remnant of Gallo-Roman architecture. The ramparts afford glorious views of elegant Renaissance mansions and narrow town alleys, not to mention the Marne and Vosges valleys and the wooded Bonnelle Valley rolling into the distance; the **Navarre et d'Orval tower** (1511–19; ☎ 03-25-87-67-67) is particularly impressive, standing 20m (65 ft.) high and 28m (90 ft.) wide, with some 20 arrow slits on four levels, and walls 7m (22

ft.) thick. On a sunny day, you can see as far as Mont Blanc in the Alps (tours of the fortifications are available daily; ask at the tourist office). Near the Porte Henri IV (gate), the **Cathédrale St-Mammès,** place Jeanne Mance (☎ 03-25-87-67-67), is a lofty, atmospheric example of the Burgundian Romanesque style. For an even wider panorama, climb 227 steps up one of the towers to admire the town's pointy red rooftops, which abruptly give way to fields and forests. Also visit the **Maison Renaissance,** 20 rue du Cardinal Morlot (☎ 03-25-87-67-67), the town's best example of Renaissance architecture (free general admission, cellars 2€; daily 9am–6pm). It is an opulent medley of Corinthian columns, ornate friezes, and rectangular windows. Langres's most famous resident was Denis Diderot, founder of the encyclopedia, born here in 1713. It took him 25 years (along with Jean d'Alembert) to write all 35 volumes, which were finished in 1772. ⏱ 1–2 days. Langres Tourist Office, square Olivier Lahalle. ☎ 03-25-87-67-67. www.tourisme-langres.com.

DOM PERIGNON
The Monk & His Bubbly BY ANNA BROOKE

THROUGHOUT THE GRAND SIECLE, from the late 17th to the early 18th centuries, kings across Europe consumed vast quantities of champagne from France. Sun King Louis XIV was the first, lavishing it upon guests during decadent banquets at the palace of Versailles. Later in the 18th century, Casanova used it to liven up his seductions of the wives and daughters of eminent Frenchmen, before they ran him out of town; Napoleon carted it to his battlefronts; and, after Bonaparte was deposed, Talleyrand imported cases of the stuff to the Congress of Vienna, to procure more favorable peace terms for France. Ironically, none of this decadent revelry would have been possible without the Benedictine monk Dom Pérignon (1638–1715); generally credited with the invention of champagne, he indisputably developed many advances in its production.

The Father of Oenology

Louis XIV's favorite winemaker, Dom Pérignon was born and died the same year as the Sun King. In 1658, at the age of 20, he entered the hilltop Abbaye St-Pierre in the tiny village of Hautvillers, south of Reims, where it was his job to tend to the vines. Soon he perfected techniques that would forever revolutionize champagne-making methods—finding just the right blend of wines; pressing red grapes in a way that prevented the skins from coloring the white juice; using chalk cellars to preserve a constant temperature; and changing the bottle's shape by hollowing out the base to limit breakages caused by the fizzing of the wine. Some say he was the first to add sugar and yeast to still wine, causing it to foam; others maintain this was a region-wide phenomenon, discovered when glass bottles replaced wooden barrels for transportation, and that Pérignon merely refined it. Either way, his finesse and perseverance earned him the title "Father of Oenology."

Making Champagne

THE GRAPES
Three grape varieties are used: pinot noir (red), pinot meunier (red), and chardonnay (white)—usually blended together. *Blanc de blancs* champagne tends to be the only *cru* made entirely from one grape variety—chardonnay.

THE HARVEST
Grapes are usually handpicked in late September and transported in small quantities, so as not to crush them, in containers called *mannequins*.

SELECTION
Unripe or rotten grapes are discarded; only the best are chosen.

WEIGHING
The grapes are weighed to obtain a *marc*—4,000kg (about 4½ tons)—the equivalent of the volume held by one traditional *champenois* grape press.

CRUSHING
The press, which is wider than it is tall, crushes the grapes quickly so that the pigment in the grapes' skin doesn't stain the juices.

FILTERING
After several hours of rest, the juice—known as *moût*—is filtered.

FERMENTING
The *moût* is placed in a fermenting barrel and kept at 18°C (64°F). Malolactic bacteria is introduced to aid the fermenting

process and diminish the wine's acidity. Once this process is over, you have a *vin tranquille* (flat wine).

THE ASSEMBLY
The taste of each house's champagne is unique, achieved by mixing (assembling) the various wines in quantities that are distinctive to the brand.

THE FIRST ADDITIVES
Just before bottling, sugar and yeast are added in the form of a liquid called *liqueur de triage,* which creates the fizz.

CELLARING
Once the *liqueur de triage* has been added, the bottles are stocked on shelves in the cellar, at a constant temperature of 10°C (50°F), for one or more years, until the second fermentation process is complete.

TURNING
During the second fermentation, deposits gather in the bottle's

base. Bottles are placed upside down on racks and turned regularly, by hand or by machine, to force the deposit into the bottleneck.

DE-DEPOSITING
Once all the deposit has fallen, the bottlenecks are plunged into a liquid at -20°C (-4°F) to freeze the sediment, which can then be removed by a process called *dégorgement.*

THE SECOND ADDITIVES
The liquid removed by the *dégorgement* is replaced by a blend of sugar and old champagne *(liqueur d'expédition),* which, depending on its sweetness, makes the champagne brut (less than 12g/½ oz. of sugar per liter) or sweet (more than 12g).

LABELING
After several more months of "rest," the bottles are labeled and sent off to be sold.

The Best Champagne Houses

Some say there are as many champagne producers in Champagne as there are bell towers. That is to say, there are hundreds of them, and all make their own champagnes according to heavily guarded methods. The most famous producers keep headquarters in Reims and Epernay and perpetuate champagne's luxurious image through well-formatted tours and clever marketing. The region's smaller producers are often family-run. This is not a tour per se, but a list of the best houses to visit in Reims and Epernay and along the vineyard-lined roads of the Sacred Triangle (see "La Route de Champagne," p. 253).

> Bubbly may be sophisticated, but there are no sumptuous châteaux in Champagne—just simple estates with endless rows of vines.

★★ **Champagne Charlier** VALLEE DE LA MARNE Within a flower-clad property, the Charlier family uses traditional *champenois* methods to make every bottle of their flavorsome, oaky champagnes—all blends of pinot meunier, pinot noir, and chardonnay grapes, matured in oak barrels. 4 rue des Pervenches, Montigny sous Châtillon (20km/12 miles west of Epernay off D24). ☎ 03-26-58-35-18. www.champagne-charlier.com. Open for visits Mon–Fri 8am–noon and 2–7:30pm, Sat 10am–noon and 3–7:30pm, Sun 10am–noon (times can change, especially during the grape harvest, so call in advance to confirm).

★★ kids **Champagne Jean Milan** COTE DES BLANCS During the harvest season, Jean Milan's family-oriented *vendages* (grape-picking

A Note on Prices

Every larger house offers champagne tastings. Tour prices (including the tastings) usually hover between 9€ and 27€, depending on how many glasses you sample. The small, family-run houses usually don't charge anything for tastings, but they do expect you to buy a bottle or two.

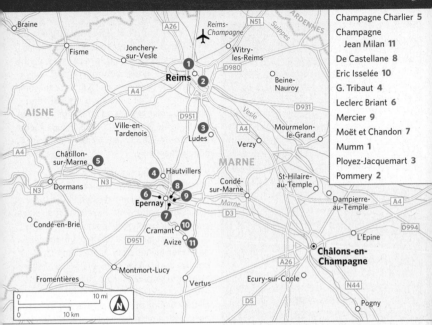

Champagne Charlier	5
Champagne Jean Milan	11
De Castellane	8
Eric Isselée	10
G. Tribaut	4
Leclerc Briant	6
Mercier	9
Moët et Chandon	7
Mumm	1
Ployez-Jacquemart	3
Pommery	2

days) are great fun and not as hard as they sound, leaving plenty of downtime for eating and drinking (40€ per person). Jean Milan is also where you can learn to *sabrer* champagne bottles (slice off the cork with a sword). The champagne you taste here is light and citrusy with a woody finish. 6 rue d'Avize, Oger (11km/6¾ miles south of Epernay on D10). ☎ 03-26-57-50-09. www.champagne-milan.com. Call in advance to arrange a visit.

★★ kids De Castellane EPERNAY

De Castellane's guided cellar tour is the only one to include a futuristic-looking assembly room where you can watch as labels are affixed to the bottles and see the gigantic stainless steel wine-fermenting barrels. As you're gazing at the barrels, think of the poor guy who has to clean them by climbing inside the tiny opening. Incredibly, nobody has ever gotten stuck inside, but it is definitely not a job for a claustrophobe. The winery's 66m-tall (216-ft.) tower—an exact copy of Paris's Gare de Lyon clock tower, designed by architect Marius Toudoire—offers excellent views over Epernay and its vineyards. 63 av. de Champagne. ☎ 03-26-51-19-11. www.castellane.com. Jan–Mar by appointment only; Apr–Nov daily 10am–noon and 2–6pm.

★★ Eric Isselée CRAMANT

As the Isselée family will explain, champagne tasting is all about swallowing, then breathing in through your nose to experience the drink's flavors. Once you've tried their Cuvée Tradition (made from the oldest vines), the velvety Rosé, and the fruity Brut Blanc de Blancs, you might decide to sleep it off at the on-site B&B (p. 261). 350 rue des Grappes d'Or (8km/5 miles south of Epernay on D40/D10). ☎ 03-26-57-54-96. www.champagne-eric-isselee.com. Call to arrange a visit.

★★★ G. Tribaut HAUTVILLERS

Come here to sample well-priced Grand Cru and Premier Cru champagnes in a panoramic garden, in the village where Dom Pérignon first created champagne. The views are stunning, the family friendly, and the champagne wonderfully velvety and fruity. 88 rue d'Eguisheim (7km/4⅓ miles north of Epernay on D386). ☎ 03-26-59-40-57. http://champagne.g.tribaut.com. Apr–Dec daily 9am–noon and 2–6pm; Jan–Mar closed Sun.

Where to Stay & Dine

For hotels and restaurants in Reims, see p. 260; elsewhere in the region, see p. 261.

Mercier's Champagne History

In 1858 Eugène Mercier was a 20-year-old upstart with grand ideas—but no money. Champagne houses were multiplying fast, and Eugène decided that his fortune was among them. After 17 years of hard slogging, he acquired a property on avenue de Champagne in Epernay; built 18km (11 miles) of wine cellar underneath the house, using more than 7,000 tons of chalk (40 times the weight of the Eiffel Tower) to do the job; and confirmed his name as a serious businessman. In 1889, for the World's Fair in Paris, he used 24 bulls and 18 horses to pull to the city a 20-ton champagne barrel, containing the equivalent of 200,000 bottles of bubbly, so that people could taste his champagne. Then, for the 1900 Paris World's Fair, he provided thousands of onlookers with the first-ever publicity film, crafted by the notorious Frères Lumières; he also rose a hot-air balloon above the Château de Vincennes, so that his public could enjoy the panorama while they tasted his wares. Eugène Mercier died just 4 years later in 1904.

★★ kids **Leclerc Briant** EPERNAY

This has to be the most original way to visit a cellar: on a rope, rappelling through a well previously used for transporting champagne-filled crates. It's not the only way down, but it is excellent fun; plus Leclerc Briant gives you an initiation certificate to take home (a nice touch for kids). Tastings take place inside the main house; choose between organic and biodynamic champagnes such as La Ravinne, a strong, rounded wine made entirely from pinot meunier grapes, and the light and floral Cuvée de Réserve Brut. **67 rue Chaude Ruelle.** ☎ 03-26-54-45-33. www.leclercbriant.com. By appointment only.

★★★ kids **Mercier** EPERNAY

On this tour, you'll see the world's largest champagne barrel and descend 30m (98 ft.) inside a panoramic elevator that displays champagne-making techniques on the way down, to explore a vast network of tunnels on a laser-guided train. More than 15 million bottles line Mercier's tunnels, and a highly protected *glacière* (secure cellar) contains Mercier's best vintages from 1923 onward. Of all the champagne houses, Mercier's story is possibly the most fascinating (see "Mercier's Champagne History"). **70 av. de Champagne.** ☎ 03-26-51-22-22. www.champagne-mercier. fr. Mid-Mar to mid-Nov daily 9:30–11:30am and 2–4:30pm. Closed Tues–Wed Feb 18–Mar 24 and Nov 16–Dec 13.

★★★ **Moët et Chandon** EPERNAY

You can practically smell the wealth of this place, founded by Jean Remy Moët in 1743. It was the favorite of Napoleon, who,

> Bottles in the chalky cellars at Mercier in Epernay are turned to force unwanted deposits into the bottleneck.

according to legend, used to lug cases of the stuff around before a battle. The tours are led in English by a staff member who spins wonderful anecdotes and makes sure you don't get lost in the 28km (17 miles) of spooky tunnels. The tour guides also provide excellent snippets of information on oenology and the savoir-faire of cellar masters. 20 av. de Champagne. ☎ 03-26-51-20-20. www.moet. com. Feb–Mar and mid-Nov to late Dec Mon–Fri 9:30–11:30am and 2–4:30pm (closed public holidays); Apr to mid-Nov daily 9:30–11:30am and 2–4:30pm; closed Jan.

★ **Mumm** REIMS

Inside Mumm's headquarters, you'll find a small museum illustrating the ancient role of the vintner and, deep down in the bedrock, a labyrinth of tunnels and storage cellars. If you had a euro for every bottle down there, you'd be a millionaire many times over—there are more than 25 million of them. The Mumm estate's gardens also contain the wonderful Foujita Chapel (p. 257). 34 rue du Champ-de-Mars. ☎ 03-26-49-59-70. www.mumm.com. Reservations required. Mar–Oct daily 9–11am and 2–5pm; Nov–Feb Sat 9–11am and 2–5pm, Sun–Fri by appointment only.

★★ **Ployez-Jacquemart** LUDES

The prestigious champagnes from the Ployez-Jacquemart house are known for their smooth, almost nutty flavor. You can also stay here in plush rooms, and wake up to the sights and sounds of a working vineyard (p. 261). 8 rue Astoin (13km/8 miles southeast of Reims on D9). ☎ 03-26-61-11-87. www.ployez-jacquemart.fr.

★★★ kids **Pommery** REIMS

This Elizabethan English–style house has an eerie, 116-step stairway that leads to an underground maze of galleries linking 120 chalk mines used during the Gallo-Roman period. Various stages of the champagne-making process are shown, including the fermentation process and riddling desks. Each year, contemporary artists are invited to fill the cellars with their weird and wacky creations, making this one of the most exciting cellars to visit. Place du Général-Gouraud. ☎ 03-26-61-62-55. www.pommery.com. Mid-Mar to mid-Nov daily 9:30am–7pm; mid-Nov to mid-Mar daily 10am–6pm. Closed Dec 25–Jan 1.

> *Eugène Mercier exhibited this champagne barrel in the 1889 World's Fair (see the box on p. 252).*

La Route de Champagne

The *route de champagne* (champagne trail) is a signposted driving route around the region's principal champagne-making villages, all within the Sacred Triangle, an area bordered by Reims, Epernay, and Châlons-en-Champagne and reputed for its Grand Cru and other top-notch champagnes. Following the route is a fine way to experience champagne alongside those who make it—and to buy bottles at lower prices. Around Reims and Epernay, there are three main circuits to follow: the Montagne de Reims and the Côte des Blancs circuits, where you'll find the best-quality champagnes, and the Vallée de la Marne circuit, known for fruity champagne blends. There is a selection of family-run champagne houses along these routes. These are small, working estates, so call before visiting to confirm that they are open. Check out www.tourisme-champagne-ardenne.com for more information.

Reims

The city of Reims (pronounced *Rhans*) is as effervescent
as the bubbly in its world-famous champagne cellars (see the Reims listings in
"The Best Champagne Houses," p. 250). Its cultural artifacts span millennia,
from Roman times to today, and its UNESCO-protected monuments are
forever linked to Christendom and French coronations. Foodies also flock here,
not just for the champagne, but for the city's excellent dining options and for
sweet delicacies such as gingerbread, *biscuits de Reims,* and champagne-filled
chocolate corks. Put aside at least 1 or 2 days to discover Reims's treasures.

> *Behind the stately walls of the former royal Abbey of St-Rémi is the Musée St-Rémi, devoted to Reims's history.*

START **Reims is 143km (89 miles) east of Paris.**

① ★★★ Cathédrale Notre-Dame de Reims.
Clovis, king of the Franks, was baptized in
Reims's original cathedral by St. Remi in A.D.
498. Since then, all the kings of France—up to
Charles X in 1825—were crowned here, in the
present cathedral, where construction started
in 1211. Now a UNESCO World Heritage site,

the building is resplendent with rich, Gothic
ornamentation and religious figures, including
smiling angels so distinctive they've earned
it the nickname "Cathedral of Angels." If the
edifice's beauty lives on today, however, it
is largely thanks to painstaking restorations
financed by John D. Rockefeller after World
War I bombs almost wiped it off the face of

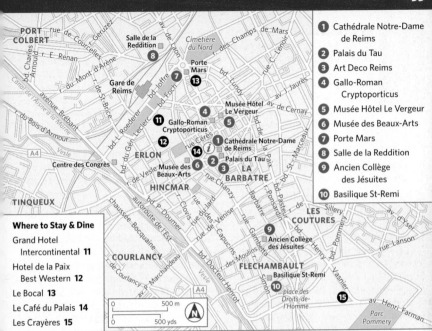

1. Cathédrale Notre-Dame de Reims
2. Palais du Tau
3. Art Deco Reims
4. Gallo-Roman Cryptoporticus
5. Musée Hôtel Le Vergeur
6. Musée des Beaux-Arts
7. Porte Mars
8. Salle de la Reddition
9. Ancien Collège des Jésuites
10. Basilique St-Remi

Where to Stay & Dine

Grand Hotel Intercontinental **11**

Hotel de la Paix Best Western **12**

Le Bocal **13**

Le Café du Palais **14**

Les Crayères **15**

the earth; fortunately, it escaped World War II relatively unharmed. Like Troyes's cathedral (p. 244, ❸), its stained-glass windows are particularly noteworthy—especially the biblical scenes by Marc Chagall, which shine an intense, deep blue and depict such scenes as the Cross, Abraham's Sacrifice, and Clovis's baptism. Some of the original statues damaged during World War I are displayed next door, in the Palais du Tau (stop ❷, below). ⏱ 45 min. 3 rue Guillaume de Machault. ☎ 03-26-47-55-34. www.cathedrale-reims.com. Free admission. Daily 7:30am–7:15pm.

❷ ★★ **Palais du Tau.** Built in 1690 as the residence of the bishops of Reims, this stone mansion beside the cathedral (a UNESCO World Heritage site) contains many statues that, until recently, decorated the cathedral facade. Also on display are holy relics associated with Reims, including a 12th-century chalice for the communion of French monarchs and a talisman supposedly containing a relic of the True Cross, which Charlemagne is said to have worn. ⏱ 1 hr. Place du Cardinal-Luçon. ☎ 03-26-47-81-79. http://palais-tau. monuments-nationaux.fr. Admission 7€ adults,

4.50€ reduced, free for ages 17 and under. May–Sept Tues–Sun 9:30am–6.30pm; Oct–Apr Tues–Sun 9:30am–12:30pm and 2–5:30pm. Closed most public holidays.

Le Biscuit Rose de Reims

In Reims, when you order champagne, you might be handed a pink, vanilla-flavored, finger-shaped naughty known as a *biscuit rose de Reims*. These cookies date from medieval times (Joan of Arc reportedly offered a few to Charles VII) when bakers, loath to waste the heat in their ovens, invented a cake that would cook slowly, at a low temperature. The word *biscuit* comes from this period, as the cookies had to be twice (*bis*) baked (*cuit*), to ensure that they were hard on the outside and fluffy in the middle. The French custom is to dip the biscuits in champagne or use them in desserts. To buy some near the cathedral, go to the pink facade of Maison Fossier at 25 cours Jean-Baptiste Langlet (☎ 03-26-47-59-84; www.fossier.fr; Mon 2–7pm, Tues–Sat 9am–7pm; MC, V), biscuit baker to the kings of France since 1756.

SITE GUIDE
PAGE 258

3 Art Deco Reims. After heavy World War I bombing destroyed 80% of its buildings, Reims lay in a heap of rubble. Urban renewal plans in the 1920s and 1930s, however, left the city with a legacy of Art Deco architecture unrivaled anywhere else in France. This hour-long itinerary leads you on foot around just some of the highlights, from the first cubic house in Reims to a reinforced concrete post office and the sumptuous Carnegie Library.

4 Gallo-Roman Cryptoporticus. This cryptoporticus (c. A.D. 200) is a semi-underground gallery once used to store grain in the Gallo-Roman period. Built below the ancient forum, the center of Roman Reims, it was originally rectangular and measured around 100m by 60m (330 ft. by 200 ft.) with one long, open side. All that remains now is the eastern gallery, which is remarkably well preserved. ⏱ 20 min. Place du Forum. ☎ 03-26-77-75-16. Free admission. June–Oct 15 Tues–Sun 2–6pm. Closed July 14.

5 ★ Musée Hôtel Le Vergeur. Just opposite the cryptoporticus, this exquisite Renaissance-era stone townhouse (with a 13th-century Gothic hall) is thoroughly charming.

Reims's Military History Museums

Aside from the Salle de la Reddition, traces of Reims's military history can be found in two museums just outside the city center. **Musée de la Base Aérienne 112 et de L'aéronautique locale (1908–2000),** 5km (3 miles) from Reims along D966 toward Vervins (☎ 03-26-79-51-86; free admission; call for hours), is dedicated to the history of Reims's 112 airbase, which helped make the region a cradle of civil and military aeronautics. **Musée Fort de la Pompelle,** 5km (3 miles) from Reims along D944 toward Châlons-en-Champagne (☎ 03-26-49-11-85; admission 4€ adults, 2€ ages 15–18, free for children 14 and under; Apr–Oct Mon–Fri 11am–6pm, Sat–Sun 11am–7pm; Nov–Mar Wed–Mon 10am–5pm; closed Dec 24–Jan 6), is a 19th-century fort that houses collections of military uniforms, hats, and weapons.

In the 19th century it belonged to photographer Hugues Krafft, who was among the first to use "instantaneous" photography, enabling him to take vivid pictures outside. Today, the period rooms contain beautiful furniture, paintings, knickknacks, and engravings, including the integral series of Albrecht Dürer's rare depictions of the Apocalypse and the Passion of Christ. ⏱ 1 hr. 36 place du Forum. ☎ 03-26-47-20-75. www.museelevergeur.com. Admission 4€ adults, 3€ students, free for ages 17 and under. Tues–Sun 2–6pm. Closed some public holidays.

6 ★★ Musée des Beaux-Arts. This fine provincial gallery, housed in the 18th-century buildings of the old Abbaye St-Denis, presents works from the 15th to the 20th centuries, including an extensive collection of 15th-century portraits by both "the Elder" and "the Younger" Cranach, and 15th- and 16th-century *toiles peintes* (light painting on rough linen) of the Passion of Christ and the Vengeance of Christ. There's an excellent series of Corot's landscapes, too. ⏱ 1 hr. 8 rue Chanzy. ☎ 03-26-35-36-00. Admission 3€ adults, free for children 15 and under, free for everyone 1st Sun of the month. Wed–Mon 10am–noon and 2–6pm. Closed some public holidays.

7 Porte Mars. These vestiges in the north of town, built to honor the emperor Augustus, are a constant reminder that Reims was once an important Roman city. The arches date from before the 3rd century A.D. but were incorporated into the city's medieval defenses before the defenses disappeared in the 18th century. The sculptures, which are rather faded, are supposed to represent Jupiter, Leda, and Romulus and Remus (the founders of Rome). From here, take nearby rue de Mars and gaze at the fantastic Art Deco, champagne-themed mosaics at no. 6 (see stop **3**, above).

8 ★★ kids Salle de la Reddition. Across the railway lines from place de Republique (via av. de Laon) this museum—a former schoolhouse near the tracks—preserves the map room of General Eisenhower's headquarters. It was here, on May 7, 1945, that the Germans surrendered, and nothing in the room has changed since then: Maps of the rail routes still line the walls, exactly as they did on that day of glory, making it a fascinating and rather moving visit. ⏱ 45 min. 12 rue Franklin-D-Roosevelt. ☎ 03-26-47-84-19. Admission 3€ adults, free for children 15 and under. Wed–Mon 10am–noon and 2–6pm. Closed some public holidays.

❾ ★★ **Ancien Collège des Jésuites.** Founded in 1606 when Henri IV granted authorization for the Jesuits to build a chapel, this architectural beauty was used as a hospital in the 18th century and contains a 300-year-old vine (brought from Palestine by one of the Jesuit fathers) that still bears fruit. The grand *refectoire* (refectory) is full of wonderful, 17th-century wooden carvings, and the underground cellar and Gallo-Roman gallery (12th century) are a feast for the eyes. There is a pretty Renaissance-style staircase that leads to an old library containing more than 18,000 books evacuated to Paris during World War I. One of the wings houses the town's planetarium (admission 3€ adults, free for children 15 and under; generally follows the same opening times as the college, but call for details). ⏱ 30 min–1 hr. 1 place Museux. ☎ 03-26-35-34-70. Mon–Fri 2–6pm.

❿ ★★★ **Basilique St-Rémi.** This UNESCO-listed church—the oldest in Reims, dating from 1007—is an example of classic medieval French masonry. Less dramatic than the cathedral, it is no less lovely. Within the complex is the former royal Abbey of St-Rémi, which once guarded the holy ampulla used to anoint the kings of France. The abbey now functions as a museum—**Musée St-Rémi,** which has an extensive collection covering the history of Reims, regional archaeology, and military history. The church's Romanesque nave leads to a magnificent choir crowned with pointed arches. The nave, the transepts, one of the towers, and the aisles date from the 11th century; the portal of the south transept is in early-16th-century flamboyant Gothic style; and some of the stained glass in the apse is from the 13th century. Don't miss the ornate tomb of St. Remi. Basilique: Place du Chanoine Ladame. Free admission. Daily 8am–7pm. Musée: 53 rue St-Simon. ☎ 03-26-85-23-36. Admission 3€ adults, free for children 15 and under, free for everyone 1st Sun of the month. Mon–Fri 2–6:30pm; Sat–Sun 2–7pm.

Foujita Chapel

In 1964, the president of Mumm, Réné Lalou, invited his friend, Japanese painter Leonard Foujita, to create the famous Rose de Champagne, which still adorns some of Mumm's champagne bottles today. Foujita went on to build and design the walls of the **Chapelle Notre-Dame-de-la-Paix** in the Mumm gardens, 33 rue du Champ de Mars (☎ 03-26-40-06-96; admission 3€; May–Oct Thurs–Tues 2–6pm; closed bank holidays). The result—a tiny, Romanesque-style church with intricate frescoes of blue, gold, green, and yellow—is a credit to Foujita's name, and all the more impressive when you think that he was 80 when he painted them. The chapel was given to the city of Reims in 1966 and has since been one of the most visited sights in town.

Reims Cafes and Bars

Whether you're looking for cocktails, coffee, beer, wine, or champagne, **place Drouet d'Erlon** (west of the cathedral) is lined with bars and brasseries, several of which (like the Café Leffe, no. 85; ☎ 03-26-40-16-32) serve food all day. Pleasant cafes also line **rue Carnot** between place Royale and the Musée des Beaux-Arts.

SITE GUIDE

3 Art Deco Reims

Built by Max Sainsaulieu between 1921 and 1928, the Ⓐ ★★★ **Bibliothèque Carnegie** (Carnegie Library) is a stunning arrangement of angular wooden paneling, marble pillars, and mosaics, at 2 place Carnegie (☎ 03-26-77-81-41; www.bm-reims.fr; Tues–Wed and Fri 10am–1pm and 2-7pm; Thurs 2-7pm; Sat 10am–1pm and 2-6pm). Its most striking feature is the lobby, with a hexagonal fountain and a cupola ceiling decorated in swirling roses. The designs represent intellectual, physical, and manual activity. From the library, take rue du Cardinal de Lorraine toward rue des Tournelles to see the angular terracotta-colored Ⓑ ★ **Cubic House** at no. 1 rue de Tournelles, near the cathedral. Architect Marc Margotin, the brainchild behind the building—the first cubic house to be built in Reims, in 1929—lived in it himself. Continue on to rue Hincmar, then turn right down rue Chanzy to the Ⓒ ★★★ **Grand Théâtre,** 1 rue de Vesles (☎ 03-26-50-03-92; www.operadereims. com). Behind a 19th-century facade, architects François Maille and Louis Sollier crafted a sumptuous Art Deco interior modeled on

Auguste Perret's Théâtre des Champs Elysées in Paris. The last public building to be rebuilt in Reims after World War I (in 1931), it's one of the most extravagant examples of an Art Deco interior in Reims today, with marble, crystal lighting, red velvet, and smart, polished woodwork. From rue de Vesles, take rue de Talleyrand to Ⓓ **No. 11 rue de Talleyrand.** Built by Emile Fanjat in 1922, this apartment block has a facade adorned in delicate blue-and-gold mosaics; wrought-iron balconies with swirling patterns inside the main balcony frame; and intricate, linear stonework. Just a short walk down rue de Vesles toward the law courts, you can fill up on hearty French cuisine at Ⓔ ★★ **Le Café du Palais** (p. 260). Jacques Simon, the artisan behind some of the Reims cathedral's stained-glass windows, created the Art Deco glass ceiling, which used to be part of a jewelry shop on rue de Talleyrand. Take rue Carnot (to the left), and cross place Royale to the Ⓕ ★★ **Hôtel des Postes,** at 3–4 rue Cérès. Built entirely from reinforced concrete by François Lecoeur between 1927 and 1930, Reims's post office stands proud

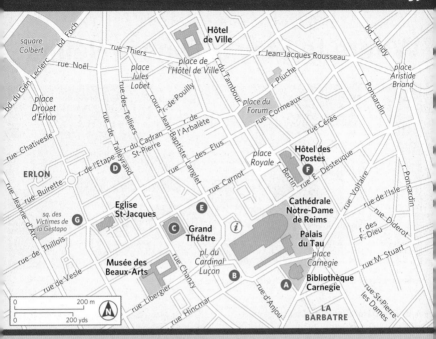

a medley of Art Deco mosaics, mirrors, and tiling, with more glass designed by Jacques Simon. Typical of the era is the mosaic floor, which states the times for the day's main meals. The mirror in the adjacent *salon de thé* (tearoom) is particularly spectacular, in orange and red tones. ⏱ 1 hr.

What Is Art Deco?

After World War I, the decorative arts moved away from the organic forms of Art Nouveau and turned toward other early-20th-century movements such as cubism, modernism, and neoclassicism. Some say Art Deco was a craving for lavish design in reaction to the forced austerity and bloodshed of the war. This would certainly explain why its popularity peaked in the Roaring Twenties and carried on well into the 1930s, especially in France and America. Art Deco traits to look out for in Reims are soft, circular forms and elongated, angular forms—not dissimilar to the shapes atop New York's Chrysler Building, built between 1928 and 1930. For more information, check out www.reimsartdeco.fr.

in curvaceous austerity. The building owes a debt to Auguste Perret, who was responsible for Le Havre's famous postwar tower-blocks and who strove to make a feature of concrete rather than conceal it. Note the frescoes in the main circular office and the latticed glass roof. Just west of the main center, toward the train lines, the 1931 **G** **Boulangerie Waïda & Fils,** 5 place Drouet d'Erlon (☎ 03-26 -47-44-49), is worth visiting even if you're not hungry for baguettes or croissants. The interior is

Where to Stay & Dine in Reims

> Rooms at Les Crayères are well worth the 5-star splurge.

★ kids **Grand Hotel Intercontinental** CENTER-WEST In this 19th-century building near the SNCF station, amid place Drouet d'Erlon's many cafes, rooms were recently renovated in neo–Art Deco and neo–Empire styles and furnished with an eclectic mix of old and new furniture. The bar area is pleasant for a drink in the evenings before or after dinner. 93 place Drouet d'Erlon. ☎ 03-26-40-39-35. www. grandhotelcontinental.com. 61 units. Doubles 95€–185€. MC, V.

★★ kids **Hotel de la Paix Best Western** CENTER-WEST This pleasant design hotel is in a handy spot between the SNCF station and the cathedral. The air-conditioned rooms are decorated in warm, earthy browns, beiges, and creams. The roof garden has a covered swimming pool, a hammam (Turkish bath), and a Jacuzzi. 9 rue Buirette. ☎ 03-26-40-04-08. www.bestwestern-lapaix-reims.com. 169 units. Doubles 155€–205€. MC, V.

★★ **Le Bocal** CENTER-NORTH SEAFOOD In an annex behind Reims's Marché des Halles, the "Fish Bowl" serves only dishes made from the day's catch, fresh from the market. On Tuesday and Wednesday, shellfish are served either hot or cold. On Thursday, Friday, and Saturday, fish fondue frequently appears on the menu—ready to be swilled down with a crisp white or, even better, champagne.

27 rue de Mars. ☎ 03-26-47-02-51. Average 15€. MC, V. Lunch and dinner Tues–Sat.

★★★ kids **Le Café du Palais** CENTER REGIONAL FRENCH Paintings, sketches (including a real Chagall), and arty photos cover every inch of the walls in this friendly, family-run restaurant. Ask for a seat at the back, under the Art Deco cupola masterly crafted by Jacques Simon (p. 258). Dishes might include a giant assiette (plate) of Reims ham, potée champensoise (a regional dish of cabbage and meat stew), and the biggest homemade desserts you've ever seen. 14 place Myron Herrick. ☎ 03-26-47-52-54. www.cafedupalais.fr. A la carte 20€–30€; fixed-price menu 32€–36€. MC, V. Breakfast and lunch Mon–Sat, dinner Tues–Sat.

★★★ **Les Crayères** SOUTH REIMS HAUTE CUISINE There is no better place to stay or dine than here, in one of the finest châteaux in eastern France, in a landscaped park opposite the Pommery champagne house. The opulent guest rooms are dressed in heavy, regal fabrics. The restaurant is an experience unto itself, with delicious dishes such as king crab with citrus fruit confit and avocado purée signed by top chef Philippe Mille. 64 bd. Henry Vasnier. ☎ 03-26-82-80-80. www.lescrayeres.com. 20 units. Doubles 325€–660€. 3 courses 90€–200€. AE, MC, V. Closed Dec 20 to early Jan.

Where to Stay in Champagne

★★★ **Château des Etoges** ETOGES *GOURMET FRENCH*   Surrounded by a moat and grounds abounding with rabbits, this classy 17th-century château offers plush rooms and fine on-site dining. Expect scrumptious red mullet and mussel roulade in saffron sauce, sage-infused rabbit, delicious desserts, and a long list of champagnes. 4 rue Richebourg (22km/14 miles south of Epernay). ☎ 03-26-59-30-08. www.chateau-etoges.com. 28 units. Doubles 90€–300€. 3 courses 35€–90€. AE, DC, MC, V.

★★ **Clos de Chassins** TRELOU SUR MARNE This lovely renovated farm has a spa and light, airy rooms. 4 rue Beethoven, Chassins, Trelou sur Marne (25km/16 miles west of Epernay). ☎ 03-23-69-36-68. www.closdechassins.com. 4 units. Doubles from 90€. MC, V.

kids **Grand Hôtel Terminus Reine** CHAUMONT CENTER *FRENCH*   In a handy spot by the Chaumont train station, this hotel has tastefully renovated, brightly colored rooms and three restaurants (a brasserie/rotisserie, a pizzeria, and a traditional French gourmet dining room). Place Charles de Gaulle. ☎ 03-25-03-66-66. www.relais-sud-champagne.com. 59 units. Doubles 68€–130€. 3 courses 18€–80€. MC, V.

★★ **La Maison de Rhodes** TROYES *FRENCH* Next to the cathedral, this half-timbered dwelling, with 12th-century foundations, once belonged to the Knights Templar of the order of Malta. Stone walls, ocher fabrics, spotless bathrooms, fireplaces, a medieval garden, and a cobbled courtyard create a sense of luxury and romance. The restaurant, La Commanderie, serves gourmet French cuisine (from 40€). 18 rue Linard Gonthier. ☎ 03-25-43-11-11. www.maisonderhodes.com. Doubles 165€–258€. MC, V.

★★ **La Villa Eugène** EPERNAY The old Jean Mercier family house is one of the best hotels in Epernay. Rooms are either classic (light colors, fireplaces, and antiques) or colonial (dark woods and earthy tones). The grounds encompass a garden and a heated pool, too. 82–84 avenue de Champagne.

> *La Villa Eugène in Epernay feels more like a family home than a hotel, with grand but cozy rooms.*

☎ 03-26-32-44-76. www.villa-eugene.com. 15 units. Doubles 100€–250€. MC, V.

★ kids **Le Cheval Blanc** LANGRES *FRENCH* A former church was transformed into this hotel in 1793. Rooms are comfortable, decorated in yellows and reds, with exposed stone walls. The restaurant offers several medieval-themed dinners throughout the year. 4 rue de L'Estres. ☎ 03-25-87-07-00. www.hotel-langres.com. 22 units. 3 courses 25€–75€. Doubles 90€–170€. MC, V.

★★★ **Les Grappes d'Or** CRAMANT Eric and Carole Isselée welcome guests with a smile and a trip around their cellars in the tiny village of Cramant, known for its prestigious Grand Cru vines. Three light-filled rooms have French country furniture, soft bedspreads, and views onto the vines. 350 rue des Grappes d'Or (7km/4⅓ miles south of Epernay on D40 and D10). ☎ 03-26-57-54-96. www.champagne-eric-isselee.com. 3 units. Doubles 45€–60€. MC, V. Closed during the grape harvest.

★★★ **Ployez-Jacquemart** LUDES This inn nestled in a vineyard in the Montagne de Reims serves home-cooked meals. Rooms have names like Azur (white and blue, with 18th-century-style furniture) and Provence (yellow and orange). 8 rue Astoin (13km/8 miles south of Reims on N51 and D26). ☎ 03-26-61-11-87. www.ployez-jacquemart.fr. 5 units. Doubles from 100€. MC, V.

Where to Dine in Champagne

> The dining room at La Table Kobus in Epernay dates to the turn of the 20th century.

★ **Au Jardin Gourmand** TROYES CENTER *AN-DOUILLETTE/FRENCH* Follow your nose and you're bound to end up here, where the most unromantic of sausages, the *andouillette*, is served with a variety of lip-smacking sauces in the most romantic courtyard. Other excellent dishes are available for less adventurous diners. 31 rue Paillot de Montabert. ☎ 03-25-73-36-13. 3 courses 25€–30€; lunch 17€. MC, V. Lunch and dinner Mon–Sat.

★ **La Cave à Champagne** EPERNAY *CHAMPENOIS* This old-fashioned restaurant serves traditional *champenois* dishes such as *potée champenoise* (cabbage and meat stew), foie gras tart, and caramelized apple pie. Each dish comes with a different glass of champagne. 16 rue Gambetta. ☎ 03-26-51-07-24. www.la-cave-a-champagne.com. Menus 17€–44€; main courses 13€. MC, V. Lunch and dinner Thurs–Mon.

★★ **La Table Kobus** EPERNAY *BRASSERIE* This lovely Belle Epoque–style brasserie serves rustic-chic cuisine along the lines of foie gras rolled in Speck with onion chutney, *magret* of duck sprinkled with sugar almonds, and gooey chocolate cake. 3 rue Dr Rousseau. ☎ 03-26-51-53-53. www.latablekobus.com. Menus 28€–48€; main courses 24€. MC, V. Lunch Tues–Sun, dinner Tues–Wed and Fri–Sat. Closed Mon.

★ **Les Caudalies** CHALONS-EN-CHAMPAGNE CENTER *FRENCH* This gourmet restaurant, set within a historic building, doubles as a lovely B&B. In a separate building, accommodations include a living room, a bathroom, and a bedroom that sleeps 2 to 4 people. In the restaurant, expect friendly service and tasty French classics such as duck and scallops. 2 rue de l'Abbé Lambert. ☎ 03-26-65-07-87. www.les-caudalies.com. 1 unit. B&B from 110€. 3 courses 25€–40€. MC, V.

Fast Facts

Arriving & Getting Around

BY CAR East of Paris, the Champagne-Ardenne region is easily accessible by car via the A5 highway through Troyes, the A4 through Reims, and the A26 past Châlons-en-Champagne. You will definitely need a car to follow the route de Champagne (p. 253). **Avis** (www.avis.com) and **Hertz** (www.hertz.com) have cars available in Reims, Epernay, and Troyes. **BY TRAIN** The region is well served by rail; from Paris, the trip to Reims takes 45 minutes (or 30 min. from Charles-de-Gaulle Airport via high-speed train); Epernay takes 1 hour and 20 minutes; and Troyes takes 1 hour and 25 minutes. **BY PLANE** The nearest airports are in Paris.

Doctors & Dentists

SOS medecin (☎ 3634) is a nationwide hotline for non-emergency medical referrals. Some (but not all) doctors speak English and are available day and night, including Sundays and public holidays. The doctor travels to your address for the consultation, but you may have to wait for several hours if your condition is not urgent.

Emergency

Police ☎ 17. Fire department and paramedics ☎ 18. Ambulance ☎ 15. For any emergency, dial ☎ 112 from a cell phone.

Internet

Most hotels will have Internet service of some kind. Or try **Cyber Games** in Reims, 52 place Drouet d'Erlon (☎ 03-26 -49-14-66; http://cybergamesreims.free.fr; Mon–Sat 10am–7pm). Ask at the tourist offices about additional cybercafes in the towns you are visiting.

Post Office

REIMS The most beautiful post office is the Art Deco **La Poste,** on rue Cérès (p. 258). The office near the convention center, at 9 place Stalingrad, is in a handy spot. Mon–Sat 8:30am–noon, 1:30–6pm. **TROYES** Try **La Poste** at 14 rue de La Republique (inside the cork-shaped town center), open Tues–Sat 10am–12:30pm, 1:45–5:30pm.

> *The post office in Reims.*

Tourist Offices

Municipal tourist offices are listed at the end of the town tour stops throughout the chapter. **REIMS** 2 rue Guillaume de Machault (☎ 08-92-70-13-51; www.reims-tourism.com). **CHAMPAGNE REGIONAL TOURIST BOARD** www.champagne-ardenne-tourism.co.uk.

Travel Tip

For more practical information, see "France Fast Facts," p. 703.

7
Alsace &
Lorraine

Favorite Moments in Alsace & Lorraine

On the banks of the Rhine River, Alsace and its western neighbor, Lorraine, may remind you of Germany, which shares a border with both French regions. The gabled houses, Christmas markets, and ubiquitous *choucroute* (sauerkraut) are conspicuous reminders that Alsace-Lorraine was an imperial province of Germany as recently as 1918. The bucolic charm of the vineyards and villages in this easternmost part of France contrasts with the regions' three fine cities—magnificent Strasbourg, capital of Alsace and seat of the European Parliament; Nancy, the birthplace of Art Nouveau; and Metz, capital of Lorraine and the new hip destination for contemporary art lovers.

> *PREVIOUS PAGE Half-timbered facades, pointy roofs, vines, and forests: Welcome to Alsace and Lorraine.*
> *THIS PAGE Loosen your belt in Strasbourg and make way for Chez Yvonne's choucroute.*

❶ Driving the Route des Crêtes. Forming an unofficial border between Alsace and Lorraine, this 42km (26-mile) stretch between Mulhouse and Colmar is one of Europe's great mountain drives. Take your time along the way to indulge in the freshest Munster cheese, enjoy the view from a ski lift, or play outdoors in a sports town such as Gérardmer. See p. 289.

❷ Deciphering the Isenheim Altarpiece. At the Musée d'Unterlinden in Colmar, Alsace, this gorgeous, multi-winged compendium of Christian allegories is one of the inspirations to come out of the early Renaissance in northern Europe. See p. 269, ❷.

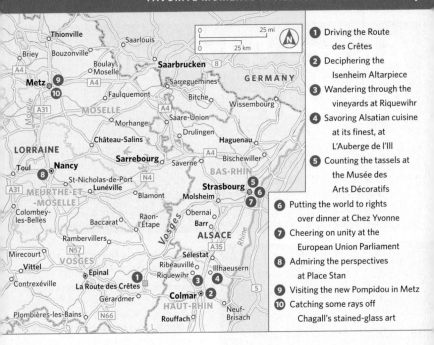

1 Driving the Route des Crêtes
2 Deciphering the Isenheim Altarpiece
3 Wandering through the vineyards at Riquewihr
4 Savoring Alsatian cuisine at its finest, at L'Auberge de l'Ill
5 Counting the tassels at the Musée des Arts Décoratifs
6 Putting the world to rights over dinner at Chez Yvonne
7 Cheering on unity at the European Union Parliament
8 Admiring the perspectives at Place Stan
9 Visiting the new Pompidou in Metz
10 Catching some rays off Chagall's stained-glass art

3 **Wandering through the vineyards at Riquewihr.** Pathways wind through the vineyards from the prettiest village on the Alsace Wine Route, where roses bloom at the ends of the vine rows. See p. 273, 2.

4 **Savoring Alsatian cuisine at its finest, at L'Auberge de l'Ill.** This restaurant in the tiny village of Illhaeusern has put Alsace on the map for gastronomes. The flavors are fine-tuned to pair beautifully with the region's distinctive wines. See p. 308.

5 **Counting the tassels at the Musée des Arts Décoratifs.** Among the treasures at the stunning Palais Rohan in Strasbourg are the restored bedrooms of the previous royal residents, which had more silk, velvet, and frills than a sultan's harem. See p. 301, 4.

6 **Putting the world to rights over dinner at Chez Yvonne.** Intellectuals used to get together in the cozy Alsatian *winstubs* (wine bistros)— Chez Yvonne in Strasbourg is the very best of these—to thrash out their ideas, and you can do the same as you tuck into a plate of *baeckeoffe* (a pork, mutton, beef, and potato stew). See p. 304.

7 **Cheering on unity at the European Union Parliament.** Plan your trip to Strasbourg so you can attend a session of Parliament during the few days a month when Europe's bigwigs and blowhards inhabit the gorgeous Louise Weiss Building. See p. 302, 6.

8 **Admiring the perspectives at Place Stan.** You may actually feel your sense of space realign as you stroll along place Stanislas in Nancy, a model of European symmetry in urban planning. See p. 294, 1.

9 **Visiting the new Pompidou in Metz.** Both the honeycomb architecture and the visiting collections from Paris's Centre Pompidou make the Centre Pompidou-Metz the region's new art highlight. See p. 275, 10.

10 **Catching some rays off Chagall's stained-glass art.** The stained-glass designed by Russian-French artist Marc Chagall is justly famous, and some of his earliest pieces are found in the windows of Metz's Cathédrale St-Etienne. But his work is just a part of the largest expanse of stained glass in the world. Aim for a sunny-weather visit. See p. 275, 10.

Alsace & Lorraine in 3 Days

Three days for three cities—international Strasbourg, medieval Colmar, and Art Nouveau Nancy. Each is culturally rich and expresses a different facet of this rigorously intellectual and artistic region. Be prepared for long days, with visits to several museums punctuated by city walks amid glorious architecture and meals of rich but satisfying food. You can do this short itinerary entirely by train, unless you want to visit a vineyard or two en route.

> With its 142m-tall (466-ft.) spire, Strasbourg's cathedral was the world's tallest building until 1874.

START Strasbourg is 489km (304 miles) east of Paris. TRIP LENGTH 216km (134 miles).

❶ ★★★ **Strasbourg.** The best place to start your tour is the capital of Alsace, Strasbourg. Spend a couple of hours in the morning at the ★★★ **Musée d'Art Moderne et Contemporain,** one of Europe's top repositories of modern art. The museum is best known for its vast collection of works by master engraver and Strasbourg native Gustave Doré; a distinctive collection of contemporary German paintings; and a permanent display of works by modern visionaries including Kandinsky, Klee, Monet, Picasso, Pissarro, and Rodin. Plan to leave the museum by noon and take the tram to the Grande Ile in time to catch the 12:30pm kids **Procession of the Apostles** on the astronomical clock at the ★★★ **Cathédrale Notre-Dame.** Then climb the 332 steps to the top of the cathedral's spire for a view that, on a clear day, encompasses three nations: the French plains, Germany's Black Forest, and the mountains of Switzerland. Taste your first authentic Alsatian cuisine over lunch at the nearby ★ **Le Tire Bouchon** before strolling to the baroque ★★ **Palais Rohan.** This palace, one of Strasbourg's architectural treasures, contains three museums devoted to decorative arts, fine arts (the pre-modern eras), and archaeology; take your pick according to preference. Spend the remainder of the afternoon in the lovely ★★★ **Petite France quarter,** Strasbourg's picturesque mini-Venice, with its waterways, cobblestone streets, 18th-century buildings, boutiques, and cafes. This is a restaurant

neighborhood, and you won't regret staying on to dine here at ★ **La Cambuse** or ★★ **Umami.**
⏲ 1 day. For detailed information on Strasbourg, see p. 298; see also p. 276, **1**.

From Strasbourg, take A35 south to Colmar (74km/46 miles; or 30 min. by train).

2 ★★★ **Colmar.** Near the fine powder–covered slopes of the southern Vosges, Colmar is Alsace's most beautiful city, full of medieval and early Renaissance buildings, half-timbered structures, gables, and loggias. In summer, window boxes are draped with geraniums, and in winter, log fires burn in cozy restaurants. Colmar's main claim to fame on the cultural front, and the focus of your visit here, is the ★★★ **Isenheim Altarpiece,** housed in the **Musée d'Unterlinden,** 1 rue d'Unterlinden (☎ 03-89-20-15-50; www.musee-unterlinden. com; admission 8€ adults, 5€ students, 3€ ages 12–18, free for children 11 and under; May–Oct daily 9am–6pm, Nov–Apr Wed–Mon 9am–noon and 2–5pm). The immense 16th-century altar screen by Matthias Grünewald depicts St. Anthony visiting the hermit of St. Paul, along with birds, monsters, and loathsome animals. Make time also for a visit to the **Musée Bartholdi,**

> *The region's wine capital, Colmar is also renowned as the most beautiful city in Alsace.*

Where to Stay & Dine

For hotels and restaurants in Strasbourg, see p. 303; in Nancy, see p. 297; elsewhere in the region, see p. 306.

30 rue des Marchands (☎ 03-89-41-90-60; www.musee-bartholdi.com; admission 5€ adults, 2.50€ children; Mar–Dec Wed–Mon 10am–noon and 2–6pm; closed Jan–Feb), a curiosity that will interest North American visitors. Statue of Liberty sculptor Frédéric-Auguste Bartholdi was born here in Colmar, and the museum contains memorabilia as well as plans and scale models of Lady Liberty.

Colmar is "the capital of Alsatian wine"; while 3 days in the region won't allow you to fully explore the Wine Route, stop in at the **Cave du Musée,** 11 rue Kléber (☎ 03-89-23-85-29), to peruse a large selection of the region's wines. Colmar's old town has many lovely shops, especially for antiques collectors, and it's well worth browsing for a while. ⏱ 1 day. Colmar Tourist Office, 4 rue Unterlinden. ☎ 03-89-20-68-92. www.colmar.fr.

From Colmar, take D415/N415 northwest, pick up N59 at Le Faing, and join N333/A33 to Nancy (142km/88 miles; or 2 hr. by train).

❸ ★★ **Nancy.** The handsome capital of Lorraine is renowned as the birthplace of Art Nouveau, but it also has medieval alleys and towers and rococo gates and fountains. It is a lively city, home to a large population of industrious students of engineering, mining, metallurgy, and finance. Head first for ★★★ **place Stanislas,** the very heart of the city and a historical achievement in urban planning. Known affectionately as "Place Stan," the square has gained UNESCO World Heritage status for the concentration of architectural gems that line its periphery. It's just a few steps from here to the ★ **Musée des Beaux-Arts,** where you can easily get lost for 90 minutes exploring works by Matisse, Modigliani, Monet, and Picasso, as well as early paintings by Rubens and late pieces by Caravaggio. By now you'll have worked up an appetite, so lunch in style at the nearby **Le Capucin Gourmand.** After lunch, discover Nancy's groundbreaking Art Nouveau movement at the ★★ **Musée de l'Ecole de Nancy,** one of the world's foremost collections of work inspired by this sweeping philosophy. If you care to shop for some Art Nouveau of your very own, you'll find plenty of pieces, both antique and new, around place Stanislas. Then sample some of the heavy local fondue at ★ **Le Bouche à Oreille.** ⏱ 1 day. For detailed information on Nancy, see p. 294.

> First admire Colmar's Isenheim Altarpiece as a whole, then get closer to see the Christ figure with two faces.

> Nancy's glorious "Place Stan" is a top spot for coffee and people-watching.

Alsace & Lorraine in 1 Week

With a week to spare, you can venture out of the city and into the lush countryside. We start this tour in the wine heartland of southern Alsace, taking in some of the jewel-like villages between Colmar and Strasbourg along the Alsace Wine Route (p. 279). After spending a day in Strasbourg, the Alsatian capital, we move west into the Lorraine region to see art treasures in Nancy and Metz and historic landmarks in Toul and Verdun.

> The half-timbered houses along Colmar's quai de la Poissonnerie typify Alsatian architecture.

START Colmar is 74km (46 miles) south of Strasbourg. **TRIP LENGTH** 432km/268 miles.

1 ★★★ **Colmar.** What better place to begin a week in this region of natural and gastronomic splendor than in the capital of Alsatian wine. Beautiful Colmar glories in its own "Little Venice," a neighborhood formed of interlocking canals. The 12m-high (39-ft.) **Statue of Liberty** at the city's north entrance stands in honor of hometown hero Frêdéric Bartholdi, who designed the original Lady Liberty; the **Musée Bartholdi** is dedicated to him. Move

on to the **Musée d'Unterlinden,** which houses the glorious ★★★ **Isenheim Altarpiece**—one of Europe's finest, largest, and most dramatic paintings from the early 16th century. 1 day. See p. 269, **2**.

The stretch from Colmar to Riquewihr meanders through some famous vineyards. On Day 2, head to Ammerschwihr on D415, turn right on rue de Kientzheim out of the village, and continue on the route de Riquewihr (14km/8¾ miles).

1 Colmar
2 Riquewihr
3 Ribeauvillé
4 Château du Haut-Koenigsbourg
5 Obernai
6 Strasbourg
7 Nancy
8 Toul
9 Verdun
10 Metz

2 ★★★ **Riquewihr.** Some say Riquewihr is the prettiest village on the Alsace Wine Route (p. 279). Vineyards run right up to its ramparts, and the ends of the vine rows are planted with roses, which serve as early parasite detectors. The village, which belonged to the counts of Wurtenberg until the French Revolution, is picture-perfect with its geranium-filled balconies, cobblestone alleys, and red roofs. Visit the old prison, the **Tour des Voleurs;** the 16th-century winemakers' home, **Maison du Vigneron,** on rue des Juifs; and the old fortifications of the **Tour du Dolder,** on rue du Général de Gaulle (☎ 03-89-86-00-92; www.musees-alsace.org; admission 5€ for both museums; Apr–June and Sept–Nov Sat–Sun 10:30am–1pm and 2–6pm; July–Aug daily 10:30am–1pm and 2–6pm). If you're lucky enough to be visiting on a Sunday or Monday, lunch at **Auberge du Schoenenbourg** (p. 306), at the edge of the vineyards; otherwise try the sublime **Le Sarment d'Or,** 4 rue du Cerf (☎ 03-89-86-02-86; main courses 24€–28€; menus 26€–37€; lunch and dinner Tues–Sun except Nov–Dec). ⏱ Half-day. Pays de Ribeauvillé-Riquewihr Tourist Office, 2 rue de la 1ère Armée. ☎ 03-89-73-23-23. www.ribeauville-riquewihr.com.

> *Pro-European Union fervor is omnipresent in Alsace, even in remote villages such as Riquewihr, on the wine route.*

Where to Stay & Dine

For hotels and restaurants in Strasbourg, see p. 303; in Nancy, see p. 297; elsewhere in the region, see p. 306.

> *L'Oussuaire in Verdun displays the names of those who died in one of World War I's bloodiest battles.*

After lunch, take D1bis north from Riquewihr to Ribeauvillé (5km/3 miles).

③ ★★ Ribeauvillé. No fewer than three ruined castles, built by the Ribeaupierre family during the Middle Ages, overlook Ribeauvillé, one of the most visited villages on the Alsace Wine Route. All three can be reached via a signposted path from the village. The Grand'rue is the main street in the village, lined with historic half-timbered houses painted in pastel colors. If you stray into the neighboring streets, you'll find squares adorned with Renaissance fountains. There is no better place to stay and eat than ★★ **Le Clos St-Vincent** (p. 308), overlooking the village. ⏱ Half-day. See p. 278, **④**.

On Day 3, take D1bis to St-Hippolyte, and pick up the Route du Haut-Koenigsbourg left out of town to the Château de Haut-Koenigsbourg (10km/6 miles).

④ ★★★ 📷 Château du Haut-Koenigsbourg. This prominent castle on the route to Obernai is straight out of a fairy tale. Towering high above a forest, it was begun in the 12th century and successively added to and besieged over centuries of war, with a massive renovation at the beginning of the 20th century. A trophy of war and diplomacy over the centuries, Haut-Koenigsbourg still conveys how a medieval fortress looked, though it now serves as a museum of weapons and furniture from the 16th to the 18th centuries. ⏱ Half-day. See p. 286, **⑦**.

Retrace your route to St-Hippolyte, and join A35 north to Obernai (35km/22 miles).

⑤ ★★ Obernai. Try to arrive in Obernai in time to lunch at ★★ **Zum Schnogalch** (p. 308), known for its *choucroute*. Obernai is the second most visited town in Alsace after Strasbourg, esteemed for its beautifully preserved medieval character and numerous festivals, events, and street performances dedicated to promoting local history. Most of the sights in Obernai are free; as you wander around, you can take in the ramparts, the Jewish quarter, the Kappellturn Belfry, the Church of St. Peter and Paul, the Renaissance Well of the Six Buckets, and 17th-century Fastinger Courtyard. ⏱ Half-day. Obernai Tourist Office, place du Beffroi. ☎ 03-88-95-64-13. www.obernai.fr. See also p. 277, **②**, and 285, **⑥**.

From Obernai, continue north on A35 to Strasbourg (31km/19 miles) for dinner.

⑥ ★★★ Strasbourg. Try to reach Strasbourg, with its wealth of excellent restaurants, in time for dinner on Day 3. On Day 4, don't miss the ★★★ **Musée d'Art Moderne et Contemporain,** the ★★★ **Cathédrale Notre-Dame,** the museums of the ★★ **Palais Rohan,** and ★★★ **La Petite France,** the canal quarter. ⏱ 1 day. For detailed information on Strasbourg, see p. 298; see also p. 276, **①**.

Early on Day 5, take A4 from Strasbourg east to Phalsbourg, and follow N4 and N333 to Nancy (156km/97 miles).

⑦ ★★ Nancy. After the 2-hour drive from Strasbourg, stretch your legs in ★★★ **place Stanislas**—one of the premier squares in Europe and a UNESCO World Heritage site—before exploring Nancy's Art Nouveau treasures. ⏱ 1 day. For detailed information on Nancy, see p. 294.

On Day 6, take A31 west from Nancy to Toul (23km/14 miles).

⑧ Toul. Toul was the primary U.S. airbase during World War I, from which two large offensives were launched. But the city's military history didn't begin in the 20th century. It was fortified by Louis XIV's military architect Vauban, and parts of its **ramparts**—which in places stand over 5m (16 ft.) high—date back even further. As one of the powerful Three Bishoprics of Lorraine, conquered by Henri II in the 16th century, Toul also has an impressive cathedral,

> *The spire of the Centre Pompidou-Metz rises 77m (253 ft.), alluding to the 1977 opening date of the Centre Pompidou in Paris.*

St-Etienne, on place Charles de Gaulle, with an arched, high-Gothic interior. We recommend stopping for lunch on your way out of town, in an old railway station on D908, at the **Auberge du Pressoir,** 7 rue Pachenottes, Lucey (☎ 03-83-63-81-91; www.aubergedupressoir.com; main courses 16€–21€, menus 12.90€–17€; lunch Tues–Sun, dinner Tues and Thurs–Sat). ⏰ Half-day. See p. 284, ❸.

From Toul, take D904 and D903 northwest to Verdun (77km/48 miles).

❾ ★ **Verdun.** "Hell cannot be so terrible as this," wrote a French soldier from the Battle of Verdun, the longest episode of combat during World War I. The battle accounted for some 360,000 French casualties, made Marshal Pétain a hero, and had future repercussions during World War II. It's little wonder that this tiny patch of land—it covers fewer than 10 sq. km (4 sq. miles)—was shunned for decades after World War I, allowing nature to overrun it. But little by little, veterans and historians began returning to erect impressive monuments in the name of peace. Forty kilometers (25 miles) north of Verdun is the immaculate **American Meuse-Argonne Cemetery** at Romagne, which contains the largest number of American military dead in Europe, all famously resting under 14,246 white crosses or stars of David, in eight geometric sections. ⏰ Half-day. See p. 282, ❶.

On Day 7 from Verdun, take A4 and A31 to Metz (81km/50 miles).

❿ ★ **Metz.** The capital of Lorraine has rapidly recovered from its tough industrial times since the 2010 opening of the ★★★ **Centre Pompidou-Metz,** 1 parvis des Droits de l'Homme (☎ 03-87-15-39-39; www.centrepompidou-metz.fr; admission 7€ adults, 4.50€ reduced; Mon, Wed, Sun 11am–6pm, Thurs–Sat 11am–8pm). Junior sibling to the Centre Pompidou in Paris (p. 61, ❹), this new contemporary art museum houses modern masterpieces heretofore only available in the City of Light. The building itself is remarkable; built of glued, laminated wood, latticed together to form a wavy hexagonal mesh, it becomes luminously transparent at night. Depending on what's on loan when you visit, you may find Picasso or Matisse, as well as exciting works in new media. After your museum visit, stroll around **place St-Louis.** Don't miss the world's largest expanse of stained glass, from the 14th-century to 20th-century windows by Marc Chagall, at the ★★ **Cathédrale St-Etienne,** 2 place de La Chambre (☎ 03-87-75-54-61; www.cathedrale-metz.fr; admission 3.50€; summer daily 8am–7pm, winter 9am–6pm). ⏰ 1 day. Metz Tourist Office, 2 place d'Armes. ☎ 03-87-55-53-76. http://tourisme.mairie-metz.fr/fr/index.php.

Alsace & Lorraine for Gourmands

"Gourmand" to English speakers means "greedy," but for the French, the term is a compliment—equally apt for the farmer tucking into his heaped plate of *choucroute* as for the epicurean swilling pricey wine in a temple of gastronomy. This region rewards travelers with a range of dining experiences from rustic to refined. Let yourself be seduced by the cozy intimacy of the *winstubs,* the delis casually purveying foie gras, and (if you can spring for it) at least one Michelin-starred blowout. This route starts in Strasbourg and from there follows the Alsace Wine Route (see the box on p. 279) through picturesque villages and flower-filled valleys—from one meal to the next.

> Diners can watch Chef René Fieger at work in his small kitchen, visible from the dining room, at Umami in Strasbourg.

START Strasbourg is 489km (304 miles) east of Paris. **TRIP LENGTH** 120km (75 miles).

❶ ★★★ Strasbourg. Alsace has more Michelin-starred chefs than anywhere else in France besides Paris, and most of them are concentrated in Strasbourg. In this administrative city, it's no surprise really: Eurocrats are known for their gastronomic tendencies. But Strasbourg's high-flying cuisine predates the European Union by centuries. It's rooted in a great intellectual tradition that can be traced back to the birth of humanism,

when Strasbourg's thinkers assembled to thrash out their ideas in the *winstubs,* wine bars serving hearty fare such as *baeckeoffe* and *choucroute,* or tasty small morsels like *grumbeerekeichle* (potato galettes) and *quenelles de foie* (pork liver patties). This tradition continues at **★★ Chez Yvonne** (p. 304), with its snug rooms stacked with books and decorated with oil paintings. If you are lucky enough to meet owner Jean-Louis de Valmigère, you are sure to be treated to a fascinating foray into Alsatian history. Together with Emile Jung,

1 Strasbourg

2 Obernai

3 Dambach-la-Ville

4 Ribeauvillé

5 L'Auberge de l'Ill, Illhaeusern

6 Riquewihr

7 Colmar

8 Turckheim

9 Eguisheim

10 Guebwiller

11 Ecomusée d'Alsace, Ungersheim

12 Mulhouse

the former chef at ★★★ **Au Crocodile** (p. 304), Valmigère started the **Food Culture** festival (www.culture-food.eu), which takes place every year in June.

Strasbourg's other culinary star is Eric Westermann, chef-owner of ★★ **Le Buerehiesel,** 4 parc de l'Orangerie (☎ 03-88-45-56-65; www.buerehiesel.fr; main courses 24€–39, menus 65€ and 88€; AE, DC, MC, V; Tues–Sat noon–1:30pm and 7:30–9:30pm). Westermann offers proof, as if anyone needed it, that Alsatian cuisine can attain an exceptional finesse that belies its porky, earthy origins. Did you know, for instance, that Alsace has its own tradition of foie gras—the food so often associated with the southwest of the country? Taste for yourself at **Artzner,** 7 rue de la Mésange (☎ 03-88-32-05-00; www.edouard-artzner.com; Mon 3–7pm, Tues–Fri 9am–7pm, Sat 8:30am–6pm; AE, DC, MC, V), which has been producing Alsatian foie gras since the early 19th century.

Finally, check out rising star René Fieger—a daring and iconoclastic chef working from his own tiny kitchen at ★★ **Umami** (p. 305). There's enough to keep you busy and full in Strasbourg for at least 2 days, before you set off on the Alsace Wine Route. ⏱ 2 days. For detailed information on Strasbourg, see p. 298.

From Strasbourg, turn right on A35, drive 15km (9⅓ miles) to D1422 and, after 2km (1¼ mile), pick up A35 again. Continue 8.5km (5⅓ miles) to D426, which leads to Obernai (30km/19 miles total).

2 ★★ **Obernai.** The meticulously restored medieval town of Obernai is the second-most-visited town in Alsace after Strasbourg. It has a well-founded reputation for good food, with 11 *winstubs* and two Michelin-starred restaurants. The Lalique-decorated dining room lives up to the elegance of Nicolas Stamm's cooking at the fabulous **La Fourchette des Ducs,** 6 rue de la Gare (☎ 03-88-48-33-38; main courses 30€–40€, menus 89€–120€; AE, DC, MC, V; Tues–Sat 7:30–9pm). In a

Where to Stay & Dine

For hotels and restaurants in Strasbourg, see p. 303; elsewhere in the region, see p. 306.

> Alsatian wines are recognizable by the elongated form of their bottles, like these in Dambach-la-Ville.

more relaxed setting, Thierry Schwartz dishes up surprising culinary inventions in a rustic old inn, **Le Bistro des Saveurs,** 35 rue de Sélestat (☎ 03-88-49-90-41; main courses 20€–30€, menus 32€–89€; Tues–Sat noon–2pm and 7:30–9pm, Sun noon–2pm). Many local wineries produce red wine, including pinot noir, which is rare in the region. Obernai is also known for hosting one of the best Christmas markets in France. We recommend spending the night, and relaxing for a while in the spa, at ★★ **Le Parc** (p. 308). ◷ Half-day. See p. 274, **5**, and 285, **6**.

Travel south from Obernai on D1422 to Dambach-la-Ville (19km/12 miles).

3 **Dambach-la-Ville.** You'll find more than 30 grape growers here, including the **Willy Gisselbrecht Winery,** 5 rte. du Vin (☎ 03-88-92-41-02; www.vins-gisselbrecht.com), and a *Grand Cru*, **Frankstein.** The town hosts two major wine fairs in summer: **Wine Night** in July and **Eurovin** in August. Dambach-la-Ville

is also renowned for its well-preserved, half-timbered houses; the 11th-century Chapelle St-Sébastien; an ancient market square; and centuries-old ramparts. ◷ Half-day. Dambach-la-Ville Tourist Office, 11 place du Marché. ☎ 03-88-92-41-05. www.dambach-la-ville.fr.

From Dambach-la-Ville, travel south on A35, D1b, and D1bis to Ribeauvillé (19km/12 miles).

4 ★★ **Ribeauvillé.** On the first weekend of September in Ribeauvillé, in celebration of an event called Piper's Day, the town fountain runs with drinkable wine. Ribeauvillé is home to three *Grand Crus*—**Geisberg, Kirschberg,** and **Osterberg**—and at least two other excellent wineries, **Trimbach** and the aptly named **Sipp.** Travel on to Illhaeusern for dinner and a good night's sleep. ◷ Half-day. Ribeauvillé Tourist Office, 1 Grand'rue. www.ribeauville-riquewihr.com. ☎ 03-89-73-23-23. See also p. 274, **3**.

From Ribeauvillé, take D106 east to Illhaeusern (9km/5⅔ miles).

5 ★★★ **L'Auberge de l'Ill, Illhaeusern.** For gastronomes, there is one reason to visit Illhaeusern: the Auberge de l'Ill—the greatest restaurant in eastern France, run by the Haeberlin family in their 19th-century farmhouse, with rooms to let. ◷ Overnight. See p. 308.

Backtrack on D106 as far as Guémar, join N83 for a few kilometers to the Ostheim junction, and follow signs for Riquewihr (13km/8 miles).

6 ★★★ **Riquewihr.** One of the few great Riesling areas, with vines running right up to the village limits, Riquewihr is a romantic stop that attracts amorous couples. Its historical architecture is film-set perfect, nearly unchanged since the 16th century. Two popular *Grand Crus* are here: **Schoenenbourg de Riquewihr** and **Sporen.** Dozens of other wineries are nearby, and walking trails lead straight out of the village, so you can take in the gorgeous scenery entirely on foot, close to the vines. The tourist office (www.ribeauville-riquewihr.com) can set you on your way. ◷ Half-day. See information for Ribeauvillé Tourist Office, **4** on this tour.

Take the route de Riquewihr south out of Riquewihr, and travel through Kientzheim and Ammerschwihr, via D415, to Colmar (13km/8 miles).

> *The Alsatian restaurant L'Auberge de l'Ill has garnered three Michelin stars since 1967.*

7 ★★★ **Colmar.** Eguisheim (**9** on this tour) may be the cradle of Alsatian wine, but Colmar is the capital and the largest town on the Alsace Wine Route. It's a good hub from which to enjoy day trips to wineries; if you want to ditch the car, organize a guided tour through the **Centre d'Information du Vin d'Alsace,** 12 av. de la Foire aux Vins, at the Maison du Vin d'Alsace (☎ 03-89-20-16-20; Mon–Fri 9am–noon and 2–5pm). Try to visit in mid-August, during the region's largest wine fair, the **Foire aux Vins d'Alsace.** See p. 269, **2**. ⏱ Half-day and overnight.

Drive east on av. de la Liberté and av. de l'Europe to Turckheim (9km/5⅔ miles).

8 ★★ **Turckheim.** This is the home of Gewürztraminer, a lychee-like grape that produces a sugary, off-dry wine that often pairs well with East Asian cuisines. **Cave Vinicole,** 16 rue des Tuileries (☎ 03-89-30-23-60; www.cave-turckheim.com), is a reputable cooperative of more than 200 wineries, guaranteeing splendid tastings. The town is distinguished by its medieval walls, with three large gates. If you arrive in spring or summer, you'll hear the songs of the town's Night Watchman, a native in period dress who strolls the city at 10pm every night, singing golden Alsatian oldies. As in many towns on the Wine Route, the quantity of beautiful flowers here is staggering. ⏱ 1 day.

Turckheim Tourist Office, rue Wickram, corps de Garde. ☎ 03-89-27-38-44. www.turckheim.fr.

Drive south from Turckheim via Wintzenheim and Wettolsheim to Eguisheim (5km/3 miles).

9 ★ **Eguisheim.** Every type of wine grown in Alsace can be found in these environs, one of the great grape-growing areas of the region. Two of the town's vineyards merit the *Grand Cru* appellation—**Eichberg** and **Pfersigberg.**

The Alsace Wine Route (Le Route du Vin d'Alsace)

The oldest designated wine route in France, the Alsace Route du Vin (www.vinsalsace.com) meanders through B-roads so insignificant they sometimes don't even have a number. Still, the route is easy to follow; it's signposted, and you can pick up maps along the way or download them from the website. For complete information on regional wine caves, visit the **Centre d'Information du Vin d'Alsace** in Colmar, 12 av. de la Foire aux Vins, at the Maison du Vin d'Alsace (☎ 03-89-20-16-20; Mon–Fri 9am–noon and 2–5pm). Tourist offices and wineries along the route will also dispense information and maps. Included in this tour are our favorite stops on the Route du Vin, listed from north to south.

Two more *Grands Crus* are nearby: **Hatschbourg,** in Voegtlinshoffen, and **Steingrubler,** in Wettolsheim. The area's reputation as the cradle of Alsatian wine country merited the construction of a number of impressive castles to protect it; three still exist and warrant a visit. Just ask directions to the rue de Trois Châteaux (Street of the Three Castles). The presentation of new wine on the last weekend of March draws a number of oenophiles, as do the area's many tasting cellars. ⏱ Half-day. Eguisheim Tourist Office, 22A Grand'rue. ☎ 03-89-23-40-33. www.ot-eguisheim.fr.

From Eguisheim, take D1bis south through Hattstatt and Pfaffenheim to Guebwiller (21km/13 miles).

⑩ ★ **Guebwiller.** At the mouth of the Lauch Valley, known as the "Valley of Flowers," this small town's main draws are its beautiful landscapes and its trio of churches: Romanesque Eglise St-Léger, Gothic Eglise des Dominicains, and the rare baroque Eglise Notre-Dame. If you have time left at the end of the day, take a walk out into the valley. Guebwiller has several wine caves in the town itself, but you'll probably gain more insight by staying with a wine producer, at ★★ **Auberge du Cheval Blanc** (p. 306). ⏱ Half-day and overnight. Guebwiller Tourist Office, 71 rue de la République. ☎ 03-89-76-10-63. www.tourisme-guebwiller.fr.

From Guebwiller, follow D430 southeast then D44 east to Ungersheim (9km/5⅔ miles).

⑪ ★★ kids **Ecomuseé d'Alsace, Ungersheim.** En route to Mulhouse, your last stop, you'll pass the biggest open-air museum in Europe. This veritable village, made up of 70 houses transplanted from all over the region, is devoted to exploring cuisine and *terroir* (the unique attributes of the particular patch of land that produces a food or wine). Visitors can take cooking lessons and learn how to make Alsatian cuisine back home. ⏱ Half-day. ☎ 03-89-74-44-74. www.ecomusee-alsace.fr. July–Aug daily 10am–7pm, Sept–June daily 10am–6pm. Admission 12€ adults, 7€ reduced.

From Ungersheim, backtrack to D430 and continue southeast to Mulhouse (19km/12 miles).

> *Riquewihr is famous for its wines, but you can also sample delicious German pretzels.*

Choucroute & Quiche

Nothing says Lorraine like quiche. This dish probably became such a local hit because of its cheap, easy-to-find ingredients: eggs, cream, cheese (Gruyère, Emmental, or Swiss), white wine–marinated pork, and a delicate pastry crust. If you want the full Lorraine experience, pair it with a Gris de Toul wine, which comes from one of the largest vineyards in the region.

Few foods are more Alsatian, on the other hand, than *choucroute* (sauerkraut), despite the condiment's association with Germany and the theory that it was actually Genghis Khan who introduced it to Europe 1,000 years ago. Here it's made from locally grown white cabbage, which is shredded and fermented for at least 2 months, first in brine, salt, and juniper berries, and then in the cook's special blend of white wine, onions, pepper, garlic, lard, and maybe pigs' feet. Delivering a burst of flavor in every bite, *choucroute* should appear on the menu wherever you go in this area, from the swankiest restaurants to the most rustic of local *winstubs*.

⓬ **Mulhouse.** Just a 20-minute drive from the southern end of the Alsace Wine Route, this small city of 118,000 people was the industrial capital of Alsace in the 19th century. Now, with its chic nightlife, contemporary decor, and thriving culture, it's a refreshing change after so many perfect chocolate-box Alsatian villages. There is steaming *choucroute* to be had at restaurants such as the *winstub* **Pic-Vit,** 8 rue Bons Enfants (☎ 03-89-45-71-17; main courses 11.50€–16€, menus 21€–22.50€; AE, DC, MC, V; Mon 11:30am–2pm, Tues–Sat 11:30am–2pm and 6:30–10pm; closed Sun), and **Aux Caves du Vieux Couvent,** 23 rue du Couvent (☎ 03-89-46-28-79; www.cavesduvieuxcouvent.com; main courses 13€–20€, menus 24€–27€; AE, DC, MC, V). For those who crave a little more nightlife, there are bars such as **Le Festival,** 2 passage de l'Hôtel de Ville (☎ 03-89-56-04-21), and **Cotton Club,** 13 rue Louise Pasteur (☎ 03-89-56-09-39). ⏱ Half-day. Mulhouse Tourist Office, place de la Reunion. ☎ 03-89-35-48-48. www.mulhouse.fr.

> *The pert, juicy grapes grown in Eguisheim are the beginnings of many Grand Cru wines.*

Alsace & Lorraine for History Buffs

The phrase "disputed territory" comes up in almost any discussion about the history of Alsace and Lorraine, coveted as these regions have been by both France and Germany over the centuries. Despite their peaceful beauty today, they have seen plenty of soldiers and innocent victims fall over the centuries. Lorraine served as one of the main killing fields of World War I, and fortifications at Toul and Neuf-Brisach testify to the region's strategic importance to France in the 17th century. The region's position as a European crossroads also gave rise to intellectual and artistic movements, from French humanism in Sélestat to Art Nouveau in Nancy. History lovers will adore this tour, where relatively small distances take you through 8 centuries of conflict and creative thinking.

> The beautiful Bibliothèque Humaniste in Sélestat contains the bust of Jean Mentel, a Renaissance printer born in Sélestat in 1410.

START Verdun is just about equidistant from Paris (260km/162 miles) and Strasbourg (238km/148 miles). **TRIP LENGTH** 7 days; 397km (247 miles).

❶ ★ **Verdun.** There is a saying that "Modern France began at Verdun." It refers to the treaty signed here in A.D. 843 among the three grandsons of Charlemagne, in which the western part of his empire, claimed by Charles the Bald, approximated to modern-day France. The treaty—a slicing of the cake that disregarded language and customs—started arguments and wars that continued into the 20th century. But Verdun has another

1	Verdun
2	Domrémy-la-Pucelle
3	Toul
4	Nancy
5	Saverne
6	Obernai
7	Château du Haut-Koenigsbourg
8	Sélestat
9	Colmar
10	Neuf-Brisach

dark resonance: One of the longest and most deadly clashes in history—the 1916 Battle of Verdun—revealed the futility of World War I, as the fight became simply a matter of prestige for two warring nations. Appallingly, more than 750,000 soldiers were killed or wounded over this tiny patch of soil, which does not even tally 10 sq. km (4 sq. miles). The battlefield was nearly deserted for years following the slaughter, and nature overran it. Humans then returned to build impressive memorials, such as the **Mémorial de Verdun,** 1 av. du Corps Européen (☎ 03-29-84-35-34; www. memorial-de-verdun.fr; admission 7€ adults, 4.50€ reduced; daily 9am–noon and 2–6pm, open during lunch in summer); the **Monument du Victoire,** rue Mazel; and the 7km-long (4⅓-mile) underground city that is the **Citadelle Souterraine,** av. du 5émes (☎ 03-29-45-77-15; www.meuse.fr; admission 5.40€ adults, 2.30€ reduced; tours every 5 min., daily 9am–noon and 2–6:30pm; shorter hours in winter). Many **old fortifications,** topped with devastating 75-mm (3-inch) gun turrets, have been reopened for tourists. The most eye-widening spectacle of them all has to be the grisly ★★ **L'Oussuaire de Douaumont** (☎ 03-29-84-54-81; www.verdun-douaumont.

com; free admission; Feb 4–29 and Dec daily 2–5pm; March, Oct, and Nov daily 9am–noon and 2–5:30pm; April daily 9am–6pm; May–Aug daily 9am–6:30pm; Sept daily 9am–noon and 2–6pm). This enormous crypt, filled with the remains of thousands of unknown soldiers, has windows that reveal unknown skulls and bones thrown together inside—the grim reapings of war. Just 40km (25 miles) north is the immaculate **American Meuse-Argonne Cemetery,** just east of the village of Romagne-sous-Montfaucon (free admission; daily 9am–5pm). The town of Verdun has other attractions, too, such as its **Cathédrale Notre-Dame,** built in A.D. 990, making it one of the oldest chapels in Europe. The impressive 18th-century Bishop's Palace near the city center is now the **World Center for Peace.** ◷ 1 day. Verdun Tourist Office, 11 av. Gén Mangin. ☎ 03-29-84-55-55. www.tourisme-verdun.fr.

From Verdun, drive south on D964 to Domrémy-la-Pucelle (93km/58 miles).

Where to Stay & Dine

For hotels and restaurants in Nancy, see p. 297; elsewhere in the region, see p. 303.

> *L'Oussuaire de Douaumont, with the remains of 130,000 unidentified soldiers, commemorates the 300-day battle of Verdun.*

2 **Domrémy-la-Pucelle.** The huge number of visitors that come to Joan of Arc's birthplace every year is testament to the enduring fascination she exerts over both the French (for whom she is the patron saint) and foreign tourists. *La Pucelle* ("the Virgin," a fond moniker) has even given her name to the village. There is not much to see, but if you are interested in the female warrior burned at the stake by the English in Rouen (see p. 224), you will appreciate the chamber where she reputedly was born at the **Maison Natale de Jeanne d'Arc,** 2 rue de la Basilique (☎ 03-29-06-95-86; Apr–Sept Wed–Mon 10am–6pm, Oct–Mar Wed–Mon 10am–noon and 2–5pm; admission 3€ adults, free for children 8 and under). A museum beside the house shows a film about her life. The adjacent **Eglise St-Rémy** was largely rebuilt, so only the baptismal font and some stonework remain from the time of Joan of Arc. On a slope of the Bois-Chenu, 1.5km (1 mile) up the hill from the village, is the **Basilique du Bois-Chenu,** begun in 1881 and consecrated in 1926. ⊕ 2 hr. Domrémy-la-Pucelle Tourist Office, 7 rue Principale. ☎ 03-29-06-90-70. www.domremy.fr.

From Domrémy-la-Pucelle, drive north on N74 to Toul (46km/29 miles).

3 **Toul.** The so-called Fortress City gets its name from its striking stone ramparts. No one knows exactly who made them or when they were first built, but historians agree there has been a fortified town here since the earliest recorded history. Built of luminous white stone and now topped with growing grass, the columns reach over 5.2m (17 ft.) in some areas. In 1700, according to the design plans of Vauban (Louis XIV's preeminent military engineer), Toul was further fortified with walls enclosing the entire city. Four gates—the **Gate of France,** the renovated **Gate of Moselle,** the decrepit **Gate of Metz,** and the newer **Joan of Arc Gate**—provide the feeling of comfort that only a 12m (40-ft.) stone door can. Thanks to such extensive defensive measures, a wealth of medieval buildings and several fine Gothic churches have survived. Extensive Gallo-Roman archaeological sites have also been uncovered here. ⊕ 3 hr. Toul Tourist Office, Parvis de la Cathédrale. ☎ 03-83-64-90-60. www.mairie-toul.fr.

Travel on to Nancy to spend the night: From Toul, take A31 east (24km/15 miles).

4 ★★ **Nancy.** For nearly 2 decades, between 1895 and 1915, Art Nouveau was one of Europe's most vibrant art movements; its swirling, almost cartoonish forms are recognized as providing the critical link between historical neoclassicism and modernism. Long a center of famed glass blowers, engravers, ceramicists, and furniture makers, Nancy served as the movement's base for practical, applied art. The ★★ **Musée de l'Ecole de Nancy** houses enough diverse works by local artists to make it one of the movement's critical repositories. *Objets d'art* of all disciplines abound: furniture inspired by natural forms; glassware designed by Emile Gallé; pioneering experiments in ironwork, stained glass, and ceramics; and lovely examples of the revolutionary Daum crystal glassware that now spans several generations. The museum building is an Art Nouveau masterpiece in itself—the mansion of Louis Majorelle, restored and preserved in the spirit of the early 20th century. In the city center, the **Villa Majorelle** now houses shops, banks, *brasseries,* and other amenities. ⏱ 1 day. For detailed information on Nancy, see p. 294.

> *Jacques Gruber, who made this fabulous window at the Musée de l'Ecole de Nancy, pioneered Art Nouveau glasswork techniques.*

From Nancy on Day 4, take A33 east (toward Strasbourg) and follow signs to Saverne on N4 (112km/70 miles).

5 ★ **Saverne.** Few areas combine nature, history, and art as impressively as Saverne, which has been a popular settlement since antiquity and is strategically important as the gateway to Lorraine. From below, the area appears as a leafy forest crowned by imposing castles, none more impressive than ★★ **Château des Rohan,** with its exquisite neoclassical facade, on place Général de Gaulle (☎ 03-88-91-06-28; www.mairie-saverne.fr; admission 6€ adults, 4.50€ reduced; Mon and Wed–Fri 2–6pm, Sat–Sun 10am–noon and 2–6pm; closed Tues). The grounds once housed the bishops of Strasbourg; they now afford the same splendor to ancient Roman and Celtic artifacts at the **Musée Archéologique de Saverne.** Another impressive castle, the 15th-century **Château Vieux,** is next to **Notre Dame de la Nativité,** on place de l'Eglise (☎ 03-88-91-08-47; free admission; daily 10am–6pm), a fine church that contains some of the region's best stained glass and sculpture outside of Metz. The 14th-century **Le Cloître des Récollets** (Recollets Cloister), decorated with 17th-century frescoes, is on rue Poincaré (☎ 03-88-91-80-47; www.ot-saverne.fr; free admission; daily 10am–6pm). Also visit **La Roseraie,** rte. de Paris (☎ 03-88-71-21-33; www.roseraie-saverne.fr; admission 2.50€; May–Sept daily 10am–7pm; closed Oct–Apr), a garden with more than 550 varieties of roses. If you're visiting in June, don't miss the annual International Contest of New Roses. ⏱ 5–6 hr. Saverne Tourist Office, 37 Grand'rue. ☎ 03-88-91-80-47. www.ot-saverne.fr.

Travel on to Obernai to spend the night: Head south on N4, turn off on D422 to Molsheim, and follow signs to Obernai (40km/25 miles).

6 ★★ **Obernai.** The essence of Alsace, Obernai is, for good reason, the second-most visited area in the province behind Strasbourg. Unlike most of the region's other towns—defensively perched high upon hills, surrounded by huge ramparts, cut off by moats—Obernai's unguardedness has allowed it to be a witness, though not a participant, in the devastating wars since the French Revolution. As such, the years are still represented in intricate layers on the city streets. You'll find an abundance of medieval-themed festivals and events; re-enactors even wander the streets threatening to levy a tax in the name of Emperor Barbarossa. You'll also find a confluence of gorgeous Renaissance buildings at the **place du Marché** (Market Square), site of a Thursday-morning market (8am–noon). Stand transfixed by the six-pail fountain, probably the best in Alsace, and make sure to walk the picturesque **butchers' quarter** to find the adorable corn exchange building. Stay and dine at ★★ **Le Parc** (p. 308). ⏱1 evening. See p. 274, **5**, and 277, **2**.

On Day 5, travel south from Obernai on A35 (toward Sélestat) to exit 17. Pass through Kintzheim, and follow signs to the Château du Haut-Koenigsbourg (30km/19 miles).

7 ★★★ kids **Château du Haut-Koenigsbourg.** Eight centuries of war haven't dimmed the brilliance of this extensive castle, on a hill atop the Alsatian plain. Quarreled over for 6 centuries and then abandoned for more than 2, it's now a major attraction on the Alsace Wine Route, in Orschwiller. It was a major fortress of the Holy Roman Empire extending as far back as the early 12th century, until it was pillaged by Swedish troops during the Thirty Years' War. Abandoned and overtaken by nature, it became a favorite site of Romantic artists until Kaiser

Wilhelm II ordered its renovation, to curry favor among his newly German subjects in Alsace. Over a period of 8 years the emperor's architect, Bobo Ebhardt, scrupulously restored the castle almost exactly to its medieval conditions, creating the cultural treasure in evidence today. The castle is famous for its fairy-tale feel and has been used in countless movies, including Jean Renoir's *The Grand Illusion*. ⏱Half-day. Rue du Château, Orschwiller. www.haut-koenigsbourg.fr. ☎ 03-88-82-50-60. Admission 7.50€ adults, 5.70€ reduced. Summer daily 9:30am–4:30pm; winter 9:30am–noon and 1–4:30pm. Hours may vary.

Take the road to the village of Orschwiller, then take D201 to Sélestat (10km/6¼ miles).

8 ★ **Sélestat.** Sélestat is the cradle of humanism in France. It was the intellectual focus of Alsace during the Renaissance, when scholar Beatus Rhenatus, a friend of Erasmus, created a center of learning based on a pragmatic approach to knowledge. The highlight of a visit here is the ★★ **Bibliothèque Humaniste,** 1 rue de la Bibliothèque (☎ 03-88-58-07-20; www.ville-selestat.fr; admission 4€ adults, 2.50€ ages 12–18, free for children 11 and under; Mon and Wed–Fri 9am–noon and 2–6pm, Sat 9am–2pm), which contains a large collection of early printed books, including the first book ever to

> *Traditional Alsatian culture and costume are regularly celebrated in Obernai.*

> *Neuf-Brisach is widely considered the finest citadel built by the Marquis de Vauban in the 17th century.*

mention America, in 1507. The 12th-century **Eglise Ste-Foy** has an octagonal belltower, while **Eglise St-Georges** features glittering colored tiles in the Burgundy tradition. ⏱ Half-day. Sélestat Tourist Office, square Albert Schweitzer. ☎ 03-88-58-87-20. www.selestat-tourisme.com.

On Day 6, travel south on N83 from Sélestat to Colmar (25km/16 miles).

⑨ ★★★ **Colmar.** The small city of Colmar is one of the best preserved in the area, having been ignored during the French Revolution, the Franco-Prussian War of 1870–71, World War I, and World War II. ⏱ 1 day. See p. 269, ②, and 272, ①.

On Day 7, take N415 east from Colmar to Neuf-Brisach (17km/11 miles).

★★★ ⑩ ★ **Neuf-Brisach.** Envisioning France as a ring of fortresses, the Marquis de Vauban designed or revamped more than 100 strongholds in the 17th century, rendering the country impregnable until the rise of artillery. The Leonardo da Vinci of France's Golden Century, Vauban was a scientist, a writer, a man of profound social conscience, and a world-renowned designer who revolutionized the face of French architecture. All these tributaries of his powerful personality are honored

at the ★ **Musée Vauban,** 7 place de la Porte de Belfort (☎ 03-89-72-03-93; www.musees-alsace.org; admission 2.50€ adults, 1.60€ reduced; May–Sept Wed–Mon 10am–noon and 2–5pm; year-round by appointment for groups). Neuf-Brisach, the last and, most historians agree, the finest of Vauban's fortresses, is Alsace and Lorraine's major contribution to the **Network of Major Vauban Sites** (www.sites-vauban.org), found in every corner of France as well as France's former overseas territories, and counting among them no fewer than 12 UNESCO World Heritage sites. Neuf-Brisach's history is not one of Gallo-Roman taverns or Frankish palaces—the city did not exist until the first stone was laid in 1699. The citadel was finished by 1702, providing the capstone to this awe-inspiring, octagon-shaped city, which was extensively fortified to intimidate the Germans across the Rhine just a mile away. Designed into 48 geometric neighborhoods with a huge central square, the city amply shows why Louis XIV said, "Of all the diamonds in the crown of France, the finest is the Rhine fortress." ⏱ 1 day. Neuf-Brisach Tourist Office, 6 place d'Armes, Palais du Gouverneur. ☎ 03-89-72-56-66. www.tourisme-paysdebrisach.com.

Alsace & Lorraine Outdoors

The Sun King himself, Louis XIV, described Alsace as a "beautiful garden," and it may have been the region's stunning natural resources that, in part, led many disparate empires to covet its treasures. Three regional parks now protect both the natural surroundings and the lifestyle of hundreds of thousands of inhabitants whose families have been here for generations. A scenic drive and a lakeside sports area are included in this roundup of the best that Alsace and Lorraine have to offer nature lovers; take your pick to supplement a history- or food-and-wine-based tour with a healthy dose of fresh air.

> One of the most beautiful cycling routes in the region is La Route des Crêtes, which separates Alsace and Lorraine.

★ kids **Gérardmer.** Picture-perfect postcard scenes are a dime a dozen in Gérardmer, but tourists have begun to flock to the town for its multitude of fun sporting activities, too. Located between Colmar and Epinal, the town is centered around **Lake Gérardmer,** which has a perimeter of nearly 7km (4⅓ miles). In summer you can rent a bike and pedal on the 240km (150 miles) of marked cycling trails, discover the **Vallée des Lacs** on horseback, go canoeing or kayaking at the harbor, fish for perch, walk miles and miles of hiking trails, and more. Nature museums are manifold here; check out the **Expo-Foret ecomuseum,** 11 rue de l'Eglise (☎ 03-29-60-82-02; www. gerardmer.net; admission 5€ adults, 3€

Gérardmer **4**

La Route des Crêtes **3**

Parc Naturel Régional de Lorraine **1**

Parc Naturel Régional des Ballons des Vosges **5**

Parc Naturel Régional des Vosges du Nord **2**

children; Tues–Sun 10am–6pm), to understand more about unique local forestry practices. Or learn about the area's flora and fauna at the [kids] **Expo Faune Lorraine,** Le Saut des Cuves, Xonrupt-Longemer (☎ 03-29-63-39-50; www.gerardmer.net; admission 6€ adults, 4.50€ children; Tues–Sun 10:30am–1:30pm and 3–6pm; closed Mon). Gain insight into a bygone era by joining some folk dancing at the [kids] **Ferme-Musée de Soyotte,** 68 chemin du Greffier, St. Marguerite (☎ 03-29-56-68-89; http://soyotte.free.fr; admission 5€ adults, 2€ children; summer Tues–Sat 10am–noon and 2–5pm, Sun 3–5pm; winter Tues–Sat 2–5pm). Or just enjoy the greenery at the **Jardines de Callunes,** chemin de la Prelle, Ban de Sapt (☎ 03-29-58-94-94; www.jardins-callunes. com; admission 7€ adults, 3€ children; Mon–Sat 10am–noon and 2–6pm; closed Sun). In winter, opportunities to hit the slopes are plentiful, as the Gérardmer **ski domain** has the longest slope (3.2km/nearly 2 miles) in the Vosges region, with night skiing until 10pm (www.gerardmer-ski-com). You can strap on snowshoes and hike the mountain trails, or opt for an easier route: Take a ski lift up and to-boggan down. The town has excellent hotels,

tranquil cafes, an endless supply of flower boxes, and a casino. Excellent restaurants are the norm. If you can afford the best, stay at the ★★ **Hostellerie Les Bas Rupts et Chalet Fleuri,** 181 rte. de la Bresse (☎ 03-29-63-09-25; www.basrupts.com; 25 units; doubles 145€–630€; AE, DC, MC, V), where mountain style meets luxury; the hotel has a top restaurant (lunch and dinner daily; lunch menu 30€; main courses 25€–33€) and offers access to nearly every sport available in the area. It's also the best spot in Gérardmer after a day on the slopes or at the waterfront. Finally, visit what used to make this town famous: the **Vosgian Clog Factory,** 189 chemin du Tour du Lac (☎ 03-29-63-08-69). Gérardmer is 53km (33 miles) west of Colmar on D417. Gérardmer Tourist Office, 4 place des Déportés. ☎ 03-29-27-27-27. www.gerardmer.net.

★★ **La Route des Crêtes.** This majestic 80km (50-mile) route functions as an unofficial border between Lorraine and Alsace, linking the **Col de Bonhomme pass** and the town of **Thann;** the "Crest Road" straddles both Latin-leaning and Germanic-oriented towns. Hop on, and you'll encounter sweeping views of the

> *Lake Gérardmer, in Alsace, is a popular place to canoe, kayak, and fish for perch.*

Vosges Mountains, sparkling lakes, dappled meadows, impressive forests, the distant Alps, and much more. A shuttle operates during the summer, stopping at several points to let part-time mountaineers choose their preferred hiking paths. The road averages an elevation of more than 1,000m (3,300 ft.), affording grand views of the Alsatian plains below, and nearly reaching the highest peak

Where to Stay

World Wildlife Federation–approved **Panda Accommodations** (B&Bs and *gîtes*), Hôtels au Naturel green hotels, and Fermes Auberges, where you stay on a working farm, can all be booked through the regional parks' visitor centers and the tourist offices within the parks. Lists of these accommodations can be downloaded from the park websites.

of the Vosges—the **Grand Ballon,** at 1,424m (4,672 ft.). The highway is a relatively recent creation but with an already violent history: The French Army charted it in World War I as a means of transporting war supplies east for battles against the Germans. If you're a war buff, you won't want to miss the haunting battlefield of **Linge,** where you can find French and German trenches that were separated by just 2.7m (9 ft.). In today's more peaceful times, the rapidly increasing popularity of the road has drawn increased efforts from the French government to make it more tourist-friendly by adding road signs and lookout points. It may seem like a short road, but there's no shortage of things to do along the way: Check out the **Haut-Chitelet botanical gardens, Freundstein Castle,** the glacial lakes of **Lac Noir** or **Lac Blanc,** and much more. One of the most beautiful passes, the **Col de la Schlucht,** is a big draw for locals during the high summer period. Skiing is the main attraction in winter, as the route provides an essentially unbroken cross-country ski trail. Small ski resorts dot the route; their chairlifts run year-round to offer great views. From the **Grand Ballon** or the **Hohneck** in La Bresse, you can see as far as Mont Blanc in the Swiss Alps on a clear day. Try to finish the route in Thann, so you can relax with a glass of the town's famed Rangen wine. With a convenient location between Munster and Gérardmer, the **Route des Crêtes** supports many restaurants and hiking opportunities in the charming towns nearby. The Route des Crêtes starts where N415 meets D148, 28km (17 miles) west of Colmar. It becomes D61, D430, and D431 before reaching Thann.

Parc Naturel Régional de Lorraine. Lakes, rivers, and marshes proliferate in this park, making it a haven for fishing and watersports enthusiasts. It covers more than 219,000 hectares (540,000 acres), which constitutes 11% of the Lorraine region. **Lake Madine,** where you can rent boats and bicycles, has many hidden romantic getaways. Don't miss the **Hattonchâtel castle** near Meuse. Maison du Parc, rue du Quai, Pont-à-Mousson (31km/19 miles northwest of Nancy, following A31 to Loisy and D120 to the park). ☎ 03-83-81-46-61. www.pnr-lorraine.com. Fall and winter 1:30–5:30pm; spring and summer 10am–2pm.

★★ Parc Naturel Régional des Ballons des Vosges. With its glacier lakes, valley pastures, and winter sports opportunities, the Ballons des Vosges is best suited to mountain-ready legs and lungs. The park, one of France's largest at more than 3,000 sq. km (1,150 sq. miles), encompasses the southern Vosges Mountains and a quarter of a million residents, who take pride in showing how the inhabitants have worked with, not against, nature; more than 60 museums are dedicated to informing visitors of their shared history. The park is west of Colmar, roughly following the Alsace Wine Route and centering on Munster. **Maison du Parc,** 1 cour de l'Abbaye, Munster (92km/57 miles southwest of Strasbourg, following A35 to Obernai, N422 to Houssen, N83 to Wintzenheim, and D417 to the park). ☎ 03-89-77-90-34. www.parc-ballons-vosges.fr. Fall and winter 1:30–5:30pm; spring and summer 10am–2pm.

> *Parc Naturel Régionel de Lorraine is land-locked, but its lakeside beaches are worthy of the seashore.*

★ Parc Naturel Régional des Vosges du Nord. In the rolling foothills of Vosges, this UNESCO World Biosphere Reserve is Alsace at its loveliest. Few areas of eastern France can claim such a glorious combination of orchards (beech, oak, alder, and pine), wetlands, and wildlife (roe deer, stags, lynx, and more). It may be the most historic of the three parks, too, with nearly 40 castles and 113 historical sites emerging from the forests. Vosges du Nord has more than 3,280km (2,000 miles) of signposted hiking trails. **Maison du Parc,** rue du Château, La Petite Pierre (57km/35 miles northwest of Strasbourg, following A4 to Hochfelden and D100 to the park). ☎ 03-88-01-49-59. www.parc-vosges-nord.fr. Daily 10am–noon and 2–6pm. Closed Jan.

L'ART NOUVEAU
Natural Forms by Industrial Means

BY ANNA BROOKE

THE ORGANIC, VIVID CURVES AND GRAPHIC FLOURISHES OF ART NOUVEAU distinguished decorative arts and architecture across Europe and in New York from the 1890s until World War I. France's take on the international style arose in Nancy in 1901, through the work of local cabinetmaker Louis Majorelle (1859–1926), painter and sculptor Victor Prouvé (1858–1943), and glassmakers Emile Gallé (1846–1904) and Jacques Gruber, from the Daum glass factory (1870–1936). These Nancy artisans employed new industrial techniques to undergird traditional artisanal skills. They also formed a school of Art Nouveau, known as l'Ecole de Nancy, where forms based on plants, nature, folklore, and mythology took shape in metal, glass, ceramics, textiles, and wood—on everyday items ranging from graphic art and jewelry to architecture and interior decor. Instantly popular, Art Nouveau designs became a defining decorative element of the Belle Epoque.

LE METRO, PARIS
by Hector Guimard
Hector Guimard (1867–1942) was among Art Nouveau's most prolific architects and interior designers. Though he studied in Paris, the School of Nancy heavily influenced his work. He is best known for his grace-

ful, twisted iron Métro stations in the capital. Porte Dauphine, Châtelet, and Abbesses have retained their original, fan-shaped glass roofs.

L'ECOLE DE NANCY
by Emile Gallé
Nancy's Art Nouveau movement was particularly recognized for its glasswork, headed by master Emile Gallé and local manufacturer Daum. Glass was a popular part of Art Nouveau interior design; with the advent of electricity, it became a veritable tool of light, taking on varying degrees of transparency to create effects and ambiances hitherto unseen.

VILLA MAJORELLE, NANCY
by Henri Sauvage & Jacques Gruber
In 1898 Louis Majorelle asked architect Henri Sauvage to build his dream home at 1 rue Louis Majorelle (p. 285), in Nancy. The result is one of the world's best-preserved Art Nouveau houses: a three-floor riot of glass, iron, wood, and stone, with pointy roofs and half-moon, stained-glass windows by Jacques Gruber.

DINING ROOM, 122 AV. MOZART, PARIS
by Hector Guimard
In May 1909 Guimard built his own Art Nouveau mansion in Paris. After the building was sold in 1948, several museums divided the spoils from the interior, whose every detail was designed by Guimard. Le Petit Palais (p. 64, ❶) currently holds the dining room—an ovoid space with wooden paneling and furniture with forms reminiscent of Paris's Métro stations.

CASTEL BERENGER, PARIS
by Hector Guimard
Another one of Guimard's creations, this apart-

ment block of 36 flats, at 16 rue la Fontaine in Paris, is both asymmetrical and balanced, with swirling lines and a mélange of building materials.

LIT AUBE ET CREPUSCULE (DAWN AND DUSK) BED), NANCY
by Emile Gallé
Gallé's *Dawn and Dusk* bed (1904) has to be one of the most beautiful and poetic beds ever made; it is now on display at the Musée de l'Ecole de Nancy (p. 296, ❺). Dawn is symbolized at the foot of the bed by two giant butterfly wings encrusted with mother of pearl; dusk is featured on the headboard as a moth, striped with the dark wood of the night sky.

LA FERMETTE MARBEUF, PARIS
by Hubert & Martineau
Paris's brasseries and bistros often bear preserved elements of their original Art Nouveau

interiors. One of the most stunning—with Art Nouveau decor that lay forgotten under plasterboard until 1978—is the Fermette Marbeuf, at 5 rue Marbeuf, just off the Champs-Elysées, with a glass cupola designed in 1898 by Hubert Martineau.

Nancy

The one-time capital of the powerful Duchy of Lorraine, Nancy has retained a sense of grandeur—culminating in the stunning place Stanislas, symbol of the city and a beloved public square for its 400,000 residents. Nancy has much more of a French feel than Alsace and many other parts of Lorraine, as it was rarely under the yoke of foreign domination for long, preserving its unique character among the cities of eastern France.

> *Place Stanislas's pearly walls and gracious buildings provide the separation point between old and new Nancy.*

START Nancy is 356km (221 miles) east of Paris.

① ★★★ **Place Stanislas.** This superbly symmetrical public square was initiated in the early 18th century by Stanislaw Leszczynski—duke of Lorraine and king of the once-mighty Polish-Lithuanian Commonwealth—to honor his son-in-law, the French king Louis XV. It features ornate fountains, gilded wrought-iron railings, and impressive colonnades, and harmoniously incorporates government edifices with the **Musée des Beaux-Arts, Opéra-Théâtre,** an impressive **Arc de Triomphe,** and two expanses known as **place de la Carrière**

and **place d'Alliance.** The square received an extensive refurbishment in time for its 250th birthday in 2005 and is especially pretty at night, thanks to innovative colored lighting. Still one of the premier royal squares in France, it is now the site of popular festivities and a great place to have a coffee. ⏲ **2 hr.** www.ot-nancy.fr.

② ★ **Musée des Beaux-Arts.** Appropriately situated on the very *beau* place Stanislas, this exceptional museum houses examples from every European school of art since the Renaissance. You'll also find sculptures from Rodin,

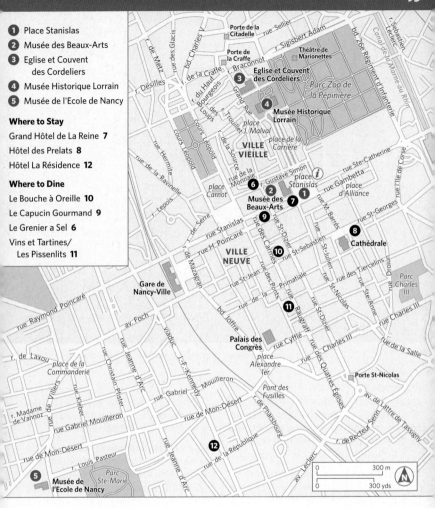

1 Place Stanislas
2 Musée des Beaux-Arts
3 Eglise et Couvent
    des Cordeliers
4 Musée Historique Lorrain
5 Musée de l'Ecole de Nancy

Where to Stay
Grand Hôtel de La Reine **7**
Hôtel des Prelats **8**
Hôtel La Résidence **12**

Where to Dine
Le Bouche à Oreille **10**
Le Capucin Gourmand **9**
Le Grenier a Sel **6**
Vins et Tartines/
    Les Pissenlits **11**

Zadkine, and Dietman and, in the print room, some of the finest engravings and prints from artists such as Callot and Grandville. The Daum glassware is so good that Louis Comfort Tiffany often traveled from New York to visit the master craftsmen in Nancy's glassworks.
🕐 2 hr. 3 place Stanislas. ☎ 03-83-85-30-72. Admission 6€ adults, 4€ reduced. Daily 10am–6pm.

3 **Eglise et Couvent des Cordeliers.** Don't be fooled by the extremely drab exterior of this church; the interior is chock-full of colorful murals, detailed sculpture, and a *trompe l'oeil* dome that is reminiscent, in its precision, of Islamic mosques. The illustrious Hapsburgs, Europe's royal family par excellence, placed this church on a par with the Medici Chapel in Florence when they claimed it as a final resting place; the Renaissance-era **tomb of Rene II** is one of many exceptional funeral monuments here. The dukes of Lorraine followed, striving to match the Hapsburgs' posthumous glamour. Unfortunately, anti-religious fervor during the French Revolution resulted in the loss of many chapel treasures, but the Hapsburgs continued to make the church important to their family: Marie Antoinette made a pilgrimage there on her way to marry her

> *The Art Nouveau facade of this building on avenue Foch has a Renaissance, château-like spin.*

future husband, Louis XVI; and, in 1951, the chapel hosted the marriage of Archduke Otto Von Hapsburg and Princess Regina of Saxe-Meiningen. ⏱ 60 min. 66 Grand Rue. ☎ 03-83-32-18-74. www.ot-nancy.fr. Admission 2.60€. Mon–Sat 10am–6pm; Sun 10am–5:30pm.

❹ Musée Historique Lorrain. Next to the Cordeliers Church is the treasured Lorraine Historical Museum, the definitive art history museum of the region. If Lorraine's artists have produced it, you'll find it here: engravings, porcelains, sculpture, glasswork, carpets, and much more. The museum makes clear that Lorraine's history as a bargaining chip for successive empires (French, German, Austrian, Polish-Lithuanian, etc.) fostered countless talents and competing artistic and intellectual currents. The museum is not very large, but its eclectic collections bring together such disparate elements as medieval church sculpture, painstakingly crafted porcelains, some of the finest tapestries in European history, the socially conscious engravings of Jacques Callot, the paintings of Georges de la Tour—the

master of indirect lighting—and much more. ⏱ 90 min. 64 Grand Rue. ☎ 03-83-32-18-74. www.ot-nancy.fr. Admission 8€ adults, 3€ children. Daily 10am–12:30pm and 2–6pm.

❺ ★★ Musée de l'Ecole de Nancy. The School of Nancy came to be one of the defining styles of the Art Nouveau movement, which reached its apogee at the turn of the 20th century. This excellent museum is one of the world's foremost repositories of work inspired by the sweeping philosophy, which rejected academic art in favor of stylized, flowing, non-linear forms applied not just to painting but to the decorative arts of everyday life as well—from architecture to furniture and beyond. The plethora of original pieces includes Emile Gallé's *Dawn and Dusk* bed, Louis Majorelle's *Death of the Swan* piano, and many other technically outstanding works that exemplified the movement. ⏱ 90 min. 36–38 rue du Sergent Blandan. ☎ 03-83-40-14-86. www.ecole-de-nancy-com. Admission 6€ adults, 4€ children. Wed–Sun 10:30am–6pm.

Where to Stay & Dine in Nancy

★★ Grand Hôtel de La Reine

This upscale hotel offers Belle Epoque interior elegance in an 18th-century building. It's also on place Stanislas, and the service is exquisite, as is the hotel bar. 2 place Stanislas. ☎ 03-83-35-03-01. www.hoteldelareine.com. 42 units. Doubles 125€–165€. AC, DC, MC, V.

★★ Hôtel des Prelats

This elegant hotel, set in a former bishop's palace built in 1609, has a superb location near place Stanislas. Every room has stained-glass windows and many have romantic four-poster beds. 56 place Monseigneur Ruch. ☎ 03-83-30-20-20. www.hoteldesprelats.com. 41 units. Doubles 100€–120€. AE, MC, V.

Hôtel La Résidence

Convenient and stylish at an affordable price, this hotel is close to the Musée de l'Ecole de Nancy and a 10-minute walk from the city center. Contemporary decor is mixed in with the 19th-century building's original style. Rooms are small; ask for one in the back (they're slightly bigger). 30 bd. Jean-Jaures. ☎ 03-83-40-33-56. www.hotel-laresidence-nancy.fr. 22 units. Doubles 60€–95€. AE, MC, V.

★ Le Bouche à Oreille *FONDUE*

This house of fondue is a city favorite for its cozy, rustic atmosphere and friendly staff, not to mention its cheese. You can choose from various cheesy offerings, from *raclette* and *tartiflette* to omelettes and goat cheese salad. 4 rue des Carmes. ☎ 03-83-35-17-17. Lunch 10€–12€, dinner 18€–20€. MC, V. Lunch Mon–Fri, dinner daily.

Le Capucin Gourmand *GASTRONOMIC*

This expensive but rewarding restaurant will not disappoint, with food, decor, and competent service to match the prime location on place Stanislas. It's a magnet for lovers of foie gras, served in a myriad of presentations. 31 rue Gambetta. ☎ 03-83-35-26-98. www.lecapu.com. Main courses 30€–40€. AE, MC, V. Lunch and dinner Mon–Sat.

★ Le Grenier a Sel *FRENCH FUSION*

The restaurant, in one of the oldest buildings

> *Seventeenth-century Catholic Primates governed all the bishops of Lorraine from the palace that is now the Hôtel des Prélats in the heart of Nancy.*

in Nancy, has contemporary decor. Fusion cuisine by chef Patrick Frechin includes beef filet paired with wasabi, caviar with crab, and chocolate rhubarb. The chef also gives classes on Saturday mornings from 10am to noon for 50€ per person. 28 rue Gustave-Simon. ☎ 03-83-32-31-98. www.legrenierasel.eu. 3-course lunch menu 25€, 5-course dinner menu 65€. AE, MC, V. Sept–June lunch Tues–Fri and Sun, dinner Tues–Sat; July–Aug lunch Tues–Sun, dinner daily.

★ Vins et Tartines/Les Pissenlits *FRENCH*

This combination restaurant offers two excellent venues with two totally different outlooks. Vins et Tartines, as the name implies, offers a great selection of wines and modest, toasted sandwiches and tapas in the basement of a former chapel. Above ground, you'll find an extremely reasonable but tasty restaurant—Les Pissenlits. If you're seeking a long night of eating and drinking, start in the basement for an extended apertif and appetizer, and work your way up, but slowly, *à la francais*. 25bis rue des Ponts. ☎ 03-83-35-17-25. www.vins-et-tartines.com. www.les-pissenlits.com. Appetizers (Tartines) 2€–11€; main courses (Pissenlits) 12€–18€. MC, V. Lunch and dinner Tues–Sat.

Strasbourg

Strasbourg means "City of Roads" in German, and indeed this urban center of nearly 300,000 people in Alsace has long been a crossroads of Europe. A dominant city during the medieval era, it was devastated by the Wars of Religion in the 16th and 17th centuries but rallied to become not just a thriving burg but the second government seat of the European Union. You may feel as though you've crossed the Rhine River into Germany here. Closer to Frankfurt and Munich than to Paris, Strasbourg did belong to Germany several times throughout its history, though now it has a strong identity all its own, founded on an intellectual and cultural dynamism that dates back to the time of Erasmus.

> One of the best times to admire Strasbourg's cathedral is at night, when the facade is illuminated.

START Strasbourg is 489km (304 miles) east of Paris.

1 ★★★ **Musée d'Art Moderne et Contemporain de Strasbourg (MAMAC).** The Strasbourg Museum of Modern and Contemporary Art, housed in an uplifting, modular-glass showcase by Adrian Fainsilber, is the city's top museum, in league with the finest cultural

institutions in Paris. MAMAC's collection ranges from important works by Monet, Picasso, Georges Braque, and native son Gustav Doré to contemporary paintings, video art, and installations. The museum is located beside the River Ill, with its own tram stop —just look for the building with the 4m (13-ft.) horse sculpture on the roof. The building itself was constructed in 1998, but

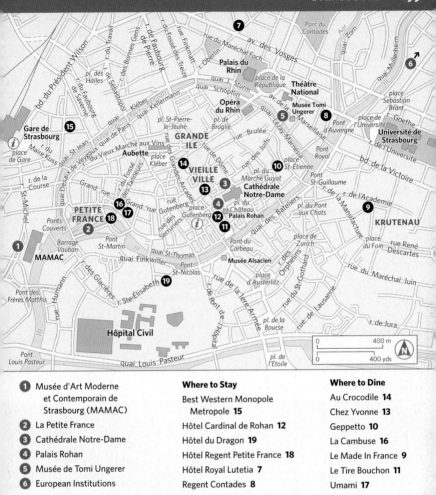

1 Musée d'Art Moderne
   et Contemporain de
   Strasbourg (MAMAC)
2 La Petite France
3 Cathédrale Notre-Dame
4 Palais Rohan
5 Musée de Tomi Ungerer
6 European Institutions

Where to Stay

Best Western Monopole
   Metropole **15**
Hôtel Cardinal de Rohan **12**
Hôtel du Dragon **19**
Hôtel Regent Petite France **18**
Hôtel Royal Lutetia **7**
Regent Contades **8**

Where to Dine

Au Crocodile **14**
Chez Yvonne **13**
Geppetto **10**
La Cambuse **16**
Le Made In France **9**
Le Tire Bouchon **11**
Umami **17**

the modern collection dates back to the early
20th century, when visionary museum director Hans Haug legitimized cubism by investing
public money on Braque's *Nature Morte* (*Still
Life)*, making it the first cubist work to enter an
institution (then housed in the Palais Rohan).
MAMAC's photography collection spans the
entire history of the shuttered image, from
images by pioneers such as Marey and Muy-
bridge to modern portraits by Mapplethorpe
and Maywald. The video art perpetuates the
museum's progressive legacy, and interactive
features help entertain children and enlighten
adults. Laminated note cards in English are

provided for Anglophone sightseers. The well-
provisioned but pricey **Art Café Restaurant,**
with a floor-to-ceiling window view of the Ill
and La Petite France district, serves snacks
and full meals. ⏰ 2 hr. place Hans Jean Arp.
☎ 03-88-23-31-31. www.musees-strasbourg.
org. Admission 6€ adults, 3€ reduced. Tues,
Wed, Fri noon–7pm; Thurs noon–9pm; Sat-Sun
10am–6pm. Closed Mon. Tram B and C: Musée
d'Art Moderne.

2 ★★★ **La Petite France.** Cool off after a stringent debate or intense artistic experience by
strolling around La Petite France, the island
heart of Strasbourg. Of all the city's many

and varied neighborhoods, this one is the prettiest—a maze of medieval streets broken up by canals that earned it the nickname "the Venice of the north." Street names such as rue du Bain-aux-Plantes (plant baths) and rue du Fossé-des-Tanneurs (tanners' ditch) are reminders of the ancient trades plied here. Cross the pont St-Martin to admire the 18th-century facades of the rue des Boucliers and the *bateau-lavoir,* a waterborne wash house, reflected in the water. This neighborhood has lots of small cafes and restaurants, including ★★ **Umami** (p. 305) on rue des Dentelles.

❸ ★★★ **Cathédrale Notre-Dame.** Mainly built between the 12th and the 15th centuries, Strasbourg's cathedral was the world's tallest building from 1647 to 1874 (after its main competitor, St-Mary's in Stralsund, Germany, burned down), and it's still the world's sixth-tallest church, at 132m (433 ft.). Originally Roman Catholic, the cathedral converted to Protestantism in 1521, only to return to Rome's jurisdiction after France incorporated Strasbourg in 1681. Leaders of the Revolution called for the tower's demolition, but an ingenious local locksmith created a fireproof protective metal cap that saved the structure. Designed by German architect Erwin von Steinbach and praised for its beauty by Goethe, Stendhal, and Hugo, the cathedral was constructed by many of the stonemasons and master builders who had worked at Chartres and is considered the epitome of late Gothic architecture. The staggering height of the spire affords views of the French plains, Germany's Black Forest, and the mountains of Switzerland, not to mention the triangular rooftops of Strasbourg. Gorgeous stained-glass windows date from the late 12th to the 14th centuries. Even more impressive is the 18m (59-ft.), 19th-century **astronomical clock,** one of the largest in the world. Long before the advent of computers, the clock could determine the precise date of Easter, leap years, equinoxes, and other key events. The 🚸 **Procession of the Apostles** mesmerizes onlookers every day at 12:30pm: On the face of the clock, sculpted figurines depict the various stages of life, an angel strikes a bell while another overturns an hourglass,

> *A view of the picturesque La Petite France.*

> *A lawn in the German quarter of Strasbourg, near the Musée de Tomi Ungerer.*

and the Apostles march in procession, among other mechanized choreographies. Admission to the clock is extra but worth the 2€ fee. ⏱ 75 min. 1 rue Rohan. ☎ 03-88-21-43-34. www.cathedrale-strasbourg.fr. Admission 4.40€ adults, 2.20€ reduced. Daily 7:30am–11:30am and 12:30–7pm (except during services). Procession of the Apostles: Daily 12:30. Cathedral platform (332 steps): Apr–Sept 9am–7:15pm, Oct–March 10am–5:15pm.

④ ★★ Palais Rohan. Justly considered one of the most beautiful creations of 18th-century French architecture east of Versailles, the palace was constructed by the Rohan family, who, after the French reconquest of Strasbourg, supplied four archbishops to the Strasbourg diocese. If the new rulers of Strasbourg built Palais Rohan to impress their new subjects, there's little doubt they succeeded: The towering facades and columns, sumptuous rococo interior, life-size statues, and delicately carved ribbons, fruit, and flowers all convey a grandeur heretofore unseen in the region. Today the *palais* houses three museums; if you have time to see only one, we recommend the **Musée des Arts Décoratifs,** which includes the lavish living quarters of the Rohans. The restored chambers gleam in all their revolution-inspiring opulence: varnished wood, carved ceilings, and enough silk, velvet, and tassels to satisfy the most sensuous sultan. Each chamber provides written descriptions

in English. Former inhabitants of the palace at one time or another have included Napoleon, Henry XV, Marie Antoinette, and other luminaries from France's late royal era. The **Musée Archéologique** is one of France's premier repositories of antiquity, with densely packed exhibits relating the past of Alsace, from prehistory up to the Middle Ages. The **Musée des Beaux-Arts** displays works by pre-modern masters such as El Greco, Goya, Monet, Rembrandt, and Renoir, to name a few. In typical Strasbourgeois fashion, the *palais* plays an important role in German history as well, serving as the main building of the University of Strasbourg during the epoch of imperial Germany from 1872 until 1898. ⏱ 2 hr. 2 place du Château. ☎ 03-88-52-50-00. www.musees-strasbourg.org. Admission (1 museum): 4€ adults, 2€ reduced. All 3 museums: 6€ adults, 4€ reduced. Wed–Mon noon–6pm.

⑤ Musée de Tomi Ungerer. Draftsman, illustrator, renowned bad boy, and Strasbourg native Tomi Ungerer has made headlines around the world for the biting nature of his political caricatures, in sharp contrast to the sensitivity of his children's stories. He donated his personal archives of nearly 8,000 drawings—taken from his work in children's books, political cartoons, advertisements, erotica, and elsewhere—and 6,000 collectible children's toys to create the fun, if perhaps slightly schizophrenic, Tomi Ungerer Museum, located

> *Louise Weiss (1893–1983), after whom this part of Europe's Parliament is named, was a French journalist and an active suffragette.*

6 ★ **European Institutions.** The long-disputed ownership of Alsace and Lorraine was just a preamble to Strasbourg's current role as the seat of the **Parliament of the European Union.** As the second home of Europe's lawmakers (the main seat being Brussels), Strasbourg has become a major bureaucratic hub for BlackBerry-wielding elected officials, ambassadors, and royal dignitaries, who work about 4 days a month in the impressive glass-and-steel **Louise Weiss Building.** The structure—inspired by Roman amphitheaters, with a 60m (200-ft.) tower reminiscent of the Colosseum—is far more impressive than its rather dull official name, Immeuble du Parlement Européen 4 (Building of the European Parliament 4); inaugurated in 1999 in the city's Wacken district, at the confluence of the Ill River and the Marne-Rhine Canal, it cuts a vital silhouette in Strasbourg's skyline. Architecture buffs will appreciate the Parliament complex, which includes the equally impressive **Winston Churchill** and **Salvador de Madariaga buildings.** News junkies will no doubt recognize the hemicycle (horseshoe-shaped) seating arrangement where members sit, debate, and vote. Visitors age 14 and older with an online reservation can attend a "plenary sitting" (Parliament is in session here for twelve 4-day sittings a year); check the calendar on the website for exact dates. Facing the Parliament buildings across the river, the Council of Europe houses the **European Court of Human Rights,** avenue de l'Europe (☎ 03-88-41-20-29; www.echr.coe.int), in a Richard Rogers building that resembles three shining gasworks towers. Here, too, the public can attend hearings after applying online in advance. The website lists upcoming cases and the stringent rules that must be obeyed (including punctuality) while hearings are in session. When Parliament is not sitting, you can request a tour of the buildings at the EP website. **European Parliament, 1 av. du Président Robert Schuman. ☎ 03-88-17-40-01. www.europarl.europa.eu. Free admission. Hours vary according to the program of debates. Visitors should check the Parliament's schedule in advance. Court of Human Rights, av. de l'Europe. ☎ 03-88-41-20-29. www.echr.coe.int. Tram E: Parlement Européen.**

in a handsome villa in the German quarter. The ground floor displays his work as a children's book illustrator, interspersed with toys; the first floor is devoted to his career as a satirical cartoonist for publications such as the *New York Times;* and the basement (inaccessible to children) is dedicated to his erotic drawings. The exhibition also includes works by some of Ungerer's contemporaries, such as Saul Steinberg, famed for his work in the *New Yorker,* and André François, best known for his zinging illustrations in the British satirical magazine *Punch.* With too many goodies to exhibit all at once, the museum routinely introduces unseen works and sections of the toy collection in special exhibitions.

🕑 90 min. 2 av. de la Marseillaise. ☎ 03-69-06-37-27. www.musees-strasbourg.org. Admission 5€ adults, 2.50€ reduced. Mon and Wed–Fri noon–6pm; Sat–Sun 10am–6pm. Closed Tues. Tram B, C and E: République.

Where to Stay in Strasbourg

Best Western Monopole Metropole GARE
This midrange hotel offers an excellent compromise between the dependability of a chain and local flavor of an independently owned establishment. For very reasonable rates, lodgers can retire to guest rooms with either traditional Alsatian decor or contemporary furnishings. 16 rue Kuhn. ☎ 03-88-14-39-14. www.bw-monopole.com. 68 units. Doubles 100€–130€. AE, MC, V.

Hôtel Cardinal de Rohan CATHEDRAL
Very close to the cathedral, this midrange hotel delivers an authentic French hotel experience. The Cardinal is housed in a gorgeous downtown building with rooms that are sometimes small but always lushly appointed. 17 rue du Maroquin. ☎ 03-88-32-85-11. www.hotel-rohan.com. 36 units. Doubles 125€–145€. AE, DC, MC, V.

Hôtel du Dragon HOSPITAL
Excellent staff and contemporary rooms in a 17th-century building make this hotel extremely popular with savvy travelers and visiting politicians who are actually trying to keep their budgets balanced. The only caveat is that it's a few minutes' walk outside the Petite France quarter. 12 rue du Dragon. ☎ 03-88-35-79-80. www.dragon.fr. 32 units. Doubles 71€–99€. AE, MC, V.

★★ Hôtel Regent Petite France PETITE FRANCE
With a riverbank view and a convenient location in the heart of the Petite France neighborhood, this hotel offers excellent accommodations to those who can afford it. Inside you'll find rooms with an elegant, contemporary decor—hewn from the building's proletariat beginnings as a multipurpose mill in the 17th century—and all the amenities you'd expect for the steep price. A champagne bar stands in for the workout room. 5 rue des Moulins. ☎ 03-88-76-43-76. www.regent-petite-france.com. 72 units. Doubles 265€–445€. MC, V.

Hôtel Royal Lutetia GERMAN QUARTER
A favorite among budget travelers, this hotel

> *Regent Contades in the German quarter occupies a mansion once owned by Kaiser Wilhelm II.*

is a little removed from the historic center but convenient to the Parliament and the train station. Spacious rooms, sunny decor, and excellent service make it a very good deal. 2bis rue du Général Rapp. ☎ 03-88-35-20-45. www.royal-lutetia.fr. 39 units. Doubles 62€–75€. AE, MC, V.

★★ Regent Contades GERMAN QUARTER
This sister hotel of the Regent Petite France is a bit cheaper for nearly the same posh digs, housed in a Haussmann-style building in the German quarter. Unlike the more modern Petite France, the Contades is steeped in plush French history; stained glass, an ornate balcony, and a grandiose staircase heighten its old-world charm. It's easy to believe the riverbank mansion was formerly owned by Kaiser Wilhelm II, the last emperor of Germany. 8 av. de la Liberté. ☎ 03-88-15-05-05. www.regent-hotels.com. 47 units. Doubles 195€–375€. AE, DC, MC, V.

Where to Dine in Strasbourg

> *Attention goes into every detail of your meal at Au Crocodile.*

★★★ **Au Crocodile** CATHEDRAL *GASTRONOMIC*
Emile Jung forged the excellent reputation of
this gastronomic restaurant that is soaring
to new heights under Philippe Bohrer, who
has earned a Michelin star for his use of local
ingredients such as Alsatian mustard in both
traditional and contemporary French cuisine.
You'll eat under a glass roof in the freshly
modernized dining room, which still gives
pride of place to a huge old-master painting
of a village *fête*. Every mouthful is divine here,
down to the *amuse-bouches, petits fours,* and
superb wine list, including some very fine
Alsatian pinot gris. 10 rue de l'Outre. ☎ 03-88-
32-13-02. www.au-crocodile.com. Fixed menu
(5-course dinner) 92€–132€. AE, DC, MC, V.
Lunch and dinner Tues-Sat.

★★ **Chez Yvonne** CATHEDRAL *FRENCH/ALSA-
TIAN* Journalists and other political dignitaries

frequent this historic Alsatian *winstub* near the
cathedral, open since 1873. Amid a cozy dining room with lots of wood and red-checked
curtains, steaming platters of well-prepared
food emerge from the kitchen, including such
appetizers as snails Alsatian or foie gras of
the house. For a main course, opt for suckling
pig or hen cooked in Riesling and served with
spaëtzle or *choucroute* (sauerkraut) with pork
products. 10 rue du Sanglier. ☎ 03-88-32-84-15.
www.chez-yvonne.net. Main courses 13€–26€.
AE, DC, MC, V. Lunch and dinner daily; reservations required.

Geppetto CATHEDRAL *ITALIAN*
This solid, family-friendly restaurant serves
good, traditional Italian food at good prices
in the Petite France district. The open kitchen
reveals the chef at work, tossing some of
the best pizzas in Strasbourg or whipping

up pastas with secret sauces. Reservations are accepted but not always a guarantee of prompt seating in this small restaurant. **1 place St-Etienne.** ☎ 03-88-36-91-05. Main courses 10€–15€. MC. Lunch and dinner Mon–Sat.

★ **La Cambuse** PETITE FRANCE *SEAFOOD*
Excellent seafood is served in French, Japanese, Thai, and Provençal style aboard this charming riverboat in the Petite France neighborhood. Reservations are necessary at this unexpectedly refined but small restaurant with just eight tables. **1 rue des Dentelles.** ☎ 03-88-22-10-22. 3-course menu 55€. MC, V. Lunch and dinner Mon–Sat.

Le Made In France UNIVERSITIES *DELI*
Craving a triple cheeseburger, double-decker club, or huge pastrami sandwich? These sandwiches may honor American excess, but expect them to be served with a unique French twist. Sandwiches such as the Big Boss Brie are served on excellent bread with fresh products and your choice of nearly 20 sauces. The place is popular with students and everyone else around lunchtime. **7 place St-Nicolas aux Ondes.** ☎ 03-88-24-07-08. Main courses 4€–9€. AE, MC, V. Lunch and dinner Mon–Sat. East of Eglise St. Guilliame, near downtown.

★ **Le Tire Bouchon** CATHEDRAL *ALSATIAN*
This centrally located restaurant may offer the best traditional Alsatian cuisine in the area. Carefully made dishes are served in rustic, 19th-century style, from *steak tartare au couteau* (hand-minced by knife instead of ground), to "Grandmother-style" vinaigrette calf's head, to multiple types of sauerkraut and more. Ask your server how to pair these unusual dishes with one of the excellent wines on hand. The place is always crowded with locals, so reservations are a must. **5 rue Tailleurs de Pierre.** ☎ 03-88-22-16-32. www.letirebouchon.fr. Main courses 14€–18€. AE, DC, MC, V. Lunch and dinner daily.

★★ **Umami** PETITE FRANCE *CONTEMPORARY*
Refinement and artistry are the hallmarks of this small restaurant named for the mysterious fifth flavor, often translated as "savory."

> *The 50€ five-course tasting menu at Umami is well worth the splurge.*

Chef René Fieger traveled the globe before returning home to open this restaurant with his wife. Working in a minuscule kitchen, visible from the equally small dining room, he turns out extraordinary, unforgettable dishes, which you can choose to sample in five small courses. **8 rue des Dentelles.** ☎ 03-88-32-80-53. www.restaurant-umami.com. Reservations required. 2-course menu 37€–4€; 5-course tasting menu 50€. AE, MC, V. Lunch Sat, dinner Mon–Sat.

Dining Tip

For additional restaurants in Strasbourg, see "Alsace & Lorraine for Gourmands," p. 276.

Where to Stay & Dine in Alsace & Lorraine

> *Hotellerie des Deux Clefs has been a hostelry for centuries: In 1540 it was called the "Statthof zum Schwartzen Adler."*

★★ **Auberge du Cheval Blanc** GUEBWILLER GASTRONOMIC A few kilometers outside Guebwiller, in the small village of Westhalten, this family-run hotel is a must for wine lovers. You'll be staying on the vineyard grounds, and Monsieur Koehler will gladly show you round his caves and vines, which produce all the major *cépages* (varietals) of the Alsace region: Edelzwicker, Sylvaner, pinot blanc, Riesling, Tokay d'Alsace, muscat, Gewürztraminer, pinot noir, and Cremant d'Alsace. With food to match and bright, comfortable lodgings, it's an all-around great choice. 20 rue Rouffach, Westhalten. ☎ 03-89-47-01-16. www.auberge-chevalblc.com. 11 units. Doubles 95€–130€. Fixed-price menu 26€–84€. AE, DC, MC, V.

★★★ **Auberge du Schoenenbourg** RIQUE-WIHR FRENCH We highly recommend this restaurant-inn surrounded by vineyards at the edge of the village. The foie gras maison is *de rigueur*, but salmon soufflé with truffle sabayon is an elegant surprise. Especially flavorful is a platter of both smoked and fresh salmon, served with creamy horseradish sauce and herb-flavored sauerkraut. The 58-room **Hôtel Le Schoenenbourg** is next door on rue du Schoenenbourg (☎ 03-89-49-01-11; www.auberge-schoenenbourg.fr). It offers comfortably furnished guest rooms on site. Doubles 97€–123€; suites 176€–232€. 2 rue de la Piscine. ☎ 03-89-47-92-28. www.auberge-schoenenbourg.com. Reservations required. Main courses 18€–32€; fixed-price menu 29€ lunch, 39€–81€ dinner. AE, MC, V. Lunch Sun–Mon, dinner Thurs–Tues; closed Jan.

★★ **Château des Monthairons** DIEUE-SUR-MEUSE GASTRONOMIC This hotel run by the Thouvenin family occupies an 1857 château crafted from blocks of pale stone. Guest rooms have luxury beds and quality linens. The property encompasses a pair of 15th-century chapels, a nesting ground for herons, and opportunities for canoeing and fishing. The gastronomic restaurant is also open to non-guests.

> *Chef Marc Haeberlin serves some of the finest partridge, pheasant, and duckling in Europe at L'Auberge de l'Ill.*

26 rte. de Verdun, Les Monthairons (12km/7½ miles south of Verdun on D334). ☎ 03-29-87-78-55. www.chateaudesmonthairons.fr. 25 units. Doubles 98€–190€. Main courses 22€–27€, fixed-price menus 40€–92€. AE, DC, MC, V. Apr to mid-Nov lunch Wed–Sun, dinner Tues–Sun; mid-Nov to Mar lunch Wed–Sat, dinner Tues–Sat. Closed Jan to mid-Feb.

★ Hostellerie Abbaye de la Pommeraie

SELESTAT This former Cistercian abbey transports lodgers back a century or five, but with modern comforts, of course. Each room is individually decorated; check the photos on the website to inform your choice: the summery garden room 100, the cozy beam-ceilinged twin room 203, or the urbane double 105. There is a choice of two restaurants: the gastronomic **La Prieuré** (lunch Tues–Sun, dinner Mon–Sat; main courses 27€–33€) or the more homey and generous **l'Apfelsteubel** (lunch and dinner daily; main courses 18€–20€). 8 bd. du Marechal Foch. ☎ 03-88-92-07-84. www.pommeraie.fr. 14 units. Doubles 165€–208€. AE, MC, V.

★ Hostellerie du Coq Hardi VERDUN

GASTRONOMIC Our favorite hotel in Verdun, composed of four connected 18th-century houses near the Meuse, is loaded with antiques, including church pews and a Renaissance fireplace. The dining room serves the best food in town. It has a painted ceiling, Louis XIII chairs, and two deactivated World War I bombshells at the entrance. 8 av. de la Victoire. ☎ 03-29-86-36-36. www.coq-hardi.com. 35 units. Doubles 99€–132€; suites 250€. Fixed-price menus 46€–97€. Lunch Sun–Thurs, dinner Sat and Mon–Thurs. AE, MC, V.

Hostellerie Le Maréchal COLMAR

This inn in a 16th-century building is an atmospheric and tranquil place to sleep. It also has a good restaurant that serves dishes beyond the standard Alsatian repertoire. 4–6 place des Six-Montagnes-Noires. ☎ 03-89-41-60-43. www.hotel-le-marechal.com. 30 units. Doubles 105€–225€. AE, DC, MC, V.

★★ Hôtel de la Cathédrale METZ

A real *hôtel de charme* in an unbeatable location overlooking the cathedral, this comfortable hotel has beams and toile de Jouy fabrics. It's worth paying extra for the nighttime view of the illuminated cathedral. 25 place de Chambre. ☎ 03-87-75-00-02. www.hotelcathedrale-metz.fr. 20 units. Doubles 75€–110€. AE, MC, V.

★★ Hôtel des Deux Clefs TURCKHEIM

The very picture of a rustic Alsatian inn, the 15th-century Hôtel des Deux Clefs has a gabled roof and half-timbered facade adorned with flowering window boxes. It's just as pretty inside, with rooms decorated in warm red and yellow tones, antique furniture, and rich fabrics. 3 rue du Conseil. ☎ 03-89-27-06-01. www.hotellerie-deuxclefs.fr. 48 units. Doubles 89€–229€. AE, MC, V.

★★ **JY's** COLMAR
Named for chef Jean Yves Schillinger, this restaurant, housed in a 17th-century building with a riverside terrace in the Little Venice quarter, is sure to please gourmands. Schillinger draws on influences from Italy, Spain, and Japan, though his roots are clearly in France. 17 rue de la Poissonnerie. ☎ 03-89-21-53-60. www.jean-yves-schillinger.com. Main courses 17€–28€, menus 32€–55€. AE, DC, MC, V. Tues–Sat noon–2:30pm and 7–10:30pm.

★★ **La Citadelle** METZ *GASTRONOMIC*
Configured from the city's restored 16th-century citadel, this hotel is the top stay in Metz. It is located n the heart of the city center and has plasma TVs, air-conditioning, and Wi-Fi access. The fabulous gourmet **Le Magasin Aux Vivres** restaurant, frequented by well-heeled locals as well as visitors, underscores the quality of the hotel. 5 avenue Ney. ☎ 03-87-17-17-17. www.citadelle-metz.com. 35 units. Doubles 165€–205€. Main courses 38€– 49€. AE, DC, MC, V. Lunch Tues–Fri, dinner Tues–Sat.

★ **La Maison des Têtes** COLMAR *GASTRONOMIC*
Colmar's leading hotel houses one of its top restaurants, near the Unterlinden Museum. The dining rooms have aged-wood beams, Art Nouveau lighting fixtures, and stained-glass windows. The excellent food includes foie gras with truffles and Rhine salmon braised in Riesling. Rooms are nicely furnished, with air-conditioning and TVs; some have Jacuzzis. 19 rue des Têtes. ☎ 03-89-24-43-43. www.la-maison-des-tetes. com. 21 units. Doubles 91€–235€. Main courses 10€–28€; menus 33€–72€. AE, DC, MC, V.

★★★ **L'Auberge de l'Ill** ILLHAEUSERN *REGIONAL*
The best restaurant in eastern France is run by the Haeberlin family in their 19th-century farmhouse, where patrons can stay the night after dinner. Chef Marc Haeberlin takes dishes of Alsatian origin and finesses them into *grande cuisine*—freshwater eel stewed in Riesling, *matelotes* (small glazed onions) in Riesling, and an inventive foie gras. His preparations of partridge, pheasant, and duckling are among the best in Europe. Some dishes require 24 hours' notice, so inquire when you make reservations. The Auberge has its own hotel in the grounds, the **Hôtel des Berges,** where the 13 rooms are very distinctively and individually decorated. The Torsado suite has painted frescoes on its wooden, curved walls and ceiling, making it feel like a 17th-century galley. 4 rue de Collonges au Mont d'Or. ☎ 03-89-71-89-00 (inn ☎ 03-89-71-87-87). www.auberge-de-l-ill.com. 13 units. Doubles 262€–520€, cottage 465€. Main courses 45€–140€; menus 117€–148€. AE, DC, MC, V. Mid-Mar to mid-Feb lunch and dinner Wed–Sun; reservations required.

Le Beau Séjour COLMAR
This inn lives up to its name, which means a beautiful place to stay. The smart, tartan-themed rooms in the eaves are particularly attractive. The outdoor dining room, hung with lilacs, is especially lovely in summer. 25 rue du Ladhof. ☎ 03-89-20-66-66. www.beausejour.fr. Doubles 80€. MC, V.

★★ **Le Clos St-Vincent** RIBEAUVILLE *GASTRONOMIC* Sitting up high, with beautiful views of the vineyards, this hotel is known for its contemporary elegance. As you linger over your food, taking in the stunning view from the restaurant terrace, you'll remember that you didn't come here to save money. A spa, a fitness center, and all the modern amenities round out the appeal. Rue Klee Osterbergweg. ☎ 03-89-73-67-65. www.leclossaintvincent.com. 24 units. Doubles 135€–285€. Main courses 18€–30€; fixed price menus 40€–55€. AE, DC, MC, V.

★★ **Le Parc Hôtel, Restaurant & Spa** OBERNAI *GASTRONOMIC* More than a hotel, this "resort spa" is quite a rarity in Alsace. It has a lot of style, from the folksy exterior and *winstub* restaurant to the warmly decorated contemporary rooms and luxurious spa with an attractive indoor pool. Try to arrive in time for an evening swim before dinner. 169 rte. d'Ottrot. ☎ 03-88-95-50-08. www.hotel-du-parc.com. 62 units. Doubles 120€–240€. Main courses 31€–40€. AE, MC, V.

★★ **Zum Schnogalch** OBERNAI *REGIONAL*
This restaurant specializes in French cuisine and German delicacies; the heaping helpings of *choucroute* (sauerkraut), served with five garnishes, are reasonably priced. 18 place de l'Etoile. ☎ 03-88-95-54-47. http://zum.schnogaloch.free. fr. Main courses 14€–18€. AE, MC, V. Lunch Tues–Sun, dinner Tues–Wed and Fri–Sun.

Fast Facts

Arriving

BY PLANE The **Strasbourg-Entzheim Airport** (Aéroport International Strasbourg; ☎ 03-88-64-67-67; www.strasbourg.aeroport.fr), 15km (9⅓ miles) southwest of the city center, receives daily flights from many European cities, including Paris, London, Rome, Vienna, and Moscow. You can get from the airport to the Strasbourg town center via shuttle bus or city trams, which run at 40-minute intervals all day long. **BY TRAIN** Direct, high-speed TGV trains from Paris reach Metz in 80 minutes; Nancy in 90 minutes; and Strasbourg in 2 hours, 20 minutes. At least 20 trains a day arrive in Strasbourg, the major rail hub in the area, from Paris's Gare de l'Est (trip time: 4 hr.). Trains link Strasbourg to Colmar, Nancy, and Mulhouse, as well as to Germany via Strasbourg, across the Rhine. For information and schedules, call ☎ 36-35 or 08-92-35-35-35. **BY CAR** The giant A35 (with occasional references to its original name, the N83) crosses the plain of Alsace, linking Strasbourg with Colmar and Mulhouse. From Paris, if you're driving to Nancy, follow N4 east (trip time: 4 hr.). Verdun is several miles north of the Paris-Strasbourg autoroute (A4).

Internet Cafes

There are numerous Internet cafes in Strasbourg, including **Net sur Cour,** 18 quai des Pêcheurs (☎ 03-88-35-66-76), which offers Wi-Fi access. In Nancy, try **E-Café,** 11 rue des Quatre Eglises (☎ 03-83-35-47-34; www.ecafe.fr) or **Médiathèque,** 10 rue Baron Louis (☎ 03-83-39-00-63). For information on other Internet cafes, check with the local tourist office in each town.

Post Office

COLMAR 36 av. de la République (☎ 03-89-24-62-00). **NANCY** 10 rue St-Dizier (☎ 03-83-39-75-20). **STRASBOURG** 5 av. de la Marseillaise (☎ 03-88-52-35-50).

Safety

Alsace and Lorraine are generally very safe. In an emergency, call 17 for the police, 18 for the fire department or paramedics, and 15 for an ambulance.

> Scenic routes abound as you drive around Alsace and Lorraine.

Tourist Offices

Municipal tourist offices are listed at the end of the town tour stops throughout the chapter. **NANCY** place Stanislas (☎ 03-83-35-22-41; www.ot-nancy.fr). **STRASBOURG** 17 place de la Cathédrale (☎ 03-88-52-28-28; www.ot-strasbourg.fr). The offices are closed on bank holidays. For information on wines, vintages, and winery visits, contact the **CIVA** (Alsace Wine Committee), Maison du Vin d'Alsace, 12 av. de la Foire-aux-Vins (☎ 03-89-20-16-20; Mon–Fri 8am–noon and 2–5pm). Make arrangements far in advance.

8
Burgundy

Favorite Moments in Burgundy

Burgundy feels rich: the lush fields, the legendary grapes, the ocher stone of its monasteries and manors. During the Middle Ages, powerful dukes and bishops governed Bourgogne, the French name for this eastern part of the country. They live on today through the region's religious buildings, art, and culinary traditions. Their legacy is yours to explore, at a gentle pace, along country back roads that meander from one *Grand Cru* winery to the next.

1 **Reveling in the Renaissance architecture of Château Ancy-le-Franc.** If you tire of all the medieval abbeys in this region, make a detour to Château Ancy-le-Franc. Designed by a 16th-century Italian architect, it was one of the first manifestations of the Renaissance in France. See p. 330, **4**.

2 **Counting all the medieval abbeys.** Bourgogne and abbeys go together like "pinot" and "noir." With a handsome monastery seemingly in every good-size town—Abbaye de Fontenay is the finest (p. 314, **2**)—Burgundy has a past clearly indebted to the history of its brotherhoods.

3 **Driving in Burgundy's pristine countryside.** As you explore the routes in these tours, you'll see that a highway rarely figures into the journey. Amid the quiet pleasures of country roads, the getting there will be its own reward.

4 **Following the Route des Grands Crus.** One of France's most celebrated wine roads, the Route des Grands Crus is renowned for its scenery, history, and aristocratic wines. See p. 322.

> PREVIOUS PAGE This church in the Côte de Nuits vineyards, has a colorful tiled roof typical of Burgundy. THIS PAGE The Loire may be most associated with Renaissance châteaux, but Burgundy has the sumptuous Château Ancy-le-Franc.

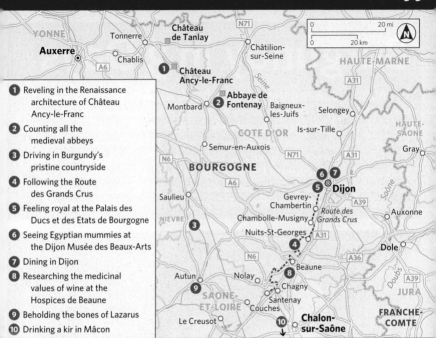

1. Reveling in the Renaissance architecture of Château Ancy-le-Franc
2. Counting all the medieval abbeys
3. Driving in Burgundy's pristine countryside
4. Following the Route des Grands Crus
5. Feeling royal at the Palais des Ducs et des Etats de Bourgogne
6. Seeing Egyptian mummies at the Dijon Musée des Beaux-Arts
7. Dining in Dijon
8. Researching the medicinal values of wine at the Hospices de Beaune
9. Beholding the bones of Lazarus
10. Drinking a kir in Mâcon

⑤ Feeling royal at the Palais des Ducs et des Etats de Bourgogne. It's good to be king, but this former royal residence of the richest bootleggers in the world proves it's not so bad to be a duke either. There aren't many royal palaces in Bourgogne, so the dukes of Burgundy built this gorgeous edifice to make sure their subjects knew who was in charge. See p. 334, ①.

⑥ Seeing Egyptian mummies at the Dijon Musée des Beaux-Arts. Like a mini-Louvre, this wonderfully wide-ranging museum assembles the treasures pillaged by dukes and kings, catalogued by the *luminaires* of the Enlightenment. The difference? It's free. See p. 334, ②.

⑦ Dining in Dijon. For a small city, Dijon has an amazing concentration of gastronomic restaurants led by chefs who combine creativity with respect for Burgundy's deeply rooted culinary traditions. See p. 337.

⑧ Researching the medicinal values of wine at the Hospices de Beaune. An architectural gem, this former hospital now combines the remains of an old apothecary's shop, religious art treasures, and the going concern of its vineyards—the fruits of which you can taste and buy. The highlight of the year is a star-studded charity auction. See p. 316, ④.

⑨ Beholding the bones of Lazarus. Coming back from the dead is no easy feat. If you're a fan of the saint who pulled it off, all we can say is, drop what you're doing and head directly to the Bourgogne region. Not one but two sites— Avallon and Autun—house relics of the corpse that died twice. See p. 331, ⑥, and 320, ⑦.

⑩ Drinking a kir in Mâcon. The ultimate aperitif, kir should be made from a good Bourgogne *aligoté* lightly dosed with Dijon's own *crème de cassis* to create a rosy (rather than black currant–colored) drink. They are sure to get it right in Mâcon, home of the dryer-than-dry *aligoté*. See p. 325, ⑥.

Burgundy in 3 Days

Burgundy, in a nutshell, is all about wine and abbeys, and the two are deeply connected. During the Middle Ages, monastic orders grew in this area as in no other, reaching unparalleled heights in Christendom and leaving a magnificent legacy of architecture and viniculture, as the monks also tended the vine. Dijon is the region's only real city; begin your tour here before venturing out to explore the three abbeys of Fontenay, Vézelay, and Cluny; the Burgundy Wine Route; and Beaune, the quintessential wine lover's town. What's more, wherever you dine, you'll find that Burgundy's reputation for fine food is justly deserved.

> The medieval cloisters at the Abbaye de Fontenay still look much as they did in the 12th century.

START Dijon is 316km (196 miles) southeast of Paris. **TRIP LENGTH** 325km (202 miles).

1 ★★★ **Dijon.** The ★★★ **Palais des Ducs et des Etats de Bourgogne** is the former palace of the supremely powerful dukes that ruled this land during the Middle Ages. Make sure to head up the palace's 316-step **Tour de Philippe le Bon** for an optimal birds-eye view of the region you're about to explore. ⏱ Half-day. For detailed information on Dijon, see p. 334.

After lunch, drive northwest from Dijon on D971 (also called N71), D6, and D19 toward Montbard. The turnoff for the Abbaye de Fontenay is in the village of Marmagne, just before Montbard (71km/44 miles total).

2 ★★★ **Abbaye de Fontenay.** Despite its remote location, this former Cistercian abbey draws more than 100,000 tourists annually. St. Bernard, founder of the order, began construction in 1119, and by 1269 Fontenay had become the royal abbey under St. Louis (Louis

1. Dijon
2. Abbaye de Fontenay
3. Abbaye de Vézelay
4. Beaune
5. Abbaye de Cluny

IX), who exempted it from taxes and lavished it with funding. Its demise came during the French Revolution, and it functioned as a paper mill until the early 20th century, when new owners fully and impeccably restored it. Now a UNESCO World Heritage site, Fontenay Abbey is probably the best example of a Cistercian abbey in Europe. All the original buildings save the long-demolished refectory have been preserved, and the grounds and gravel *parterres* are near-perfect examples of medieval landscaping, so what you see is nearly the same Abbaye de Fontenay as the one inhabited by 12th-century Cistercian monks. Hourly guided tours are in French; there are self-guided tour leaflets available for English speakers. Stay the night nearby at the **Château de Malaisy** (p. 333). ⏱ 2 hr. Rte. de Dijon, Marmagne. ☎ 03-80-92-15-00. www. abbayedefontenay.com. Mar–Sept daily 11am–11pm; Oct–Apr daily 10am–6pm.

Where to Stay & Dine

For hotels and restaurants in Dijon, see p. 337; along the Wine Route, see p. 326; elsewhere in the region, see p. 333.

> *Colorful roof tiles like these in Dijon are as emblematic of Burgundy as are wine and good food.*

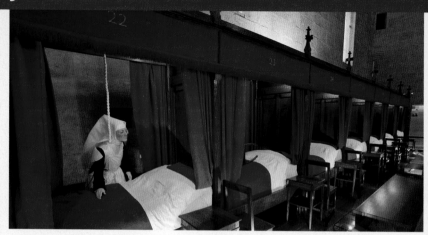

> *The Hôtel-Dieu de Beaune was a hospital until the 20th century, which is illustrated in the museum's mock period wards.*

On Day 2, set out from Montbard on D980 south. Turn right after only 1km (⅔ mile) toward Quincerot and Quincy-le-Vicomte, continue west for 14km (8⅔ miles) to pick up D957 south to Avallon, and follow signs to Vézelay (56km/35 miles total).

③ ★★★ **Abbaye de Vézelay.** The Benedictine abbey of Vézelay was an important stop on the Santiago de Compostela pilgrimage route from its beginnings in the 9th century. In the 11th century the monks here claimed that the abbey contained the relics of St. Mary Magdalene. Several papal bulls confirmed that her body and relics had been removed from the tombs at St-Maximin in Provence and relocated to Vézelay, and the story was widely accepted as fact. The influx of pilgrims this generated necessitated a larger church, resulting in the beautiful **Basilique Ste-Marie-Madeleine,** place de la Basilique (☎ 03-86-33-39-50; www.vezelay.cef.fr; admission free; guided tours 3.20€; July–Aug 7am–9pm, Sept–June sunrise–sunset), now a UNESCO World Heritage site. A dominant ecclesiastical power for centuries, the church was a nexus of activity for the Second and Third Crusades and provided exile for the English archbishop Thomas Becket, who in 1166 excommunicated supporters of King Henry II, the first king of England, but not the king himself. In the 16th century, rioting Protestant Huguenots burned the abbey and turned it into a storehouse and stable. A good portion of the basilica's exterior facade was

also defaced during the anti-religious fervor that swept France during the Revolution. Yet the church remains one of Europe's largest. It's also among the continent's best-preserved Romanesque churches, filled with superb sculptures and priceless relics looted from the Middle East before the Crusades. ⏱ 2½ hr. Vézelay Tourist Office, rue St-Etienne. ☎ 03-86-33-23-69. www.vezelaytourisme.com.

Retrace your route to Avallon, and take A6 southeast for 117km (73 miles).

④ ★★ **Beaune.** Spend the rest of the afternoon driving along the **Route des Grands Crus** (p. 322), north of Beaune. Explore the vineyards of **Gevrey-Chambertin** or **Nuits-St-Georges** (p. 322, ②), before returning to the walled precincts of Beaune, perhaps the premier wine town in France (see p. 324, ③). Here you can load up on wine and food souvenirs. In November a famed charity wine auction takes place at the ★★ **Hospices de Beaune,** also known as the **Hôtel-Dieu de Beaune,** rue de l'Hôtel-Dieu (☎ 03-80-24-45-00; www.hospices-de-beaune.com; 6.50€ adults, 4€ reduced; March to mid-Nov daily 9am–6:30pm, mid-Nov to March daily 9am–11:30am and 2–5:30pm), which owns some of the region's best vineyards and sells its wines year-round. The building itself is an architectural delight, with Flemish-influenced designs and perhaps the best tiled roof in a region full of them. Inside, a museum exploring the history of this former hospital displays medieval medical instruments that will make you glad you live in the 21st century.

For original gastronomic cuisine with its roots in the Burgundy tradition, dine at ★★ **Le Bénaton** (p. 327), and then spend the night at ★★ **Hôtel de la Clôche** (p. 326) to enjoy a lovely breakfast in the walled garden.

The morning of Day 3 gives you time to admire Beaune's historic town center, and perhaps buy some wines. You can explore the full range of Burgundy wines at the 15th-century **Marché aux Vins** tasting cellar, 2 rue Nicholas-Rollin (☎ 03-80-25-08-20; www.marcheauxvins.com; admission 10€; July–Aug daily 9:30am–5:30pm, Sept–June 9:30–11:30am and 2–5:30pm). ⏱ Half-day in Beaune. Beaune Tourist Office, 6 bd. Perpreuil. ☎ 03-80-26-21-30. www.beaune-tourism.com. See also p. 319, ③, and 324, ③.

From Beaune on Day 3, take A6 south to N80 (exit 26, Cluny is indicated), and drive 11km (6¾ miles) to D981, which leads to Cluny (81km/50 miles total).

⑤ ★★ **Abbaye de Cluny.** The ruins of the 10th-century Benedictine **Abbaye de Cluny** are a mere 10% of what was once the largest, most prestigious Christian building in the world, until it was surpassed by St. Peter's Basilica in Rome in 1626. All that remains is the 14th-century **Hôtel de Cluny** (now a fine museum), a 12th-century transept, 15th-century abbots' residences, a few 18th-century convent buildings, and the gardens. But what stood before was for more than 400 years the lynchpin of medieval French culture and the widely acknowledged leader among the monastic orders. The monastery gained its power largely through patronage from Western European kings, as well as a well-guarded meritocracy. Exempted from taxation by the dukes of Burgundy, it was able to retain its vast coffers and hire managers and workers to tend to quotidian affairs, thus freeing the monks to perform liturgy and charity. This, combined with the fact that the order prohibited itself from holding land by feudal service, garnered the monks greater and greater esteem, among both ecclesiastical brethren and laypeople, who were content to overlook the fine food, wine, and clothing the monks enjoyed despite their vows of poverty. The abbey's prominence began to decline in the 12th century, due to financial problems, the rise of other monastic orders, and an increase in papal authority. The Wars of Religion also took their toll. When Protestant Huguenots sacked the abbey in 1562, they destroyed the library, which was one of the richest and most important storehouses of information in all of Europe. But it was the local residents, fuming over the monks' close ties with the Ancien Régime, who delivered a staggering *coup de grâce* to the monastery and sacked it during the French Revolution. Knowledge of the history of Cluny is a must to understand medieval France; this "empire" of 10,000 monks was declared "the light of the world" by an 11th-century pope. Unfortunately, its best works were removed to Paris, at the Thermes de Cluny, also known as **Musée National du Moyen Age** (National Museum of the Middle Ages; p. 55, ⑪). ⏱ 2 hr. Place Jean de Bourbon. ☎ 03-85-59-07-30. www.cluny.monuments-nationaux.fr. Admission 7€ adults, 4.50€ reduced. May–Aug 9:30am–6:30pm; Sept–Apr 9:30am–noon and 1:30–5pm.

> *In the 11th century, the monks of the vast Abbaye de Cluny were so powerful, the abbey was dubbed the "light of the world."*

Burgundy in 1 Week

You are in for a treat: no rushing from place to place, no six-lane highways—just rolling countryside, small towns and villages, sumptuous meals, and soft beds to fall into. Before you venture into Burgundy's delightful back roads and villages, it is worth spending a day in Dijon, the regional capital. From there, you'll travel through the legendary vineyards of Nuits-St-Georges, Gevrey-Chambertin, Mercuréy, and Givry; visit the historically important Abbey of Cluny; and then change direction to head northeast where Roman ruins, a fortified town, and Renaissance châteaux reveal the region's lesser-known side.

> *Burgundy's countryside looks particularly pretty in autumn, when its forests show an earthy, golden hue.*

START Dijon is 316km (196 miles) southeast of Paris. **TRIP LENGTH** 424km (263 miles).

① ★★★ **Dijon.** Great wine accompanies good food here in the ancient capital of Burgundy. Between meals, you'll find plenty of art and architecture to explore. ⊙ 1 day. For detailed information on Dijon, see p. 334.

From Dijon on Day 2, take N74 (the Route des Grands Crus) south to Nuits-St-Georges (28km/17 miles).

② **Nuits-St-Georges & the Route des Grands Crus.** From this point on, you'll be driving the N74, the **Route des Grands Crus** (see "The Burgundy Wine Routes," p. 325), all the way south to the threshold of the Rhône-Alps region (p. 340). These next several days will be a joy ride. As soon as you exit Dijon, you'll enter the **Marsannay-la-Côte** region; before

you know it, you'll be in **Gevrey-Chambertin.** It's a scant 28km (17 miles) from Dijon to **Nuits-St-Georges,** but take your time.

A great place for lunch, in the center of Nuits-St-Georges and with a fine wine selection, is the innovative and reasonable **La Cabotte** (p. 326). After lunch, get back on N74, inhale the country air, allow your mind to be soothed by the never-ending straight rows of tiny vines, and permit yourself to range just southwest of Beaune to the winery-filled villages of **Pommard** and **Meursault.** ⊙ Half-day. See p. 322, **②**.

Beaune is 25km (16 miles) south of Nuits-St-Georges on N74.

Where to Stay & Dine

For hotels and restaurants in Dijon, see p. 337; along the Wine Route, see p. 326; elsewhere in the region, see p. 333.

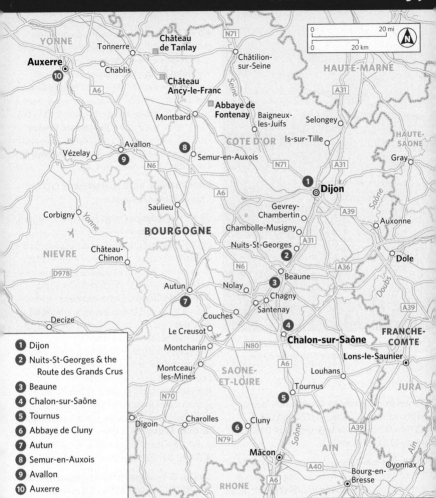

1 Dijon
2 Nuits-St-Georges & the Route des Grands Crus
3 Beaune
4 Chalon-sur-Saône
5 Tournus
6 Abbaye de Cluny
7 Autun
8 Semur-en-Auxois
9 Avallon
10 Auxerre

3 ★★ **Beaune.** When you arrive in town, check into the three-star **Hôtel de la Clôche** (p. 326). Spend the afternoon and the following morning exploring the bonny city of Beaune. There's plenty to do in this tourism capital, with its museums on wine and mustard and the beautiful 15th-century ★★ **Hôtel-Dieu de Beaune,** also called the **Hospices de Beaune.** Here you'll find a collection of buildings set in a rectangular format, several of them displaying the splendid, glazed-tile roofs that are so prevalent in Bourgogne. As beautiful on the inside as it is on the outside, this hospital was originally created to treat casualties of the 16th-century Wars of Religion. Now

it houses a museum with an eclectic collection, from apothecaries' jars to 15th-century art, and it sells wine from its own vineyards.

After lunch on Day 3 (for recommendations, see p. 326), have a quick look at the last great Romanesque church in Bourgogne, the **Collégiale Notre-Dame,** 21 place du Général Leclerc (☎ 03-80-24-77-95; Admission 2.50€ adults, 1.90€ reduced; June–Sept Mon–Sat 9am–7pm, Sun 2–7pm; Oct–May Mon–Sat 9am–12:30pm and 2–7pm, Sun 2–7pm). It's home to some of the finest medieval tapestries produced in Europe, illustrating the life of the Virgin Mary. ⏱ 1 day. For more on Beaune, see p. 316, 4, and 324, 3.

> You can see gently trestled vines growing all around the pretty town of Chalon-sur-Saône.

To get from Beaune to Chalon-sur-Saône, either continue south on N74 and D981 (37km/23 miles) or take the quiet D18/19 route (30km/19 miles).

4 Chalon-sur-Saône. Continuing on the Wine Route, you can visit more superb wineries in the villages of **Mercuréy** and **Givry.** Just to the east is Chalon-sur-Saône. Bunk there for the night, keeping in mind that this town is just south of the Côte d'Or region, so the wines farther south aren't quite as impeccable. Chalon-sur-Saône is a charming riverboat city with a lovely port, however, so spend the morning walking around the waterfront before heading over to the city center's excellent shopping district, full of high-end shops as well as local wares. If you've had regrets about not buying a certain bottle of wine, head over to the comprehensive **Maison des Vins** on promenade Ste-Marie, and you can probably find it there. ⏱ Half-day. See p. 324, **4**.

From Chalon-sur-Saône on Day 4, take N6 south to Tournus (27km/17 miles).

5 ★★ Tournus. Even though you're still on the Wine Route, take a break from tasting and spend some time exploring Tournus. Visit the **★★ Hôtel Dieu,** a former hospital that now houses a fine arts museum, the **Musée Greuze,** and an old apothecary shop. Afterward, head to one of the many excellent restaurants in this lovely town, such as **★★ Restaurant Greuze** (p. 327). Several castles are nearby; if we had to choose one, we'd recommend the **Château de Cormatin.** ⏱ 2 hr. See p. 324, **5**.

From Tournus, head southwest on D15 to Cluny (35km/22 miles).

6 ★★★ Abbaye de Cluny. Far from cloistered, the medieval monks of Cluny orchestrated politics across Europe, bore the standards of Catholic doctrine, and steered monasticism from its remote independence to community-based charity work. What remains of the **Abbaye de Cluny** is just a fragment of what it used to be, but the museum at the **Hôtel de Cluny** provides reminders of the place of importance it held for centuries; this gives visitors an understanding of both medieval France and the anti-religious sentiment the church ultimately engendered, which led to the sacking of this gigantic abbey during the French Revolution. A delightful place to stay near Cluny, in Le Rousset, is **★★ La Fontaine du Grand Fussy** (p. 333). ⏱ Half-day. See p. 317, **5**. Cluny Tourist Office, 6 rue Mercière. ☎ 03-85-59-05-34. www.cluny-tourisme.com.

On Day 5, head north from Cluny on D980 and N80 to Autun (80km/50 miles).

7 ★★ Autun. Autun was one of the shining cities of Roman Gaul, and numerous examples of that heritage abound. There are the two Roman gates, **Porte St-André** and **Porte d'Arroux,** and the huge Gallo-Roman **Temple de Janus** is just outside town, but the town's pride is the **★★ Théâtre Antique,** the largest Roman amphitheater in France, which could accommodate 20,000 people.

One of the finest Cluniac churches in France is the 12th-century **★ Cathédrale St-Lazare,** place du Terreau (☎ 03-85-86-80-38; www. autun-tourisme.com; admission 3€ adults, 1.50€ reduced; daily 10am–7pm). The sculpture at the cathedral is well known—especially the tympanum of the Last Judgment—thanks

> *The Roman Porte St-André in Autun once opened out onto the Roman road to Langres and Besançon.*

to the work of the sculptor **Gislebertus.** Like Avallon (9 , below), Autun Cathedral contains relics of Lazarus. ☉ 1 day. Autun Tourist Office, 13 rue Général Demetz. ☎ 03-85-86-80-38. www.autun-tourisme.com.

On Day 6, drive north from Autun on D980 to Semur-en-Auxois (71km/44 miles).

8 **Semur-en-Auxois.** As you resume heading north, a different side of Bourgogne opens up, though the Côte d'Or scenery remains superlative. In less than an hour, you'll find yourself gazing at the pink granite bluff on which rests the fortified village of Semur-en-Auxois. Legend has it that Hercules built Semur upon his return from Spain, but it wasn't until the late 15th century that the rulers of Bourgogne decided to take advantage of the natural defensive attributes of this plateau by modernizing the fortress, which now dominates the town and provides the draw for tourists. With restored ramparts that make for an excellent stroll, several towers, medieval gates, and the **Collégiale Notre-Dame,** it's little wonder this picturesque town is full of sketching artists. ☉ Half-day. Semur-en-Auxois Town Hall, 7bis place François Mitterrand. ☎ 03-80-97-01-11. www.ville-semur-en-auxois.fr.

To get from Semur-en-Auxois to Avallon, take D954 west to Cussy-les-Forges, and switch to N6 (43km/27 miles).

9 **Avallon.** You're in for another pleasant countryside drive—this time to the charming town of Avallon—so you can compare two different walled cities. A must-see here are the holy relics of Lazarus, believed to cure leprosy, stored at the fine **Eglise St-Lazare.** Keep in mind that Avallon is the closest town to the entrance of **Parc Naturel Régional du Morvan** (Morvan Regional Park; www.parcdumorvan. org), the biggest national park in Burgundy. ☉ Half-day. See p. 331, 6 .

From Avallon on Day 7, take N6 northwest to Auxerre (60km/37 miles).

10 **Auxerre.** An excellent place to spend the last day of your trip, Auxerre has tremendous character and affords easy access to many great sites nearby. ★★★ **Château Ancy-le-Franc** (p. 330, 3) and **Château de Tanlay** (p. 331, 5) are two of the finest but least-visited castles in France. The nearby town of ★ **Tonnerre** is home to the unique **Fosse Dionne** (Pit of Diane, p. 330), with its picturesque fountain. ☉ 1 day. See p. 328, 1 .

The Wine Route

Burgundy has six wine routes. Here we cover two of them, the Route des Grands Crus, which extends into the Route des Grands Vins. Running south from Dijon, roughly following N74 to Beaune and then N6 to Mâcon, these two routes are easy to follow and can claim 24 of Burgundy's 33 *Grand Crus* along the way. *Cru* means "growth place," and these are the prime soils of Burgundy, toiled for untold generations since the time when Cistercian monks first delineated their plots. You'll also be enjoying some of the finest food that Burgundy can produce—a fitting complement to these unforgettable wines.

> *This vineyard in Nuits-St-Georges is where some of the world's best wines start life.*

START Dijon is 316km (196 miles) southeast of Paris. **TRIP LENGTH** At least 5 days; 152km (94 miles).

❶ ★★★ **Dijon.** The city of Dijon is the region of Burgundy in its fullest expression, with the area's highest concentration of excellent restaurants and culture. The vast majority of wineries in Dijon are actually just south of the city along N74, beginning in the town of Marsannay-la-Côte. **Château du Marsannay** (☎ 03-80-51-71-11; www.chateau-marsannay.com) exemplifies the small but high-quality approach that is so common among vineyards in this area, with superlative wines effectively explained by the vineyard's English-speaking experts. ⏱ 1 day. For detailed information on Dijon, see p. 334.

From Dijon, take N74 south to Nuits-St-Georges (28km/17 miles).

❷ **Nuits-St-Georges.** Côte de Nuits territory is part of the **Côte d'Or** (Golden Slope) department that makes its way south from Dijon to Beaune. The pinot noir here is some of the best red in the world, and some gamay grapes, usually found farther south in Beaujolais, grow here as well. The only two white grapes that vineyards in Bourgogne are permitted to grow—chardonnay and *aligoté*—can also be found here. You won't be the only tourists, as more than a few of the biggest wine sellers are located on the main road in the center of this busy town. An historic winery worth visiting is **Morin Père & Fils,** 9 quai Fleury (☎ 03-80-61-19-51; www.morinpere-fils.com;

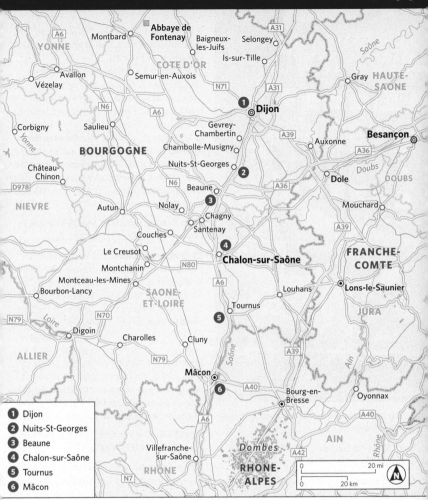

1 Dijon
2 Nuits-St-Georges
3 Beaune
4 Chalon-sur-Saône
5 Tournus
6 Mâcon

free admission; daily 9am–noon and 2–6pm), which originated in 1822 and receives more than 30,000 visitors yearly.

There are plenty of shops back in town where you can gather some food to accompany your wines, including jam, crackers, cheese, and foie gras. If money is not an object, head north to the **Romanée-Conti** vineyards to fork over a few thousand dollars for a bottle. A bit farther north is the more reasonable but also famous town of **Gevrey-Chambertin,** rue Gaston Roupnel (☎ 03-80-34 38-40; www.ot-gevreychambertin.fr), which offers its own red *Grand Cru*. The attractions here are the nine

vineyards that produce Chambertin pinot noir wines, which Napoleon could not do battle without. Many fine restaurants are located right next to the wine centers in town. ⏱ 1 day. Nuits-St-Georges Tourist Office, 3 rue Sonoys. ☎ 03-80-62-11-17. www.ot-nuits-st-georges.fr. See also p. 318, 2.

Alternate Route

From Dijon, you can easily reach all the stops on the Route des Grands Crus. Even the southernmost city of Mâcon is only 125km (78 miles) away.

> *Wine tasting and buying opportunities abound all across Burgundy.*

3.50€ reduced; Jan–Nov 9:30am–6pm, Dec 9:30am–5pm), for a look at local winemaking through the centuries.

Although it's synonymous with *Grands Crus,* Beaune has plenty to offer besides wine: hotels of all size and cost, walking and biking trails, idyllic driving conditions, and fabulous dining. The nearby town of Ladoix-Serrigny is famed for its summertime **Balades Gourmandes** (www.baladesgourmandes.com), a gastronomic trail that showcases superb dining, *Premier Cru* wines, and pristine, vine-filled natural surroundings. ⏱ 1 day. See p. 316, ④, and 319, ③.

From Beaune, take N74 and D981 south to Chalon-sur-Saône (37km/23 miles).

④ **Chalon-sur-Saône.** The largest town in the **Saône-et-Loire** department of southern Bourgogne, Chalon-sur-Saône serves as an excellent hub for those who tire of bed-and-breakfasts and country scenery. At the **Maison des Vins,** promenade Ste-Marie (☎ 03-85-41-64-00; www.maisonvinsbourgogne.com; Mon–Sat 9am–7pm), you can taste all the wines the region has to offer: nearly 150 reds, whites, rosés, and sparkling wines. ⏱ 1 day. Chalon-sur-Saône Tourist Office, 4 place du Port Villiers. ☎ 03-33-85-48-37-97. www.uk.chalon-sur-saone.net. See also p. 320, ④.

From Chalon-sur-Saône, take N6 south to Tournus (27km/17 miles).

⑤ ★★ **Tournus.** In the heart of southern Bourgogne, between Chalon-sur-Saône and Mâcon, is Tournus, one of the most enchanting towns on the Routes des Vins, where the white wines of Burgundy begin to develop. It's probably the most authentic and convenient base for travels on this part of the route. This town of fewer than 6,000 people has high-end hotels, Michelin-starred restaurants, and fabulous village scenery. The 17th-century ★★ **Hôtel de Dieu,** which houses the fine-arts **Musée Greuze,** 21 rue de l'Hôpital (☎ 03-85-51-23-50; www.musees-bourgogne.org; admission 4€ adults, 2€ children; Wed–Mon 10am–1pm and 2–6pm; closed Tues), is one of the area's best-known buildings. Its gilded decor, two chapels, and medieval apothecary transport you back to a time when leeches were considered good medicine. Tournus

From Nuits-St-Georges, take N74 south to Beaune (25km/16 miles).

③ ★★ **Beaune.** The heart of wine country, Beaune is the sleepy, picturesque town that draws the most tourist attention along the Wine Route. Surrounded by the **Côte de Beaune** as well as the **Côte de Nuits** vineyards, Beaune produces both excellent reds and the most prestigious whites. The sunny microclimate and the shale-and-limestone soil perfected by erosion make this simply the best place in Burgundy to grow vines. The ★★ **Hospices de Beaune** is an excellent place to test wines; it is also the finest architectural site in town. Perhaps the best place to buy wine is the **Marché aux Vins,** but don't expect table wine prices. Take a break at one of the top museums on wine in the world, the **Musée du Vin de Bourgogne,** Hôtel des Ducs, rue d'Enfer (☎ 03-80-22-08-19; admission 5.50€ adults, is also home to a gorgeous abbey, the 12th-century **Abbaye St-Philibert,** a masterwork of Romanesque architecture.

Several castles lie in the outskirts of town, the finest being **Château de Cormatin,** rue du Château (☎ 03-85-50-16-55; www.chateaudecormatin.com; admission 9€ adults, 5.50€ reduced, free under 7; April–Nov 15 10am–noon and 2–5:30pm, with extended hours in summer), about a 10-minute drive south of Tournus. This sumptuous palace was built during the reign of Louis XIII, just as

> *Gracious wine châteaux like this one pop up all around Beaune in the Côte de Beaune and Côte de Nuits territory.*

The Burgundy Wine Routes
(Les Routes des Vins de Bourgogne)

The Route des Grands Crus and the Route des Grands Vins are just two of Burgundy's six Wine Routes; each is signposted with brown "Route des Vins" signs. **The Route des Vignobles de l'Yonne** is the northern, and less swanky, extension of the Route des Grands Crus. If you prefer chablis and other white wines, this Yonne area may be more to your liking. The new **Route du Crémant** (Sparkling Wine Route), in the Châtillon-sur-Seine area north of Dijon, is an option for those who prefer Champagne-style wines. The **Route des Grands Vins** can be continued into the **Route des Vins Mâconnais-Beaujolais** and on into the Beaujolais region of the Rhône-Alps (p. 353). Finally, due west of Dijon, outside the official Burgundy appellation but still in the region, is the **Route du Vin des Côteaux de Pouilly-Sancerre** (Pouilly-Sancerre Wine Route), which explores the Burgundian part of the Loire Valley. The **Route des Grand Crus,** which we explore here, is considered the Champs-Elysées of the Burgundy Wine Route. First-time wine enthusiasts normally make Beaune their center, but those in the know understand that staying in the small villages is the best way to get away from it all and into the heart of wine country. Copious information, with maps and places to stay, is available on the **Burgundy Tourism** website (www.burgundy-tourism.com; go to "Downloadable documents," then "Good food and wine") and the official **Burgundy Wines** website (www.burgundy-wines-tourism.fr).

French decadence was starting to rise; decadence is on display here in the gold-embossed wall decorations, rich tapestries, and baroque gardens with a maze of flowers. ⏲ 1 day. Tournus Tourist Office, 2 place de l'Abbaye. ☎ 03-85-27-00-20. www.tournugeois.fr.

From Tournus, take N6 south to Mâcon (35km/22 miles).

❻ Mâcon. Mâcon is the terminus of the Côte Chalonnaise, which extends south from Chalon-sur-Saône. The wines produced here are not quite as prestigious as those from up north, but they're still pleasant and they're cheaper; there are no *Grands Crus,* but the area is home to a large number of *Premier Crus* vineyards. Mâcon used to be associated with red wine, but now it's the largest overall producer of white wine in Burgundy. In fact, the *aligoté* in the village of Bouzeron is probably the best you can find in France. The towns of Rully, Mercurey, and Givry produce the best grape stuff here, and plenty of caves and châteaux line the route. ⏲ 1 day. Mâcon Tourist Office, 1 place St-Pierre. ☎ 03-85-21-07-07. www.macon-tourism.com.

Where to Stay & Dine on the Wine Route

> Order a bottle of local white to be delivered to your classy room at Hôtel Le Rempart in Tournus.

Chez Guy GEVREY-CHAMBERTIN *REGIONAL FRENCH* The affordable fixed-price menus at this local spot feature many Burgundy favorites. Try the *oeufs en meurette* as an appetizer: a runny poached egg with a splash of Burgundy wine. As you would expect, there's a very good wine list. 3 place Mairie. ☎ 03-80-58-51-51. www.chez-guy.fr. Fixed-price menus 29.50€–39€. MC, V. Lunch and dinner daily.

★★ Hôtel de la Clôche BEAUNE
This Hôtel de la Clôche (not to be confused with the Sofitel-run hotel of the same name in Dijon) is independently run and housed

in a restored 16th-century inn with a walled garden that makes an alfresco breakfast sheer pleasure. 40 rue Faubourg Madeleine. ☎ 03-80-24-66-33. www.hotel-lacloche-beaune.com. 22 units. Doubles 61€–102€. AE, MC, V.

★ Hôtel des Remparts BEAUNE
A fine three-star hotel, Hotel des Remparts is located right in the heart of the city inside a 17th-century mansion. Exposed beams, stone floors, and oak furniture add to its rustic appeal. 48 rue Thiers. ☎ 03-80-24-94-94. www.hotel-remparts-beaune.com. 22 units. Doubles 92€–108€. MC, V.

★★ Hôtel Le Rempart TOURNUS *GASTRONOMIC*
This traditional hotel provides comfortable accommodation and a superb restaurant, where you'll eat either in a baronial-style dining room or the interior courtyard. Burgundy snails, Bresse chicken, and Charolais beef are the specialties. 2 av. Gambetta. ☎ 03-85-51-10-56. www.lerempart.com. 23 units. Doubles 100€–115€. Fixed-price menus 32€–68€. AE, DC, MC, V. Lunch and dinner daily.

★ Hôtel Le Richebourg NUITS-ST-GEORGES
FRENCH Just 2.5km (1½ miles) from Nuits-St-Georges, this purpose-built luxury hotel in the midst of the vineyards offers spacious contemporary rooms and a spa. Ruelle du Pont, Vosne Romanée. ☎ 03-80-61-59-59. www.hotel-lerichebourg.com. 26 units. Doubles 135€–260€. Main courses 15€–18€. AE, DC, MC, V. Lunch and dinner daily.

Ibis Nuits St-Georges NUITS ST-GEORGE
Another quality budget hotel from the Ibis chain, this hotel offers a central location, a restaurant, a bar, and the opportunity to put your savings toward more wine. 1 av. de Chamboland. ☎ 03-80-61-17-17. www.accorhotels.com. 55 units. Doubles 55€–62€. AE, MC, V.

★ La Cabotte NUITS-ST-GEORGES *CONTEMPORARY FRENCH* With stone walls and

contemporary art, this bistro puts great effort into presentation as well as flavor. The inventive cuisine is served on slates or hand-made crockery. 24 Grande Rue. ☎ 03-80-61-20-77. Fixed-price menus 28€–48€. AE, MC, V. Lunch Tues–Fri, dinner Mon–Sat.

★★ La Montagne de Brancion MARTAILLY-LES-BRANCION *GASTRONOMIC*

The superb restaurant is the draw here, in this small town just west of Tournus (the hotel is good but not great). With a view of the vineyards, you will enjoy fabulous wines and the quintessence of Burgundian cuisine. Martailly-les-Brancion. ☎ 03-85-51-12-40. www.brancion.com. Fixed-price menus 48€–75€. MC, V. Lunch Fri–Mon, dinner daily.

★★★ Le Bénaton BEAUNE *GASTRONOMIC*

The canon of luxury ingredients—lobster, scallops, foie gras, truffles—are treated with flair and delicacy at this Burgundy restaurant. Pigeon, *pot au feu*, and Angus steak provide more earthy options. 25 rue du Faubourg Bretonnière. ☎ 03-80-22-00-26. www.lebenaton.com. Main courses 29€–52€; 3-course menu 28€–95€. AE, DC, MC, V. Apr–Nov lunch Mon, Thurs, Fri, Sun and dinner Thurs–Tues; Dec–Mar lunch and dinner Fri–Tues.

★★ L'Ecusson BEAUNE *GASTRONOMIC*

Husband-and-wife team Thomas and Virginie Compagnon run this very pleasant restaurant, with outdoor seating in summer. The cuisine here is innovative, with enough nods to the regional cuisine to keep the neighbors returning. 2 rue du Lieutenant Dupuis. ☎ 03-80-24-03-82. www.ecusson.fr. Main courses 27€–37€. Lunch menu 25€. Fixed-price menu 39€–65€. AE, DC, MC, V. Lunch and dinner Mon–Tues and Thurs–Sat.

★★★ Maison Lameloise CHALON-SUR-SAONE *GASTRONOMIC*

This luxury inn outside Chalon-sur-Saône has a gastronomic restaurant where three generations of chefs from the same family have been garnering Michelin stars since 1925. Come in expecting excellence—odds are high that you'll leave satisfied. 36 place d'Armes, Chagny. ☎ 03-85-87-65-65. www.lameloise.fr. 30 units. Doubles 125€–175€. Main courses 45€–73€. Fixed-price menus 100€ and 130€. AE, DC, MC, V. Lunch and dinner Thurs–Mon.

> Lip-smacking Michelin-starred cuisine and impeccable service await you at Maison Lameloise in Chalon-sur-Saône.

★★★ Pierre MACON *GASTRONOMIC*

One of the highlights of the Burgundy restaurant scene, Pierre features a diverse and exquisite menu that makes inventive use of classic base ingredients such as sea bass, scallops, and Bresse chicken. A selection of wines by the glass means you can taste a different one with each course. 7 rue Dufour. ☎ 03-85-38-14-23. www.restaurant-pierre.com. Fixed-price menus 47€–74€. AE, DC, MC, V. Lunch Wed–Sun, dinner Tues–Sat.

★★ Restaurant Greuze TOURNUS *GASTRONOMIC*

In a warm dining room with beams and stone walls, you'll find the best of traditional Burgundian cuisine, with an emphasis on game in season. 1 rue A. Thibaudet. ☎ 03-85-51-13-52. www.restaurant-greuze.fr. Main courses 38€–40€. Fixed-price menus 35€–80€. AE, DC, MC, V. Lunch and dinner daily.

Burgundy for Art & History Buffs

The feudal history of Burgundy, whose rich Dukes amassed a treasure trove of art and financed magnificent religious buildings, has left an enormous legacy throughout the region. As the first two tours in this chapter already cover Dijon and the abbeys, we here explore the lesser-known northwest area of Burgundy, which may not have the vineyards or monasteries of its rich neighbors, but is perhaps even better endowed with superlative castles, cathedrals, and fascinating historic sites.

> It took just 8 years, from 1542 to 1550, to build and decorate this Renaissance beauty, the Château Ancy-le-Franc.

START Auxerre is 170km (106 miles) south-east of Paris. **TRIP LENGTH** 393km (244 miles).

① **Auxerre.** The capital of the Yonne department, best known as the home of chablis (see "The Burgundy Wine Routes," p. 322), Auxerre is nearly a city, with almost 90,000 people. Its Yonne River location has served it well: It has been an important trade hub since Roman times. Base yourself here for stops ①

and ② of this tour. In 1567, the area was captured by Huguenots, who severely damaged many of its Catholic churches, but the ★ **Cathédrale St-Etienne,** rue Fourier (☎ 03-86-64-15-27; www.cathedrale-auxerre.com; free admission; daily 7:30am–6pm), still exemplifies the distinctive Burgundian Gothic style of the 12th century. While the cathedral has a few Renaissance additions, it's best known for its stained glass and for statues that

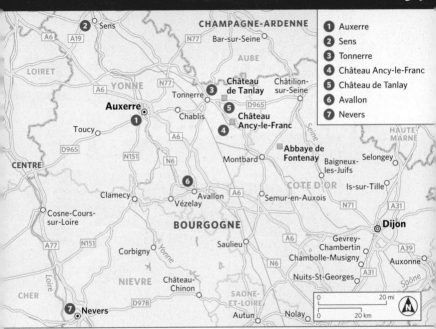

1 Auxerre
2 Sens
3 Tonnerre
4 Château Ancy-le-Franc
5 Château de Tanlay
6 Avallon
7 Nevers

were decapitated by rampaging Huguenots. The Romanesque **Abbaye de St-Germain,** 2 place St-Germain (☎ 03-86-18-05-50; www. auxerre.culture.gouv.fr; free admission; Wed–Mon 10am–12:30pm and 2–6:30pm), contains some of France's oldest frescoes. Dating back to A.D. 500, it is still an important pilgrimage site for Catholics, thanks to relics such as the preserved tunic of St. Germain.

Rented miniboats, gliding past expensive river yachts, are a fun way to explore Auxerre. The lovely **Passarelle footbridge,** next to the train station, is also a treat. ⏱ 1 day. Auxerre Tourist Office, 2 quai de la République. ☎ 03-86-51-03-26. www.ot-auxerre.fr. See also p. 321, 10.

From Auxerre, take A6 northwest and switch to A19 at Courtenay to Sens (80km/50 miles).

2 **Sens.** Practically a suburb of Paris, this large town played a prominent role in early medieval architecture, as its **Cathédrale St-Etienne,** place de la République (☎ 03-86-64-46-22; admission 4€; daily 10am–6pm), is one of the very first Gothic cathedrals in France. Well-read lovers of romance everywhere may be interested to know that the cathedral was the site of the trial of Peter Abelard, the renowned theologian and soon-to-be castrated

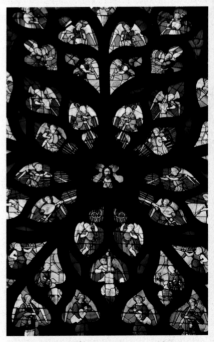

> *These petal-shaped stained-glass windows at the Cathédrale St-Etienne in Sens are works of art from the Renaissance period.*

> *Tonnerre's Fosse Dionne fountain has been the source of many local legends involving the devil.*

monk, best known for his affair and written correspondence with the equally brilliant nun Héloïse. In 1234 King Louis IX was married to Marguerite of Provence at the cathedral. Louis IX, whose prosperous reign is referred to as the "golden century of St. Louis," was the only canonized king of France, so all those places named St-Louis (or San Luis) are named after him. The cathedral itself is reputed not for its beauty, but for its massive solidity. ⏱ 1 day. Sens Tourist Office, place Jean Jaurès. ☎ 03-86-65-19-49. www.office-de-tourisme-sens.com.

Backtrack to Auxerre for the night; from there, travel east on D965 to Tonnerre (36km/22 miles).

❸ ★ **Tonnerre.** This town's top attraction is the unique **Fosse Dionne** (Pit of Diane), a natural fountain in the shape of a cauldron. It has been in use since pagan times; for centuries, as its name suggests, it was thought to be a bottomless pit and the entrance to hell. In later times, it became Tonnerre's water source and headquarters of the town's washwomen. Now it's a popular postcard site, thanks to its

emerald waters and Burgundian tiles. Tonnerre's architectural gem is the **Hôtel Dieu** (Old Hospital), which is one of the earliest and largest medieval hospitals in France; it was built in just 3 years, a staggeringly efficient achievement back in 1293. Several Gothic churches are found here, including the stained-glass adorned **Eglise St-Peter,** sitting high above the city. The **Cathédrale Notre Dame** has been rebuilt but still shows scars from World War II bombs. The best place to stay here is the **Abbaye St-Michel** (p. 333), where you can base yourself for visits to the nearby châteaux (stops ❹ and ❺, below). ⏱ 1 day. Tonnerre Tourist Office, Le Cellier, place Marguerite de Bourgogne. ☎ 03-86-55-14-48. www.ville-tonnerre.com.

From Tonnerre, take D905 southeast to Ancy-le-Franc (18km/11 miles).

❹ ★★★ **Château Ancy-le-Franc.** Two of the finest and most architecturally significant castles in France are also the least visited: **Château Ancy-le-Franc** and **Château de Tanlay** (stop ❺). What's more, they deliver you from

> *Avallon's Eglise St-Lazare is a 12th-century marvel, with twisted stone columns that seem elastic.*

the ecclesiastical Middle Ages and into the exuberant, Italianate Renaissance. Château Ancy-le-Franc was built in the 16th century for Diane de Poitiers, the notorious mistress of King Henri II. If the castle seems out of place, that's because it's an outgrowth of the Italian Renaissance in France, designed by the Italian architect Sebastiano Serilo, whose theories guided the construction of the famed Fontainebleau outside Paris (p. 134). The inside is sheer decadence, with wall paintings, also the work of Italian artists, to rival those at Fontainebleau. ⏱ 1 hr. 18 place Clermont-Tonnerre. ☎ 03-86-75-14-63. www.chateau-ancy.com. Admission 9€ adults, 6€ reduced, free for children 5 and under. Apr–Nov 14 Tues–Sun by guided tour only; closed Nov 15–Mar.

From Ancy-le-Franc, take D12 north to Pimelles, then D965 west to Tanlay (16km/10 miles).

⑤ **Château de Tanlay.** Built shortly after Château Ancy-le-Franc, this castle shows how quickly French architects adopted the new Italian ideas but modified them to suit French tastes. Tanlay is much closer to nature, surrounded by moats, forests, and a fine courtyard and garden. Inside, the trompe-l'oeil frescoes of the Grand Galerie are astounding. ⏱ 1 hr. Place du Château–Tanlay. ☎ 08-92-56-56-28. www.chateaux-france.com. Admission 8.50€ adults, 3.50€ reduced. April–Nov Wed–Mon by guided tour only.

Return to Tonnerre on D65a (9.5km/6 miles). From Tonnerre, follow D944 south to Avallon (53km/33 miles; don't take the autoroute, or you'll miss out on lovely scenery).

⑥ **Avallon.** For centuries, Avallon served as the walled gateway to western Bourgogne. As you walk the medieval streets of this picturesque town, you'll see 7th-century watchtowers, turreted ramparts, huge defensive walls and fortifications, and the 15th-century clock tower. The walls that encircle the city were almost entirely rebuilt in the 15th century. In keeping with other churches in Bourgogne, Avallon's Burgundian Romanesque **Eglise St-Lazare,** Rue Bocquillot (☎ 03-86-34-07-85; www.ville-avallon.fr; daily 8am–7pm), made itself a center of pilgrimage in the 12th century, when it obtained a piece

of the skull of Lazarus, believed to cure leprosy. Avallon is also one of the chief producers of France's beloved *pain d'épices* (gingerbread), so make sure to try some here.
⏱ 1 day. Avallon Tourist Office, 6 rue Bocquillot. ☎ 03-86-34-14-19. www.avallonnais-tourisme.com. See also p. 321, ❾.

From Avallon, take D957 toward Vézelay to St-Père, and then D958 and D977 to Nevers (100km/62 miles).

❼ **Nevers.** It's a pity tourists rarely visit this town on the western border of Bourgogne; as the principal city of the former province of Nivernais, it has a rich history. The area's medieval history and abundant Romanesque architecture have been well preserved on the banks of the Loire River, and the old quarter encompasses many religious buildings, old houses, and winding streets. ★ **Cathédrale**

St-Cyr et Ste-Juliette is a national monument, thanks to its stunning combination of Romanesque and Gothic styles, culminating in the huge and ornate 16th-century southern tower. Its mélange of influences was further compounded when, after the cathedral was damaged during World War II, the stained glass expanses were remade in modern style. **Eglise St-Etienne** is a rare 9th-century chapel, built in the Romanesque style and consecrated by the Cluniac monastery. Nevers is an important pilgrimage spot; its **Sanctuaire Ste-Bernadette in Couvent St-Gildard** is the home of the reliquary of Bernadette Soubirous, a nun who saw the Virgin Mary 18 times in 1858. Soubirous was born in Lourdes (p. 502), where she reportedly witnessed the apparitions. ⏱ 1 day. Nevers Tourist Office, 4 rue Sabatier. ☎ 03-86-68-46-00. www.nevers-tourisme.com.

> *The Cathédrale St-Cyr et Ste-Juliette in Nevers has two choirs—one Gothic and one Romanesque.*

Where to Stay & Dine for History Buffs

Abbaye St-Michel TONNERRE *REGIONAL FRENCH* This 10th-century Benedictine abbey surrounded by parkland was converted into a comfortable hotel. A splendid living room with a huge chimney and a large vaulted restaurant suggest that the monks lived on a grand scale. Montée St-Michel. ☎ 03-86-55-05-99. www.abbaye-saint-michel-tonnerre.federal-hotel.com. 17 units. Doubles 69€–98€. Main courses 20€–26€. Fixed-price menus 25€–70€. DC, MC, V. Lunch Tues–Sun, dinner Tues–Sat.

Château de Malaisy FAIN-LES-MONTBARD (FONTENAY) For the price of a B&B, you get the run of a 15-hectare (37-acre) deer park. The decor needs an uplift, but the wonderful restaurant—open to nonguests—is ample compensation. Rue du Château, Fain-les-Montbard. ☎ 03-80-89-46-54. http://chat-malaisy.ifrance.com. 24 units. Doubles 65€–120€; half-board 99€–119€ per person. AE, MC, V.

★★ **Hostellerie de la Poste** AVALLON *REGIONAL FRENCH* This inn dates back to 1707. Guests are greeted with modern luxury and historic charm. The restaurant serves delicious regional cuisine. 13 place Vauban. ☎ 03-86-34-16-16. www.hostelleriedelaposte.com. 12 units. Doubles 108€–132€. Main courses 18€–20€. Menus 25€–48€. DC, MC, V. Lunch and dinner Tues–Sat.

Hôtel le Maxime AUXERRE In the heart of Auxerre, this graceful town-house offers clean and comfortable accommodations, a private garage, and a wine cellar and tasting room. 2 quai de la Marine. ☎ 03-86-52-14-19. www.lemaxime.com. 26 units. Doubles 83€–145€. AE, DC, MC, V.

Inter-hotel Clos Ste-Marie NEVERS This three-star hotel is full of warmth and comfort for leisure travelers. It has a lovely garden with water features. 25 rue du Petit-Mouesse. ☎ 03-86-71-94-50. www.inter-hotel.fr. 17 units. Doubles 75€–115€. AE, DC, MC, V.

★★ **La Fontaine du Grand Fussy** LE ROUSSET (CLUNY) The owner is an interior designer

> You can't beat a plate of piping hot snails in garlic butter washed down with a Burgundy red.

and exquisitely decorated this old manor house with lime-washed, paneled rooms; frescoes; and antique furniture. The self-catering *gîtes* are like Russian *dachas*. ☎ 03-85-24-60-26. www.fontaine-fussy.com. 5 units plus *gîtes*. Doubles 68€; *gîte* prices available upon request.

★ **Le Bourgogne** AUXERRE *REGIONAL FRENCH* This attractive bistro—with its sunny dining room, a blackboard menu, and a collection of farm tools on the wall—is the place to go for snails in parsley, ox tail and foie gras terrine, *tête de veau*, and thyme-flavored roast lamb. We love the chef's chutney, made with chablis. 15 rue de Preuilly. ☎ 03-86-51-57-50. www.lebourgogne.fr. Menus 29€ and 38€. MC, V. Lunch Tues–Sat, dinner Tues–Wed and Fri–Sat.

★★ **Moulin des Ruats** AVALLON *REGIONAL FRENCH* This former flour mill has been converted into a darling country inn. The three-star hotel has a riverbank terrace from which you can eat at the superb restaurant. Vallée du Cousin, rue des Iles Labaunes. ☎ 03-86-34-97-00. www.moulindesruats.com. 24 units. Doubles 82€–102€. 4-course menu 47€. AE, DC, MC, V. Lunch Sun, dinner Tues–Sun. Closed Mon.

Dijon

Dijon is the capital of both the famed, wine-rich region of Burgundy and the Côte d'Or *département*. The city is small, with fewer than a quarter of a million residents, but for centuries it has been a settlement rich in culture, learning, and commerce. Its age-old food traditions, rooted in the Burgundy *terroir,* now find their expression in a hub of gastronomic restaurants competing to be the flavor of the month. Many tourists visiting Europe easily find their way to Dijon, as it's a halfway point between Paris and Lyon. Also known as the "City of Bell Towers," Dijon features some of the finest examples of French architecture to come out of the past millennium.

> *The Hôtel de Vogüe's colorful tiled mosaic rooftop stands out on Dijon's cityscape.*

START Dijon is 316km (196 miles) south of Paris.

❶ ★★★ Palais des Ducs et des Etats de Bourgogne. The most visited site in Dijon, the Ducal Palace was the seat of authority of many a powerful duke of Burgundy. The first Duke of Valois vastly expanded the original Gallo-Roman fort in the 14th century, but it wasn't until the 17th century that the palace began to resemble the current prestigious edifice. The palace is huge enough to house most of Dijon's tourist sites, as well as the administrative offices of the city and region. You can see many magnificent rooms, including the ducal kitchens, where it is easy to imagine the gargantuan feasts that were prepared here. The 15th-century **Tour de Philippe le Bon** (Tower of Philip the Good) affords superlative views of what are probably the richest vineyards in the world—once you climb the 316 steps to the top. ⏱ 1 hr. Rue de la Liberté. ☎ 03-80-74-52-70. www.ot-dijon.fr. Admission 2.30€ adults, 1.20€ children. Summer daily 9am–noon and 1:45–5:30pm; otherwise Mon–Tues and Thurs–Fri 11am–1:30pm and 2:30–5:30pm, Wed 11am–1:30pm.

❷ ★★ Musée des Beaux-Arts. Housed in a wing of the Ducal Palace complex, this is one of the oldest museums in France. Unlike the majority of the country's art museums, it is free—such is the largesse of Dijon's *mairie* (city council). A massive renovation program is ongoing until 2017, but it's taking place bit by bit, so while one part of the museum may

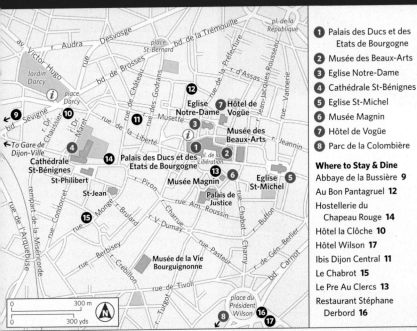

> Originally acquired by the wealthy dukes of Burgundy, the vast holdings of Dijon's Musée des Beaux-Art now belong to the city, which grants the public free entry.

be closed when you visit, there will still be plenty to see. The encyclopedic collection was amassed by the rich dukes themselves, saved by the *luminaires* of the Enlightenment, and added to over the years by donations and acquisitions; it covers a vast range of subjects, from Egyptian to local medieval and 20th-century art. As with the Louvre in Paris (p. 50, 1), a good strategy is to pick a department that interests you and head

> *Gargoyles watch over the city, staving off evil spirits at Eglise St-Michel.*

for it, whether it's the Flemish Masters, the Renaissance Italians, the Impressionists, or the vast low-key but fascinating collection of drawings. ⏱ 2 hr. Rue de la Liberté. ☎ 03-80-74-52-09. http://mba.dijon.fr. Free admission. Tues–Sun 10am–5pm.

③ Eglise Notre-Dame. In the heart of Dijon's protected historic Notre-Dame quarter, the fine 13th-century Gothic church is the home of a rare 12th-century **Black Virgin Mary statue,** one of the oldest representations in France of a dark-skinned Mary. The **Jacquemart Clock** sitting atop the church was actually looted from Belgium in the 14th century. ⏱ 30 min. 9 place Notre Dame. ☎ 03-80-30-40-42. Free admission. Daily 9am–7pm.

④ ★★ Cathédrale St-Bénignes. This Gothic cathedral is one of the top works of medieval architecture in Burgundy. Built on the site of a

6th-century basilica housing the sarcoph of St-Bénignes, it is one of the oldest Chri tian sanctuaries you can visit in France. ⏱ 1 hr. place St-Béninges. ☎ 03-80-30-39- www.diocese-dijon.com. Admission 4€ ad 2.50€ reduced. Daily 9am–7pm (except du services).

⑤ ★ Eglise St-Michel. In this city of churc you also can't miss the Italianate sculpte cade of St-Michel. In the Renaissance ca over the porch, angels and biblical motifs gle with mythological ones. ⏱ 30 min. Pla St-Michel. Free admission. Daily 9am–7pm

⑥ ★★★ Musée Magnin. Dijon has not on two fine-arts museums. This one, with a collection of French Renaissance and Ro tic art, Italian Renaissance and Flemish p ings, and sculpture, is housed in the gorg Hôtel Lantin, the former home of Mauric Jeanne Magnin, who built up the magnifi private collection. There's an elegant tea in the courtyard. ⏱ 1½ hr. 4 rue des Bons fants. ☎ 03-80-67-11-10. www.musee-mag fr. Admission 3.50€ adults, 2.50€ reduced 1st Sun of the month. Tues–Sun 10am–noo 2–6pm.

⑦ Hôtel de Vogüe. A distinctive architec feature of Burgundy is its *toits bourguigno* (Burgundian roofs), composed of glazed cotta tiles arranged in unique geometric terns. One of the best instances of this (a one of the most precious examples of a 1 century *hôtel particulier* in France) is now architecture and culture service of Dijon. can't visit the inside unless you have a pr sional reason, but you're bound to admir exterior as you walk around the city. 8 ru la Chouette.

⑧ ★ Parc de la Colombière. This expans (33 hectares/82 acres) park was sculpte by Antoine de Maerle, a pupil of Le Nôtre who created the gardens of Versailles. It is approached from the city center via th majestic avenue **cours du Parc,** which Lo XIV deemed the most beautiful street in kingdom. Highlights include the 17th-cen Temple of Love, a zoo, and restored path of the Via Agrippa, the ancient Roman ro that runs through the park. ⏱ 1½ hr. Sumr daily 7am–10pm, winter daily 8am–8pm.

Where to Stay & Dine in Dijon

> Fine views and fine food: You get both at Le Pre Au Clercs' *gastronomique* restaurant.

★★ Abbaye de la Bussière *GASTRONOMIC*

Where better to stay in this region of abbeys than in one that was built in the 12th century? By far the premier place to stay near Dijon, the abbey has creamy stone walls that enclose rooms decorated with impeccable French flair. Baronial-style lounges, a magnificent restaurant as well as a lunchtime bistro, exquisite grounds, and excellent service all live up to the Relais & Châteaux ideal. Bussière-sur-Ouches, on D33 outside Dijon. ☎ 03-80-49-02-29. Gastronomic restaurant: main courses 52€–58€. Bistro: fixed-price menus 22€–30€. www.abbaye-dela-bussiere.com. 17 units. 2-room doubles 215€. AE, MC, V. Gastronomic restaurant lunch Sun, dinner Wed–Sun; bistro lunch Wed–Sat.

Au Bon Pantagruel *REGIONAL FRENCH*

This is the place to find traditional rural Bourguignon cuisine for low prices, which is probably why it's so popular with locals. You can get all the old favorites here: pigs' feet and tails, frog legs, snails, and (gulp!) more. 20 rue Quentin. ☎ 03-80-30-68-69. 3-course menu 24€. MC, V. Lunch and dinner daily.

★★ Hostellerie du Chapeau Rouge *CONTEMPORARY FRENCH*

This superb, Michelin-starred restaurant offers modern fusion cuisine, such as shellfish soup with a miso base, tea-flavored duck, and beautifully concocted desserts. 5 rue Michelet. ☎ 03-80-50-88-88. www.chapeau-rouge.fr. Main courses 41€–99€. AE, DC, MC, V. Lunch and dinner Tues–Sat.

★★ Hôtel la Clôche *TRADITIONAL FRENCH*

Housed in a grand 19th-century mansion with a garden, this Sofitel hotel offers every luxury: high thread counts, sumptuous fabrics, a fabulous restaurant with alfresco dining in summer, library bar, fitness room, and sauna. The whole top floor is given over to suites. 14 place Darcy. ☎ 03-80-30-12-32. www.hotel-lacloche.com. 68 units. Doubles 190€–240€. Main courses 22€–30€. AE, DC, MC, V. Lunch and dinner daily.

★ Hôtel Wilson

A 17th-century staging post arranged around a central courtyard (available for parking) was converted into this gorgeous hotel with exposed beams in some of the rooms. In winter a real fire burns in the chimney of the comfortable salon. Place Wilson. ☎ 03-80-66-82-50. www.wilson-hotel.com. 27 units. Doubles 82€–106€. AE, MC, V.

Ibis Dijon Central *ROTISSERIE*
This hotel from the Ibis chain is in the heart of the historic center of Dijon on an attractive square. Its rôtisserie restaurant, with an open kitchen where you watch various meats grilling on a spit, is popular with locals. 3 place Grangier. ☎ 03-80-30-44-00. www.hotel-ibiscentral-dijon.com. 90 units. Doubles 62€–93€. AE, DC, MC, V. Lunch and dinner Mon–Sat.

Le Chabrot *REGIONAL FRENCH*
Excellent Burgundy cuisine, a strong wine list, and a great plaza view make this one of the best reasonably priced restaurants in Dijon. 36 rue Monge. ☎ 03-80-30-69-61. Main courses 16€–20€; 3-course menu 31€. AE, MC, V. Lunch Tues–Sat, dinner Mon–Sat.

★★★ Le Pre Au Clercs *GASTRONOMIC*
The most celebrated gastronomic restaurant in Dijon is situated opposite the Palais des Ducs—and if the dukes were alive today, they would surely be eating here. Jean Pierre Billoux and his son Alexis present *billets-doux* (love letters) of Burgundy gastronomy, such as a gâteau of guinea fowl with artichoke, or *perche* (pike perch) poached in mustard. Le Bistrot des Halles opposite the covered market is their budget-friendly offshoot. 15 place de la Libération. ☎ 03-80-38-05-05. www.jeanpierrebilloux.com. Lunch menu 35€; dinner menu 50€–95€. AE, MC, V. Lunch Tues–Sun, dinner Tues–Sat.

★★ Restaurant Stéphane Derbord *GAS-TRONOMIC* Next to Hôtel Wilson, chef Stéphane Derbord runs his gastronomic restaurant with his wife, serving various cuts of meat and choice morsels in creations that demonstrate the couple's modern creativity and love of the Burgundy *terroir*. 10 place Wilson. ☎ 03-80-67-74-64. www.restaurantstephanederbord.fr. Main courses 32€–44€. Lunch menu 25€, dinner menu 66€–88€. AE, DC, MC, V. Lunch and dinner Tues–Sat.

Bourguignon Cuisine

Burgundy's wines and distinctive cuisine make it one of the regions most closely associated with traditional French gastronomy. The region's vineyards mainly grow pinot noir and chardonnay grapes, putting their wines on the drier end of the spectrum (see p. 680). Just as popular in France is Dijon's contribution to the aperitif menu, *crème de cassis,* which is combined with **Bourgogne aligoté** (the driest white wine of all) to form kir, a sweet preprandial drink enjoyed throughout France. Burgundy was the birthplace of numerous French culinary staples, such as *boeuf bourguignon, coq au vin, escargots bourguignon, gougère* (a light pastry stuffed with cheese), *jambon persillée* (terrine-cooked ham flavored with parsley and served cold), and *pain d'épices* (gingerbread). Of course, it's also the home of Dijon mustard, although that strong stuff is just one of the many atypically flavored mustards produced in Dijon. You can check out everything you ever wanted to know about the mustard seed, and buy some exotic variations on the condiment, at the **Musée de la Moutarde,** 48 quai Nicolas Rolin (☎ 03-80-44-44-52; www.dijon-tourism.com; free admission; June–Aug Mon–Sat 2–6pm; Sept–May Tues–Sat 2–6pm). The **Foire International et Gastronomique de Dijon** (Dijon International Gastronomic Fair; www.foirededijon.com) takes place every autumn at the Parc des Expositions, drawing nearly a quarter million connoisseurs each year to sample even more fine food and beverages.

Fast Facts

Arriving & Getting Around

BY TRAIN For train information, call ☎ 08-92-35-35-35. For information on rail passes for France, see p. 697. Many trains between Paris (Gare de Lyon) and Lyon stop at towns in Burgundy. From Paris, high-speed TGV trains arrive in Dijon in about 1 hour, 45 minutes; Auxerre in 2 hours; Beaune in 2 hours; Avallon in 2 hours 30 minutes; and Vezelay (via Auxerre to Sermizelles) in 2 hours, 30 minutes. To reach Autun from Paris, take a train to Montchanin–Le Creusot, 40km (25 miles) south of Autun, and from there, take a 45-minute bus connection to Autun (for bus information, call ☎ 03-85-86-92-55). To reach Saulieu from Paris, take the train to Montbard, 48km (30 miles) north of Saulieu, and then take a bus to town. From Lyon, trains arrive in Beaune in 1 hour, 30 minutes; Dijon in 2 hours; and Auxerre in about 4 hours. BY CAR Although you can reach the main cities by train, a car is imperative for getting around Burgundy. The main highways in the region are the A5 (Paris–Sens–Dijon); A6 (Paris–Sens–Auxerre–Avallon–Saulieu–Pouilly-en-Auxois–Beaune–Chalon-sur-Saône–Tournus–Mâcon); A38 (Pouilly-en-Auxois–Dijon); A39 (Bourg-en-Bresse–Dole–Dijon); A31 (Luxembourg–Dijon–Beaune); A36 (Mulhouse–Besançon–Beaune); and A77 (Paris–Cosne-sur-Loire–Nevers). To reach Dijon from Paris, follow A6 southeast to Pouilly-en-Auxois, and then go east along A38 into Dijon. Auxerre is near A6/E1 (Autoroute du Soleil). To reach Vézelay, take A6 south to Auxerre, then continue south along N151 to Clamecy and turn east on D951 to Vézelay. To reach Avallon from Paris, travel south along A6 to Auxerre, and then take N6 south to Avallon. To reach Autun, take D944 south from Avallon to Château-Chinon and follow D978 east into Autun. Beaune is a few miles from the junction of four highways—A6, A31, A36, and N6.

ATMs/Cashpoints

See p. 703, France Fast Facts.

Emergencies

See p. 704, France Fast Facts.

> Burgundy's back roads are popular with cyclists.

Internet Cafes

AUXERRE **Speed Informatique 89,** 32 rue du Pont. DIJON **Cybersp@ce21,** 46 rue Monge (☎ 03-80-30-57-43; www.cyberspace21.fr). For other towns check with the local tourist office.

Police

See "Emergencies," France Fast Facts, p. 704.

Post Offices

AUXERRE Place Charles-Surugue (☎ 03-86-72-23-00). AVALLON 9 rue Des Odeberts (☎ 03-86-34-91-05). BEAUNE 7 bd. St-Jacques (☎ 03-80-26-29-50). DIJON Place Grangier (☎ 03-80-50-62-19). VEZELAY 17 rue St-Étienne (☎ 03-86-33-26-35)

Safety

Burgundy is pretty safe. Even so, use common sense and watch over your possessions. In an emergency, call 17 for the police, 18 for the fire department or paramedics, and 15 for an ambulance.

Tourist Offices

Municipal tourist offices are listed at the end of the town tour stops throughout the chapter. BURGUNDY ☎ 03-80-28-02-80; www.burgundy-tourism.com). DIJON Place Darcy (☎ 08-92-70-05-58; www.dijon-tourism.com).

9
Lyon & the
Rhône-Alps

Favorite Moments in the Rhône-Alps

This large and breathtakingly beautiful region of south-eastern France was crafted by two tremendous forces of nature: the Rhône River and the Alps mountain range. From the glaciers and mountain flowers of Savoie to the lavender of the Drôme, you will keenly feel the transition from Alpine to Mediterranean climes as you travel around. With a wealth of top-quality produce and famous wines, the Rhône-Alps is one of the most gastronomic corners of France, culminating in its dynamic capital, Lyon—the world's top destination for fine French cuisine.

> PREVIOUS PAGE *The French Alps are home to some of the world's most awe-inspiring ski slopes.*
> THIS PAGE *This cable car from Chamonix Sud ascends Mont Blanc.*

① Exploring the Presqu'île of Lyon. Lyon is France's second-largest metropolis (after Paris), but the majority of the city's best museums and monuments, including the Musée des Beaux-Arts (p. 381, ⑤), are conveniently located on this small peninsula, extending from the city's Croix Rousse neighborhood into the union of the Rhône and Saône rivers. It's splendidly lit at night and full of too many great restaurants to choose from.

② Staring at the walls in Lyon. In Lyon, graffiti reaches a new level of refinement. More than 150 stunning murals make the streets a work of art. With so many elegant renderings adorning the walls, you'll wonder if France's talented taggers haven't all relocated to the Rhône-Alps. See "Lyon's Murals" on p. 383.

③ Bird-watching in the Dombes Wetlands. Everyone thinks about the mountains when

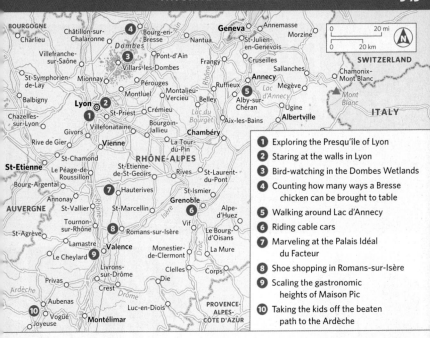

the conversation turns to the Rhône-Alps region, but do they think about a thousand ponds dug by Trappist monks, which now provide a rare wildlife habitat? The bird park at Villars-des-Dombes is one of the Rhône-Alps' best-kept secrets. See p. 360.

④ Counting how many ways a Bresse chicken can be brought to table. France's finest chickens are the strictly regulated AOC cluckers from Bourg-en-Bresse, and restaurants throughout the region know just how to bring out the firm flesh and great flavor of these birds. See p. 346, **③**.

⑤ Walking around Lac d'Annecy. The Alps' purest and most mirrorlike lake is Annecy. It's at its most poetic in the still of winter. See p. 346, **④**.

⑥ Riding cable cars. A symbol of the city, Grenoble's cable cars take you to the hilltop Bastille, with its stunning view of the streets below, the Isère River, and the mountains. The cable cars up to the slopes of Mont Blanc or the funicular to Lyon's Basilique are just as much fun. See p. 374, **①**.

⑦ Marveling at the Palais Idéal du Facteur Cheval. This stunning castle made from found objects and broken tiles is amazing enough— but it's all the more astounding when you learn that a French postman built it piece by piece during his off-hours over the course of 3 decades. See p. 357, **⑫**.

⑧ Shoe shopping in Romans-sur-Isère. A history of shoemaking in Romans-sur-Isère has lured some of Europe's most select designers to manufacture here, resulting in a fascinating shoe museum and southern France's biggest factory shopping outlet, selling fancy footwear and more at knockdown prices. See p. 355, **⑨**.

⑨ Scaling the gastronomic heights of Maison Pic. Anne-Sophie Pic just happens to be the only woman in France to have won three Michelin stars. But her restaurant's renown has more to do with her use of superb ingredients and its exquisite setting on the Northern Côtes du Rhône Wine Route. See p. 367.

⑩ Taking the kids off the beaten path to the Ardèche. If you're traveling with kids, this sports paradise will probably provide them with their best memories. The prehistoric caves and gorges that seem purpose-built for kayaking are a side of France frequently bypassed by epicurean travelers. See p. 370.

The Rhône-Alps in 1 Week

Lyon is the undisputed food capital of France, with more sites of interest than any city besides Paris, so it should be the initial focus of any trip to the Rhône-Alps. Staying within a 200km (125-mile) radius of the city, this itinerary leads you from Lyons through architecturally rich Pérouges and Bourg-en-Bresse, also famous for its AOC chicken; explores the lakes and spa towns of Haute-Savoie; and returns via Vienne, the gateway to the Rhône Valley.

> Annecy's quai de l'Ile has a distinct Italian feel, and makes a plum spot for an alfresco lunch.

START Lyon is 470km (292 miles) south of Paris. **TRIP LENGTH** 392km (244 miles).

① ★★★ **Lyon.** Lyon has so much to see, it makes sense to begin and end this 7-day tour here. The views are stunning from Lyon's hilltop ★★★ **Basilique Notre-Dame,** accessible by cable car, so make it the focus of your first morning, followed by an afternoon exploring ★★★ **Vieux Lyon** and its *traboules* (covered passageways). Dine at **Chez Mounier** for the authentic bustling atmosphere, or choose from one of the several gastronomic restaurants vying to please your palate. ⏱1 day. For detailed information on Lyon, see p. 378.

On Day 2, take A42 from Lyon to Pérouges (40km/25 miles).

Where to Stay & Dine

For hotels and restaurants in Lyon, see p. 384; in the Rhône Valley, see p. 368; in the French Alps, see p. 358.

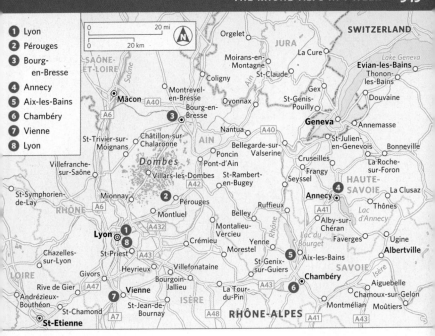

1 Lyon
2 Pérouges
3 Bourg-en-Bresse
4 Annecy
5 Aix-les-Bains
6 Chambéry
7 Vienne
8 Lyon

2 Pérouges. Pérouges is a stunning example of a medieval town built around a church, the impressive stone **Eglise Forteresse.** It stands proudly on a high plateau, replete with surrounding walls, restored homes, and two impressive stone gates. The village was a sort of Silicon Valley of the medieval era, filled with free craftsmen and linen weavers. It fought often against Lyon to retain its special status and did not officially become incorporated into France until 1601. Never a big burg, it nonetheless enjoyed boom times once more when the Industrial Revolution hit France in full swing during the 18th century. After that it was essentially abandoned until, beginning in the early 20th century, denizens of Lyon rediscovered and restored the city. Pérouges is now a common site for French period movies. Lunch outside at **Les Terrasses de Pérouges,** Porte d'En-Bas (☎ 04-74-61-38-68; www.terrassesperouges. free.fr; main courses 9€–15€; MC, V; Thurs–Tues noon–2:30pm and 7–10pm, closed Wed). ⏱ 4 hr. Pérouges Tourist Office, at the village entrance. ☎ 04-74-46-70-84. www.perouges.org.

> With two rivers running through its center, Lyon has miles of riverbanks overlooked by stately, peachy-toned buildings.

> *The stunning Gothic Eglise de Brou in Bourg-en-Bresse has painted roof tiles more typical of Burgundy.*

From Pérouges, follow D22 north via Chalamont to Bourg-en-Bresse (39km/24 miles).

❸ ★ Bourg-en-Bresse. Bourg-en-Bresse is small, but it features two splendid cathedrals: the Gothic-Renaissance **Cathédrale Bourg-en-Bresse** and the especially impressive ★ **Eglise de Brou,** one of the most visited churches in France. Dedicated craftsmanship went into creating this stunning masterpiece of Flamboyant Gothic style—such as the stained-glass windows inspired by an Albrecht Dürer engraving and the finely sculpted tombs of Philibert II, Duke of Savoie, and Margaret of Austria, daughter of Holy Roman Emperor Maximilian. Part of the church and monastery complex is the **Musée de Brou,** 63 bd. de Brou (☎ 04-74-22-83-83; admission 7€ adults, 4.50€ reduced; daily 9am–noon and 2–5pm), which features a fine collection of mainly French paintings, European sculptures, and international exhibitions. For lunch, seek out the town's signature dish, which features *Bresse bleu* cheese atop free-range chicken. Bresse farmers preserve the flavor of their chicken as seriously as their neighbors cultivate wine grapes; each chicken has an appellation, to denote where it was raised, and is governed by some of the strictest free-range regulations in the world, which justifies prices over 20€ per chicken. To enjoy these local cluckers in a lovely setting try ★ **l'Auberge Bressane,** 166 bd. de Brou (☎ 04-74-22-22-68; www. aubergebressane.fr). It's easy to find as it faces l'Eglise de Brou. Spend the night at **Le Logis de Brou** or **Hôtel du Prieuré** (p. 368). ⏱ Half-day. Bourg-en-Bresse Tourist Office, 6 av. Alsace-Lorraine. ☎ 04-74-22-49-40. www.bourg-en-bresse.fr.

On Day 3, take A40 east from Bourg-en-Bresse; at junction 14 join A41 to Annecy (128km/80 miles).

❹ ★★ Annecy. Just 35km (22 miles) from Geneva, Switzerland, Annecy is on the northern tip of Europe's cleanest lake, **Lac d'Annecy.** In summer, it's a bustling tourist town, full of people enjoying watersports. In colder seasons, the idyllic landscapes of **Les Forêts du Semnoz** (Semnoz Forest) are the main draw. Year-round, it's worth visiting the **Château d'Annecy** (☎ 04-50-33-87-30; http://musees. agglo-annecy.fr; admission 5.90€ adults, 2.30€ reduced; Tues–Sun 10:30am–6pm), a restored castle in all its medieval, many-towered splendor. Home of the counts of Geneva, this 12th-century château was abandoned until 1953, when the city acquired the castle, restored it, and installed several fine museums. The **Tour de la Reine** (Queen's Tower) has a gorgeous view of the town and water below. It's worth spending at least 1 night in Annecy just to see the ★ **Palais de l'Isle** after dark; set on an island in the Thiou River, this former prison is one of France's most photographed monuments, and it's stunning when illuminated at night. Eat and stay at the regal ★★★ **l'Impérial Palace** (p. 359), which offers superlative dining with views of the lake. ⏱ 1 day. Annecy Tourist Office, 1 rue Jean-Jaurès. ☎ 04-50-45-00-33. www.lac-annecy.com.

On Day 4, take A41 south to Aix-les-Bains (50km/31 miles).

5 Aix-les-Bains. This small city takes its name from the healing waters that make it the second-most visited spa town in France. If you want to enjoy thermal spa waters without spending a fortune, follow the French to **Thermes d'Aix-les-Bains,** place Maurice Mollard (☎ 04-79-35-38-50; www.thermaix.com; admission 12€, session in leisure spa 18€ after 5:45pm; V; daily 10am–7:45pm). As a government-run facility, it is very reasonably priced, though in peak holiday periods it may be more crowded than a deluxe spa. After you've spent the morning at the spa, stroll serenely into town while seeking a spot for lunch; you'll pass by an abundance of fine Belle Epoque buildings and facades, and possibly rub elbows with a few of the many rich and famous Europeans who have a residence here. Spend the afternoon discovering some of the most picture-perfect peaks of the western Alps in the low mountains of **Crêt de Châtillon.** As the sun sets, traverse some of the area's many trails and parks before returning to town for the night. Like most French spa towns, this one has a casino, but few are as architecturally and historically significant as the **Casino Grand Cercle,** 200 rue du Casino (☎ 04-79-35-16-16; www.casinograndcercle.com; daily noon–2pm and 7–11pm). Built in 1850, it features a splendid mosaic of more than 3½ million pieces of gold-encrusted glass. If you want to stay the night, we recommend **Hostellerie Le Manoir**

(p. 358). ⏱ 1 day. Aix-les-Bains Tourist Office, place Maurice-Mollard. ☎ 04-79-88-68-00. www.aixlesbains.com.

From Aix-les-Bains on Day 5, follow the lake road south, then take N201 to Chambéry (17km/11 miles).

6 ★ Chambéry. This picture-perfect Alpine city is dominated by the 13th-century **Château de Chambéry**, but it's the outlandish **Fontaine des Eléphants** that is its most beloved landmark. For lunch, head to local favorite **l'Hypotenuse** (p. 359) or try an Italian restaurant, a good option here, as Chambéry's culture can fairly be called a mix of French and Italian. Then spend the afternoon wandering among the well-preserved medieval city center, the ancient capital of the dukes of Savoie, which features museums, mansions, and a maze of Dark Age alleys. ⏱ 1 day. See p. 355, **7**.

From Chambéry on Day 6, take A43 west; at junction 5 pick up D75 (toward Heyrieux) to Vienne (100km/62 miles).

7 ★★ Vienne. This town is rich in ancient Roman history; there are many Roman monuments in the small but pretty old quarter. You can grab a dinner to suit any budget here, before driving back to Lyon to spend the night. Alternatively, stay and dine at the delightful ★★ **La Pyramide** (p. 368) if you can get a room; during peak season, it tends to book up early with Parisians making their way down to the Riviera. ⏱ 1 day. See p. 364, **1**.

From Vienne, take A7 north to Lyon (33km/21 miles).

8 ★★★ Lyon. You will probably want to spend at least part of your last day in one of the city's great museums: The ★★★ **Musée des Beaux-Arts** is second only to the Louvre, while the ★★ **Musée d'Art Moderne** (MAM) provides an excuse to walk through the lovely ★ **Parc de la Tête d'Or.** For lunch, stop in most any cafe to sample the *mâchons*, snacks of cold cuts famously munched upon by Lyon's silk workers. For dinner, we say scrape up your few remaining *centimes* and spend them all on a blowout dinner in one of the world's top restaurant towns. ⏱ 1 day. For detailed information on Lyon, see p. 378.

ALPINE CHEESES
Tradition-Bound Cultures of the Rhône-Alps
BY NATHALIE JORDI

ALPINE CHEESE MAKING is a tradition that dates back more than a thousand years. Alpine pastures, rife with wildflowers and herbs, lend a unique flavor to each wheel of raw-milk cheese produced here. Cold temperatures in the mountains allow for production of larger cheeses, which can age without spoiling and provide nourishment through the long, hard winters. The larger cheeses required milk from more animals, which led to a cooperative-based system that still thrives in the Alps today, producing large cheeses like Beaufort, Abondance, and Comté, but also smaller ones such as Reblochon and Chevrotin. While 21st-century technology has crept into production methods in the region—particularly surrounding microbacterial control—many cheese makers still employ ancient tools and ingredients such as wood fires, copper kettles, and animal rennet.

LA DENT DU CHAT
Raw, hard cow's milk cheese; fruity and nutty. Named after a nearby mountain (French for "cat's tooth"), this über-local cheese is made only in Yenne by one local cheese cooperative.

BEAUFORT
Raw, hard cow's milk cheese; nutty and fruity. Made exclusively with uncooled milk within 2 hours of milking.

Beaufort d'ete is made only from the summer milk of grass-fed cows. *Beaufort d'hiver*, made in winter from cows fed on hay, is the cheese most traditionally used in *fondue savoyarde*. *Beaufort chalet d'alpage*, the

most elevated and expensive of the three, is made only in summer on the high prairie, above 1,500m (4,921 ft.); it tastes the most aromatic, with notes of wildflower and herb. If sold grated, the Beaufort AOC appellation is lost.

TOME DES BAUGES
Raw, hard cow's milk cheese; mild and sweet. This cheese of 17th-century origin is covered in a mold called *mucor*, otherwise known as *poil de chat*, or "cat hair." About 25% of production is farmstead, the rest industrial. Paradoxically, the farmstead version is often less expensive than the industrial.

CHEVROTIN DES ARAVIS
Raw goat's milk cheese; mild and savory. The goat's milk equivalent to Reblochon, this rare cheese is made

exclusively in season from the milk of one specific race of

alpine goats and then pressed. It's made only on a few farms in the Chaine des Aravis.

ABONDANCE
Raw, hard cow's milk cheese; milder than Beaufort, and sweet. Originating in the 14th century from the Abondance monastery near the Swiss border, this cheese is similar to Beaufort but made exclusively with milk from Abondance cattle. Like Beaufort, the wheels have concave sides, owing to the molds in which they are pressed; you can still see the imprints of the pressing cloth on the cheese's surface many

months after pressing takes place. About a third of production is farmstead, made by the same folk who raise the animals; the rest is artisanal or industrial, but made to the same specifications (that is, raw, with Abondance milk, etc.).

REBLOCHON
Raw, washed-rind cow's milk cheese; mushroomy and creamy. The name comes from *re-blocher*—the 13th-century practice of re-milking a cow once the tax collector had already paid his visit for the milk. The second milking, scarcer

in quantity but higher in butterfat, was (and is) perfect for this creamy cheese.

12 Popular French AOC Cheeses by Region

AOC, or *Appellation d'Origine Contrôlée*, is an official designation that guarantees the geographical origin and traditional production methods of cheeses, wines, and other French food products.

BLEU D'AUVERGNE
Auvergne, cow

BRIE DE MEAUX
Ile-de-France, cow

CAMEMBERT
Normandy, pasteurized cow

CANTAL
Auvergne, cow

EPPOISES
Burgundy, cow

MONTRACHET
Burgundy, goat

MORBIER
Franche-Comté, cow

EMMENTAL
Savoie and Franche-Comté, cow

MUNSTER
Lorraine, cow

NEUFCHATEL
Normandy, cow

ROQUEFORT
Midi-Pyrénées, sheep

ST-NECTAIRE
Auvergne, cow

The Rhône-Alps in 10 Days

Think big if you're exploring the Rhône-Alps, on the border of Italy and Switzerland, in the southern half of the country. The region covers eight French *départements* and 43,700 sq. km (16,870 sq. miles), encompassing Mont Blanc, the highest peak in France, on the Italian border; three major cities including Lyon, the national capital of gastronomy; great, wide rivers including the Rhône; and huge lakes such as Lake Geneva. This ambitious itinerary circles north, east, and south of Lyon to take in the region's various distinctive landscapes.

> Ruin upon ruin: The 12th-century Château de Crussol in Valence was built on the site of a Roman temple.

START **Lyon** is 467km (290 miles) south of Paris. TRIP LENGTH 573km (356 miles).

❶ ★★★ **Lyon.** With its vibrant population, dynamic history, and powerful economy, Lyon is really on the level of better-known cities such as Athens or Mumbai. Unlike Marseille to the south, which is only slightly more populated, Lyon has no second-city complex. Take your pick of great restaurants for dinner—you just can't visit enough Lyonnais restaurants—and spend the night in the city. ⏱ 1 day. For detailed information on Lyon, see p. 378.

On Day 2, follow the Saône River north out of Lyon along quai Geoges Clemenceau and cross at the pont de Collonges (8km/5 miles).

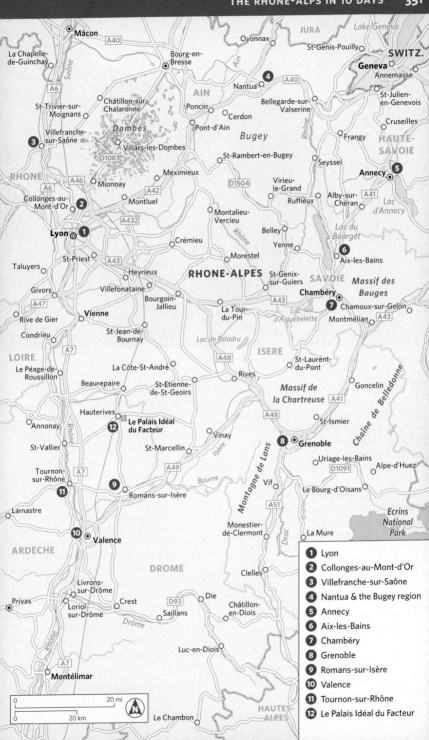

> *Step back in time along St-Romain-au-Mont-d'Or's deserted, narrow medieval streets.*

2 Collonges-au-Mont-d'Or. Immediately upon exiting Lyon, you'll enter the **Massif Mont d'Or,** a small mountain chain blessed with extremely pure water; an abundance of yellow limestone, which was used to build Lyon and gave the area its name; and a plethora of charming villages. Despite their proximity to the big city, the villages in this area—such as **St-Romain-au-Mont-d'Or, Couzon-au-Mont-d'Or,** and **Rochetaillee-sur-Saône**—have retained an authentic medieval character. You'll find centuries-old stone buildings still inhabited by residents and shopkeepers, perhaps a Romanesque or Gothic cathedral, stunning sights such as historic **Couzon Bridge,** and a wealth of other surprises. Stop at **Collonges-au-Mont-d'Or** for lunch at the eponymous restaurant of world-renowned chef ★★★ **Paul Bocuse** (p. 386). At lunch you can experience his extraordinary food without blowing your entire dining budget on one meal. ⏱ Half-day. Collonges-au-Mont-d'Or Tourist Office, place de la Marie. ☎ 04-78-22-02-12. www.collongesau-montdor.fr.

Continue following the Saône north, on its left bank this time, to A46, which brings you to Villefranche-sur-Saône (27km/17 miles).

3 Villefranche-sur-Saône. Considered the wine capital of Beaujolais, Villefranche gets its name from its "free town" status (meaning it's a town free of customs duties), established in 1140. Rue National ("the Nat," as locals call it) is lined with 16th- and 17th-century bourgeois and patrician mansions, revealing its wealthy past. Spend the afternoon visiting a few of the nearby vineyards (see "Beaujolais Route du Vin"); the **visitors' center** has plenty of information on them. ⏱ Half-day and overnight. Villefranche Tourist Office, 96 rue de la Sous-Prefecture. ☎ 04-74-07-27-50. www.villefranche-beaujolais.fr.

On Day 3, follow D936, a Roman road, to Bourg-en-Bresse (p. 346, **3**), and pick up the winding D979 to Nantua (101km/63 miles).

4 Nantua & the Bugey region. For centuries, travelers heading from Lyon to the south of France, the Alps, Switzerland, or Italy have stopped to relax in this town full of panoramic views and excellent eats. In fact, the entire region of Bugey, the historical term for the area between Geneva and Lyon, is full of lush green landscapes. The area is well fed by a myriad of waterfalls, lakes, and ponds, making it true to its description as a vast English garden raised to the hundredth power. Nantua's beauty stems from its steep bluffs in the north and south and the lovely Lac Nantua to the west. It's a great area for strenuous outdoor sports or slow nature walks. The food here is usually topped with the famed Nantua sauce, a mixture of butter and crayfish. Nearby villages such as Oyonnax, Izernore, and Bellegarde are all worth visiting, but be sure not to miss the **Fort l'Ecluse** in Collonges (www.cc-pays-de-gex.fr/fortlecluse; admission 5€ adults, 3.50€ children; daily 10am–6:30pm; lower fort open summer only). Perched high above the Rhône in the Gex gorge, the fort was finished by Vauban, the famed military architect of the Golden Siècle. Even if you can't visit the lower fort, you'll find rewarding (but difficult) hiking trails that permit access to the upper fort with breathtaking views of the Jura Mountains

Beaujolais Route du Vin

The best and most pleasurable way to see this region is to cruise the 22km (14-mile) **Beaujolais Route du Vin** (www.route-vins. com), featuring some 30 villages and more than 150 castles and architectural sites. If you're lucky enough to be visiting the region on the third Thursday of November, you'll be in time for what has become perhaps the premier wine holiday: the release of **Beaujolais Nouveau.** Beaujolais Nouveau wines tend to peak in just 2 to 10 years. The short shelf life and rapid maturation process of this abundant and adaptable, but often mundane, wine is what motivated the recent and massive propaganda effort behind this "holiday." In the eyes of many wine enthusiasts it's something of a scam, yet it's celebrated around the world. But don't judge the whole region by Beaujolais Nouveau; besides the massive vineyards full of machine harvesters, there are nearly a dozen *Cru* and *Grand Cru* vineyards. For wine lovers, we recommend adding a day to your tour to visit several wineries, as well as the gorgeous Azergues Valley and the village of **Oingt,** considered one of the most beautiful in the world, thanks to its fully restored buildings and its château made of honey-colored stone.

> *Legend has it that lovers who kiss in the middle of Annecy's pont des Amours will stay together for life.*

above and the Rhône Valley below, which the fort was built to protect. For the more adventurous there is also a *via ferrata* between the two forts. Drive to Annecy to spend the night. ⏱ 1 day. Nantua Tourist Office, place de la Déportation. ☎ 04-74-75-00-05. www.nantua-tourisme.com.

Drive to Annecy, via A40 south (83km/53 miles) to spend the night.

⑤ ★★ **Annecy.** The serene lake city of Annecy is a lovely place to spend an evening. Eat in one of the town's Belle Epoque restaurants and enjoy a restful day walking around the glassy lake in the morning, and visiting the **Château d'Annecy** (p. 346, ④) in the afternoon. **La Ferme de la Charbonnière** (p. 359) will provide you with one of the most unique evening meals of your trip, or simply soak up the luxury of the ★★★ **Imperial Palace** (p. 359) and its casino. ⏱ 1 day. See p. 346, ④.

From Annecy on Day 5, take A41 to Aix-les-Bains (35km/22 miles).

⑥ **Aix-les-Bains.** On the eastern edge of Lac du Bourget, modern Aix-les-Bains is the largest and most fashionable spa town in eastern France, yet it's still affordable to relax in the thermal waters here. ⏱ 1½ days. See p. 347, ⑤.

Chemin de Fer de La Mure

The 19th-century Chemin de Fer de La Mure is one of the most beloved tourist railway lines in Europe. Now electric-powered, the train creeps over 31km (19 miles) of dams, tunnels, lakes, and spectacular mountain scenery at about 32km (20 miles) per hour. At its terminus, a former mining town on the Matheysin Plateau, travelers are afforded a gorgeous panorama of **Mont Aiguille** and **L'Aiguille Percée** (Pierced Needle). Historical sites—such as former coal installations, workshops, a forge, and the **Musée de Matheysin,** Maison Caral, rue Colonel Escallon (☎ 04-76-30-98-15; http://musee.matheysine.com; admission 2.30€ adults, 1.50€ reduced; May 2–Aug 31 Wed–Mon 1–6:30pm; closed Sept–Apr)—open a window onto a bygone era. La Mure still has many restaurants that used to serve the mining communities, which thrived until the 1960s. *La Mure Railway Station, St-Georges-de-Commiers (23km/14 miles south of Grenoble on A51; leave at exit 12 for St-Georges-de-Commiers).* ☎ *04-76-73-57-35. www.trainlamure.com. Reservations limited. Round-trip 19.20€ adults, 9.70€ ages 15 and under. Call for departure times.*

After lunch on Day 6, take A41 south from Aix-les-Bain to Chambéry (17km/11 miles).

❼ ★ Chambéry. The dukes of Savoie, long the kingmakers and kings of Europe, built the esteemed Château de Chambéry in the 13th century (it's closed to the public), cementing this city with an Alpine feel as the historical capital of the region. The symbol of the city, however, is the **Fontaine des Eléphants,** constructed in 1838 to commemorate France's man in India, Benoit de Boigne. With four life-size elephants carved into the base, it was initially met with disapproval from local residents, known for their general impassivity, but it won their affection over time. You'll find plenty of opportunities to indulge in fondue here, sharpened by crisp white Savoie wines, or enjoy the local feel of the popular theater-restaurant **L'Hypotenuse** (p. 359). A very special place to stay and dine is the **★★★ Château de Candie** (p. 358). It's definitely not to be missed if fine dining is one of your priorities. ⏱ Half-day. Chambéry Tourist Office, Town Hall. ☎ 04-79-60-20-20. www.chambery.fr.

On Day 7, take A41 south from Chambéry to Grenoble (57km/35 miles).

❽ ★★★ Grenoble. The premier city of the Alps, Grenoble offers an array of fun activities, even if you're not there to ski on the nearby slopes, which are some of the world's best. ⏱ 2 days. For detailed information on Grenoble, see p. 374.

On Day 9, head north from Grenoble on A48 and pick up A49 (toward Valence) to Romans-sur-Isère (77km/48 miles).

❾ Romans-sur-Isère. You're now dipping into the *département* of Drôme (p. 357). Romans-sur-Isère, redolent of the local peach and apricot orchards, will ease you into these fragrant southern climes. You'll find great food here, including the excellent local ravioli and the produce and nuts sold at the city center market on Friday and Saturday mornings. It's also worth checking out the **Musée Internationale de la Chaussure** (International Museum of Shoes), 2 rue Ste-Marie (☎ 04-75-05-51-81; www.ville-romans.com; admission 5€ adults, 2.50€ reduced; Mon–Sat 10am–5pm). You'll find everything from Second Empire silk evening boots to high-fashion exhibits from the likes of Roger Vivier and Raymond Massaro, both of which continue to produce locally. Romans-sur-Isère has the biggest factory shopping outlet south of the Loire—**Marques Avenue,** in the city center at 60 avenue Gambetta (☎ 04-75-05-85-29; www.marquesavenue.com), with

> *The elephants on Chambéry's famous fountain are nicknamed* les quatre sans cul *(the four without behinds).*

> *A cobbler demonstrates his craft at the International Museum of Shoes in Romans-sur-Isère.*

67 brands housed in an old police barracks redesigned by Jean-Michel Wilmotte, one of France's most famous architects. ⏱ Half-day. Pays de Romans Tourist Office, Le Neuilly, place Jean Jaurès, Romans. ☎ 04-75-02-28-72. www. romans-tourisme.com.

From Romans-sur-Isère, take N532 southwest to Valence (20km/12 miles).

⑩ ★ **Valence.** Serving as a gateway to both the gorges of Ardèche and the decadent beaches of the Midi, Valence is first and foremost the capital of the Drôme. The 10th-century **Château de Crussol,** St-Peray (☎ 04-75-40-30-15; free; daily 11am–7pm), lies mostly in ruins atop Crussol Mountain, but the natural setting and views are glorious. Valence was an important military training ground—hence the **Champs de Mars,** home of the **Peynet Kiosque** (the bandstand made famous by French illustrator Raymond Peynet's decidedly unmilitant drawings called *The Lovers*). Napoleon served in his first garrison here, where he also heard his last *"Vive l'Empéreur!"* on his way to exile on the island of Elba. The **Cathédrale St-Appolinaire,**

place des Ormeaux (no phone; free admission; daily 8am–7pm), features a museum dedicated to the town's extensive Roman history. Valence also has an **Armenian Heritage Center,** 14 rue Louis Gallet (☎ 04-75-80-13-00; free admission; Apr–Sept Tues–Sun 2:30–6:30pm, Oct–Mar Tues–Sun 2–5:30pm; closed Dec 25–Jan 6); the town welcomed exiles after the genocide of 1918 to 1921, and one in ten Valentinois are now of Armenian extraction. Valence was a textile, leather, and jewelry capital for centuries, and it still holds special appeal for shoppers. Be sure to try *le Suisse,* an orange-flavored cookie shaped like one of the Vatican's Swiss guards, and the Drôme's most famous drink, a sparkling wine called **Clairette de Die** from the village of Die. You'll also find great Rhône Valley wines in this town. ⏱ 1 day. Valence Tourist Office, 11 bd. Bancel. ☎ 08-92-70-70-99. www.valencetourisme.com.

From Valence on Day 10, take A7 to Tournon-sur-Rhône (20km/12 miles).

⑪ ★ **Tournon-sur-Rhône.** You're now in the heart of the most prestigious Côtes du Rhône

> *This surreal palace was built single-handedly by a postman, Ferdinand Cheval.*

vineyards, so don't miss tastings of the Crozes Hermitage and Tain-l'Hermitage wines (see "The Northern Cotes du Rhône Wine Route," p. 366). Tournon also has the ★★ **Kids** **Château de Ventadour** and some beautiful walks in the surrounding hills. ⏱ **Half-day. See p. 367, ③.**

Leave Tournon-sur-Rhône on D532; after Chano-Curson make a left onto D67, and at

The Drôme

The southern Rhône-Alps *département* of the Drôme (see stops ⑨ and ⑩) has much in common with the luscious Provence region to the south. The home of three rivers, including its namesake, the Drôme is infused with a sunny Mediterranean feel. Here, unlike in the northern reaches of the region, you'll see those quintessentially Provençal fields of lavender and olive trees, and Mediterranean ingredients start appearing in the local cuisine. Driving is a pleasure on quiet roads between the region's feudal-era villages.

Charmes-sur-l'Herbasse pick up D66 and then D538 to Hauterives (42km/26 miles).

⑫ ★★ **Le Palais Idéal du Facteur Cheval.** Before you head back to Lyon, take a small detour to witness one of France's greatest follies, Le Palais Idéal du Facteur Cheval. Cheval was a late-19th-century postman who spent 33 years delivering the mail and picking up loads of rocks on the rural roads of Hauterives. He would return home with pockets full of stones and, often working by lamp at night, fashioned them into a veritable castle of art, now a national monument. The themes, inspired by the Bible, Hindu mythology, and much more, reveal this humble mailman's fervent imagination. This monument to the will of a single human being ends your trip on an unforgettable note. ⏱ 1 hr. At the junction of D538 and D51, Hauterives. ☎ 04-75-68-81-19. www.facteurcheval.com. Admission 5.50€ adults, 4.50€ reduced. Daily 9:30am–12:30pm and 1:30–4:30pm (or later).

To return to Lyon, go north to join D519 and A7 at Chanas (83km/52 miles).

Where to Stay & Dine in the Rhône-Alps

> In Aix-les-Bains, when the chips are down you can still fill up in the casino's Bar Restaurant Koupol'.

Bar Restaurant Koupol' (Casino Grand Cercle)
AIX-LES-BAINS *FRENCH* At this beautiful Beaux Arts restaurant in the town casino, diners have a close-up view of blackjack and roulette players testing their luck. The menu offers conservative but flavorful dishes of veal, beef, and chicken, with a scattering of terrines, soups, and salads. Rue du Casino. ☎ 04-79-35-16-16. Fixed-price menu 12€–21€. AE, DC, MC, V. Lunch and dinner daily.

★★★ **Château de Candie** CHAMBERY *GAS-TRONOMIC* In this former Savoyarde fortified manor, from the time of the Knights Templar, in the woods above Chambéry, you'll find fine food and luxury rooms with toile de Jouy taffeta fabrics, antique furniture, and splendid bathrooms; the three-floor tower has circular rooms and a Jacuzzi for two. The elegant, paneled Orangerie restaurant serves up the finest local products in delicate and inspired flavor combinations, with a choice of variations on foie gras for starters. Rue du Bois de Candie, Chambéry-le-Vieux. ☎ 04-79-96-63-00. www.

chateaudecandie.com. 25 units. Doubles 160€–600€. Main courses €35–62€. AE, DC, MC, V. Lunch Tues–Fri and Sun, dinner Tues–Sat.

Hostellerie Le Manoir AIX-LES-BAINS
This converted 19th-century stable has paths weaving through turn-of-the-20th-century gardens with outdoor furniture under shade trees. Midsize to spacious guest rooms have unique and old-fashioned decor—with antique and provincial furniture; most have terraces. You can order breakfast or dinner on a terrace bordering the garden. 37 rue Georges 1er. ☎ 04-79-61-44-00. www.hotel-lemanoir.com. 73 units. Doubles 99€–169€. AE, DC, MC, V.

kids Hôtel Campanile Valence Sud VALENCE
This hotel in the Campanile chain is an excellent value for families. It is furnished in a

For hotels and restaurants in Lyon, see p. 384; in Grenoble, see p. 376; in the Rhône Valley, see p. 368; in the Ardèche, see p. 373.

contemporary style, the buffet restaurant is open for all three meals, and the playground will keep the kids happily occupied. 9 rue Henri Abel. ☎ 04-75-56-92-80. www. campanile-valence-sud.fr. 54 units. Doubles 65€–85€. MC, V.

Hôtel de Lyon VALENCE
Close to the train station but also near the downtown shopping district, this hotel offers basic modern comfort at very good prices. 23 av. Pierre Semard. ☎ 04-75-41-44-66. www. hoteldelyon.fr. 50 units. Doubles 59€–68€. V.

★ Hôtel La Demeure de Chavoire CHAVOIRES (LAC ANNECY) About 3km (1¾ miles) east of Annecy, this intimate and cozy inn is one of the area's most charming, with well-chosen Savoy antiques, a garden overlooking the lake, and thoughtful staff. Each guest room has wood beams and unique decor. 71 rte. d'Annecy, Veyrier-du-Lac. ☎ 04-50-60-04-38. 13 units. Doubles 126€–195€. AE, DC, MC, V.

★★ Hôtel Mercure Ariana AIX-LES-BAINS
Tunnel-like glass walkways connect this hotel's sports facilities to its main core, drawing a spa-oriented crowd. The loggia-dotted glass exterior, surrounded by a park, opens into an Art Deco interior. The guest rooms come in a range of sizes and styles, each comfortable and well appointed. **Café Adelaïde** is both a cafe and a restaurant. 111 av. de Marlioz, à Marlioz. ☎ 04-79-61-79-79. www.mercure.com. 60 units. Doubles 100€–144€. AE, DC, MC, V.

★★★ L'Imperial Palace LAC ANNECY GASTRONOMIC
This grand, Belle Epoque–era hotel houses Annecy's casino and an upscale restaurant with terraces overlooking the lake. Balcony rooms afford an equally splendid view. A wellness center is a 2-minute walk away. Allée de l'Imperial. ☎ 04-50-09-30-00. www.hotel-imperial-palace.com. 99 units. Doubles 190€–250€. AE, DC, MC, V. Lunch and dinner daily.

La Ferme de la Charbonnière MENTHON-ST-BERNARD REGIONAL FRENCH
At this unique restaurant, 8km (5 miles) from Annecy, you'll likely dine on *reblochonnade:* A personal oven hauled to your table grills ham and potatoes above and broils cheese below. Through a plexiglass floor in the rustic dining room, diners can see the restaurant's cows being milked. Col de Bluffy. ☎ 04-50-02-82-59. www. lafermedelacharbonniere.com. Menus 18€. MC, V. Lunch and dinner Tues–Sun.

La Petite Auberge VALENCE REGIONAL FRENCH
This rustic but elegant restaurant features authentic Valence cuisine, such as *rumsteak charolais,* and Mediterranean fish plates, such as grilled *gambas* (king prawns). The selection of cheeses is well worth sampling. 1 rue Athenes. ☎ 04-75-43-20-30. www.lapetiteauberge. net. Lunch menu 25€; fixed-price menu 49€. V. Lunch Mon–Sat; dinner Tues and Thurs–Sat.

★ Le Belvédère LAC ANNECY FRENCH/SEAFOOD
From a belvedere above Annecy, about 1.5km (1 mile) west of the town center, the views extend 8km (5 miles) over mountains and lakes. Try the salad of Breton lobster with freshwater crayfish and strips of foie gras; a platter of scallops and red mullet with shellfish-flavored butter sauce; and foie gras with a purée of figs and vanilla-flavored bourbon sauce. 7 chemin du Belvédère. ☎ 04-50-45-04-90. www. belvedere-annecy.com. Main courses 16€–40€; fixed-price lunch menu 28€; fixed-price dinner 42€–85€. AE, MC, V. Lunch Thurs–Tues, dinner Mon and Thurs–Sat. Closed Jan. From downtown Annecy, follow signs leading uphill to Le Semnoz.

★ Le Bistrot du Kiosque VALENCE TRADITIONAL FRENCH
Sunny in the day, filled with jazz at night, and looking out upon the inspirational Peynet Kiosk, this quaint bistro is perfect for two. Try the veal kidneys or the excellent *cassolette,* a Provençal specialty cooked in the oven in a shallow dish (not *cassoulet*). 11 place Jules Nadi. ☎ 04-75-05-24-71. Main courses 12€–22€. MC, V. Lunch and dinner Tues–Sun.

L'Hypotenuse CHAMBERY REGIONAL FRENCH
A hub of Chambéry's social scene, L'Hypotenuse is also a theater, showing a lively program of comedy, dramas, and jazz, while serving generously under-priced menus of delicious local specialties. We particularly recommend the dessert of pears with Aprémont wine. 141 carrée Curial. ☎ 04-79-85-80-15. www.restaurant-hypotenuse.com. Lunch menu 16€. Fixed-price menus 24€–34€. MC, V. Lunch and dinner Thurs–Sun. Reservations recommended.

The Rhône-Alps for Nature Lovers

The Rhône-Alps is home to six natural regional parks and two national parks. Here we give a sampling of four of them, with their varied seasonal activities, from cross-country ski trails to beautiful drives, craft workshops, or wildlife hikes. We strongly recommend abandoning the mountains for a while to see the majestic herons and egrets, as well as more exotic birds, in Les Etangs de la Dombes (the Dombes Wetlands), a wilderness area close to Lyon and unique to the region.

> *Villages, hidden by forests and beautiful steep mounds, pop up all over the Rhône-Alps' dramatic countryside.*

★★ **Les Etangs de la Dombes** (near Lyon). Bordered by the Rhône and Saône rivers, in the northern part of the Rhône-Alps region, the Dombes Wetlands are one of the area's most interesting wildlife spots. If you don't like the weather here, wait five minutes and it will change. France's Land o'Lakes, this gently sloping plateau is covered by small, man-made rainwater lakes, mostly created by Trappist monks who dug up the area to access the region's fine building clay. The pride of the area is **Villars-les-Dombes,** home of one of the world's ornithological treasures: the 14-hectare (35-acre) **Parc des Oiseaux,** rte. 1083s (www. parcdesoiseaux.com; admission 13€ adults, 10€ kids; daily 10am–6pm). A natural bird habitat, the park has been safeguarded and stocked

Where to Stay & Dine

For hotels and restaurants in Lyon, see p. 384; in Grenoble, see p. 376; in the Rhône Valley, see p. 368; in the French Alps, see p. 358; in the Ardèche, see p. 373.

Les Etangs de la Dombes **1**

Parc Naturel Régional du Haut Jura **2**

Parc Naturel Régional du Pilat **5**

Parc Naturel Régional Massif des Bauges **3**

Parc Naturel Régional Vercors **4**

with more than 2,000 birds from 400 species, representing all continents. The best way to explore the Dombes is by car on the **Route des Etangs,** which splits into north and south routes (both start at Villars-les-Dombes). The northern route wends its way through many charming villages, some with Romanesque churches and beautiful walking paths that allow you to see the Dombes up close. The southern route features fewer walking paths and more Gothic or modern churches. Agriculture in the Dombes follows an ancient practice evolved by the monks: Every 3 years, the ponds are drained and the manure-rich soil is used to raise crops for a year, before returning to aquaculture. When full, they're used to raise fish and are teeming with carp; fishing is best between October and March. There are many *gîtes* and charming bed-and-breakfasts around the Dombes. If you prefer a hotel, seek one in Villars-les-Dombes, Pérouges, or Trevoux. You'll find an ample supply of decent inexpensive hotels around the Dombes region, and good regional cuisine for all budgets. The main entrance to the Dombes Wetlands is on A46, Villars-les-Dombes exit, 38km (24 miles) north of Lyon. Villars-les-Dombes Tourist Office, 3 place de l'Hôtel de Ville. ☎ 04-74-98-06-29. www.villars-les-dombes.com.

Parc Naturel Régional du Haut Jura (near Nantua). This large regional natural park is on the Swiss border in the Jura Mountain range; only the bottom tip of the park falls within Rhône-Alps territory. Its geography is extremely diverse—including forests, grasslands, plateaus, bogs, lakes, and valleys—and the generally low height of the mountains makes them ideal for sports enthusiasts. Three grand, dedicated trails—hiking, cross-country skiing, and mountain biking—run through the park. Indeed, no park in France is so accommodating of cross-country skiers, and the **Transjurassienne long-distance ski race** takes place here every February, drawing more than 150,000 spectators. In summer the region's many lakes and rivers feature sailing of all types, and there's fishing year-round. As French parks go, this one is not densely populated, but its denizens are industrious: There are several themed routes—including ones devoted to cheese, toys, woodcarving, and glassware—that draw visitors to local workshops for shopping. The park is full of waterfalls; the most breathtaking is **La Billaude,** near Champagnole. Hiking paths also abound. Start at the **Flumen River** hike, beginning next to the campsite of St-Claude, and then cross over to the **Queue**

> *You can do much more than ski when the French Alps are topped with powdery snow.*

de Cheval (Horse Tail) trail, departing from Chaumont, just 5km (3 miles) from St-Claude. The top drive in the park is **Route de Geneve,** a serpentine road that wends slowly through St-Claude valley and its gorges. Two especially fine perches for panoramic views are **Chalam Crest,** the highest point of the southern Haut-Jura, near La Pesse, and Belvédère de la Roche Blanche, between the villages of Septmoncel and Les Moussières. There aren't many places to stay in the park, and the better hotels are in the outskirts; St-Claude offers a central location and good accommodations. You can also rent WWF Panda huts via the park's website. Haut Jura is the wettest French national park, so bring raingear if you're visiting during the warm seasons. The park begins just a few kilometers north of Nantua at Montréal-la-Cluse. St-Claude is 50km (31 miles) northeast of Nantua in the region of Franche-Comté. Maison du Parc (Park Headquarters): ☎ 03-84-34-12-27; www.parc-haut-jura.fr.

Parc Naturel Régional du Pilat (near Vienne). Crossing from the Loire into the Rhône area, near Vienne, this reserve is the major park closest to Lyon, so you're bound to encounter day-trippers. An ample 710 sq. km (274 sq. miles), the park covers most of the relatively squat **Pilat Massif.** It is exceptionally geared toward leisurely walking, owing to the 180km (112-mile) **Tour du Parc** circle trail. The trail is not totally flat, but it is easy going and surprisingly uncrowded, making for fine, multiday jaunts through the countryside. Come prepared with clothes for multiple seasons, however, as the climate varies wildly from Mediterranean in the Rhône Valley to nearly Alpine in the higher reaches. The village of Pelussin, a former silk center, is a charming and historic town to visit, with multiple cathedrals and castles, plus excellent food and lodging. The village of St-Croix-en-Jarez is a postcard in itself; inhabitants have moved into the former Carthusian monastery. From Vienne, take D502 west for 8km (5 miles). www.parc-naturel-pilat.fr. Vienne Tourist Office, cours Brillier. ☎ 04-74-53-80-30. www.vienne-tourisme.com.

Parc Naturel Régional Massif des Bauges (near Chambéry). This region's newest natural park was designed to preserve the gorgeous Savoie countryside in the foothills of the French Alps. It features swaths of pasture, lush valleys, and a few surprisingly dramatic limestone cliffs. Few parks are as colorful and fragrant in springtime, thanks to the presence of more than 1,600 Alpine plants and flowers. Amateur botanists will adore the wild carnations, lilies, orchids, blue thistles, and more. Running from Annecy to Lac du Bourget, the park is high on easy adventure, with gentle hiking trails and, in winter, copious cross-country routes. In the villages inside the park, cheese lovers will find a plethora of excellent Savoie cheeses, from Gruyère and Emmental to rarer finds such as Mont-d'Or or Tamie. Indeed, the renowned flavors of **Savoie cheeses** originate from these unique plants ruminated upon by dairy cows. The **Abbaye de Tamié** houses a small community of cheese-making Cistercian monks and is a popular spot in Bauges. The park is surrounded by more than a handful of fine, thriving cities and is easily accessible via six roads. Annecy, Aix-les-Bains, or Chambéry would make an excellent base for day trips or longer stays. Ski slopes here are modest. The park is 30 minutes east of Chambéry on D912 northeast to D911 southeast. Maison du Parc, Le Châtelard. ☎ 04-79-54-86-40. www. parcdesbauges.com.

Parc Naturel Régional Vercors (near Grenoble). Crossing the Drôme into Isère, this vast, 2,000-sq-km (772-sq.-mile) park in the **Vercors Mountains** has high mountains but also milder lowland areas. The northern plateau is most popular with tourists, mainly from Grenoble (just 10 min. away), seeking Nordic and alpine skiing. Go west and you'll find the beginning of the plateaus; they overlook gorgeous vistas of canyons, meadows, and the plains below. The northwest Columes part of the park is the most thickly forested, and the villages have an Italian feel to them, thanks to waves of immigrant coal miners in the 19th century. The southeastern region is especially wild and remote, full of desert scrub. **Grand Veymont** is the highest peak, at 2,341m (7,680 ft.), near the eastern town of Gresse-en-Vercors. It's popular despite the fact that it's about 16km (10 miles) from paved roads. Driving in this park is not easy,

> *The western parts of the Parc Naturel Régional Massif des Bauges are nicknamed Petit Canada.*

as suggested by the aptly named **Les Routes du Vertige** (Vertigo Roads). If you don't mind letting the passengers have most of the fun, slowly traverse the Combe Laval on D76, Les Grand Goulets (the Great Gullies) on D518, or Gorges du Nant (Nant Gorges) on D22. Vercors also offers great opportunities for spelunking, including the **Grotte du Thais,** which features prehistoric paintings. From Grenoble, take D531 south for 10km (6¼ miles) to the park entrance in Lans-en-Vercors. Maison du Parc (Park Headquarters), 255 chemin des Fusillés, Lans-en-Vercors. ☎ 04-76-94-38-26. www. parc-du-vercors.fr.

The Rhône Valley

The Rhône River, which flows from Geneva all the way to the Mediterranean via Avignon and Arles, has created a magnificent valley that has attracted travelers and trade since ancient times. This stretch of land, south of Lyon from Vienne to Valence, is home to some of the finest Côtes du Rhône wines. A continental climate prevails, and the vineyards, clinging to granite hillsides, produce deep and rounded reds as well as a few rich whites. What make the Rhône Valley a particularly rewarding destination are these fabulous wines and the concentration of ancient Roman sites.

> *Vines thrive on the steep, terraced hills of the Rhône Valley.*

START Vienne is 33km (21 miles) south of Lyon.
TRIP LENGTH About 5 days; 113km (70 miles), more if you travel the meandering Northern Côtes du Rhône Wine Route (see p. 366).

1 ★★ **Vienne.** The Romans recognized the geographic and strategic value of the natural basin between the Rhône and the hills, and so they established Vienne there. They left behind a legacy of superb architecture as well as the first northern Côtes du Rhône vines. The 1st-century **Temple d'Auguste et de Livie** (Temple of Augustus and Livia) marks the

center of the old Roman town, on place du Palais. Not far off place de Miremont is the **Jardin Archéologique de Cybèle,** the remains of another temple devoted to the Phrygian earth-mother goddess. The **pyramid of the Roman Circus** is an Egyptian-style obelisk on the site of the ancient city racetrack. A marvelous view of the city and the Rhône can be had by hiking up **Mont Pipet,** at the foot of which is the ★★ **Théâtre Antique,** on rue Circus (☎ 04-74-85-39-23; admission 2.30€ adults, 1.70€ reduced; Mon–Fri 9:30am–12:30pm and 3–7pm, Sat–Sun 1:30–5:30pm). With a seating capacity

> *The 1950s stained-glass windows inside Vienne's Gothic Cathédrale St-Maurice are an anachronistic but beautiful addition.*

of 13,000, it is the second-largest ancient amphitheater in France and is still in use today, most notably during the superb **Jazz à Vienne** (www.vienne.fr). If you're lucky enough to visit in July, experience this annual jazz festival, one of the best in Europe. The town has several churches of exceptional interest: the Romanesque basilica of **Eglise St-Pierre,** the Gothic **Cathédrale St-Maurice,** and the 12th-century church and cloister of **St-André-le-Bas.** You'll find plenty of fine places to eat in Vienne's compact and charming old quarter. Vienne Tourist Office, cours Brillier. ☎ 04-74-53-80-30. www.vienne-tourisme.com. See also p. 347, **7**.

From Vienne, take D502 the short distance west to St-Romain-en-Gal (3.5km/2¼ miles).

2 St-Romain-en-Gal. If you are not hellbent on tasting as many Côtes du Rhône as you can during your brief trip here, take the time to cross the river to Vienne's neighboring town

of St-Romain-en-Gal, where an archaeological dig in 1967 uncovered the remains of a significant Roman community. At the site, where excavation is ongoing, you can walk the streets

Bottled Perfection

Just south of Vienne, at Ampius, Côtes du Rhône producer **E. Guigal** (☎ 04-74-56-10-22; www.guigal.com; open to visitors by reservation only Sept–July Mon–Fri 8am–noon and 2–6pm except public holidays; 2-hr. guided tours available for groups of 15–20 by reservation only) has generated a cultlike following among serious wine collectors. Wine guru Robert Parker described the estate's Côte Rôtie "La Landonne" 2005 as "utter perfection." It retails at around 390€, but Guigal's less rarified bottles are affordable to all. Even its classic Côtes du Rhône, at under 10€, is a treat.

The Côtes du Rhône Tourist Trails

For additional information on vineyards in the Rhône Valley, contact Rhône Wines Tourism, www.vins-rhone-tourisme.com.

of the ancient settlement and see the footprint of shops, baths, and villas, including the House of the Ocean Gods, whose magnificent mosaic floor depicts Neptune and his waterborne cohorts. The **Musée Gallo-Romain,** rte. départmental 502 (☎ 04-74-53-74-01; www. musee-gallo-romain.com; admission 4€ adults, 2.50€ reduced, free for ages 18 and under;

Tues–Sun 10am–6pm; closed public holidays), contains finds from both here and Vienne. For more information, contact the Vienne Tourist Office, cours Brillier, Viennes. ☎ 04-74-53-80-30. www.vienne-tourisme.com.

Return to Vienne, and from there take A7 south to Tournon-sur-Rhône (60km/37 miles, or longer via the Wine Route).

The Northern Côtes du Rhône Wine Route

While the entire Rhône River corridor is justly famed for its wines, it's worth remembering that the northern and southern regions are viticulturally and geographically distinct. There are 12 separate Côtes du Rhône wine routes in the southern Rhône Valley, mainly in the region of Provence (p. 390). But the **Northern Côtes du Rhône Route du Vin** is exceptional, providing beautiful scenery as well as some of the most famous wines of the appellation, including Côte Rôtie, Condrieu-Château Grillet, Hermitage, Crozes Hermitage, and Cornas. Côtes du Rhône runs the gamut, from a simple AOC wine available by the box to vintages that grace the tables of the world's finest restaurants. The route runs from Vienne to Valence, passing through Tournon-sur-Rhône and nearly 100 wineries along the way. The tortuously steep hills

of the northern Rhône have made growing grapes a significant challenge, but this has also assured that hand-picking has prevailed over mass harvesting. Nearly 90% of the wines in this area are reds; the main varietals are grenache, mourvèdre, and syrah. The spicy grenache grape, hardy enough to withstand the region's cooler winters, is what usually gives northern Côtes du Rhône red wines their celebrated intense flavor. The great walking trails along the vineyards of the Hermitage can be found exiting from the village Tain-l'Hermitage, near Tournon-sur-Rhône. You'll find plenty of signs pointing the way, and superb dining and lodging options up and down the road, which follows routes D4 and D86 south along the Rhône River. Find more information at www.rhone-wines-tourism.com.

❸ ★ **Tournon-sur-Rhône.** You won't find many castles like the 10th-century ★★ kids **Château de Ventadour.** This stone giant, looming high above the Fontolière and Ardèche rivers, features a drawbridge, vaulted rooms, towers, and other elements typical of pre-Renaissance castle architecture. A vast restoration project has been in place since 1969, but the castle's very dilapidation, after lying dormant for centuries, is part of its charm. As the gateway to the Ardèche *département,* the town below has a distinctly Ardéchois feel, making it an ideal spot in which to enjoy the region's celebrated Crozes Hermitage and Tain-l'Hermitage wines. A network of pleasant walking trails lead through charming countryside, lush hills, and vineyards that offer tastings. The **Sentier des Tours** (Path of the Towers) affords a view of three towers (one in ruins) that stand like sentries for the town. Nearby vineyard ★ **Cave de Tain,** 22 rte. de Lamage (☎ 04-75-08-91-86; www.cavedetain.fr; year-round daily 10am–12:30 and 2–6pm, with extended hours in summer), has the area's biggest wine cellar and a store with bilingual sales attendants and plenty of wines to suit every budget. Gastronomy is of vital importance in Tournon-sur-Rhône, and meals are much more affordable than in Lyon. **Tournonais Tourist Office,** Hôtel de la Tourette. ☎ 04-75-08-10-23. www.ville-tournon.com.

From Tournon-sur-Rhône, take D86 and D533 south to Valence (19km/12 miles, or longer via the Wine Route).

❹ ★ **Valence.** At the end of the Northern Côtes du Rhône Wine Route, Valence opens up like a typical southern town, with its neatly clipped, gnarly rows of plane trees providing essential shade for residents. In 1942 Parisian illustrator Raymond Peynet captured the romantic spirit of this town with his now-celebrated drawings *Les Amoureux (The Lovers),* inspired by a bandstand (now renamed the **Peynet Kiosk**) in Champ de Mars, a former military parade ground. To take in some of the local history, visit the **Cathédrale St-Appolinaire,** which houses a museum dedicated to the town's extensive Roman history, and then head over to nearby **Maison des Têtes,** a medieval mansion with sculpted busts of famed figures such as Homer and Aristotle. See p. 356, ❿.

Maison Pic

Drawing gastronomes and sophisticates from miles around, including gourmands from Lyon and Paris, Maison Pic is a culinary and design phenomenon in the Rhône-Alps. The only female chef in France to garner three stars in the Michelin guide, Anne-Sophie Pic capitalizes on four generations' worth of family tradition in the kitchen. With designer Bruno Borrione, she has also created an exquisite place to stay, featuring the purest lines and contemporary furniture. It doesn't come cheap—menus run from 85€ at lunchtime to 320€ for the eight-course dinner, which runs through the finest local vegetables with Parmigiano and truffles, to lobster, line-caught sea bass with caviar, Bresse chicken, and soufflé Grand Marnier. If you want to splurge on one exceptional meal on your trip, make it this one. For smaller budgets, Pic's **Bistro 7** is also good, plus she runs a cookery school for those who want to try some of her tricks at home. *285 av. Victor Hugo, Valence.* ☎ *04-75-44-15-32. www.pic-valence.com. Menus 90€–210€. Bistro 7 menus 19€–29€. AE, DC, MC, V. Restaurant Pic lunch and dinner Tues–Sun. Bistro 7 lunch and dinner daily.*

Where to Stay & Dine in the Rhône Valley

Best Western Plaisance VILLEFRANCHE-SUR-SAONE *REGIONAL FRENCH* If you don't opt for a B&B in one of the villages around Villefranche (bookable through its tourist office), you can't go wrong with this Best Western hotel, which offers all the comforts you can expect from this chain. Colorful curtains and furnishing fabrics have been used to lend a personalized touch to the rooms at this modern hotel, with free Wi-Fi and a frescoed restaurant serving local specialties. 96 av de la Libération, Villefranche-sur-Saône. 04-74-65-33-52. www. hotel-plaisance.com. 68 units. Doubles 90€–142€. Fixed-price menus 24.50€–58€. AE, MC, V. Lunch Mon, Tues, Thurs, and Fri; dinner daily.

★ kids **Castel d'Espéranche** ST-GEORGES D'ESPÉRANCHE *MEDIEVAL FRENCH* This restaurant-and-cabin combination, 24km (15 miles) east of Vienne along D75, in bucolic and sporty St-Georges d'Espéranche, is unique: Few 13th-century guard towers have been partially converted into restaurants. Next to the restaurant are the restored castle gardens. The medieval-themed menus are reasonable, diverse, and fun. Rue de Mezet. ☎ 04-74-59-18-45. www.castel-esperanche. com. 3-course lunch 18€, 4-course dinner 33€. 16 units. Large cabin €80 per night. MC, V.

kids **Hôtel Azalées** TOURNON-SUR-RHONE Clean and dependable, this friendly hotel is in the town center with private parking. Its self-catering facilities and family rooms will attract those with young kids. 6 av. de la Gare. ☎ 04-75-08-05-23. www.hotel-azalees.com. 37 units. Doubles 59€–69€. MC, V.

Hôtel Central à Vienne VIENNE Typical of French rural family-run accommodations, this decent, reasonably priced provincial hotel cannot claim designer decor, but it is in the center of Vienne and staff are extremely helpful. 7 rue de l'Archevêché. ☎ 04-74-85-18-38. www.hotel-central-vienne.com. 25 units. Doubles 49€–65€. MC, V.

★★ **Hôtel du Prieuré** BOURG-EN-BRESSE Erected in 1982, this is the town's most gracious hotel. The angular structure sits on 0.4 hectare (1 acre) of gardens surrounded by 500-year-old stone walls. The place is especially alluring in spring, when forsythia, lilacs, roses, and Japanese cherries bloom. Most guest rooms are large and tranquil, outfitted in Louis XV, Louis XVI, or French country style. 49–51 bd. de Brou. ☎ 04-74-22-44-60. 14 units. Doubles 85€–105€. AE, MC, V.

★★ **La Pyramide** VIENNE *GASTRONOMIC* This restaurant-and-hotel combination is the height of fancy in Vienne, with sumptuous and decadent dining and lodging options. Eating here is not cheap, but the French beef dishes such as *boeuf salers* are divine and worth every *centime*. 14 bd. Fernand Point, Vienne. ☎ 04-74-53-01-96. www.lapyramide. com. Doubles 200€. Main courses 55€–65€. AE, DC, MC, V. Lunch and dinner Thurs–Mon.

★ **Le Château** TOURNON-SUR-RHÔNE *REGIONAL FRENCH* This riverbank hotel has a beautiful locale with a view of the Hermitage vineyards. The elegant on-site restaurant is favored by locals. 12 quai Marc Seguin. ☎ 04-75-08-60-22. www.hotel-le-chateau.com. 44 units. Doubles 64€–72€. Main courses 13€–20€. Fixed-price menus 26€–46€. AE, MC, V. Lunch and dinner daily.

Le Logis de Brou BOURG-EN-BRESSE This four-story property has landscaped grounds near the road fronting the church. Each comfortable guest room has reproductions of antique furniture, plus a small, shower-only bathroom. Jacqueline and Gérard Roger run a fine inn and employ an especially helpful staff. 132 bd. de Brou. ☎ 04-74-22-11-55. www.logisdebrou.com. 30 units. Doubles 68€–78€. AE, MC, V.

> On the bank of the river in Tournon-sur-Rhône, Le Château affords guests views of the prestigious 10th-century Hermitage vineyards.

★★★ **Les Cèdres** GRANGES LES BEAUMONT *GASTRONOMIC* With three Michelin stars, this enchanting restaurant in an elegant village house is well worth the effort it takes to get here. Brothers Jacques and Jean-Paul Bertrand cut their teeth in several renowned restaurants in the Rhône-Alps and abroad before setting up in this idyllic spot. Dishes include melted baby leeks in locally produced olive oil, fresh truffles from the Drôme, roasted pigeon on toast, and much more. Rue Le Village, 11km (6¾ miles) east of Tournon-sur-Rhône via rte. D532. ☎ 04-75-71-50-67. www.restaurantlescedres.fr. Lunch menu 40€, fixed-price menus 80€–100€. AE, MC, V. Lunch Wed–Sun, dinner Wed–Sat. Reservations required.

Le Tournesol TOURNON-SUR-RHONE *FRENCH* Le Tournesol (French for "the sunflower") offers simply prepared, fresh market produce at reasonable prices. Ask to dine on the terrace. 44 av. Marechal Foch. ☎ 04-75-07-08-26. www.letournesol.net. Lunch menu 10€–15€, fixed-price menus 16€–34€. V. Lunch and dinner Mon–Sat.

Saveurs du Marche VIENNE *CONTEMPORARY FRENCH* Ten minutes south of the city center, this bustling restaurant is popular for its affordable prices and ever-interesting menu that changes with the seasons. 34 cours de Verdun. ☎ 04-74-31-65-65. www.lessaveursdumarche.fr. Lunch menu 14€, fixed-price menus 19€–31€. MC, V. Lunch and dinner Mon–Fri.

The Ardèche

Taking its name from the river that makes its way through the *département,* this area, nestled between Lyon and Avignon, is full of geological and archaeological wonders. It's sunny year-round, as it is throughout the Rhône-Alps, but prices are lower in this deeply rural region. The Ardèche has retained its French character, and Anglophones are something of a rarity, so pack your phrasebook. Also prepare for a sparser selection of restaurants here, compared to other parts of France.

> *The largest natural arch in Europe, the pont d'Arc is a fine spot for a quick splash.*

START Privas is 40km (25 miles) southwest of Valence. **TRIP LENGTH** About 4–5 days; 85km (53 miles).

1 Privas. With a population of only 9,000, Privas, prefecture of the Ardèche, is the second-smallest administrative center of any *département* in France. What it lacks in size, however, it makes up for in historical significance: The Protestant town's inhabitants fought to the death in France's bloody Wars of Religion, and in 1629 the town was virtually destroyed in a siege. Two

15th-century remnants include the **Tour Diane Poitiers** on place de la République and the **Louis XIII bridge** over the Ouvèze, one of the town's three rivers. You'll soon realize that chestnuts are the main industry here. In autumn they litter the streets, and in October the **Castagnades d'Autumne festival** celebrates this fruit that sustained the Huguenots and *Résistants* during World War II. You'll find chestnut spreads, chestnut spice breads, chestnut liqueurs, and chestnut sausages on sale at the Saturday market, and the chestnut is ubiquitous on

1. Privas
2. Vogüé
3. Joyeuse
4. Vallon-Pont-d'Arc

> *The gorgeous village of Vogüé tumbles into the Ardèche River.*

restaurant menus. On the edge of the **Parc Naturel Régional des Monts d'Ardèche,** Privas is a perfect starting point for hiking, dog sledding, snowshoeing (in season), canyoning, and rock climbing; several shops sell and rent equipment. ⏱ 1 day (or 2 days if you add a hike). Privas Tourist Office, 3 place Général de Gaulle. ☎ 04-75-64-33-35. www.paysdeprivas.com.

Vogüé is 39km (24 miles) southwest of Privas via N304 (to Aubenas) and D579.

❷ ★★ **Vogüé.** One of the most beautiful villages in France (certified by its "Les Plus Beaux Villages de France" label), this riverfront settlement is best known for its magnificently preserved **Château de Vogüé** (☎ 04-75-37-01-95; www.chateaudevogue.net; admission 4€ adults, 2€ reduced; Apr–Nov Wed–Sun 10:30am–12:30pm and 2–6pm, closed Dec–Mar), a former medieval fort that became a château in the 17th century. The castle grounds encompass hanging gardens; a Romanesque chapel with stained-glass windows; the Hall of Vogüé, which details the lineage of the local marquis's family; a dungeon; and a fine-arts museum, with copious paintings, sculptures, engravings, and more. The village is a great place to have a relaxing lunch, with river views and an enormous castle at your back. ⏱ 1 day.

Vogüé Tourist Office, place de Heyd. ☎ 04-75-37-01-17. www.ot-vogue.com.

Joyeuse is 21km (13 miles) southwest of Vogüé. For the more scenic route, follow the Ardèche south on D579 to Ruoms, and turn right onto D4 and left onto D104.

❸ ★ **Joyeuse.** Named for the famed sword of Charlemagne, this fortified town could have put the "picture" in picturesque, with its stone houses and cobbled streets perched high on a hill overlooking the river. Ramparts and stout defensive walls surround the Renaissance-style **Château de Joyeuse** (www.chateau-des-ducs.com), which now serves as the City Hall. Joyeuse's main gifts to the world are its supremely cultivated chestnut trees, celebrated at the **Musée de la Chataîgneraie** (Chestnut Museum). Joyeuse has several other museums, including the superb **Eglise St-Pierre,** as well as outstanding architecture. It's also an excellent place to shop, with plenty of artisans working in leather, jewelry, and silk. ⏱ 1 day. www.joyeuse.fr.

Vallon-Pont-d'Arc is 25km (16 miles) east of Joyeuse via Ruoms on well-signed roads.

❹ ★★ Vallon-Pont-d'Arc. The most famous landmark in Ardèche, and the largest natural

Caves of the Ardèche

The Ardèche is defined by its status as a dormant volcano, which in hotter times forged black basalt cliffs and domes of petrified lava, and burned through the area to create gorgeous waterfalls, vast gorges, and awesome caves. Tourists can visit only seven *grottes* (caves) and *aven-grottes* ("potholes"; different from a cave in that the entrance is vertical and not horizontal), but all are exceptional and unique. The **Aven-Grotte Orgnac** (Orgnac Pothole) is one of the largest in Europe, with 46m (151-ft.) ceilings spanning nearly 3 sq. km (1¼ sq. mile). The **Aven-Grotte de Marzal** features a prehistoric zoo and museum dedicated to caves. The other potholes and caves include the **Aven-Grotte de la Forestière, Grotte de la Madeleine, Grotte de St-Marcel d'Ardèche,** and **Grotte des Huguenots.** Admission to the caves runs between 7€ and 10€; operating hours are roughly 10am to 6pm. All are within a 30km (19-mile) radius of Vallon-Pont-d'Arc.

arch in Europe, the **pont d'Arc** stands 66m (217 ft.) high and spans more than 34m (112 ft.). It's near the town of Vallon-Pont-d'Arc, and serves as the natural entry into the Ardèche and a threshold to the gorges below. Tourists are no longer permitted to cross this natural bridge, but the site is a nexus of prehistoric and cultural significance. The town, featuring a mild and almost semi-arid climate, comes alive in the spring as tourists descend to take advantage of some of the best kayaking and canoeing in France. Pont d'Arc was the site of many battles during France's Wars of Religion, thanks to the area's status as a Protestant stronghold, and losers were often pushed off the arch into the river below. Prior to the internecine Christian wars, as late as the 10th century, the town was continually raided for slaves by Middle Eastern marauders. Little wonder, then, that the Crusades were staffed by area inhabitants, as illustrated by the impressive **Aubusson tapestries** at the **Hôtel de Ville** (Town Hall), 1 place de la Resistance (☎ 04-75-88-02-06; www.vallon-pont-darc.com; admission 2€; Mon–Fri 9am–noon and 2–5pm). In 1994 three explorers came upon one of the greatest finds in modern spelunking, unearthing **Chauvet-Pont-d'Arc Cave,** home to the oldest known cave paintings in the world. Few prehistoric art sites have yielded such treasure: hundreds of animal paintings, abstract art, hand stencils, and (above the painting site) fossilized remains of animals, some now extinct. The art, despite being more than 32,000 years old, is far from crude and can't help but awe the viewer. One reason the paintings are so well preserved is the technological advancement of the artists: They scrubbed the walls clean before painting. The cave is not open to visitors, as scientists are still studying the site, but the **Exposition de la Grotte Chauvet,** 1 rue Miarou (☎ 05-75-37-17-68; www.culture.gouv.fr/culture/arcnat/chauvet; admission 4€; Tues–Sun 10am–1pm and 3–7pm), is an informative experience, thanks to full-scale reconstructions of prehistoric dwellings and animals, more than 70 engravings taken from caves around Ardèche, and an exhibit dedicated solely to Chauvet Cave. ⏱ 2 days, to enable you to visit some of the caves (see "Caves of the Ardèche"). Town Hall, Vallon-Pont-d'Arc. ☎ 04-75-88-04-01. www.vallon-pont-darc.com.

Where to Stay & Dine in the Ardèche

★★ kids **Hôtel Chaumette** PRIVAS *REGIONAL FRENCH* Five minutes on foot from the center of Privas, this 36-room hotel is an ideal base for families, as it has a swimming pool, a game room, and a play area. The owner, Monique Teyssier, has taken a modern hotel and transformed it with a decor inspired by Morocco. The fine local specialties served on the terrace are another pleasure. Av. du Vanel. ☎ 04-75-64-30-66. www.hotelchaumette.fr. 36 units. Doubles 75€–94€. Lunch menu 23€. Fixed-price menus 35€–65€. MC, V. Lunch Mon–Fri, dinner daily.

kids **Hôtel La Falaise** VOGUE *REGIONAL FRENCH* Perched up on the rocks overhanging the Ardèche in the charming village of Vogüé, the restaurant and ice cream parlor here will delight the kids. It's a great location if you're here for outdoor activities in the Ardèche. 1 Grand Rue. ☎ 04-75-37-72-59. 34 units. www.la-falaise.com. Doubles 47€.

★ **Hôtel Relais du Vivarais** VIVIERS *REGIONAL FRENCH* Exemplary local cuisine, such as 8-hour marinated lamb and locally produced Picodon goat cheese, the premiere cheese of the Ardèche, are the main draw here. There are also 5 hotel rooms and a swimming pool. 31 Fauborg des Sautelles. ☎ 04-75-52-60-41. www.relaisduvivarais.fr. 5 units. Doubles 75€–92€. Lunch menu 27€, dinner menu 45€. MC, V. Lunch daily, dinner Mon–Sat.

kids **L'Auberge des Gorges** ST-MARTIN D'ARDECHE Facing the Ardèche River gorges, this hotel is geared toward families looking to play outdoors. Just outside St-Martin-de-l'Ardèche, following signs to Vallon-Pont-d'Arc. ☎ 04-75-04-65-35. www.aubergedesgorges.com. 38 units. Doubles 53€–63€. MC, V.

Le Clos Charmant VALLON-PONT-D'ARC *REGIONAL FRENCH* This cozy country hotel with a lovely terrace restaurant under

the trees serves local specialties. 66 bd. Peschaire Alizon. ☎ 04-75-88-13-36. www.lecloscharmant.com. 9 units. Doubles 65€–68€. Main courses 11€–19€. MC, V. Lunch and dinner daily.

kids **Le Grand Virage** PONT DE LABEAUME In the southern Ardèche, 40km (25 miles) south of Vallon-Pont-d'Arc, this hotel offers spacious and clean accommodation for reasonable prices. Each room has its own terrace. Its family suites are ideal for large families looking for a longer vacation, and there's a brasserie serving basic fare. 1 rue Le Grand Virage. ☎ 04-75-38-05-20. www.legrandvirage.com. 19 units. Doubles 40€. MC, V.

Le Place Gourmande PRIVAS *TRADITIONAL FRENCH* In the heart of Privas, this brasserie offers basic cuisine but excellent chocolates and desserts. 14 place de l'Hôtel de Ville, Privas. ☎ 04-75-64-08-77. www.laplacegourmande.com. Main courses 10€–15€. MC, V. Breakfast, lunch, and dinner Mon–Sat.

L'Ormeau CHALENCON *REGIONAL FRENCH* In a picturesque village 34km (21 miles) north of Privas, L'Ormeau features the twin stars of the region's cuisine: sausages and chestnuts. You'll find plenty of sweet stuff to tantalize your tongue here, and there's a shop selling locally produced preserves. Rue Royale. ☎ 04-75-59-99-57. www.lormeau.fr. Fixed-price menu 29€. V. Lunch Thurs–Mon, dinner Fri and Sat.

Grenoble

As modern a city as you'll find in France, Grenoble is the seat of the Isère *département* and the unofficial "Capital of the Alps." It's known for technology and ski slopes; unless you're here on business, the odds are you've come for the latter. One of the few areas of France with a sizable Protestant population, Grenoble was a crucible of conflict during the country's Wars of Religion in the 16th century. The city retains its northern perspective, due to an abundance of English speakers. It is also known for *les beaux gosses—* good-looking guys—so ladies, consider yourselves warned.

> *Nicknamed* les bulles *(the bubbles), Grenoble's cable cars date to 1934 and hold up to 6 people.*

START Grenoble is 573km (356 miles) southwest of Paris.

❶ ★★★ **Bastille.** For an optimal introduction to Grenoble, ride a **cable car** up to the Bastille for the impressive city view. You can find the cars at quai Stephane Jay, on the left bank of the Isère River, next to the impressive **Jardin de Ville**—a great green space in which to relax for a bit. ⏲ 1 hr. Quai Stephane Jay. www. bastille-grenoble.fr. Admission 6.60€ adults, 4.05€ reduced. 11am–11:45pm (hours may vary).

❷ Cathédrale Notre-Dame. The Roman Catholic cathedral was built between the 12th and 15th centuries, giving it an appealing mishmash of Romanesque, Gothic, and Renaissance elements. The discovery in 1989 of a 4th-century Christian baptistery in the Bishop's Palace has drawn recent attention. ⏲ 30 min. Place Notre-Dame. ☎ 04-76-55-76-68. www.diocese-grenoble-vienne.fr. Free admission. Daily 10am–6pm.

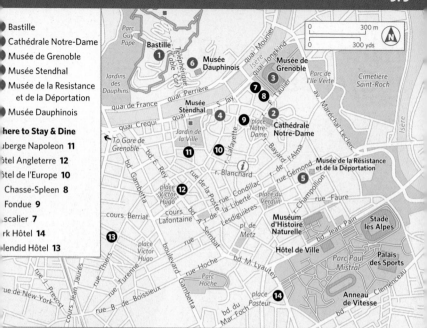

★★★ **Musée de Grenoble.** Grenoble's fine-
rts museum is one of the best in Europe, with
n especially important Egyptian collection.
his museum, which grew from the roots
anted by a tenacious drawing teacher dur-
g the French Revolution, encompasses work
om the Renaissance to the modern era. It has
particularly rich collection of Matisse paint-
gs. ⏱ 2 hr. 5 place de Lavalette. ☎ 04-76-63-
4-44. www.museedegrenoble.fr. Admission
€ adults, free for ages 17 and under. Wed–Mon
am–6:30pm.

Musée Stendhal. Grenoble's favorite son is
arie-Henri Beyle, better known by his pen
ame: Stendhal. Even if you're not particularly
terested in the collection of manuscripts,
ortraits, and rare editions dedicated to one of
e first realist writers, you may be intrigued
y the museum's stunning home in the **Palais
e Lesdiguieres,** full of carved woodwork
nd antique furnishings, which are part of the
storic artisan history of Grenoble. ⏱ 1 hr.
rue Hector Berlioz. www.bm-grenoble.fr. Free
dmission. Tues–Sun 2pm–6pm.

★★★ **Musée de la Resistance et de la Dépor-
tion.** The compelling Museum of Resistance

and Deportation documents Grenoble's
victims of the Nazi Holocaust, and details
the role of the French Resistance in the Vercors region. The museum also dispenses a
self-guided Stendhal itinerary. ⏱ 1½ hr. 14 rue
Hebert. ☎ 04-76-42-38-53. www.resistance-
en-isere.fr. Free admission. Mon 10am–1:30pm;
Tues–Sun 10am–6pm.

★ **Musée Dauphinois.** In the 17th-century
convent Ste-Marie-d'en-Haut, enhanced by
the convent's cloister, gardens, and baroque
chapel, this museum lies on the north side of
the Isère River, unlike most of the city's attractions with the exception of the Bastille.
Ethnographic and historical mementos of the
Dauphine region are on display, along with
folk arts and crafts. No other museum gives
such a detailed view of the people of the Alps,
through furnishings, tools, artifacts, and replicas of Alpine settings. Check out the special
exhibition on skiing, which traces the development of the sport from its origins to the 21st
century's high-tech innovations. ⏱ 1½ hr. 30
rue Maurice-Gignoux. ☎ 04-57-58-89-01. www.
musee-dauphinois.fr. Free admission. June–Sept
Wed–Mon 10am–7pm; Oct–May Wed–Mon
10am–6pm. Closed Jan 1, May 1, and Dec 25.

Where to Stay & Dine in Grenoble

> *La Chasse-Spleen's regional dessert is a Baba Chartreuse, made with Chartreuse liqueur instead of rum and lashings of cream.*

★★★ Auberge Napoleon TRADITIONAL FRENCH
One of Grenoble's best and most celebrated restaurants, the Napoleon is so named because the Emperor spent the night here at the beginning of his 100-day reign that ended at the Battle of Waterloo. Foie gras is served in multiple forms, all of them a delight. Crayfish-and-shrimp cream soup and beef filet in game sauce are other highlights that take their cue from traditional recipe sources. The menus are more reasonably priced than the a la carte options. 7 rue Montorge. ☎ 04-76-87-53-64. www.auberge-napoleon.fr. Main courses 25€–35€. Fixed-price menus 35€–69€. AE, DC, MC, V. Dinner Mon-Sat.

Hôtel Angleterre
Next to place Victor Hugo gardens, the Angleterre is said to have the city center's best view of the Vercors Mountains. Rooms are comfortable, spacious, and soundproofed. The Balneo rooms in the eaves are attractive, with whirlpool baths. Overnight parking, in a nearby underground lot, is free. 5 place Victor Hugo. ☎ 04-76-87-37-21. www.hotel-angleterre-grenoble.com. 62 units. Doubles 115€–185€. AE, MC, V.

Hôtel de l'Europe
An excellent value for the price, the oldest hotel in Grenoble has plenty of historic feel but modern decor in the soundproofed rooms. It's conveniently located just a few feet from the cable cars to the Bastille. 22 place Grenette. ☎ 04-76-46-16-94. www.hoteleurope.fr. 45 units. Doubles 70€–90€. MC, V.

★ La Chasse-Spleen CONTEMPORARY FRENCH
Named after a Médoc wine, with Baudelaire poems printed on the walls and a glass ceiling, La Chasse-Spleen is one of Grenoble's

> The Park Hôtel is near the city center on the edge of Paul Mistral Park.

best-known restaurants. The *nouvelle cuisine* will titillate your taste buds, and there are fine wines for those willing to spend. **6 place Lavalette. ☎ 04-38-37-03-52. Lunch menu 20€. Fixed-price menus 28€–34€. AE, MC, V. Lunch Tues–Fri; dinner Mon–Sat.**

La Fondue *REGIONAL FRENCH*
You know what you're getting with a name like this: cheese—and lots of it. Five types in big vats, to be precise. They also serve *raclette:* roast slabs of meat and cheese. You may want to think about walking home in a roundabout way, to burn off dinner. **5 rue de la Brocherie. ☎ 04-76-15-20-72. Main courses 15€. MC, V. Dinner Mon–Sat.**

★ L'Escalier *REGIONAL FRENCH*
Another local legend, and justifiably so: a peerless location matched with superlative regional cuisine and a refined atmosphere. Ask for the terrace if the weather is fine. **6 place de Lavalette. ☎ 04-76-54-66-16. www.aurestaurant.com. Reservations required. 3-course menu a la carte 32€–65€. MC, V. Lunch Mon–Fri; dinner daily.**

★★ Park Hôtel *GASTRONOMIC*
At the edge of Parc de Paul Mistral, on the first four floors of a mid-1960s tower mostly devoted to private condominiums, this hotel is the most prestigious and opulent in the city. Rooms are considerably more traditional than the Louis 10 restaurant, which glories in an unabashedly Austin Powers '60s decor and serves fabulous traditional French cuisine and raw fish at the sushi bar. **10 place Paul Mistral. ☎ 04-76-85-81-23. www.park-hotel-grenoble. fr. 50 units. Doubles 160€–199€. Main courses 28€–35€. AE, DC, MC, V. Lunch Mon–Fri, dinner Mon–Sat. Tram: A to Chavant.**

Splendid Hôtel
If you want tranquility in the city, choose this family-run hotel with its relaxing garden for alfresco breakfasts. It's a 15-minute walk to the city center. **22 rue Thiers. ☎ 04-76-46-33-12. www.splendid-hotel.com. 45 units. Doubles 59€–75€. AE, MC, V.**

Lyon

The second-largest metropolitan area in France, Lyon is one of the world's great culinary capitals. Even cheap table wine can be pleasing in Lyon, sandwiched as it is between two of France's major wine-growing regions— Beaujolais in the north and Côtes du Rhône in the south. This city is also the cultural center of the Rhône-Alps region, with beguiling architecture, stunning scenery, and a lively history that almost rivals that of Paris. Speaking of rivalries, while the Paris St-Germain soccer squad has fallen on tough times, the success of Olympique Lyonnais has only raised the second city's international status.

> The gracious and stately center of Lyon, with allegorical fountains and Italianate facades.

START Lyon is 467km (290 miles) south of Paris.

❶ ★★★ **Basilique Notre-Dame.** A standout even in a country full of stunning cathedrals, the hilltop Lyon Basilica presides like a fairy-tale castle over the city below. Just like Paris's Sacré-Coeur, whose architectural style it echoes, it was funded by subscription. The Basilique was completed in 1896, as a memorial to the victory of Christian values over the socialist Lyon commune of 1870. It is one of the most-visited sites in Lyon and has become the unofficial symbol of the city. Its design is a rare mixture of Romanesque and Byzantine styles, featuring no fewer than five towers, stained-glass windows, mosaics, and a crypt dedicated to St. Joseph. To get there, take the cable car which leaves from opposite St-Jean Cathedral, at the corner of avenue Adolphe-Max and pont Bonaparte. The **Musée d'Art Sacrée,** adjacent to the Basilica, with an emphasis on representations of Mary, keeps the same hours (admission 5€). ⏱ 2½ hr. 8 place de Fourvière. ☎ 04-78-25-86-19. www.fourviere. org. Free admission. Daily 8am-7pm. Métro: Vieux Lyon.

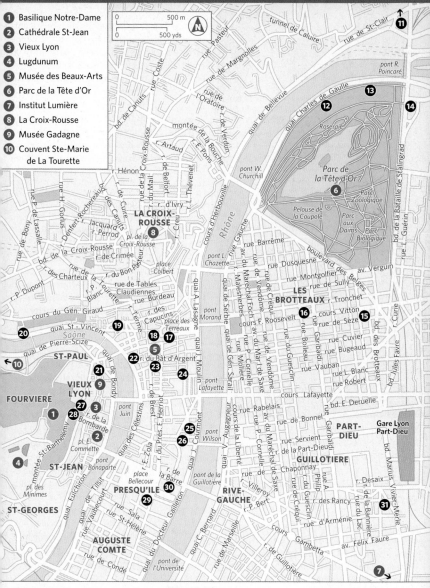

1 Basilique Notre-Dame
2 Cathédrale St-Jean
3 Vieux Lyon
4 Lugdunum
5 Musée des Beaux-Arts
6 Parc de la Tête d'Or
7 Institut Lumière
8 La Croix-Rousse
9 Musée Gadagne
10 Couvent Ste-Marie
   de La Tourette

Where to Stay

Boscolo Grand Hôtel 25

Grand Hôtel
  des Terreaux 22

Hôtel de la
  Cite Concorde 13

Hôtel Saint Paul 14

Le Royal Hôtel 29

Villa Florentine 28

Where to Dine

Chez Mounier 30

Le Bouchon des Filles 19

Le Gourmet de Sèze 15

Leon de Lyon 23

Les Terrasses de Lyon 27

Nicolas Le Bec 26

Paul Bocuse 11

Pierre Orsi 16

Lyon Nightlife

Le Bar Evolution 24

Le Fridge 31

Le Transbordeur 14

New Albion 18

Opéra de Lyon 17

UGC Ciné
  Cité Lyon 12

Yes 20

> *During World War II, the French Resistance used Lyon's traboules (medieval covered passages, ❸) as escape routes and meeting points.*

❷ **Cathédrale St-Jean.** The archbishop of Lyon used to be housed in this cathedral, a mix of Gothic and Romanesque styles, reflecting continuous upgrades from the 11th to the 15th centuries. It's a testament to Lyon's historic influence that the pope granted the archbishop primacy over all the churches in Gaul in the 11th

Getting Around

Lyon's public transportation system, the TCL (Transports en Commun Lyonnais), is excellent, including a subway network of four lines and a tram system. During peak hours, subway trains run every 2 minutes, so be sure to take advantage of the system.

century. The flying buttresses are reminiscent of those in Paris's Notre-Dame Cathedral, but the 12th-century apse at the south end is one of the gems of Lyonnais Romanesque architecture. As you'd expect, the stained glass is excellent. The 14th-century astronomical clock is a mesmerizing treasure; it chimes at noon, 2pm, 3pm, and 4pm, with an attendant rooster crow and herald of angels. ⏱1½ hr. 70 rue St-Jean. ☎ 04-78-54-76-21. www.cathedrale-lyon.cef.fr. Free admission. Mon–Fri 8:15am–12:05pm and 1:45–7:30pm; Sat–Sun 8:15am–12:05pm and 1:45–7pm. Métro: Vieux Lyon.

❸ ★★★ **Vieux Lyon.** Vieux Lyon is divided into several quarters: the **St-Jean Quarter** was the power center, where the **Cathédrale St-Jean** housed the archbishop of Lyon, formerly the most powerful man in northwestern Europe. You'll also find the **Musée Gadagne,** 1 place du Petit College (❾ on this tour), which houses the Lyon Historical Museum and the International Museum of Puppets. The **St-Paul Quarter** was dominated by Italian bankers during the Renaissance, and here you'll find their luxurious residences, called *hôtels particuliers,* such as **Hôtel Bullion.** In this section you'll note the impressive spire of the Romanesque **Eglise St-Paul,** one of Lyon's oldest churches. The **St-George Quarter** is where silk from the East was delicately refashioned for several medieval centuries. If you're fit enough to handle a lot of stairs, twists, and turns, make sure to traverse the *traboules* (passageways), which are an integral part of Lyon's architectural history. These corridors connect building to building, allowing visitors an intimate look at courtyards, galleries, spiral staircases, and hidden alleys. Your hotel will likely offer maps of the *traboules,* but don't miss the winding passage beginning at the door marked 27 rue de Boeuf or the one at 24 rue St-Jean, which takes you to the garden of a 15th-century mansion. For more information on the 230 *traboules* and their five main rounds, contact www.lyontraboules.net. ⏱2 hr. Métro: Vieux Lyon.

❹ ★★ **Lugdunum.** This is the ancient Roman name for Lyon, a city that hails back to 43 B.C. As capital of the province Gallia Lugdunensis, Lyon was the most important city in northwestern Europe for more than 3 centuries. Extensive and well-preserved ruins lie scattered throughout the city; the best is the **Théâtre Antique,** atop Fourvière Hill near the basilica. To reach it take the **cable car,** opposite Cathédrale St-Jean, at the corner of avenue Adolphe-Max and pont Bonaparte. A museum and a theater adjacent to the amphitheater have separate entrances, and the theater is free. The **Musée Gallo-Romain,** 17 rue Cleberg (☎ 04-72-38-49-30; www.musees-gallo-romains.com; admission 7€ adults, 4.50€ reduced, free every Thurs; Tues–Sun 10am–6pm), exhibits a trove of Roman, Celtic, and pre-Roman objects, including jewelry, sculpture, bronze chariots, mosaics, writing implements, and quotidian objects; the miniature scale model of ancient Lugdunum is a special treat. The impressive remains of the outdoor **Amphithéâtre des Trois Gaules** are also atop Fourvière Hill, in the popular **Croix-Rousse** section. Take the cable car back to Vieux Lyon, or amble down via the **Montée St-Barthélemy** footpath to enjoy the hanging gardens. ⊙ 2 hr. Métro: Vieux Lyon.

5 ★★★ **Musée des Beaux-Arts.** Lyon's fine-arts museum contains the largest and most important public art collection in France after the Louvre. It is housed in a suitably beautiful building, the 17th-century former Benedictine abbey of St-Pierre, on the south side of place des Terreaux. Entering through a courtyard graced with statuary and shady trees, you step into a peaceful world where the monastic architecture enhances the meditative pursuit of art appreciation. On the ground floor, admire the statue-encrusted baroque refectory before wandering, in the former chapel, between sculptures from the French Romanesque through the Italian Renaissance to the 19th century. The first floor houses an extensive collection of antiquities, coins, and decorative arts. The second floor is where the paintings are displayed, under glass roofs. Here you'll find Spanish and Dutch old masters as well as Veronese, Tintoretto, and Rubens through to Braque, Bonnard, and Picasso. Look for Joseph Chinard's bust of Mme. Récamier, the Lyon beauty who charmed Napoleonic Paris merely by reclining. ⊙ 2 hr. 20 place des Terreaux. ☎ 04-72-10-17-40. www.mba-lyon.fr. Admission 9€ adults, 6€ reduced. Daily 10am–6pm. Métro: Hôtel de Ville–Louis Pradel.

> Lyon's Roman amphitheater predates the Christian era, but the acoustics are still impressive.

> *You can learn about the origins of cinema and see old cameras like this one at Lyon's Institut Lumière.*

6 ★★ **Parc de la Tête d'Or.** Golden Head Park dominates Lyon and deserves the same status accorded the other great city parks of the world. Modeled on the Bois de Boulogne in Paris, the park dates to 1857 and spreads over 100 hectares (247 acres), making it the largest urban park in France. Check out the **Zoo de Lyon,** the **Jardin Botanique,** or the famed **Jardin des Roses,** with more than 350 varieties of roses and 30,000 bushes. Lyon's ★★ **MAC** (Musée d'Art Contemporain), 81 quai Charles de Gaulle (☎ 04-72-69-17-17; www.mac-lyon.com; admission 8€ adults, 6€ reduced; Wed–Fri noon–7pm, Sat–Sun 10am–7pm), which recalls New York's MoMA (Museum of Modern Art), is also housed in the park, on the northern edge. Try to enter from the southeast corner to enjoy the enormous, wrought-iron **Porte des Enfants du Rhône** (Children of the Rhône Gate), which opens onto a lake with boats for rent during the summer months. Like many other old cities in France, Lyon was not originally built with many green spaces, so expect a lot of visitors in this one. ⏱ 2 hr. Tête d'Or. ☎ 04-78-89-02-03. Mon–Sat 9am–6pm. Métro: Masséna.

7 **Institut Lumière.** The favored sons of Lyon are Auguste and Louis Lumière, credited by some as the inventors of the moving picture. Surprisingly, the brothers Lumière said cinema had no future—a misstep, certainly—but they went on to patent the dominant color photography process of the next several decades. You can see some of their earliest footage at their movie theater, the interactive **Château de Lumière** (Castle of Light). ⏱ 90 min. 25 rue du Premiere-Film. ☎ 04-78-78-18-94. www.institut-lumiere.org. Tickets 6€ adults, 5€ reduced. Tues–Sun 11am–6:30pm. Métro: Sans Souci, Grange Blanche.

8 **La Croix-Rousse.** The historic district of La Croix-Rousse is rich with traces of Lyon's former claim to fame as the silk capital of the world. This once purely proletariat area is now Lyon's chic spot on the hill, full of places to grab a tasty lunch. The factories have relocated, but you can find stores with some of the best silk in the world here. To work off the calories, take a walking tour of the area's fascinating *traboules* (**3** on this tour), keeping in mind that during the 19th century, more than

60,000 people squeezed daily through these narrow streets. ⏲ 90 min. Métro: Hénon.

❾ Musée Gadagne. Reopened in June 2009 to great acclaim after 10 years of renovation, the **Musée Gadagne** in fact houses two museums in a gorgeous Renaissance building: the **Musée d'Histoire de Lyon** (Lyon Historical Museum) and the **Musée des Marionnettes du Monde** (International Museum of Puppets). In the history museum, you'll find interesting Romanesque sculptures, 18th-century

> *Cafe terrace–loving Lyon folk are much more laid back than Parisians, so pull up a chair.*

Lyon's Murals

More than 150 murals liven up the streets of Lyon. A far cry from the amateur graffiti that litters many cities, the rendering of these murals is consistently excellent—in the superb portraits as well as the fantasy scenarios and intricate *trompe l'oeils*—and effective in telling the city's history. Even if you don't take a guided tour, you will no doubt stop in your tracks more than once to admire these exemplary illustrations. Begun in the 1970s and owing a large debt to Mexican muralist Diego Rivera, the paintings are mainly the result of a dedicated artist cooperative. Indeed, you may find yourself attempting to walk through a fake door; some of the murals are painted with faux storefronts and windows with inhabitants peering out, making a blank wall look like any average building. Highlights include the giant bookcase on the Mur des Ecrivains (Writers' Wall) where rue de la Platière meets quai de la Pêcherie and the Mur des Canuts (Canuts' Wall) in the Croix Rousse neighborhood. Few urban beautification projects have been as successful as this one, which lends even more cosmopolitan chic to an already hip city. The best guided tour is run by the **Musée Urbain Tony Garnier,** 4 rue des Serpollieres (☎ 04-78-75-16-75; www.museeurbaintonygarnier.com; admission 6€ adults, 4€ ages 5–16, free for children 4 and under; year-round Tues–Fri and Sun 2–6pm; Apr–Oct Sat 11am–7pm, Nov–Mar 2pm–6pm), but you can also pick up a self-guided tour at the tourist office, place Bellecour (☎ 04-72-77-69-69; www.en.lyon-france.com; daily 9am–6pm), or print up your own from www.lyon-visite.info/murs-peints.

Lyonnais furniture and pottery, antique ceramics from the town of Nevers, a pewter collection, and numerous paintings and engravings of Lyon. The puppet museum has three marionettes by Laurent Mourguet, creator of Guignol, the best-known French puppet character. The museum also displays marionettes from other parts of France (Amiens, Lille, and Aix-en-Provence) and from around the world. ⏲ 90 min. 1 place du Petit College. ☎ 04-78-42-03-61. www.gadagne.musees.lyon.fr. Admission 6€ adults, 4€ reduced. Wed–Sun 11am–6:30pm. Métro: Vieux Lyon.

❿ Couvent Ste-Marie de La Tourette. Modern architecture aficionados may want to make a trip to the suburbs to see the brutally stark Couvent Ste-Marie de La Tourette, designed by Le Corbusier. Finished in 1960 and considered a vital example of late modernist architecture, it's the master architect's last major work in Europe. Eveux-sur-Arbresle. ☎ 04-72-19-10-90. www.couventlatourette.com. Admission 7€ adults, 5€ reduced. 10:30am–6pm daily; tours in English daily at 4pm.

Where to Stay in Lyon

> City life doesn't get better than at Villa Florentine, in a former convent.

★ Boscolo Grand Hôtel PRESQU'ILE

This four-star hotel caters to those who come to Lyon to lap up the luxury. Located next to place Bellecour, with soundproofed rooms, huge chambers, and an Art Deco bar, it's an excellent value for the price. 11 rue Grolée. ☎ 04-73-40-45-45. www.boscolohotels.com. 140 units. Doubles 98€–136€. AE, MC, V. Métro: Cordeliers Bourse.

Grand Hôtel des Terreaux HOTEL DE VILLE

Close to both the Presqu'île and the modern city center, this hotel is an excellent value for the price. All the rooms feature individualized decor, with superb linens, gorgeously tiled bathrooms, and blissfully restful beds. The suites are especially affordable. 16 rue Lanterne. ☎ 04-78-27-04-10. www.grand-hotel-terreaux-lyon.federal-hotel.com. 53 units. Doubles 115€–147€. AE, MC, V. Métro: Hôtel de Ville–Louis Pradel.

Hôtel de la Cité Concorde PARC DE LA TETE

D'OR An alternative to the city center is offered by this hotel bordering the Parc de la Tête d'Or, right beside the Musée d'Art Contemporain. The light rooms, with contemporary decor, have views of the park or the river. Free shuttle service bridges the distance to the city center, 3.2km (2 miles) away. 22 quai Charles de Gaulle. ☎ 04-78-17-86-86. http://lyon.concorde-hotels.com. 164 units. Doubles 175€–225€. AE, DC, MC, V. Bus: C1.

Hôtel Saint Paul VIEUX LYON

This hotel proudly, and accurately, offers four-star services for two-star prices right in the center of Vieux Lyon, making it a great value. The building dates to the 13th century, but the rooms are renovated with gorgeous paintings, marble sinks, and hardwood floors. Owner Dominique Krawczyk speaks perfect English, and he's as helpful as a tour guide. 6 rue Lainerie. ☎ 04-78-28-13-29. www.hotelstpaul.fr. 20 units. Doubles 74€. MC, V. Métro: Vieux Lyon.

★★★ Le Royal Hôtel PRESQU'ILE *TRADITIONAL FRENCH* This grand hotel on the lovely place Bellecour was built by Lyon's most famous architect, Prosper Perrin, in 1888. It is now handsomely decorated in blue or red toile de Jouy fabrics, with gorgeous public areas, too. What makes Le Royal unique is that it is also the Institut Paul Bocuse hotel school, guaranteeing eager and exemplary service and good food at the all-day Côté Cuisine restaurant. 20 place Bellecour. ☎ 04-78-37-57-31. www.lyonhotel-leroyal.com. 76 units. Doubles 190€–250€. Main courses 17€. AE, DC, MC, V. Lunch and dinner daily. Métro: Bellecour.

★★★ Villa Florentine FOURVIERE

This unforgettably beautiful hotel, in a former convent halfway up the Fourvière Hill, between Cathédrale St-Jean and the Basilique, is the pinnacle of luxury, with prime views of the city below. There are so many things that make this hotel exceptional: its Michelin-starred restaurant, Les Terrasses des Lyon (see the restaurant listing); the original frescoes adorning the lobby; the rigorous conservation of the two buildings; the full roster of amenities. Prices aren't low, but they provide an excellent value, all things considered. 25 montée St-Barthélemy. ☎ 04-72-56-56-56. www.villaflorentine.com. 28 units. Doubles €195€–555€. AE, DC, MC, V. Métro: Vieux Lyon.

Where to Dine in Lyon

> *Nicolas Le Bec shook up traditional Lyon when, at the age of 30, he won his first Michelin star for his innovative cuisine.*

Chez Mounier PRESQU'ILE *BOUCHON LYONNAIS* One of the best *bouchons* in Lyon is also one of the cheapest. It's good enough to draw plenty of locals, even though it's located on a street that's popular with tourists. 3 rue des Marron-niers, 2nd. ☎ 04-78-37-79-26. 3-course menu a la carte 20€–30€. Lunch Tues–Sun; dinner Tues–Sat. Métro: Bellecoeur.

★ **Le Bouchon des Filles** HOTEL DE VILLE *BOUCHON LYONNAIS* You'll have no problem finding greasy, heavy food all over town, but this restaurant lends a feminine delicacy to the gen-erally hyper-masculine *bouchon* scene. Its take on local favorites, such as *quenelles* and *croustille de boudin,* renders these dishes superbly light. The restaurant is far from the tourist scene but just two short blocks from the *Fresque de Lyon-nais Celebres (Mural of Famous Lyon Locals),* one of the city's great murals. 20 rue Serg Blandan, 1st. ☎ 04-78-30-40-44. 3-course menu 25€. V. Lunch Tues and Thurs–Sun; dinner Tues and Thurs–Sat. Tram: La Feuillée.

★★ **Le Gourmet de Sèze** GUILLOTIERE *GAS-TRONOMIC* This Michelin-starred restaurant

typifies modern Lyonnaise cuisine, upholding traditional standards but augmenting them with flavors and techniques from other cul-tures. The minimalist decor deflects attention toward chef Bernard Marillier's stunningly flavorful food, made from the best French ingredients, such as shrimp from Lake Geneva, Brittany lobster, or Nantes pigeon. Romantic and intimate, it's a great spot for couples. 129 rue de Sèze, 6th. ☎ 04-78-24-23-42. www.le-gourmet-de-seze.com. Lunch menus 35€; dinner menus 47€–110€. AE, DC, MC, V. Lunch and dinner Tues–Sat. Métro: Masséna.

Leon de Lyon HOTEL DE VILLE *BRASSERIE* Another mainstay of Lyon's culinary scene, this luxuriant *brasserie* serves Lyonnais staples with a modern twist, such as the filet mignon with chorizo sauce. The menu changes six times a year to offer the freshest ingredients, so even if you've eaten here before, it's well worth going again. 1 rue Pleney, 1st. ☎ 04-72-10-11-12. www. leondelyon.com. Lunch menu 20€–24€; dinner menu 28€–36€. MC, V. Lunch and dinner daily. Métro: Hôtel de Ville–Louis Pradel.

★★★ **Les Terrasses de Lyon** FOURVIERE *GAS-TRONOMIC* It's hard to decide what's better here: chef Davy Tissot's *tour de force* spices or the views of Lyon from halfway up Fourvière Hill. With the red rooftops of the city below and the clouds just above, you'll dine on stellar French products, such as Limousin lamb and Dordogne veal, rendered with more exotic delicacies such as coconut, curry, and North African spices. The service is formal and attentive, befitting the kitchen staff's immaculately presented, imaginative creations. The impressive marble floors and other elements of architectural craftsmanship extend from the adjacent five-star Villa Florentine hotel. 25 montée Saint Barthélémy, 5th. ☎ 04-72-56-56-02. www.villaflorentine.com. Main courses 44€–56€. Lunch menus 38€–48€; dinner menus 95€. AE, DC, MC, V. Lunch and dinner Tues–Sat. Métro: Vieux Lyon.

Dining Tip

Traditional Lyonnais restaurants are known as *bouchons* and feature a fatty cuisine, heavy on sausages and roast pork, and an unpretentious atmosphere. The city's gift for gastronomy has also created an intensely competitive, multicultural environment, where famous chefs arrive to vie for the respect of their lucky diners.

★★ **Nicolas Le Bec** PRESQU'ILE *CONTEMPORARY* This eponymous restaurant of a celebrity chef delivers the best, from decor to demitasse. The seasonal menu has only one constant: excellence, whether in the form of traditional Lyonnais sausage-centered cuisine or fusion gems. Le Bec is considered one of the most innovative chefs around. His diverse menu features everything from Angus steaks from Kansas to oysters Gillardeau. 14 rue Grolée, 2nd. ☎ 04-78-42-15-00. www.nicolaslebec.com. Main courses 20€–75€. AE, MC, V. Lunch and dinner Tues–Sat. Métro: Cordeliers Bourse.

★★★ **Paul Bocuse** COLLONGES-AU-MONT-D'OR *LYONNAIS* World-renowned Chef Paul Bocuse's temple of gastronomy has borne three Michelin stars since 1965. Begin your meal with the famous black-truffle soup, and then try one of the most enduring dishes in the Bocuse repertoire: Bresse chicken cooked in a pig's bladder. Or sample the roast pigeon in puff pastry with baby cabbage leaves, or the red snapper served in a potato casing. A boutique sells Bocuse's preferred wine, cognac, jams and jellies, coffees and teas, and cookbooks. 9km (5¾ miles) north of Lyon on N433. 40 quai de la Plage, Pont de Collonges, Collonges-au-Mont-d'Or. ☎ 04-72-42-90-90. www.bocuse.fr. Main courses 48€–84€; fixed-price menu 130€–210€. AE, DC, MC, V. Lunch and dinner daily. Reservations required as far in advance as possible.

★★★ **Pierre Orsi** GUILLOTIERE *GASTRONOMIC* Few chefs are more beloved than Pierre Orsi, whose passion and *joie de vivre* inspire his talented staff, infuse his food, and convey themselves to all his customers. Since 1975 his Michelin-starred restaurant has been offering some of the finest formal cuisine in Lyon. Call ahead for a free tour of his famed wine cellar, featuring more than 20,000 bottles and standouts that include cognac from the Napoleonic era. If you're not impressed by the silver plate cover, which unveils Orsi's delectable creations such as lobster in the shell, then head over to **Le Cazenove,** the chef's Belle Epoque brasserie, which showcases his romance with his Lyonnais roots, at 75 Rue Boileau (☎ 04-78-89-82-92; www.le-cazenove.com). 3 place Kléber, 6th. ☎ 04-78-89-57-68. www.pierreorsi.com. Menus 45€–115€. AE, DC, MC, V. Lunch and dinner Tues–Sat. Métro: Masséna.

Lyon Nightlife

Bars & Clubs

★ **Le Bar Evolution** CROIX-ROUSSE
The trendiest bar in Lyon is packed on weekends with a thronging crowd who come here
to drink designer cocktails thrown by the
showmen behind the bar. The party spills out
onto the huge terrace on summer nights. 10bis
rue de la Bourse, 2nd. ☎ 04-78-39-51-08. www.
evolution-bar.com. Métro: Cordeliers Bourse.

Le Fridge GUILLOTIERE
Burn up the large dance floor here to keep
cool. The music is a mix of danceable oldies,
rhythm and blues, hip-hop, and techno. 67 rue
des Rancy, 3rd. ☎ 04-72-61-13-61. Cover w/1
drink 10€–12€. Métro: Garibaldi.

New Albion HOTEL DE VILLE
One of the first English pubs in Lyon, this
popular hub features a huge selection of draft
beers, big-screen televisions, dartboards, and
a rousing, convivial atmosphere. 12 rue Ste-
Catherine, 1st (1 block north of the Musée des
Beaux-Arts de Lyon). ☎ 04-78-28-33-00. Métro:
Hotel de Ville–Louis Pradel.

Yes CROIX-ROUSSE
The hip Lyonnais chill at this new bar—a hit,
thanks to its intimate vibe, its themed rooms,
and the tight hold the techno deejays keep on

the volume. 12 quai St-Vincent, 1st (along the
river, north of the Basilique). ☎ 06-29-16-14-15.
www.yeshotspot.com. Tram: La Feuillée.

Film

UGC Ciné Cité Lyon PARC DE LA TETE D'OR
Anglophone tourists like to take a break from
French at this cinema with the largest English-
language program in Lyon. Quai Charles de
Gaulle, 6th (north end of Parc de la Tête d'Or,
near the river). ☎ 04-72-69-70-70. www.ugc.fr.
Tram: Musée d'Art Contemporain.

Music

★ **Le Transbordeur** VILLEURBANNE
This club in a converted water station features
two performance stages—one geared toward
local bands, and the other for well-known
acts that pass through Lyon. 3 bd. Stalingrad,
6th (southern border of Parc de la Tete d'Or).
☎ 04-72-50-97-13. www.transbordeur.fr. Tram:
Vitton-Belges.

Opéra de Lyon HOTEL DE VILLE
The best of opera, classical music, jazz, and
dance are performed here in a stunning, modern architectural setting. Tours are offered
daily from 1pm to 6pm. 1 place de la Comedie,
1st. ☎ 04-72-00-45-00. www.opera-lyon.com.
Métro: Hotel de Ville–Louis Pradel.

> *Like a jeweled crown, this glass drum roof by Jean Nouvel caps the original neoclassical structure of the
Opéra de Lyon, from 1826.*

> The winged arches of Santiago Calatrava's TGV station, at the Lyon airport, prepare passengers to fly by train at up to 320kmph (200 mph).

Fast Facts

Arriving & Getting Around

BY PLANE The easiest way to reach the region is to fly into Lyon. From Paris, it is a 45-minute flight to Lyon's **Aéroport Saint-Exupéry** (☎ 08-26-80-08-26), 25km (16 miles) east of the city. **Satobuses** (☎ 04-72-68-72-17) run from the airport into the center of Lyon every 20 minutes during the day. Flights arrive at Grenoble's **Aéroport Grenoble-Isère** (☎ 04-76-65-48-48), 41km (25 miles) northwest of the city center, from London and Bristol (England). You can also fly Air France directly from Paris's Orly airport to the Alps via a small airport in the hamlet of Meythet (near Annecy), **Aéroport Annecy-Haute-Savoie-Mont-Blanc** (☎ 04-50-27-30-06). **BY TRAIN** Lyon is a rail hub that connects to many other cities in the region. If you're arriving in Lyon from the north by train, don't get off at the first station, Gare La Part-Dieu; continue to Gare de Perrache; the high-speed TGV takes only 2 hours from Paris. From Lyon, trains connect to Vienne in 20 minutes; to Valence in 35 minutes; to Bourg-en-Bresse in about 45 minutes; and to destinations in the Alps, including Chamonix (in 4 hr.) and Annecy (in 5 hr.). There is also TGV service from Paris's Gare de Lyon to Bourg-en-Bresse (2 hr.), Grenoble (3½ hr.), Aix-les-Bains (4½ hr.), Annecy (5 hr.), and Chamonix (7 hr.). Annecy is a train hub that connects many towns in the Alps, including Aix-les-Bains and Evian-les-Bains. For train information and schedules, call ☎ 36-35 or 08-92-35-35-35, or visit www.voyages-sncf.com. **BY CAR IN THE RHONE** A car is useful for getting around the Rhône. To reach Lyon from Paris, head southeast on A8/E1 into Lyon; from Grenoble or the French Alps, head northwest on A48 to A43, which will take you northwest into Lyon. From Lyon, you can drive to Pérouges (take rte. 84 northeast and exit near Meximieux), Bourg-en-Bresse (take A42 or N83), Vienne (take N7 or A7), or Valence (take A7 south). **BY CAR IN THE ALPS** A car is useful but not essential in the Alps, as most of the towns are well-connected by rail or bus. If you're driving from Paris, you can reach **Annecy** (take A6 southeast to Beaune and connect with A6/N6 south to Mâcon-Nord, then follow A40 southeast to Seyssel, connecting with N508 southeast to Annecy; 5 hr.), **Evian-les-Bains** (take A6 south, and look for signs to the turnoff for Thonon-Evian, then follow N5 to Evian; 5½ hr.), **Grenoble** (take A6 to Lyon, and continue on A48 into Grenoble; 6 hr.), and **Chamonix** (take A6 to Lyon, and then take A40 toward Geneva but turn south before the city along A40, which runs to Chamonix). From Geneva, you can reach Annecy in 30 minutes (follow A40W to St-Julien and take RN201 south toward Annecy) and Evian-les-Bains in 50 minutes (take N5 east along the southern rim of the lake).

Internet Cafes

ANNECY Planète Telecom, 4 rue Jean-Jaurès (☎ 04-50-33-92-60). **GRENOBLE** Celsiuscafe.com, 11 rue Gutéal (☎ 04-76-46-43-36; www.celsiuscafe.com). **LYON** Raconte Moi la Terre, 14 rue du Plat (☎ 04-78-92-60-22; www.racontemoilaterre.com).

Post Offices

ANNECY 4 rue des Glières (☎ 04-50-33-68-00). **CHAMONIX** Place Balmat (☎ 04-50-53-15-90). **GRENOBLE** 12 rue de la Republique. **LYON** 10 place Antonin Poncet.

Safety

Lyon and the Rhône-Alps are pretty safe. In an emergency, call 17 for the police, 18 for the fire department or paramedics, and 15 for an ambulance.

Tourist Offices

Municipal tourist offices are listed at the end of the town tour stops throughout the chapter. **ARDECHE CHAMBER OF COMMERCE** Chemin La Temple BP 215, Aubenas (☎ 04-75-35-85-00; www.ardeche-tourisme.com). **DROME** 8 rue Baudin, Valence (☎ 04-75-82-19-26; www.drome-tourism.com). **GRENOBLE** 14 rue de la République (☎ 04-76-42-41-41; www.grenoble-isere-tourisme.com). **LYON** place Bellecour (☎ 04-72-77-69-69; www.lyon-france.com). **RHONE-ALPS** 8 rue Paul Montrochet, Lyon (☎ 04-26-73-31-59; www.rhonealpes-tourisme.com).

Favorite Moments in Provence

Inland Provence is a wondrous region graced by fields of lavender, Roman ruins, sun-drenched olive groves, sloping vineyards, and medieval villages. It woos you on its coastline too, with sandy beach resorts, gastronomic restaurants, and the clear waters of the Mediterranean. Then there's the Camargue, where the Rhône River meets the sea; it's a stunning region, with its rice paddies, salt marshes, white horses, black bulls, and pink flamingos. It is this landscape that has inspired generations of artists and continues to attract visitors from all over the world today. Here are some of our favorite Provençal moments.

> *PREVIOUS PAGE Medieval Gordes, cascading down a foothill of the Vaucluse Mountains, has withstood the Plague, two earthquakes, and bombing during World War II. THIS PAGE Le Miramar's scrumptious bouillabaisse is best enjoyed alfresco.*

① **Visiting the Roman Arena in Nîmes.** Even if you've seen Roman Arles, you'll be bowled over by the grand fortitude of Nîmes's 1st-century amphitheater, built to stage bloody gladiatorial battles and chariot racing. It's a marvel of ancient civil engineering. See p. 432, **①**.

② **Riding the white horses of the Camargue.** The desolate, marshy flatlands of the Rhône Delta are home to pink flamingos, black bulls, and white horses ridden by salty French cowboys called *gardians*. Saddle up at La Bergerie de Maguelonne or Mas de Peint, and you'll discover a world of rare birds, salt lagoons, and sweeping panoramas that are unreachable by car. See p. 413, **②**, and "A Night with the *Gardians*," p. 415.

1 Visiting the Roman Arena in Nîmes
2 Riding the white horses of the Camargue
3 Experiencing the tranquility of St-Paul-de-Mausolée
4 Ambling through the streets of Avignon at night
5 Tasting Châteauneuf-du-Pape wine
6 Sifting through antiques in L'Isle-sur-la-Sorgue
7 Visiting the Abbaye de Sénanque in bloom
8 Eating bouillabaisse in Marseille's Le Miramar
9 Bathing in the Calanques

3 **Experiencing the tranquility of St-Paul-de-Mausolée.** Vincent van Gogh had himself committed here after lopping off his ear in Arles. The tormented artist whiled away many an hour silently painting the medieval cloisters and monastery gardens. A series of illustrated panels show his paintings on the very sites where he painted them. For fans, it is a moving experience. See p. 395, 2.

4 **Ambling through the streets of Avignon at night.** Pretty by day but even more striking by night, the former papal city comes into its own on a summer evening. Arty cafe patrons flood the streets, and the air rings with lively conversation, lending even medieval alleyways a contemporary sophistication. See p. 422.

5 **Tasting Châteauneuf-du-Pape wine.** France's most famous product grows in the green, vineyard-studded hills around Châteauneuf-du-Pape. When you're driving around the Vaucluse, don't hesitate to pop into one of the many châteaux whose Côte du Rhône wines are among the best the country has to offer. See p. 406, 1.

6 **Sifting through antiques in L'Isle-sur-la-Sorgue.** A bargain is a rarity nowadays, but whether you covet an original Louis XIV chair or just fancy perusing other people's junk in search of hidden treasure, pretty L'Isle-sur-la-Sorgue, with its crystalline river and old waterwheels, is a paradise for antique lovers of every stripe. See p. 408, 4.

7 **Visiting the Abbaye de Sénanque in bloom.** It's possibly the most clichéd symbol of summer in Provence, but that doesn't make the seas of lavender surrounding the 12th-century Cistercian monastery any less breathtaking, especially when approached from Gordes. See p. 409, 6.

8 **Eating bouillabaisse in Marseille's Le Miramar.** As the light shimmers off the old port, grab a table on Le Miramar's sunny terrace, order a crisp white wine, and wait for the bouillabaisse to arrive. This rich, ancient traditional recipe—made from many kinds of impeccably fresh fish, saffron, and orange zest—is reason alone to visit Marseille. See p. 431.

9 **Bathing in the Calanques.** Explore the hidden splendor of creeks and beaches snuggled against the jagged, white cliffs between Marseille and Cassis. En-Vau, the prettiest *calanque*, is known for its sandy beach and needle-like rock formations. See p. 415, 9.

Provence in 3 Days

From the seaside salt flats of the Camargue to the *villages perchés* spilling down the rocky plateaus of the Lubéron, Provence's landscapes are so varied that you don't have to travel far for a dramatic change of scenery and atmosphere. Yet the region's compact scale is a blessing if you have just 3 days to explore it. This tour covers four requisite stops: Avignon, Provence's elegant cultural capital; the chocolate-box town of St-Rémy and the nearby cloisters where Vincent van Gogh convalesced during his final years; the gravity-defying Les Baux; and Arles, with its Roman vestiges, bullfights, and other strong Provençal traditions that reveal a Spanish twist.

> Avignon's place de l'Horloge (Clocktower Square), near the carousel and the Palais des Papes, is one of the liveliest meeting places in town.

START Avignon is 684km (425 miles) south of Paris, 81km (50 miles) northwest of Aix-en-Provence, and 106km (66 miles) northwest of Marseille. **TRIP LENGTH** 65km (40 miles).

1 ★★★ **Avignon.** Contained within medieval ramparts, beautiful, UNESCO-protected Avignon is easy to explore on foot. Most sites surround **place de l'Horloge,** named after the 15th-century clock that dominates the square. From there, it's easy to reach the fortresslike

kids **Palais des Papes** (Popes' Palace). This Gothic castle was built as the headquarters of Christendom when the papacy fled to Avignon—officially from 1309 until 1376, followed

Where to Stay & Dine

Avignon (see p. 425 for hotel and restaurant recommendations) makes a good base for your first 2 nights, then spend the third night in Arles.

by the reign here of two antipopes that lasted until 1417. Equally emblematic is Avignon's half-fallen, 12th-century kids **Pont St-Bénézet** (Pont d'Avignon), just outside the city walls. The city also has several excellent art museums housing works ranging from medieval times to the avant-garde movements. And there are fine shopping opportunities here. After a meal and a wondrous night of roaming through Avignon's floodlit streets, bed down and then head out early to St-Rémy. ⏱1 day. For detailed information on Avignon, see p. 422.

From Avignon early on Day 2, take N570 (av. de Tarascon) to D570N, cross the pont de Rognonas (bridge), and at the next island, turn left onto D571, which leads to St-Rémy, via Châteaurenard and Eyragues (21km/13 miles).

❷ ★★ **St-Rémy-de-Provence.** Arrive in this affluent, quintessentially Provençal town as early as possible. In the morning, visit the 14th-century **Collégiale St-Martin,** bd. Marceau (☎ 04-90-92-10-51; free admission; daily 9–11am and 3–5pm, but check with tourist office); walk past **Nostradamus's birthplace** on rue Hoche; and explore the 20th-century art collections of the stunning 18th-century **Hôtel Estrine,** rue Estrine (☎ 04-90-92-34-72;

> Wander through St-Rémy's medieval streets to find rue Hoche, where the great seer Nostradamus was born.

> *If you're in Les Baux with kids, inquire about the medieval weapon reenactments that involve contraptions like this mean machine.*

admission 3.20€ adults, 2.30€ reduced; Thurs–Sun and Tues 10am–12:30pm and 2–6pm, Wed 10:30am–6pm). Also worth a look is the 16th-century galleried courtyard of the **Musée des Alpilles,** 1 place Flavier (☎ 04-90-92-68-24; admission 3€ adults, 2€ reduced; Mar–Jun and Sept–Oct Tues–Sat and 1st Sun of the month 10am–noon and 2–6pm; July–Aug Tues–Sat and 1st Sun of the month 10am–12:30pm and 2–7pm; Nov–Feb Tues–Sat and 1st Sun of the month 2–5pm).

After lunch, continue simply exploring St-Rémy, or consider focusing on one of two fascinating options. Take D5 for 1.5km (1 mile) south from town, following signs for *"les antiques,"* to the nearby Gallo-Roman ruins at **Glanum** (av. van Gogh/Rte. des Baux; ☎ 04-90-92-23-79; http://glanum.monuments-nationaux.fr; admission 7€ adults, 4.50€ reduced; Apr–Sept daily 10am–6:30pm, Oct–Mar Tues–Sun 10:30am–5pm). Alternatively, van Gogh fans will not want to miss the **St-Paul-de-Mausolée** monastery, where the artist convalesced and painted some of his best-loved works during the final year of his life, north of Glanum on D5 (av. van Gogh; ☎ 04-90-92-77-00; www.cloitresaintpaul-valetudo.com; admission 5€ adults, 3.50€ reduced, free for children 11 and under; Apr–Oct daily 9:30am–7pm, Nov–Mar daily 10:30am–4:45pm). ⊙ Half-day. St-Rémy Tourist Office, place Jean Jaurès. ☎ 04-90-92-05-22. www.saintremy-de-provence.com.

Drive to Les Baux in the midafternoon: Take D5 from St-Rémy for 6km (3¾ miles), then turn right onto D27 to Les Baux (10km/6¼ miles total).

❸ ★ **Les Baux.** Wander in awe through the center of this medieval engineering marvel, tee-tering on a steep, bare-bauxite ridge. Les Baux is small, so even if you arrive in the late afternoon, you'll have time to see the former **Hôtel de Ville** (city hall and 16th-century chapel); the 12th-century **Eglise St-Vincent,** a church with stained glass windows by Max Ingrand; the present city hall in the **Hôtel de Manville;** and **place St-Vincent,** which affords panoramas over the Fontaine valley, Les Alpilles mountain range, and Val d'Enfer (Hell's Valley). If you have the time and can bear the crowds, don't miss the sunset from place St-Vincent.

Baux's ruined chapel, towers, and **citadel** (☎ 04-90-54-55-56; www.chateau-baux-provence.com; admission 7.80€ adults, 5.80€ reduced; daily 9am to sundown) are fascinating, especially when actors in period costume are assailing the buildings with medieval catapults (four times a day, usually at 11am, 12:30pm, 2:30pm, and 4:30pm; check times when you arrive). The village is famous for its olive oils; purist chefs swear that only oils from Baux impart traditional Provençal flavor. **Terre des Huiles,** Grande Rue (☎ 04-90-54-37-62), sells a wide selection. Wine, too, is a specialty here; reds and rosés dominate, but a few whites slip through. To try some of Baux's wines, head to Kids **Château Romanin** (☎ 04-90-92-45-87; www.romanin.fr), just outside the village. Its cellar is an eerie troglodyte cathedral. ⏱ Half-day. Les Baux Tourist Office, rue Porte Mage. ☎ 04-90-54-34-39. www.lesbauxdeprovence.com.

At the end of the day head back to Avignon. Rise early on Day 3 and take N570 toward Arles (it is well signposted); at the pont de Rognonas, pick up D570N to Arles (36km/22miles total).

④ ★★ **Arles.** Be prepared for a jam-packed day. Before you visit Arles's Roman vestiges, stop in at the Kids **Musée d'Arles Antique,** Presqu'île du Cirque Romain (☎ 04-90-18-88-88; www.arles-antique.cg13.fr; admission 7.50€ adults, 5.50€ reduced; Wed–Mon 10am–6pm; closed some public holidays), to get a grasp on how Arles would have looked in ancient times. From here, make sure to tour the 1st-century Roman arena, **Les Arènes,** Rond-Point des Arènes (☎ 08-91-70-03-70; www.arenes-arles.com; admission 6€ adults, 5€ reduced; Mar–Apr and Oct daily 9am–5:30pm, May–Sept daily 9am–6pm, Nov–Feb daily 10am–4:40pm), once the site of bloody gladiatorial battles and now the region's leading bullfight venue. Other requisite stops include such ancient landmarks as the 4th-century Roman baths, **Thermes de**

Constantin, rue Dominique Maïsto (☎ 04-90-49-59-05), and the **Théâtre Antique** (Roman theater), rue de la Calade (☎ 04-90-49-36-25; admission 3.50€ adults, 2.20€ reduced; Mar–Apr and Oct 9–11:30am and 2–5:30pm, May–Sept 9am–6pm, Nov–Feb 10am–4:30pm).

Art fans can see the graveyard van Gogh painted, **Les Alycamps,** av. des Alycamps (admission 3.50€ adults, 2.60€ reduced; Mar–Apr and Oct 9–11:30am and 2–5:30pm, May–Sept 9am–6pm, Nov–Feb 10am–4:30pm), and must also visit the **Espace van Gogh,** place du Dr Félix Rey (☎ 04-90-49-37-53; free admission; daily 7:30am–7pm), one of the former Provençal hospitals that sheltered the artist and became a subject of his paintings. The **Fondation van Gogh** is a tribute museum in town, at 24bis Rond-Point des Arènes (☎ 04-90-49-94-04; www.fondationvangogh-arles.org; admission 6€ adults, 4€ reduced; Apr to mid-Oct daily 10am–7pm, mid-Oct to Mar 9:30am–noon and 2–5:30pm). The **Musée Réattu,** rue Grand Prieuré (☎ 04-90-49-37-58; www.museereattu.arles.fr; admission 7€ adults, 5€ reduced; July–Sept 10am–7pm, Oct–Jun Tues–Sun 10am–12.30pm and 2–6pm), includes dozens of works by Picasso, Dufy, and Zadkine. ⏱ 1 day. Arles Tourist Office, esplanade Charles de Gaulle/bd. Craponne. ☎ 04-90-18-41-20. www.tourisme.ville-arles.fr.

> *Horses and crowds fill Arles's Roman arena during the April Feria.*

Provence & the Riviera in 1 Week

With a full 7 days, you can dip down to the Mediterranean coast and still have time to explore the diverse inland regions of Provence. This trip begins in Avignon and takes you into the Roman heart of Nîmes, with its ancient amphitheater; Aigues-Mortes, ensconced by ramparts and salt marshes; Arles, known for its Roman vestiges and bullfights; chichi Aix-en-Provence, birthplace of Paul Cézanne and former capital of the region; and gritty, exotic Marseille, where you will spend 2 days exploring the city and surrounding coastal attractions. For a more leisurely rhythm, you could take up to 2 weeks to cover this route.

> *The Notre-Dame-de-la-Garde basilica presides over the 2,600-year-old port of Marseille.*

START Avignon is 684km (425 miles) south of Paris, 81km (50 miles) northwest of Aix-en-Provence, and 106km (66 miles) northwest of Marseille. **TRIP LENGTH** 253km (157 miles).

❶ ★★★ **Avignon.** At one time Avignon was the capital of not just Provence but all Christendom. Today it remains one of France's important cultural centers, with a world-renowned theater festival. It is also celebrated for its sumptuous town houses, its medieval streets, and the centuries-old children's song *Sur le Pont d'Avignon,* inspired by its tumbledown 12th-century bridge. ⏱ 1 day. For a 1-day itinerary in Avignon, see p. 394, ❶. For detailed information on Avignon, see p. 422.

Exit Avignon via la Porte de l'Oulle, join N100 for 20km (12 miles) to A9, and follow signs to Nîmes, exiting at junction 24 (45km/28 miles total).

❷ ★★ **Nîmes.** Although it's technically outside Provence, within the Languedoc region, Nîmes is essentially Provençal. The city is famed for its **Roman amphitheater,** a two-storied vestige more complete than the Colosseum in Rome; but it also wows crowds with the miraculously conserved **Maison Carrée** (Roman temple); the **Carré**

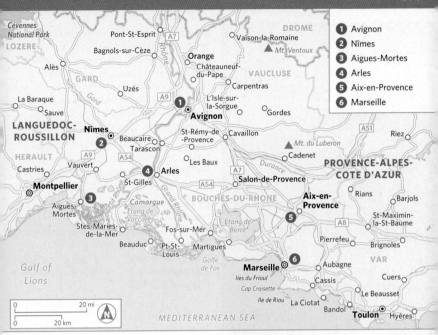

1. Avignon
2. Nîmes
3. Aigues-Mortes
4. Arles
5. Aix-en-Provence
6. Marseille

d'Art, a modern architectural take on the Maison Carrée that houses the contemporary art museum; the stunning **Jardin de la Fontaine,** gardens lined with trees and more Roman and pre-Roman ruins; and the **Castellum,** a Roman water tower. While here, sample the food specialties such as *croquants* (almond biscuits) and *brandade de morue,* a cod-and-potato purée that is one of the region's best dishes. (In supermarkets, authentic *brandade* comes in a tin to take home; the best brand is Brandade Raymond.) ⏲ 1 day. For detailed information on Nîmes, see p. 432.

Leave Nîmes early on Day 3 for Aigues-Mortes: Take A9 toward Montpellier, exit at junction 26, and follow signs to Aigues-Mortes, via N313, D6313, and D979 (42km/26 miles).

3 Aigues-Mortes. This medieval, grid-patterned settlement is spellbinding in the way its ancient battlements and defense towers rise

> In Nîmes's Jardin de la Fontaine, this peaceful ruin, the Temple de Diane, may once have held a Roman library.

Where to Stay & Dine

For hotels and restaurants in Avignon, see p. 425; in Nîmes, see p. 436; in Aix-en-Provence, see p. 421; in Marseille, see p. 431.

> This Vincent Van Gogh painting depicts the room where he stayed in Arles.

simple working salt farm and information center, its awe-inspiring marshes harbor endangered flora and 200 species of birds, including elegant pink flamingos. You could also opt for a relaxing **boat tour** along La-Grau-du-Roi canal. ⏱ 1 day. Aigues-Mortes Tourist Office, place St-Louis. ☎ 04-66-53-73-00. www.ot-aiguesmortes.fr. See also p. 404, **5**.

Head to Arles for the night: From Aigues-Mortes, take D979 and (after Aimargues) D6572, and follow signs to Arles, via D572N, N572, and N113 (55km/34 miles).

4 ★★ **Arles.** Vincent van Gogh once found inspiration in Arles; and it's not hard to see why. This town offers a breathtaking Roman arena and museum, postcard-perfect streets, and cafe terraces galore. ⏱ 1 day. For detailed suggestions on how to make the most of Arles in a day, see p. 397, **4**.

On Day 5, follow N113 from Arles for 19km (12 miles) and pick up A54 near St-Martin-de-Crau; follow signs to Aix-en-Provence via A7 and A8, exiting at junction 30A toward Les Milles (77km/48 miles total).

5 ★★★ **Aix-en-Provence.** This tony spa town was once the home of Paul Cézanne and Emile Zola, whose legacies have helped to shape France today. The town still encompasses the best Provence has to offer: gorgeous 17th- and 18th-century town houses, medieval streets, bustling markets, fine food, thronging cafes, and Roman baths. Once you've checked into your hotel, you can easily spend the day just wandering through the streets. **Cours Mirabeau** is the main drag, dotted with fountains; **rue Gaston-de-Saporta** is littered with shops; and the **Mazarin Quarter** is the peaceful, grid-patterned district of Aix's former bourgeoisie. ⏱ 1 day. For detailed information on Aix-en-Provence, see p. 418.

From Aix, join A8 and follow signs to Marseille, via A51 and A7 (35km/22 miles).

6 ★★★ **Marseille.** Spend at least 2 days in France's fascinating oldest town, the European Capital of Culture 2013. Granted, Marseille has all the undesirable trappings of any big city—crowds, commerce, crime, and car fumes—but it is also home to fabulous monuments, restaurants, bars, cafes, and markets. Marseille's

sharply from the melancholy, salty flatlands of the Camargue. Aigues-Mortes is tiny and easy to cover on foot. Much of its charm comes from narrow streets teeming with art galleries, cafes, and craft shops. As you wander around, look out for the beautiful baroque **Chapelle des Pénitents Blancs;** the 17th-century **Chapelle des Pénitents Gris;** and the **Eglise Notre-Dame-des-Sablons,** a Gothic church once used as a salt warehouse. The ramparts encircle the entire town, but they're accessible from place Anatole France (Porte de la Gardette). You can enter the **Tour de Constance**—a humongous, circular keep once used as a prison. Also look out for the grisly **Tour des Bourguignons,** a 15th-century tower that housed the salted bodies of dead Bourguignon soldiers during the Hundred Years' War.

If you have time in the afternoon, jump into the car and head 3km (1¾ miles) along the route du Grau-du-Roi to the **Salins du Midi** (☎ 04-66-73-40-02). Much more than a

> *From Basilique de Notre-Dame-de-la-Garde's panoramic viewing points, you can see the offshore Frioul Islands (p. 429, ⑩).*

nerve center, its ancient port, crackles with energy and change. Fishing and pleasure boats are crammed in rows like pretty sardines, and the waters are watched over from above by Marseille's emblematic **Notre-Dame-de-la-Garde** basilica, high on a hill. To get the best out of the city, spend the first day downtown, exploring the endless museums, monuments, and districts, each with its own atmosphere. Then on Day 2, head for the coastline. If you don't mind sharing sand with droves of sunbathers, the kids **Prado beaches** foot the bill nicely. Boats frequently leave the **Vieux Port** for excursions to the kids **Château d'If** island fortress and the wild **Frioul Islands. Les Calanques** (p. 415, ⑨), the stretch of picturesque rocky creek valleys between Marseille and Cassis, are truly hypnotic; north of town, **L'Estaque** (see "Top Stops for Art & Architecture Buffs," p. 430) is the fishing port prized by many Impressionist and fauvist painters. ◷ 2 days. For detailed information on Marseille, see p. 426.

A Romantic Stay En Route

Imagine waking up inside a little house on a working, organic vineyard, surrounded by vine-trestled hills blanketed with ripening syrah, cabernet sauvignon, and grenache grapes. Sound tempting? If you want to slow the pace, and there's just the two of you, the **Villa Minna Vineyard**—between Aix-en-Provence and Arles (near St-Cannat) in the shadow of Montagne Ste-Victoire (immortalized by Cézanne)—is the perfect spot for winding down with a few days of romance. There are oodles of walking, picnicking, and cycling opportunities on-site—plus wine tasting, of course, with both red and whites lovingly produced by the friendly owners. *Villa Minna Vineyard, just off D17, Roque-Pessade, St-Cannat. ☎ 04-42-57-23-19. www.villaminnavineyard.fr.*

Provence for Architecture Buffs

As the Roman Empire's first transalpine conquest, Provence has a wealth of ancient architectural wonders. In the Middle Ages, as Christendom took root, a wave of Romanesque abbeys and churches were erected here, followed by structures built in France's own homegrown Gothic style. From the 16th to the 18th centuries, the fortified walls and gates that protected many cities during the religious wars gave way to sumptuous châteaux and classical town houses.

> Gordes—the setting for Ridley Scott's movie A Good Year—has to be one of Provence's prettiest villages perchés (perched villages).

START Vaison-la-Romaine is 56km (35 miles) north of Avignon. **TRIP LENGTH** 228km (142 miles).

1 ★★ kids **Vaison-la-Romaine.** Vasio Vocontiorum (the Roman name of Vaison-la-Romaine) flourished under Roman rule for centuries. Today, in a 15-hectare (37-acre) park below Vaison's pretty, medieval upper town, you can see what's left of the **courthouse** (praetorium) and **temples.** There's also the impressive 1st-century **Théâtre Antique,** with 34 semicircular rows of stone benches that would have seated 6,000. Admission to all sites is 8€ adults, 3.50€ reduced. Times vary. ⏱ 3-4 hr. Vaison-la-Romaine Tourist Office, place du Chanoine Sautel. ☎ 04-90-36-02-11. www.vaison-en-provence.com.

From Vaison, take D938 to Carpentras, and then follow D4 (for 12km/7½ miles), D177, D224, and D15 to Gordes (67km/42 miles total).

Cévennes
National Park
LOZERE

Pont-St-Esprit

DROME

① Vaison-la-Romaine

Mt Ventoux

Bagnols-sur-Cèze

Alès

GARD

Uzés

Orange
Châteauneuf-
du-Pape

VAUCLUSE

Carpentras

L'Isle-sur-
la-Sorgue

③

Avignon

② Gordes

La Baraque
Sauve

LANGUEDOC-
ROUSSILLON

Nîmes

④

Beaucaire
Tarascon

St-Rémy-de-
Provence

Cavaillon

Mt. du Luberon

Riez

HERAULT

Vauvert

Castries

Montpellier

Aigues-
Mortes

⑤

Camargue
Etang de
Vaccares

A54

Les Baux

A7

St-Gilles

⑥ Arles

Cadenet

PROVENCE-ALPES-
COTE D'AZUR

Durance

Salon-de-Provence

BOUCHES-DU-RHONE

Aix-en-
Provence

Rians

Barjols

St-Maximin-
la-St-Baume

A8

Stès-Maries-
de-la-Mer

Fos-sur-Mer

Beauduc

Pt-St-
Louis

Martigues

Golfe
de Fos

Etang de
Berre

Pierrefeu

Brignoles

VAR

Marseille

Gulf of
Lions

Iles du Frioul
Cap Croisette
Ile de Riou

Aubagne

Cassis

La Ciotat

Bandol

Le Beausset

Cuers

Toulon

Hyères

MEDITERRANEAN SEA

0   20 mi
0   20 km

① Vaison-la-Romaine
② Gordes
③ Palais des Papes,
   Avignon
④ Les Arènes de Nîmes
⑤ Aigues-Mortes
⑥ Arles

② ★★ **Gordes.** This chic "perched village" has a fine **Renaissance château** (see p. 408, **⑤**), built on the site of a 12th-century fortress. But Gordes's real intrigue lies along the D2 at the **Abbaye de Sénanque** (p. 409, **⑥**), which, set in a valley of lavender fields, is an almost perfect example of Romanesque Cistercian architecture, with plain windows and barrel-vaulted ceilings. Also fascinating is the nearby **kids Village des Bories** (☎ 04-90-72-03-48), an architectural conundrum from the Bronze Age; its peculiar, corbel-vaulted, dry-stone huts (bories) were used for more than 3,000 years for housing or storage. ⊙ 3–4 hr. Gordes Tourist Office, place Château. ☎ 04-90-72-02-75. www.gordes-village.com.

From Gordes, take D2 to La Coustellet, and then take D900 (for 18km/11 miles), D907 (for 185m/600 ft.), and N7 (near Noves) to Avignon (40km/25 miles total).

③ ★★★ **kids Palais des Papes, Avignon.** The jewel of the Vaucluse capital is the Palais des Papes—a testimony to the immense power of the papacy in the 14th century—built by Popes Benedict XII and Clement VI (1335–52). It soars 50m (164 feet) above the town in a massive ensemble of stone towers and sheer

> The face of this Roman statue is wonderfully pre-served, much like the rest of Vaison-la-Romaine.

Where to Stay & Dine

For hotels and restaurants in Avignon, see p. 425; in Nîmes, see p. 436.

> *Some of the 3,000-year-old stone bories near Gordes were inhabited until the 19th century.*

walls that hide a maze of passages, chapels, and galleries. Two styles reign: Cistercian (from the era of Benedict XII) and Gothic (Clement VI). Their most visible meeting point is in the Cour d'Honneur, with its machicolated conclave wing and irregular gothic openings across the facade. ⏱ 2–3 hr. For detailed information on Avignon, including the palace, see p. 422.

Leave Avignon via the Porte de l'Oulle, pick up N100 (for 20km/12 miles) to A9, and follow signs to Nîmes (45km/28 miles total).

④ ★ **kids** **Les Arènes de Nîmes.** This city's *arènes* (arena) is more complete than Rome's Colosseum and bears two small carvings of Romulus and Remus, the mythological founders of Rome who were raised by a she-wolf. You can still sit on the original stone benches and make out the holes that would have held awning poles that helped shield the crowds from the sun. For an explanation of the origin

Blood on the Sand

The name *arènes* derives from the Latin word for sand, which was used to soak up the blood of combatants in the central oval space, the *vomitorias* (exits), and the corridors.

of the word *arènes*, see the box "Blood on the Sand." ⏱ 45 min. For detailed information on Nîmes, including the arena, see p. 432.

From Nîmes, take A9 toward Montpellier, exit at junction 26, and follow signs to Aigues-Mortes (42km/26 miles).

⑤ ★ Aigues-Mortes. South of Nîmes, this city of the "dead waters" (*aigues mortes* in Provençal) stands alone in the middle of the Camargue's lagoons. Louis IX and his crusaders once set forth from this former thriving port; today it is France's most perfectly preserved medieval walled settlement, with ramparts (1272–1300) punctuated by 10 gates, 6 towers, a watch path, and overhanging latrines. ⏱ 1 day. See p. 399, ③.

From Aigues, follow D979 and cross Aimargues; then turn right onto D6572 and follow signs to Arles, via D6572N, N572, and N113 (55km/34 miles).

⑥ ★★★ Arles. This town, once known as the "little Rome of the Gauls," possesses some of France's best-preserved Gallo-Roman legacies. The 136m x 107m (446-ft. x 351-ft.) *arènes* is a complex structure of arches, corridors, vomitorias, seating for 20,000 spectators, and underground passages for machinery, animals, and gladiators. ⏱ 1 day. See p. 397, ④.

> Beautifully preserved frescoes in
the 14th-century Palais des Papes
in Avignon.

Vaucluse & the Luberon

Villages perchés (perched villages) spring up like mushrooms in the hills of Provence's northernmost region. It's an idyllic, kaleidoscopic landscape, adorned by grape vines and fields of lavender and poppy, and dotted with bountiful village markets. Avignon, capital of the Vaucluse and briefly the seat of Christendom, is a fine cultural center with a world-famous annual theater festival. Some of Provence's best wines come from Châteauneuf-du-Pape, near Avignon. Vaison-la-Romaine is rich with Roman ruins. L'Isle-sur-la-Sorgue is a mother lode for antiques lovers. And don't miss the pretty village of Fontaine-de-Vaucluse, with its mysterious water source.

> *The Sorgue River originates in pretty Fontaine-de-Vaucluse (see "View from the Top," p. 409) and turns the village's waterwheel.*

START Châteauneuf-du-Pape is 565km (351 miles) from Paris and 16km (10 miles) from Avignon. **TRIP LENGTH** 230km (142 miles).

1 ★★ **Châteauneuf-du-Pape.** This village gave the most famous Côte du Rhône wine its name. Some 350 domains now constitute the *appellation contrôlée.* The tastefully restored medieval village rolls up a hill toward the old ruin of the Château des Papes. Built in 1317 by Pope John XXII, who first planted the surrounding vineyards, the castle was destroyed during the wars of religion in the 16th century. But the ruins still commands a wonderful view of Avignon and the surrounding countryside. Besides the pretty streets, the main attraction here is the **Musée du Vin,** Le Clos

(☎ 04-90-83-70-07; www.brotte.com; call in advance to arrange a visit). Its displays are relatively interesting, but the highlight is the tasting at the end of the tour. ⏲ Half-day. Châteauneuf-du-Pape Tourist Office, place Portail. ☎ 04-90-83-71-08. www.chateauneuf.com.

From Châteauneuf, follow D17 to join D507 at the island (2nd exit), and follow signs to Avignon, via D225 (17km/11 miles).

② ★★★ **Avignon.** Stunningly beautiful Avignon is deservedly one of France's top tourist magnets. ⏲ 1½ days. For detailed information on Avignon, see p. 422.

From Avignon, take D225 (Rte. Touristique du Docteur Pons) for 5km (3 miles) and pick up D942 to A7 (toward Orange); exit A7 at junction 22, and follow signs to Vaison-la-Romaine (56km/35 miles total).

③ ★★ **Vaison-la-Romaine.** This town is a symbiosis of ancient Rome, the Middle Ages, and modernity. ⏲ 3 hr. See p. 402, **①**.

Where to Stay & Dine

Avignon (p. 425) makes a good base for this area.

> A wine bar in Châteauneuf-du-Pape, where Pope John XXII planted the region's first vineyard in the 14th century.

Two Beautiful Villages

On your way south, between Vaison-la-Romaine and L'Isle-sur-la-Sorgue, spend an hour in the exquisite, quintessential Provençal village of **Séguret,** where a rabbit's warren of sloping streets lead to a ruined castle that provides sweeping vistas over the peaks of Les Dentelles (p. 409); contact Vaison's tourist office for information (p. 402, ❶). Also worth a detour is **Venasque,** former seat of the Avignon Comtat bishopric, with a baptistery dating fromthe mid-5th to the mid-8th centuries—one of France's oldest religious edifices. *Venasque Tourist Office, Grande Rue. ☎ 04-90-66-11-66. www.venasque.fr.*

From Vaison, take D938 and cross Malaucène and Carpentras (about 30km/19 miles). At the first island join D235, at the second join D49, and at the third join D31 to L'Isle-sur-la-Sorgue (47km/30 miles total).

❹ ★ **L'Isle-sur-la-Sorgue.** This attractive town owes its name to the Sorgue River, whose crystalline source starts at nearby Fontaine-de-Vaucluse (p. 409). Seventy watermills once pressed the grains and oil that made the town so prosperous. Only nine inoperative wheels remain, but the money rolls in from the antiques industry, thanks to 300 or so dealers. Shops are concentrated around avenue de la Libération, avenue des Quatres Otages, and the station, but beware: they're expensive. On Sundays, *brocanteurs* join in, plying their wares along the water's edge. While in town, don't miss the temporary art exhibitions at the **Maison Rene Char,** 20 rue du Dr Tallet (☎ 04-90-38-17-41; www.maison-renechar.fr), a stately 18th-century mansion devoted to the French surrealist poet who was born here. ◷ 3 hr. L'Isle-sur-la-Sorgue Tourist Office, place de la Liberté. ☎ 04-90-38-04-78. www.oti-delasorgue.fr.

From L'Isle-sur-la-Sorgue, head back to Avignon for the night: Follow D938 and D900 (past Les Vignères), then take D907 and N7 (28km/17 miles) into Avignon. The following day, drive to Gordes: Take N7 and D907 (toward Cavaillon for 300m/¼ mile) to D900. Cross Le Coustellet and follow D2, which twists and turns regularly, to the island and then follow D102 for 38km (24 miles) to Gordes (66km/41 miles total).

❺ ★ **Gordes.** Gordes is a startlingly steep "perched village," with prices to match. Its beauty has attracted many a film director—including Ridley Scott, who used the village as the setting for his romantic comedy, *A Good Year,* starring Russell Crowe. Gordes is crowned by the 16th-century **Château de Gordes** (contact the tourist office for information), which houses a collection of Pol Mara paintings. West of Gordes, you should visit the strange kids **Village des Bories** (p. 403, ❷), populated with beehive-shaped, dry-stone huts. ◷ 2–3 hr. Gordes Tourist Office, place Château. ☎ 04-90-72-02-75. www.gordes-village.com.

View from the Top

The Luberon region of the Vaucluse is largely a national park abounding with rocky limestone massifs, crags, gorges, and rolling hills—a fine destination for walking and cycling (see "Hiking Around Saignon & Apt," p. 411). **Fontaine-de-Vaucluse** (on D25) is a pretty village with a waterwheel, decent restaurants, and an eerie panoramic castle ruin. The Sorgue River springs here, in a cascade called the *fontaine* (fountain), but strangely, no one has ever determined the source of the water. Vast white-capped **Mont Ventoux** rises 1,912m (6,273 ft.) above sea level. During the Tour de France, hundreds of professionals huff and puff up the steep slopes to the top. Because it's windy year-round, moisture rarely has time to condense, which means the views from the summit are often unobstructed by clouds. **Les Dentelles de Montmirail** are the region's most picturesque mountains, formed by three chalk ridges topped with ragged crowns; they look more like sharp teeth than the lace (*dentelle*) suggested by their name.

From Gordes, take D15/D177 north, following signs to the nearby Abbaye de Sénanque (4km/2½ miles).

6 ★★ **Abbaye de Sénanque.** In the zenith of summer, this tranquil Cistercian abbey is engulfed by a carpet of perfumed lavender, rendering it one of the most photographed sites in Provence. But the abbey's harmonious yet austere Romanesque architecture, offset by lovely gardens, makes it worth facing the crowds. ⏱ 2 hr. ☎ 04-90-72-05-72. www.senanque.fr.

Return to Gordes and backtrack to Avignon for the night (38km/24 miles). The following day drive to Roussillon: Take D907 to N7 (toward Cavaillon), then rejoin D907 again (for 300m/¼ mile) to D900. Take D900 for 32km (20 miles), turn left onto D149 and drive 48km (30 miles) to Roussillon (86km/53 miles total).

7 ★★ kids **Roussillon.** The ocher soils and strangely eroded red outcrops surrounding Roussillon lend it an otherworldly romanticism. You'll enjoy simply wandering around the peach-colored town center. Note the

> *Gordes's Neolithic beehive bories were likely built as shelters for shepherds and their flocks.*

Fine Dining in L'Isle-sur-la-Sorgue

Le Vivier has food critics across the world raving about its pigeon pie with foie gras and John Dory with artichoke purée. But whatever the season, you won't be disappointed; the food is consistently good. In hot weather, the terrace overlooking the Sorgue is a godsend. *800 Cours Fernande Peyre.* ☎ *04-90-38-52-80. levivier-restaurant.com. Menus 28€–70€. AE, MC, V. Lunch Tues–Thurs and Sun, dinner Tues–Sat.*

> *Dramatic red ocher outcroppings distinguish Roussillon from its neighbors between the mountains of the Vaucluse and the Luberon.*

> *Pretty stone cottages line the sloping streets of Séguret (see "Two Beautiful Villages," p. 408).*

belfry sundial of the Eglise St-Michel. But the real fun is to be had at the Sentiers des Ocres (left of the village cemetery, above the parking area; closed Nov–Mar)—an educational path through an old ocher quarry, taking you past weird and wonderful rock formations. ⏱ 3 hr. Roussillon Tourist Office, place Poste. ☎ 04-90-05-60-25. www.roussillon-provence.com.

From Roussillon, follow D105 and D104, turn right at the island onto D149, right onto D900, left at the island onto D36, and pick up D943 to Lourmarin (26km/16 miles).

8 ★★ **Lourmarin.** Easily one of Provence's most charming towns, Lourmarin is dominated by its hilltop Renaissance château, famed for its chimneys, ornamented with Corinthian columns. The main staircase is a splendid work, ending abruptly with a thin stone pillar and a cupola. Literary buffs might want to visit the town cemetery, where lie the remains of former resident Albert Camus, author of *L'Étranger (The Stranger)* and *La Peste (The Plague).* ⏱ 2 hr. Lourmarin Marie (City Hall), av. Philippe de Girard. ☎ 04-90-68-10-77.

Truffles & Melons

Carpentras contains France's oldest synagogue (from 1367) and has a wonderful winter truffle market. **Cavaillon** is famed for its cantaloupe melons. Although not covered here, both towns are signposted en route.

Hiking Around Saignon & Apt

If you're looking to freshen up your town tours with a dose of country air, consider this 3-hour, 7.5km (4.6-mile), nonstrenuous hike. The charming village of Saignon and the market town of Apt present an ideal opportunity to visit someplace new while taking in the dramatic Vaucluse countryside, including panoramas over Mont Ventoux and the distant, snow-capped Alps. This itinerary is also ideal if you have older children in tow (just make sure they've got the stamina for a 3-hour walk). Some of the trail is on roads, so look out for traffic. Apt dates back to ancient Roman times, when it was a prosperous city. Remnants of its days as a Christian bishopric are also visible in its gorgeous 11th-century **Cathédrale Ste-Anne d'Apt,** which you should visit before you set off. Today the town is loved for its crystallized fruits, jams, lavender essence, and truffles, and for a colorful market that teems with Provençal produce on Saturday mornings.

Park your car in the cours Lauze-de-Perret parking area on the east end of town; from the island, take avenue de Saignon onto D48. Farther along, on your left, take the well-surfaced **Auriane track,** then cross the bridge over the Rimayon River, and as the road sweeps left, go straight ahead along the path that climbs the hill (you can just make out the remains of old terraces). Then follow a tarmac path left for 50m (164 ft.) until you get to the **Ginestière crossroads.** Here,

take the right-hand road for 30m (98 ft.), then go up the track on the left, which turns into a cobbled road leading to the bottom of **Saignon.** Follow D174 right to get to the village entrance, which leads to the pretty **place de la Fontaine** (a square named after its fountain). Saignon is little known by tourists, yet it has no fewer than three château ruins and a wonderful lookout point. To get there, go left down **rue du Bourget** and walk for 100m (328 ft.) to a cobbled path (on the left) that leads to a square by a parking area. At the bottom of the parking area, you'll find the path that winds around the village's ramparts. After the last house, huff and puff your way up the steps to the main castle ruins, and marvel at the vistas from the lookout point. Then go back down and continue around the ramparts, before turning left to join D174. At **place de la Fontaine** again, backtrack to the Ginestière crossroads, but this time head right. After the bend, keeping the Tourel settlement on your left, shortcut the next bend and go straight on. Then continue along the road again for 200m (656 ft.). At the following bend, go left along a dirt track, and head straight through an oak forest, which leads to a residential area. Go straight on again, then cross the old N100, and use the steps to join the cycle path. Keep going, over the Cavalon River; then head up a ramp on the right to follow D22 back to Apt, where refreshments await you.

Bouches du Rhône & the Rhône Delta

Most of the Bouches du Rhône's attractions lie inland, on the Rhône River, which fans into the sea via the saltwater marshes of the Camargue—French cowboy country. In ancient times, the Romans inhabited much of the Rhône Valley; their legacy endures in cities such as Arles, Aix-en-Provence, and Nîmes. Farther inland toward the Alpilles mountain range, St-Rémy is quintessentially Provençal, and neighboring Les Baux teeters atop a rocky outcrop. Back along the coast, Marseille and the fishing town of Cassis are popular destinations, linked by dozens of stony creek valleys and limestone cliffs called Les Calanques.

> The 1st century B.C. Pont du Gard is one of the world's best-preserved Roman aqueducts.

START Nîmes is 127km (79 miles) from Marseille and 719km (447 miles) from Paris.
TRIP LENGTH 7–10 days; 275km (171 miles).

❶ ★★ Nîmes. An incredibly sturdy set of Roman ruins will be the highlight of this tour for many historical architecture lovers. While you're in Nîmes, don't miss the **★★★ Pont du Gard** (25km/16 miles northeast along N86

and D6086), the tallest of all Roman aqueducts (48m/157 ft.). **For detailed information on Nîmes, see p. 432.**

From Nîmes, take A54 (toward Arles), exit at junction 4, and follow signs to Stes-Maries-de-la-Mer, the capital of the Camargue (65km/40 miles).

1. Nîmes
2. Camargue
3. Arles
4. St-Rémy-de-Provence
5. Les Baux
6. Salon-de-Provence
7. Aix-en-Provence
8. Marseille
9. Cassis & Les Calanques

2 ★★★ **Camargue.** Unique to the region in every way, the Camargue has its own traditions—and France's only cowboys, *les gardians.* They herd and care for white horses and black bulls, and live in distinctive, low, whitewashed *mas,* or farmhouses. A haunting, flat region of rice paddies and salt marshes, the Camargue attracts rare birds, including pink flamingos. One of the best places to observe our feathered friends is in the **Parc Ornithologique du Pont-de-Gau,** off D570 (☎ 04-90-97-82-62; www.parcornithologique.com; Apr–Sept daily from 9am, Oct–Mar from 10am; closing time varies by season); more than 400 species of migrating birds visit the park annually. Just 4km (2½ miles) south of here is the region's capital, **Stes-Maries-de-la-Mer.** It is named after the three Marys (Mary Magdalene; her sister, Mary Jacobeal; and Mary Salome, mother of the apostles James and John) who supposedly set sail after the crucifixion, landing with their servant Sarah in Stes-Maries. Their arrival is celebrated in May and October, when residents carry a statue to the sea for a blessing. Worth a visit is the Romanesque **Eglise de Notre-Dame-de-la-Mer.** This gem of a fortified church has a rooftop walkway that affords breathtaking views over the sea and the Camargue plains. The church also contains the three Marys' boat, which locals parade around town during the celebrations. Don't leave the Camargue without visiting **Aigues-Mortes** (p. 399, **3**), 32km (20 miles) west of Stes-Maries (take D570, then go left on D38c and follow signposts). The town's turreted, defensive curtain wall rises gallantly from the flat plains and is especially beguiling at sunset. Built to stave off outsiders, the wall now welcomes them into the town's grid-patterned streets via a series of ancient *portes* (gates).

The best way to fully appreciate the strange beauty of this region is to go off the beaten track, whether on foot or on a bike (ask for maps at the tourist office in Nîmes, Arles, Aigues-Mortes, or Stes-Maries). Or, to ride a white Camargian horse, call **La Bergerie de Maguelone,** D570, Stes-Maries-de-la-Mer (☎ 06-26-39-54-01). Stes-Maries-de-la-Mer Tourist Office, 5 av. Van Gogh. ☎ 04-90-97-82-55. www.saintesmaries.com/us.

Where to Stay & Dine

Nîmes (p. 436), Aix-en-Provence (p. 421), and Marseille (p. 431) make good bases for this itinerary.

From Stes-Maries, follow D570 and N113 to Arles (38km/24 miles).

❸ ★★★ Arles. The Romans left behind an arena, a theater, relics, and ruined baths in this former port town on the Rhône. Vincent van Gogh memorialized its street life, waterfront, and surrounding landscapes when he lived there in the late 1880s. See p. 397, **❹**.

From Arles, take D570n for 15km (9⅓ miles), and turn right onto D99 to St-Rémy (25km/16 miles total).

❹ ★★★ St-Rémy-de-Provence. This quintessentially Provençal market town, dotted with 15th- and 16th-century mansions, was the birthplace of Nostradamus, who later lived in Salon-de-Provence (stop **❻**, below). Van Gogh's presence is felt here, too, in the nearby Monastère St-Paul-de-Mausolée (5km/3 miles along D5), where he convalesced after cutting off his ear in Arles. See p. 395, **❷**.

From St-Rémy, take D5 for 7km (4⅓ miles), and pick up D27 to Les Baux (10km/6¼ miles total).

> *Rising from the Camargue plains, 13th-century Aigues-Mortes is France's best-preserved medieval walled settlement.*

❺ ★ Les Baux. Possibly the most dramatic fortified village in France, Les Baux commands spectacular views across Val d'Enfer and the Alpilles mountains. Just opposite the village stands an old quarry where, in 1822, mineralogist Pierre Berthier discovered bauxite (the principle component of aluminum), naming it after the town. Today, part of the quarry has become the **Cathédrale d'Images,** rte. de Maillane (D27; ☎ 04-90-54-38-65; www.cathedrale-images.com)—a spectacular light-and-sound show inside an old tunnel. See p. 396, **❸**.

From Les Baux, take D27 for 2km (1¼ miles), and turn right onto D5 to Maussane-les-Alpilles. Pick up D17 out of town, rejoin D5 after Mouriès, and at the island, join D113 to Salon-de-Provence (32km/20 miles total).

❻ Salon-de-Provence. Salon's most famous inhabitant was the physician and astrologer Nostradamus, best-known for his celebrated book of predictions, *Les Propheties* (*The Prophecies),* first published in 1555. The house in which the seer spent the last 19 years of his life is now a kitschy waxwork museum, the **Maison de Nostradamus,** rue Nostradamus (☎ 04-90-56-64-31; admission 4.50€ adults, 3€ reduced; Mon–Fri 9am–noon and 2–6pm; Sat–Sun 2–6pm). You can also pay a visit to his tomb, just outside the city wall, in the Gothic **Collégiale de St-Laurent.** Salon is in the shadow of the medieval kids **Château de l'Emperi,** Montée du Puech (☎ 04-90-56-22-36; admission 4.50€ adults, 3€ reduced; Wed–Mon 10am–noon and 2–6pm), which houses an interesting military museum, covering the history of the French army from the reign of the Sun King to 1918. For a taste of life in Salon, head to the shops on **cours Gimon** and the cafes on **place Croustillat.** Salon-de-Provence Tourist Office, 56 cours Gimon. ☎ 04-90-56-27-60. www.visitsalondeprovence.com.

From Salon, follow D538 and A54 toward Aix, then take A7 for 10km (6¼ miles) to A8; exit A8 at junction 31 and follow signs to Aix center (40km/25 miles total).

❼ ★★★ Aix-en-Provence. This former Roman spa town, nestled beneath Mont Ste-Victoire, was once the capital of Provence. Today, it is a chic jamboree of fountains, Renaissance

> *Cassis's fishermen make the most of the low tide to maintain their fishing boats.*

mansions, medieval streets, cafes, restaurants, and boulevards shaded by plane trees. For detailed information on Aix-en-Provence, see p. 418.

From Aix, join A8 and follow signs to Marseille, via A51 and A7 (35km/22 miles).

8 ★★★ Marseille. France's oldest city has been a trading hub and an immigration magnet for millennia. You need at least 2 days to get a feel for the place. Make sure you grab a boat from the Vieux Port on quai des Belges to visit the Île d'If, dominated by the 16th-century fortress that inspired Alexandre Dumas to write *Le Comte de Monte-Cristo (The Count of Monte Cristo)*. For detailed information on Marseille, see p. 426.

The direct route from Marseille to Cassis (30km/19 miles) is along D559. Along the coastline, you will notice the Calanques; access is signposted.

9 ★★★ kids Cassis & Les Calanques. The attractive fishing port of Cassis, sheltered by the Cap Canaille outcrop, is famous for its pretty streets and excellent seafood. A summer resort coveted by artists such as Dufy and Matisse, it continues to inspire artists today. The tourist office can organize guided walks over the spectacular limestone cliffs—Les Calanques—between Marseille and Cassis. They

are the craggy sea edges of a 5,000-hectare (12,355-acre) national park, home to rare flora, fauna, and birdlife. The only calanque fully accessible by car on the Cassis side is Port Miou. It has the longest beach and is nearly always invaded by pleasure boats. Two of the prettiest calanques are En-Vau and Port-Pin (the latter surrounded by pines). At sunset, don't miss the heart-stopping views over the Calanques along the **Route des Crêtes** (take D559 east from Cassis and watch for a signposted road on your right; then turn left at Pas de la Colle). For walking and rock climbing, ask at the Cassis Tourist Office. To see the Calanques by boat, try **Cassis Calanques,** which has a large fleet (☎ 04-42-01-90-83; www.calanques-cassis.com). Cassis Tourist Office, quai des Moulins. ☎ 08-92-25-98-92. www.ot-cassis.com.

A Night with the *Gardians*

White horses, black bulls, and genuine cowboys *(les gardians)* wander around **Le Mas de Peint**—a beautiful 500-hectare (1,235-acre) *auberge* with plush rooms, a gourmet restaurant, and excellent horseback excursions into the Camargue. *Le Sambuc, via D570 and D36.* ☎ 04-90-97-20-62. www.masdepeint. com. 11 units. Doubles 235€–435€. Half-board available. MC, V.

CAMARGUE WETLANDS
The Bouches du Rhône's Salty Inhabitants

BY KATHRYN WILLIAMS

THE VAST PLAIN OF THE CAMARGUE WETLANDS, encompassing the triangular delta between the Rhône River's two branches and the Mediterranean Sea, has been a designated Regional Nature Park since 1970. Dotted with reedy marshes and briny lagoons called *étangs*, the 863-sq.-km (333-sq.-mile) park is a habitat for almost 400 species of birds, including the pink flamingo, and more than 1,000 species of plants. Since the Middle Ages, the region's greatest natural resource has been sea salt, which brought wealth first to the Cistercian "salt abbeys" and since the 19th century to large salt and chemical corporations. Today, the Camargue is a popular destination for sustainable tourism.

PINK FLAMINGOS
An estimated 7,500 to 20,000 pink flamingos nest in the Camargue. The birds get their pink color from carotenoids, pigments found in their algae-and-crustacean diet.

CAMARGUE HORSES
This ancient breed of semi-wild horse is born brown or black but becomes white (or gray, in

horse terminology) by adulthood. Small, at only 13 to 14 hands (about 1.4m/4½ ft.), they are hardy and even-tempered.

CAMARGUE CATTLE

Black Camargue cattle are smaller than other breeds, making them faster and more agile, and thus ideally suited to the Provençal form of bull-fighting known as *courses camarguaises*.

MOSQUITOES

Drawn to the moist, warm climate, 40 species of this pesky insect swarm the delta, inciting heated debate for and against extermination programs.

HUMANS

Gardians are the region's "saltwater cowboys," who corral herds of *manades* (Camargue cattle) over the marshy plain, some of the bulls destined for rings in southern France and Spain. The *gardian* can be recognized by his mount, the small white Camargue horse, and his iron trident on a long staff. These guardians of the native bull and horse populations are also the keepers of traditional Camargue culture. The Camargue has few towns to speak of, beyond Arles to the north, Stes-Maries-de-la-Mer on the sea, and Aigues-Mortes, a popular tourist town in the Petite Camargue to the west. Still, evidence of human intervention is apparent in the region's dams, dikes, saltworks, and rice paddies.

Aix-en-Provence

With its elegant 17th- and 18th-century mansions, graceful fountains, and exquisitely detailed facades, Aix has long inspired artists and writers. Both Paul Cézanne and Emile Zola lived here, and visitors can follow in their footsteps via themed walks organized by the tourist office. For centuries, the University of Aix-en-Provence has infused the town with intellectual energy; today, the large student population congregates on busy cafe terraces, soaking up the sun between classes. Aix is also a renowned spa town, built over a natural spring, and the largest center in France for processed almonds, used to make the delicious local specialty, Calissons d'Aix.

> Ornate mansions from the 18th and 19th centuries attest to the prosperity of Aix, a spa town and former capital of Provence.

START Aix is 80km (50 miles) southeast of Arles and 32km (20 miles) north of Marseille.

1 ★★ **Cours Mirabeau.** This fountain-clad boulevard is lined with 17th-century aristocratic mansions (*hôtels*) famed for their baroque doorways and wrought-iron balconies. The opulent **Hôtel d'Espagnet** (no. 38), whose balcony is supported by giant sculptures of Atlas, reflects the social rise of its former owner, Pierre Maurel, whose booming textile business allowed him to join France's noble classes. Next to passage Agard, you'll find Cézanne's childhood home (now a shop called La Plume d'Or). And at no. 53 stands the **Café des Deux Garçons** (☎ 04-42-26-00-51), the former hangout for Cézanne and Zola. Built over a natural hot spring, Aix has always been associated with water (*aix*, in fact, means "water source"). Some of this hot water issues forth at a steaming 34°C (93°F) on cours Mirabeau at the moss-coated **Fontaine Moussue** (rue de Nazareth and rue Laroque).

2 ★★ **Quartier Mazarin.** Archbishop Mazarin designed this grid-patterned district in the 17th century as a luxury housing estate for Aix's haute bourgeoisie. Today its restful squares and exquisite facades hide art galleries, antique shops, and Aix's first Gothic building, the late 13th-century ★ **St-Jean-de-Malte Priory,** now part of the **Musée Granet** (**3** on this tour). Rue Cardinale and rue du 4 Septembre.

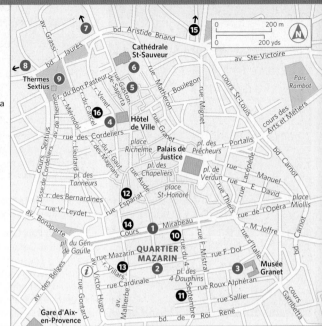

1. Cours Mirabeau
2. Quartier Mazarin
3. Musée Granet
4. Hôtel-de-Ville
   (City Hall)
5. Rue Gaston-de-Saporta
6. Cathédrale St-Sauveur
7. Atelier Paul Cézanne
8. Fondation Vasarely
9. Thermes Sextius

Where to Stay & Dine

Grand Hôtel
  Nègre Coste **10**

Hôtel des
  Augustins **14**

La Villa Gallici **15**

Le Formal **12**

Le Papagayo **16**

Le Passage **13**

28 A Aix **11**

❸ ★ **Musée Granet.** Housed in a former commander's palace, the Palais de Malte (1676), this museum displays major painting collections from the great European schools, including works by Ingres, Rembrandt, and Cézanne. ⏱ 1 hr. Place St-Jean-de-Malte. ☎ 04-42-52-88-32. www.museegranet-aixenprovence.fr. Admission 4€ adults, free for ages 17 and under. June–Sept Tues–Sun 11am–7pm; Oct–May Tues–Sun noon–6pm. Closed Jan 1, May 1, Dec 25.

❹ **Hôtel-de-Ville (City Hall).** The city hall is a 17th-century masterpiece by Pierre Pavillon, with classical pilasters separating the buildings. Outside, the square is dominated by a stunning 16th-century belfry with an astronomical clock, built in 1661 and embellished by four wooden statues that represent the seasons. Place de l'Hôtel-de-Ville.

❺ ★★ **Rue Gaston-de-Saporta.** This former Roman road heaves with shops and sumptuous mansions. Louis XIV stayed at no. 19, the Hôtel du Châteaurenard, in 1660. No. 17, distinguished by elegant Corinthian pilasters, is the stunning **Estienne de St-Jean Museum** (☎ 04-42-21-43-55; admission 4€; Feb–Mar and Oct–Dec Tues–Sun 10am–5pm, Apr–Sept Tues–Sun 10am–6pm), formerly the Musée du Vieil Aix.

> Aix's astronomical clock by the city hall still chimes every hour on the hour.

> The Musée Granet houses the peaceful St-Jean de Malte Priory chapel.

Dating to the 17th century, this former home of the St-Jean family wows visitors with intricate friezes, majestic staircases, paintings, screens, ceramics, and wooden puppets.

6 ★★★ **Cathédrale St-Sauveur.** Built between the 5th and 18th centuries on what was believed to be the site of a temple to Apollo, Aix's lovely cathedral has a 12th-century Romanesque gate joined to a Roman wall. To the north, a huge 14th-century bell tower flanks a richly carved Gothic gate (15th c.–16th c.). Inside, the pillared galleries of 12th-century cloisters cast dramatic shadows on the floor.

Aix's Markets

Aix's vast street markets take over place des Prêcheurs and place de la Madeleine on Tuesday, Thursday, and Saturday mornings. Also on these days, a wonderful flower market showers color onto the square in front of the Hôtel-de-Ville (**4** on this tour), and an antiques fair fills place Verdun. A daily farmers market, selling fresh local produce, sets up beneath the plane trees on place Richelme.

Montagne Ste-Victoire

Once you see it, it's easy to understand why this limestone ridge, 1,011m (3,317 ft.) tall and 7km (4⅓ miles) wide, obsessed Cézanne. He painted it more than 60 times. Picasso, however, got the final word: The Spaniard is buried on the mountain's north slopes at the Château de Vauvenargues, where he lived until his death in 1973. From Aix, Vauvenargues is 15km (9⅓ miles) northeast along D10.

🕐 30 min. Place de l'Université. ☎ 04-42-23-45-65. Free admission. Daily 7:30am–noon, 2–6pm.

7 ★ **Atelier Paul Cézanne.** The major forerunner of cubism, Cézanne lived and worked in this unassuming house uphill from the cathedral. It remains much as he left it in 1906. Here he painted his celebrated *Les Baigneuses* (The Bathers). 🕐 1 hr. 9 av. Paul-Cézanne (head north along rue Pasteur). ☎ 04-42-21-06-53. www.ateliercezanne.com. Admission 5.50€ adults, 2€ ages 13–25, free for children 11 and under. Apr–June and Sept daily 10am–noon and 2:30–6pm; July–Aug daily 10am–6pm; Oct–Nov and Mar daily 10am–noon and 2–5pm; Dec–Feb Mon–Sat 10am–noon and 2–5pm. Closed public holidays.

8 ★ **Fondation Vasarely.** Designed by Hungarian artist Victor Vasarely, this black-and-white metal structure from the 1970s houses his fascinating avant-garde collections, which explore the boundaries between art and architecture. 🕐 1 hr. 1 av. Marcel Pagnol. ☎ 04-42-20-01-09. www.fondationvasarely.fr. Admission 9€ adults, 6€ reduced. Jan–Mar Wed–Sun 10am–1pm and 2–6pm; Apr–Dec Tues–Sun 10am–1pm and 2–6pm.

9 ★★★ **Thermes Sextius.** Aix lies on the site of a 10,000-year-old hot spring, enriched with calcium and magnesium, which served as the baths of Aix's founder, Roman emperor Augustus Sextius, in 122 B.C. If you're feeling flush, pamper yourself at the modern spa, where remains of the original thermal pool are visible at the entrance. 55 av. des Thermes. ☎ 04-42-23-81-82. www.thermes-sextius.com. Basic treatments: 30€–156€. Mon–Fri 8:30am–7:30pm; Sat 8:30am–6:30pm; Sun 9:30am–2:30pm (autumn and winter), 9am–8pm (spring and summer).

Where to Stay & Dine in Aix

★ **Grand Hôtel Nègre Coste** COURS MIRABEAU
This 17th-century townhouse is popular with musicians who flock to Aix for the summer festivals. 33 cours Mirabeau. ☎ 04-42-27-74-22. www.hotelnegrecoste.com. 37 units. Doubles 85€–145€. MC, V. Parking is available.

★ **Hôtel des Augustins** COURS MIRABEAU
History lovers appreciate this quirky hotel—first a 12th-century chapel, then an auberge where Martin Luther stayed after his excommunication from Rome. 3 rue de la Masse. ☎ 04-42-27-28-59. www.hotel-augustins.com. 29 units. Doubles 110€–250€. AE, MC, V.

★★★ **La Villa Gallici** NORTH OF HISTORIC CENTER This relentlessly chic inn has a pool, Aix's finest restaurant (Le Clos de la Violette), and charming rooms richly imbued with the decorative traditions of Aix. Av. de la Violette (impasse des Grands Pins). ☎ 04-42-23-29-23. www.villagallici.com. 22 units. Doubles 230€–945€. AE, DC, MC, V.

★★ **Le Formal** COURS MIRABEAU *FRENCH*
Join food-savvy locals for succulent foie gras, locally produced cheeses, fresh lobster, and a solid wine list. 32 rue Espariat. ☎ 04-42-27-08-31. Menus 36€–65€. AE, MC, V. Lunch Tues–Fri, dinner Tues–Sat.

★ **Le Papagayo** HISTORIC CENTER *SALADS*
Cheap food and copious salads are served with a smile on this bustling, sun-filled square. 22 place Forum des Cardeurs. ☎ 04-42-23-98-35. Menus 14€–18€, salads 10€. No credit cards. May–Aug lunch and dinner daily; Sept–April lunch daily.

★ **Le Passage** QUARTIER MAZARIN *FRENCH FUSION* This converted warehouse combines fun design with great, often organic food, art exhibitions, live music, and even cooking classes. 10 rue Villars. ☎ 04-42-37-09; www.le-passage.fr. Menus 13€–35€; a la carte 40€. AE, MC, V. Breakfast, lunch, and dinner daily (until midnight). Closed public holidays.

★★★ **28 A Aix** COURS MIRABEAU
This chic B&B, set in an 18th-century Aix mansion, has charming rooms richly infused with the decorative traditions of Aix, plus a tearoom, an art gallery, and a decorating workshop. 28 rue du 4 Septembre. ☎ 04-42-54-82-01. www.28-a-aix.com. 4 units. Doubles 200€–500€. AE, DC, MC, V.

An Almond Caress

Try André Genis's divine **Calissons d'Aix.** Legend has it that Good King René of Aix concocted this almond dessert in 1473 to win the trust of his young second wife, Jeanne. Until she was ready, he sublimated his advances with a symbolic, petal-shaped *calisson*—which literally means "sweet caress." *1 rue Gaston de Saporta.* ☎ 04- 42-23-30-64.

Avignon

Once the center of Christendom, Avignon is still one of Europe's most elegant and captivating medieval cities, bordered by the Rhône River and encircled by fortified ramparts. The papacy was headquartered here in the 14th century—an era dubbed the Babylonian Captivity—centered on the Palais des Papes (Popes' Palace). Avignon's city walls encompass architectural treasures, petite but bustling squares, and animated cafe culture. Its festivals, museums, and progressive, contemporary attitude toward film and theater earned it the distinction of being the European Capital of Culture in 2000.

> *Year-round, street performances enliven the place du Palais des Papes, in front of the Popes' Palace in Avignon.*

START Avignon is 37km (23 miles) northeast of Arles and 45km (28 miles) east of Nîmes.

1 ★★★ kids **Palais des Papes.** Dominating Avignon from a hilltop, this 14th-century monument—headquarters of a schismatic group of cardinals who came close to destroying the authority of the popes in Rome—is one of the most notorious palaces in the Christian world. See p. 403, **3**, for more details. ⏱ 1 hr. Place du Palais des Papes. ☎ 04-90-27-50-00. www.palais-des-papes.com. Admission (including audio-guide) 10.50€ adults, 8.50€ reduced. Mar 1-15 daily 9am-6:30pm; Mar 15-June and Sept 16-Oct daily 9am-7pm; July and Sept 1-15 daily 9am-8pm; Aug daily 9am-9pm; Nov-Feb daily 9:30am-5:45pm.

2 ★★★ kids **Pont St-Bénézet (Pont d'Avignon).** Spanning the Rhône, much of this

1 Palais des Papes
2 Pont St-Bénézet
3 Musée du Petit Palais
4 Musée Angladon
5 Rue des Teinturiers
6 Musée Calvet
7 Collection Lambert
8 Villeneuve-lez-Avignon

Where to Stay & Dine

A l'Ombre du Palais 9
Christian Etienne 12
Hiély-Lucullus 13
Hotel de Garlande 14
La Mirande 11
Restaurant Brunel 10

12th-century monument was washed away during floods several hundred years ago. Today it has only 4 of its original 22 arches. On one pier is the two-story Chapelle St-Nicolas—one story in Romanesque style, the other in Gothic. There is also a small space recounting the history of the song *Sur le Pont d'Avignon*. ⏱ 45 min. Pont St-Bénézet. ☎ 04-32-74-32-74. www.palais-des-papes.com. Admission 4.50€ adults, 3.50€ reduced. Mar 1–15 daily 9am–6:30pm; Mar 16 to June and Sept 16 to Oct daily 9am–7pm; July and early Sept daily 9am–8pm; Aug daily 9am–9pm; Nov–Feb daily 9:30am–5:45pm.

3 **Musée du Petit Palais.** Overshadowed by the Palais des Papes, this wonderful museum contains an important collection of paintings from the Italian and Avignon schools of the

---

Money-Saving Tip

Buy a combined ticket for the Pont d'Avignon and Palais des Papes; or get an Avignon Pass (at any attraction) and pay full rate for your first visit, then a reduced rate at all other museums in Avignon and Villeneuve-lez-Avignon.

13th to the 16th centuries, as well as Roman and Gothic sculptures. ⏱ 45 min. Place du Palais des Papes. ☎ 04-90-86-44-58. www.petit-palais.org. Admission 6€ adults, 3€ reduced, free for ages 17 and under. Wed–Mon 10am–1pm and 2–6pm. Closed public holidays.

4 ★★ **Musée Angladon.** Jacques Doucet (1853–1929) was a Belle Epoque dandy, dilettante, and designer of Parisian haute couture. He also collected works of art. He died a pauper, but his former home contains 6th-century Buddhas, Louis XVI chairs, and canvases by Cézanne, Sisley, Degas, Modigliani, Picasso, Max Jacob, and van Gogh. ⏱ 45 min. 5 rue Laboureur. ☎ 04-90-82-29-03. www.angladon.com. Admission 6€ adults, 4€ reduced. Winter Wed–Sun 1–6pm; rest of year Tues–Sun 1–6pm.

5 ★ **Rue des Teinturiers.** Named after the textile workers and dyers who lived here in the medieval era, this cobbled street, shaded by plane trees, is one of the city's most atmospheric spots. Waterwheels still wind while locals relax in cafes, secondhand bookstores, and art galleries.

6 ★ **Musée Calvet.** This wonderful fine arts museum has lovely colonnaded rooms that

> *Displays at the Musée Calvet show the intricate handiwork that went into creating Gobelin's tapestries.*

surround a courtyard. Inside, tapestries by the Manufacture des Gobelins, French paintings from the 18th and 19th centuries, silverware, and clocks make up part of a wide-ranging collection of artifacts, including Impressionist and modern works. ⏱ 45 min. 65 rue Joseph Vernet. ☎ 04-90-86-33-84. www.musee-calvet.org. Admission 6€ adults, 3€ reduced. Wed-Mon 10am–1pm and 2–6pm.

7 ★★★ **Collection Lambert.** Created in 2000 by Parisian art dealer Yvon Lambert, this remarkable gallery presents more than 350 works from several art movements—from minimal, conceptual, and land art from the 1960s and 1970s, to painting from the 1980s, and photography and video from the 1990s. ⏱ 1 hr. 5 rue Violette. ☎ 04-90-16-56-20. www.collectionlambert.com. Admission 6€ adults, 4€ reduced. July–Aug daily 11am–7pm, Sept–Jun Tues–Sun 11am–6pm.

8 ★★ **Villeneuve-lez-Avignon.** This sleepy village opposite Avignon, just across the Rhône, contains some architectural gems built by the pope's cardinals. These include France's largest Carthusian monastery, the **Chartreuse du Val-de-Bénédiction,** rue de la République (☎ 04-90-15-24-24; www.chartreuse.org; admission 7€ adults, 4.50€ reduced, ages 18 and under free; Mon–Fri 9:30am–5pm, Sat–Sun 10am–5pm, extended hours in summer); the hauntingly beautiful **Eglise Notre-Dame,** place Meissonier (☎ 04-90-25-46-24; free admission; Apr–Sept daily 10am–12:30pm and 2–6:30pm; Oct–March daily 10am–noon and 2–5pm), built in 1333; and the **Fort and Abbaye St-André,** Mont Andaon (☎ 04-90-25-45-35; www.abbaye-saint-andre.com; admission to abbey 8€; to gardens 5€ adults, 4€ reduced, free for ages 12 and under; Oct–Mar 31 Tues–Sun 10am–noon and 2–5pm; Apr–Sept 10am–12:30pm and 2–6pm), founded in 1360 by Jean-le-Bon to serve as a symbol of might to the pontifical powers across the river. The region's richest repository of medieval painting and sculpture is housed in the **Musée Pierre de Luxembourg,** 3 rue de la République (☎ 04-90-27-49-66; admission 3€; Oct–Jan and Mar 10am–noon and 2–5:30pm, Apr–Sept 10am–12:30pm and 3–7pm; closed Feb).

Where to Stay & Dine in Avignon

> The Belle Epoque dining room of the Hiély-Lucullus on place de l'Horloge.

A l'Ombre du Palais CENTER
Nowhere in Avignon will you get better views of the Palais des Papes than in this B&B on the main square. Sabine, the friendly, eccentric owner, will cook for you in the evening, too (40€). **6 rue de la Vielle Juiverie. ☎ 06-23-46-50-95. www.alombredupalais.com. 5 units. Doubles 125€–165€. MC, V.**

★★ Christian Etienne PALAIS DES PAPES
PROVENÇAL This 12th-century dining room, still clad in early-16th-century frescoes honoring the marriage of Anne de Bretagne to the French king in 1491, reaches new culinary heights. If you're on a budget, opt for the half-price lunch menu. **10 rue Mons. ☎ 04-90-86-16-50. www.christian-etienne.fr. Reservations required. Fixed-price lunch 31€; fixed-price dinner 65€–125€. AE, MC, V. Lunch and dinner Tues–Sat. Closed early Aug and late Dec–Jan.**

★★★ Hiély-Lucullus HORLOGE CONTEMPO-
RARY FRENCH Stunning Belle Epoque decor enhances grand, innovative cuisine such as St. Jacques scallops in a coconut crust, and lychee mousse served with raspberries and Sauterne jelly. **5 rue de la République. ☎ 04-90-86-17-07. www.hiely-lucullus.com. Reservations required. Fixed-price menu 30€–50€. Menu gastronomique (including wine) 90€. AE, MC, V. Lunch and dinner daily.**

★ Hotel de Garlande CENTER
Near the Palais des Papes and place de l'Horloge, you can't ask for a location more central, nor for accommodations more charming for your money. All 12 rooms are dressed in warm and cozy tones, and the staff are friendly. **20 rue Galante. ☎ 04-90-80-08-85. www.hoteldegarlande.com. 12 units. Doubles 80€–118€. MC, V.**

★★★ La Mirande PALAIS DES PAPES GOURMET
FRENCH This nest of opulence displays 2 centuries of decorative art, from the 1700s Salon Chinois to the Salon Rouge. Rooms are huge, the garden adorable, and the restaurant Avignon's finest. Sign up for cooking lessons with the region's top chefs, who give classes in the vaulted basement kitchens (80€–135€). **4 place de la Mirande. ☎ 04-90-85-93-93. www.la-mirande.fr. 21 units. Doubles 310€–690€. AE, MC, V. Parking 25€.**

★★ Restaurant Brunel CENTER
MEDITERRANEAN A refreshingly modern setting for delectable dishes such as tarte Tatin of tomatoes, duck moussaka, and tasty homemade patisseries. The 15€ lunch menu (a glass of wine, a main, coffee, and cakes) is a particular steal. **46 rue de la Balance. ☎ 04-90-85-24-83. www.restaurantbrunel.fr. Main courses from 11€; menus 15€–32.50€. AE, MC, V. Lunch and dinner Tues–Sat.**

Marseille

France's first city has been a crossroads of culture, trade, and immigration since the Phoenicians founded it in 600 B.C. Today Marseille remains a fast-paced, forward-thinking port where Provençal traditions meet exotic influences from North Africa and the Middle East; it's no wonder the city has been named European Capital of Culture 2013. Flanked by white cliffs and facing the sea, its stepped streets and tranquil squares contrast with bustling 19th-century thoroughfares, souk-like markets, chic shops, and the colorful Vieux Port where fishmongers animate the boat-lined quayside.

> *Fresh cockles, mussels, and other sea creatures are prepared and sold at the fish market in Marseille's Vieux Port.*

START Marseille is 32km (20 miles) south of Aix-en-Provence and 30km (19 miles) west of Cassis.

① ★★★ **Basilique de Notre-Dame-de-la-Garde.** This Romanesque-Byzantine–style church, crowning a limestone mount, is the symbol of Marseille, built by Henri Espérandieu in the mid-19th century and topped by a 9m (30-ft.) gilded statue of the Virgin. Get your camera ready for the sweeping panoramas from its terrace. ⏱ 1 hr. Rue

Fort-du-Sanctuaire. ☎ 04-91-13-40-80. Free admission. Summer daily 7am–7pm; winter daily 7:30am–5:30pm. Métro: Vieux Port.

② ★★★ **Vieux Port.** The histories of Marseille and the Vieux Port are inseparable. Greek-Phoenicians landed here in 600 B.C., taking over a small Celto-Ligurian settlement. In 1666, Louis XIV built two emblematic forts at the harbor entrance. In 1943, most of the restaurant-rich quai du Port was dynamited by the Nazis. The only building to survive was

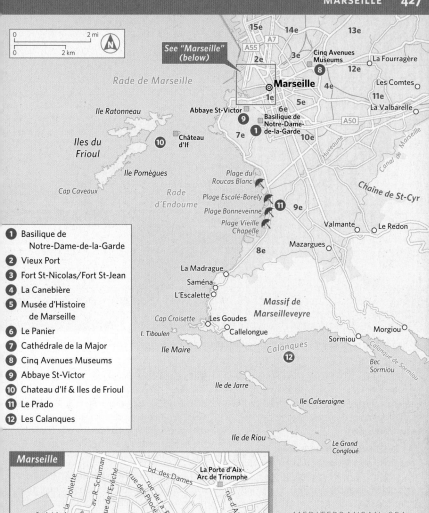

1 Basilique de Notre-Dame-de-la-Garde
2 Vieux Port
3 Fort St-Nicolas/Fort St-Jean
4 La Canebière
5 Musée d'Histoire de Marseille
6 Le Panier
7 Cathédrale de la Major
8 Cinq Avenues Museums
9 Abbaye St-Victor
10 Chateau d'If & Iles de Frioul
11 Le Prado
12 Les Calanques

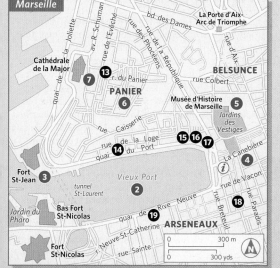

Marseille After Dark
La Caravelle **18**
Opéra de Marseille **21**
Trolley Bus **22**

Where to Stay & Dine
Chez Madie les Galinettes **17**
La Maison du Petit Canard **16**
Le Miramar **20**
Residence du Vieux Port **19**

> *The Sun King reinforced the 12th-century Fort St-Jean at the north entrance of Marseille's Vieux Port.*

the 17th-century La Mairie (City Hall). Every morning from 8am to 1pm, head to quai des Belges and listen to the velvety drawl of Provençal fishmongers hawking their catches. **Métro: Vieux Port.**

3 ★ **Fort St-Nicolas/Fort St-Jean.** The Sun King built Fort St-Nicolas (closed to visitors), near today's Le Pharo gardens, to control the city's defenses and contain rebels. He later reinforced the 12th-century Fort St-Jean, on the north entrance, which is now the MUCEM, a state-of-the-art museum that focuses on Mediterranean civilizations. ⏱ **2 hr.** Fort St-Jean, 201 quai du Port. ☎ 04-96-13-80-90. www.musee-europemediterranee.org. Admission 5€ adults, 3€ reduced. Wed–Mon 1–7pm. Closed public holidays. **Métro: Vieux Port.**

Marseille Tips

A cheap, user-friendly subway (Métro) and modern tramway cover most sites. For a tour with a local, **Marseille Greeters** sets you up with a volunteer who'll show you around his or her neighborhood. Sign up online: www.marseilleprovencegreeters.com.

4 **La Canebière.** Marseille's illustrious thoroughfare, lined with fine 19th-century Haussman-style buildings, was nicknamed "Can a' Beer" by American soldiers during WWII, but the name really stems from *canebe* (canibis), the hemp used to make rigging for boats. **Métro: Vieux Port.**

5 **Musée d'Histoire de Marseille.** Hidden away behind the Bourse shopping mall, this museum and garden (where 1st-century Greek fortifications have been revealed) tells the story of Marseille from prehistory to Gallo-Roman times, through archaeological finds and models. The museum is closed for renovations until Jan 2013. ⏱ **1 hr.** Centre Bourse, square Belsunce. ☎ 04-91-90-42-22. Admission 2€ adults, 1€ reduced. Mon–Sat noon–7pm. Closed public holidays. **Métro: Vieux Port.**

6 ★★ **Le Panier.** The hill on the north side of the Vieux Port is where the Phoenicians first settled, and it has remained a magnet for immigration ever since. The 17th-century Vieille Charité, 2 rue de la Charité (☎ 04-91-14-58-59; www.marseille.fr; admission 3€ for both museums; Oct–May Tues–Sun 10am–5pm,

June–Sept Tues–Sun 11am–6pm; closed public holidays), is a former workhouse; its arcaded galleries contain the Musée d'Archéologie Méditerranéenne (Mediterranean Archaeological Museum) and the Musée d'Arts Africains, Océaniens, et Amérindiens (Museum of African, Oceanic, and Native American Art), France's only primitive arts museum outside Paris. ⏱ 2½ hr. Métro: Joliette.

7 ★★ **Cathédrale de la Major.** This white-and-blue neo-Byzantine beauty, built between 1852 and 1893, was modeled on Saint Sophia of Constantinople and houses the tombs of the bishops of Marseille. Regular organ concerts take place here. ⏱ 30 min. Place de la Major. ☎ 04-91-90-53-57. Daily 10am–6pm (closed some Mon). Métro: Joliette.

8 ★★ **Cinq Avenues Museums.** The stately Cinq Avenues quarter is home to the Second Empire **Palais Longchamp**, 21 bd. Claude Charles Guillaume Philippon (☎ 04-91-55-25-51; www.museum-marseille.org; 4€ adults, 2€ reduced; Tues–Sun 10am–5pm), which contains the Natural History Museum, a fine arts museum, and a pretty park. Its giant fountain symbolizes the Durance River, surrounded by allegories of vine and wheat, on a chariot drawn by bulls from the Camargue. Just over the road, the **Musée Grobet-Labadie,** 140 bd. Longchamp (☎ 04-91-62-21-82; Oct–May

Marseille Shopping

Check out the souk market area on place du Marché des Capucins; then the high-street and designer offerings on rue St-Ferréol, rue Sainte, and rue de la Tour; then head to the quirky boutiques and galleries around cours Julien, a fine, bohemian spot for a coffee break, lunch, or dinner.

> The Panier neighborhood is where the Phoenicians first settled Marseille in 600 B.C.

Tues–Sun 10am–5pm; June–Sept 11am–6pm), is a sumptuous bourgeois home that contains salons, bedrooms, boudoirs, and libraries laden with treasures, including paintings by Fragonard, local painter Monticelli (see "Top Stops for Art & Architecture Buffs," p. 430), and Constable. Métro: Cinq Avenues.

9 ★★ **Abbaye St-Victor.** Founded in A.D. 416, this fortified abbey contains among its crypts that of the Black Virgin, brought out each February 2 in a procession commemorating the legendary arrival by boat of the three Saint Marys. To celebrate this event, orange-flavored cookies in the shape of boats, called *navettes,* are sold. The best are from **Le Four des Navettes,** 136 rue Sainte (☎ 04-91-33-32-12; www.fourdesnavettes.com), the oldest bakery in Marseille, dating from 1731. ⏱ 30 min. Place St-Victor. ☎ 04-96-11-22-60. Admission to crypt 2€. Daily 9am–7pm.

10 ★★★ **Château d'If & Iles de Frioul.** From Marseille's mainland you can see the mysterious silhouettes of four limestone islands: The **Ile d'If** is world-famous for its 16th-century fortress, a fine example of military architecture and the setting for Alexandre Dumas's *The Count of Monte Cristo.* The untamed environment of the Frioul Islands constitutes a refuge for flora and fauna such as sea lavender, the sand lily, and the yellow-legged gull. Summer concerts are held in the Hôpital Caroline on the island of **Ratonneau**—a former hospice for yellow fever patients. **Pomègues** houses the world's first official organic fish farm, and **Port Frioul** accommodates pleasure boats and

> The best way to admire the Château d'If's austere ramparts is by boat, launched from the Vieux Port.

yachts. Make the crossing by boat with Frioul If Express (crossing time 20 min.). ☉ Half-day to 1 day. Quai des Belges. ☎ 04-91-46-54-65. www.frioul-if-express.com. Open all year; times vary (call for details). Métro: Vieux Port.

⓫ ★ kids **Le Prado.** These beaches are where the locals work up a tan. **Roucas Blanc** beach has a bike track, children's play area, volleyball court, and solarium. By day, **Escalé Borely** beach is a fine spot for windsurfing, before it reels in the party crowds at night. The pebbled **Bonneveine** beaches are for water-skiers and sea-scooters, and **Plage de la Vieille Chapelle** (La Vieille Chapelle Beach) has yet more kids' facilities. Métro: Castellane/Rond Point du Prado, then bus no. 19.

⓬ ★★★ **Les Calanques.** Just 15 minutes from the city, you're into the Calanques massif—a stretch of rocky creeks along the coastline between Marseille and Cassis. See p. 415, ❾.

Top Stops for Art & Architecture Buffs

In the 1950s, Le Corbusier changed the face of modern architecture with his **Cité Radieuse,** 280 bd. Michelet (☎ 04-91-16-78-00; www.marseille-citeradieuse.org; Metro: Rond Point du Prado, then bus no. 21S or 22S to Le Corbusier)—a revolutionary 18-story village of 337 apartments, schools, shops, sports facilities, a theater, and a hotel. It can be visited today (check with the tourist office or go it alone) and will thrill amateurs of modern architecture with its artful use of concrete and color. In the northernmost part of Marseille, Impressionist artists flocked to **L'Estaque** fishing port between 1860 and 1920 to paint the eclectic scenery. A signposted walking tour begins at the harbor's jetty. Take bus no. 35 from the Vieux Port; or drive from place de la Joliette to bd. Dunkerque, then onto the Littoral highway and follow the Estaque exit. Don't miss the **Fondation Monticelli,** Pointe de Corbières (5 min. by car on RN568 toward Corbières, just off a parking area on your left; ☎ 06-82-87-69-07; www.associationmonticelli.com; free admission; Wed–Sun 10am–5pm, except public holidays), dedicated to local painter Adolphe Monticelli, who inspired van Gogh.

Marseille After Dark

For a late-night boogie, the **Trolley Bus,** 24 quai de Rive-Neuve (☎ 04-91-54-30-45; www.letrolley.com), plays an eclectic selection of music. Fight for a spot on the balcony at ★★ **La Caravelle**, 34 quai du Port (☎ 04-91-90-36-64), and enjoy the vintage surroundings, a breathtaking port view, and free tapas. For highbrow entertainment, the operas and music concerts at the **Opéra de Marseille,** 2 rue Molière (☎ 04-91-55-11-10; www.marseille.fr; tickets 8€–80€; Métro: Vieux Port), are always top-notch.

> *Outside Marseille, the craggy coves of Les Calanques attract sporty urban hipsters.*

Where to Stay & Dine in Marseille

★ kids **Chez Madie les Galinettes** VIEUX PORT
PROVENCALE Dreamy cuisine, including *ali-bofis* (sweet breads) and fish grilled to perfection. The atmosphere is relaxed so kids feel welcome. 138 quai du Port. ☎ 04-91-90-40-87. Lunch 15€; dinner 22€–28€. MC, V. Lunch Mon–Fri, dinner Mon–Sat. Métro: Vieux Port.

La Maison du Petit Canard PANIER
The "House of the Little Duck" bursts with character. Choose between self-contained apartments or a B&B plan. Hearty meals for 18€ on request. 2 Impasse Sainte Françoise. ☎ 04-91-91-40-31. http://maison.petit.canard.free.fr. 4 independent studios, 1 room. Doubles 60€–80€. No credit cards. Métro: Joliette.

★★★ **Le Miramar** VIEUX PORT *BOUILLABAISSE*
Chef Christian Buffa's bouillabaisse may be the culinary highlight of your trip. 12 quai du Port. ☎ 04-91-91-10-40. www.bouillabaisse.com. Reservations required (48 hr. in advance). Main courses 30€–50€; bouillabaisse from 55€ per person (minimum 2). AE, MC, V. Lunch and dinner Tues–Sat. Métro: Vieux Port.

★★ **Residence du Vieux Port** VIEUX PORT
Decor is based on Le Corbusier's Cité Radieuse (see "Top Stops for Art &

> *Hearty, saffron-tinted bouillabaisse is Marseille's signature dish.*

Architecture Buffs, p. 430") with lots of 1950s-inspired furniture. Eat breakfast on your own balcony overlooking the old port. 18 quai du Port. ☎ 04-91-91-91-22. www.hotel marseille.com. 44 units. Doubles 180€–200€ w/breakfast. AE, MC, V. Métro: Vieux Port.

Nîmes

On the edge of the Camargue plain, the ancient town of Nemausus (Nîmes) grew to prominence during the reign of Emperor Caesar Augustus (27 B.C.-A.D. 14). It possesses some awe-inspiring Gallo-Roman relics, including one of the world's best-preserved Roman amphitheaters, where bullfights now take place. An honorary part of Provence, due to its Provençal atmosphere and culture, the city is technically in the nearby region of Languedoc (p. 510). Spain's influence is also palpable—especially when cafes serving paella and sangría spill onto the streets at night.

> The toreador statue in front of Nîmes's Roman arena is a reminder that bullfights still take place here.

START Nîmes is 51km (32 miles) west of Avignon and 31km (19 miles) northwest of Arles.

① ★★★ kids **Les Arènes de Nîmes.** With its perfect classical proportions, Nîmes's Arena is a more complete amphitheater than Rome's Colosseum. It has two stories, each with 60 arches, and was built of huge stones painstakingly fitted together without mortar. Concerts, ballets, and bullfights now take place where

Romans once staged fearsome gladiatorial combats. ⏱ 45 min. Amphithéâtre Romain de Nîmes. ☎ 04-66-21-82-56. Admission 7.80€ adults, 5.90€ reduced, free for children 6 and under. Mar and Oct daily 9am–7pm; Apr–May and Sept daily 9am–6:30pm; June–Aug daily 9am–7pm; Nov–Feb daily 9:30am–5pm.

② ★★★ **Maison Carrée.** Built during the reign of Emperor Caesar Augustus and consisting of a raised platform with tall, finely fluted

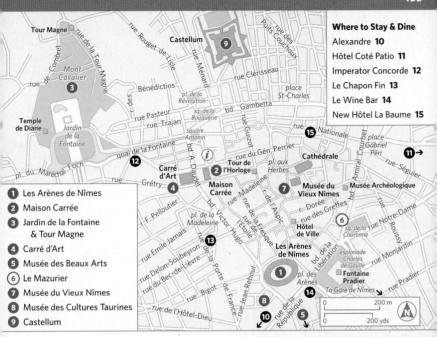

Where to Stay & Dine

Alexandre **10**
Hôtel Coté Patio **11**
Imperator Concorde **12**
Le Chapon Fin **13**
Le Wine Bar **14**
New Hôtel La Baume **15**

1. Les Arènes de Nîmes
2. Maison Carrée
3. Jardin de la Fontaine & Tour Magne
4. Carré d'Art
5. Musée des Beaux Arts
6. Le Mazurier
7. Musée du Vieux Nîmes
8. Musée des Cultures Taurines
9. Castellum

Corinthian columns and friezes of acanthus leaves, this temple is one of Europe's most beautiful and best-preserved Roman structures. It was the inspiration behind Eglise de la Madeleine in Paris (p. 44, ⑧) and today houses art exhibits, presented beneath an authentically preserved roof. ⏱ 45 min. Place de la Maison Carrée. ☎ 04-04-66-21-82-56. Admission 4.50€ adults, 3.70€ reduced, free for children 6 and under. Mar daily 10am–6pm; Apr–May and Sept daily 10am–6:30pm; June daily 10am–7:30pm; July–Aug daily 10am–8pm; Oct daily 10am–1pm and 2–6pm; Nov–Feb daily 10am–1pm and 2–5pm.

③ ★★★ kids **Jardin de la Fontaine & Tour Magne.** The stunning Jardin de la Fontaine (Fountain Garden) is planted with rows of trees; adorned with statues; and intersected by grottoes, canals, and a natural spring that inspired Nîmes's ancient name—Nemausus, after the Roman river god. The grounds

> The stonework preserved on the Maison Carrée, built in 19 B.C., is among the finest of Roman remains in Europe.

encompass the ruined Temple de Diane, Roman baths, and the sturdy bulk of the **Tour Magne** (10 min. north through the park), the city's oldest Roman monument. Climb 140 steps for views over the Alpilles mountains. Admission 2.70€ adults, 2.30€ reduced. Apr–Sept daily 7:30am–10pm; Oct–Mar daily 7:30am–6:30pm.

Money-saving Tip

Buy a combined ticket for the Arena, Maison Carrée, and Tour Magne for 9.90€ (7.60€ reduced).

> *The Tour Magne is the only tower remaining from the original city built by Caesar Augustus.*

4 ★ **Carré d'Art.** Opposite the Maison Carrée stands its glass-and-metal, modern-day twin, where the Musée d'Art Contemporain displays French art from the 1960s to the present. The terrace affords a panorama of most of Nîmes's ancient monuments and medieval churches. ⏱ 45 min. Place de la Maison Carrée. ☎ 04-66-76-35-70. www.nimes.fr. Admission 5€, 3.70€ reduced. Tues–Sun 10am–6pm.

5 ★ **Musée des Beaux Arts.** This early-20th-century building exhibits French paintings and sculptures from the 17th to the 20th centuries, as well as Flemish, Dutch, and Italian works from the 15th to the 18th centuries. ⏱ 45 min. Rue de la Cité-Foulc. ☎ 04-66-67-38-21. www.nimes.fr. Admission 5.20€ adults, 3.80€ reduced, free for children 9 and under. Tues–Sun 10am–6pm; July–Aug Thurs until 9pm; Sept–June 2nd Thurs each month until 9pm.

6 🍴 **Le Mazurier.** Grab a seat at one of the many terrace-cafes on place aux Herbes, just off rue de la Madeleine; or head straight for Le Mazurier, a tasteful Belle Epoque brasserie with a zinc bar and a terrace that inspires France's greatest pastime: people-watching. 9 bd. Amiral Courbet. ☎ 04-66-67-27-48.

7 **Musée du Vieux Nîmes.** Housed in an Episcopal palace from the 1700s, this museum opened in the 1920s. It preserves regional antiques and workday objects from the 18th and 19th centuries in mock-up interiors illustrating daily life in Nîmes. ⏱ 40 min. Place aux Herbes. ☎ 04-66-76-73-70. Free admission. Tues–Sun 10am–6pm.

8 **Musée des Cultures Taurines.** This small museum, in an annex of the Musée du Vieux Nîmes, is devoted to tauromachy (bullfighting) and the role it plays in Nîmes. ⏱ 30 min. 6 rue Alexandre Ducros. ☎ 04-66-36-83-77. Admission 5.20€ adults, 3.80€ reduced. Tues–Sun 10am–6pm.

9 **Castellum.** In rue Lampèze (north of center), archaeologists recently unearthed these remnants of a Roman water tower, which received water from the Pont du Gard aqueduct (see "Bridge to the Past," below). Huge lead pipes, the holes for which are still visible, distributed the water across town.

Shopping in Nîmes

You'll find plenty of spending opportunities on rue du Général-Perrier, rue des Marchands, rue du Chapître, and the pedestrian rue de l'Aspic. At 13 rue de la Madeleine look out for **Maison Villaret** (☎ 04-66-67-41-79), which bakes and sells Nîmes specialty cookies (*croquants*). The covered market in Les Halles (rue des Halles) is open daily from 7am until 1pm. Ironically, it's not the best place to buy jeans. It was a blue cotton textile called *serge de Nîmes*, made here in the 18th century, that came to be called "denim" (literally, "from Nîmes").

Bridge to the Past

Dating to 19 B.C., the **Pont du Gard** aqueduct stands strong, spanning the Gard River, 23km (14 miles) northeast of Nîmes. Its huge stones, fitted together without mortar, form three tiers of arches arranged gracefully into symmetrical patterns. One of the region's most vivid Roman achievements, it is now a UNESCO World Heritage site. Frédéric Mistral, poet and native son of Provence and Languedoc, recorded a legend touting that the devil himself constructed the bridge after being promised that he could claim the soul of the first person to cross it. *From Nîmes, take N86 for 3km (1¾ miles) from the village of Remoulins, and follow signs.*

> Don't miss Nîmes's Musée des Beaux Arts if you're into sculpture and fine art.

Where to Stay & Dine in Nîmes

> Le Chapon Fin is known for its brandade de morue (codfish pie), a specialty of Nîmes.

★★★ Alexandre OUTSKIRTS TRADITIONAL FRENCH Just 8km (5 miles) south of Nîmes, chef Michel Kayser wows the palate with dishes like *île flottante*—a playful, savory variation on the French dessert, with truffles and *velouté* of *cèpe* mushrooms. The dessert trolley and wine list are irresistible. Rte. de l'Aéroport de Garons. ☎ 04-66-70-08-99. www.michelkayser.com. Reservations required. Main courses 28€–54€; menus 64€–134€. AE, DC, MC, V. Lunch and dinner Tues–Sat. Closed 2 weeks in Feb. Take rue de la République southwest to av. Jean-Jaurès; then head south and follow signs to the airport, toward Garons.

★ Hôtel Coté Patio CENTER A 10-minute walk from Les Arènes, this brightly colored, friendly hotel is an excellent value. Rooms are small but modern and airy, and 11 of them open out onto a large patio (hence the hotel name)—a fine spot for breakfast. 31 rue de Beaucaire. ☎ 04-66-67-60-17. www.hotel-cote-patio.com. 17 units. Doubles 63€–77€. MC, V. Parking 9€.

★★ Imperator Concorde CENTER This grand hotel in ancient Nîmes, adjacent to Les Jardins de la Fontaine, has cozy but ample rooms. Order a meal in the verdant rear gardens or in the stately L'Enclos de la Fontaine dining room. Quai de la Fontaine. ☎ 04-66-21-90-30. www.hotel-imperator.com. 62 units. Doubles 130€–250€. AE, DC, MC, V. Parking 13€.

★★ Le Chapon Fin CENTER TRADITIONAL/RE-GIONAL This eating institution's best dishes include foie gras with truffles, casserole of roasted lamb and eggplant, sauerkraut, and a Nîmes specialty: *brandade de morue* (codfish pie). 3 rue du Château-Fadaise. ☎ 04-66-67-34-73. www.chaponfin-restaurant-nimes.com. Reservations required. Main courses 16€; menus 22€–30€. MC, V. Lunch Mon–Fri, dinner Mon–Sat.

★ Le Wine Bar ARENA TRADITIONAL FRENCH Come to this mahogany-paneled place for more than 300 varieties of wine, many of which owner Michel Hermet makes at his family vineyards. Foodwise, expect top-notch beefsteaks and fresh fish. 1 place des Arènes. ☎ 04-66-76-19-59. www.winebar-lechevalblanc.com. Main courses 11€–25€; lunch menu 12€–21€; dinner menu 18€–30€. AE, MC, V. Lunch Tues–Fri, dinner Tues–Sat.

★ New Hôtel La Baume CENTER A magnificent staircase ornaments this 17th-century mansion's interior courtyard, lending it a wonderful sense of grandeur. Guest rooms are hyper-contemporary, decorated in tones of soft reds, oranges, and ochers. 21 rue Nationale. ☎ 04-66-76-28-42. www.new-hotel.com. 34 units. Doubles 140€–260€. AE, DC, MC, V.

Fast Facts

Arriving & Getting Around

BY PLANE All major airlines fly to Paris from the U.S. and the U.K. Once you fly into Paris's Orly or Charles de Gaulle, **Air France** (☎ 800/237-2747 (U.S.), ☎ 0871 66 33 777 (U.K.); www.airfrance.com) covers most destinations in Provence. From Orly and Charles de Gaulle, there are several flights per day to the airports of Marseille (www.marseille.aeroport.fr), Avignon (www.avignon.aeroport.fr), and Nîmes (www.nimes-aeroport.fr). The following airlines also fly directly to the region from the U.K. To Marseille: **Easyjet** (☎ +44/870-6000-000 (from outside U.K.); ☎ 08-99-65-00-11 in France; www.easyjet.com); **Ryanair** (☎ 0871-246-0000; www.ryanair.com); **British Airways** (☎ 0844-493-0-787; www.britishairways.com). To Avignon: **Jet2** (☎ 0871-226-1737; www.jet2.com); **Flybe** (☎ 0871-700-2000; www.flybe.com). To Nîmes: **Ryanair.** From the airports you can hire a car, grab a taxi, or ask about public transport into the nearest town. **BY TRAIN** Direct, high-speed TGV trains from Paris arrive in Avignon (2 hr. 15 min.), Aix-en-Provence (3 hr.), Aix Centre (3 hr. 30 min.; the better option if you're not hiring a car), and Marseille (3 hr. 15 min.). Train travel is one of the most efficient ways to get to the region. Reserve online at www.voyages-sncf.com, or see p. 697. While you can see the main cities by train, you will need a car to explore the heart of Provence's *arrière-pays* (backlands) and quaint villages. **BY CAR** Cars can be hired at most large train stations, from **Avis** (www.avis.com), **Europcar** (www.europcar.co.uk), or **Hertz** (www.hertz.fr). A series of highways link most major points. The A9 goes past Nîmes, the A7 descends past Avignon and Salon-de-Provence toward Marseille, the A54 covers Arles, and the A8 goes past Aix and onward along the Riviera.

Internet Cafes

AIX LogiDrake, 34–36 place Miollis (☎ 04-42-93-47-88; www.logidrake.com). **AVIGNON Cybernet@84,** 8 place Jerusalem (☎ 04-32-74-17-59). **MARSEILLE Cyber Café de la Friche Friche de la Belle de Mai,** 41 rue Jobin (☎ 04-

> *The post office in Villeneuve-lez-Avignon.*

95-04-95-11). **NIMES Net m'Eating,** 38 rue Porte de France (☎ 04-66-21-09-70; www.restaurant-netmeating.com).

Post Offices

AIX 1 rue des Cordeliers (old center, north of cours Mirabeau). **AVIGNON** 2 rue de la Petite Meuse (old center). **MARSEILLE** 1 cours Jean Ballard (Old Port). **NIMES** 9 place Belle Croix (old center, north of cathedral).

Safety

Provence is a pretty safe region. Even Marseille isn't as rough as its reputation would have you believe. Still, be wary of pickpockets. In an emergency, as always, call 17 for the police, 18 for the fire department or paramedics, and 15 for an ambulance.

Tourist Offices

Municipal tourist offices are listed at the end of the town tour stops throughout the chapter. **AIX-EN-PROVENCE** 2 place Général de Gaulle (☎ 04-42-16-11-61; www.aixenprovencetourism.com). **AVIGNON** 41 cours Jean Jaures (☎ 04-32-74-32-74; www.ot-avignon.fr). **MARSEILLE** 4 la Canebière (☎ 04-91-13-89-00; www.marseille-tourisme.com). **NIMES** 6 rue Auguste (☎ 04-66-58-38-00; www.ot-nimes.fr). Also consult www.visitprovence.com.

Favorite Moments on the Riviera & Corsica

The Roman ruins, perched villages, and glamorous coastal towns of France's southeast coastline—the Côte d'Azur (Azure Coast), also known as the Riviera—bask in sunshine more than 300 days a year. Inland, the Var and Haute-Provence harbor some of the region's most dramatic mountains and gorges. And then there's the island of Corsica, floating in the Mediterranean Sea between Nice and Sardinia. Alternately French and Italian in spirit, this wild and beautiful island exudes a Mediterranean warmth that, in places, seems unchanged by the centuries. Here are some of our favorite moments on the Riviera and Corsica.

> PREVIOUS PAGE *The secluded creeks and shallow waters of Cannes's Lérins Islands are perfect for lazy, summer dips.* THIS PAGE *La Turbie's impressive Roman ruin (7 B.C.) celebrates Rome's victory over the Alpine populations.*

① Recharging body and mind at Le Couvent des Minimes. As the sun sets over the Haute-Provence hills, let the masseuses at the Couvent des Minimes knead away your tensions in the spa (the only one in France to use L'Occitane en Provence products), then soothe your soul with the hotel restaurant's fine Mediterranean cuisine, washed down with a crisp rosé. See p. 459.

② Eating a picnic lunch on Porquerolles. The most Edenlike of the Hyères islands is a must for nature lovers, who will adore the expanses of pine forests, olive groves, vineyards, and glorious beaches. See p. 442, **①**, and 454.

③ Following the Mimosa Trail. Between January and March, the Côte d'Azur comes alive with sweet-scented balls of yellow mimosa flowers—a unique event celebrated with lively festivals in Mandelieu and along the fabulous 130km (80-mile) fragrant trail over the hilly backlands between Bormes-les-Mimosas and the capital of perfume, Grasse. See p. 692.

1. Recharging body and mind at Le Couvent des Minimes
2. Eating a picnic lunch on Porquerolles
3. Following the Mimosa Trail
4. Stealing kisses at Château de la Napoule
5. Filling up at Antibes's Provençal market
6. Indulging in a gastronomic meal at a Provençal *table d'hôte*
7. Basking in the glory of Rome in La Turbie
8. Raising the stakes at the Casino de Monte Carlo
9. Stepping back in time in Bastia
10. Sunbathing at Rondinara beach

④ Stealing kisses at Château de la Napoule. There is something hopelessly romantic about Mandelieu's mock-Gothic château—a labor of love by artists Marie and Henry Clews, who fled America in 1918. Is it the topiary-filled gardens? Henry's fantastical sculptures and gargoyles? You decide; then steal a kiss on the turreted terraces overlooking the sea. See p. 462.

❺ Filling up at Antibes's Provençal market. Colorful, bustling, and bursting at the seams with delicious produce, charcuterie, and olives, Antibes's covered market makes a plum spot to stock a picnic basket. See p. 462, ④.

❻ Indulging in a gastronomic meal at a Provençal *table d'hôte*. When you're dining at Michelin-starred Château de la Chèvre d'Or, in the village of Eze, perched 429m (1,407 ft.) above the Mediterranean, life doesn't get much better. See p. 471.

❼ Basking in the glory of Rome in La Turbie. The gigantic Trophée des Alpes was erected to celebrate Emperor Augustus Caesar's victory against the Ligurians in 13 B.C. The monument used to mark the frontier between Italy

and Gaul, and it still affords triumphant views over Cap-Ferrat and Eze. See p. 462, ❼.

❽ Raising the stakes at the Casino de Monte Carlo. You may not even mind losing money at this beautiful palace on the Riviera. Play blackjack in the opulent Salons Privés, spin the roulette wheel in the Belle Epoque Salon Europe, try your luck on the slot machines, or sip champagne beneath the Belle Epoque ceiling of the Salle Blanche. See p. 465, ❸.

❾ Stepping back in time in Bastia. Corsica's laid-back, northern hub feels as though it hasn't changed in 100 years. Soak up its old-world atmosphere in the Vieux Port (Old Port), and admire its crumbling beauty from the Jetée du Dragon, a jetty from which you can take in the seafront in one breathtaking sweep. See p. 472, ❶.

❿ Sunbathing at Rondinara beach. South of Porto-Vecchio in Corsica, it's all about you, the turquoise water, the white sand, and a good book. This pine-lined cove is sheltered from the wind, so you won't find a better spot for soaking up the sun and relaxing. See p. 455.

The Riviera & Monaco in 1 Week

This tour takes you along France's sunshine coast through the pretty port of Hyères (and its offshore islands), glamorous St-Tropez, quaint Fréjus, star-studded Cannes, and buzzing Nice, to the principality of Monaco. For a more leisurely rhythm, allow 10 days. You can easily combine these destinations with a tour in Provence (see chapter 10), or extend your trip by catching a boat from Toulon or Nice to explore Corsica's lesser-known treasures (p. 472).

> St-Tropez's yacht-filled port harbored modest fishing boats before World War II.

START Hyères is 63km (39 miles) from Marseille, 111km (69 miles) from Nice, and 700km (435 miles) from Paris. **TRIP LENGTH** 186km (116 miles) on both fast and country roads.

1 ★ **Hyères.** Famous for its palm trees and mild climate, this winter resort has been popular since the 19th century. In the steep medieval town, **place Massillon** has a daily market near the **Tour St-Blaise** (a 12th-c. tower linked to the Templar Knights). **Place St-Paul,** by the Collégiale St-Paul (12th and 17th c.), affords some fine views. On one of the highest points, you'll find the **Villa Noailles,** famous for extravagant parties thrown here by such artists as Picasso and Dalí in the 1920s, and now a cutting-edge art exhibition space. Back in the new town, don't miss the faded but beautiful **Godillot District,** with its Belle Epoque hotels and villas—testimony to Hyères's popularity among aristocrats.

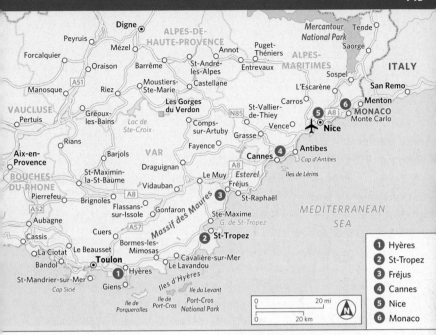

Map legend:
1. Hyères
2. St-Tropez
3. Fréjus
4. Cannes
5. Nice
6. Monaco

Hyères's unspoiled islands, ★★★ **Les Iles de Hyères,** make for an excellent afternoon trip. The largest, `kids` **Porquerolles,** is famed for its pine forests, beaches, wines, and bumpy bicycle paths. You can hire a bike from **Le Cycle Porquerollais,** 1 rue de la Ferme (☎ 04-94-58-30-32; www.velo-porquerolles.fr). **Port-Cros** is a rugged national park with fabulous marine life and walking routes through lush, green forests. If you have a snorkel, goggles, and flippers, you can follow an underwater swimming route and observe the sea creatures in their natural habitat (visit the park office in the Port-Cros port for details). The ★★ **Ile de Levant** was formerly inhabited by Cistercian monks. Nowadays, the French Navy prohibits access to much of the island, but in the west, the village of Héliopolis is coveted by nudist bathers. During high season, diving activities are open to the public (inquire at the tourist office in Hyères). Boats to the islands can be caught at the tip of Hyères at la Tour Fondue (along D97). ⏱1 day. Hyères Tourist Office, av. Ambroise Thomas. ☎ 04-94-01-84-50. www.hyeres-tourisme.com.

From Hyères, join N98 (past Bormes-les-Mimosas), and at Port Grimaud, turn right onto D98A to **St-Tropez** (50km/31 miles).

> *A fish market by the port in St-Tropez.*

Where to Stay & Dine

For hotels and restaurants in Nice, see p. 471; in Monaco, see p. 467; elsewhere along the Riviera, see p. 459.

> *On the cliff's edge, Monaco's Le Rocher district is home to the Grimaldi palace.*

② ★★ St-Tropez. At its most Bacchanalian, between May and September, St-Tropez is as steamy and sun-kissed as ever. The Brigitte Bardot vehicle *And God Created Woman* certainly put the town on the tourist map, and in summer, artists, composers, novelists, and the film colony still drop anchor here in extortionately expensive yachts. The rest of the year, however, St-Tropez goes back to what it knows best: being a down-to-earth port for simple (if not moneyed) folk, with a darling historic center. Spend the morning wandering through the **Vieux Port** and its tiny fish market, and around the former fisherman's quarters, known as the **Ponche district,** behind quai Jean Jaurès. Don't miss the **Château Suffran** (remains of the former St-Tropez Seigneurs' castle) on place de l'Hôtel de Ville, or the views from the lofty heights of the Citadelle ramparts. One of the best spots for coffee or a meal is place des Lices—a tree-shaded square prized by *boules* players and market-goers alike. Afterward, if you have a sweet tooth, try St-Tropez's specialty cake with vanilla cream, *la tarte Tropézienne,* sold by a bakery of the same name on the square.

Art fans should explore the **Musée de l'Annonciade,** place Grammont (☎ 04-94-17-84-10; admission 6€ adults, 4€ ages 12–18, free for children 11 and under; Dec–Oct Wed–Mon 10am–noon and 3–7pm; closed Nov and public holidays). Its fantastic modern art collection includes works by Maurice Utrillo and Georges Braque. The **Maison des Papillons,** 9 rue Etienne-Berny (☎ 04-94-97-63-45; http://maisondespapillons.ifrance.com; admission 3€ adults, free for ages 9 and under; Wed–Mon 10am–noon and 3–7pm), is an old-world Provençal house entirely given over to pinned butterflies. St-Tropez also has some of the best beaches on the Riviera (p. 454). ⏱ 1 day. St-Tropez Tourist Office, quai Jean Jaurès. ☎ 08-92-68-48-28. www.ot-saint-tropez.com.

From St-Tropez, take D98A to Port Grimaud and pick up N98; cross Ste-Maxime, and join D1098 (on the left) to Fréjus (36km/22 miles).

③ Fréjus. This pleasant resort has a quaint historic center, charming cafes, and boutiques. There are also Roman amphitheater ruins and an aqueduct on the outskirts of town. ⏱ 1 day. See p. 457, **④**.

Leave Fréjus on D37, then join A8 to Cannes, exiting at junction 40 (38km/24 miles).

④ ★ Cannes. Thanks to Cannes's world-famous film festival, the rich and famous flock there like bees to honey. There are three parts to the city: La Croisette, Le Suquet, and Les Iles des Lérins. **La Croisette** is where you'll find the flashy shops, restaurants, beaches, and palace hotels such as the Carlton and the Majestic. The modern **Palais des Festivals** (nicknamed the "Bunker"), with its famous red carpet and surrounding allée des Stars, is also in this part of Cannes. It is in the old town of **Le Suquet** where you'll find authentic Cannes. Here, visit the **Forville market** and the **Musée de la Castre,** place de la Castre (☎ 04-93-38-55-26; www.cannes.com; admission 3.50€ adults, 2.20€ ages 18–25, free for ages 17 and under; Sept–Jun Tues–Sun 10am–1pm and 2–5pm [until 6pm Apr–Jun and Sept]; Jul–Aug daily 10am–7pm). The museum's collection of ethnic and 19th-century art includes a 12th-century watch tower and the Chapelle Ste-Anne (chapel), which houses a small collection of musical instruments. Adjacent to the museum is the pretty 17th-century church, Notre-Dame de l'Esperence. Just a 15-minute boat ride offshore, **Les Iles des Lérins** are Cannes's peaceful offshore islands. **Ile St-Honorat** is a striking, pine-studded religious backwater, founded in the 4th century and now home to Cistercian monks who make and sell their own liquors. kids **Ile Ste-Marguerite** is ideal for a hike, swim, and picnic. The star attraction here is the kids **Musée de la Mer** (Marine Museum, ☎ 04-93-43-18-17; 3.40€ adults, 2.20€ reduced, free for ages 18 and under; June–Sept daily 10am–5:45pm; Apr–May Tues–Sun 10:30am–1:15pm and 2:15–5:45pm; Oct–Mar Tues–Sun 10:30am–1:15pm and 2:15–4:45pm), set inside the Fort Royal prison that Alexandre Dumas made famous in his novel *The Man in the Iron Mask.* Nature trails, known as *sentiers,* are well indicated all around the island. The **Plongée Club de Cannes** (☎ 04-93-38-67-57; www.plongee-sylpa.com) takes tourists diving around the island to see the wealth of aquatic flora and fauna. Catch **Trans Côte d'Azur** boats to both islands from quai Laubeuf (☎ 04-92-98-71-30; www.trans-cote-azur.com; tickets 11.50€ adults, 6€ children 9 and under; MC, V); the first departure from Cannes is usually at 7:30am, and the last boat usually departs for Cannes at 6pm, but always check before you set out. ⊙ 1 day. Cannes Tourist Office, Bureau Palais des Festivals, La Croisette. ☎ 04-92-99-84-22. www.palaisdesfestivals.com.

Leave Cannes along D6285 past Le Cannet, and head for A8 to Nice, exiting at junction 54 (41km/25 miles).

⑤ Nice. Founded by the ancient Greeks, who called it Nike (Victory), Nice attracted the Victorian upper class and tsarist aristocrats during the 19th century, but these days it's the most affordable of all the major French resorts. It's also extremely accessible, especially if you're dependent on public transportation; from the Nice airport, the second largest in France, you can travel by train or bus along the entire coast. ⊙ 2 days. For detailed information on Nice, see p. 468.

From Nice, rejoin A8 and follow signs to Monaco (21km/13 miles).

⑥ Monaco. The principality of Monaco impresses visitors with its opulence, cleanliness, and friendliness. ⊙ 1 day. For detailed information on Monaco, see p. 472.

Cannes Film Festival

In 1939, French minister Jean Zay chose Cannes's sunny shores as the venue for an international film festival. World War II broke out, however, and delayed his plans. The first Festival de Cannes (www.festival-cannes.fr) didn't take place until 1946, in the specially built Palais des Festivals on the present-day site of the Hilton hotel. According to legend, architects forgot to include a projection window and had to chisel out a hole in front of crowds of impatient VIPs. The festival's popularity and renown grew to include star-studded juries presided over by the likes of Jean Cocteau, Marcel Pagnol, and, more recently, Tim Burton. For 2 weeks in May each year, in the new Palais des Festivals, celebrities confront frenzied hordes to promote their films and their image, meet directors, and party until sunrise.

LA NOUVELLE VAGUE

France's Postwar Cinematic Breakthrough BY ANNA BROOKE

ALTHOUGH THE FRENCH INVENTED CINEMA—movie camera pioneers Auguste and Louis Lumière held the first public film screening in 1895—it was not until after World War II that French filmmakers made their biggest splash with the *Nouvelle Vague* (New Wave) movement. Their low-budget, realistic, and sociological movies rejected the narrative conventions of expensive, studio-based, classic Hollywood pictures, using improvised dialogue, fast scene changes, long tracking shots, and hand-held cameras. They kept budgets low by shooting in friends' apartments or in the street, and by frequently using friends and family as cast and crew. Their subjects reflected the philosophical preoccupations of postwar France, particularly existentialism, producing narratives and aesthetics hitherto unseen on the silver screen.

Les Auteurs

The New Wave's greatest directors (below) all started out as journalists for the *Cahier du Cinéma* magazine. Their artist-driven approach became known as *cinéma d'auteur* (author theory), in which the director's personality and creative vision imbues each picture with its unique character.

JEAN-LUC GODARD (b. 1930)
The New Wave's most radical filmmaker, Godard made pictures infused with his Marxist ideals and existentialist outlook. His films—such as *A bout de souffle* (*Breathless*, 1960) and *Le mépris* (*Contempt*, 1963)—have inspired Quentin Tarantino and Steven Soderbergh.

FRANÇOIS TRUFFAUT (1932–84) "The Gravedigger of French Cinema," Truffaut was an unforgiving critic of traditional film. He frequently adapted novels, including Henri-Pierre Roché's 1953 work, *Jules et Jim*.

CLAUDE CHABROL (1930–2010) The most mainstream New Wave director averaged one film a year until his death. Chabrol is known for an experimental edge and dense suspense thrillers. His first commercial success was *Les cousins* (1959), a tragedy about love and jealousy.

ERIC ROHMER (1920–2010)
The last director to join the movement set his films apart by filling them with dialogue, rarely filming close-ups, and often omitting music. A good example of his stark, often mundane realism is found in *La collectionneuse* (*The Collector*, 1967).

1958
Louis Malle's *Ascenseur pour l'échafaud* (*Elevator to the Gallows*) features a young Jeanne Moreau and a legendarily sexy soundtrack by Miles Davis.

1959
Chabrol's *Les cousins* brings a love triangle involving family members to the screen.

1959
Truffaut's *Les quatre cent coups* (*The 400 Blows*) reveals the unjust treatment of juvenile offenders and earned Truffaut Best Director at Cannes.

1960
Godard's *A bout de souffle* (*Breathless*), an entirely improvised tragedy about love and crime, becomes the emblem of the *Nouvelle Vague*.

1962
Truffaut's *Jules et Jim* brings a *ménage à trois* to the screen.

1963
Godard's *Le mépris* (*Contempt*), starring Brigitte Bardot, treats infidelity and the disintegration of marriage.

1964
Godard's *Bande à part* (*Band of Outsiders*) contains an audacious 36 seconds of silence—no text, no music, just the two main characters sitting in a bar.

1966
Claude Lelouch wrote, shot, and directed *Un homme et une femme* (*A Man and a Woman*), about a widow and a widower who fall in love in Deauville.

1967
Eric Rohmer's *La collectionneuse* (*The Collector*) tells a tale of desire, fidelity, and friendship between a man and a woman.

1970
Eric Rohmer's *Le genou de Claire* (*Claire's Knee*) explores sexual obsession and repressed desire.

The Riviera for Art Lovers

Like moths to a flame, artists have gravitated toward the Riviera's vivid sunlight and vibrant landscape for centuries. Impressionists Claude Monet and Auguste Renoir eased the world into modernism with their treatment of light, and Raoul Dufy, Pierre Bonnard, and Paul Signac carried the torch decades later. Both Pablo Picasso and Henri Matisse settled here, and Jean Cocteau spent much of his life on the Côte d'Azur, creating his own museum in Menton, the start of our tour.

> *The Musée Matisse in Nice, where the artist lived from 1917 to 1954.*

START Menton is 30km (19 miles) east of Nice. **TRIP LENGTH** 101km (63 miles) on both fast and country roads.

1 Menton. Parisian-born artist, dramatist, and surrealist filmmaker Jean Cocteau (1889–1963) was a big fan of Menton and left the town two important legacies: his sublime murals in the **Salle des Mariages** (Wedding Room), in Menton's City Hall, including the famous *Noce Imaginaire;* and the **Musée Jean Cocteau,** a ruined 17th-century fort that he painstakingly restored with self-designed

window and floor mosaics and wrought-iron, zoomorphic window decorations. ⏱ 1 day. For detailed information on Menton, see p. 463, **8**.

From Menton, drive west onto A8, turn off at junction 55, and follow signs to Nice (30km/19 miles).

Where to Stay & Dine

For hotels and restaurants in Nice, see p. 471; in Monaco, see p. 467; elsewhere along the Riviera, see p. 459.

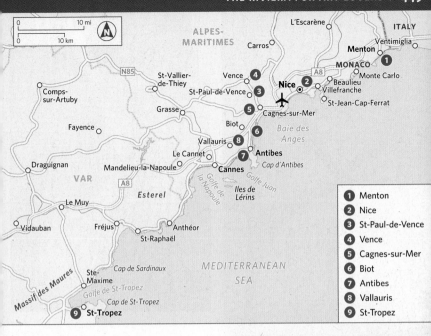

Map legend:

1. Menton
2. Nice
3. St-Paul-de-Vence
4. Vence
5. Cagnes-sur-Mer
6. Biot
7. Antibes
8. Vallauris
9. St-Tropez

2 Nice. The fifth-biggest city in France attracted several 19th- and 20th-century artists, including Henri Matisse (1869–1954), who loved Nice's "crystalline, limpid" light. He bequeathed the city a vast collection of paintings, sculptures, drawings, engravings, paper cutouts, and illustrated books, displayed today in the **Musée Matisse.** Russian-born Marc Chagall (1887–1985) also bequeathed Nice his paintings and sculptures, a mosaic, and three huge stained-glass windows, on show today in the **Musée National Message Biblique Marc Chagall.** Fauvist painter Raoul Dufy (1877–1953) made revolutionary use of light and color in Nice, choosing the town as the background and inspiration for his works. A small but fine selection of paintings hangs on the walls of the **Musée des Beaux Arts.** One of the best contemporary art museums outside Paris is Nice's **MAMAC** (Musée d'Art Moderne et d'Art Contemporain), which presents French and American avant-garde art from the 1960s onward. ⊙ 2 days. For detailed information on Nice, see p. 468.

From Nice, take A8 (toward Cagnes), exit at junction 48, and follow signs for Vence/Cagnes-sur-Mer; as soon as possible pick up D2 (Route de Serres) to St-Paul (28km/17 miles).

> You can walk on works of art at Menton's Musée Jean Cocteau, where the surrealist created numerous floor mosaics.

> *A Calder sculpture at the Fondation Maeght in St-Paul-de-Vence.*

> *A live glassblowing demonstration in Biot.*

3 **St-Paul-de-Vence.** This fortified medieval settlement—presiding over the Vence countryside amid orange and olive trees—was rediscovered in the early 1900s by painters such as Amedeo Modigliani, Pierre Bonnard, Chaim Soutine, and Paul Signac. Since then, hundreds of artists have followed suit, along with serious art dealers whose boutiques and galleries flank the narrow, often teeming cobblestone streets. No art buff should miss the **Fondation Maeght** (☎ 04-93-32-81-63; www.maeght. com; admission 14€ adults, 9€ reduced, children 9 and under free; July–Sept daily 10am–7pm; Oct–June 10am–12:30pm and 2:30–6pm), where works by Chagall, Matisse, and Joan Miró stand alongside an Alexander Calder stabile, which rises from the lawn like a futuristic monster. ⏱ 4 hr. St-Paul-de-Vence Tourist Office, 2 rue Grande. ☎ 04-93-32-86-95. www.saint-pauldevence.com.

From St-Paul, continue on D2 north to Vence (4km/2½ miles).

4 **Vence.** This resort town's historic core is charming enough, but don't miss the Matisse-designed **Chapelle du Rosaire** (also known as Chapelle Matisse) on its outer edges, at 466 av. Henri Matisse (☎ 04-93-58-03-26; admission 3€ adults, 2€ reduced; Mon, Wed, and Sat 2–5:30pm, Tues and Thurs 10–11:30am and 2–5:30pm; closed Nov). It's the artist's complete and final work, and he called it his "masterpiece, despite all its imperfections." Undoubtedly it's one of the most exquisite pieces of 20th-century art on the Riviera. ⏱ 2–3 hr. Vence Tourist Office, 8 place Grand Jardin. ☎ 04-93-58-06-38. www.ville-vence.fr.

From Vence, take D236 for 2km (1¼ mile), and pick up D36 to Cagnes (10km/6¼ miles total).

5 **Cagnes-sur-Mer.** Renoir deemed the perched old town of Cagnes-sur-Mer "the place where I want to paint until the last day of my life." He got his wish in 1919, when he died, leaving a still life behind to dry, in his family home—today's **Musée Renoir,** 19 chemin des Collettes (☎ 04-93-20-61-07; admission 4€ adults, 2€ reduced; May–Sept Wed–Mon 10am–noon, 2–6pm; Oct–Apr Wed–Mon 10am–noon and 2–5pm). The museum has

20 portrait busts and portrait medallions that constitute the largest collection of Renoir sculpture in the world. In his atelier are his wheelchair, easel, and brushes. ⏱ 2 hr. **Cagnes-sur-Mer Tourist Office**, place du Dr. Maurel. ☎ 04-93-20-61-64. www.cagnes-tourisme.com.

From Cagnes, take D6007 for 4km (2½ miles), and pick up D4 to Biot (10km/6¼ miles total).

6 Biot. Famous for its bubble-flecked glass known as *verre rustique,* Biot was where Fernand Léger (1881–1955) painted until the day he died. A magnificent collection of his work is on display at the **Musée Nationale Fernand Léger,** chemin du Val-de-Pome (☎ 04-92-91-50-30; www.musee-fernandleger.fr; admission 5.50€; June–Oct and Dec–Apr daily 10am–6pm, Nov–May 10am–5pm). ⏱ 2 hr. **Biot Tourist Office**, rue St-Sébastien. ☎ 04-93-65-78-00. www.biot.fr.

Take D4 out of Biot and at the island pick up D6007 to Antibes (6km/3¾ miles).

7 Antibes. This unpretentious port town with a bustling covered market is home to the Château Grimaldi, which shelters the world-class **Musée Picasso,** Château Grimaldi, place du Mariejol (☎ 04-92-90-54-20; admission 6€ adults, 3€ reduced; June–Sept Tues–Sun 10am–6pm; Oct–May Tues–Sun 10am–noon and 2–6pm). In addition to Picasso's works, a contemporary art gallery exhibits Léger, Miró, Max Ernst, and Calder. ⏱ 2–3 hr. See p. 462, **4**.

Take D6107 out of Antibes and follow signs to Vallauris (7km/4⅓ miles).

8 Vallauris. The tacky ceramics capital of the Riviera still attracts lovers of pottery and Picasso with its three-in-one **Musée National Picasso La Guerre et La Paix, Musée Magnelli,** and **Musée de la Céramique,** in the village castle, place de la Libération (☎ 04-93-64-71-83; www.musee-picasso-vallauris.fr; admission 4€ adults, 2€ reduced, free for ages 17 and under; mid-June to mid-Sept Wed–Mon 10am–6pm; mid-Sept to mid-June Wed–Mon 10am–5pm). From 1948 to 1955 Picasso lived in Vallauris, where he created some 4,000 ceramic pieces and decorated a rough stone chapel with two fabulous contrasting paintings: *La Paix (Peace)* and *La Guerre (War),* on view here. ⏱ 3 hr. **Vallauris Tourist Office**, av. Frères Roustan. ☎ 04-93-63-21-07. www.vallauris-golfe-juan.com.

St-Tropez is on the coast, 85km (52 miles) southwest of Vallauris.

9 St-Tropez. Well-off or well-connected artists have long flocked to St-Tropez. Painter Paul Signac (1863–1935) was one of them, and he inspired a host of others bent on capturing the Riviera's light. The **Musée de l'Annonciade,** opened in 1955 within a 16th-century chapel on the old port, displays striking works by Signac and other post-Impressionist artists. ⏱ 2 hr. See p. 444, **2**.

> *Picasso's* War *and* Peace *works are installed in a chapel that is now the Musée National Picasso La Guerre et La Paix in Vallauris.*

The Riviera & the Var with Kids

Through a child's eyes, the castles and fortified hill towns of the Var look as if they have come straight from a Disney movie. Then there's the great outdoors, which provides a host of activities, both on land and on sea, for the whole brood, as well as chances to learn about wildlife and flora.

> *From domed underground lookout posts, kids get down with tortoises in Gonfaron.*

START Antibes is 913km (567 miles) south of Paris, 21km (13 miles) southwest of Nice, and 11km (6¾ miles) northeast of Cannes. TRIP LENGTH 108km (67 miles) on both fast and country roads.

1 **Marineland, Antibes.** Just outside Antibes, Marineland, RN 7 (☎ 08-92-30-06-06; www. marineland.fr; admission from 36€ adults, from 29€ ages 3–12; May–Sept 10am–6pm), is a multitasking adventure park with excellent live dolphin, killer whale, and sea lion shows: **Aquasplash** is the Riviera's biggest water-slide park, with 13 giant toboggans; next door, the **Petite Ferme du Far West** also amuses pre-teens with cowboy-themed pony rides and

obstacle courses; and the **Adventure Golf** section is a crazy, Jurassic-themed golf course with a mean-looking Tyrannosaurus. You can buy combined and 2-day tickets. ⏱ 1 day. For more on Antibes, see p. 462, **4**.

From Antibes, take D35 (toward Cannes) to A8, exit at junction 38, and follow signs to Fréjus (50km/31 miles).

2 **Fréjus.** After exploring Fréjus's beaches and **Roman amphitheater,** you and your children might want visit the 20-hectare (50-acre), safari-style **Parc Zoölogique,** zone du Capitou, off A8 (☎ 04-98-11-37-37; www.zoo-frejus. com; admission 14€ adults, 9.50€ ages 3–9;

1. Marineland, Antibes
2. Fréjus
3. Village des Tortues, Gonfaron
4. Aoubré, Flassans

Mar–May and Sept daily 10am–5pm, June–Aug daily 10am–6pm, Nov–Feb daily 10am–4:30pm). More than 150 different species—part of a permanent breeding program to help maintain endangered animals—roam the park. They range from cute and fluffy mammals to big Asian elephants, wild cats, birds, and reptiles. ⏱ 1 day. For more on Fréjus, see p. 457, ④.

From Fréjus, take DN7 to A8 (toward Aix-en-Provence) for 30km (19 miles) to A57; exit A57 at junction 13 (toward Le Luc), and follow DN7 through Le Luc, then join N97 and follow signs to Gonfaron (49km/30 miles total).

❸ **Village des Tortues, Gonfaron.** At the foot of the Massif des Maures mountains, amid fields of lavender and oak, this sanctuary cares for 2,500-plus species of tortoise—particularly the Hermann tortoise, which is almost extinct in France. A series of shaded paths and bridges lead you and your kids through the village and into the clinic, where staffers nurse sick tortoises back to health before releasing them into the wild. In the hatching room, your kids might be lucky enough to see baby tortoises and terrapins. ⏱ 3–4 hr. Quartier les plaines, Gonfaron. ☎ 04-94-78-26-41. www.villagetortues.com. Admission 8€ adults, 5€ children. Mar–Nov daily 9am–7pm; Dec–Mar daily 9am–6pm.

From Gonfaron, take D39 (Route de Flassans) to Flassans-sur-Issole and follow signs for Parc des Cèdres (9km/5⅔ miles).

❹ **Aoubré, Flassans.** Within this 30-hectare (74-acre) cedar forest, the whole family can pretend to be primates for the day and move from tree to tree between platforms hoisted high above the forest floor. A small farm provides plenty of cooing opportunities with cute rabbits, guinea pigs, and dwarf goats; meanwhile, the Parc Animalier (Animal Park) contains larger deer, wild boar, and donkeys. ⏱ 1 day. Parc des Cèdres, Flassans. ☎ 04-94-86-10-92 or 06-12-58-02-26. www.aoubre.fr. Admission 19€ adults, 16€ ages 8–11, 11€ ages 5–7. No credit cards. Sat–Sun by reservations only; public holidays and school holidays 9am–8pm. Closed Nov–Feb.

Food on the Farm

Graine & Ficelle is a wee farm, in the flower-strewn hills beyond Vence, where small kids can fawn over baby rabbits and hens or take a cooking class, while parents wait for owner Isabella Sallusti to prepare a delicious vegetarian meal. *670 chemin des Collets, St-Jeannet. ☎ 06-85-08-15-64. Lunch and farm visit 35€ adults, 19€ ages 17 and under. 2-hr. farm visit 11€ adults, 8€ children. Cooking classes 25€. No credit cards. Requires advance reservation by phone or e-mail, graine.ficelle@wanadoo.fr or online www.graine-ficelle.com.*

Best Beaches

Contrary to the French Riviera's film and tabloid image, it's not just about bronzed stick figures and celebrities hiding behind Chanel shades. The coastline from the Hyères to Nice is lengthy and varied enough to satisfy a range of beachcombers—whether you seek solace and tranquility in a secluded cove, wild nature, family activities, or a hotspot in which to see and be seen. The island of Corsica, too, is famed for its shorelines. Access to the listed beaches is free. Unless otherwise noted in the following reviews, assume there are no facilities on-site and pack food, drink, towels, and sunscreen before you head for the *plage*.

> Brigitte Bardot made a legend of this inviting stretch of sand at Plage de Pampelonne in St-Tropez.

Ile de Porquerolles (Hyères). A short boat crossing from the Hyères peninsula leads you to an island of pine trees, vineyards, walking and cycling trails, and several small, sandy beaches—the landscape that reportedly inspired Robert Louis Stevenson to write *Treasure Island*. Rent a bicycle and choose a destination: the silvery sands of the **Plage d'Argent; Plage de la Courtade,** ideally situated by Fort Ste-Agathe; or beautiful **Plage Notre Dame,** the island's biggest beach, bordered by pines and furnished with a seasonal restaurant. Maps are available at the information center in the village, **Carré du Port,** Ile de Porquerolles (☎ 04-94-58-33-76; www.porquerolles.com; opening times vary so call to check or call Hyères tourist office). To rent a bike, try **Le Cycle Porquerollais,** 1 rue de al Ferme (☎ 04-94-58-30-32; www.cycle-porquerollais.com; 14€ day, 11€ children). **TLV-TVM** runs boats to the island (☎ 04-94-58-21-81; www.tlv-tvm.com; from 17€; daily 7:30am–6pm; times subject to change). Embark south of Hyères at the Tour Fondue on the peninsula of Gien, at the bottom of D97. Hyères Tourist Office, 3 av. Ambroise Thomas, Le Forum Casino. ☎ 04-94-01-84-50.

Iles de Lérins (Ste-Marguerite & St-Honorat). Away from the glitter of Cannes, two offshore islands, called the Iles de Lérins, offer sanctuary to those wishing to escape the Riviera's glamour queens and

Ile de Porquerolles **1**
Iles de Lérins **4**
Plage de Pampelonne **2**
Plage de Rondinara **5**
Plage de St-Aygulf **3**

kings. **Ile St-Honorat** is the smaller of the two, dominated by a fortified Cistercian monastery that is still occupied by monks. Its remote creeks and beaches are peaceful and inviting. No nipples or bare bottoms are permitted while swimming and sunbathing. **Ile Ste-Marguerite** is an Eldorado for those wishing to break up their beach time with hikes through pine and eucalyptus woods. There's also an old fortress, built by Cardinal Richelieu and reinforced by Sébastien de Vauban in the early 18th century, which contains a marine museum. **Trans Côte d'Azur** boats leave from quai Laubeuf (☎ 04-92-98-71-30; www.trans-cote-azur.com; tickets 11.50€ adults, 6€ ages 5–10; MC, V; first departure from Cannes 9am, last return to Cannes 6pm, subject to change and weather).

Plage de Pampelonne (St-Tropez). St-Tropez's public image was forged and burnished on this 9km (5⅔-mile) stretch of white sand. A galaxy of stars have bronzed their busts and butts to perfection on this beach, and the mega-wealthy and famous continue reserving places in the exclusive beach clubs. Certain stretches are reserved for nudists. Gays and families also have their own designated areas.

Plage de Rondinara (South of Porto-Vecchio, Corsica). The horseshoe-shaped Rondinara beach—with its fine, white sand; clear, shallow turquoise water; and resident cows in the off season (tourists chase them away in the summer months)—is one of Corsica's most beautiful bays. It has a desert island–like quality to it; bathing here in spring or autumn can make you feel as though you've found your own slice of paradise. In summer, however, the hordes arrive, so choose your season. Along N198 btw. Bonifacio and Porto-Vecchio.

Plage de St-Aygulf (Fréjus). Just outside of Fréjus, St-Aygulf beach is encircled by rocks inside the nature preserve **Les Etangs de Villepey,** which affords a lovely view over the Fréjus bay. The preserve protects both fresh- and saltwater lagoons and is home to more than 217 species of birds. The most exciting time to visit is spring, when pink flamingos and gray herons fly overhead while you soak up the sun. Chair rentals are about 10€ a day. Restaurants and public facilities are available onsite. From Fréjus take D1098 (5km/3miles). For more information on Fréjus, see p. 457, **4**.

The Var & Haute-Provence

Bordered by the southernmost Alps to the east, the Bouches du Rhône to the west, and the Mediterranean to the south, the landscape of the Var is a patchwork of rocky outcrops, luscious vineyards, undulating hills, and fine beaches; no two areas offer the same attractions. The Var is home to some of the Côte d'Azur's most famous port towns—St-Tropez, St-Raphaël, and Fréjus. But if you tire of seaside frivolity, head north to mountainous Haute-Provence, where the chocolate-box capital of *faïence* pottery, Moustiers-Ste-Marie, provides a dramatic gateway to the Gorges du Verdon.

> *In contrast to the rest of the Côte d'Azur, the Massif de l'Estérel is composed of red-hued volcanic rock.*

START Hyères is 63km (39 miles) from Marseille, 111km (69 miles) from Nice, and 700km (435 miles) from Paris. TRIP LENGTH 340km (211 miles) on both fast and country roads.

1 Hyères. The oldest winter resort on the coast has 35km (22 miles) of sandy beaches, a charming town center lined with palm trees, and three offshore islands waiting to be explored. ⏱ 1 day. See p. 442, **1**.

From Hyères, follow N98 for 2km (1¼ miles) and pick up D559, via La Lond-les-Maures, to Bormes (20km/12 miles).

2 ★ Bormes-les-Mimosas. Postcard-perfect Bormes is famous for mimosa flowers, which it cultivates for export all over the world. As steep as it is pretty, the old town twists and turns through cobbled slopes, including one precipitous lane with 83 steps known in Provençal as rue Rompi-Cuou, or "Neck-Breaker Street." If you fancy a tipple in a working winery, stop by the **Château de Bregançon** (☎ 04-94-64-80-73; www.chateau-de-bregancon.fr), which offers samples of its Côte de Provence rosés. ⏱ 1 day. Bormes-les-Mimosas Tourist Office, 1 place Gambetta. ☎ 04-94-01-38-38. www.bormeslesmimosas.com.

1. Hyères
2. Bormes-les-Mimosas
3. St-Tropez
4. Fréjus
5. St-Raphaël
6. Manosque
7. Moustiers-Ste-Marie
8. Les Gorges du Verdon

Where to Stay & Dine

Hostellerie du Cigalou 13
Hotel La Ponche 15
L'Arena 16
La Bastide de Moustiers 10
Le Couvent des Minimes 9
Le Haut du Pavé 12
L'Hostellerie de l'Abbaye de La Celle 11
Pastis 14

Exit Bormes on D559, and at La Garrigue, turn right onto N98; after 30km (19 miles), make a left onto D98a and an immediate right to D61; at Gassin, rejoin D98a to St-Tropez (40km/25 miles total).

3 ★ St-Tropez. The birthplace of Riviera glamour is a requisite stop-off. ☉ 1 day. See p. 444, **2**.

From St-Tropez, take D98 to Ste-Maxime, then join N98 (on the right) to Fréjus (36km/22 miles).

4 Fréjus. Once an important center for Roman merchants, Fréjus still has a **Roman amphitheater** (☎ 04-94-51-34-31) and the remains of an aqueduct. The upper town, painted in ocher and peach tones, houses small boutiques, cafes, restaurants, and artists' ateliers. Make sure you set aside an hour to visit the unusual, fortified **Groupe Episcopal** (baptistry, cathedral, cloisters, and archaeological museum) in the old town. Other unique buildings are linked to Fréjus's military role as a center for colonial troops from Africa and Asia at the start of the 20th century. Exotic architectural legacies include the red-brick **Mosquée de Missri** (leave Fréjus on av.

de Verdun and take D4 toward Fayence for 3km/1¾ miles), built by Senegalese soldiers as an exact replica of the Missiri de Djenne mosque in Mali; and the **Hông Hiên Buddhist pagoda,** along N7 (☎ 04-94-53-25-29), surrounded by an Asian garden with sacred animals and mythological guardians. The beach area of Fréjus is a long stretch of fine sand known as **Fréjus Plage,** bordered by tacky bars and amusements. ☉ 1 day. Fréjus Tourist Office, 249 rue Jean Jaurès. ☎ 04-94-51-83-83. www.frejus.fr.

Av. du Maréchal de Lattre de Tassigny (D98c) in Fréjus leads to rue Anatole France (D37) in St-Raphaël (3km/1¾ miles).

5 St-Raphaël. A continuation of Fréjus Plage, this post–World War II resort lacks the historical charm of Fréjus's center. What it does have is 36km (22 miles) of coastline with 30 beaches and creeks, making it a brilliant spot for bathing, watersports, and beach games. It also lies at the foot of the magnificent **Massif de l'Estérel**—a red, porphyry (volcanic rock) mountain prized by nature enthusiasts and hikers. For watersports, **Terrescale** (☎ 04-94-19-19-79; www.terrescale.com; June–Sept) runs sea kayaking and diving trips from

Dramont beach. To explore the Massif de l'Estérel on foot, ask at the tourist office about English-speaking guides. ⏱ 1 day. St-Raphaël Tourist Office, quai Albert 1er. ☎ 04-94-19-52-52. www.saint-raphael.com.

Return to Fréjus and follow signs to A8 (toward Toulon/Aix-en-Provence). After 112km (70 miles), take N296 (toward Gap) for 7km (4⅓ miles), A51 for 48km (30 miles), and follow signs to Manosque (178km/111 miles total).

6 Manosque. The largest town in Haute-Provence is industrial and sprawling. There are some quaint medieval streets in the old center, but Manosque's main attraction is the **L'Occitane** cosmetics factory (p. 440, **1**). It makes for a fascinating visit, as you watch workers mixing, labeling, and packaging perfumes, creams, and candles. After a whirl around the shop, follow your nose 26km (16 miles) northeast (along D4096 and N100) to the medieval village of Forcalquier, crowned by the octagonal, 19th-century Notre-Dame-de-Provence chapel. The **Couvent des Cordeliers** (☎ 04-92-72-50-68; www.uess.fr), a former Franciscan convent and home to the Université Européenne Saveurs & Senteurs (European Scent & Flavor University), offers eye-opening fragrance workshops. Call for more information. ⏱ 5 hr. Manosque Tourist Office, place du Dr Joubert. ☎ 04-92-72-16-00. www.manosque-tourisme.com.

Follow allée de la Ponsonne from Manosque and make a left onto D4096; at the island join D907; at the next island, take the first exit onto D4; continue to D554, and after Vinon-sur-Verdon, pick up D952 to Moustiers (57km/35 miles).

7 ★★★ Moustiers-Ste-Marie. Moustiers clings to its gorge-torn cliffside in medieval splendor. The steep, labyrinthine streets are watched over by the eerie, 13th-century Notre-Dame chapel and by a golden star that swings on a cord over the gorge. According to a legend popularized by Provençal poet Frédéric Mistral, the star was mounted by crusading knight Bozon de Blacas in the 10th century, but no one actually knows its true origins. From the 17th century onward, the village has been a center for *faïence* pottery,

a tradition carried on today by several artists, who sell their original designs in the village shops. If you're into hiking, follow the signposted trails out of town and over the gorge, or see the tourist office about guided walks. Moustiers is also a fine base for discovering the Gorges du Verdon (stop **8**, below). ⏱ 1 day. Moustiers Tourist Office, place de l'Eglise. ☎ 04-92-74-67-84. www.moustiers.fr.

8 ★★★ kids Les Gorges du Verdon. Reputedly the most beautiful canyon in Europe, the Verdon's clear, turquoise waters and theatrical gorges provide an awe-inspiring backdrop for hiking, cycling, and watersports. Inquire at the **Moustiers tourist office** (☎ 04-92-74-67-84; www.moustiers.fr). Nearby, the 22km (14-mile) manmade **Ste-Croix Lake** is utterly breathtaking, especially when seen from the village of Ste-Croix-de-Verdon, which juts out of a rocky promontory above the azure water to afford marvelous views over the mountains. ⏱ Half-day. www.verdon-en-provence.com.

Worthy Detours

Although not covered here, medieval Brignoles and the winemaking port of Bandol are worth an hour or two of your time, as are Draguignan, gateway to the Var's wild truffle woods and vineyards, and Toulon, France's second-largest naval port.

Where to Stay & Dine in the Var & Haute-Provence

★ **Hostellerie du Cigalou** BORMES-LES-MIMOSAS *FRENCH* Exceptionally well situated in the medieval village, this simple hotel has pleasant rooms and a decent restaurant, which doubles as a tearoom by day. Decor is distinctly Provençal. **Place Gambetta.** ☎ 04-94-41-51-27. www.hostellerieducigalou.com. 8 units. Doubles from 108€. Menus 30€. MC, V.

Hotel La Ponche ST-TROPEZ *PROVENCALE GOURMET* At this hotel-restaurant near St-Tropez's La Ponche beach, expect high-end dishes such as filet mignon of pork, red mullet with saffron rice, and stuffed lobster. Rooms in the adjoining hotel are lovely. **Place du Revelin.** ☎ 04-94-97-09-29. www.laponche.com. 18 units. Doubles from 189€ (up to 655€ in high season). Fixed-price menus 40€. AE, MC, V.

★★ **L'Arena** FREJUS *GOURMET FRENCH* Three handsome, typical Provençal-style buildings make up this hotel-villa in Fréjus's old town. The restaurant serves delicacies such as fricassee of lobster. **145 rue Général de Gaulle.** ☎ 04-94-17-09-40. www.hotel-frejus-arena.com. 36 units. Doubles 70€–160€. Menus from 30€. AE, MC, V. Closed Oct 31–Dec 5.

★★★ **La Bastide de Moustiers** MOUSTIERS *GOURMET FRENCH* Service at this country *auberge* is five-star, the rooms are an ode to comfort, and the cuisine created by Alain Ducasse protégé Alain Souliac is deeply satisfying. **Chemin de Quinson, Moustiers-Ste-Marie.** ☎ 04-92-70-47-47. www.bastide-moustiers.com. 12 units. Doubles 190€–400€. Meals from 55€. AE, MC, V.

★★ **Le Couvent des Minimes** MANE This cozy hotel is set in a medieval converted convent with neo–Art Deco rooms, two excellent gourmet restaurants, and France's only L'Occitane spa. **Chemin des Jeux de Maï.** ☎ 04-92-74-77-77. www.couventdesminimes-hotelspa.com. 46 units. Doubles 170€–415€. AE, MC, V.

> *Alain Souliac brings out the best in every ingredient at La Bastide de Moustiers.*

★★ **Le Haut du Pavé** HYERES *PROVENCAL* Think perfectly cooked fish, Provençal specialties, fine wine, medieval vaults, and friendly service. This is one of the best restaurants in Hyères. **Place Massillon.** ☎ 04-94-35-20-98. Menus 20€–30€. Lunch and dinner Wed–Sun.

★★ **L'Hostellerie de l'Abbaye de La Celle** LA CELLE *GOURMET FRENCH* This 18th-century Benedictine abbey, now a country inn, offers Michelin-starred Provençal cuisine and verdant gardens that contain 80 varieties of vine. **10 place du Général de Gaulle.** ☎ 04-98-05-14-14. www.abbaye-celle.com. 10 units. Menus 40€–82€; main courses 27€–43€. Doubles 250€–450€. AE, MC, V.

★★★ **Pastis** ST-TROPEZ This boutique hotel overlooking the Bay of St-Tropez has a gorgeous pool surrounded by palms as well as smart rooms filled with artful touches and crisp, cotton bedsheets. **61 av. du General Leclerc.** ☎ 04-98-12-56-50. www.pastis-st-tropez.com. 9 units. Doubles from 175€ (up to 650€ in high season). AE, MC, V.

The Riviera

The Riviera encompasses the best and the worst of the south of France. On the one hand, there are all those tall, concrete, postwar constructions monopolizing the sea views along some of the country's most spectacular coastline. On the other, there's the definitive glamour of towns such as Cannes and St-Jean-Cap-Ferrat; the legacy of artists such as Henri Matisse, Auguste Renoir, Jean Cocteau, and Pablo Picasso; and the subtropical climate that suports some of France's most extraordinary gardens and citrus groves. It is this varied landscape that makes the region so stimulating and beguiling.

> Offshore from Cannes, Les Îles des Lérins are still inhabited by monks, providing a peaceful, down-to-earth alternative to the glittery city.

START **Cannes** is 905km (562 miles) south of Paris, 163km (101 miles) east of Marseille, and 26km (16 miles) southwest of Nice. TRIP LENGTH 124km (77 miles) on both fast and small roads.

1 Cannes. This epicenter of wealth, fame, and adulating stargazers is a fine spot for shopping and salivating over designer merchandise, before winding down over a cocktail in a trendy bar or hotel. ⏱ 1 day. See p. 445, **4**.

Leave Cannes via Le Cannet district on D6285; at the Rond-Point Winston Churchill, join D3 and follow signs to Mougins (7km/4⅓ miles).

2 ★ Mougins. As with most of the Riviera's hilltop villages, medieval Mougins was adopted in modern times by artists—in this case, surrealists Francis Picabia and Jean Cocteau. Picasso also came here, first as a poor artist who resorted to painting the walls of his room just to pay his rent, and again in 1961 when he

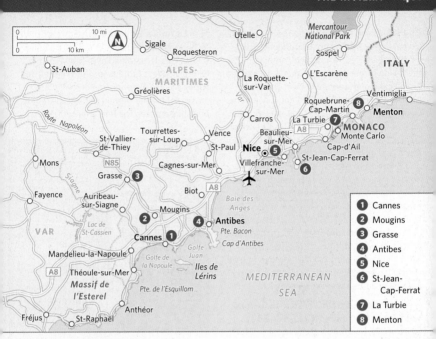

1	Cannes
2	Mougins
3	Grasse
4	Antibes
5	Nice
6	St-Jean-Cap-Ferrat
7	La Turbie
8	Menton

bought **L'Antre du Minotaur** (the Minotaur's Lair). You can still see the house, opposite the pretty Notre-Dame-de-Vie chapel just southeast of the village. Art lives on in Mougins inside the numerous galleries and at the **Musée de la Photographie André Villiers,** 67 rue de l'Eglise/Porte Sarrazine (☎ 04-93-75-85-67; free admission; July–Aug daily 10am–8pm; Sept–June Mon–Fri 10am–6pm, Sat–Sun 11am–6pm), where lesser-known works by celebrated photographers such as Robert Doisneau are exhibited. ⏱ Half-day. Mougins Tourist Office, 96 av. Moulin de la Croix. ☎ 04-93-75-87-67. www.mougins.fr/tourisme.

Leave Mougins on av. du Moulin de la Croix, turn left onto D35, and at the Rond-Point de Tournamy, turn right onto av. St-Martin; after 100m (328 ft.), pick up D6185 and follow signs to Grasse, via D9 and D4 (13km/8 miles total).

3 Grasse. The fragrance capital of the world has been making scents since the Renaissance. You could easily spend a languorous half-day in the famous perfume factories of Fragonard and Molinard, 60 bd. Victor-Hugo (☎ 04-93-36-01-62; www.molinard.com; free admission; May–Sept daily 9am–6pm, Oct–Apr Mon–Sat 9am–12:30pm and 2–6pm),

where you can learn to make your own scent. The **Musée International de la Parfumérie** (MIP), 8 place du Cours (☎ 04-97-05-58-00; www.museesdegrasse.com; admission 3€ adults, 1.50€ reduced; May–Sept daily 10am–7pm; Oct and mid-Dec to Apr Wed–Mon 11am–6pm; closed Nov to early Dec), recounts the history of perfume over the last 1,000 years. Grasse's colorful, often flaking *centre-ville* may charm you away from the scent of Fragonard for a spell. Wander the narrow streets, linked by old arches, steep ramps, and staircases, before entering the **Cathédrale Notre-Dame-du-Puy** (www.cathedraledupuy. org)—a magnificent example of Lombard-influenced Romanesque architecture. ⏱ 1 day. Grasse Tourist Office, 22 cours Honoré Cresp. ☎ 04-93-36-66-66. www.grasse.fr.

From Grasse, follow D4 toward Nice, Cabris, and then Cannes to A8; exit A8 at junction 44, and follow signs to Antibes (28km/17 miles).

Where to Stay & Dine

For hotels and restaurants in Nice, see p. 471; in Monaco, see p. 467; elsewhere along the Riviera, see p. 459.

4 ★★ Antibes. The picturesque streets of this former Greek trading post (founded in 500 B.C.) are lively year-round and contain one of the region's best produce markets, **Le Marché Provençal** (June–Sept daily 6am–1pm; Oct–Mar Tues–Sun 6am–1pm), on cours Masséna. Overlooking the town, the Château Grimaldi houses the **Musée Picasso** (p. 451, **7**), which displays a collection of works donated by the artist; and over the port, the **Fort Carré,** av. du 11 Novembre (☎ 04-92-90-52-13; www.antibes-juanlespins.com; admission 3€ adults, 1.50€ reduced, ages 17 and under free; off season Tues–Sun 10am–4:30pm, June 15–Sept 15 Tues–Sun 10am–5.30pm), is a fine example of the star-shaped defenses designed in the 17th century by Marquis de Vauban, Louis XIV's military genius. ⏱ 1 day. Antibes Tourist Office, 11 place Général de Gaulle. ☎ 04-97-23-11-11. www.antibesjuanlespins.com.

From Antibes, take D6007 (bd. du Général Vautrin) to A8 (toward Nice), exit A8 at junction 44, and follow signs to Nice-Centre (30km/19 miles).

5 Nice. Thanks to its stunning setting in the Baie des Anges, an ideal climate, and wonderful culinary and cultural traditions, Nice is one of the most charming cities on the Riviera. ⏱ At least 2 days. For detailed information on Nice, see p. 468.

From Nice, follow D6098 for 8km (5 miles), via Villefranche-sur-Mer, to join D125 and then D25 to Cap-Ferrat (11km/6¾ miles).

6 St-Jean-Cap-Ferrat. Snuggled between the resorts of Beaulieu and Villefranche, the Cap-Ferrat peninsula affords some of the best views over the sea from its coastal roads and footpaths. The main town, St-Jean-Cap-Ferrat, is a former fishing village with old houses overlooking the pleasure boats in the harbor. The peninsula is lined with some of the coast's grandest villas, like Villa Ephrussi-de-Rothschild, av. Denis-Séméria (☎ 04-93-01-33-09; www.villa-ephrussi.com). ⏱ 1 day. St-Jean-Cap-Ferrat Tourist Office, 59 av. Denis Senaria. ☎ 04-93-76-08-90.

Leave St-Jean-Cap-Ferrat on D25; at av. Jean Monnet, join D125 to Beaulieu, and then pick up D6098 to La Turbie (18km/11 miles).

7 ★ La Turbie. Built upon the Grande Corniche road, at the base of the Tête de Chien (Dog's Head) headland over Monaco, this hilltop village is famous for the **Trophée des Alpes** (Alpine Trophy), one of the tallest and most spectacular Roman ruins in the region. If possible, come in the late afternoon to climb

Château de la Napoule

In 1918, after a scandalous love affair, rich Americans Marie and Henry Clews moved to France to shun society and invent their own world. The result is this magical castle, rebuilt from medieval ruins and entirely decorated in their own artistic creations—a grotesque, sculpted menagerie of gargoyles, monkeys, gnomes, and mythological creatures. *7km/4½ miles west of Cannes, in Mandlieu-la-Napoule.* ☎ *04-93-49-95-05. www.chateau-lanapoule.com. Admission 6€ guided visit at 11:30am, 2:30pm, 3:30pm, and 4:30pm; 4€ ages 7–17. Mar–Oct daily 10am–6pm; Nov–Feb Mon–Fri 2–6pm, Sat–Sun 10am–5pm.*

Two Unforgettable Places to Stay on the Coast

For a memorable splurge, there is no finer establishment than the **Grand Hôtel du Cap-Ferrat,** 71 bd. du Général de Gaulle, Cap-Ferrat (☎ 04-93-76-50-50; www. grand-hotel-cap-ferrat.com; 73 units; doubles from 250€–1,550€ with a balcony sea-view; AE, DC, MC, V), where chef Didier Anies cooks Michelin-starred cuisine (such as lasagna with Aquitaine caviar) and service is irreproachable. The spa will dissipate your worries. The outdoor heated swimming pool overlooks the sea, alongside a garden path that leads to Cap-Ferrat's lighthouse. A more affordable option, in Antibes, is the wonderful **La Jabotte,** 13 av. Max Maurey (☎ 04-93-61-45-89; www.jabotte.com; 10 units; doubles from 69€–201€; MC, V) —a gem of a hotel with exquisite, personalized decor. It's a 10-minute walk from the old town, opposite the beach, and Tommy the dog is the star of the house.

> *Antibes's lively, fragrant market is a fine place to find delicious finger food and fruit for a picnic on the beach.*

the trophy, and then stay for sunset when the lights of Monaco begin to twinkle over the jagged coastline. ⏱ **Half-day.** La Turbie Tourist Office, place Detras. ☎ 04-93-41-21-15. www.ville-la-turbie.fr.

From La Turbie, take D2564 to A8 and follow signs to Menton (17km/11 miles).

⑧ Menton. The warmest spot on the Riviera is the lemon capital of France, with an annual lemon festival in February that draws in crowds of onlookers. Shops, cafes, and houses with Belle Epoque facades line the main pedestrian thoroughfare, rue St-Michel. A stroll through the bustling covered market, where luscious local produce is sold, will stimulate your senses. The **Basilique St-Michel-Archange,** Parvis St-Michel (☎ 04-93-35-81-63; open daily 10am–6pm), with its fine medley of Baroque ornamentations, is the largest church of its kind in the region. Jean Cocteau is associated with Menton, thanks to the **Salle des Mariages** (Wedding Room) he decorated in the City Hall, Place Ardoïno (☎ 04-92-10-50-00; admission 1.50€, reduced 1.15€; Mon–Fri 8:30am–12:30pm and 1:30–5pm). Devoted to his art is the **Musée Jean Cocteau,** Bastion du Vieux Port (☎ 04-93-57-72-30; admission 3€ adults, 1.50€ reduced; Wed–Mon 10am–noon and 2–6pm except public holidays). ⏱ **1 day.** Menton Tourist Office, 8 av. Boyer. ☎ 04-92-41-76-76. www.tourisme-menton.fr. For more on Menton, see p. 448, ①.

The Riviera's *Villages Perchés*

For information on the Riviera's other wonderful hilltop villages—Vallauris, Biot, St-Paul-de-Vence, Vence, and Cagnes-sur-Mer—see "The Riviera for Art Lovers," p. 448.

Monaco

Glamorous coastal Monaco is a feudal anomaly. Controlled by the Grimaldi family since 1297, it's the only European state outside of the Vatican with an autocratic leader. It's exempt from all taxes, gaining most of its revenues from gambling and tourism. Its world-famous casino, exclusive boutiques, luxury hotels, and annual Formula 1 Grand Prix make the principality a veritable playground for international jet-setters and the yachteratti.

> Flip-flops and shorts are prohibited in the Belle Epoque Casino de Monte-Carlo.

START Monaco is 939km (583 miles) south of Paris, and 18km (11 miles) east of Nice.

1 ★★★ **Les Grands Appartements du Palais.** The royal Grimaldis, whose ancestors have ruled Monaco since the 13th century, reside here at the Palais du Prince, which dominates the principality from La Rocher. Tour the sumptuous royal quarters, and get a glimpse of the dazzling red **Throne Room.** To see the **Relève de la Garde** (Changing of the Guard), arrive in front of the palace at 11:55am. ⏱ 1½ hr. Place du Palais. ☎ 93-25-18-31. www.palais. mc. Admission 8€ adults, 3.50€ reduced. Apr–Oct daily 10am–6:15pm. Closed Nov–Apr.

2 ★★★ kids **Musée Océanographique.** Albert I founded this museum in 1910 to display exotic specimens he collected during 30 years' worth of expeditions. The underground aquarium is one of Europe's finest. It contains more than 90 tanks of rare and wonderful species and a shark lagoon. ⏱ 2–3 hr. Av. St-Martin.

Shopping with Billionaires

For glitz, glamour, and designer style, the **Galeries du Métropole** (av. de la Madone, below the hotel; see the Monaco hotel listings) is unrivaled.

0 ⎯⎯⎯⎯ 1/4 mi
0 ⎯⎯⎯⎯ 1/4 km

LA TURBIE

FRANCE

BEAUSOLEIL

MONEGHETTI

Gare de Monaco

MONTE CARLO

LA CONDAMINE

MONACO-VILLE

Palais du Prince

Cathédrale

FONTVIEILLE

Stade Louis II (AS Monaco)

Parc Paysager de Fontvieille

Roseraie Princesse Grace

ST-ROMAN

TENAO

LARVOTTO

Plage de Larvotto

Monte Carlo Sporting Club

MONACO

place du Casino

Casino de Monte Carlo

Port de Monaco (Port Hercule)

Musée Océanographique

Jardins St-Martin

Port de Fontvieille

MEDITERRANEAN SEA

Jardin Exotique

1 Les Grands Appartements du Palais
2 Musée Océanographique
3 Casino de Monte Carlo
4 Le Café de Paris
5 Jardin Exotique

Where to Stay and Dine
Avenue 31 **7**
Hotel Columbus **13**
Hotel de France **12**
Métropole **10**
Mozza **9**
Quai des Artistes **11**

Shopping
Galeries du Metropole **10**

Where to Sunbathe & Party
Jimmy'z **6**
Plage de Larvotto **8**

☎ 93-15-36-00. www.oceano.mc. Admission 13€ adults, 6.50€ reduced, free for children 3 and under. Apr–June and Sept daily 9:30am–7pm; July–Aug daily 7:30am–7:30pm; Oct–Mar daily 10am–6pm. Closed during Grand Prix.

3 ★★★ **Casino de Monte Carlo.** Built between 1878 and 1910, this ornate Charles Garnier–designed palace is the draw for wealthy visitors. Smart dress (jacket and tie for men) is de rigueur. ⏲ At least 1 hr. Place du Casino. ☎ 98-06-21-21. www.montecarlocasinos.com. ID required; must be 18 to enter. Admission 10€ min. Winter Mon–Fri from 2pm; summer Sat–Sun from noon.

Driving in Monaco

Monaco is split into five districts: Monaco-Ville (the old town on La Rocher, "the Rock"), Fontvieille (west), Moneghetti (northwest), Monte-Carlo (the central hub of luxury around the casino), and La Condamine (the port area). Only cars registered in Monaco or with a 06 license plate (Alpes-Maritimes) are allowed access to La Rocher. Other vehicles should park at Chemin des Pêcheurs parking area, which is linked to Monaco-Ville by a lift.

> Monaco's fabulous Musée Océanographique features skeletons of rare sea creatures and a shark lagoon.

④ 🍲 **Le Café de Paris.** Along with the casino and the sublimely rococo Hôtel de Paris, this turn-of-the-century cafe is a Monégasque institution. The upstairs salon affords fine views over the coastline. Place du Casino. ☎ 98-06-76-23. Main courses 30€–50€; fixed-price menu 35€. AE, DC, MC, V.

Where to Sunbathe & Party

All VIPs frequent **Jimmy'z,** in the exclusive Le Sporting Club seaside complex (av. Princesse-Grace; ☎ 98-06-70-68; daily 10:30pm–late), while beach beauties work up a tan on avenue Princesse-Grace's beaches. For free sunbathing, head just off avenue Princesse-Grace to **Plage de Larvotto** (☎ 93-30-63-84).

Prince Albert II of Monaco

When Prince Rainier III died in 2005, his title went to his son Albert II—one of the children (along with sisters Caroline and Stephanie) of the late American film legend Grace Kelly. A descendant of the family that has ruled Monaco for more than 7 centuries, Albert has two illegitimate children on record but no official heir—although that may change with his July 2011 marriage to swimming champion Charlene Wittstock. A fervent environmentalist, Albert is the only monarch to have explored both the North and South poles.

⑤ ★★ kids **Jardin Exotique.** These gardens, clinging precariously to cliffs overlooking the principality, are known for their cactus collection, their dolomite limestone grottoes, and the **Musée d'Anthropologie Préhistorique** (☎ 93-15-80-06), with its collection of Stone Age tools and mammoth bones. ⏱ 1–2 hr. Bd. du Jardin-Exotique. ☎ 93-15-29-80. www.jardin-exotique.mc. Admission (includes museum) 7€ adults, 3.70€ reduced. Daily 9am–6pm (or sundown); closed Nov 19, Dec 25.

Where to Stay & Dine in Monaco

> *Chef Joël Robuchon (right), at his Japanese restaurant Yoshi in the Métropole, is the world's most Michelin-starred chef, with 26 stars (at press time).*

★ **Avenue 31** LES PLAGES *INTERNATIONAL*
In a prime spot near the beaches, this good-value eatery covers food for all tastes, with salads, brasserie fare, fish dishes, and sushi. And it pulls it off with flair. 31 av. Princesse-Grace. ☎ 97-70-31-31. www.avenue31.mc. Reservations recommended. Lunch from 14 €, dinner from 39€. AE, DC, MC, V. Lunch and dinner daily.

★★ **Hotel Columbus** FONTVIEILLE
This contemporary address with big, luxurious leather furnishings is a coveted crash pad, so to speak, for Formula 1 drivers and fans. Check the website for special offers. 23 av. des Papalins. ☎ 92-05-90-00. www.columbushotels.com. 184 units. Doubles 295€–325€. AE, MC, V.

★ **Hotel de France** CONDAMINE PORT
A small, old-fashioned, but welcoming hotel, all dressed up in bright yellows and checkered fabrics. Rooms are a good value for the money in Monaco. 6 rue de la Turbie. ☎ 93-30-24-64. www.monte-carlo.mc/france. 26 units. Doubles 85€. MC, V.

★★★ **Métropole** MONTE CARLO CASINO
Impeccably discreet yet utterly luxurious, this is a timeless palace, with a pool, a solarium, a fabulous luxury spa (ESPA), and two Michelin-starred restaurants run by Joël Robuchon, the world's most Michelin-starred chef: the traditional French Restaurant Joël Robuchon, and Yoshi, which serves delicious, gourmet Japanese cuisine. 4 av. de la Madone. ☎ 93-15-15-15. www.metropole.com. 169 units. Doubles 385€–1,300€. AE, DC, MC, V.

★★★ **Mozza** MONTE CARLO/PLAGES *ITALIAN*
Fifteen types of certified Italian mozzarella cheeses, Parma ham to die for, and *the* best pasta in Monaco. 11 rue d Portier. ☎ 97-77-03-04. Mozza platter 18€; main courses 15€–29€. MC, V. Lunch and dinner daily.

★★★ **Quai des Artistes** CONDAMINE PORT *BRASSERIE* Wonderful, traditional French cuisine in a Parisian-style brasserie. On a warm day, tuck into a giant seafood platter under the arcades overlooking the port. 4 quai Antoine 1er. ☎ 97-97-97-77. www.quaidesartistes.com. Lunch menu 25€, dinner menu 53€–65€. AE, MC, V. Lunch and dinner daily.

Nice

Tracing the pebbled shores of the Baie des Anges (Angel Bay), and creeping its way up into the surrounding hillside, the capital of the Riviera balances old-world decadence with modern urban energy. Founded by the Greeks in the 4th century B.C., it fell to the Romans and, subsequently, the House of Savoy in the Middle Ages, until Napoleon made it part of France in 1860. By the late 19th century, the upper class and czarist aristocrats were flocking here in winter. Nice's spectacular light also caught the attention of artists such as Henri Matisse. Nowadays, with its wonderful markets and an age-old cultural respect for good eating, Nice has become a paradise for foodies.

> This seafront in Nice, quai des Etats Unis (America quay), commemorates American assistance during World War I.

START Nice is 21km (13 miles) west of Monaco and 37km (23 miles) east of Cannes.

❶ ★★★ **Vieux Nice.** The old town is a maze of narrow, medieval streets spreading out below the Colline du Château—Nice's former stronghold. The fish market takes place Tuesday to Sunday from 6am to 1pm at place St-François. At the same time, the great **cours Saleya** market is a flamboyant bustle of bright flowers, fresh fruit, and appetizing vegetables (Tues–Sun 6am–1:30pm). Monday it becomes an antiques market, and by evening it's the focal point of Nice's nightlife. Vieux Nice is home to three of the Riviera's most beautiful baroque churches: the flamboyant **Chapelle de la Miséricorde** (cours Saleya), the heavily gilded **Chapelle de l'Annonciation** (1 rue de la Poissonnerie), and the stucco-and-marble-clad **Cathédrale de St-Réparte** (place Rossetti). The nearly invisible **Palais Lascaris,** 15 rue Droite (☎ 04-93-62-72-40; free admission; Wed–Mon 10am–6pm), is an eerie 17th-century town house with elaborate ornaments and ceilings frescoed with mythological scenes. A pharmacy, built around 1738, complete with many of the original Delftware accessories, is also on the premises. ⏱ 3–4 hr.

❷ ★ **Promenade des Anglais.** This world-famous promenade owes its existence to English aristocrats who, after a bad orange crop in 1822, occupied their idle workers with the construction of this wide boulevard fronting the bay. Stretching for about 7km (4⅓ miles) between the pebbled beach and the town, it is lined by rows of grand cafes; famous hotels, including the wildly palatial

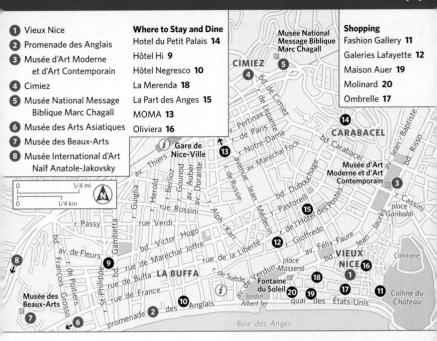

1. Vieux Nice
2. Promenade des Anglais
3. Musée d'Art Moderne et d'Art Contemporain
4. Cimiez
5. Musée National Message Biblique Marc Chagall
6. Musée des Arts Asiatiques
7. Musée des Beaux-Arts
8. Musée International d'Art Naïf Anatole-Jakovsky

Where to Stay and Dine
Hotel du Petit Palais 14
Hôtel Hi 9
Hôtel Negresco 10
La Merenda 18
La Part des Anges 15
MOMA 13
Oliviera 16

Shopping
Fashion Gallery 11
Galeries Lafayette 12
Maison Auer 19
Molinard 20
Ombrelle 17

and kitschy Hôtel Negresco; and villas. Farther east, the promenade becomes quai des Etats-Unis, the original boulevard, lined with more restaurants and nightclubs.

3 ★★★ Musée d'Art Moderne et d'Art Contemporain. This modern building—recognizable by its gargantuan cube-head statue near the entrance—is home to exceptional artworks that trace the avant-garde movement from the 1960s to the present. U.S. pop artists and European neo-realists are particularly well represented. ⏱ 2–3 hr. Promenade des Arts. ☎ 04-97-13-42-01. www.mamac-nice.org. Free admission. Tues–Sun 10am–6pm. Closed public holidays.

4 ★★★ Cimiez. Five kilometers (3 miles) north of Nice's *centre-ville* lies the once-aristocratic hilltop quarter of Cimiez, where Queen Victoria used to stay in winter, in the Hôtel Excelsior. Founded by the Romans, who called it Cemenelum, Cimiez was the capital of the Maritime Alps province. Ruins from this era include a 5,000-seat **amphitheater** still used for Nice's **Festival du Jazz** (☎ 04-97-13-36-86; www.nicejazzfestival.fr); artifacts are on display in the **Musée d'Archéologie,** 160 av. des Arènes (☎ 04-93-81-59-57; www.musee-archeologique-nice.org; admission

> *Sacha Sosno's square head, in front of Nice's Musée d'Art Moderne et d'Art Contemporain.*

Nice Shopping

Avenue Jean Médecin is the main high-street shopping drag, where you'll find the **Galeries Lafayette** (☎ 04-92-17-36-36; www.galerieslafayette.com) department store. For designer labels, target rue Paradis and **avenue de Suède**. Vieux Nice is cluttered with food shops, markets, and clothing creators. **Fashion Gallery,** 5 rue St-Suaire (☎ 04-93-80-33-73), brings together several brands in a hip, cavelike shop, dressed in chandeliers. **Molinard,** 20 rue St-François-de-Paule (☎ 04-93-62-90-50; www.molinard.com), sells perfume and offers lessons on scent. **Ombrelle,** 17 rue de la Préfecture (☎ 04-93-80-33-13; http://bestagno.exen.fr), has been selling marvelous umbrellas, parasols, and canes since 1850. And **Maison Auer,** 7 rue St-François-de-Paule (☎ 04-93-85-77-98; www.maison-auer.com), is renowned for its chocolate and Belle Epoque boutique.

gingko trees. ⏱ 1–2 hr. 405 promenade des Anglais. ☎ 04-92-29-37-00. www.arts-asiatiques.com. Free admission. May to mid-Oct Wed–Mon 10am–6pm; mid-Oct to Apr Wed–Mon 10am–5pm.

❼ ★★ Musée des Beaux-Arts. This fine collection is devoted to the masters of the Second Empire, with works by J. B. Carpeaux, François Rude, and Auguste Rodin. Paintings include treasures by the Dutch Vanloo family dynasty, including Carle Vanloo, Louis XV's premier painter. ⏱ 1–2 hr. 33 av. des Baumettes. ☎ 04-92-15-28-28. www.musee-beaux-arts-nice.org. Free admission. Tues–Sun 10am–6pm.

❽ Musée International d'Art Naïf Anatole-Jakovsky. This unique museum, set in the dazzling, pink-faceted Château Ste-Hélène, offers a rare panorama of naïve and primitive art from the 18th century to the present. ⏱ 1–2 hr. Château St-Hélène, av. de Fabron. ☎ 04-93-71-78-33. Free admission. Wed–Mon 10am–6pm.

free; Wed–Mon 10am–6pm). The next-door Italianate villa in the heart of a public olive-tree garden is the **Musée Matisse,** 164 av. des Arènes-de-Cimiez (☎ 04-93-81-08-08; www.musee-matisse-nice.org; free admission; Wed–Mon 10am–6pm except public holidays), where some of the artist's finest works are on display. ⏱ 4 hr. Take the Grand Tour tourist bus or catch bus no. 15 or 17 from place Masséna.

❺ ★ Musée National Message Biblique Marc Chagall. This handsome museum, surrounded by pools and a garden, contains the most important Chagall collection of biblical themes ever assembled, with some 450 oils, drawings, gouaches, pastels, lithographs, sculptures, and ceramics. ⏱ 1–2 hr. Av. du Dr. Ménard. ☎ 04-93-53-87-31. www.musee-chagall.fr. Admission 7.50€ adults, 5.50€ reduced, free for ages 17 and under. July–Sept Wed–Mon 10am–6pm; Oct–June Wed–Mon 10am–5pm.

❻ ★ Musée des Arts Asiatiques. In a swanky, minimalist, glass-and-metal construction near Nice's airport, this museum is a tribute to the sculpture and paintings of Cambodia, China, India, Tibet, and Japan. Of special interest are the accoutrements associated with Japanese tea ceremonies, in the tea pavilion shaded by

Mardi Gras of the Riviera

More than a million visitors from around the world flock to the 3-week Nice Carnaval (www.nicecarnaval.com) in February for a dose of sunshine during the gray winter months. Festivities traditionally include spectacularly colorful, bulbous *corsi* (floats); *veglioni* (masked balls); confetti tossing; and glorious battles in which young women fling flowers. The climax is a fireworks display on Shrove Tuesday that lights up the Baie des Anges.

Where to Stay & Dine in Nice

> Vibrant colors play off crisp white linens and fixtures in rooms at the Hôtel Hi in Nice.

Hotel du Petit Palais CIMIEZ
Actor Sacha Guitry lived in this Belle Epoque building in the 1930s. The decor is plain but pretty, with fine views and a relaxing garden. 17 av. Emile Bieckiert. ☎ 04-93-62-19-11. www.petitpalaisnice.com. 25 units. Doubles 100€–180€. AE, MC, V.

★★ Hôtel Hi NEW TOWN
The avant-garde Hi offers nine different high-tech room "concepts" that range from hospital white-on-white to birchwood veneer and acid green. 3 av. des Fleurs. ☎ 04-97-07-26-26. www.hi-hotel.net. 38 units. Doubles 200€–700€. AE, DC, MC, V. Parking 20€.

★ Hôtel Negresco PROMENADE DES ANGLAIS
No other palace hotel on the Riviera can boast such a wildly kitschy assemblage of European art treasures (think Louis XIV portraits hanging near psychedelic Niki de Saint Phalle statues). There's also a carousel-themed breakfast room and a Michelin-starred restaurant, the **Chantecler** (main courses 48€–80€; fixed-price lunch 50€–130€, dinner 90€–130€; AE, MC, V; lunch Sun, dinner Wed–Sun). 37 promenade des Anglais. ☎ 04-93-16-64-00. www.hotel-negresco-nice.com. 145 units. Doubles 280€–650€. AE, DC, MC, V.

★★ La Merenda VIEUX NICE TRADITIONAL NIÇOIS This bustling, rustic restaurant wows clients with Niçois classics such as *tarte aux blettes* (made from Swiss chard, pine nuts, raisins, and Parmesan). 4 rue Raoul Bosio. No phone. Menus 25€. No credit cards. Lunch and dinner Mon–Fri (or when the owner feels like it). Closed Aug 1–15 and public holidays.

★ La Part des Anges VIEUX NICE WINE BAR
The sommelier-owner of this intimate wine bistro delights his regulars with fine wines and hearty regional fare. 17 rue Gubernatis. ☎ 04-93-85-71-53. Menus 25€. AE, MC, V. Breakfast, lunch, and dinner Mon–Sat (until 2am).

★★★ MOMA NORTH OF CENTER
The arty Arboireau family renovated their vintage Belle Epoque house into this gorgeous little B&B, which also doubles as artists' work-shops and an events space. 5 av. des Mousqu-etaires. ☎ 06-60-57-49-59. www.moma-nice.com. 2 units. Doubles 90€. No credit cards.

★★★ Oliviera VIEUX NICE MEDITERRANEAN
This shop/cafe serves delicious salads and pastas with oils so good you can't stop sop-ping them up. 8bis rue du Collet. ☎ 04-93-13-06-45. www.oliviera.com. Main courses 9€–17€; menu 35€. No credit cards. Breakfast, lunch, and dinner Tues–Sat.

A Table & A Room with a View

For a gastronomic escapade just 15 min-utes from Nice, serious foodies flock to the narrow, medieval streets of Eze and the **Château de la Chèvre d'Or** (Golden Goat Castle), a sumptuous hotel with Michelin-starred food, impeccable service, and dizzying views over the jagged cliffs and the azure sea. *Eze is east of Nice on D6007.* ☎ 04-92-10-66-66. www.chevredor.com. *Menus from 130€. Rooms from 290€. AE, MC, V. Closed late Nov–early Mar.*

Corsica

The birthplace of Napoleon Bonaparte has a wildness that's never been tamed. Many of the island's inhabitants still speak the Corsican language (as well as French), and there is still a strong separatist movement. Yet for visitors, La Corse is a paradisiacal land of contrasts: From lush vineyards, fish-rich rivers, and citrus groves to the sun-parched *maquis* (mountainous scrublands), where an aromatic breeze blows through herb- and-flower-speckled hills, the island's wild beauty has been preserved in ways unseen elsewhere in the Mediterranean.

> *The ragged cliffs around Porto change colors throughout the day, depending on the intensity of the light.*

START Bastia is accessible by plane via Paris, Lyon, Marseille, and Nice, and by boat via Marseille, Toulon, and Nice. TRIP LENGTH 480km (298 miles) on mostly narrow, winding roads.

① Bastia. As Corsica's second-biggest city and capital of Haute-Corse, the port town of Bastia is both fetching and authentic, with striking Italianate architecture and a Genoese **citadel.** The huge, cafe-strewn **place St-Nicolas** is the city's fashionable promenade zone—a fine spot for sipping cool *aperitifs* and, on Sundays, rummaging through antiques at the flea market. Pop into the tourist office here to grab a map of Bastia's chapels and churches. Many, like the rococo **Chapelle Ste-Croix,** with its black Christ, are pure architectural gems. The ocher-and-blue-shuttered streets around the **Hôtel de Ville** (the site of a daily food market) swarm with shops selling Corsican liquors, wines, olive oils, honeys, and other local specialties. At the end of the day, watch the sun set over the **Old Port** (head to the Jetée du Dragon for the best views), and take your pick of the many seafood restaurants near the jetty. ⏱ 1–2 days. Bastia Tourist Office, place St-Nicolas. ☎ 04-95-54-20-40. www.bastia-tourisme.com.

Driving Tips

A car is the best way to explore the island. Carry a spare tank of gas, as service stations are infrequent. Also, beware of the many tortuously twisting roads, although the views from these are more than rewarding.

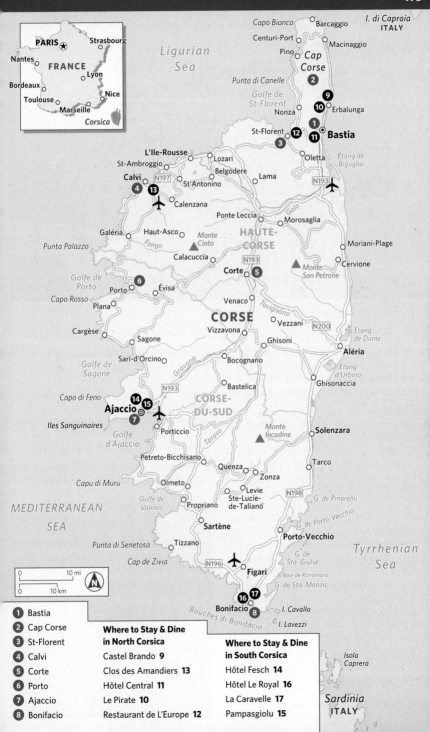

Inset map of France:
PARIS ★
Strasbourg
Nantes
FRANCE
Lyon
Bordeaux
Nice
Toulouse
Marseille
Corsica

Map labels:
Ligurian Sea

Capo Bianco
Barcaggio
Centuri-Port
Macinaggio
Pino
Cap Corse ❷
Punta di Canelle
Golfe de St-Florent
❾
Nonza
❿ Erbalunga
❶
St-Florent ⓬
❸ ⓫ **Bastia**
Oletta
Étang de Biguglia

L'Ile-Rousse
Lozari
St-Ambroggio
Belgodere
Lama
Calvi ❹
St'Antonino
⓭
N197
Calenzana
N193
✈
Ponte Leccia
Morosaglia
Galéria
Haut-Asco
Monte Cinto ▲
HAUTE-CORSE
Moriani-Plage
Calacuccia
Cervione
Punta Palazzo
Fango
Golo
Corte ❺
▲ *Monte San Petrone*

Golfe de Porto
❻
Évisa
Porto
Venaco
Vezzani
N200
Étang de Diane
CORSE
Capo Rosso
Plana
Tavignano
Vizzavona
Ghisoni
Étang d'Urbino
Cargèse
Sagone
Sari-d'Orcino
Bocognano
Aléria
Golfe de Sagone
Ghisonaccia
Capo di Feno
N193
Bastelica
CORSE-DU-SUD
Ajaccio ⓮ ⓯
✈
❼
Monte Incudine ▲
Solenzara
Iles Sanguinaires
Porticcio
Golfe d'Ajaccio
Tavaro
Petreto-Bicchisano
Tarco
Quenza
Capu di Muru
Zonza
Olmeto
Levie
N198
Ste-Lucie-de-Taliano
G. de Pinarellu
Golfe de Valinco
Propriano
G. de Porto-Vecchio
Sartène
Porto-Vecchio
Punta di Senetosa
Tizzano
G. de Sta. Giulia
Cap de Zivia
N196
✈
Figari
Baie di Rondinara
G. de Sta. Manza
⓰ ⓱
Bonifacio
❽
I. Cavallo
Bouches di Bonifacio
I. Lavezzi

MEDITERRANEAN SEA

Gravona

Tyrrhenian Sea

I. di Capraia
ITALY

Isola Caprera

Sardinia
ITALY

Scale: 0 — 10 mi / 0 — 10 km
N

❶ Bastia
❷ Cap Corse
❸ St-Florent
❹ Calvi
❺ Corte
❻ Porto
❼ Ajaccio
❽ Bonifacio

Where to Stay & Dine in North Corsica

Castel Brando **9**
Clos des Amandiers **13**
Hôtel Central **11**
Le Pirate **10**
Restaurant de L'Europe **12**

Where to Stay & Dine in South Corsica

Hôtel Fesch **14**
Hôtel Le Royal **16**
La Caravelle **17**
Pampasgiolu **15**

> Bastia's Old Port, viewed from the Jetée du Dragon.

From Bastia, D80 north loops around Cap Corse, while D81 heads west to St-Florent. From Bastia, it's 10km (6¼ miles) to Erbalunga and 23km (14 miles) to St-Florent.

2 Cap Corse. The geography of Corsica's northernmost tip, north of Bastia—a peninsula 40km (25 miles) long and never more than 14km (8⅔ miles) wide—has earned it the nickname "island on the island." Separated by a ridge of mountains, Cap Corse is dotted with divine old villages, some precipitously perched on rocky outcrops and others nestled into sea-side coves. One of the prettiest is **Erbalunga,** an old fishing port on the eastern shore (D80). If you're into hiking, take D80 from the coastal village of **Lavasina** and join D54 to **Pozzu,** where a 5-hour hike takes you 1,307m (4,288 ft.) to the top of **Monte-Stello,** the Cap's highest peak (ascent is not recommended during fog or heat waves). From its breezy heights, unsullied by time, war, or tourism, you can see the Italian island of Elba, where Napoleon was exiled—so close, he could smell Corsica's *maquis.* Another picture-perfect village is **Centuri,** on the west side of the peninsula's head. More than just pretty, it's also a prime spot for a seafood platter. From here, don't

miss **Pino,** whose church is packed with model ships placed there by locals in honor of the Virgin who protects them while at sea. Farther south, the black sands of **Nonza** (on the west side) are particularly haunting at sunset. ⏱ 2–3 days. For more information, contact the Maison du Cap Port, Toga.☎ 04-95-31-02-32. www. destination-cap-corse.com.

3 St-Florent. Lord Nelson relentlessly bombarded St-Florent's 15th-century **citadel** long

A Wine Route from Bastia

Between Bastia and St-Florent (along D81), around the village of Patrimonia, a myriad of *cavistes* (wine producers) coax you in with the promise of wine tasting—and inevitably, purchasing—of their AOC sun-kissed reds, whites, rosés, and muscats. About 95% of the region's red and rosé wines are made from the nielluccio grape variety, while the whites are usually 100% vermentino. For a stopover en route, **L'Hôtel du Vignole,** in Patrimonio (☎ 04-95-37-18-48. www.hotel-du-vignoble. com), offers simple rooms from 60€, and there's wine tasting in the cellar.

before the Battle of Trafalgar. But it survived, and it stands today as an excellent example of Genoese military architecture, lending its thick, stone walls to art exhibitions every summer. In August it is also used for the annual Latino music festival, **Porto Latino** (www. porto-latino.com). Rather like St-Tropez, St-Florent attracts the island's most moneyed crowd, with its yacht-lined pleasure port and twisting, glamorous alleys that lead to the main **place des Portes**—an elegant square where white-haired *pétanque* players merrily rub shoulders with bronze-bodied beauties. ⏱1 day. St-Florent Tourist Office. ☎ 04-95-37-06-04. www.corsica-saintflorent.com.

From St-Florent, take D81 for 28km (17 miles), turn right onto N1197, and after 9km (5⅔ miles), pick up N197 to Calvi (68km/42 miles total).

❹ **Calvi.** Part holiday resort, part military port, this town is where Lord Nelson lost his eye in 1794. It is also purportedly where Christopher Columbus was born, but there is no supporting evidence for this. In the streets below Calvi's looming 15th-century citadel, listen to the chatter and clinking of glasses emanating from lively cafe terraces; contemplate the fishermen hauling in their fresh catches on quai Adolphe Landry; or hit the shops on rue Clémenceau or boulevard Wilson. When the crowds get to be too much, the secluded beaches of Arinella and Restitude to the south beckon (take the train from Calvi's station, if you don't want to drive). Certified divers can also explore the wreckage of a World War II B-17 bomber, inside which a huge moray eel is rumored to be living in between the seats. ⏱1–2 days. Calvi Tourist Office, Port de Plaisance de Calvi. ☎ 04-95-65-16-67. www.balagne-corsica.com.

From Calvi, take N197 for 27km (17 miles), join N1197 at Belgodère, and after 31km (19 miles), rejoin N197 to Ponte Leccia; then take N193 (3rd exit) to Corte (86km/53 miles total).

❺ **Corte.** Smack-bang in the center of Corsica, perched high on a crag, beautiful Corte is the intellectual capital of Corsica, with a university and an anthropology museum set snugly inside yet another 15th-century citadel (☎ 04-95-45-25-45; www.musee-corse.com; admission 5.50€ adults, 3.80€ reduced; June–Sept

For Beach Lovers

Corsica has more than 200 beaches, the best of which have been photographed by local paper *Corse Matin* and compiled into the bilingual guide *Les Plages de Corse* (10€ from newsstands). In Haute-Corse, beaches near the main resorts teem with bronzing bodies, but there are isolated paradisiacal stretches that can be reached only on foot, via bike, or by boat. One of the best is **Plage de Sallecia,** whose crystalline water and fine, white sand were the backdrop for the invasion scenes of the movie *The Longest Day.* You can drive there from D81, but the track is very bumpy; most people hike or cycle the 12km (7½ miles) from St-Florent (p. 474, ❸). In Corse-du-Sud, Porto-Vecchio's beaches are legendary: **Rondinara** (p. 455) is one of the prettiest, and **Palombaggia** is bordered by bright green pines that contrast with the beach's white sand and red rocks. In high season, shuttle buses run to Palombaggia; ask at Porto-Vecchio's tourist office (rue du Docteur Camille de Rocca Serra; 04-95-70-09-58; www.ot-portovecchio.com).

> *High on a rocky knoll, Corte's old citadel has housed the Musée de la Corse (Corsica Museum) since 1997.*

> *Napoleon's bust presides over a fireplace inside Maison Bonaparte, where the conqueror was born in 1769.*

daily 10am–8pm, Oct–May Tues–Sun 10am–5pm). The town tumbles down the mountain in a cascade of artists' workshops, old houses, and secret passageways, and makes a delightful base for exploring the surrounding mountains—especially Corsica's celebrated hiking trails (see p. 477). ⏲ 1 day. **Corte Tourist Office, La Citadelle.** ☎ 04-95-46-26-70. www.corte-tourisme.com.

From Corte, take N193 to Francardo, turn left on D84, and after 78km (48 miles), turn right onto D81 to Porto (92km/57 miles total).

⑥ **Porto.** At the tip of the UNESCO-protected **Golfe de Porto** (one of Europe's most beautiful Mediterranean bays), this sea-facing town bustles year-round. Its Genoese watchtower contains the fragrant **Musée de la Bruyère** (Heather Museum), place de la Marine (☎ 04-

95-26-10-55; admission 2.50€; Apr–June and Sept daily 11am–7pm, July–Aug 11am–9pm). It's the best place to be as the sun slides below the horizon, igniting everything in hues of fiery red, orange, and mauve. The grandiose cliff and mountains surrounding Porto are best viewed by boat. From the port, **Nave Va,** quartier de la Marine, Hôtel Cyrnée (☎ 04-95-26-15-16 or 04-95-21-83-97; www.naveva.com), runs regular excursions (Apr–Oct) to the red granite **Calanche** cliffs and the tiny, goat-inhabited hamlet of **Girolata,** reached only by sea, on foot, or via mule track. ⏲ 1 day. **Porto Tourist Office, quartier de la Marine.** ☎ 04-95-26-10-55. www.porto-tourisme.com.

From Porto, take D81 to Ajaccio (80km/50 miles).

Hiking on Corsica

Corsica is laced with easy-to-follow **Grande Randonnée** (GR, long-distance) hiking trails that stretch up from the jagged coastline into the alternately arid and fertile inland peaks. The most famous tracks are the GR20 (for fit, seasoned hikers) and the Mare e Monti and Mare e Mare routes (more accessible to amateur ramblers). Make sure you take plenty of water and food, as you'll encounter few places to replenish en route. For the following hiking trails, we recommend you check out **Parc Naturel Régional de Corse,** or PNRC (Natural Park of Corsica), 2 rue du Sergent-Casalonga (☎ 04-95-51-79-00; www.parc-naturel-corse.com); it covers more than one-third of the island. Or try the **Fédération Française de Randonnée Pédestre** (FFRP), 64 rue du Dessous des Berges (☎ 01-44-89-93-93; www.ffrandonnee.fr). Both provide detailed maps.

The GR20 Trail. Hikers often refer to this 200km (124-mile) trail as the most beautiful long-distance route in the world, with its flower-strewn plateaus and pine forests; cascading waterfalls; snow-peaked mountains; white cliffs dropping into the sea; and moonlike, granite landscapes. The GR20 traverses Corsica on a northwest/southeast axis, from Calenzana (in the Balagne region) to Conco (just north of Porto-Vecchio), at an altitude of 1,000 to 2,000m (3,281–6,562 ft.). It generally takes 15 days, in 5- to 8-hour stretches, to walk the entire length of the route. A perfect fitness level and confidence

on a variety of rugged terrains are crucial. Weather conditions are changeable, so it is important to bring proper hiking equipment (including a tent) and enough food to last several days. Along the way, the PNRC provides *refuges,* which are no-frills shelters with a stove, places to wash, and beds or space for camping. It is recommended that you reserve the *refuges* online before you leave. If you'd rather walk the GR20 with a guide, try **Corsica Nature** (☎ 04-95-10-83-16; www.corsicanatura.fr).

Mare e Monti & Mare e Mare Trails. For fit hikers who want the views without the strain of the **GR20,** the Mare e Monti and Mare e Mare encompass five trails that cross the PNRC in the north and south of the island. While the GR20 stays up in the mountains, these trails take you through numerous pretty hamlets and villages with *gîte* accommodation (a cut above the GR's *refuges*), and each trail can be covered in 5 to 10 days. The route stretching from Moriani on the east to Cargèse in the west takes 10 days and passes through Corte (p. 475, **⑤**)—a fine stop-off point, and a chance to punctuate your walk with a day or two of culture. A good place to stay in Corte is Kyrn Flor, U San Gaviru, RN 193 (☎ 04-95-61-02-88; www.chambresdhotes-kyrnflor.com)—a holiday estate with *gîtes* from 70€ per night for up to four people (bring your own sheets and towels), a shared swimming pool, and an essential-oil distillery.

> *Bonifacio's boat-filled port at the southern tip of Corsica, closer to Sardinia than mainland France.*

❼ Ajaccio. Unlike its most famous progeny, Napoleon Bonaparte, Ajaccio has no complex about being petite. It's also mellower than most other French provincial capitals—with wide, tree-lined avenues and a gorgeous open bay. Culture lovers can heave a sigh of relief here. **Cathédrale Notre-Dame de la Miséricorde** (where Napoleon was baptized in 1771) contains Delacroix's *Vierge au Sacré Coeur* (Virgin of the Sacred Heart) masterpiece. On nearby rue St-Charles, **Maison Bonaparte** (☎ 04-95-21-43-89; www.musees-nationaux-napoleoniens.org; admission 7€ adults, 5€ reduced; Apr–Sept Tues–Sun 10am–noon and 2–6pm, Oct–Mar Tues–Sun 10am–noon and 2–4:45pm), where the emperor was born, contains period rooms and family portraits. Art lovers also flock to the **Musée Fesch,** 50 rue Cardinal Fesch (☎ 04-95-21-48-17; www.musee-fesch.com), to see the largest collection of Italian primitive art outside Paris's Louvre (p. 50, ❶). Most of the treasures, by artists such as Botticelli and Giovanni, were looted by Napoleon's uncle, Cardinal Fesch,

during the Italian campaign. ⏱ 2 days. Ajaccio Tourist Office, 3 bd. du Roi Jérôme. ☎ 04-95-51-53-03. www.ajaccio-tourisme.com.

From Ajaccio, take N193 and N196, following signs to Bonifacio (130km/81 miles).

❽ Bonifacio. Jutting out into the sea atop a limestone cliff, Bunifazui, as the locals know it, is a veritable jewel. In the summer months, its narrow streets throng with sightseers. The harbor is a handsome sight, abounding with shops, cafes, and restaurants. Steep stairs inch their way up from here to the 12th-century Genoese bastion via the fortified **Old Town.** The St-Roch steps (which begin as the *montée Rastello*) take you past the little **Chapelle St-Roch,** edified on the spot where the last person died of the plague in 1528. In the cliff below Bonifacio's tower a mysterious, 187-step staircase, **Escalier du Roi d'Aragon** (King of Aragon's Steps), is rumored to have been dug by hand, by Alphonse V's soldiers during the 1420 siege, though it was more likely the work of Franciscan monks. West of the citadel, a pebbly plateau called the

Diving on Corsica

Surrounded by sea, with no intensive fishing and very little pollution, Corsica is an Eldorado for divers, with an underwater landscape as rich and varied as its above-ground scenery. Marine life is abundant, and there are plenty of wrecks to explore (mostly World War II ships and bombers). To shake fins with the fishes, call the following companies, or check with your closest tourist office:

AJACCIO
Maeva Plongée, Les Marines de Porticco (☎ 04-95-25-02-40 or ☎ 06-23-13-35-39; www.maeva-plongee.com).

BASTIA
Club de Plongée Bastiais, Vieux Port (☎ 06-18-39-96-37 in Thierry, or ☎ 06-26-42-90-53 in Stephane; www.plongee-bastia.com).

CALVI
Stareso (lessons on Corsica's marine life), Pointe Revellata (☎ 04-95-65-06-18; http://stareso.com).

CAP CORSE
Dollfin, Marine de Sisco (☎ 09-71-28-49-10 or ☎ 06-07-08-95-92; www.dollfin-plongee.com).

PORTO
Centre de Plongée du Golde de Porto (☎ 04-95-26-10-29 or ☎ 06-84-24-49-20; www.plongeeporto.com).

PORTO-VECCHIO
Plongée Nature, 9 rte. de l'Ancienne Douane de Port (☎ 06-64-43-26-04 or ☎ 06-19-26-26-51; www.plongee-nature.com).

ST-FLORENT
Actisub, quai de l'Aliso (☎ 04-95-46-06-53 or ☎ 06-12-10-29-71; http://actisub.com).

Bosco houses two old windmills and the ruins of a Franciscan monastery. Several companies run boat trips out of the marina, going past Bonifacio's cliffs and hidden limestone caves, as well as excursions to the nearby islands of Lavezzi and Cavallo. ⊙ 2 days. Bonifacio Tourist Office, 2 rue Fred Scamaroni. ☎ 04-95-73-11-88. www.bonifacio.fr.

Corsica & Napoleon

Corsica's most famous native, Napoleon Bonaparte (born in Ajaccio in 1769), is celebrated here in every way, from statues to street names. The son of petty Corsican aristocrats, he left the island at the age of 9 to attend military school in Brienne. In 1793 he rebuffed the royalists in Toulon as an artillery chief and defended Corsica from the English. Then, after the Revolution and a Parisian coup in 1799, Napoleon declared himself consul, and eventually, emperor of the new French republic. Seven years later, he made Corsica the newest French *département*, binding it irretrievably to France.

NOT TONIGHT, NAPOLEON!

The Emperor's Personal Waterloo

BY TONY PERROTTET

DESPITE HIS BEST EFFORTS TO BE REMEMBERED AS A CONQUEROR, Napoleon was the modern era's first mega-celebrity—a man who rose like a meteor from total obscurity to terrorize the whole of Europe—and his every romantic encounter was followed in detail by both proud French patriots and mocking British propagandists. Since his death in 1821, historians have shown the same enthusiasm, as they discover, with some ironic glee, that Napoleon was not quite as successful in the boudoir as he was on the battlefield.

The Conquests

1787 The 18-year-old Corsican lieutenant claims to lose his virginity to a prostitute in the Palais Royale in Paris.

1796 Now an up-and-coming general, Napoleon falls in love with Marie-Joséphe-Rose de Beauharnais—a 33-year-old widow he calls "Joséphine." They quickly marry, but the comely mother of two soon takes up with a young cavalry officer.

1797 London tabloids report that Joséphine has dubbed Bonaparte *"bon-pour-rien"* (good for nothing), and dwell on rumors about his prowess.

1798 On campaign in Egypt in 1798, Napoleon learns of Joséphine's adultery. According to his secretary, Bourienne, "A wild look came into his eyes, and several times he struck his head with his fists."

1799 Napoleon forgives his wife. But in a stunning role reversal, Joséphine becomes a devoted wife while the general takes a parade of lovers over the ensuing decade.

1805 After his coronation at Notre Dame, Emperor Napoleon I of France confesses that he has conquered Europe for love: As the world's most powerful man, he can sleep with any woman he desires.

1810 Napoleon divorces Empress Joséphine, who has failed to produce an heir, and marries 19-year-old Austrian princess, Marie-Louise. She gives birth to an heir, Napoleon François-Joseph Charles.

1816 After his exile to St-Helena, rumors suggest Napoleon is having affairs with the wives of the loyal generals who join him in prison.

1821 Before dying of stomach cancer, Napoleon utters his last words: "France, the army, the head of the army, Joséphine!"

"The Honeymoon Letters"

After a whirlwind courtship, Napoleon and Joséphine had 36 hours together before the young general departed for Italy, for his first important campaign. Napoleon's missives to Joséphine are known as "the honeymoon letters"—though his new wife, while cuckolding him in Paris, refused invitations to join him in Italy.

WEEK 1
"Citizeness Bonaparte, My imagination exhausts itself wondering what you are doing."

WEEK 2
"My imagination frightens me: You love me less, you will find consolation elsewhere."

WEEK 4
"To live through Joséphine—that is the story of my life."

WEEK 6
"You let many days go by without writing to me. What, then, are you doing?"

WEEK 7
"There is no one else, no one but me, is there?"

WEEK 8
"You will come [to Italy], won't you?"

WEEK 12
"My life is a perpetual nightmare. A fatal premonition stops me from breathing. I am no longer living."

WEEK 14
"Mock me, stay on in Paris, take lovers, let all the world know it, never write to me—and then? And then I shall love you ten times more than I did before!"

The Family Jewels

As reported in the book *Napoléon's Privates*, Napoleon's Corsican doctor, Francesco Antommarchi, "souvenired" the vanquished ruler's "sword" at the postmortem in St-Helena. The preserved body part traveled the globe for 200 years until 1977, when the world's top urologist, Dr. John Kingsley Lattimer, bought it at an auction in Paris. To this day, Napoleon's reputed privates are part of a collection of military artifacts at the late doctor's family home in Englewood, New Jersey.

Where to Stay & Dine in North Corsica

> The warm, 19th-century interior of the Hôtel Central in Bastia.

★★ **Castel Brando** ERBALUNGA
A resplendent, isolated, bougainvillea-covered hotel in a 19th-century American-style house. Erbalunga, 10km (6¼ miles) north of Bastia. ☎ 04-95-30-10-30. 44 units. www.castelbrando.com. Doubles from 105€. MC, V.

Clos des Amandiers CALVI
This charming, higgledy-piggledy collection of no-frills bungalows is set in an orchard, 15 minutes on foot from Calvi's center and beach. Rte. de Pietramaggiore, Calvi.

☎ 04-95-65-08-32. www.clos-des-amandiers.com. 24 units. Doubles 65€–165€. MC, V.

★ **Hôtel Central** BASTIA
This hotel is calm, discreet, and impeccably 19th-century in style. Rooms are large, and there are six fully equipped family apartments on the top floor. 3 rue Miot. ☎ 04-95-31-71-12. www.centralhotel.fr. 21 units. Doubles 62€–137€; apartments 97€–137€. MC, V.

★★★ **Le Pirate** ERBALUNGA *CONTEMPORARY CORSICAN* An unrivaled seaside setting and Michelin-starred cuisine such as octopus risotto and veal piccata. The 35€ lunch menu is a steal. Erbalunga port. ☎ 04-95-33-24.20. www.restaurantlepirate.com. Menus 65€–90€. MC, V. June–Sept lunch and dinner daily, Oct–May lunch and dinner Wed–Sun.

★★ **Restaurant de L'Europe** ST-FLORENT *SEAFOOD/FRENCH* There's an unpretentious hotel upstairs, but the stars here are oven-baked sea bass and garlic lamb chops. Quai du Port de Plaisance. ☎ 04-95-35-32.91. www.hotel-europe2.com. Doubles 50€–110€. MC, V. 3 courses 40€. Lunch Wed–Sun, dinner Wed–Sat.

Opening Hours on Corsica

Note that in Corsica, many hotels close between November and March, so check when booking. Ditto for restaurants, which may even close in peak season if the owners decide to do so on a whim (for a family member's birthday, for instance).

North or South?

We recommend splitting your time between North Corsica (Haute-Corse) and South Corsica (Corse-du-Sud), or choosing one area and staying there to relax on beaches and sightsee at a leisurely pace. Ajaccio, Bastia, and Calvi make good bases for a long weekend if you're combining this tour with mainland spots on the Riviera.

Where to Stay & Dine in South Corsica

> *Alfresco diners at night in Bonifacio.*

★ Hôtel Fesch AJACCIO
Rooms are simple, with antique touches, in this hotel on a boutique-lined pedestrian street within walking distance of Ajaccio's museums. 7 rue Cardinal Fesch. ☎ 04-95-51-62-62. www.hotel-fesch.com. 77 units (some rooms sleep 5). Doubles 78€–117€. MC, V.

★ Hôtel Le Royal BONIFACIO PIZZA
In a prime spot in the heart of the Old Town, this hotel has unfussy rooms, and there's a handy pizzeria on the ground floor. 8 rue Fred Scamaroni. ☎ 04-95-73-00-51. www.hotel-leroyal.com. 14 units. Doubles 55€–115€. MC, V. Pizzeria open daily for lunch and dinner.

★★ La Caravelle BONIFACIO SEAFOOD
Here's the place to splurge on glorious seafood, such as lobster in basil butter, followed by sticky sweet desserts. There are chic rooms upstairs, too, from 78€ to 270€. 37 quai Camparetti. ☎ 04-95-73-00-03. www.hotel-caravelle-corse.com. 3-courses 80€. AE, MC, V.

★★ Pampasgiolu AJACCIO CORSICAN
Book ahead, and try the local *spuntini* (mixed platters of fish and local charcuteries) and the scrumptious chestnut fondants. 15 rue de la Porta. ☎ 04-95-50-71-52. www.upampasgiolu. fr. 3 courses 30€. AE, MC, V. Dinner Mon–Sat.

Corsican Delicacies

CHARCUTERIES
Salted, dried meats—especially *cochon coureur* ham, from domesticated, semi-wild pig. The pigs are raised in the mountains, where they feast on acorns and chestnuts, which gives their meat a rich, nutty flavor.

LE BROCCIU
A creamy white cheese eaten with honey, *eau de vie*, and vinaigrette, or used in soups, pasta dishes, and desserts.

CHATAÎGNE
Chestnuts—used to make flour, *pulenta* (chestnut dumplings), or *crème de marron* (chestnut cream).

OLIVE OILS
Six varieties of olive make smooth flavorful oils, scented with *maquis*, a fragrant local shrub.

BEERS
Amber-colored **Pietra** (made with chestnuts), pale **Serena**, and **La Colomba,** perfumed with herbs from the *maquis*.

Riviera & Monaco Fast Facts

> The world's finest cars are a common sight in Monte Carlo, whose streets become a racetrack during the Formula One Grand Prix.

Arriving & Getting Around

BY PLANE From the U.K., you can catch regular flights to the Toulon-Hyères airport with **Ryanair** (☎ 0871 246 0000; www.ryanair.com); while Nice–Côte d'Azur is served by several companies: **Ryanair, BMI Baby** (☎ 0905 828 2828; www.bmibaby.com), **British Airways** (☎ 0844 493 0787; www.britishairways. com), **Jet2** (☎ 0871 226 1 737; www.jet2. com), and **Flybe** (☎ 0871 700 2000; www. flybe.com). From the U.S., all major airlines fly to Paris; from there, your connecting flight will probably land in Nice's international airport, **Aéroport Nice-Côte d'Azur** (☎ 04-89-88-98-28; www.nice.aeroport.fr). **Air France** (☎ 800/237-2747 U.S. or ☎ 0871 66 33 777 U.K.; www.airfrance.com) covers most destinations on the Riviera from Paris. **Delta Airlines** (☎ 800/241-4141; www.delta.com) flies nonstop to Paris from Atlanta, Cincinnati, and New York, and has one nonstop service from New York to Nice. **BY TRAIN** The major rail transportation hub along the French Riviera is Nice, although Cannes also enjoys good train connections. Nice and Monaco are linked by frequent service, and in summer about eight trains per day connect Nice with the rapid TGV train from Paris to Marseille. The website for the national rail service is **www. voyages-sncf.com**. Otherwise, call ☎ 36-35, or ☎ 33-08-92-35-35-35 when outside France. For information on rail passes for France, see

p. 697. The main cities are accessible by train, but a car is imperative for Haute-Provence, much of the Var, and the Riviera's perched villages. **BY CAR** Cars can be rented in most cities and at train stations, from **Avis** (www. avis.com), **Europcar** (www.europcar.co.uk), or **Hertz** (www.hertz.fr). A series of highways link most major points. The A8 follows the coast inland along the Riviera to Monaco.

Internet Cafes

NICE Cyber Point Nice, 10 av. Felix Faure (☎ 04-93-92-70-63; www.cyberpoint-nice.com). For other towns check with the tourist office.

Post Offices

NICE 12 rue Botero (New Town). **MONACO** Palais de la Scala, 1 av. Henry Dunant (Monte Carlo).

Safety

The Riviera, and particularly Monaco, is generally very safe. Pickpockets circulate in tourist cities, however, so be mindful of your belongings. In an emergency, call 17 for the police, 18 for the fire department or paramedics, and 15 for an ambulance.

Tourist Offices

Municipal tourist offices are listed at the end of the town tour stops throughout the chapter. **CÔTE D'AZUR RIVIERA** Côte d'Azur Tourism, 400 Promenade des Anglais, Nice (☎ 04-93-37-78-78; www.cotedazur-tourisme.com). **MONACO** 2a bd. Moulins (☎ 77-92-16-61-16; www.visitmonaco.com). **NICE** 5 promenade des Anglais (☎ 08-92-70-74-07; www.nicetourisme.com). Also consult www.terre-mediterranee.com, www.alpes-haute-provence.com, www.visitvar.fr, www. cotedazur-tourisme.com, and www.monaco-tourisme.com. **THE VAR** Var Tourism (☎ 04-94-18-59-69; www.visitvar.fr).

Monaco Dialing Tips

To call Monaco from outside its borders, add 00-377 at the beginning of the number. Swimwear is prohibited in the street, and suitable attire is required in all public places and religious buildings.

Corsica Fast Facts

> A ferry runs passengers to St-Nicolas Harbor in Bastia, in northern Corsica.

Arriving

BY PLANE Corsica has four airports: Bastia, Ajaccio, Calvi, and Figari. From outside Europe, the easiest way to get there is via Paris; or, if you're already in France, from Lyon, Marseille, or Nice airport. **Air France** (www.airfrance.com) and **Air Corsica** (www.aircorsica.com) fly internally to all four airports. Air Corsica even covers other French cities, such as Bordeaux and Nantes. Low-cost airline **Easyjet** (www.easyjet.com) has regular flights from Paris Charles de Gaulle and London Gatwick to Ajaccio; and from Bristol, London Gatwick, Manchester, Lyon, and Paris CDG to Bastia. **BY BOAT** Ferries leave from Marseille, Toulon, and Nice to various ports in Corsica (Bastia, Calvi, Ajaccio, Propriano, Bonifacio, and Porto-Vecchio). The three main companies are **Corsica Ferries** (☎ 04-95-32-95-95; www.corsica-ferries.fr) from Toulon and Nice; **La Méridonale** (☎ 08-10-20-13-20; www.lameridionale.fr), with overnight crossings from Marseille; and **SNCM** (☎ 32-60 or ☎ 08-25-88-80-88; www.sncm.fr) from Marseille, Toulon, and Nice. Prices vary according to the season. Always check the websites for special offers.

Getting Around

BY CAR & MOTORBIKE By far the best way to get around the island is on two or four wheels, but be prepared for steep slopes and sharp, hairpin bends. Due to insurance technicalities, it is usually impossible to rent a car in mainland France and take it on the ferry to Corsica. The following car rental companies have offices on the island, however: www.avis.com, www.ada.fr, www.budget-en-corse.com, www.hertzcorse.com, www.citer.fr, and www.sixt.fr. Be prepared to barter for a good deal, or contact **Autoescape** (☎ 08-00-92-09-40; www.autoescape.com), which compares car-rental prices and often offers the best rates. Always check that you have enough petrol. Stations are few and far between, so carry extra fuel in the trunk if you can. **BY TRAIN** The **Chemins de Fer de la Corse** (CFC; www.ter-sncf.com/corse) cover four routes year-round: Ajaccio-Bastia, Bastia-Corte, Ajaccio-Calvi, and Calvi-Bastia. Trains are a fine way to see some of the island's exceptional landscapes, but be prepared for long journeys; Bastia-Ajaccio, for example, takes 4 hours. **BY BUS** It is difficult, but not impossible, to cover Corsica by bus. The tourist offices will have up-to-date information on bus times and routes. We advise you to reserve your tickets in the towns with bus stations (Ajaccio, Calvi, Bastia, Corte, and Porto-Vechio) or check **www.corsicabus.org**—an unofficial site that does its best to obtain up-to-date bus timetables and display them online.

Tourist Office

Corsica Tourist Board, www.visit-corsica.fr/en.

12

The Basque Country, Pyrenees & Languedoc

Favorite Moments

This chapter explores three distinct regions of southern France that extend from the Atlantic to the Mediterranean: the Basque Country, the Pyrenees, and Languedoc. What do they all have in common? A border with Spain, a passion for rugby, and a fun-loving, friendly people, for a start. Whether you decide to stick to the most frequented sites in France's deepest south, such as Carcassonne and Toulouse, or venture off the beaten track to snowshoe, surf, or follow the art trail, you will likely be met with hearty cuisine and a warm welcome.

> PREVIOUS PAGE A UNESCO World Heritage site, Carcassonne's medieval citadel sits on a hill that has been fortified since the 6th century B.C. THIS PAGE Ease into the laidback pace of local life and dine at Le Zaza Club, on the beach around Perpignan. .

① **Savoring bonbons at the Atelier du Chocolat, Bayonne.** Portuguese Jews fleeing the Inquisition brought their chocolate-making skills to Bayonne, and the tradition has endured to this day. Learn all about it, and then have a taste at this chocolate museum and workshop. See p. 491, **①**.

② **Making waves in Biarritz.** Any heated seawater pool is a luxury, but the one at **Sofitel Biarritz** also has a view of the breakers crashing on Miramar Beach just below. See p. 498.

③ **Hiking the Kakuetta Gorges.** Experience the wildness of the Pays Basque—raging waters, caves, and a beautiful waterfall—as you trek through these deep Pyrenean gorges. See p. 496, **⑫**.

④ **Riding through Tarbes in style.** There's really only one way to travel in equestrian Tarbes: by horse-drawn carriage. You'll see why Napoleon loved this town. See p. 501, **②**.

⑤ **Swinging up the cable car to Pic du Midi.** The thrill of this 15-minute ride culminates in the majesty of the domed observatory appearing through the clouds. You'll feel ecstatic before you even reach the top, where the view is sublime. See p. 504, **⑥**.

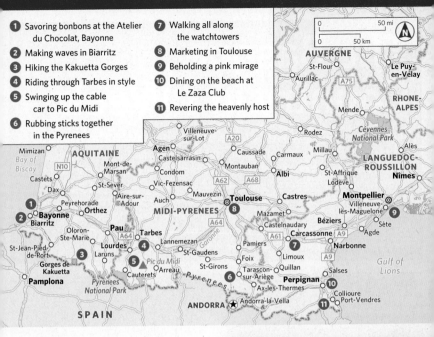

1. Savoring bonbons at the Atelier du Chocolat, Bayonne
2. Making waves in Biarritz
3. Hiking the Kakuetta Gorges
4. Riding through Tarbes in style
5. Swinging up the cable car to Pic du Midi
6. Rubbing sticks together in the Pyrenees
7. Walking all along the watchtowers
8. Marketing in Toulouse
9. Beholding a pink mirage
10. Dining on the beach at Le Zaza Club
11. Revering the heavenly host

6 Rubbing sticks together in the Pyrenees. We all know it's possible to start a fire with flint, but would you actually be able to do it? The **Parc de la Préhistoire** shows you how. See p. 506, 11.

7 Walking all along the watchtowers. Your first sight of the medieval citadel of Carcassonne will take you back 900 years. It's the finest example of such a fortress in Europe. See p. 521, 6.

8 Marketing in Toulouse. This city of art is no museum: dive in to its jovial, bustling, boozy heart at **Marché Victor Hugo,** a covered market. See p. 541, 4.

9 Beholding a pink mirage. No you're not dreaming. Those really are flamingos you're seeing in the marshes south of Montpellier. See "Two-Wheel Adventure," p. 533.

10 Dining on the beach at Le Zaza Club. The sand is fine, the mood is relaxed, and the day's catch is cooked Catalan-style at this beach club east of Perpignan. See p. 517.

11 Revering the heavenly host. Put a coin in the slot and the gilded, floor-to-ceiling altarpiece at Notre-Dame des Anges in Collioure lights up. This piece of religious folk

> *A detail from the baroque altarpiece at Notre-Dame des Anges in Collioure.*

art expresses all the hope and despair of a seafaring community. See p. 516, 10.

The Basque Country in 1 Week

From the rolling waves of the Bay of Biscay to the deep mountain villages of its eastern reaches, the French Basque Country *(Pays Basque)* makes you keenly aware of the forces of nature that have pulled against each other for centuries along this coast, long before it became chic. The first three stops on this tour—Bayonne, Biarritz, and St-Jean-de-Luz—are connected by train along the coast (and thus virtually roll into one another, making for an ideal itinerary if you have only a long weekend). From there, you'll need a car to venture deep into the heart of the Pyrenees Mountains, close to the Spanish border.

> On the Atlantic, just over the border from Spain, Biarritz is the surfing capital of Europe.

START Bayonne is 775km (482 miles) south of Paris and 190km (118 miles) south of Bordeaux. TRIP LENGTH 286km (178 miles).

❶ ★★ **Bayonne.** The coast is 6km (3¾ miles) away, but there is still a waterfront splendor to this cultural capital of French Basque Country, along the Ardour and Nive rivers. During General Franco's fascist purges in Spain, Bayonne provided a sanctuary for Spanish Basques. Indeed, the Petit Bayonne neighborhood remained a crucible of Basque nationalism until the French government repressed its sometimes violent ways. The visual look of

the city—with its timber buildings swathed in the Basque colors of green and red—is an about-face from the stone buildings that predominate in southwestern France. The **Musée Basque et de l'Histoire de Bayonne** (Basque and Bayonne History Museum), 37 quai des Corsaires (☎ 05-58-46-61-90; www. musee-basque.com; admission 5.50€ adults, 3€ reduced; daily 10am–6:30pm; closed Mon), illuminates Basque culture through its superb compendium of crafts, games, *pelotas* (balls), and other artifacts. Bayonne also is home to the region's top art museum, the **Musée de**

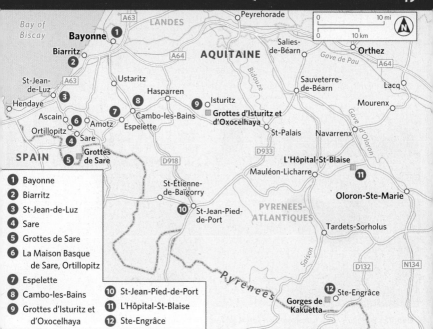

1. Bayonne
2. Biarritz
3. St-Jean-de-Luz
4. Sare
5. Grottes de Sare
6. La Maison Basque de Sare, Ortillopitz
7. Espelette
8. Cambo-les-Bains
9. Grottes d'Isturitz et d'Oxocelhaya
10. St-Jean-Pied-de-Port
11. L'Hôpital-St-Blaise
12. Ste-Engrâce

Bonnat, 5 rue Jacques-Laffitte (☎ 05-58-59-08-52; www.musee-bonnat.com; admission 5.50€ adults, 3€ reduced; May–Oct daily 10am–6:30pm, Nov–Apr 10am–12:30pm and 2–6pm). The collection features an array of schools and periods (from Delacroix to Rembrandt to El Greco), portraits by native hero Léon Bonnat, archaeological finds, and artifacts worked from gold and ceramics. When it comes to food, Bayonne is best associated with its eponymous ham, similar to Italian prosciutto. You'll find plenty of it in the market along the Nive River, as well as local cheese, cider, and honey; plenty of hanging red peppers; and more. One of the best of the chocolate workshops in a town full of them is **l'Atelier du Chocolat,** 7 allée de Gibéléou (☎ 05-59-55-00-15; admission 6.30€ adults, 2.60€ reduced; Mon–Sat 9:30am–12:30am and 2–6pm). Here you can view confectioners at work, learn about the origin of chocolate, and taste the goods at the end of the tour. ⏱ 1 day. Bayonne Tourist Office, place des Basques. ☎ 08-20-42-64-64. www.bayonne-tourisme.com.

On Day 2, follow signs out of Bayonne southwest to Biarritz (8km/5 miles), or take the train (10 min.).

② ★★★ **Biarritz.** As a long-established getaway for royalty from around the world, this seaside town is synonymous with luxury. But before Biarritz become a royal playground, it made money from the whaling and fishing industries. The town's connection with the sea is celebrated at the **Musée de la Mer,** plateau de l'Atalaye (☎ 05-59-22-33-34; admission 8€ adults, 5.50€ reduced; July–Aug 9:30am–midnight; Sept–June shorter hours), which has 2 dozen aquariums containing sharks, seals, and more. On land, Biarritz is full of great architecture. Its jewel is undoubtedly the **Chapelle Impériale,** rue Pellot (☎ 05-59-22-37-10; www.biarritz.fr; July–Aug Tues, Thurs, and Sat 3–7pm; Sept–June hours vary), constructed by Empress Eugénie, the wife of Napoleon III. It's a stunning mix of Roman, Byzantine, and Hispano-Mauresque styles, dedicated to Our Lady of Guadalupe in Mexico. The **Musée d'Art Asiatique** (Museum of Asian Art), 1 rue Guy Petit (☎ 05-59-22-78-78; www.museeasiatica.com; admission 7€ adults, 5€ reduced; July–Aug Mon–Fri 10:30am–6pm, Sat–Sun 2–6pm; Sept–June daily 2–6pm), is a great respite from all things Basque, with its collection of precious objects from across the Orient: stylized jade

> *Biarritz's popularity as a 19th-century resort is evident in the town's turn-of-the-century seaside hotels.*

> *Get to St-Jean-de-Luz's beaches early to rent a deck chair and parasol before everyone else does.*

tigers from China, mandalas from Tibet, and bronze ritual objects from Nepal. Another exotic but integral part of the city's skyline is the blue dome of the **Eglise Alexandre Newsky,** 8 av. de l'Impératrice (free admission; daily 10am–6pm). This Russian Orthodox Church was constructed in the 19th century for visiting Russian aristocrats. ⏱ 1 day. Biarritz Tourist Office, square d'Ixelles. ☎ 05-59-22-37-00. www. biarritz.fr. See p. 525 for beaches in Biarritz.

On Day 3 head for St-Jean-de-Luz, 14km (8⅔ miles) southwest of Biarritz on A63, or take the train (12 min.)

❸ ★★ kids **St-Jean-de-Luz.** This pretty seaside town and working port has an entirely different atmosphere from Biarritz. It doesn't attract quite such a glitzy crowd, and it's on a bay sheltered from the vast sea swells. Sardine boats cluster in the port, in the heart of the restaurant area, and the pleasure beach is flanked by a lovely boardwalk where you can shop for swimwear and buy ice cream. Historically, St-Jean prospered from the excellency of its shipbuilders and from state-supported piracy in the 16th century; as a result, the beautiful old town houses often feature maritime motifs. You'd do well to spend your day on the golden sands here (see "Best Beaches," p. 524), emerging only to shop and eat in the attractive streets behind the beach. If you want to explore town, check out one of the finest Basque churches, **Eglise St-Jean-Baptiste,** place du Maréchal Foch (☎ 05-59-26-03-16; www.ville-saintjeandeluz.fr; free admission; daily 8am–noon and 2–6:30pm). The interior is heavily gilded and has three balconies, in sharp contrast to the building's simple stone wall and wood beam construction. The church was the site of one of the most important marriages in French and European history: the union of Louis XIV and Marie-Thérèse of Spain, which concluded the Franco-Spanish War. Another treat is **l'Ecomusée Basque** (Basque Ecomuseum), rte. 10 (2km/1¼ miles from town), Sortie Nord (☎ 05-95-51-06-06; www.jean-vier.com/ecomusee.aspx; admission 6.30€ adults, 2.60€ reduced; Apr–Oct 10am–6:30pm). This renovated 19th-century farmhouse presents Basque crafts through more than 500 amazing reconstructions, revealing the richness of the Basque identity. For family fun, climb aboard **La Petit Train de la Rhune** (Little Train of the Rhune), Col de St-Ignace, Sare (☎ 08-92-39-14-25; www.rhune.com; Mar–Nov). From a station 10km (6¼ miles) from St-Jean, between the Basque villages of Ascain and Sare, this former mining train takes you 905m (2,969 ft.) up to the Rhune summit, affording gorgeous views of the Basque countryside and the Pyrenees. While the coast's high-end dining rooms are in Biarritz, St-Jean has more than a smattering of good restaurants. It's a great town for seafood lovers; tuna, sardines, and anchovies caught in the morning by the local fishing crews show up later that day, with a Spanish twist, on local menus. Spas are another draw. With its healthy climate and fresh sea breezes, St-Jean started using the sea's curative properties to attract visitors in the 19th century, and today it has several leisure spas, including the gorgeously arrayed, vaulted complex under the **Grand Hôtel Loréamar** (p. 529). ⏲ 1 day. St-Jean-de-Luz Tourist Office, 20 bd. Victor Hugo. ☎ 05-59-26-03-16. www.saint-jean-de-luz.com.

On Day 4, follow D918 southeast from St-Jean-de-Luz to Ascain and pick up D4 to Sare (14km/8⅔ miles).

❹ ★ **Sare.** Named one of "Les Plus Beaux Villages de France" (the Most Beautiful Villages in France), this hilltop town is full of authentic Basque charms, in the shadow of La Rhune, the iconic mountain of Basque Country.
⏲ Half-day. Sare Tourist Office, Place du village. ☎ 05-59-54-20-14. www.sare.fr.

Basque Cuisine

In northern Basque Country, there's a big difference between the fish-centered coastal cuisine and the cured meats, pigeon, and vegetables of the more inland areas. What you'll see labeled as *basquaise* is usually a dish that contains the sweet or hot **red peppers** the region produces, most notably in the town of Espelette. But there are actually more than a few Basque specialties that are well known and widely appreciated. Perhaps the star dish is **Bayonne ham,** an air-dried, salted pork that is one of the best in the world, often served as **tapas.** As this is still France, cheese is a priority, and most of the cheese here is made from sheep's milk; **Idiazabal** is the most notable, as is the artisanal **brebis blue cheese.** The main wine of the region is **Txakoli,** a dry white that is low in alcohol content and served as a before-dinner drink. **Basque cider,** prevalent in the region, is unusual in that it isn't sparkling. For dessert there's **chocolate;** Bayonne's chocolate industry is extremely well developed. Few places serve better traditional hot chocolate than **Cazenave,** just north of Cathédrale St-Marie, 19 rue du Port Neuf, Bayonne (☎ 05-59-59-03-16; www.chocolats-bayonne-cazenave.fr; Tues–Sat 9am–noon and 2–7pm; closed Sun–Mon).

> *Espelette takes its name from a local chili pepper, which is commonly hung out to dry on facades throughout town.*

⑤ kids Grottes de Sare. Just 6km (3¾ miles) south of Sare on D306 are the caves of Grottes de Sare, where a mesmerizing sound-and-light show educates viewers not just in geology but in the genesis, mythology, and beliefs of the Basque people. The bears were run out of these caves long ago, but beware the 13 species of bats. ⏱ 1½ hr. ☎ 05-59-54-21-88. www.sare.fr/grottes_sare.html. Admission 7€ adults, 5€ reduced. July–Aug daily 10am–7pm; Sept–Oct and Jan–June shorter hours; Nov–Dec Sat–Sun only. Closed Jan.

⑥ La Maison Basque de Sare, Ortillopitz. This farmhouse at the town of Ortillopitz, just 3km (1¾ miles) north of Sare on D4, shows what aristocratic Basque life was like in the 17th century. The 16th-century building, vineyard, and fields of flax are beautiful and enlightening, and far more interesting than you might at first think. ⏱ 1 hr. ☎ 05-59-26-30-74. www.ortillopitz.com. Admission 7€ adults, 3€ reduced. July 11–Aug 20 daily 10:45am–6pm; Aug 21–Oct 21 and Apr 1–July 10 afternoons only. Closed Oct 22–Mar 31.

From Sare, follow D4, D305, and D20 east to Espelette (17km/11 miles).

⑦ Espelette. On your way to Cambo-les-Bains, make sure to swing through Espelette, famed for the quality of its red peppers, which hang from the town's red-and-white houses in summer. The peppers are used in the production of Bayonne ham and inspire as much local pride as French wines and cheeses do in other regions of France. ⏱ 1 hr. Espelette Tourist Office: ☎ 05-59-93-95-02; http://espelette.com.pagesperso-orange.fr.

Continue to Cambo-les-Bains for the night, 6km (3¾ miles) away on D918.

⑧ Cambo-les-Bains. As its name implies, Cambo-les-Bains is first and foremost a spa town, with a long history of treating tuberculosis patients. It's home to many traditional houses and flower-filled gardens, but the big draw is **Villa Arnaga** (☎ 05-59-29-83-92; www.arnaga.com; admission 6€ adults, 3€ reduced; July–Aug daily 10am–7pm, Sept–Oct and Mar–June shorter hours; closed Nov–Feb), the home of *Cyrano de Bergerac* author Edmond Rostand, who was a patient in the area. The villa has become an emblem of Basque craftsmanship, thanks to its ornate wood engravings and huge windows. The capper is a splendid garden in the formal French style, with sculpted *parterres* and water everywhere. ⏱ Overnight. Cambo-les-Bains Tourist Office, 3 av. de la Mairie. ☎ 05-59-29-70-25. www.cambolesbains.com.

On Day 5, spend the morning in Cambo-les-Bains. In the afternoon, take D10/D22 to Hasparren, pick up D22 to Bonloc and D14 to St-Esteben, make a left on D251, and follow signs from the village (25km/15 miles).

⑨ kids Grottes d'Isturitz et d'Oxocelhaya. These caves are part of the Pyreneo-Cantabria painted caves system and are actually two different caves. **Grotte d'Isturitz,** inhabited for more than 80,000 years, has been famous since guano miners came upon it in the 19th century. The best drawings are of semicircular sticks with lines and other markings. **Grotte d'Oxocelhaya,** accidentally stumbled upon in 1929, is impressive more for its geologic splendor. You'll see plenty of huge, pointed stalagmites and stalactites as well

> *Visit St-Jean-Pied-de-Port on Monday or Thursday to shop in its colorful market.*

as rimstone pools. You won't see the finger-painted artworks themselves, but the replicas are worth a look. A man-made tunnel links the two caves. ⏱ 5 hr. St-Martin-d'Arberoue. ☎ 05-59-29-64-72. www.grottes-isturitz.com. Admission 7.50€ adults, 3.60€ reduced. July–Aug daily 10am–1pm and 2–6pm (guided tours every 20 min.); Mar 15–June 30 and Sept 1–Nov 15 shorter hours.

From Isturitz, take D251 south to Hélette, and pick up D22, following signs to St-Jean-Pied-de-Port (34km/21 miles).

Chemin de St-Jacques Pilgrimage Route

St-Jean-Pied-de-Port is just south of the convergence point, in Ostabat, for the routes of the St. James pilgrimage route (Santiago de Compostela, or St-Jacques-de-Compostelle), which begins in Paris, Vézelay, and Le Puy. If you are a pilgrim, make sure to visit the dedicated office for passports, special discounts, maps, and other tips to make your journey easier.

🔟 **St-Jean-Pied-de-Port.** This village is the old capital of the former Basque province of Lower Navarre; it takes its name from its location at the foot of the mountain pass that leads to Spain, just a few kilometers from the town is the essence of Basque charm, built of pink sandstone. After being nearly leveled by Spaniards in the 16th century, it became the lucky recipient of the attentions of Vauban, the legendary French military architect. Vauban rebuilt the area with modern defenses; the **Citadelle de Vauban** is the best site to visit here. **Porte Notre Dame** is perhaps the finest of the town's four gates, and the stone seats carved into the walls were for poor pilgrims to rest upon while they waited for the distribution of alms from the hospital on the other side. There's just one main street, **rue de la Citadelle,** on which there is an excellent market on Monday (Thurs, too, in high season). Shepherds drive cattle and sheep into the town, and you can find some of the excellent brebis blue cheese the area is known for. ⏱ Half-day. St-Jean-Pied-de-Port Tourist Office, 14 place Charles De Gaulle. ☎ 05-59-37-03-57. www.saintjeanpieddeport-paysbasque-tourisme.com.

> *A rarity in France, the Romanesque Hôpital-St-Blaise displays both Moorish and Christian decorative influences.*

Spend the morning of Day 6 in St-Jean-Pied-de-Port. In the afternoon, take D933 northeast as far as Larceveau-Arras-Cibits, and pick up D918 over the Osquich pass to Mauléon-Licharre; from there follow D25 to l'Hôpital-St-Blaise (52km/32 miles).

11 L'Hôpital-St-Blaise. In a tiny hamlet of fewer than 100 people, the 12th-century Romanesque Hôpital-St-Blaise served as a resting place for pilgrims and is now a UNESCO World Heritage site. The church has been remarkably well preserved, mostly due to its state of extreme isolation. Its remoteness adds to the splendor of the scene: a harmoniously proportioned church in a wooded valley, with beautifully ornate Moorish decor. Indeed, it can be said that Christian and Muslim arts in France never converged better than in this church. We recommend heading to Ste-Engrâce, the next stop on our list, to spend the night. ⏱ 2 hr. ☎ 05-59-66-11-12. www.hopital-saint-blaise.fr. Admission 4€ adults, 2.70€ reduced. Daily 10am–7pm.

Retrace your route to Mauléon-Licharre, then take D26 south through Licq-Athéray. About 2km (1¼ mile) outside of town, turn left on D113 to Ste-Engrâce (44km/27 miles).

12 Ste-Engrâce. No trip to this region is complete without spending ample time in the **Kakuetta Gorges,** the great canyons of Basque Country. Plunging into the limestone are some of the wildest canyons in Europe, filled with dense vegetation and a raging river. There's a great footpath that runs through the area, and the terminus is signaled by both a foreboding cave with intimidating stalactites and stalagmites and an enchanting waterfall. Make sure to walk through the **Grand Etroit** canyon; it's more than 200m (656 ft.) deep but only 3 to 10m (10–33 ft.) wide. The tiny hamlet of **Ste-Engrâce** sits amid countless acres of beautiful and variegated trees, flora, and fauna. It provides great hiking options and has a finely restored Romanesque church. ⏱ 1 day. Tourist Office, Ste-Engrâce Town Hall. ☎ 05-59-28-60-83. www.sainte-engrace.com.

For the round trip, retrace your route to Mauléon-Licharre, Larceveau-Arros-Cibits, and St-Jean-Pied-de-Port, then take D918 and D932 to Bayonne (124km/77 miles).

Into the Mountains

To continue into the Pyrenees (p. 500), take D26 to Laguinge-Restoue, turn right on D918 and D919 to Oloron-Ste-Marie, and take N134 to Pau (77km/48 miles).

Where to Stay in Basque Country

> Besides these stately bedrooms, the Hôtel du Palais in Biarritz has a gourmet restaurant with a panoramic view and a luxury spa.

★★ Château d'Urtubie URRUGNE
The 14th-century Château d'Urtubie has featured prominently in Basque history. With splendidly restored ramparts, fortifications, and huge gardens, it makes for an unforgettable stay. The rooms feature 18th- and 19th-century paintings. The owner, beloved of guests, provides impeccable service. 10 rue Bernard de Coral. ☎ 05-59-54-31-15. www.chateaudurtubie.fr. 10 units. Doubles from 90€. AE, MC, V.

Hostellerie du Parc Cambo CAMBO-LES-BAINS
An especially good value, this two-star hotel has tasteful decor, little pretension, and a comfortable and welcoming feel. It's the little touches that make it memorable: a buffet-style breakfast, varied dinner menus, and a catered lunch basket, available upon request. ☎ 05-59-94-54-54. www.hotel-parc-cambo.com. 12 units. Doubles 61€–68€ in high season. AE, MC, V.

Hôtel Amaia BIARRITZ
If you're looking for an affordable hotel in pricy Biarritz, you can't beat this charming place near the Côte des Basques Beach. Recently renovated, in a traditional red-and-white Basque house, it is very clean, bright, and comfortable. 35 av. du Maréchal Joffre. ☎ 05-59-23-09-49. www.amaia.fr. 19 units. Doubles 59€–85€. AE, MC, V.

★★★ kids Hôtel du Palais BIARRITZ
This is one of the finest hotels in Europe. The building dates from 1854, when Napoleon III commissioned it as a private villa for Eugénie. The hotel has an ideal beachfront, in view of the rocky shoreline; a golf course; an indoor pool; and a dining room with sea views. Suites are elaborate, but even the double rooms have period furniture and silk drapes. Try to book a room facing west for views of the sunsets over

the Basque coast. 1 av. de l'Impératrice. ☎ 05-59-41-64-00. www.hotel-du-palais.com. 154 units. Doubles 375€–575€; suites 700€–1,750€. AE, DC, MC, V.

★★★ Grand Hôtel Loreamar Thalasso Spa

ST-JEAN-DE-LUZ *GASTRONOMIC* This turn-of-the-20th-century hotel has nostalgic charm, with Impressionist paintings in the rooms and vintage trunks in the corridors. At the English-style bar, a Paris Ritz–trained barman mixes jazz-era cocktails. The country house–style restaurant serves prize-winning French dishes on a seaside terrace. Guests soak and relax by candlelight in the spa. See p. 529.

> Stay at the Villa Vauréal in Biarritz and you'll have access to its secluded garden.

Hôtel Loustau BAYONNE

This three-star hotel is close to the city center and the train station. It's a great value, with a riverfront view and pleasantly decorated rooms. The restaurant serves a good meal for a low price, and the bar is relaxing and convivial. 1 place de la République. ☎ 05-59-55-08-08. www.hotel-loustau.fr. 45 units. Doubles from 82€. AE, DC, MC, V.

★★ La Villa Bayonne BAYONNE

On a hill overlooking the Nive River, this lovely 1905 villa is a peaceful place to stay, surrounded by an Italianate garden. The rooms, either on the ground floor or in the eaves, are exquisitely decorated in mauve, gray, and gold, and the reception rooms make the place feel like your own splendid home. 12 chemin de Jacquette. ☎ 05-59-03-01-20. www.bayonne-hotel-lavilla.com. 10 units. Doubles 90€–150€. AE, MC, V.

★★★ Les Pyrénées ST-JEAN-PIED-DE-PORT

GASTRONOMIC One of the best restaurants in southwestern France is also a three-star hotel. Basque specialties—such as rabbit terrine with cherries, scampi fritters with red pepper ketchup, and egg with cod cream—have garnered two Michelin stars. The wine list is extensive, with plenty of local varietals, such as Irouleguy. 19 place Charles de Gaulle. ☎ 05-59-37-01-01. www.hotel-les-pyrenees.com. Menus 40€–100€. Doubles from 100€. AE, DC, MC, V. Lunch and dinner daily.

★★★ Sofitel Biarritz Le Miramar Thalassa

BIARRITZ *GASTRONOMIC* The sound of the waves, effects of the spa, and service from top-notch staff here will soothe you. And the food is amazing, whether you opt for the full-calorie or reduced-fat menu items. 13 rue Louison Bobet. www.sofitel.com. 126 units. Doubles 275€–372€. Main courses 20€–30€. AE, DC, MC, V. Lunch and dinner daily.

★ Villa Vauréal BIARRITZ

This guesthouse is an excellent value, within walking distance of the center and close to the sea. Breakfast is served outside on a terrace shaded by lime trees. Rooms are neat and tidy, with traditional furnishings and a kitchenette. 14 rue Vauréal. ☎ 06-10-11-64-21. www.villavaureal.com. 5 units. Doubles 108€–187€. AE, MC, V. Parking 5€.

Where to Dine in Basque Country

★ **Auberge du Cheval Blanc** BAYONNE *BASQUE/ FRENCH* This Michelin-starred family restaurant serves excellent cuisine in an elegant environment. Basque favorites include gazpacho, pigeon, fish, local foie gras, chocolate, and salted pork. 68 rue Bourgneuf. ☎ 05-59-59-01-33. Menu 27.50€–80€. AE, MC, V. Lunch Tues–Fri and Sun, dinner Tues–Sat.

★★ **Auberge Kaïku** ST-JEAN-DE-LUZ *BASQUE/ FRENCH* Auberge Kaïku is the best restaurant in town (outside of the hotel restaurants), and it's in the oldest building, dating from 1540. Under hand-hewn beams and chiseled masonry, you'll dine on roast suckling Pyrenean lamb, grilled shellfish, filet of beef with truffle essence, and duckling in honey. 17 rue de la République. ☎ 05-59-26-13-20. Main courses 20€–25€, fixed-price lunch 25€, fixed-price dinner 32€. MC, V. July–Aug lunch and dinner daily; Sept–June lunch and dinner Thurs–Mon.

Café de la Grande Plage BIARRITZ *BASQUE/ FRENCH* This restaurant in the Casino Biarritz is a great value, with a view of the beach, delicious dishes such as duck pie and piquillo peppers, and great pastries. 1 av. Edouard VII. ☎ 05-59-22-77-88. www.lucienbarriere.com. 3-course meal 30€. AE, MC, V. Daily.

★★ **Clos Basque** BIARRITZ *BASQUE/FRENCH* This Basque kitchen serves savory dishes made from local ingredients, such as *maigre* (Atlantic whitefish), sea scallops, and a codfish platter with chorizo and artichokes. Rack of lamb and duck are often featured as well. 12 rue Louis Barthou. ☎ 05-59-24-24-96. Main courses 13€; fixed-price menu 24€. MC, V. Lunch Tues–Sun, dinner Tues–Sat. Closed June 25–July 6, Oct 22–Nov 9, and Feb 18–Mar 18.

La Vieille Auberge ST-JEAN-DE-LUZ *BASQUE/ SEAFOOD* On one of the oldest streets in town, this tavern specializes in seafood—most notably the fish soup and grilled seafood platter. The fixed-price menu is a good value. The food, especially mussels *à la crème*, goes well with the local wine. 22 rue Tourasse.

> Lightly fried calamari with lemon is a staple along the coast.

☎ 05-59-26-19-61. Reservations required. Main courses 12€–24€; fixed-price menu 13€–30€. MC, V. May–Sept lunch and dinner daily; Oct–Nov and Feb–Mar lunch Wed–Sun, dinner Wed–Sat. Closed mid-Nov to mid-Dec.

★ **Restaurant Ibaia** BAYONNE *BASQUE* The great Basque tapas mesh divinely with the cool sangria served here. Yet it's the warm, friendly atmosphere that makes this place a bit more of a wine bar than a restaurant by some standards. 45 quai l'Amiral Jauréguiberry. ☎ 05-59-59-86-66. Tapas 3€–6€. Main courses 9€–15€. MC, V. Lunch and dinner Tues–Sat.

The Pyrenees in 10 Days

The Pyrenees stretch a full 435km (270 miles) from coast to coast and count no fewer than 35 peaks that reach heights of more than 3,000m (almost 10,000 ft.). They're less famous and not quite as high as the Alps, so you won't find any Alpine ski resort snobbery here. Amid the wealth of cultural heritage nestled in the valleys below, you'll be able to play indoors or outdoors as long as you like.

> Ride a cable car up to the Observatoire du Pic du Midi for stargazing and endless views over the Pyrenees.

START Pau is 871km (541 miles) south of Paris and about equidistant from Bordeaux and Toulouse (200km/124 miles). **TRIP LENGTH** 600km/373 miles (slightly less if you take the mountain passes).

1 ★★★ **Pau.** The city of Pau is the capital of the Pyrénées Atlantiques department in the region of Aquitaine. But speak to any Palois (as residents are called) and you'll find the city's inhabitants identify themselves as Béarnais: Béarn is the old province of which Pau was the capital, with its own language and cuisine, most famously the sauce *béarnaise*

made with tarragon, shallots, eggs, and butter. The **Château de Pau** (☎ 05-59-82-38-00; www.musee-chateau-pau.fr; admission 5€ adults, 3.50€ reduced, free 1st Sun of the month; June 15 to Sept 15 daily 9:30am–12:15pm and 1:30–5:45pm, Sept 16–June 14 daily 9:30am–11:45pm and 2–5pm) surveys the majestic Gave River, whose source is in the **Cirque de Gavarnie** (**4** on this tour). This was the birthplace of Henri IV, France's beloved sovereign, who unified the country by converting to Catholicism with the famously pragmatic statement, "Paris is worth a Mass." Recently restored, it has

1. Pau
2. Tarbes
3. Cauterets
4. Cirque de Gavarnie
5. Luz-St-Sauveur
6. Observatoire du
   Pic du Midi
7. Bagnères-de-Bigorre
8. Loudenvielle &
   La Vallée du Louron
9. St-Bertrand-de-Comminges
10. St-Lizier
11. Tarascon-sur-Ariège
12. Toulouse

fabulously regal interiors, including magnificent tapestries. Ascend via the historic funicular for your first glimpse of the snowtopped Pyrenees from the Ville Haute (Upper City), 30m (98 ft.) up from the Ville Basse (Lower City), the château, and the train station. Beautiful exotic gardens filled with banana trees and palms fill the gap in between, leading up to the **Promenade des Pyrénées,** an elegant avenue built for the English, French, and Russian bourgeoisie who came here in the 19th century to "take the air." At one end the **Palais Beaumont,** built as a casino and winter garden, now hosts concerts, theater, and exhibitions. Pau is also famous for its **Haras National** (National Stud), 1 rue du Maréchal Leclerc, Gelos (☎ 05-59-35-06-52; www.haras-nationaux.fr; tickets 5€ adults, 3€ reduced, free for children 5 and under; tours Nov–Apr Mon–Fri 2pm; May–June and Sept–Oct 2pm and 4pm; July–Aug 10am, 2pm, and 4pm), created by Napoleon and, for the equine-minded, worth a visit (see also the **Haras National de Tarbes,** ② on this tour). ⊙ 1 day. Pau Tourist Office, place Royale. ☎ 05-59-27-27-08. www.pau-pyrenees.com.

Follow A64 east from Pau to Tarbes (43km/27 miles).

> *On a clear day, you can see the Pyrenees mountains from Pau's town center.*

② **Tarbes.** Tarbes is the capital of the Hautes-Pyrénées, and those glistening mountains form a backdrop to this equestrian and military city also known for its parks and fountains. Take a trip around the city by horse-drawn *calèche* (a light carriage): The tour leaves from the cafe at the glorious Jardin

> Cheeky-looking creatures peek down from facades in Cauterets.

Massey (call Philippe Daunis, ☎ 06-83-09-11-03 to reserve), and travels past the birthplace of World War I hero Maréchal Foch, the barracks that were home of the dashing Hussards, and the fountains of place Marcadieu. In the afternoon, visit the **Haras National de Tarbes** (Tarbes National Stud), Chemin de Mauhourat (☎ 05-62-56-30-80; admission 5.50€ adults, 3.50€ ages 4–12, free for children 3 and under; tours July–Aug 2pm, 3pm, and 4pm; other times by reservation). These buildings, also established by Napoleon, and a national monument surrounded by parkland but in the center of town, show that in the 19th century, some horses got better accommodations than most humans. You can see a collection of horse-drawn carriages, watch equine demonstrations, and visit the exhibitions in the Maison du Cheval, devoted to the history of horses in the Bigorre area, which goes back to prehistory. Throughout August the **Equestria Festival**

(www.festivalequestria.com) is the big event in Tarbes, with parades through the streets, a festival village, shows, competitions, and music. ☺ Half-day. Tarbes Tourist Office, 3 cours Gambetta. ☎ 05-62-51-30-31. www.tarbes.com.

From Tarbes, go south on N21, bypassing Lourdes; at the large roundabout, take D821 to Argelès, then D921 to Pierrefitte-Nestalas and D920a to Cauterets (50km/31 miles).

❸ ★ **Cauterets.** Cauterets is a 19th-century spa town, and its elegant buildings, seemingly held up by caryatids, are emblematic of the age when high society flocked to enjoy the "cures" of the thermal waters. The best buildings are on boulevard Latapie-Flurin, where the Résidence l'Angleterre houses a private museum of period costumes, **Musée 1900** (☎ 05-62-92-02-02; admission 6€ adults, 3€ ages 5–14; call in advance for reservations). Today no trains pass through the quaint wooden rail station, *Le Gare,* but it is an original exhibit from the Norwegian Pavillion of the Paris Exhibition of 1889, which served as a real station here for a short time. As for the casino—well, if you've been to Las Vegas or Monte Carlo, you'll likely be unimpressed. Still, you may find Cauterets more to your liking. Besides its old-fashioned charm, it has a new leisure spa complex, **Les Bains du Rocher** (p. 530), with outdoor thermal pools; a cable car that ferries skiers up the slopes; and, a little farther up the valley, the beautiful **pont d'Espagne,**

Lourdes

A 23km (14-mile) drive south from Tarbes on N21, Lourdes (www.lourdes-infotourisme.com) may not have much appeal for non-Catholics, but it still attracts six million visitors a year and is classed as a *Grand Site Touristique* for the Midi-Pyrénées region (www.grandsites.midipyrenees.fr). If you visit, be prepared for crowds. A signed interpretation path through town takes you in the steps of Bernadette Soubirous, the peasant who saw an apparition of the Virgin Mary in 1858. You can visit the grotto, two 19th-century basilicas, the underground basilica Ste-Pie-X (from 1958), and Ste-Bernadette church. The summer torchlight parade is a sight to behold for visitors of any denomination.

> *Views from the Cirque de Gavarnie mountain range will leave you speechless (not least from the climb up).*

once a trading point between France and Spain. Cauterets refused to allow hydroelectric power dams here, and so waterfalls gush in summer and freeze into sculptural forms in winter. ⏲ Half-day. Cauterets Tourist Office, place Foch. ☎ 05-62-92-50-50. www.cauterets.com.

On Day 3, follow D920 north from Cauterets to Pierrefitte-Nestalas, and pick up D921 south to Gavarnie, via Luz-St-Sauveur (41km/25 miles).

④ ★★★ kids Cirque de Gavarnie. Rise early to encounter one of the Pyrenees' most spectacular sights. The Cirque de Gavarnie is a mountain amphitheater encompassing 15 peaks that are more than 3,000m (9,850 ft.) high. In the center is the **Cascade de Gavarnie,** a 420m (1,378-ft.) waterfall that forms a white streak in the mountain wall. In winter, the waterfall freezes, and brave ice-climbers can hack their way up; you may be more inclined to take a gentle walk around the bottom in boots or snowshoes (rent these in Gavarnie), or simply

to admire it from **La Chaumière** (☎ 05-62-92-48-08; http://lachaumiere.gavarnie.free.fr), a bed-and-breakfast with a cafe for snacks (4€–12€) and the very best view. Remember: Beyond that wall of rock is Spain, *mi amigo.* ⏲ Half-day. Gavarnie Tourist Office: ☎ 05-62-92-49-10; www.gavarnie.com.

Backtrack on D921 to Luz-St-Sauveur (19km/12 miles).

⑤ Luz-St-Sauveur. Luz is another spa town that was favored by Empress Eugénie, the wife of Napoleon III. The 11th-century fortified church of St-André was designed to be big enough to hold the entire population of the village when under siege. A real Pyrenean mountain village, Luz celebrates the return of shepherds from the high pastures in September with a big sheep auction and meat fest. There is also a cosmopolitan jazz festival here in mid-July. ⏲ Half-day. Luz-St-Sauveur Tourist Office, place du 8 mai 1945. ☎ 05-62-92-30-30. www.luz.org.

On Day 4, head into the mountains. Under the right conditions, you can cross the Tourmalet pass to La Mongie on D918 (about 20km/12 miles). But the pass is closed during winter and in bad weather, necessitating a 76km (47-mile) round trip back through Lourdes, then east on D937, south on D935, and finally into the mountains on D918.

6 ★★★ [kids] **Observatoire du Pic du Midi.** It's impossible to convey how brilliant this observatory is—you just have to go there. It looks like a fortress in the sky, and the museum tells the story of its early-20th-century construction by brave mountaineers working under frightful conditions. The swing up to the observatory via a 15-minute cable-car ride is scary, but once there you have a panorama of the entire Pyrenean range. The observatory houses a telescope so powerful, you could read the time on Big Ben if the earth weren't round; another telescope, which NASA used for the Apollo missions; and the original chronograph designed by Bernard

> *In Bagnères-de-Bigorre, the naturally warm water at Aquensis spa (p. 528) is known for its therapeutic properties.*

Lyot. Book in advance to stay the night, in basic but clean rooms, so you can stargaze with an astronomer and watch the dawn rise over the peaks. ⏱ Half-day. Cable car from La Mongie. ☎ 08-25-00-28-77. www.picdumidi.com. Admission 32€ adults, 21€ ages 7–12, free for ages 3–6. See website for hours.

Descend from La Mongie to Bagnères-de-Bigorre via D918 and D935 (22km/14 miles).

7 ★ **Bagnères-de-Bigorre.** Lovely Bagnères retains its 19th-century charm and is one of the few towns in the area to provide some culture, as well as winter sports and a delectable spa (p. 528). Situated over the 1783 baths, with the casino right beside it, the **Musée Saliès,** place des Thermes (☎ 05-62-91-07-26; www. museesbagneres.fr; June–Oct Wed–Fri 10am–noon and 4–6pm, Sat–Sun 3–6pm; admission 4€ adults, 3€ students), houses a collection of Orientalist painters (Chasseriau, Vigneron), Barbizon landscapes, and works by local flower painter Blanche Odin. The folk art **Musée du Vieux Moulin** is just over the river, and the **Musée d'Histoire Naturel** and **Musée du Marbre** (Bagnères was an important marble quarrying area) are a little bit out of town, with the botanical gardens. ⏱ Half-day. Bagnères Tourist Office: ☎ 05-62-95-50-71. www. bagneresdebigorre-lamongie.com.

From Bagnères-de-Bigorre on Day 5, go north on D936 and after 7km (4⅓ miles) right onto D938 (signposted Avezac-Prat-Lahitte). Pick up D929 south at La-Barthe-de-Neste, make a left onto D929 at Arreau, and follow D919 (another left) and D618 to Loudenvielle (63km/39 miles total). Alternatively, take the scenic route south via the Aspin pass (see "Travel Tip," p. 506).

8 ★ **Loudenvielle & La Vallée du Louron.** Strung out along the Louron Valley are eight frescoed churches built in the 11th century, when the Pyreneans had finally driven out the marauding Saracens. In the 16th century, itinerant artists from Aragon, notably Maître Rodrigis, filled the churches with vivid frescoes that depict the bloodthirsty combat of local saints Calixte and Mercurial against the Saracens. Although the churches are desperately in need of funds to shore up their leaky roofs and fight the rising damp, they are a jewel that may well stay in your memory forever. In Loudenvielle, the **L'Arixo visitor center** (☎ 05-62-99-97-70) features an exhibition on the frescoed churches; manager Yoann Lemonnier is also a mountain guide (☎ 06-01-92-37-58; www.pachamama-pyrenees.com). For visitors who would rather relax than sightsee, Loudenvielle has a good spa (p. 529). ☺ 1 day. Loudenvielle Tourist Office, Chemin de Cazalis (☎ 05-62-99-95-35). Bordères-Louron Tourist Office, Maison de la Vallée (☎ 05-62-99-92-00; www.lelouron.com).

From Loudenvielle, go north on D618, D929, and A64 (toward Toulouse) for 17km (11 miles), take exit 17, and follow A645 for 5km (3 miles); continue on D825 and D26 to Valcabrère, where a left and a right lead to St-Bertrand-de-Comminges (68km/42 miles total). Alternatively, take the scenic route via the Peyresourde pass (see "Travel Tip," p. 506).

⑨ ★ St-Bertrand-de-Comminges. Between the first mountain crests and the Garonne River, St-Bertrand is an important stop on one of the St-Jacques-de-Compostelle pilgrim routes. It's also inscribed as one of the Most Beautiful Villages of France and named a UNESCO World Heritage site. Two millennia of Christianity are preserved in the architecture here: a 1st-century **Roman settlement** with a Paleo-Christian basilica; the 11th-century **Basilica of St-Just,** which looks like a Tuscan church in its landscape; and the grandiose Renaissance **Cathedral of Ste-Marie** (☎ 05-61-95-44-44; www.cathedrale-saint-bertrand.org; admission 4€ adults, 1.50€ reduced; May–Sept Mon–Sat 9am–7pm, Sun 2–5pm; Oct–Apr Mon–Sat 10am–noon and 2–6pm, Sun 2–5pm). But it's not all old relics: The **Olivétains** tourist and cultural center has contemporary art exhibitions, and the **Festival of Comminges** in July premiers new classical music compositions in the hallowed buildings. ☺ 1 day. Tourist and Cultural Center of Olivétains. ☎ 05-61-95-44-44. www.tourisme-stgaudens.com/web/en/84-saint-bertrand-de-comminges.

At the end of Day 6, we recommend driving 67km (42 miles) east to St-Lizier to spend the night. Follow signs to Toulouse on A645 and A64 to exit 20, and then follow signs to Foix for 24km (15 miles) until you reach St-Lizier. Alternatively, take the scenic route via the Monté and Aspet passes (see "Travel Tip," p. 506).

> *The Cathedral of Ste-Marie in St-Bertrand-de-Comminges.*

⑩ ★★ St-Lizier. Like St-Bertrand-de-Comminges, St-Lizier receives hundreds of modern-day pilgrims following in the footsteps of their forerunners, and the tourist office takes the stamping of their *credencial* very seriously (see "The Road to Compostela," p. 507). The historic village, crawling in a spiral to the **archbishop's palace complex** at the very top, is a richly encrusted cultural jewel with two cathedrals. The upper one—the **Eglise Notre-Dame de la Sède**—along with the museum in the archbishop's palace, is due to reopen in 2011 after renovation. In the lower village, near the tourist office, the **Eglise St-Lizier** is a huge 11th-century Byzantine-style edifice filled with frescoes; its Gallo-Roman cloisters are beautiful, and you can also visit the 18th-century pharmacy, complete with its bottles of poisons and potions (entrance to these three attractions is free but must be arranged through the tourist office). ☺ 1 day. St-Lizier Tourist Office, place de l'Eglise. ☎ 05-61-96-77-77. www.st-lizier.fr/accueilen.html.

Travel Tip

The drive over the Pyrenean mountain passes—famous challenges along the Tour de France— offers exhilarating climbs with breathtaking views around each hairpin bend. It also enables you to avoid D929 with its rattling trucks hurtling toward the Bielsa tunnel. If you take these routes in spring or fall, you will experience an immediate change of season as you emerge from the mountain forests of the Hautes-Pyrénées into the gentler Ariège countryside. Check the weather conditions with locals before setting off: It is not advisable to drive the route in fog, snow, or heavy rain. A stick-shift car is better for this kind of driving, and be sure to use gear braking as you descend the passes.

From St-Lizier, take D117 and N20 east, via Foix, to Tarascon-sur-Ariège (45km/28 miles).

⑪ ★★★ kids **Tarascon-sur-Ariège.** Like Dordogne (p. 598), the Ariège has its share of prehistoric caves—more than in any other *département* in France. If you see but one, don't miss the marvelous line drawings of bison, horses, and ibex from 13,000 years ago

> *For centuries, Compostela pilgrims have wandered the cobbled lanes at St-Lizier.*

at the **Grotte de Niaux,** 5km (3 miles) south of Tarascon on D8 (☎ 05-61-05-10-10; www.ariege.com/niaux; admission 9.40€ adults, 7.50€ students, 7€ ages 13–18, 5.70€ ages 5–12; guided tours only [in English Apr–Sept 1pm]; daily except Mon Nov–Mar during school holidays). The fact that you have to walk 800m (2,625 ft.) into the cave by torchlight just adds to the sense of wonder when you behold the mystical menagerie for the first time. There are more than 100 drawings, mainly in the vast Salon Noir, as well as mysterious red symbols and signs. After or before your visit, try to spend at least 2 hours at the ★★★ **Parc de la Préhistoire,** a kilometer or so out of Tarascon on the rte. de Banat (☎ 05-61-05-10-10; www.sesta.fr; admission 9.50€ adults, 7.50€ students, 7.20€ ages 13–18, 5.90€ ages 5–12; Apr and June

> *Toulouse is known as "Pink City" for its red brick center, which is uncommon in France.*

Mon–Fri 10am–6pm and Sat–Sun 10am–7pm; May and Sept–Oct Tues–Fri 10am–6pm and Sat–Sun 10am–7pm; July–Aug daily 10am–8pm; closed Nov–Mar). Armed with an audio-guide in English, you'll take a voyage in space and time at this imaginative interpretation center, which even explores crossovers between pre-historic and modern art. The 13-hectare (32-acre) park is peopled with actors who demonstrate Cro-Magnon skills such as making a fire from flint. Children will be transfixed. You can easily spend a day here if you have time, and adults will enjoy the fine food in the restaurant. ⏱ 1 day. See www.paysdetarascon.com.

From Tarascon, take N20, A66, and A61 north to Toulouse (104km/65 miles).

⑫ ★★★ **Toulouse**. Spare some time to explore the Pink City and enjoy a noisy, convivial meal above the covered market, before leaving by plane or train from Toulouse. Alternatively, stop by **Foix** (p. 518, ❶), **Mirepoix** (p. 521, ❸), and **Carcassonne** (p. 521, ❻), and then head on into Languedoc-Roussillon (p. 510). ⏱ 2 days. For detailed information on Toulouse, see p. 540.

The Road to Compostela

Pilgrims have made their way across the Pyrenees to the shrine of Santiago de Compostela in Galicia continuously since the 8th century. St. James (St-Jacques to the French, Santiago to the Spanish) was the apostle brother of John the Evangelist and is commonly thought to have been the first Christian martyr. Several routes through the mountains follow ancient trade routes and are punctuated by stops at churches along the way. Today, the journey is as popular as ever, among Christian and secular travelers alike. All, however, must ostensibly undertake the journey with a spiritual purpose in order to benefit from the pilgrims' accommodations (*gîtes*, refuges, and host families) along the way. To do this you need to apply for a *crédencial*, a kind of pilgrim's passport that is stamped by tourist offices at each stop. English-speaking visitors can find information in English at www.americanpilgrims.com. The French website www.chemins-compostelle.com tells you how to apply from abroad.

Where to Stay & Dine in the Pyrenees

> *Exposed stone walls in the rooms at Château de Beauregard.*

★★ **Au Fin Gourmet** PAU BASQUE
This family-run restaurant, near the railway station, is a great value. The postmodern, circular dining room has soaring windows overlooking a park. The best dishes, based on regional ingredients, include grilled scallops with fennel, duckling foie gras with mushrooms, rack of lamb, and braised stuffed trout. 24 av. Gaston-Lacoste. ☎ 05-59-27-47-71. www.restaurant-aufingourmet.com. Main courses 22€–25€, fixed-price lunch 27€–76€, dinner 38€–76€. AE, DC, MC, V. Lunch Tues and Thurs–Sun, dinner Tues–Sat. Reservations recommended.

★★ **Château de Beauregard** ST-GIRONS (NEAR ST-LIZIER) ROTISSERIE Two kilometers (1¼ miles) from St-Lizier is this romantic hotel, restaurant, and spa in a 19th-century château. The regular rooms are decorated with antiques (including a piano in the Victor Hugo unit). Prestige suites have contemporary decor and a deck. The restaurant serves extremely generous portions. The spa is set in a converted barn with stone walls and a fireplace. Av. de la Résistance. ☎ 05-61-66-66-64. www.chateaubeauregard.

net. 10 units. Doubles 60€–180€ (high season 80€–200€). Fixed-price menus 29€–33€. AE, MC, V. Lunch and dinner daily.

★ **Hôtel de Gramont** PAU
In the heart of Pau, this hotel dating from around 1880 is artfully restored to evoke grand-scale country living. Elegant woodwork adorns the street-level salons, and guest rooms are uniquely decorated with late-19th-century antiques. Lots of restaurants are nearby. 3 place Gramont. ☎ 05-59-27-84-04. Fax 05-59-27-62-23. www.hotelgramont.com. 34 units. Doubles 77€–126€; suites 140€–180€. AE, DC, MC, V.

Hôtel du Lion d'Or CAUTERETS TRADITIONAL FRENCH Owner Madame Lasserre takes your luggage and shows you a choice of rooms, each one charming in its old-fashioned way. Her son, a ski instructor, runs the bar and

Additional Hotels & Restaurants

For hotels and restaurants in Toulouse, see p. 543.

restaurant, where the four-course menu is a great value and diners can leave their half-drunk bottle corked on the table for the following night's meal. This place has many repeat visitors. 12 rue Richelieu. ☎ 05-62-92-52-87. www.liondor.eu. 19 units. Doubles from 70€. Fixed-price menus 20€–28€. AE, MC, V. Lunch and dinner daily.

Hôtel Le Saint Vincent BAGNERES-DE-BIGORRE
TRADITIONAL FRENCH This family-run hotel is clean, friendly, and attentive to guests. The restaurant is a local favorite for its sunny yellow dining room serving up reasonably priced classic French cuisine, including a superlative *crème caramel maison*. 31 rue du Maréchal Foch. ☎ 05-62-91-10-00. www.hotel-saint-vincent.com. Doubles 44€–46€. Fixed-price menus 12€–28€. MC, V. Lunch and dinner Tues–Sun.

Hotel Restaurant Panoramic LUZ-ST-SAVEUR
REGIONAL FRENCH Come to this mid-19th century inn, on the outskirts of town near the baths, for the panoramic views from the dining room. Most of the modest but clean and quiet guest rooms have views of the mountains as well. 30 av. Empératrice Eugénie. ☎ 05-62-92-80-14. www.hotel-panoramic-luz.com. Doubles 55€. Fixed-price menus 13€–18€. MC, V. Lunch and dinner Tues–Sat.

★★★ Le Carré de l'Ange ST-LIZIER *GASTRO-NOMIC* Opened in 2010 in the archbishop's palace, this restaurant has an exquisite setting, whether you're on the terrace with views of the mountains, in the stone-walled interior, or in the intimate wine bar. The chefs lovingly coax out the flavor of John Dory, lobster, pigeon, or Pyrenean lamb. Palais des Evêques. ☎ 05-61-65-65-65. www.lecarredelange.com. Fixed-price menus 24€–70€. AE, DC, MC, V. Lunch daily, dinner Wed–Sat. Closed Mar and Nov.

Les Cimes ESTARVIELLE (NEAR LOUDENVIELLE)
REGIONAL & FRENCH FUSION The charismatic owners of this hotel-restaurant work the place for 9 months (closed Sept to mid-Dec) and then set off for adventures, returning with souvenirs, which they display in the exotically themed rooms. Journalists covering the Tour de France used to wire their stories from the old relay station. All the rooms have views over the valley, and some have a balcony; a few cheaper rooms share bathrooms. Rte. du Col de Peyresourde, Estarvielle, Louron Valley. ☎ 05-62-99-67-21. www.hotel-les-cimes.net. 8 units. Fixed-price menus 18€–33€. Doubles from 43€. MC, V. Lunch and dinner daily. Closed Jan and Feb.

Le Manoir d'Agnès TARASCON-SUR-ARIEGE
REGIONAL FRENCH This beautifully restored 19th-century pink stone manse evokes an English manor, surrounded by a 100-year-old park. Inside it's more hip, with spare contemporary decor. The manor has its hammam and enjoyable restaurant serving local specialties. 2 rue Saint Roch. ☎ 05-61-02-32-81. www.manoiragnes.com. 15 units. Doubles 95€–120€. Fixed-price menus 18€–50€. MC, V. Lunch Tues–Sun, dinner Tues–Sat.

Résidence Le Domaine du Palais ST-LIZIER
French architect Jean-Michel Wilmotte's renovation of historic buildings belonging to the archbishop's complex has resulted in 86 beautifully appointed tourist apartments with marvelous views of the valley. Their contemporary style highlights the stark beauty of the ecclesiastical architecture, and they are well equipped with top-quality kitchens. Rte. de l'Evêché. ☎ 05-34-14-49-49. www.domainedupalais.fr. 86 units. Doubles 105€–125€. MC, V.

★★ Tentations ST-GIRONS (NEAR ST-LIZIER)
ICE CREAM & MODERN CUISINE A fourth-generation ice-cream maker, Philippe Faur decided to experiment with savory flavors, and his foie gras, caviar, espelette pepper, and truffle ice creams have found their way onto top tables around France. Chef Jean-Marc Granger devises the perfect dishes to go with them, and the ice creams are served on the side. 8 rue Gambetta. ☎ 05-61-04-88-60. www.philippefaur.com. Main courses 21€; tasting menu 25€. MC, V. Lunch and dinner Mon–Sat.

★ Villa Rose BAGNERES-DE-BIGORRE
Interior designer and antiquarian Marie-Christine Mécoën has paid homage to the 19th-century ladies who came here to "take the waters" at this gorgeous *chambres d'hôtes* furnished with antiques and local marble. The *salon du chocolat* has a library with antiquarian books on the art of skiing. 54 rue George Lassalle. ☎ 05-62-34-09-84. www.villarose65.com. 2 units. Doubles 135€–160€. V.

Languedoc-Roussillon in 10 Days

Rabbit-shaped Languedoc-Roussillon is a hugely diverse region. This land of ancient cities runs from Roman Nîmes (p. 432) via Montpellier and the Mediterranean down to Perpignan, and into the Pyrénées Orientales. The coast of Languedoc has an almost continuous strip of sand stretching west from the Rhône toward the Pyrenees. Ancient Roussillon is French Catalonia, a small region of Languedoc inspired more by Barcelona than by Paris. This weeklong trip takes you down the coast and into the mountains.

> With its rowboats and cafe terraces, Quai de la Résistance in Sète has a Venetian feel.

START Montpellier is 750km (466 miles) south of Paris and 240km (149 miles) east of Toulouse. TRIP LENGTH 367km (228 miles).

1 ★★ **Montpellier.** A large part of Montpellier's city center is pedestrianized, and street parking is almost nonexistent, so arrive by train or leave your car in the park-and-ride (www.ot-montpellier.fr/en/stationnement). Start your day with a coffee and a newspaper in **place de la Comédie.** You might take this opportunity to pop in to the Opéra-Comédie to see if there's an evening performance that catches your fancy. Then walk up rue de La Loge into Montpellier's Old Town, and wander the streets and pretty squares such as **place**

St-Ravy with its fountain. ⏱ 1 day. For detailed information on Montpellier, see p. 532.

From Montpellier, follow A9 and D300 southwest to Sète (36km/22 miles).

2 ★ **Sète.** Sète was made famous in France by the prize-winning 2007 movie *La Graine et le Mulet (The Secret of the Grain),* in which shipyard worker Monsieur Slimani tries to achieve his dream of opening a restaurant. Rent the DVD if you're planning this trip—it says much about this hardworking fishing port that was the first stop for thousands of immigrants from Italy and Morocco. Almost an island, with sea on virtually all sides, it is the biggest

1	Montpellier
2	Sète
3	Pézenas
4	Béziers
5	Narbonne
6	Carcassonne
7	Villefranche-de-Conflent
8	Prades
9	Céret
10	Collioure
11	Perpignan

fishing port on the Mediterranean. Go early in the morning to the **Criée** (wholesale fish market), where 800 lots of fish sell per hour. It's situated in the Vieux Port; the tourist office nearby can book you a tour. Following the canal that slices the Vieux Port in half north to south, you'll get to the old boatbuilding area, where an association of enthusiasts carries on building the ancient **Voile Latine** fishing boats with their brightly painted hulls, at 24 rue des Chantiers (☎ 04-67-74-32-60; www.voilelatine-sete.fr). In July and August, the canal is the scene of nautical jousting—a sight to be seen. Typical of Sète, instead of vaunting high art credentials, it offers the **Musée**

If You Have Only 3 Days

With just a long weekend in Languedoc-Roussillon, you'll have enough time for a day in each of the region's top three tourist towns: Montpellier, Carcassonne, and Perpignan. Carcassonne is 150km (93 miles) west of Montpellier on A9 and A61; a direct train takes at least 1½ hours, depending on the service. Perpignan is 113km (70 miles) southeast of Carcassonne on A61 and A9; a direct train takes from 1 hour, 22 minutes, depending on the service. For detailed information, see p. 532; 521, **6**; and 536.

> *Pézenas's picturesque Jewish Ghetto lies beyond the medieval porte Faugères.*

International des Arts Modestes, 23 quai du Maréchal de Latte de Tassigny (☎ 04-67-18-64-00; www.miam.org; admission 5€ adults, 2€ ages 10–18, free for children 9 and under, free for everyone 1st Sun of the month; Apr–Sept daily 9:30am–7pm, Oct–Mar Tues–Sun 10am–noon and 2–6pm), a humorous collection of bibelots, kitsch, and contemporary art. The **Cimetière Marin,** where poet Paul Valéry is buried, has fantastic views. If you've managed to pack even half of that into your day, you deserve a good meal. Reward yourself with a fish feast at any one of the restaurants on quai Général Durand. ⊕ 1 day. Sète Tourist Office, 60 Grand'rue Mario Roustan. ☎ 04-99-04-71-71. www.ot-sete.fr.

From Sète, head west on N300 and N113 to Pézenas (38km/24 miles).

❸ Pézenas. Sète's more high-minded cousin, Pézenas is part of an archipelago of historic villages set amid the vineyards. None other than Molière, the future court playwright to Louis XIV, came here with his troupe of players when he was a young man, staying for several months each time and taking inspiration from Pézenas's local characters for some of his most famous comedies. In the tourist office, at place des Etats du Languedoc, the **Scénovision Molière** (☎ 04-67-98-35-39; www.scenovisionmoliere.com; admission 7€; 6€ reduced; daily) is a 55-minute 3-D show on Molière's life that will delight children and adults alike. It was the town's merchant wealth and importance as a seat of local government that drew Molière and other playwrights here. Walking around, you'll see plenty of evidence of this former glory in the courtyards of grand 17th-century houses such as the **Hôtel des Barons de Lacoste,** rue François Oustrin (☎ 04-67-90-19-06). Just within the 14th-century porte Faugères is the old **Jewish Ghetto.** Visit some of the Val de l'Hérault vineyards, where you can buy reasonably robust reds and Clairette, a sweet white wine perfect as an aperitif, before moving on. ⊕ 1 day. Pézenas Tourist Office, place des Etats du Languedoc. ☎ 04-67-98-36-40. www.ot-pezenas-valdherault.com.

From Pézenas, follow N9 southwest to Béziers (24km/15 miles).

❹ Béziers. This small city of nearly 60,000 was the site of the biggest massacre of the Albigensian Crusade (see "Who Were the Cathars?" p. 520). When the Cathar locals refused to submit, nearly 20,000 were summarily wiped out, with lenience refused to women, children, and those in churches. The Crusades commander made no distinction between Catholics and Cathars, famously

The Local Lingo

This region's eponymous antique language, Oc (*langue d'oc*), still survives in a quaint, reliquary way. Although there are stirrings to bring it back in schools and literature, it is mostly honored on street signs, and pulled from the closet and dusted off for traditional festivals.

> *Part of the movie* Robin Hood: Prince of Thieves, *starring Kevin Costner, was filmed in the medieval city of Carcassonne.*

saying, "Kill them all; God will know His own." The crusaders torched the original cathedral and in its place built the immense 14th-century Gothic **Cathédrale St-Nazaire,** place du Cathédrale (☎ 04-67-76-47-00; free admission; daily 9am–6:30pm). The frescoes, baroque choir, and 15th-century arch of the sacristy are all highlights. The cathedral is on the highest point in the town and affords great views. Béziers is a fascinating mixture of beefy machismo (rugby, bullfighting) and cultural refinement, as seen in the **Musée des Beaux-Arts,** in the Hôtel Fabrégat on place de la Révolution (☎ 04-67-28-38-78), and in the Hôtel Fayet on rue de Capu (☎ 04-67-49-04-66). The **Arènes de Béziers,** av. Emile Claparède (☎ 04-67-76-13-45; www.arenes-de-beziers.com), is a huge 19th-century arena that hosts concerts and operas as well as *corridas* (bullfights). In the month of August, Béziers goes 100% bullfighting, attracting nearly one million visitors a year to its Feria, which includes the spectacle of men running through the streets pursued by angry bulls.

About 10km (6¼ miles) east of Béziers (take D11 and D162) is the **Oppidum d'Ensérune** (http://enserune.monuments-nationaux.fr; last admission 1 hr. before closing; May–Aug daily 10am–7pm; Apr and Sept Tues–Sun 10am–12:30pm and 2–6pm; Oct–Mar Tues–Sun 9:30am–12:30pm and 2–5pm), the superb remains of a Roman hill town that existed from the 6th century B.C. to the 1st century A.D. You can see streets, columns, the foundations of houses and shops, a grain silo, and a necropolis. The on-site museum shows many fine archaeological finds. ⏱ 1 day. Béziers Tourist Office, 29 av. St-Saëns. ☎ 04-67-76-84-00. www.beziers-tourisme.fr.

From Béziers, follow N9 southwest to Narbonne (28km/17 miles).

❺ ★ **Narbonne.** Wine and water have dictated Narbonne's history. It started as a major Roman port and then became a prosperous medieval town and important bishopric. Then, after the Aude River changed its course, the Narbonnais built the canal de la Robine and once again became the main depot for the Corbières wine industry. With demand for reasonably priced French wine in decline, Narbonne is now capitalizing on its past grandeur, pulling in the tourists with both its heritage and its beach (12km/7½ miles away). Starting with the oldest site, there's the **Horreum,** 7 rue Rouget de Lisle (☎ 04-68-32-45-30), an underground warren of granaries and grain chutes built by the Romans in the 1st century B.C.; situated in the restored medieval quarter, it's now filled with attractive shops and restaurants. In the center of town, the huge palace and cathedral complex, built from the 12th to the 14th centuries, reveals vaunting ecclesiastical ambitions. The **Cathédrale St-Just et St-Pasteur,** rue Armand Gautier (☎ 04-68-32-09-52; free admission; daily 9am–noon and 2–6pm), is just the chancel

of the original cathedral plan, but it is still huge, decorated with 14th-century statues, stained glass, and Aubusson tapestries. Cloisters join it to the **Palais des Archevêques** (Archbishop's Palace), which contains several museums, including the **Archaeology Museum** and the **Museum of Art and History.** There are pleasant walks by the canal, which is lined with 18th-century houses and *chais* (wine warehouses). ☉ 1 day. Narbonne Tourist Office, 31 rue Jean Jaurès. ☎ 04-68-65-15-60. www.mairie-narbonne.fr. All Narbonne museums have the same opening hours and prices: Admission to one museum 6€ adults, 4€ reduced; pass for all museums 9€ adult, 6€ reduced. April–July 14 Wed–Mon 10am–noon and 2–5pm; July 15–Oct 31 daily 10am–1pm and 2:30–6pm; Nov–Mar Wed–Mon 2–5pm.

From Narbonne, head west on D168, E80, and D6113 to Carcassone (63km/39 miles).

❻ ★★★ kids **Carcassonne.** The magnificent walled **Cité de Carcassonne** is the largest medieval walled city in Europe. It's also in mint condition, largely thanks to the efforts of writer Prosper Mérimée, who doubled as inspector of national monuments, and Napoleon III's architect Viollet-le-Duc, who saved this now world-famous piece of heritage from plans to demolish it. ☉ 1 day. See p. 521, ❻.

From Carcassonne, head south on N113, A61/E80, A9/E15, D900, and N116 to Villefranche-de-Conflent (162km/101 miles).

❼ ★ kids **Villefranche-de-Conflent.** However many of Vauban's citadels you've seen, they continue to inspire awe. This virtually perfect walled city, on the UNESCO World Heritage site list, was built by Louis XIV's military architect on the site of Spanish fortifications, to protect France's borderland. A walk around the **ramparts** takes about an hour; it's worth getting the audio-guide (3€) or taking a guided tour to understand the genius of the city's siege-proof architecture. As you walk around, you'll see arrow slits, watchtowers, and amazing drops down to the rushing river. Enter the ramparts at 32bis rue St-Jacques (☎ 04-68-96-16-40; www.villefranchedeconflent.com; admission 4€ adults, 3€ reduced, free for children 11 and under; July–Aug daily 10am–8pm, June and Sept 10am–7pm, Mar–May

St-Martin-du-Canigou

The little village of Casteil, 8km (5 miles) south of Villefranche-de-Conflent and 18km (11 miles) south of Prades via Taurinya, is the starting point for the climb to the 11th-century Abbaye St-Martin-du-Canigou, on Mount Canigou. Not for the fainthearted, this mile-long trek climbs to 1,000m (3,281 ft.) above sea level but is rewarded by a spiritual high. The abbey in the clouds was home to a Benedictine community from its foundation until the French Revolution. Since 1988 it has again housed Benedictine monks, who move silently among the ancient buildings. You can visit by guided tour only; allow at least 40 minutes for the climb, and plan to arrive at the abbey 15 minutes before the tour begins. ☎ 04-68-05-50-03. www. stmartinducanigou.org. Admission 5€ adults, 3.50€ ages 12–18, free for children 11 and under. MC, V accepted with 15€ minimum. Tours June–Sept Mon–Sat 10am, 11am, noon, 2pm, 3pm, 4pm, and 5pm; Sun 10am and 12:30pm only; Oct–May no 5pm tour.

> *Picasso loved the shaded squares of Céret.*

and Oct 10:30am–12:30pm and 2–6pm, Feb and Nov 10:30am–12:30pm and 2–6pm, Dec 2–5pm, closed Jan).

The medieval streets within are filled with shops and restaurants. In the afternoon, unless you want to make the climb to the **Abbaye St-Martin-du-Canigou** (see the box, at right), take a leisurely ride on the **Petit Train Jaune** (www.trainstouristiques-ter.com; admission 3.50€–18.10€ one way, depending on trip length), which travels 63km (39 miles) from Villefranche-le-Conflent to Latour-de-Carol Enveitg on the border with Spain. The world's first electric train, it opened in 1927, powered by hydroelectricity generated by a barrage across the Têt; 650 feats of engineering were needed to carve this route through the eastern Pyrenees. Soaring viaducts, audacious tunnels, and France's highest station, at Bolquère (1,593m/5,226 ft.), make it one of the most breathtaking train rides in the world. There are 22 stations, and you can cover as many as you want; the whole route takes just over 2 hours (one way). ☉1 day. Friends of the Villefranche Conflent, www.villefranchedeconflent.com.

From Villefranche-de-Conflent, follow N116 northeast to Prades (7km/4⅓ miles).

❽ Prades. In Prades, you'll find a friendly, down-to-earth Catalan town with a few locals enjoying an aperitif and tapas on cafe terraces. From late-July to mid-August, however, you'll see an unusual number of people wheeling cellos, for this is the home of the **Festival Pablo Casals** (www.prades-festival-casals. com), the international chamber music festival begun by the cellist who adopted Prades as his home after escaping here during the Spanish Civil War. Concerts are held in Romanesque churches in Prades and its nearby villages, including the **Abbey of St-Michel-de-Cuixa** with its beautiful rose marble cloister. ☉1 day. Prades Tourist Office, 10 place de la République. ☎04-68-05-41-02. www.prades-tourisme.fr.

Céret is 57km (35 miles) southeast of Prades: Take N116 as far as Ille-sur-Têt, then D615 to Tuir, before cutting through country roads on D615.

❾ ★★ Céret. Céret, only 9km (5⅔ miles) from the Spanish border, nestles among the cherry

> *Perpignan has been French since 1659, but it was once Catalan's second city, after Barcelona.*

orchards that gave the town its name. Architectural heritage from the time of the kings of Majorca includes two tall entrance arches, the **porte de l'Espagne** and **porte de France.** The **Musée d'Art Moderne,** 8 bd. Maréchal Joffre (☎ 04-68-87-27-76; www. musee-ceret.com; 8€ regular, 6€ reduced; free for children 11 and under; May–June and Sept 16–30 daily 10am–6pm, July 1–Sept 15 daily 10am–7pm, Oct–Apr Wed–Mon 10am–6pm), is devoted to Picasso, who made the town his home, and to other artists of the cubist movement. ◷ Half-day. Céret Tourist Office, 1 av. Georges Clemenceau. ☎ 04-68-87-00-53. www.ot-ceret.fr.

From Céret, take D618 and D914 east (to exit 13) to Collioure (33km/21 miles).

🔟 ★★ **Collioure.** A half-hour drive takes you past the beaches of Argelès (p. 524) to Collioure, a former fishing village beloved of the fauvist painters. The joyous colors of their canvases are still seen in the steep streets full of brightly painted houses covered in bougainvillea. The views are superb from the **Château Royal** (☎ 04-68-82-06-43; June–Sept

10am–5:15pm, Oct–May 9am–4:15pm) and **Fort St-Elme** (☎ 06-64-61-82-42; Apr–Sept guided tours 2:30–7pm). The **Eglise de Notre-Dame-des-Anges** (daily 9am–noon and 2–6pm) is the town's most famous monument; half lighthouse, half church, it looks austere from the outside but inside features a floor-to-ceiling altarpiece dripping with gold. The village is now entirely given over to tourism, but it's impossible not to enjoy its charm, and small hotels and restaurants are plentiful. ◷ Half-day. Collioure Tourist Office, place 18 Juin. ☎ 04-68-82-15-47. www.collioure.com.

From Collioure, take D914 northwest to Perpignan (30km/19 miles).

⓫ ★★ **Perpignan.** This town is the former continental seat of the kings of Majorca. In the 13th and 14th centuries, these powerful monarchs from the Balearic island left a wealth of impressive architecture in distinctive pink Roussillon stone, including the **Palais des Rois de Majorque,** the **Castillet** tower, and several religious buildings. ◷ 1 day. For detailed information on Perpignan, see p. 536.

Where to Stay & Dine in Languedoc-Roussillon

> Sardines drizzled in garlic butter and lemon juice is a popular aperitif in Languedoc-Roussillon.

Domaine de la Tannerie PRADES
This hotel is housed in a spacious 1780 tannery building. Each of the five rooms is decked out in honor of a different country, including Morocco and India. And the sports-loving hosts have installed a heated swimming pool in the garden, a sauna and hammam, and a game room. 6 rue St-Martin. ☎ 04-68-97-16-76. www.domainedelatannerie.com. 5 units. Doubles 69€–99€. MC, V.

★ Hôtel L'Orque Bleue SETE
In a *fin-de-siècle* Hausmannian building, L'Orque Bleue is right on the busy harbor. One of the top hotels in Sète, the roomy chambers feature air conditioning, plush beds, and (for just 3€ extra) breakfast-in-bed service. The rooms with a view of Canal Royal are worth the reasonable prices. 10 quai Aspirant Heber. ☎ 04-67-74-72-13. www.hotel-orquebleue-sete.com. 30 units. Doubles from 85€. AE, MC, V.

★ Le Marie Jean SETE *FISH*
Just across the Grand Canal from L'Orque Bleue is one of Sète's top restaurants. The fish doesn't get any fresher than the day's catch prepared with a creative twist by chef Gilles Balaguer, such as sea bass with Roquefort sauce or a tantalizing oyster and mussels appetizer with creamy garlic sauce. 26 quai Général. ☎ 04-67-46-02-01. 3-course menu 15€–27€. AE, MC, V. Lunch and dinner Thurs–Tues.

Le Zaza Club TORREILLES *SEAFOOD*
Impeccably fresh seafood is prepared with a Catalan twist at this restaurant with beach service on the Mediterranean Gulf of Lions, between the traditional villages of Le Barcarès and Canet. Plage Sud Torreilles. ☎ 04-68-59-21-45. www.restaurant-lezazaclub.com. June–Sept 15 daily 10am–2am.

Villa Lafabrègue PRADES
Pablo Casals used to compose in this Florentine-style villa built by a Catalan banking family in the 19th century. Run by an English family now, it has a lovely garden and a swimming pool. 15 av. Louis Prat. ☎ 04-68-96-29-90. www.villafrench.com. 5 units. Doubles 65€–75€. Cash or check only.

On the Cathar Trail

This 5-day tour will take you around the areas where the 12th-century Cathar cult of religious separatists was at its most powerful. The term "Cathar castles" is really a tourist invention. The Cathars themselves built no fortifications but merely sought refuge in existing castles, under the protection of local lords. Cathars exist today only in history books—and in the fascinating myths, conspiracies, and doomsday scenarios that have enveloped this band of religious purists who set the stage for the Protestant Reformation.

> Nestled in the Ariège hills, Foix is known for its three-towered Cathar castle, the Château de Foix.

START Foix is 85km (53 miles) south of Toulouse and 200km (124 miles) west of Perpignan. TRIP LENGTH 258km (160 miles).

① Foix. Today's administrative capital of the Ariège *département* was formerly the seat of the Comtes de Foix—counts whose protection was vital to the Cathars but paradoxically a nail in their coffin, as it turned them from simple heretics into a political threat for the Vatican. For Raymond-Roger de Foix, it was a family affair: His sister, wife, and illegitimate daughter Esclarmonde were all Cathars. But Raymond-Roger himself was able to do more to protect his family and subjects by

remaining a Catholic and wielding his sword, as Cathars took a vow of pacifism. He fought against the Albigensian Crusade, sustained four sieges before losing the **Château de Foix** in 1214, and died at the siege of Mirepoix—relatively happy, as he'd gotten the castle and the rest of his land back by then. The **château** itself (☎ 05-61-05-10-10; www.sesta.fr; admission 4.50€ adults, free for children 4 and under; July–Aug daily 9:45am–6:30pm, Sept–June 10:30am–noon and 2–5:30pm) is a dramatic symbol of resistance and power, with its unusual three towers, which are especially imposing when illuminated at night. The climb up the hundreds of steps to the top

1. Foix
2. Château de Montségur
3. Mirepoix
4. Rennes-le-Château
5. Château de Peyrepertuse
6. Carcassonne
7. Châteaux de Lastours

of the towers is rewarded with a fabulous view over Foix and the Ariège River. Inside, displays include a permanent exhibition on the Comtes de Foix, including the bed of Henri IV (the Protestant count who became king of France). Resistance—a thread that runs through Foix's history right up to World War II—is the theme of a 10-day film festival each July, the **Festival Résistances** (www.festival-resistances.fr). ☉ 1 day. Foix Tourist Office, 29 rue Delcassé. ☎ 05-61-65-12-12. www.tourisme-foix-varilhes.fr.

From Foix, take N20 south (toward Lavel-anet) to exit 12 and D117; 5km (3 miles) past Nalzen, turn right to Villeneuve-d'Olmes and right again onto D9. Pass the first parking area and continue to the second, large one at the foot of the path to the château (30km/19 miles total).

2 ★★ **Château de Montségur.** More than 1,200m (3,937 ft.) high, on a rock formation known as a *pog* (peak), this fortress repre-sents the Cathars' last stand. After 10 months of siege in 1244, 220 people were burned alive after refusing to renounce their religion. The castle you see was not the place the Cathars died defending—that was destroyed by the victorious French forces. What stands now

is an amalgamation of mostly 13th- but some 17th-century French architecture; still, you can see the remains of the Cathar village spread out around it, reclaimed by brambles and gorse. This castle is surrounded by myths: It's the resting home of the Holy Grail . . . a Cathar treasure trove . . . a center of Nazi archaeologi-cal research . . . and other fantastical claims to fame. Whether you believe them or not, this place at the top of the world, where hell caught up with those in search of heaven, cer-tainly has a mystical vibe. Below, in the village of Montségur, a free museum—open Febru-ary to May and October to December in the afternoons, and June through September also in the mornings—shows archaeological finds from the château and village. ☉ 3 hr. ☎ 05-61-01-06-94. www.montsegur.org. Admission 4.50€ adults, 2€ reduced. Feb–Dec times vary; May–Sept optional guided tours included; Feb–Apr and Oct–Dec arrange private tours with Fabrice Chambon (number above). The château is a strenuous 20-min. hike, up from the road level—only for the fit and well shod.

From Montségur, head north on D6 to Lavelanet then pick up D625 to Mirepoix (32km/20 miles).

Who Were the Cathars?

Across 12th-century Christendom, with adherents from Catalonia to the Rhineland, the religious sect known as the Cathars flourished in Languedoc until they were annihilated by the Catholic Church and the nobles of northern France. ("Cathar" is a moniker bestowed upon the group, who called themselves simply *Good Men and Good Women* or *Good Christians*.) The Cathars were strongly influenced by Persian and Byzantine dualistic beliefs. They believed that the physical world was evil, created by *Rex Mundi* (King of the World), and the world of spirit was pure love, although adherents differed on whether one's purpose was to transcend corrupted physical matter or to redeem it. Either way the Catholic Church was united in calling Catharism heresy. The attempt to re-convert the Cathars was at first peaceful—the **Dominican Order** was created for this purpose—but it turned violent in 1209 with the full-fledged **Albigensian Crusade,**

which divided northern and southern France. The zeal of the crusaders wasn't entirely pure: This was really a northern land grab sanctioned by the pope. Cathar centers such as **Carcassonne** were besieged, and a notorious massacre followed at **Béziers.** When it was all over, the areas of Toulouse and Languedoc were part of the northern French empire, no longer independent or allied with Spanish Aragon. The first appearance of the **Inquisition,** an institution established to suppress heresy that lasted into the mid-14th century, was to ferret out the remaining Cathar faithful. In France, what was once considered *Pays Cathare* (Cathar Country) is now the *département* of Aude, the eastern part of the Ariège *département,* embodied by the fortifications at Carcassonne and Montségur. The Cathar movement was important not just for the way it shaped French history but also because it was a clear precursor to the Protestant Reformation.

❸ ★ **Mirepoix.** Before the crusaders besieged this town of 3,000, Catharism was freely practiced here under the protection of the lords of Mirepoix, and a council of 600 church leaders was held here in 1204. What was left after the crusaders had ravaged it was then destroyed by a terrible flood, but the pretty "new" town of 1289 shows exemplary grid planning. **Place du Maréchal-Leclerc** is one of the finest medieval squares in France, full of historic buildings and all the architectural garnishing Mirepoix could muster. The carvings of people and animals on the beams of the arcaded Maison des Consuls will raise a smile. The covered market here on Mondays is especially fine; you will find all the ingredients required to make the famed **Mirepoix,** a fragrant combination of chopped onions, carrots, and celery that serves as a base in many a French dish. The Gothic sandstone **Cathédrale St-Maurice** is the second-largest single-naved church in Europe, measuring 20.26m (66½ ft.) high. Mirepoix's main draws today are eating, drinking, and shopping for antiques. ⏱ Half-day. Mirepoix Tourist Office, place Maréchal Leclerc. ☎ 05-61-68-83-76. www.tourisme-mirepoix.com.

From Mirepoix, head east on D626 to Limoux, south on D116 to Couiza, and pick up D52 to Rennes-le-Château (53km/33 miles).

❹ **Rennes-le-Château.** If you're into conspiracies, you can consider this village France's version of Roswell or Loch Ness. In the 1950s, a restaurant owner in this hamlet of fewer than 100 people exhumed a local mystery about the village priest in order to drum up business. Where did Abbé Saunière get the money (the equivalent of $3 million today) to renovate his church in fantastical style and build a tower and luxury villa? Though he was convicted for selling Masses, the suggestion that he'd found Visigoth treasure and documents that could bring down the entire Catholic Church fueled the public imagination and found its way into many fiction thrillers, such as *The Da Vinci Code.* Even if you're skeptical of such stories, it's worth visiting Rennes-le-Château to marvel at the bucolic countryside and the Victorian megalomaniac's domain, including the **Eglise Ste-Marie-Madeleine.** Rennes-le-Château's only true link with the Cathars is its locality, but it's still a lot of fun.

⏱ 2 hr. La Domaine de Rennes-le-Château. ☎ 04-68-31-38-85. www.rennes-le-chateau.fr. Daily, times vary (see website for details). Admission 4.50€ adults, 3.50€ reduced. The village is closed to traffic July–Aug, when there is a park-and-ride from the first parking area.

From Rennes-le-Château, retrace your route to Couiza, then pick up D613 east for 6km (3¾ miles), and turn right onto D14, passing through pretty Rennes-les-Bains, to Duilhac-sous-Peyrepertuse (46km/29 miles total).

❺ **Château de Peyrepertuse.** The hamlet of Duilhac is the closest to Château de Peyrepertuse. The two castles here, linked by a vast staircase, constitute one of the finest of the Cathar forts. Peyrepertuse seems suspended in the air, placed at an elevation of 780m (2,559 ft.) on a jagged, vertiginous cliff. You can reach it by car or on foot—a rather rigorous hour-long climb—and the panoramic view of the area is astounding. ⏱ 4 hr. ☎ 04-68-45-69-40. www.chateau-peyrepertuse.com. Admission 7.50€ adults, 3€ reduced. June–Sept daily 8:30am–8:30pm; Oct–Nov and Feb–May shorter hours. Closed in Jan.

Carcassonne is 80km (50 miles) north of Duilhac-sous-Peyrepertuse. We recommend this scenic route, which follows D804, D410, D123, D39, D613, and D23: Head north to Rouffiac-des-Corbières, turn right, and pass through Montgaillard and Maisons, where you take a right and then your first left. Continue on to Villerouge-Terminès; then, after 5km (3 miles), take a left at the fork. At Lagrasse, pick up D3 to Carcassonne.

❻ ★★★ 🅺🅸🅳🅂 **Carcassonne.** The medieval walled city of Carcassonne is the largest in Europe and the most meticulously preserved. The Cathars had a powerful friend in the ruling Trencavel family, who built the inner wall of the Cité, but even this could not stand the full force of the Albigensian Crusade (see "Who Were the Cathars?"). Raymond-Roger Trencavel (de Foix) was a hero of their cause: As a result of his efforts to save Carcassonne's inhabitants, he was excommunicated and then imprisoned in his own dungeon, where he died of dysentery. His son Raymond won Carcassonne back, but was besieged again, and hundreds were burned at the stake. You can still see the Maison de

> *The hour-long hike up to the Château de Peyrepertuse is worth the effort for the views.*

l'Inquisition within the city walls. King Louis IX built the second wall, bringing Carcassonne's fortifications to nearly 6km (3¾ miles) of ramparts with more than 50 watchtowers. The main entrance—porte Narbonne, on the eastern side—is the most spectacular. Just to the right of the entrance is the tourist office, which runs excellent guided tours in multiple languages. Three main sights within the city walls are the UNESCO World Heritage site, **Château Comtal** (☎ 04-68-11-70-70; carcassonne.monuments-nationaux.fr; admission 8.50€ adults, 5€ reduced; Apr–Sept daily 9:30am–6:30pm, Oct–Mar daily 9:30am–5pm), a fortress within a fortress, housing the aforementioned tourist office and a museum on the architecture and restoration of Cité (from which you can access the ramparts); the Gothic **Basilique St-Nazaire,** Place Auguste Pierre Pont (free admission; summer daily 9am–7pm, winter shorter hours), whose organ, gleamingly restored, is the oldest in France; and the **Théâtre Jean Deschamps,** an open-air amphitheater seating 5,000 within the medieval walls. It is only 100 years old, but the surrounding walls and towers lend a performance here the same appeal as a show in the ancient Nîmes arena or Athens's antique theater. In July, the **Festival des Deux Cités** (www.festivaldecarcassonne.fr) attracts international stars of rock, jazz, opera, and dance. ⏱1 day. Carcassonne Tourist Office, 28 rue de Verdun. ☎ 04-68-10-24-30. www.carcassonne-tourisme.com.

From Carcassonne, take D201 at the roundabout 6km (3¾ miles) out of town, then D101 after Conques-sur-Orbiel north to Lastours (17km/11 miles).

7 ★ **Châteaux de Lastours.** This set of four interconnected castles, on a rocky hillside atop the village of Lastours, was originally built in the 11th century and controlled by the independent lords of Cabaret. The castles provided protection to the Cathar *parfaits* (perfects), monks who were extremely devout in following a path of strict renunciation, which endeared them to the area's residents. But the French royalty was hellbent on destroying this Cathar refuge. The original forts were torn down, and the castles you see today are 13th-century constructions. During the Wars of Religion the castles were occupied by Protestants, making this a home of many a Catholic dissenter. **Cabaret** is the primary castle, surrounded by ramparts that keep watch over the Cabardès and the Montagne Noire regions. **Surdespine** is the most dilapidated of the four, noted for its *meurtrières,* or murder-holes, in which defenders rained down oil, arrows, and rocks on the attackers. **Tour Régine,** the newest, is mainly just a tower and a large cistern. A bit farther south is **Quertineux,** which contains the ruins of a Romanesque church. Get a fine view of all four from the other end of the Gresillon Valley, at Montfermier Belvedere. ⏱ Half-day. Châteaux de Lastours. ☎ 04-68-77-56-02. www.chateaudelastours.com. Admission 4€ adults, 2€ reduced. July–Aug daily 9am–8pm; Sept–Dec and Feb–June shorter hours. Closed Jan.

Where to Stay & Dine on the Cathar Trail

★ **Hôtel de La Cité** CARCASSONNE
This hotel in the citadel provides the fullest possible experience of old Carcassonne, and the views are breathtaking. As soon as you see the richness of your room, you'll be glad you paid to stay here. The service, attention, and care offered by the staff are impeccable. Place Auguste Pont. ☎ 04-68-71-98-71. www.hoteldelacite.com. 61 units. Doubles from 225€. AE, DC, MC, V.

Hôtel La Maison des Consuls MIREPOIX
An official *Monument Historique*, this three-star hotel in a 13th-century building has the finest sculpted arcades in town. Rooms are in the style of Louis XIV, Louis XVI, and the 1950s. 6 place du Maréchal-Leclerc. ☎ 05-61-68-81-81. www.maisondesconsuls.com. 8 units. Doubles from 110 in July–Aug. AE, MC, V.

★ **Hôtel Restaurant Costes** MONTSÉGUR *ORGANIC FRENCH*   This charming hotel has a sunny garden, a restaurant that favors organic produce, and rooms with four-poster beds and Jacuzzis with chromo- and aromatherapy. 52 Le Village. ☎ 05-61-01-10-24. www.chez-costes. com. 12 units. Doubles from 46€. Menus 15€–35€. MC, V. Lunch and dinner Tues–Sat.

★ **La Barbacane** CARCASSONNE *GASTRONOMIC*
The only Michelin-starred restaurant in Carcassonne, La Barbacane serves delicacies such as lobster, crayfish, Bayonne ham, octopus cooked in its ink, and chestnut parfait. Rue

> *Step back in time at the Logis de Mirepoix, where guests dine heartily in medieval style.*

de la Barbacane. ☎ 04-68-71-98-71. Menus from 70€. AE, DC, MC. Dinner Thurs–Mon.

★★★ **Le Ciel d'Or** MIREPOIX *GASTRONOMIC*
The cuisine served at this Relais & Châteaux hotel is sublime. Try the magret of Barbary duck, with its accompaniment of blanched spinach and a cake of beetroot pureé. Then retire in one of the inn's eight lovely bedrooms. 8 rue de Maréchal Clauzel. ☎ 05-61-60-19-19. www.relaisroyal.com. Doubles 200€–300€. Main courses 26€–34€; menus 35€–90€. AE, DC, MC, V. Easter–Nov lunch Tues–Thurs and Sat, dinner Tues–Sun; Nov–Easter lunch Wed–Thurs and Sat, dinner Wed–Sun. Closed Jan.

kids **Logis de Mirepoix** MIREPOIX *MEDIEVAL BANQUET*   Feast at a medieval banquet here, with the owners donning traditional garb and welcoming guests in their refurbished 18th-century home and inn. 2 cours du Docteur Chabaud. ☎ 05-61-68-21-63. www.logisdemirepoix. com. Guest house 80€. Main courses 12€–18€. MC, V. High season lunch and dinner Tues–Sun; low season lunch and dinner Sat, lunch Sun.

Tips on Lodging in Carcassonne

Guest hotels tend to be a better value on the other side of the Aude River, in the **Bastide St-Louis** or *Basse Ville* (Lower City), built by King Louis XI in 1247. If you choose to stay in the Lower City, don't miss the many beautiful *hôtels particuliers* from the 16th to 18th centuries, including the **Musée des Mémoires,** 53 rue de Verdun (☎ 04-68-72-45-55; free admission; Tues–Sat 9am–noon and 2–6pm). The Basse Ville also has a lively Saturday market, close to beautiful **place Carnot** and its centerpiece, **Fontaine de Neptune.**

Best Beaches

The Pyrenees may be 435km (270 miles) long, but

eventually they reach down to the sea on either end. On the Atlantic side, the Pays Basque has only 45km (28 miles) of coast, but it's almost all beach—a continuation of the longest stretch of sand in Europe, known as the Côte d'Argent. If you've got the *argent* (money), you've caught the surfing bug, or you don't like too much hoi polloi, this is the place to visit. If you're with your family, opt for the other end, along the warmer Mediterranean Sea, whose resorts are some of the most laid-back in France.

> The 7km (4⅓-mile) Blue Flag stretch of pristine sand at Argelès Beach, in Argelès-sur-Mer, near Perpignan.

Argelès-sur-Mer PYRENEES

South of Perpignan (p. 536) is the longest beach in the Pyrénées-Orientales *département*. Argelès has a historic village and a more modern beach resort, with 7km (4⅓ miles) of wide, sandy beaches that are well-staffed with lifeguards and other necessary provisions (such as pizzerias). The beaches here have won various awards for their quality, in large part due to their meticulous upkeep. Ever heard of four-star camping? This beach stretch is a favorite for those wishing to get back to nature—but not too far back. There's a plethora of places that offer camping sites and caravans, such as **Camping Le Soleil** and **La Sirene,** set amid swimming pools, restaurants, and evening entertainment. Argelès is at the northern end of the **Côte Vermeille** (Vermillion Coast), which inspired the fauvist painters. After Le Racou, the beaches turn pebbly and then become cliffs and coves. You can visit four castles in the area. The best is the 19th-century **Château de Valmy.** The 14th-century **Eglise Notre-Dame del Prat**

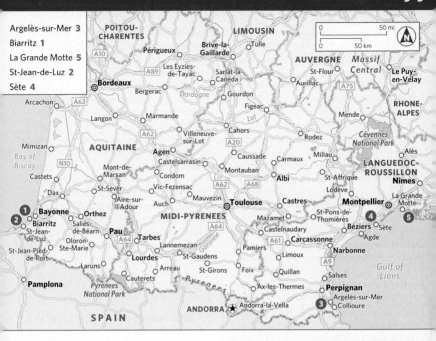

is no minor church, with a huge bell tower and more than 100 fully restored paintings depicting more than 30 saints. Prehistory abounds here in the form of the huge rocks that have been amassed to form dolmens, mass graveyards dating to 2500 B.C. **23km (14 miles) southeast of Perpignan. www.argeles-sur-mer.com.**

★★★ Biarritz BASQUE COUNTRY

Famed as the summer home for many of the world's rich and famous, the opulent town of Biarritz (p. 491, ②) is synonymous with indulgence. But it's also Europe's surfing capital, and the powerful waves of the Atlantic Ocean provide the perfect test of mettle during the **Biarritz Surf Festival,** attended by more than 150,000 people every July. The first surfer here was a Hollywood producer, on location making a movie; he was so thrilled by the huge swells, he had his surfboard shipped from California and wowed the locals. Biarritz has more than a half dozen different beaches, totaling more than 6km (3¾ miles) of shoreline. **La Grande Plage** (Grand Beach) is in the center of town, close to the casino and shopping. Crowded with both surfers and bathers during high season, it is definitely

> Come to the Basque coast in July to catch the Biarritz Surf Festival—an international event attended by thousands.

the place to be seen hanging ten. Long, wild, and backed by scrubby cliffs, the **Côte des Basques Beach** is popular with surfers, too, but it's also known as the beach the Basques themselves frequent. You can walk south from here along other beaches toward Bidart. If you're looking to avoid those pesky board-skimmers, head to the strong currents of **Plage de Miramar,** where surfing is forbidden while swimming is permitted under the gaze of lifeguards. The pool of the **Sofitel Biarritz Le Miramar Thalassa** spa hotel (p. 531) has fabulous views of this beach and, farther out to sea, of the famous **Roche Percée,** formerly a diving point but now a nature reserve for seabirds. If you're with children, opt for **Plage du Port Vieux,** a small, shady beach near the city center. **Plage de Marbella** is very pretty, and, due to the many steps that lead from a rather difficult access point, it's the most intimate stretch of sand in Biarritz. Biarritz Tourist Office, square d'Ixelles. ☎ 05-59-22-37-00. www.biarritz.fr.

kids **La Grande Motte** LANGUEDOC
This resort east of Montpellier (p. 532) was purpose-built in the 1960s to lure French holidaymakers back from sunny Spain. Its architecture is, well, out there—in the way that only 1960s architecture can be. Jean Balladur based it on the pyramids of Chichén Itzá, Mexico, which looks rather incongruous fronted by a yachting marina. What this resort offers are impeccably clean beaches (even dogs get their own patch of sand), showers, safe swimming, and a cornucopia of activities to keep children happy. It's therefore very popular with families. It's one of the most active beach towns in France, a perfect locale for water skiing, jet skiing, windsurfing, speed boating, and more. In case building sand castles isn't enough for the kiddies, there's a theme park with fun water slides and rides. If you've got a *coup de soleil* (sunburn) and need shade, you'll find it on hiking trails and picnic sites in the leafy forest preserves adjacent to the town. 22km (14 miles) east of Montpellier. www.ot-lagrandemotte.fr.

★★ kids **St-Jean-de-Luz** BASQUE COUNTRY
Considered by some to be the loveliest old port town on the French Atlantic, St-Jean-de-Luz (p. 492, ❸) has not succumbed to the Rolex-and-Porsche crowd. Fishing boats

> *Families who enjoy playing games on the beach covet the golden sands of St-Jean-de-Luz.*

> *Beachgoers dine on the sands of Toreilles Beach at Le Zaza Club, near Perpignan.*

still ply their trade in this fantastic natural harbor. The glorious bay sweeps around from headland to headland in a swath of sandy beach backed not by cotton candy or casinos, but by the festive-looking red-and-white wooden villas built by beachgoers at the beginning of the 20th century. The beach may be grand, but it's not overcrowded; quiet is the key to St-Jean. As is true of the entire Atlantic coast, the climate includes some chilly breezes, although St-Jean, in its bay, is a little more sheltered. **14km (8⅔ miles) south of Biarritz. www.saint-jean-de-luz.com.**

Sète LANGUEDOC

Known as the "Venice of Languedoc," Sète (p. 510, ❷) is a historic town full of things to do and see, and the largest fishing port on the French Mediterranean. From beaches to port it's a beautiful setting, with its boathouses painted in dense azures and rusts. Sète offers more than 12km (7½ miles) of beaches; they begin on the south side of town with Lazaret (ideal for paddling toddlers) and Corniche, continue to the newly widened Fontaine and Lido, and extend all along the causeway to Marseillan Plage. Villeroy has several beach bars, but large stretches of this causeway sand have nothing at all: just sea, sand, and lots of space. You must take a sunshade, though, as temperatures can be scorching in August. **36km (22 miles) southwest of Montpellier. www.en.ot-sete.fr.**

Torreilles PYRENEES

This 4km (2½-mile) Blue Flag beach backed by dunes east of Perpignan, in the traditional Catalan village of Torreilles on the Gulf of Lions, is considered one of the wildest stretches of sand on the Mediterranean. Stop at the tourist office in town for information on tennis, petanque, rugby, golf, hiking, horseback riding, and even go-carting opportunities. Bus service runs several times daily from the beach to the village of Torreilles and the center of Perpignan. **20km (12 miles) east of Perpignan, btw. Le Barcarès and Canet. Tourist Board of Torreilles, Place de l'Europe. ☎ 04-68-28-41-10. www.torreilles.fr.**

Best Spas

Up until the 19th century, destination spas were as popular among travelers as seasides and cities are today. Royals, writers, and celebrities of the day flocked to ancient thermal springs for their health-giving properties but also for the free-and-easy atmosphere of the resorts. After languishing for decades as institutional establishments, a new breed of leisure spa, aimed at well-being rather than medical healing, is attracting a younger—dare we say, healthier?—crowd to take the waters. Thalassotherapy reaches its zenith on the Basque coast.

> Enter these top-floor pine cabins at Aquensis, in Bagnères-de-Bigorre, for intensive beauty treatments and pampering at a relatively reasonable price.

★★ **Aquensis Bagnères-de-Bigorre** BAGNÈRES-DE-BIGORRE, PYRENEES In 2003, the Pyrenean spa town of Bagnères-de-Bigorre (p. 504, ⑦) made the smart move of adding a leisure spa to its thermal offering: the delectable Aquensis. On the ground floor, under a cathedral-like carapace of soaring wooden beams, is a magnificent pool with cascades, jets, and currents. To the right is a musical pool with Roman-style mosaics, where you hear surreal sounds under water, and a Moroccan hammam. On the second floor are pine cabins for beauty treatments and the outdoor terrace, where you can languish like a seastar in a warm *lit d'eau* (bed of water seen from below through the glass roof), bask in a Jacuzzi surrounded by the snowy mountains and forest, or take a serious sauna (the Finnish one is at 90°C/194°F). For a spa of this quality, Aquensis is an amazing value. Rue du pont d'Arras (191km/119 miles east of St-Jean-de-Luz and 66km/41 miles southeast of Pau). ☎ 05-62-95-86-95. www.aquensis.fr. Admission (2 hr., with towel and bathrobe) 22€; 3.40€ every additional half-hour. Treatments from 28€. MC, V. Mon and Wed–Sat 10:30am–8pm; Tues and Sun 1–8pm.

Aquensis Bagnères-de-Bigorre 5
Balnéa 6
Central Thermal 8
Grand Hôtel Loreamar Thalasso Spa 2
Les Bains de Llo 7
Les Bains du Rocher 3
Luzéa at Les Thermes de Luz 4
Sofitel Biarritz Le Miramar Thalassa 1

Balnéa LOUDENVIELLE, PYRENEES In the Vallée du Louron (p. 504, 8), the thermal springs were not exploited until the 19th century, but Balnéa now offers a major attraction to complement the valley's frescoed churches. With no curative ambitions at all, it's about luxuriating in the Roman-style baths: caldarium, frigidarium, and tepidarium. A second space for families has a tropical ambiance, with waterfalls and jets; there is a floor dedicated to massages and beauty treatments; and the restaurant serves dishes from around the world (ginger, coconut, and mango, found on the menu here, are otherwise rare in the Pyrenees). A word of warning: Avoid Wednesday afternoons during term time, when noisy school parties descend. On D25 just outside Loudenvielle (77km/48 miles east of Luz-Saint-Sauveur, or less on mountain roads—see "Travel Tip," p. 506.) ☎ 08-91-70-19-19. www.balnea.fr. Mon-Fri 2-7:30pm, Sat-Sun 10:30am-8pm; school holidays daily 10am-9pm. Admission 12€ Mon-Fri, 15€ Sat-Sun and holidays; 10€ ages 12-14; 9€ ages 3-11; family pass 33.50€ Mon-Fri, 40€ Sat-Sun and holidays.

Central Thermal BAGNOLS-LES-BAINS, GORGES DU TARN At Bagnols-les-Bains, north of the small but lively town of Florac in the Tarn Gorges, the water that springs forth at 107°F (41.5°C) from the depths of the earth has drawn bathers since Roman times, as suggested by a nearby ancient temple. This attractive mountain spa facility, designed for cures, has everything you need for an enjoyable spa day: Included in the standard fee are an outdoor and indoor swimming pool, a Jacuzzi, a hammam, alternating hot and cold baths (which they bizarrely call "Scottish baths"), different types of therapeutic showers, and a gym. A tantalizing selection of specialized treatments, from chocolate wraps to water jets to Shiatsu massage, cost extra. 213km (132 miles) north of Montpellier and 40km (25 miles) north of Florac. ☎ 04-66-47-60-02. www.bagnols-les-bains.com. Admission (2 hr., with towel and robe) 22€-28€, depending on season. Apr 5-late Oct Mon-Sat 9am-12:30pm and 2-6:30pm; Nov-Dec and Feb 9-Apr 4 Mon-Sat 2-6:30pm. Closed Jan 1-Feb 8.

★★★ Grand Hôtel Loreamar Thalasso Spa
ST-JEAN-DE-LUZ, BASQUE COUNTRY This unique five-star hotel encompasses a Belle Epoque palace decorated in traditional English style, a Michelin-starred restaurant, and a

> *The Pyrenean town of Llo is famous for two things: delicious smoked ham and this relaxing thermal pool.*

state-of-the-art spa whose decor is as much part of the therapy as the treatments. The underground, vaulted relaxation room is supported by marble columns and lit by candles and changing mood lights. Pebble steps lead down to the seawater pool lit by fiber-optic stars at night. A *Star Trek* corridor with 1960s-style round windows leads to the treatment rooms—each a Zen capsule lined in slate. Massage techniques from around the world supplement the various thalassic treatments. 43 bd. Thiers, St-Jean-de-Luz (14km/8⅔ miles south of Biarritz). ☎ 05-59-26-35-36. www.luzgrandhotel.fr. 55 units. Doubles 170€–620€. Spa treatments from 50€. AE, DC, MC, V. Restaurant: main courses 29€–34€; lunch and dinner daily. For information on St-Jean-de-Luz, see p. 492, ③.

Les Bains de Llo LLO, PYRENEES The happiness quotient is high in this village just southwest of Font-Romeu ski resort; Llo has a Bonzon et Fils smokery, serving the best jambon east of the Pays Basque, and this lovely local spa with an outdoor pool, where you can lounge in the thermal water against a snowy backdrop. Friendly staff offer relaxation and beauty treatments using the spa's own natural products. It's the perfect end to a day of skiing on the Font-Romeu range. Rte. des Gorges (256km/159 miles east of Loudenville, 96km/60 miles south of Foix, 90km/56 miles southwest of Perpignan). ☎ 04-68-04-74-55. www.lesbainsdello.com. Admission 9€ adults, 7.50€ ages 3–11. MC, V. Daily 10am–7:30pm. Closed Nov 6–Dec 19 and first 2 wk. in June.

Les Bains du Rocher CAUTERETS, PYRENEES In the historic spa town of Cauterets (p. 502. ③), Les Bains du Rocher is a new leisure spa that makes good use of the sulphurous thermal waters, hitherto only available for "cures." The waters do have a slight eggy smell, but you'll feel so good after bathing in them that you won't even notice. There's a fabulous outdoor lagoon, an indoor pool, hydromassage jets, tropical showers, a 40°C (104°F) bath, waterfalls, Jacuzzis, a hammam, and saunas. In terms of treatments, the Dead Sea mud wrap seems to suck out every toxin and leave you feeling ready to take on the world. Thermes de Cauterets (50km/31 miles southwest of Bagnères-de-Bigorre). ☎ 05-62-92-14-20. www.bains-rocher.fr. Admission (2 hr., with towel and bathrobe) 22€; 4€ for every additional half-hour. Treatments from 25€; day formulas with treatments and gym available. MC, V.

Luzéa at Les Thermes de Luz LUZ-ST-SAUVEUR, PYRENEES Luz (p. 503, ❺), with its reputedly fecund waters, was the favorite spa of Napoleon III's wife, Eugénie, and her marble bath is preserved at the Luz spa. Even though the Luzéa space hasn't made a big song and dance about the transition from a curative spa to one that promotes general well-being, it has long been used by locals for leisure bathing with a view of the mountains. It offers a 32°C (90°F) pool, a Jacuzzi, a sauna, and a hammam with a relaxation area fit for a queen, equipped with Philippe Starck sofas and plenty of expert treatments on demand. 31 av. de l'Impératrice Eugénie (22km/14 miles east of Cauterets). ☎ 05-62-92-81-58. http://thermes.luz.org. Admission (2 hr.) from 18€. Treatments from 33€. AE, MC, V.

★★★ **Sofitel Biarritz Le Miramar Thalassa** BIARRITZ, BASQUE COUNTRY This purpose-built thalassotherapy resort is all about what's

> *Like this happy threesome at Les Thermes de Luz, Napoleon's wife Eugenie favored the 32°C (90°F) waters at Luz-St-Sauveur.*

The Truth About Napoleon III

Emperor Napoleon III, nephew of Napoleon I, played on his lineage to secure the continuation of the imperial dynasty in France. But, as many in Cauterets will tell you, this Napoleon was not a blood relation of France's first emperor. Cauterets witnessed the visit of Napoleon's stepdaughter Hortense de Beauharnais in 1807—without her husband Louis, King of Holland. Nine months later the future Emperor Napoleon III was born, said to have been conceived in a mountain refuge near Cauterets, by either an aristocratic lover or one of the Pyrenean shepherds who worked as masseurs in the thermal baths. Napoleon III had a deep love of the region and brought his wife, Eugénie, here to bathe in the fecund waters. She gave birth to a son, commemorated by the pont Napoléon near Barèges.

on the inside. Most of the west-facing rooms have terraces where guests can watch the sun go down over the fantastic breakers of Miramar Beach. The crashing waves set a nice pace as you plow through the huge, heated outdoor seawater pool, and they lull you to sleep on the loungers. The vast, smoothly run Thalassotherapy Institute encompasses a gym, indoor pools with hydromassage, a hammam, a sauna, a DeadSea lagoon, and treatment rooms. If you like padding around in a robe and slippers, this relaxed hotel is for you, though you'll want to dress for dinner, as the cuisine and service are top-notch. Each meal offers a choice of rich gastronomic dishes and equally delicious lighter options, all prepared by chef Robert Job, who also offers cooking lessons. 13 rue Louison Bobet, Biarritz. ☎ 1 800-SOFITEL (toll-free from U.S.). www.sofitel.com. 126 units. Doubles 275€–372€. Spa packages available. AE, DC, MC, V. For information on Biarritz, see p. 491, ❷.

Montpellier

The capital of the Languedoc-Roussillon region is the fastest-growing city in France. A clean and efficient tram service, a state-of-the-art conference center, and the gleaming neoclassical apartments and offices of the Antigone quarter make it the provincial city of choice for many professionals. What has never changed is the beauty of Montpellier's old town, with its lovely 17th-century mansions and fountain squares. Yet this city's old streets thrum with life, owing to a vibrant student population.

> The fountain at place de la Comédie shows the Three Graces: Aglaea (splendor), Eurphrosyne (mirth), and Thalia (good cheer).

START Montpellier is 750km (466 miles) south of Paris and 240km (149 miles) east of Toulouse.

1 Place de la Comédie. Nicknamed "The Egg," this ovoid-shaped city center is the heart of Montpellier, filled with tourists, cafes, and magnificent buildings (including the **Opéra-Comédie,** a replica of the Opéra Garnier in Paris). At the center you'll find **La Fontaine des Trois Grâces** (Three Graces Fountain), built in 1790. It's especially beautiful when illuminated at night. Tram: Line 1, Comédie station.

2 ★★ Musée Fabre. This museum was built by the generous donations of native son François-Xavier Fabre. Fabre's works are supplemented by artists from around the world who were inspired to donate their own works, and the result is a superb art museum. There are more than 800 paintings, presented chronologically, by a range of European artists. The museum received an extensive 62.5 million euro renovation in 2007. ⏱ 2 hr. 39 bd. Bonne Nouvelle. ☎ 04-67-14-83-00. http://museefabre.montpellier-agglo.com. Admission 7€ permanent collections and decorative arts,

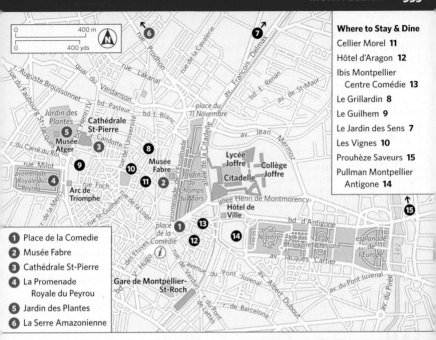

1 Place de la Comedie

2 Musée Fabre

3 Cathédrale St-Pierre

4 La Promenade
   Royale du Peyrou

5 Jardin des Plantes

6 La Serre Amazonienne

8€ temporary exhibitions; 5€ and 6€ students 6–25; free for children 5 and under; 12€ and 15€ family ticket; free for everyone 1st Sun of the month. Tues, Thurs, Fri, and Sun 10am–6pm; Wed 1–9pm; Sat 11am–6pm. Tram: Line 1, Comédie station or Line 1 or 2, Corum station.

❸ **Cathédrale St-Pierre.** The rise of this church personifies the underdog spirit of Montpellier. The cathedral began as a part of the 14th-century monastery of St-Benoît. It was raised to cathedral status as Montpellier began to exceed its pirate-besieged neighbor, the Roman-era city of Marguelonne. Montpellier wasn't on top for too long, though, and the cathedral was almost completely destroyed by Protestant Huguenots during the Wars of Religion. It was rebuilt in the 17th century. The

> The construction of Montpellier's gargoyle-clad Cathédrale St-Pierre was ordered by Pope Urbain V in the 14th century.

two medieval towers and battlements are all that's left standing of the old "Fort St-Pierre," which received extensive renovations in the 19th century. ⏱ 45 min. 6 rue de l'Abbé Marcel Montels. ☎ 04-67-66-04-12. Free admission. Daily 9am–12:30pm and 2:30–7pm. Tram: Line 1, Place Albert 1er station.

Two-Wheel Adventure

Consider renting a bike at the tourist office (2€ a day) and following the path along the river to Villeneuve-les-Maguelone (13km/8 miles). You'll pass through salt marshes filled with flamingos as you cross to the island that harbors the medieval **Cathédrale de Maguelone,** once considered the "second church of Rome."

❹ ★★ **La Promenade Royale du Peyrou.** Situated on the highest point in the city, this is a great place to rest a bit in grassy splendor, surrounded by the sound of flowing water. The first thing you'll notice is Montpelliéret—the other hill on which the city is built—and Louis XIV's branding stamp: a mini **Arc de Triomphe,** one of many he erected all around France to remind people who was king. The promenade was created at the end of the 17th century, designed to be a place suitable for a bronze equestrian statue of the Sun King, which was toppled during the Revolution but later rebuilt. Tram: 15-min walk from Line 1, Place Albert 1er station. Bus: 6, 7, and 16 from the city center.

❺ **Jardin des Plantes.** This is the oldest botanical garden in France, opened in 1593. It is maintained by the **Université de Montpellier,** one of the oldest universities in Europe. The gorgeous gardens were modeled after the Botanical Garden of Padua, and in turn inspired the Jardin des Plantes in Paris. You'll find more than 2,600 plant species here, from all around the world but with an emphasis on Mediterranean natives. ⏱ 2 hr. 163 rue Auguste Broussonnet. ☎ 04-67-63-43-22. www.ot-montpellier.fr./parcs-et-jardins. Free admission. June–Sept Tues–Sun noon–8pm; Oct–May Tues–Sun noon–6pm. Tram: Line 1, Place Albert 1er station.

❻ kids **La Serre Amazonienne.** About 3 km (1¾ miles) north of the city center, and part of the **Montpellier Zoo,** is an Amazonian greenhouse with 500 animals and 8,000 plants, all a few thousand miles from their usual habitats. ⏱ 2 hr. ☎ 04-67-29-88-35. http://zoo.montpellier.fr. Admission 6€ adults, 4€ reduced. Summer Tues–Sun 10am–6:30pm; winter Tues–Sun 9am–5pm. Tram: Line 1 to the St-Eloi stop, then transfer to the "La Navette" bus toward Agropolis and get off at the Zoo stop.

Where to Stay & Dine in Montpellier

Cellier Morel REGIONAL FRENCH
Furnished in a contemporary style but located in a 13th-century building, this is a great place for gourmet food at reasonable prices. Dishes contain local ingredients, such as peppers, tomatoes, and seafood; desserts, such as peach mousse, are scrumptious; and the sommelier knows his Languedoc wines. 27 rue de Aiguillerie. ☎ 04-67-66-46-36. www.celliermorel.com. Menus from 30€, 47€, and 49€. AE, DC, MC, V. Lunch Tues and Thurs–Sat, dinner Tues–Sat.

★ **Hôtel d'Aragon**
Near the historic district, this three-star boutique hotel has personalized decor, sound-proofing, flatscreen TVs, multi-jet showers, and more. Its great historic buliding makes up for its small size. Breakfast on the veranda is a pleasure from spring through fall. 10 rue Baudin. ☎ 04-67-10-70-00. www.hotel-aragon. fr. 12 units. Doubles 89€–118€. AE, MC, V.

Ibis Montpellier Centre Comédie
This two-star chain hotel near place de la Comédie costs half the price of swanker digs in the area. The rooms are clean, dependable, and air-conditioned, furnished in modern style. No frills here, but convenient location and value. Allée Jules Milhau. ☎ 04-99-13-29-99. www.ibishotel. com. 100 units. Doubles 69€–95€. AE, DC, MC, V.

★ **Le Grillardin** REGIONAL
This local restaurant is quiet and discreet. It's mostly regional fare, such as Mediterranean-style steaks and, as the name implies, various grills. A good wine menu and great desserts.

Montpellier's Trams

Montpellier's modern trams are quick, clean, and efficient, and they have a certain style; some have been decorated by Christian Lacroix. The two lines run diagonally across the city, meeting in the middle at Corum. You can buy tickets from machines, *tabacs,* and news agents, or get a Montpellier City Card from the tourist office.

> *Le Grillardin's rustic dining room is a romantic spot for dinner.*

3 place de la Chapelle Neuve. ☎ 04-67-66-24-33. 3-course menu 28€. AE, MC, V. High season lunch Mon–Sat, dinner daily; winter lunch Mon and Thurs–Fri, dinner daily.

★ Le Guilhem

This hotel is right in the heart of it all, next to the Promenade de Peyrou and the Jardin des Plantes. Set in a 16th-century building, the rooms are individually decorated, and most have a garden view. A standard room isn't huge, but it does net you a satellite TV and Wi-Fi access. 18 rue Jean Jacques. ☎ 04-67-60-67-67. 35 units. www.leguilhem.com. Doubles 96€–139€. AE, DC, MC, V.

★★★ Le Jardin des Sens MODERN FRENCH

This restaurant with two Michelin stars is the undisputed champ of fine dining in Montpellier. It's called "Garden of the Senses" for good reason—between the cuisine and the setting, there's something to titillate all five of them. The menu offers unusual delights, such as wolf filet or local pigeon in pear compote. The attached four-star hotel is just as luxurious, with superb paintings, a swimming pool, and a tennis court. 11 av. St-Lazare. ☎ 04-99-57-38-38. www.jardindessens.com. 12 units. Doubles from 170€. 3-course dinner 125€–175€. DC, MC, V. Lunch Tues and Thurs–Sat, dinner Mon–Sat.

Les Vignes REGIONAL

A small restaurant with a Provençal feel, this is a surprisingly swanky dining area with a vaulted ceiling; there is also a patio for outdoor dining. Fare includes local cheeses, lamb, and vegetables used to make traditionally light Mediterranean fare. Point of pride goes to the extensive wine list, with vintages from around southern France. 2 rue Bonnier d'Alco. ☎ 04-67-60-48-42. www.lesvignesrestaurant.com. Menus from 21€–49€. AE, MC, V. Closed Sun.

Prouhèze Saveurs REGIONAL FRENCH

Conveniently located in the historic center, this intimate restaurant (with a cozy patio) has a Mediterranean ambience, a regional menu, and an excellent wine list. 728 av. de la Pompignane. ☎ 04-67-79-43-34. www.prouheze-saveurs.com. Menus from 30€–60€. AE, MC, V. Closed Sun.

★ Pullman Montpellier Antigone MEDITERRANEAN

One of the finest hotels in Montpellier is this four-star with plush decor near the Fabre Museum. The elegant **Ciel d'Azur** restaurant serves Mediterranean cuisine and offers a panoramic view of the city. 1 rue des Pertuisanes. ☎ 04-67-99-72-72. www.pullmanhotels.com. 89 units. Doubles 143€–180€. AE, DC, MC, V. Lunch and dinner daily.

Perpignan

To say this region has close ties with Spain is an understatement: Catalan is a common language here, and the 2012 opening of a high-speed rail link to Barcelona will bring even more Spanish flavor to Perpignan. Over the years, the population has embraced many émigrés from the south; refugees from the Spanish Civil War, Spanish gypsies, repatriated French Algerians, and Arabs help make this a diverse and eclectic city that parties until the wee hours.

> *The peach-painted streets of sunny Perpignan remind you that you're just across the border from Spain.*

START Perpignan is 850km (528 miles) south of Paris, 153km (95 miles) southwest of Montpellier, and 192km (119 miles) north of Barcelona.

① ★ **Le Palais des Rois de Majorque.** The Palace of the Kings of Majorca is the best site in Perpignan and a premier example of medieval architecture in southern France. Perpignan's apex came during the 13th and 14th centuries, when it served as the continental capital of the Kingdom of Majorca. Things went downhill for Perpignan beginning in 1344 when it was annexed by the counts of Barcelona, and then went even further south when the Black

Plague (1348–50) wiped out half the city. Frilly and sophisticated Moorish ornamentation distinguishes this vast complex, which was completed in 1309. The Gothic chapel of **Ste-Croix Marie-Madelene,** with its *Grande Salle* (Great Room) and massive fireplaces, is a highlight. Surrounding the palace are walls built by the military architect and 17th-century genius, Vauban. The music-loving locals hold several excellent summer music festivals at the palace each year, including **Festival des Guitares** (Guitar Festival) and **Festival Eté 66** (Summer Festival 66), the largest in the area. ⏲ 1½ hr. Rue des Archers. ☎ 04-68-66-30-30.

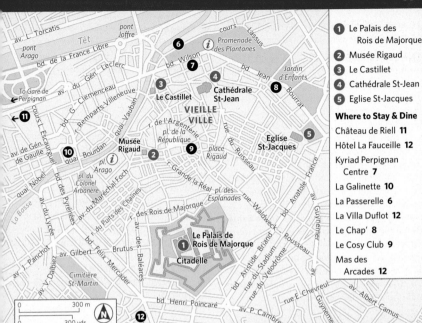

www.perpignantourisme.com. Admission 4€ adults, 2€ reduced. June–Sept daily 10am–6pm; Oct–May daily 9am–5pm.

2 Musée Rigaud. The main collection of Perpignan's art museum is from native son Hyacinthe Rigaud, the official court painter of Versailles, who painted four generations of Bourbons. There's plenty of modern art as well, including works by Picasso and Maillol. ⏱ 1 hr. 16 rue de l'Ange. ☎ 04-68-35-43-40. www.mairie-perpignan.fr. Admission 4€ adults, 2€ reduced. Wed–Mon noon–7pm.

3 ★ Le Castillet. One of the finest gates in France, if not all of Europe, is this twin-towered, 14th-century hulk. Le Castillet sits over place de la Victoire and is the emblem of Perpignan. Made of pink brick and topped by gorgeous Moorish crenellations, this defensive construction once had impressive walls and a drawbridge. You can ascend to the top for a view of the city. In later years it served as a prison; it now houses the **Casa Pairal,** a museum of Catalan folk culture, showcasing quotidian objects from across the centuries, traditional dress, religious folk art, and the like. ⏱ 1 hr. Place de Verdun. ☎ 04-68-35-42-05. www.mairie-perpignan.fr. Museum admission

> In the 13th and 14th centuries, the kings of Majorca strolled the colonnaded arcades of Le Palais des Rois de Majorque in Perpignan.

4€ adults, 2€ reduced. May–Sept daily 10am–6:30pm; Oct–Apr daily 11am–5:30pm.

4 ★ **Cathédrale St-Jean.** This immense 14th-century Gothic church is best known for the juxtaposition of its ornate Catalan altarpieces, as well as a gorgeous wrought-iron campanile, in a setting of rather gloomy shadows. The Dévôt Christ cross, which hails from the Low Countries, is as about as tortured a depiction of Jesus Christ as you'll find. Definitely resist the temptation to climb into the enormous 11th-century marble baptismal font near the door. The cathedral's exterior is an amalgam of river stones and brick. Next door is one of France's oldest cemeteries, the **Campo Santo.** Its marble funerary niches, or *enfeus,* of the Catalan nobility are gorgeously carved and marked with shields bearing the family's coat of arms. ⏱ 30 min. 1 rue de l'Horloge. ☎ 04-68-51-33-72. www.mairie-perpignan.fr. Free admission. Daily 9am–1pm and 3–7pm.

5 **Eglise St-Jacques.** A scallop shell symbol over the gate shows that this is indeed a stop on the St-Jacques-de-Compostelle pilgrim route (see "The Road to Compostela," p. 507). The dark and mysterious Catholic church, which dates back to the 13th century, is also the starting point for a Semana Santa (Holy Week) procession of cloaked penitents on Good Friday, similar to that seen in Spanish cities. The **Jardin de la Miranda** next door has a view to the Corbières Mountains on a clear day. The streets descending from the church, known as the **Quartier St-Jacques,** are the part of the Old Town that is home to a large Romany and Arab population—a colorful slice of life that you won't find anywhere else, though looking too much like a gawking tourist is obviously a bad idea. ⏱ 30 min. Eglise St-Jacques, rue de la Miranda. ☎ 04-68-66-30-30. Free admission. Mid-June to mid-Sept Mon–Sat 9am–7pm, Sun 10am–4pm; mid-Sept to mid-June Mon–Sat 9am–6pm, Sun 10am–1pm.

Where to Stay & Dine in Perpignan

★ **Château de Riell** MOLITG-LES-BAINS *REGIONAL* Surrounded by luxuriant gardens, this Baroque folly of a castle 50km (30 miles) west of Perpignan houses 12 suites and an exquisite on-site spa. All suites are spacious and decorated in sunny Mediterranean colors; those in the Gardener's House, Pigeon House, and Old Cedar House afford more privacy and individual terraces. A log fire and family portraits make the large living rooms feel welcoming. Locally produced lamb, poultry, fish, and vegetables are served in the on-site restaurant overlooking the garden and swimming pool. ☎ 04-68-05-04-40. www.chateauderiell.com. 12 units. Doubles from 281€. Menus from 49€. AE, MC, V. High season lunch and dinner daily; call ahead for hours in low season.

Hôtel La Fauceille
If you don't mind staying outside the city center, you can enjoy four-star delights here for excellent prices. The rooms are modern with balcony views. Amenities include a swimming pool, a spa, a gourmet restaurant, a fitness center, and rental cars. 860 chemin de la Fauceille. ☎ 04-68-21-09-10. www.lafauceille.com. 35 units. Doubles from 120€. AE, MC, V.

Kyriad Perpignan Centre
This popular three-star business hotel is in the heart of Perpignan. The rooms are contemporary, with bright colors and flatscreen TVs. 8 bd. Wilson. ☎ 04-68-59-25-94. www.kyriad-perpignan-centre.fr. 49 units. Doubles from 90€. AE, DC, MC, V.

★★★ **La Galinette** *VEGETARIAN*
This may be the best non-vegetarian vegetarian restaurant you'll ever attend. Chef Christophe Comes is an accomplished botanist. While his menu features teriyaki pigeon, Thai-style Angus beef, and sushi treats, it's the shockingly fresh and diverse vegetables that make it a find. The lunch menu is a steal, but make it here for dinner. 23 rue Jean Payra. ☎ 04-68-35-00-90. Lunch menu 19€, dinner menus from 58€. MC, V. Lunch and dinner Tues–Sat.

> With its piano bar and eclectic mix of patrons, with ties to nearby Spain and northern Africa, Le Cosy Club is one of Perpignan's liveliest nightclubs.

La Passerelle *SEAFOOD*
This is another fine seafood place, this time with great waterfront scenery. The graciousness of the host family adds to the experience. The Murano glass chandelier is an elegant touch. 1 cours Palmarole. ☎ 04-68-51-30-65. www.restaurant-perpignan-lapasserelle.com. 3-course menu 33€–46€. AE, DC, MC, V. Lunch Tues–Sat, dinner Mon–Sat.

★ **La Villa Duflot** *MODERN FRENCH*
Perpignan's most luxurious hotel, located outside the city center, is styled like an Italian villa. It features terracotta-colored walls, palm-filled gardens, a swimming pool, and spacious rooms arranged around a courtyard. The restaurant is gourmet, and a sommelier helps guests explore local wines from the wine library, stocked with some 5,000 bottles. Rond-point Albert Donnezan. ☎ 04-68-56-67-67. www.villa-duflot.com. 24 units. Doubles from 150€. Menus from 20€. AE, DC, MC, V. Lunch and dinner daily.

★ **Le Chap'** *FRENCH*
This restaurant offers superbly made traditional cuisine in a contemporary setting. You'll find all the local favorites on the menu, but with creative twists, such as lamb with mango purée. Make sure to try the escargots—the snails of Perpignan are some of the best in France. 18 bd. Jean Bourrat. ☎ 04-68-35-31-16. www.parkhotel-fr.com. Main courses 19€–30€. AE, MC, V. Lunch Tues–Fri, dinner Tues–Sat.

★ **Le Cosy Club**
The nightlife of Perpignan, as zesty as nearby Barcelona's, makes a nightclub stop a must. This piano bar offers the elegance and warmth promised by its name, with a great bar and soothing lighting. 4 rue du Théâtre. ☎ 04-68-66-02-57. www.lecosyclub.com. Daily 6pm–2am.

Mas des Arcades *TRADITIONAL FRENCH*
A 10-minute walk from the city center, set high on a hill overlooking Mont Canigou, this three-star hotel is calm and filled with greenery. It was recently renovated, and the rooms have been stylishly decorated in contemporary fashion. The hotel is especially senior-friendly, with plenty of 24-hour services such as prepared meals and shopping. The adjacent restaurant, Jacques 1er, offers tasty French cuisine at reasonable prices. 840 av. d'Espagne. ☎ 04-68-85-11-11. www.mas-arcades.com. 60 units. Doubles from 85€. Menus 20€–35€. MC, V. Lunch and dinner Tues–Sat.

Toulouse

You can't help but feel a warm welcome in France's fourth-largest city, with its palm trees, clement weather, and rosy-hued stone architecture. Toulouse has boomed in recent years, but it hasn't compromised its relaxed, inviting pace. The gorgeous historic center is extremely pedestrian-friendly, making it a great city to walk in, and it's an even better city for dining. After your trip, you'll easily understand why it's often voted the best place to live in France.

START Toulouse is 678km (421 miles) south of Paris, 245km (152 miles) southeast of Bordeaux, and 240km (149 miles) west of Montpellier.

1 **Place du Capitole.** This is the hub of town, with markets almost daily, high-end shopping, and ritzy cafes. This is Midi (Southern) France, so you'll see plenty of people enjoying long lunches and extended coffee breaks. Surrounded by a maze of winding streets, you'll find yourself returning to this square again and again In your wanderings, you'll come across **place Wilson,** named after U.S. president Woodrow Wilson; **place St-Etienne,** better appreciated for the city's oldest fountain than for the architecturally schizophrenic

cathedral; and **place Arnaud-Bernard,** frequented by the student crowd. **Métro:** Capitole station.

2 ★★ **Eglise des Jacobins.** This Gothic church made of pink brick isn't huge, but it's notable for having housed the crypt of St. Thomas Aquinas, until his remains were relocated to the nearby Jacobins cloister (also open to visitors). With its vast ceilings, its seven enormous columns, its frescoes, and the medieval musicians playing outside, it will take you back in time. ⏱ 30 min. 69 rue Pargaminières. ☎ 05-61-22-21-92. www.jacobins.mairie-toulouse.fr. Free admission. Daily 10am–6pm. **Métro:** Capitole.

3 ★★★ **Basilique St-Sernin.** There are a few fine cathedrals in Toulouse, but the most impressive is this

> Basilique St-Sernin's filigree bell tower dominates Toulouse.

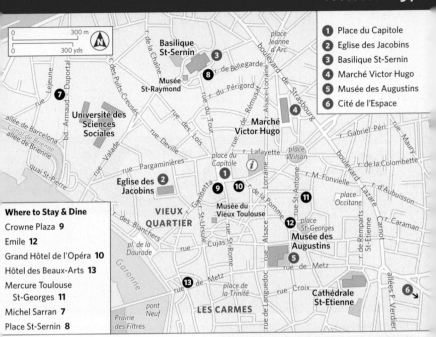

Where to Stay & Dine

Romanesque 11th-century former abbey, built to honor the first bishop of Toulouse. It dates back to the 3rd century, and it grew enormously thanks to the popularity of relics donated by Charlemagne, which made it an important pilgrimage spot as well as a stop on the Santiago de Compostela route. The cathedral also plays in important role in the Albigensian Crusade; the stone that killed the hated Simon de Montfort, who grotesquely mutilated many Cathar dissenters, was launched from the basilica. The huge bell tower and stunning stained glass are a powerful spectacle as you emerge from the narrow medieval streets. ⏱ **30 min.** Place St-Sernin. ☎ 05-61-21-80-45. www.basilique-st-sernin-toulouse.fr. Free admission to church; combined admission to the crypt and ambulatory 2€. Church Mon–Sat 10:30am–6:30pm; Sun noon–6:30pm; off season Mon–Sat 10am–noon and 2–6pm; Sun 2–6:30pm. Crypt and ambulatory summer Mon–Sat noon–6:30pm; off season Mon–Sat 10am–noon and 2–6pm. Métro: Capitole or Jeanne d'Arc.

❹ ★★★ **Marché Victor Hugo.** This covered market brims with amazing produce and meats—whole hares, quail, tripe, enormous fish, crustaceans—but it also gives a real taste of

> The Basilique St-Sernin is a stop on the Santiago de Compostela pilgrimage route.

> *The pont Neuf has been delivering visitors over the River Garonne to the warm and inviting pink-bricked city of Toulouse since the 16th century.*

Toulouse's convivial spirit. If the Irish are in town for a rugby match, this is where you'll find them. The in-house wine bars are packed with hulking guys sipping white wine and talking tries and tackles. The upper floor is entirely occupied by restaurants where cooks use impeccably fresh ingredients to whip up *cassoulet,* paella, and griddled fish in a bustling, noisy atmosphere. Place Victor-Hugo. Tues–Sun 6am–1pm. Métro: Capitole or Jeanne d'Arc.

5 ★★ **Musée des Augustins.** This fine-arts museum houses a bevy of medieval artifacts from Toulouse's golden era, when it was independent of the northern royalty. The building is a former Augustinian convent, with a fine courtyard garden. Its Romanesque sculptures compose the finest collections, but the paintings are grand as well, consisting of works confiscated from nobles after the French Revolution. ⏱ 1 hr. 21 rue de Metz. ☎ 05-61-22-21-82. www.augustins.org. Admission 3€ adults; 1.50€ reduced; free for children 17 and under; free for everyone 1st Sun of the month. Mon–Tues and Thurs–Sun 10am–6pm; Wed 10am–9pm. Métro: Esquirol station.

6 ★ kids **Cité de l'Espace.** With much prodding from the national government, Toulouse has become the home of the European aerospace industry, with major players such as the EU Galileo global satellite system, EADS, and airplane giant Airbus. The Space City theme park features amazing exhibits that will change the way you look at the universe. You'll crawl through a Mir Space Station replica, gaze at a life-size model of the Ariane 5 rocket (53m/174 ft. high), and watch a stunning 3-D IMAX film based on the construction of the International Space Station (the audio is in French, but it's still an astounding experience). The rides here aren't exceptional, but you'll leave exhilarated enough by our amazing universe. ⏱ 1 day. Av. Jean Gonord. ☎ 05-61-80-74-70. www.cite-espace.com. Admission 22€ adults (high season), 15.50€ reduced. July–Aug daily 9:30am–7pm, Sept–Dec and Feb–June hours vary. Closed most of Jan. By car, follow signs from the city center in the direction of Castres (15 min.). By public transport, take bus no. 37 from Joliment metro station (direction: La Plaine) to stop Cité de l'Espace; Sat–Sun and public holidays, take metro line A to Marengo and bus no. 37 as before.

Where to Stay & Dine in Toulouse

Crowne Plaza
If you want a chichi place du Capitole address, this recently renovated four-star luxury hotel should suit you. Rooms have a workspace and views of the lovely courtyard or teeming square. The more expensive Club Plaza rooms will gain you access to the private fifth-floor Club Lounge. 7 place du Capitole. ☎ 05-61-61-19-19. www.crowne-plaza-toulouse.com. 162 units. Doubles from 176€. AE, DC, MC, V.

Emile *REGIONAL FRENCH*
This popular restaurant with a terrace serves plenty of local favorites, such as spiced pigeon, Pyrenean lamb, *zarzuela catalane* (a grilled seafood platter), and bowls of duck *cassoulet*. The wine list is excellent and could lead you to linger on the terrace. 13 place St-Georges. ☎ 05-61-21-05-56. www.restaurant-emile.com. Menus 36€–55€. AE, DC, MC, V. Lunch Tues–Sat, dinner Mon–Sat.

★★★ Grand Hôtel de l'Opéra *MODERN FRENCH*
All the rooms are stunning in this four-star boutique hotel, housed in a converted 17th-century convent on the place du Capitole. Amenities include a sauna, hammam Turkish baths, and two restaurants: the affordable Le Grand Café de l'Opéra and the pricier Les Jardins de l'Opéra. You'll be hobnobbing with the rich and famous here. 1 place du Capitole. ☎ 05-61-21-82-66. www.grand-hotel-opera.com. 50 units. Doubles from 190€. AE, DC, MC, V. Lunch and dinner daily.

★ Hôtel des Beaux-Arts *BRASSERIE*
This three-star hotel in the historic city center is totally nonsmoking. Rooms are snug, renovated, and air-conditioned; some have a view of the river; and all have satellite TV and individualized decor. Les Beaux Arts is also the name of the restaurant, which features regional cuisine and Belle Epoque furnishings. 1 place du Pont Neuf. ☎ 05-34-45-42-42. www.hoteldesbeauxarts.com. 20 units. Doubles from 110€. Main courses 14€–22€. Menus 23€–32€. AE, DC, MC, V. Lunch Mon–Sat, dinner Tues–Sat.

> Eat, sleep, and make yourself at home but don't light up at the smoke-free Hôtel des Beaux-Arts.

★ Mercure Toulouse St-Georges
This three-star chain hotel has a city center location—just 500m (1,640 ft.) from the Capitole—and gorgeous contemporary decor. You'll enjoy air-conditioning, satellite TV, and free Wi-Fi access. Rue Saint-Jérôme. ☎ 05-62-27-79-79. www.mercure.com. 148 units. Doubles from 100€. AE, DC, MC, V.

★★★ Michel Sarran *GASTRONOMIC*
One of the best in Toulouse, this restaurant received two stars from Michelin. The emphasis isn't on elegant dining but on interesting food such as foie gras éclairs, saffron chiffon, and a *menu surprise* that varies according to the chef's whims. 21 bd. A. Duportal. ☎ 05-61-12-32-32. www.michel-sarran.com. Menus 98€–165€. AE, DC, MC, V. Lunch and dinner Mon–Fri.

Place St-Sernin *MODERN FRENCH*
This restaurant's name is the same as its address, so it's easy to remember and find. As you may expect, it's in front of St-Sernin Basilica, making it a great place to go after visiting the church. The setting is homey, and the food is regional with modern updates. 7 place St-Sernin. ☎ 05-62-30-05-30. www.7placesaintsernin.com. Menus 33€–75€. AE, MC, V. Lunch Mon–Fri, dinner Mon–Sat.

> *Every town in France brandishes a French flag, like this one here in Sète, on quai de la Résistance.*

Fast Facts

Arriving

BY PLANE The best way to reach the Pyrenees and Basque Country by air is to fly into Pau's **Pau-Uzein Airport,** which is 12km (7½ miles) north of town; call ☎ 05-59-33-33-00 for flight information. To reach the Languedoc-Roussillon region by air, fly into the **Toulouse-Blagnac International Airport,** which lies in the city's northwestern suburbs, 11km (6¾ miles) from the center; for flight information, call ☎ 08-25-38-00-00. **Air France** (☎ 08-20-80-28-02) has about 25 flights a day from Paris, and flies to Toulouse from London twice a day. From either of these airports, you can take trains or cars to connect to other major towns in the region. **BY TRAIN** The best way to reach Basque Country from Paris is to take the train to Bayonne (trip time: 5 hr.). From Bayonne, it is easy to connect to other towns in the region, including Biarritz (10 min.) and Lourdes (2 hr.). The Biarritz rail station, 3km (1¾ miles) south of the town center, in La Négresse, is a hub that connects to St-Jean-de-Luz (15 min.) and Pau (90 min.). From Paris, it is easy to reach the Languedoc-Roussillon region by train, reaching Narbonne (4 hr.), Perpignan (5 hr.), Toulouse (6 hr.), and Montpellier (9 hr.). There is also one daily high-speed TGV train that arrives in Montpellier from Paris in less than 3½ hours. For rail information, call ☎ 36-35 or 08-92-35-35-35, or visit www.voyages-sncf.com. **BY CAR** The drive from Paris to Toulouse takes 6 to 7 hours; take A10 south to Bordeaux, connecting to A62 to Toulouse. From Toulouse, it is easy to access the other towns nearby. The N117 roadway is the major thoroughfare for Basque Country; among other towns, it connects to Bayonne, Biarritz, Lourdes, Pau, and Toulouse.

ATMs/Cashpoints

See p. 703, France Fast Facts.

Emergencies

See France Fast Facts, p. 704.

Internet Cafes

BIARRITZ Formatic, 15 Av. de la Marne (☎ 05-59-22-12-79). **Zen'zibar,** 117 av. Kennedy (☎ 05-59-41-20-95). **MONTPELLIER Cafe Cyberia,** 16 rue St-Ferreol (☎ 04-68-55-35-72; www.cafe-cyberia.com). **PAU C Cyber,** 20 rue Lamothe (☎ 05-59-82-89-40). **TOULOUSE Alerte Rouge Network Café,** 21 place St Sernin (☎ 05-61-23-17-39).

Post Offices

BIARRITZ 17 rue de la Poste (☎ 05-59-22-41-12). **MONTPELLIER** 15 rue Rondelet (☎ 04-67-34-50-00). **PAU** 21 Cours Bosquet (☎ 05-59-98-98-98). **TOULOUSE** 9 rue Lafayette (☎ 05-34-45-70-82).

Safety

Basque Country, the Pyrenees, and Languedoc-Roussillon are all generally very safe. In an emergency, call 17 for the police, 18 for the fire department or paramedics, and 15 for an ambulance.

Tourist Offices

Municipal tourist offices are listed at the end of the town tour stops throughout the chapter. **BASQUE COUNTRY** 2 allée des Platanes, Bayonne (☎ 05-59-30-01-30; www.bearn-basquecountry.com). **LANGUEDOC** 954 av. Jean Mermoz, Montpellier (☎ 04-67-20-02-20; www.sunfrance.com). **MONTPELLIER** place de la Comedie/esplanade Charles de Gaulle, 30 allée Jean de Lattre de Tassigny (☎ 04-67-60-60-60; www.ot-montpellier.fr). **PERPIGNAN** Palais des Congrès, place Armand-Lanoux (☎ 04-68-66-30-30; www.perpignantourisme. com). **PYRENEES TOURISM FEDERATION** 10 rue des Arts, Toulouse (☎ 05-34-40-78-40; www.lespyrenees.net/en). **TOULOUSE** Donjon du Capitole, place de Général de Gaulle (☎ 05-61-11-02-22; www.ot-toulouse.fr).

13
Bordeaux & the Atlantic Coast

Favorite Moments in Bordeaux & the Atlantic Coast

The southwest corner of France, along the mighty Atlantic, provides a spectacular backdrop for a relaxing holiday. From La Rochelle in Poitou Charentes down to the Bassin d'Arcachon, spreading inland toward Poitiers, Cognac, Bordeaux, and the peaceful, pine-clad Landes forest, the region woos foodies, beachgoers, bird-watchers, and families. There are long sandy beaches, enough châteaux to start a theme park, and a long-standing tradition of fine seafood. And then there's the wine and the brandy—both considered the best in the world.

> *PREVIOUS PAGE Bordeaux's 18th-century place de la Bourse is reflected in Claire and Michel Corajoud's Miroir d´eau (water mirror) at dusk. THIS PAGE The record-breaking Dune du Pilat is perpetually moving, its contours changing with the weather, especially the wind.*

1 Taking the kids to Futuroscope theme park. Kids and parents alike will have a ball exploring visual technology and the environment through the wild rides, 3-D movies, water games, and simulators at this educational amusement park near Poitiers. See p. 569, **3**.

1. Taking the kids to Futuroscope theme park
2. Ripping apart a tasty crab and slurping oysters
3. Flexing your mussels at the port of La Rochelle
4. Visiting the oyster farms on Ile d'Oléron
5. Exploring the Phare de Cordouan Lighthouse near Royan
6. Feeling the velvet burn of cognac on your throat
7. Wine tasting in St-Emilion
8. Strolling along the banks of the Garonne in Bordeaux
9. Sleeping in an 18th-century Bordeaux mansion
10. Sunbathing on the Plage du Grand Crohot near Arcachon
11. Canoeing along the Leyre River
12. Climbing to the top of Dune du Pilat

2 Ripping apart a tasty crab and slurping oysters. Set on a road lined with wooded oyster huts, **La Cabane de Lauzières** overlooks semi-industrial flats to the bridge linking La Rochelle to the Ile de Ré, but the seafood is some of the best and cheapest you'll taste on the coast. See p. 596.

3 Flexing your mussels at the port of La Rochelle. Briny delights are cooked to perfection in this picturesque harbor. If you'd rather see the sea creatures alive, head to La Rochelle's pioneering **aquarium,** awash in local and exotic species. See p. 588.

4 Visiting the oyster farms on Ile d'Oléron. Growing oysters requires care akin to

cultivating grapes. The Marennes basin, around the Ile d'Oléron, is the only place that cultivates them with a bright green tinge, a result of the mollusks' diet. See p. 595, 11.

5 Exploring the Phare de Cordouan lighthouse near Royan. This marvelous feat of Renaissance architecture and engineering is the oldest lighthouse in France. It contains both royal apartments and a chapel—not to mention some of the most stupendous views on the coast. See p. 556, 8.

6 Feeling the velvet burn of cognac on your throat. The town of Cognac has lent its name to the most noble of strong alcohols. Dating back to the Viking era, **Cognac Otard,** set

> *Wine-tasting opportunities abound in medieval St-Emilion.*

inside a 15th-century château, runs one of the best distillery tours, which ends with a glass of the brand's finest. **See p. 579, ②**.

⑦ Wine tasting in St-Emilion. This UNESCO-protected medieval village is set amid steep cobblestone streets and surrounded by vines as far as the eye can see. Several of the surrounding *Grands Crus* wine châteaux produce some of the world's most famous and delectable reds. **See p. 562, ①**.

⑧ Strolling along the banks of the Garonne in Bordeaux. With its glorious 18th-century mansions, decorated with the masks of Bacchus and river gods, and its neoclassical squares along the quays, Bordeaux has justly been called the great urban aesthetic triumph of western France. **See p. 582**.

⑨ Sleeping in an 18th-century Bordeaux mansion. The owner of **Le Petit Hôtel Labottière** is a fervent historian and has reconstituted his house exactly as it was when Bordeaux was a thriving merchants' port.

Some of the antiques are so rare the only other models are in famous museums. **See p. 587**.

⑩ Sunbathing on the Plage du Grand Crohot near Arcachon. Get here early in the morning, and you'll be sharing endless expanses of fine, beige sand with nothing but the breeze and migrating birds for company. On the right day, this is also a plum spot for surfing. **See p. 573**.

⑪ Canoeing along the Leyre River. The Leyre's alternately rusty and gray-colored waters are teeming with wildlife and supply 80% of the Bassin d'Arcachon's water. You're in for some heart-stopping, unspoiled scenery as you paddle past bulrushes, frogs, dragonflies, and kingfishers. **See p. 576, ④**.

⑫ Climbing to the top of Dune du Pilat. Europe's largest dune, this vast mass of sand is 110m (361 ft.) tall and around 3km (1¾ miles) long. From the top, you'll feel as though you're in another world—a remote, hilly desert where the sea and pine trees could be a mirage. **See p. 574, ①**.

> These fine de claire oysters were matured in shallow basins to make them fleshier than those straight from the sea.

The Atlantic Coast in 1 Week

Fortified cities, offshore islands, oyster farms, beaches, and lighthouses are the highlights of this itinerary, so get ready for a busy week. If you have time and prefer to discover the area at a more leisurely pace, take 10 days to see everything listed here. Or, extend your trip by continuing south to spend a few days in the Bassin d'Arcachon (p. 574), where you'll find seafood, sand, and watersports aplenty.

> With a rich maritime history, La Rochelle holds one of France's biggest yachting harbors today.

START La Rochelle is 467km (290 miles) southwest of Paris, 145km (90 miles) southeast of Nantes, and 183km (114 miles) north of Bordeaux. **TRIP LENGTH** 156km (97 miles) overland.

1 ★★★ **La Rochelle.** Looking out across the sea, past three formidable medieval towers, beautiful La Rochelle seduces with arcaded streets, the biggest yachting center on France's Atlantic coast, the country's best aquariums, and a medieval harbor. ⏱ 2 days. For detailed information on La Rochelle, see p. 588.

Leave mainland La Rochelle on av. du 8 Mai 1945. At the Lagord island, take the second exit onto N237, then take D735, crossing the toll bridge, to St-Martin-de-Ré, on the Ile de Ré (24km/15 miles).

2 ★★ **Ile de Ré.** It's worth spending a whole day exploring La Rochelle's most famous island, with its wild landscapes of sand dunes, pretty fishing towns, cliffs, and pines. Ile de Ré also offers rich birdlife and multiple cycling opportunities. ⏱ 1 day. See p. 592, **8**.

Retrace your route to N237 (toward Rochefort), and then join D137/E602 (toward

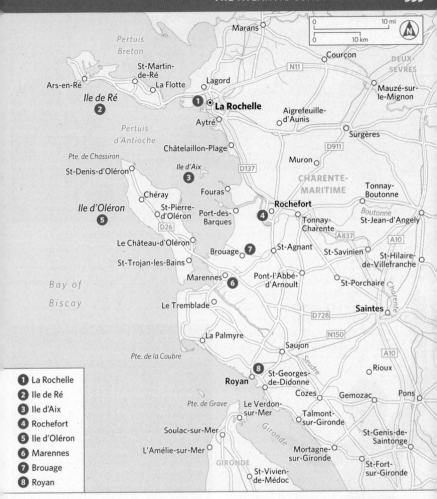

1 La Rochelle
2 Ile de Ré
3 Ile d'Aix
4 Rochefort
5 Ile d'Oléron
6 Marennes
7 Brouage
8 Royan

D937/Fouras) and D937 to Fouras (34km/21 miles). Park and catch a ferry (30 min. crossing from Pointe de la Fumée) to the Ile d'Aix.

3 ★★ **Ile d'Aix.** This little island (just 3km/1¾ miles long and 600m/⅓ mile wide) has a relaxed, old-world feel, due to the absence of cars, the blue-and-white fishermen's huts, and weeds that grow willy-nilly between the paving stones. You can walk or hire a bike and ride around the isle's perimeter, and discover its beaches and creeks in a few hours. ⏱1 day. See p. 593, **9**.

Take the ferry back to your car, pick up D937c from the rue du Docteur Boutiron, and join D137, following signs to Rochefort (13km/8 miles).

> *Well-signposted routes make Ile de Ré an ideal destination for cyclists.*

> *Pine trees provide welcome shelter from the sunshine on several of Ile d'Oléron's beaches.*

4 ★ **Rochefort.** Rochefort has a pleasant 17th-century town center and several decent museums. It's home to a replica of the frigate ★★★ kids *Hermione,* Arsenal maritime, place Amiral Dupont (☎ 05-46-82-07-07; www.hermione. com; admission 6€ adults, 5€ ages 16–25, 2.50€ ages 6–15, free for children 5 and under; Apr–Sept daily 9am–7pm, Oct–Mar daily 10am–12:30pm and 2–6pm; closed most of Jan and some public holidays), the ship that in 1780 took Marquis de Lafayette to America to join George Washington in the struggle for American independence. Since 1997, the galleon has been painstakingly rebuilt according to period methods, and it makes for a fascinating visit—especially if you're traveling with kids, who'll love imagining they're pirates or explorers. ⏱1 day, or 2–3 hr. if you concentrate on the *Hermione.* See p. 593, **10**.

> *This neo-classical wooden sculpture, at the Centre International de La Mer in Rochefort, once graced the prow of a galleon.*

The Great *Hermione*

"From the first moment I heard the name of America, I loved it; from the instant I knew it struggled for freedom, I was consumed with the desire to shed my blood for her. I will count the days I got the chance to serve it, everywhere and anytime, among the happiest days of my life."

— MARQUIS DE LAFAYETTE

The American Revolution, which set the precedent for the French Revolution in 1789, is forever tied to Rochefort, thanks to General Lafayette. He boarded the original *Hermione* here on March 21, 1780, to support the independence of the English colonies in North America. Construction had started in 1778 near the domineering **Corderie Royale** (p. 593, **10**); the huge ship measured more than 64m (210 ft.) from stern to bow and had three masts and 1,486 sq. m (15,995 sq. ft.) of sail. The *Hermione* was a light frigate, characterized by its speed and agility and fitted with 26 cannons that shot 12-pound cannonballs (hence its nickname "frigate of 12"). The whole vessel took 11 months to build, employing 100 or so carpenters, blacksmiths, drillers, caulkers, and convicts (for labor).

At the end of Day 4, take D733 from Rochefort (toward D123/Ile d'Oléron/Marennes), then follow signs to the Ile d'Oléron via Marennes (39km/24 miles). Spend the night on Île d'Oléron or Marennes (off D123 on the mainland, just opposite the island.

5 ★★ kids **Ile d'Oléron.** France's second-largest island is ideal for a day at the seaside. If you're traveling with kids, take the miniature 1916 steam train from St-Trojan through a pine wood to **Pertuis de Maumusson** beach, before visiting Oléron's fascinating oyster farms. ☺ Half-day. See p. 595, **11**.

6 **Marennes.** Here you can climb 289 steps to the top of the steeple at the **Eglise St-Pierre-de-Sales** (July–Aug 10am–12:30pm and 2–7pm, Sept–June by appointment) for breathtaking views over shiny gray oyster basins, and visit the **Cité de l'Huître** (p. 559, **2**). Or let your brood climb trees and rope bridges at **Châteaubranche,** an adventure park in the gardens of the kids **Château de la Gataudière,** 19 rue de la Gataudière (☎ 05-46-85-01-07; www.gataudiere.com; admission 19€ adults, 17€ students 16 and older, 14€ ages 4–15 or taller than 140cm/55in., 11€ children 3 and under or 140cm/55 in. or shorter)—a regal throwback from the days when Marennes was on the crossroads of the waterways used for the salt and wine trades. ☺ Half-day. Marennes Tourist Office, place Chasseloup-Laubat. ☎ 05-46-85-04-36. www.ile-oleron-marennes.com.

On Day 6, leave Ile d'Oléron on D26, which becomes D728 before Marennes; at Marennes, take D3 to Brouage (10km/6¼ miles).

7 ★ **Brouage.** Brouage was a thriving harbor until the sea receded in the 18th century, leaving it stranded amid salty marshes. Today, the walled town has a haunting, isolated appeal (especially on a misty morning when a white

> The tree ropes at Châteaubranche near Marennes vary in height and difficulty, so that any kid over 3 years of age can play.

haze envelopes the Vauban ramparts), making it a fine spot to while away an hour or two. Walk around the ramparts and visit the vaulted **Halle aux Vivres,** where salt was once traded, and the **Maison Champlain,** on place du Canada. The former home of Pierre de Comminges, founder of Quebec, now houses a small virtual museum on his explorations into Canada. You can also tour a working salt farm at **La Saline de Brouage,** rte. de Tirançon (☎ 06-20-44-03-65; http://lessalinesdebrouage.pagesperso-orange.fr; admission 2.50€; visit with seafood tasting 9.50€–50€; Thurs-Tues 10:30am–10pm). Brouage's ramparts exist thanks to Cardinal Richelieu, who based his soldiers here during

Tip

Boats sailing to the Phare de Cordouan from Royan (**8** on this tour) leave either in the morning or in the early afternoon according to the tides, and not every day—so call ahead to check (p. 556). If necessary, change the order of these next two stops to visit the lighthouse before Brouage (**7**).

> *Brouage was on the coast until the sea receded, leaving behind these salty marshes, which are a haven for wildlife.*

the siege of La Rochelle in 1627–28. Later, the Sun King, Louis XIV, stayed here overnight on his way back from his wedding to the Infanta of Spain. Louis XIV was still so in love with Marie Mancini, however, that he stayed alone in her former room in Brouage—where she had been exiled by her uncle, Cardinal Mazarin—and nursed his broken heart while preparing himself for a life with a woman he did not yet know. ⏱ 2–3 hr. **Brouage Tourist Office, 2 rue de Québec.** ☎ 05-46-85-19-16.

From Brouage, take D3 to Marennes, and leave Marennes heading left on D728. After

Shortcut Across the Water

If you wish to continue south down the coast from Royan to Arcachon (p. 560, ❸, and 575, ❷), avoid a long detour into Bordeaux by taking the **Royan Atlantique car ferry** across the Gironde Estuary to Le Verdon. Crossing time is 20 minutes; fares are 23€ per car (3.10€ per passenger in the car; free for children 3 and under). *19 avenue du Phare de Cordouan, Le Verdon-sur-Mer.* ☎ 05-56-73-37-73.

10km (6¼ miles), turn right onto D131, and at Le Gua, join D733 to Royan (36km/22 miles total).

❽ **Royan.** This seaside resort was heavily bombed during World War II and has little to offer besides sandy beaches and the soaring reinforced concrete Notre-Dame church (built 1955–58). So, after a quick wander around, head to Royan's port. The **Croisières La Sirène** kiosk on quai du Monastir, near the carousel (☎ 05-46-05-30-93; www.croisierelasirene.com; 35€ adults, 26€ ages 17 and under), runs 4-hour cruises aboard the *Sirène (Mermaid)* to the ★★★ kids **Phare de Cordouan,** France's oldest lighthouse, built in 1584. A Renaissance-style tower was added in 1611 by Henri IV. In 1786 its height was increased to 67.5m (221 ft.), making the whole place so châteaulike, it was nicknamed the "Versailles of the Sea." A 311-step grand spiral staircase leads to the king's former apartments and a chapel adorned in 19th-century stained glass. After your visit, you'll have plenty of time to take a quick dip or laze on the rocks. ⏱ 3 hr. **Royan Tourist Office, Av. des Congrès.** ☎ 05-46-23-00-00. www.ot-royan.fr.

Where to Stay & Dine on the Atlantic Coast

★ **La Corderie Royale** ROCHEFORT *CONTEMPO-RARY FRENCH* Ignore the old-fashioned decor in this hotel. Its setting is sublime, in the shadow of the Corderie Royale and the Charente River, and the restaurant is a haven for gastronomes. Relax at the end of the day in the outdoor pool and spa. Rue Audebert. ☎ 05-46-99-35-35. www.corderieroyale.com. 50 units. Doubles 82€–270€. MC, V. Restaurant: lunch Tues–Sun, dinner Tues–Sat. Hotel and restaurant closed mid-Dec to mid-Jan.

★★ kids **Le Clos St-Martin** ST-MARTIN-DE-RE This chic spot in Ile de Ré's main town, St-Martin-de-Ré, cleverly caters to couples and families thanks to large, well-furnished rooms and separate pools for adults and kids. The building is a typical Ile de Ré villa that opens out onto a network of cobblestone streets lined with hollyhocks, just 5 minutes from the harbor. Serious pampering takes place in the Clarins spa. Cours Pasteur. ☎ 05-46-01-10-62. www.le-clos-saint-martin.com. 33 units. Doubles 135€–265€. AE, MC, V.

★★ **Le Serghi** ST-MARTIN-DE-RE *SEAFOOD* Locally caught seafood—much of it from the boat bobbing in front of the restaurant—gets cooked up in this trendy seafarers' haunt. On a fine day, sit outside and tuck into fresh mussels and *frites, vanets* (La Rochelle's specialty cockles), or an extravagant seafood platter. 15 quai Clémenceau. ☎ 05-46-09-03-92. www.le-serghi.fr. 3-course menu 30€. MC, V. Apr–Sept 20 daily 24 hr. Sept 21–Mar lunch Wed–Sun, dinner Wed–Sat.

★★★ **Les Jardins d'Alienor** CHATEAU D'OLERON *HAUTE CUISINE* Rooms here are lovely, with a warm mix of period and contemporary touches, but the star of the show is the cuisine. Sea bass *goujons* with pistachio and asparagus, beef roasted with pink garlic, and *mille-feuille* of chocolate and salted butter caramel are served in a chic dining room or, on a sunny day, in the flower-clad garden. 11 rue du Maréchal Foch. ☎ 05-46-76-48-30.

> *Le Clos St-Martin is a 5-minute walk from the harbor in St-Martin-de-Ré.*

www.lesjardinsdalienor.com. 4 units. Doubles 87€–147€. Menus 32€–40€. MC, V.

★★ kids **Maison Marennes** MARENNES In a handy location between the Ile d'Oléron and Rochefort, this two-story town house, set on a winding road, is perfect if you're looking to self-cater for the week. It easily sleeps two families or four couples, and it has a big kitchen, a dining room that seats up to 12, a plasma TV, a computer, and a heated pool. 2 rue Dubois Meynardie. www.maisonmarennes.co.uk. 450€–1,850€ per week, depending on season. No credit cards: Check or transfer prior to arrival.

The Atlantic Coast for Seafood Lovers

Traveling southward from the port of La Rochelle, past the *fine de claire* oyster capital of Marennes and onward to the sandy Bassin d'Arcachon, the Atlantic coast is awash in locally fished delights such as sea bass, turbot, langoustines, prawns, and lobsters. Whether you're looking for Michelin-starred cuisine or shellfish on the beach, you'll be dining on some of the country's best fruits of the sea. This tour can be followed in 3 to 5 days or dipped into at will. *Bon appétit!*

> Oysters aren't the only shellfish to thrive near La Rochelle; you'll find mussels too, clinging to rocks at low tide.

START La Rochelle is 467km (290 miles) southwest of Paris, 145km (90 miles) southeast of Nantes, and 183km (114 miles) north of Bordeaux. **TRIP LENGTH** 273km (170 miles).

1 ★★★ **La Rochelle.** This striking port, guarded by three medieval towers, is epicurean heaven, with a varied abundance of restaurants that specialize in seafood. ★★ **Les Flots** (p. 596) is excellent and affordable. For the most rustic seaside dining experience, go the extra mile to ★★★ **La Cabane de Lauzières** (p. 596), an oyster hut just outside town, in Nieul-sur-Mer. ⏱ 1–2 days. For detailed information on La Rochelle, see p. 588.

From La Rochelle, take N237 (toward Rochefort) and join D137. At Vergerous, take D733 and follow signs to Marennes, via D123 and D728 (60km/37 miles total).

1 La Rochelle
2 Marennes
3 Arcachon & the Bassin d'Arcachon

> *If you buy oysters straight from their producers, they're usually packed in a wooden box like this.*

2 ★★ **Marennes.** Where the Seudre Estuary meets the Atlantic Ocean, opposite the Ile d'Oléron (p. 595, 11), you'll find a land of sandy flats, wooden causeways, and oyster farms, known as the Marennes-Oléron basin. This unique ecosystem yields more than 60,000 oysters each year—some 45% of France's entire oyster production. Watching proudly over it all, on the mainland, is the town of Marennes—a mishmash of waterways, bourgeois houses, and brightly colored wooden fishing huts (p. 555, 6). The place to visit here is the huge ★ kids **Cité de l'Huître** (☎ 05-46-36-78-98; www.cite-huitre.com; admission 9€ adults, 5€ ages 6–16, 23€ family ticket; Feb–Mar and Oct–Dec daily noon–7pm, Apr–June and Sept daily 10am–7pm, July–Aug daily 10am–8pm), a park and interactive oyster center that explains every step of oyster farming. You can taste oysters

Where to Stay & Dine on the Atlantic Coast

For places to stay and dine in La Rochelle, see p. 596; in Bassin d'Arcachon, see p. 577; elsewhere, see accommodations listed in the previous tour (p. 557).

> *These huts at L'Herbe, on the Bassin d'Arcachon, are used by oyster farmers; many sell them fresh onsite with wine.*

at ★★ **La Claire,** voie du chenal de la Cayenne (☎ 05-46-36-78-92; menus 12€–19€, oyster platters 8€–25€; MC, V; lunch Wed–Sun, dinner Fri–Sat), or sign up for the **Atelier des Sens** workshop (☎ 05-46-36-78-98; 6€) to learn how to differentiate their textures and

flavors (rather like wine tasting). A fun way to get around is by bike, which you can rent at the park entrance. ⏲ 2½ hr. Marennes Tourist Office, place Chasseloup-Laubat. ☎ 05-46-85-04-36. www.ile-oleron-marennes.com.

For a shortcut across the water, see p. 556. Overland, take D728E from Marennes, which becomes D728. After St-Just-Luzac, pick up D150 to Saintes, and follow signs to A10 (toward Bordeaux); exit A10 at junction 1, and follow signs to Bassin d'Arcachon (213km/132 miles total).

Aquitaine Caviar

Unbeknown to most, the Atlantic coast produces its own caviar. Following the disappearance of local species of sturgeon from the Gironde Estuary in the 1980s, the French National Institute for Agricultural Research introduced Russian breeds to local waters. Today, Aquitaine's caviar is likened to beluga, and lovers of these black pearls can visit a working caviar farm in the western corner of the Bassin d'Arcachon, the **Moulin de la Cassadotte,** in Biganos (☎ 05-56-82-64-42; www.caviardefrance.com). Watch some 70,000 sturgeons poke their black noses out of the ponds, before sampling their eggs and learning about how they're raised.

❸ ★★★ **Arcachon & the Bassin d'Arcachon.**
If you were to fly over Arcachon's horseshoe-shaped bay, on the southern side of the Gironde Estuary, you'd look down upon neat rows of oyster parks, split by the irregular lines of water channels and sand banks—a landscape that looks rather like the underwater ruins of a city. More than 400 families produce more than 16 million kilograms (18,000 tons) of oysters here each year. In fact, 60% of spat comes from Arcachon before it's sent up to places such as Marennes

for fattening. Remarkably, for a destination that receives hundreds of thousands of visitors each year, Arcachon's oyster-farming villages still feel authentic—and they don't just specialize in oysters: No fewer than 15 surrounding villages serve such delicacies as clams, prawns, sole, and bass. One such place, ★ **Gujan Mestras,** on the south side of the bay (p. 576, ❸), is famed for its seven quaint ports. At **Larros** port you'll find the **Maison de l'Huître** (☎ 05-56-66-23-71; www.maisondelhuitre.fr; admission 4.50€ adults, 2.50€ ages 5–15; July–Aug daily 10am–12:30pm and 2:30–6pm, Sept–June Mon–Sat 10am–12:30pm and 2:30–6pm), a small museum about oyster production. From here

> Oysters are kept in wooden crates in the water to preserve their freshness.

The Lowdown on Oysters

- Oysters reproduce in summer. Each oyster lays at least a million eggs in open water; once fertilized, these become oyster larvae known as "spat."

- If water conditions are good, the larvae develop into tiny oysters, which attach themselves to purposefully laid tiles and feed on microscopic algae.

- Once they are attached to the tiles, the oysters can be transported to other geographical areas for maturation.

- A year later, oysters go through *detroquage* (detachment from their tiles), a delicate task carried out mainly by women.

- Once detached, oysters are put into special bags in oyster parks, where they grow for another 2 years.

- Finally, the oysters are "finished" in *claires,* shallow pools (previously used for salt farming) that are replenished by the tides. These are what you see all around Marennes and Arcachon.

- By the time an oyster makes it onto your plate, the oyster farmer will have handled it at least 30 times in order to check on its development throughout its lifetime.

- Marennes's famous oysters are often tinged with green due to their diet of microscopic, blue-hued plankton that grow only in these waters.

it's just a short walk to **Les Pavois** restaurant, 113 Port Larros (☎ 05-56-66-38-71; www.restaurant-lespavois.com; menus 16€–36€; MC, V; lunch and dinner Wed–Sun), a large wooden house on stilts with heartwarming views over the water. Here you can tuck into fresh oysters served with shallot vinegar, bread, and butter, and savor dishes such as stuffed crab flambéed in Armagnac, *cassolette* of squid with chorizo, and sea bass with pesto. Or, if the idea of a simple platter of fresh oysters in a portside shack appeals, try the working oyster farm **Cap Noroît,** 14 Port Larros (☎ 05-56-66-04-15; 6 oysters 6€, 12 oysters 10€; cash only). To eat with your toes in the sand, head to the opposite side of the bay, to the **Cap-Ferret Peninsula** (p. 577, ❺), where narrow lanes and whitewashed houses in the tiny fishing village of **L'Herbe** lead to the beach. Here, **Cabane 83** (☎ 06-17-08-11-20; www.huitrenherbe.com; call ahead for hours), a wonderful no-frills wooden hut, lays out chairs and tables so you can indulge in fresh oyster platters or fish pâté with a glass of wine (11€–15€) while enjoying uninterrupted views over the **Ile aux Oiseaux** (p. 576)—a glorious island of sand frequented by 300 species of birds. ⏱ At least 2 days. For detailed information on the Bassin d'Arcachon, see p. 574.

Bordeaux for Wine Lovers

Covering half of Gironde (the biggest *département* in France), the Bordeaux region is without a doubt the wine capital of the world, with 57 wine appellations, more than 8,000 châteaux, and around 120,000 hectares (296,526 acres) of vines. It would take weeks to visit each wine-growing area here, so this tour concentrates on two of the best: St-Emilion and the Médoc Châteaux Route. Whether you fancy a short, epicurean excursion, or you plan to snake your way along the vine-rich roads for several days, both areas are easy to reach from the city of Bordeaux (p. 582). For more information on Bordeaux wines and grape varieties, see "Wine Tasting in Bordeaux," p. 587.

> *The impressive tree-lined drive that leads to Châteaux Margaux.*

START St-Emilion is 40km (25 miles) northeast of Bordeaux. **TRIP LENGTH** About 4 days, depending on how long you linger in each vineyard; 200km (124 miles).

① ★★★ **St-Emilion.** Set on a limestone plateau overlooking the Dordogne valley, this pale gold, Romanesque village is famed for its wine and its steep medieval stone *escalettes* (stairways), which gave rise to the modern word for "stairs" (*escaliers*). Surrounding the village,

miles of low, trestled vineyards produce no fewer than 74 *Grand Cru Classé* red wines, the most famous being Cheval Blanc and Ausone. You'll be able to walk to all the wineries listed here for tastings. (For a full list of châteaux, ask at the St-Emilion tourist office.)

Start your day at the awe-inspiring ★★ **Eglise Monolithe,** place de l'Eglise Monolithe (☎ 05-57-55-28-28; daily year-round; admission 6.70€ adults, 4.20€ students, free for

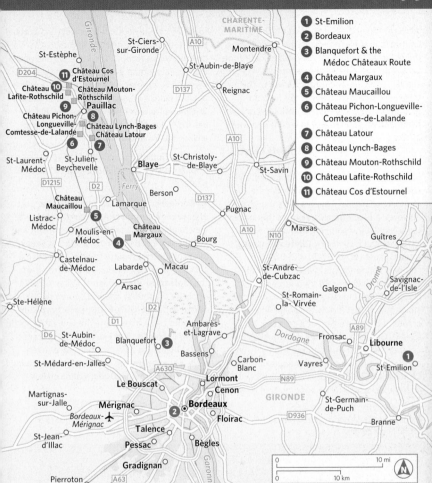

1. St-Emilion
2. Bordeaux
3. Blanquefort & the Médoc Châteaux Route
4. Château Margaux
5. Château Maucaillou
6. Château Pichon-Longueville-Comtesse-de-Lalande
7. Château Latour
8. Château Lynch-Bages
9. Château Mouton-Rothschild
10. Château Lafite-Rothschild
11. Château Cos d'Estournel

children 11 and under), the largest underground church in Europe, carved by Benedictine monks during the 9th to 13th centuries. It can be visited only as part of a tour organized by the tourist office. The tour also takes you deep into the belly of the Benedictine catacombs, the 13th-century ★ **Chapelle de la Trinité,** and its underground grotto—a site known as the Hermitage—where St. Emilion, who founded the village, reportedly sequestered himself. For sweeping views over the vineyards, head to the Eglise Monolithe's medieval ★ **Belfry,** place des Créneaux, the second-highest tower in La Gironde, or to the ★ **Tour du Château du Roy,** the only remaining part of the fortress built in the 13th

> *From a distance, St-Emilion's medieval center looks like an island rising up from a sea of vines.*

century. Today the King's Tower is used by La Jurade, a society dedicated to maintaining the highest standard for local wine. Each June, La Jurade's members, dressed in silk hats and scarlet robes, parade through town to the tower and pronounce their judgment on the new wine. Admission to both towers is 1.25€ and must be reserved with the tourist office.

After lunch, stop by ★ **La Grande Cave,** place du Clocher (☎ 05-57-24-14-24; daily 9am–8pm), where knowledgeable staff talk you through their wines, many from the surrounding châteaux. This is a wine merchant, however, and etiquette presumes that if you taste, you'll buy (shipping available). From here, you can walk to ★★ **Château Guadet,** 4 rue Guadet (☎ 05-57-74-40-04; www. chateau-guadet-saintemilion.com; by appointment only; tour 8€), a bourgeois, antiques-filled hideaway sitting over a former stone quarry that is now the cellar where the estate's bottles are kept at a constant 12°C (54°F). Guadet's wines are delicious, characterized by their ripe tannins and berry and currant flavors. Finally, end the afternoon at **Château La Clotte** (☎ 05-57-24-66-85; www. chateaulaclotte.com; by appointment only;

tour 10€). Head south of the village via Porte Brunet, then go straight; it's in the Bergat district, with a tower, a tasting area, and endless views over the sloping vines and garden. Wines are complex yet smooth, with notes of toasted cinnamon and fine tannins. ⏱ 1 day. St-Emilion Tourist Office, Le Doyenné, Place des Créneaux. ☎ 05-57-55-28-28. www.saint-emilion-tourisme.com.

From St-Emilion, take D243, D1089, N89/E70, and A631 west to Bordeaux (47km/29 miles).

② **Bordeaux.** On the Garonne River, the port of Bordeaux, capital of Aquitaine, is the gateway to one of the world's most important and notoriously exclusive wine-producing areas. Plan your trip with maps, guides, and advice about local wines, all available for free from the **Maison du Vin** (House of Wine; p. 587), opposite the tourist office (12 cours du 30 Juillet; ☎ 05-56-00-66-00; www.bordeaux-tourisme.com). To explore the vineyards north of town, consider alternative forms of transport: You can go by bus or bicycle, or even walk. For wine tasting in the city of Bordeaux, see p. 587. For detailed information on Bordeaux, see p. 582.

> *The Route du Médoc is littered with stately wine châteaux like this one, where vines have replaced a traditional garden.*

③ Blanquefort & the Médoc Châteaux Route.
Just northwest of Bordeaux, in Blanquefort, begins **La Route du Médoc** (aka the D2), which wends its way northward toward Pauillac through the appellations of Haut-Médoc, Margaux, Médoc, St-Julien, Pauillac, and St-Estèphe, and past dozens of famous châteaux—Margaux, Latour, Lafite-Rothschild. The Médoc covers around 300,000 hectares (741,315 acres) from the north of Bordeaux right to the coast at Pointe de Grave. Most of Bordeaux's prestigious *Grands Crus Classés* are grown here, along with some lip-smacking *Crus Bourgeois*. A mix of clay, gravel, and sandy soils; a mild climate; and more than 2,000 years of experience account for the excellence of Médoc's wines, created mainly from cabernet sauvignon, cabernet franc, and merlot grape varieties. ⏱1–2 days on the Wine Route.

④ Château Margaux. In 1776, a 1771 Châteaux Margaux was the first Bordeaux vintage to appear in a Christie's catalogue, as "an excellent claret with a fine flavour." Known as the Versailles of the Médoc, this Empire-style château was built in the 19th century near the village of Margaux. The estate covers more than 263 hectares (650 acres), of which 80 hectares (198 acres) produce Château Margaux and Pavillon Rouge du Château Margaux; almost 12 hectares (30 acres) are devoted to producing Pavillon Blanc du Château Margaux. To see the vat rooms and wine cellars, make an appointment by letter or phone. **Margaux.** ☎ 05-57-88-83-83. www.chateau-margaux.com. Visits by appointment only Mon–Fri 10am–noon and 2–4pm. Closed Aug–Oct.

> *Before you leave Pauillac (⑥), stop by the tourist office, which sells eight Médoc appellations.*

⑤ ★★★ Château Maucaillou. This 19th-century ocher winery is nestled near a train track and endless verdant trestles at Moulis-en-Médoc. It's one of the most visitor-friendly châteaux on the stretch, with 1- to 3-day oenology courses, helicopter rides, and an interesting museum on wine growing. The visit finishes in the *chais* (wine storage rooms) with a *dégustation* of one of the château's full-bodied, oaky wines. If you can't bear to leave, stay on-site in one of five lovely pastel bedrooms (doubles from 75€–95€). Moulis-en-Médoc is north of Margaux, following D2 north and D5 west. ☎ 05-56-58-01-23. www.chateau-maucaillou.eu. Museum and tasting 7€. Daily summer 10am–5pm, winter 10am, 11am, 2pm, 3pm, and 4pm.

⑥ ★ Château Pichon-Longueville-Comtesse-de-Lalande. Fairy-tale turrets, a moat, and a particularly impressive collection of glassware distinguish this vineyard. The wines here are characterized by their strong legs, deep ruby-red hue, and fresh black-currant aromas. The 2006 Pichon-Longueville is especially delicious, with a dense purple, almost black tone and a hint of cherry. **Pauillac.** ☎ 05-56-73-17-17. www.pichonlongueville.com. Tasting 8€. Visits by appointment only daily 9am–12:30pm and 2–6:30pm.

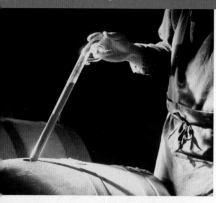

> *The quality of wine is tested throughout the fermenting process.*

7 Château Latour. This famous chateau takes its name from the 14th-century Tour Lambert (Lambert Tower) on its grounds, which has watched over vines for more than 700 years. St-Lambert. ☎ 05-56-73-19-80. www.chateau-latour.fr. Visits by appointment only Mon–Fri.

8 ★ Château Lynch-Bages. The owners of this historic vineyard have a penchant for contemporary art and offer visitors the chance to admire works by famous artists. You can take wine-tasting courses here, but the standard visit is educational, with a tour of the estate and in-depth explanations of the wines you taste. In addition to reds, Lynch-Bages makes an excellent sauvignon blanc that shines a light gold and explodes on the palate with a citrusy burst before tailoring off at the end into a light oaky, almost vanilla flavor. Pauillac. ☎ 05-56-73-19-33. www.lynchbages.com. Tasting 8€. Visits by appointment only daily 9am–1pm and 2–6:30pm.

9 ★★ Château Mouton-Rothschild. Owned by the Rothschild family since 1853, this great Bordeaux institution has achieved *Premier Grand Cru* status since 1973. The main draws here are the cellars and a museum exhibiting 3 centuries' worth of wine-related antiques. The wine-label collection is particularly impressive, with several designs by Picasso and Jean Cocteau. Le Pouyalet, 1km (⅔ mile) north of Pauillac. ☎ 05-56-73-21-29. www.bpdr.com. Visits by appointment only; to tour the cellars, make an appointment well in advance; for a tour that does not include the cellars, call a week ahead.

10 Château Lafite-Rothschild. This house offers an interesting free tour of the wine-making facilities, but visits are by appointment only (2-week minimum advance notice), and there are no direct sales. The *vinothèque* contains many vintage bottles, several dating from 1797. The Rothschilds purchased the château in 1868. Pauillac. ☎ 05-56-59-26-83. www.lafite.com. Visits by appointment only.

11 ★★ Château Cos d'Estournel. Surrounded by 91 hectares (225 acres) of cabernet sauvignon (60%) and merlot (40%) vines, this château was constructed in the early 19th century by Louis-Gaspard d'Estournel, nicknamed "Maharaja of St-Estèphe" after his trade with India and eccentric taste in architecture. Under the St-Estèphe appellation, the estate produces excellent red and white wines, each singular in strength and complexity. You can taste a few on the visit, which also includes a tour of the cellars. ☎ 05-56-73-15-50. www.estournel.com. By appointment only Mon–Fri 9am–12:30pm and 2–5:30pm; weekend visits possible upon request.

What's Your Wine Sign?

Before venturing into wine country, consider stopping at France's biggest wine cellar for a buyer's guide tailored to your taste profile. Do you prefer reds or whites? Oaky or fruity flavors? In an hour-long session, you'll taste six very different wines and express the way you feel about them using an electronic panel. This information is analyzed by a computer to determine your "wine sign." Whether you turn out to be "gourmet," "trendy," or "adventurous," you'll leave the session with a personalized wine book adapted to your tastes and budget. Three different sessions—Discovery (16€), Terroirs and Crus (29€), and Prestige (89€)—take place daily, at 11am, 3pm, and 5pm; an appointment is required, so ask in the shop or call ahead. The cellar itself, in a vast glass building that has been likened to an upside-down greenhouse, is state-of-the-art. *From Bordeaux, take D2 north, and after the village of Bern (before Labarde) head left along the rte. d'Arsac to Arsac.* ☎ 05-56-39-04-90. http://wine-tourism-france.winery.fr. Daily 10am–7pm.

Where to Stay & Dine for Wine Lovers

Château Guittot-Fellonneau MACAU *FRENCH*
This is a gorgeous, family-run vineyard whose wines are aged in traditional oak barrels. Meals here use local ingredients (plenty of duck confit and Bordelaise sauce), and the wines are of excellent quality. Rooms are simple and rustic, with views over the garden or vines. Off D2 at Bern (toward the Gironde) on the Wine Route. ☎ 05-57-88-47-81; www. guittot-fellonneau.com. Doubles from 45€. Meals from 19€. MC, V.

Clos du Roy ST-EMILION *FRENCH*
Chef Nikhola Lavie-Combot trained with France's greatest chefs and now pairs creative dishes, such as red mullet with sweet 'n' sour eggplant or roasted pigeon with foie gras, with a generous wine list. Diners have a view over the village's towers. 12 rue de la Petite Fontaine. ☎ 05-57-74-41-55. www.leclosduroy.fr. Lunch 22€–29€, dinner 39€–80€. MC, V. Lunch and dinner Wed–Sun; closed Jan–Feb 10.

★★ Cordeillan-Bages PAUILLAC *GASTRONOMIC*
This region's most consistently celebrated hotel and restaurant is set in a 18th-century manor house where most guests come to dine but end up spending the night after drinking wine with dinner. Menu items may include foie gras on confit of peaches with a port wine reduction or roasted sea bass with essence of cockles and braised, licorice-flavored leeks. Spacious guest rooms have formal curtains, upholstered walls, and antiques. Rte. D2. ☎ 05-56-59-24-24. www. cordeillanbages.com. 28 units. Fixed-price menus 90€ lunch, 170€ dinner; a la carte main courses 32€–60€. Doubles 199€–292€; junior suite 392€; 2-bedroom apt. for four 517€. AE, DC, MC, V. Closed Dec 15–Feb 14.

Le Logis de la Cadène ST-EMILION
Rooms in this town house are exceptionally charming with high ceilings, plush fabric, and rustic touches. For longer stays, a stone cottage overlooking the vines sleeps four, with a fully equipped kitchen and an open stone fireplace. **Place du Marché au Bois.**

> *In the heart of the Médoc vineyards, the 18th-century Cordeillan-Bages makes a stylish retreat, with fine rooms, wine, and dining.*

☎ 05-57-24-71-40. logisdelacadene.com. 5 units. Doubles from 100€; *gîte* 650€ per week, 250€ per weekend. MC, V.

★★ Hostellerie de Plaisance ST-EMILION *FRENCH* This 200-year-old stone building, on 14th-century foundations, is the best lodging-and-dining choice in town. Stylish rooms, some with views of stone monuments and towers, host wine tasters and buyers from all over the world (the best doubles have terraces). Chef Philippe Etchebest's menu includes salad of grilled quail with avocados, civet of sturgeon cooked with local red wine, and filet mignon of veal with wild mushrooms. Place du Clocher. ☎ 05-57-55-07-55. www. hostelleriedeplaisance.com. 21 units. Fixed-price menus 58€ lunch, 40€–135€ dinner. Half-board 80€; doubles 350€–510€; suites 670€. AE, DC, MC, V. Closed Dec 21–Feb 11.

Poitou-Charentes with Kids

From beaches and aquariums to zoos and theme parks, Poitou-Charentes is heaven for kids—whether yours are just out of diapers or in their terrible teens. This section takes you to four family-orientated attractions, all reachable from Poitiers, Bordeaux, and La Rochelle. It's not a tour per se; you can dip into these stops while following our other itineraries around Poitou-Charentes. You should put aside a day for each, except La Rochelle's aquarium, which you can explore in just a few hours.

> Let your kids' imaginations run wild amid the alleys and weird contraptions at Le Nombril du Monde in Pougne-Hérisson.

START Pougne-Hérisson is 68km (42 miles) west of Poitiers off N149. **TRIP LENGTH** 178km (110 miles).

① ★★ Le Nombril du Monde, Pougne-Hérisson. This tiny, story-themed park is founded on a local legend: Every fairy tale that has ever existed came out of a mysterious hole, the *Nombril du Monde* (Bellybutton of the World), in Pougne-Hérisson. In the beginning, a huge explosion (a kind of Big Bang), caused by a giant, supposedly came out of the *nombril* (bellybutton), spreading "sparks" of fairy stories all over the globe. In time, the sparks became full-fledged stories, which, from time to time, traveled back to Pougne on a flame. Once the fire fanned down, the stories were set in stone inside the Fairy Tale Mine, where they have stayed ever since. Local lore has it that medieval troubadours from across Europe came to meet and tell stories here, but after the Hundred Years' War, the tradition and the legend were forgotten—almost. During World War II, in 1944, an American

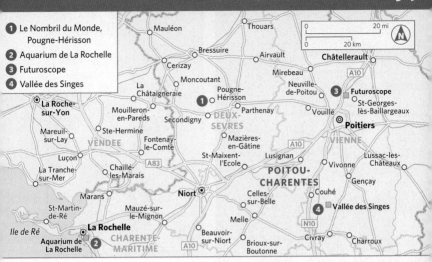

1. Le Nombril du Monde, Pougne-Hérisson
2. Aquarium de La Rochelle
3. Futuroscope
4. Vallée des Singes

soldier, anthropologist Barney Fergusson, accidentally landed in Pougne. After the French liberation, he stayed behind to research the fairy-tale myth. He befriended Robert Jarry, the village blacksmith, and together they set about creating imaginary machines and excavating the stones from the forgotten Fairy Tale Mine. This is the fabulous imaginary backdrop for this story-themed park, a living, breathing landscape of weird and wonderful contraptions and games for kids. The actual stories (straight from the Fairy Tale Mine), recounted by actors throughout the day, are less accessible for non-French speakers, but that doesn't detract from the fun of sitting in makeshift rockets, whacking pots and pans together to make music, or finding your way out of a mysterious labyrinth. ☎ 05-49-64-19-19. www.nombril.com. Admission 6€ adults; 3€ ages 4–12. Apr–June and Sept–Oct Sat–Sun 1:30–7:30pm; July–Aug daily 1:30–7:30pm. Closed Nov–Mar.

La Rochelle is 116km (72 miles) southwest of Pougne-Hérisson.

❷ ★★★ **Aquarium de La Rochelle.** In the heart of La Rochelle, children love watching the brightly colored multitude of sea creatures in what is easily the best aquarium in France. See p. 591, ❹.

Head north on A10 from Poitiers (12km/7½ miles).

❸ ★★★ **Futuroscope.** On the northern outskirts of Poitiers, Futuroscope is an amusement park—the second biggest in France, after Disneyland Paris (p. 136)—with a moving image and technology theme, including giant screens, dynamic cinema shows, and interactive experiences that keep kids (and adults) occupied for hours. Aside from being fun, it's educational: 3-D presentations, for instance,

> Kids aged 4 to 10 are entitled to their own audio-guides at La Rochelle's aquarium.

> *Futuroscope's interactive attractions are bound to put a smile on everyone's face.*

> *The Vallée des Singes is home to 350 apes.*

include *Fly Me to the Moon,* where you experience the Apollo 11 moon landing alongside Neil Armstrong and Buzz Aldrin, and *Cosmic Collisions,* which looks at how our universe has been shaped by meteorites. A recent addition is *Arthur, the 4-D Adventure,* based on Luc Besson's hit film *Arthur et les Minimoys (Arthur and the Invisibles).* Climb onto the back of a ladybuggy and jolt your way through the fairy-tale world in 3-D glasses. For younger kids, *Children's World* is an outdoor play area with water bikes, mini–electric cars, and climbing frames. As night falls, the park's lake becomes a theater for a musical water-and-light show designed by Yves Pépin, artistic advisor of the 2008 Beijing Olympics closing ceremony. Ten hotels are within a 10-minute walk of the park (check the park website for reservations and details). Exit 28 on the A10-E5 motorway (Paris-Bordeaux) is 2 min. from the Parc du Futuroscope main entrance, near Jaunay-Clan. ☎ 05-49-49-59-06. www.futuroscope.com. 1-day

ticket 35€ adults, 26€ ages 5–16; evening ticket (after 5pm) 17€ adults, 10€ ages 5–16; 2-day ticket 66€ adults, 47€ ages 5–16. Free for children 4 and under. Early Feb to early Jan daily 10am–nightfall; evening shows start btw. 6pm and 10:45pm, depending on season.

The Vallée des Singes in Romagne is 50km (31 miles) south of Poitiers off DN10, N10, D7, and D27.

❹ ★★ **Vallée des Singes.** Man's closest relatives live amid the trees, lakes, and shaded alleys of this primate zoo. Kids love wandering along the paths, which are completely open to many of the park's furry residents. More than 350 primates live here, from muscular gorillas and cheery chimps to long-maned Ethiopian geladas and Diana monkeys (one of the most threatened species in the world). Particularly interesting is feeding time, when the monkeys come to feast on fruits and leaves. This is also a chance to see some of the babies, who cling to their mother's necks. Each year around 30 babies are born—a sure sign that the animals are quite happy in their French habitat. Parents with younger kids have plenty of photo ops in the Petite Ferme, home to pygmy goats, cute ducks, and long-coated alpacas. Le Gureau. ☎ 05-49-87-20-20. www.la-vallee-des-singes.fr. Admission 14€ adults, 9€ ages 5–12. Late Mar–June and Sept daily 10am–6pm, July–Aug 10am–7pm, Oct–Nov 10am–5pm.

Where to Stay & Dine

★★★ **kids Château de la Couronne** MARTHON
Southeast of Angoulême, this old stone château packs a few surprises. Inside you'll find artful, contemporary design with large rooms reminiscent of a 1960s James Bond movie. There are also plenty of facilities: a cinema, a swimming pool, 2 hectares (5 acres) of parkland, and a billiard room. ☎ 05-45-62-29-96. www.chateaudelacouronne.com. 5 units. Doubles 145€–315€; whole castle for 2,000€ per night. AE, MC, V.

★★ **Hostellerie Les Pigeons Blancs** COGNAC
FRENCH Sleep above one of the best restaurants in Cognac, housed in a former post office, where chef Jacques Tachet creates delights such as St. Jacques scallops with spinach and crispy chorizo, and Pauillac lamb in merlot. Upstairs rooms have antique furniture, toile de Jouy wallpaper, and impeccably clean bathrooms. 110 rue Jules Brisson. ☎ 05-45-82-16-36. www.pigeons-blancs.com. 7 units. Doubles 80€–95€. 3-course menus 23€–58€. Restaurant: lunch Tues–Sun, dinner Mon–Sat. MC, V.

★ **Hôtel du Palais** ANGOULEME
You won't find a more central location in Angoulême than the Hôtel du Palais, on the pretty place Francis Louvel, just around the corner from the cartoon capital's bar and restaurant area. Rooms are dressed in deep reds, pinks, and oranges, reminiscent of a French boudoir. It's a good value for the money. 4 place Francis Louvel. ☎ 05-45-92-54-11. www.hotel-angouleme.fr. 45 units. Doubles 53€–169€. MC, V.

★★★ **La Rotonde** SAINTES
This beguiling B&B, in the heart of Saintes, overlooks the Charente River. Rooms are clad in antiques and yielding fabrics; bathrooms are spotless; and breakfast is copious. For some grandeur at bathtime, book the alcove room,

> *The dining room at the Hostellerie Les Pigeons Blancs, a hotel-restaurant housed in a former coaching inn from the 17th century.*

where a free-standing tub overlooks the river. Two studios also offer a kitchenette. 2 rue Monconseil. ☎ 05-46-74-74-44. www.chambres-hotes-saintes.com. 8 units. Doubles 100€; studio 100€ per night, from 350€ per week. MC, V.

La Ruelle ANGOULEME *CONTEMPORARY FRENCH* Stone masonry and chic white furniture create the smart backdrop for chef Guillaume Veyssière's top-notch French cuisine with a modern twist. Specialties include lobster roasted with citronella, pigeon roasted in ginger, and iced strawberry and pepper frommage blanc. 6 rue Trois-Notre-Dame. ☎ 05-45-95-15-19. Reservations recommended. Fixed-price menus 38€–60€. MC, V. Lunch Tues–Fri, dinner Mon–Sat.

★★ **La Table de Marion** SAINTES *FRENCH MARKET* This is one of Poitou-Charente's most innovative tables, and the chef runs excellent cooking classes most Saturday mornings (50€). Whatever's fresh from the market makes it onto the menu, which might include anything from mackerel with quinoa and cucumber pâté to almond ravioli with roasted peaches. 10 Place Blair. ☎ 05-46-74-16-38. http://latabledemarion.unblog.fr. Lunch menu 25€, 3-course menus 37€–47€. Lunch and dinner Thurs–Mon, lunch only Tues. MC, V.

Travel Tip

For hotels and restaurants in Bordeaux, see p. 586; in La Rochelle, see p. 596.

The Silver Coast Beaches

With silvery beaches backed by sand dunes, pines, and bike paths, the Côte d'Argent is the longest, sandiest, and straightest shoreline in France. Between Pointe de Grave on the Gironde Estuary in the north and the Bassin d'Arcachon in the south, you'll find modern holiday resorts intermingled with old establishments, and many a fine spot to spend hours contemplating the vivacious Atlantic waves.

> Côte d'Argent dunes, peppered with grasses, create a rich habitat for birds and great bathing opportunities for humans.

★ **Lacanau-Océan.** Surfers know this place well. Its huge waves, crashing rhythmically on 15km (9⅓-mile) stretches of sun-warmed sand, are the theater for numerous world surfing championships. In summer, the beaches—especially kids **Plage Centrale,** which buzzes with ice-cream gobblers and beach balls—are swarming with families from nearby campsites. Off season, however, the sand is pretty much your own—long, deserted straights interrupted only by the occasional man-made sea wall and lined with early-20th-century villas. Lacanau-Océan lies 61km (38 miles) west of Bordeaux. Lacanau Tourist Office, place de l'Europe. ☎ 05-56-03-21-01. www.medococean.com.

> Bay Watch à la Française: *Lacanau-Océan has a decent set of coast guards surveying beach activity.*

★★ Plage du Grand Crohot. Just north of the Cap-Ferret Peninsula of the Bassin d'Arcachon, this sandy spot feels like a secret seaside garden—a beach that only a handful know about. Sure, the holidaymakers come in high season, but everyone here tends to respect the peacefulness. Off season, the whole place is yours, so bring a good book and some binoculars for bird-watching, and relax on the sand as the sun disappears into the horizon. Plage du Grand Crohot lies 60km (37 miles)

southwest of Bordeaux and 20km (12 miles) north of Cap-Ferret.

★ Soulac-sur-Mer. Nestled between the ocean and the Gironde Estuary, this pine-scented, early-20th-century resort has four lovely, sandy beaches with uninterrupted sea views. It's also home to the 12th-century Romanesque **Notre-Dame-de-la-Fin-des-Terres Basilica,** Rte. de Bordeaux (☎ 05-56-09-83-99; free admission; daily 9am–6pm), part of the St-Jacques de Compostelle pilgrimage route between Britain and Spain. In high season, **kids Plage Centrale** is best for kids, with games and activities, while **★★ Plage de l'Amélie,** to the south, with its steep, pine-topped dunes and strong sea currents, feels more untamed. Soulac-sur-Mer lies 15km (9⅓ miles) southwest from Royan (across the Gironde estuary) and 94km (58 miles) northwest of Bordeaux. Soulac-sur-Mer Tourist Office, 68 rue de la Plage. ☎ 05-56-09-86-61. www.soulac.com.

The Côte d'Argent's Lakes

The seaside isn't the only attraction on this stretch: Just a few miles inland, **Lac d'Hourtins-Carcans,** off D101 and D3 (tourist office ☎ 05-56-09-19-00), is one of the largest in France, with about 7,284 hectares (18,000 acres). It's famed for its wildlife and carnivorous, fly-catching plants such as pitcher plants and sundews. Just east of Lacanau-Océan, **Lac de Lacanau,** off D3 and D6, is prized for its watersports and bike paths that lead you through pine and mimosa forests. For more information, contact the Lacanau tourist office (see p. 572).

Bassin d'Arcachon

Sandwiched between Europe's largest sand dune (Dune du Pilat) and the Côte d'Argent (p. 524), this horseshoe-shaped bay is fun, family-friendly, and fascinating, with plenty of sand, birdlife, oysters, and biking opportunities. At low tide, the waters retreat to reveal salt marshes, muddy flats, fishing huts on stilts, and sandbanks frequented by common curlews and cormorants. At high tide, boats bob in the ports of 15 surrounding fishing villages, all famous for their oysters (p. 560, ❸). You could easily spend your entire vacation here—and many people do—but it's also perfect for a weekend trip from Bordeaux (p. 582) or La Rochelle (p. 588).

> Bring binoculars to Le Teich's bird park, where you can observe our feathered friends in their natural habitat.

START Dune du Pilat, off D218, south of the bay. TRIP LENGTH 54km (34 miles).

❶ ★★★ **Dune du Pilat.** Europe's biggest sand dune (also known as Pyla) is a whopper, standing tall at 110m high (361 ft.) and 3km (1¾ miles) long. And it's getting bigger: The wind piles on layers of sand every day, sculpting the dune with cream-colored undulations so continuous that you'll feel humbled by the sight. You need plenty of leg power to get to the top, but when you do, the vistas across the pine forest and over the inky blue and turquoise ocean are awe-inspiring. Botanists will

appreciate the dune's flora, too, including occasional tufts of beach grass, blue-purple sea holly, and sea pinks. This is also a prime spot for parascending. **Wagga School,** rte. de Biscarrosse (☎ 06-32-04-32-07; www.waggaschool.com; from 120€), runs 1-day initiation courses between April and September. ☉ Half-day to 1 day. Pyla sur Mer Tourist Information Point, Rond-Point du Figuier. ☎ 05-56-54-02-22. www.tourisme-latestedebuch.fr.

From Pyla, take D218 and D259 to La Teste-de-Buch, then follow N250 to Arcachon (10km/6¼ miles).

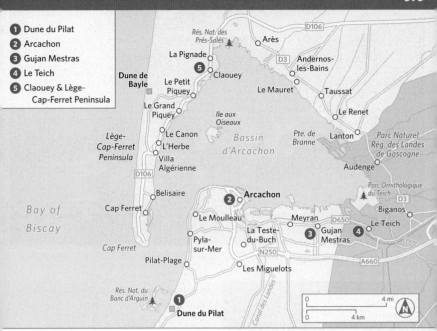

1 Dune du Pilat
2 Arcachon
3 Gujan Mestras
4 Le Teich
5 Claouey & Lège-
Cap-Ferret Peninsula

2 ★ **Arcachon.** It was Napoleon III's love for Arcachon that turned this fishing port into a prized 19th-century resort for European aristocracy. Legacies from that era live on at the Château Deganne, 163 bd. de la Plage, now a **casino** laden with slot machines; and in the **Ville d'Hiver** (Winter Town), with its ostentatious mishmash of mock Swiss chalets, Moorish villas, and neo-Gothic manors. The tourist office runs guided visits of this area between April and October. Other parts of the town center are named after the seasons, too. Jetties, beaches, and modern seafront promenades line the **Ville d'Eté** (Summer Town). The old fishing port is in **Ville d'Automne** (Autumn Town); its most easterly tip, la Pointe de l'Aiguillon, shows what pre-19th-century Arcachon would have looked like with its authentic fishermen's houses. **Ville de Printemps**

Rental Bikes

The distances between the stops on this tour are short and ideal for cyclists. Rent a bike (or electric scooter) from 10€ per day at **Locabeach,** 326 bd. de la Plage, in Arcachon (☎ 05-56-83-39-64; www.locabeach.com).

> *Europe's largest sand pile, the Dune du Pilat is still growing, with the help of strong winds.*

> *The quaint fishing port in Biganos is linked by rail to Bordeaux and the southern part of Bassin d'Arcachon.*

Around the Bassin d'Arcachon by Boat

UBA, from the Eyrac jetty, just off boulevard de la Plage on Arcachon's seafront (☎ 05-57-72-28-28; www.bateliers-arcachon.com; tickets 14€, 10€ ages 3–18, free for children 2 and under), runs excellent 1¾-hour boat tours around the mysterious ★★★ **Ile aux Oiseaux,** a sandy island named after the hundreds of birds that land here, and past oyster farms and pine-dotted fishing villages. En route, look out for *tchanques*, wooden houses on stilts whose name derives from the Gascon term *maison tchanquée* (literally, "house on stilts"), and for long, flat boats called *pinasses*, specially designed to navigate the bay's shallow waters.

(Spring Town) is home to the popular Perière beach. ◔ Half-day to 1 day. Arcachon Tourist Office, Esplanade Georges Pompidou. ☎ 05-57-52-97-97. www.arcachon.com.

From Arcachon, take D650 to Gujan Mestras (10km/6¼ miles).

③ ★ Gujan Mestras. This oyster village has seven picturesque ports, an oyster museum, and several appetizing places to eat. ◔ Half-day. Gujan Mestras Tourist Office, 19 av. de Lattre de Tassigny. ☎ 05-56-66-12-65. www.gujanmestras.com.

From Gujan Mestras, take D650 to Le Teich (5km/3 miles).

④ ★★★ kids Le Teich. This village in the southeast corner of the Bassin is a must for nature lovers. Spend the morning in the ★★★ **Parc Ornithologique du Teich,** Maison de la Nature (☎ 05-56-22-80-93; www.parc-ornithologique-du-teich.com; admission 7.20€ adults, 5.10€ ages 5–14, free for children 4 and under; daily 10am–6pm), a paradise for bird-watchers. Its brackish meadows attract more than 260 species of birdlife including herons, bluethroats, Canadian geese, ospreys, and bar-tailed godwits, all of which can be observed from within concealed observation points set along three paths. In the afternoon, rent a boat through the **Maison de la Nature** (www.canoesurlaleyre.fr; from 17€) and canoe along the ★★★ **Leyre River.** The patchwork of landscapes—alternately rustic, aquatic, and forested—comes alive amid tall grasses and branches hanging over the

The Southern Bassin by Rail

Trains run roughly every 30 minutes along the Bassin's southern stretch between Arcachon, past Gujan and Le Teich, to Biganos. From Biganos, there are direct trains to Bordeaux. A single fare is about 3.80€. For more information, call ☎ 36-35 or log on to www.voyages-sncf.com.

> *From the end of Cap-Ferret, the Bassin d'Arcachon lies to the east, but the next stop westward is America.*

taupe-color waters. Some parts of the area are so thick with vegetation that it's been nicknamed "France's Amazon." ⏱ 1 day.

From Le Teich, continue east on D650 to Biganos, and pick up D3 north to Lège-Cap-Ferrat (29km/18 miles). From here, D106 covers the peninsula.

❺ ★★★ Claouey & Lège-Cap-Ferret Peninsula. The long, narrow, generously wooded Cap-Ferret Peninsula is a coveted destination for wealthy vacationers, many of whom have second homes here. On its eastern stretch are lovely, sheltered coves and beaches overlooking the **Ile aux Oiseaux** (p. 576). The best are at **Claouey, Grand Piquey,** and **Petit Piquey,** just off D106. The peninsula's oyster villages are also seductively authentic, especially **Le Canon** and **L'Herbe,** also off D106, whose narrow, sandy alleys, lined with colorful, wooden fishermen's huts, can be explored on foot. At L'Herbe, it's worth spending a half-hour at the **Villa Algérienne,** a Moorish-style chapel that was once part of a grand estate covering the entire peninsula. The chicest resort town by far is **Cap-Ferret,** on the point. Its small, charming market (Oct–May Wed and Sat mornings, June–Sept daily) sells plenty of regional produce, and you can climb the 258 steps to the top of its lighthouse, the **Phare du Cap-Ferret** (☎ 05-57-70-33-30; www.lege-capferret.com;

admission 4.50€; daily year-round during daylight hours), for a panoramic sweep over the bay, the Dune du Pilat, and beyond. ⏱ 1 day. Lège-Cap-Ferret Tourist Office, 1 av. du Général de Gaulle, Claouey. ☎ 05-56-03-94-49. www.lege-capferret.com.

Where to Stay & Dine in the Bassin d'Arcachon

If you're traveling with kids, try the **Hôtel La Fregate,** 32–34 av. de l'Océan (☎ 05-56-60-41-62; www.hotel-la-fregate.net; 28 units plus 2 apartments; doubles 49€–157€; apartments 655€–920€ per week, from 300€ per weekend; MC, V), a simple, family-run hotel ideally situated on the Cap-Ferret Peninsula. Rooms are bright and airy, with beige, white, or yellow walls; the two small apartments each sleep up to 4. There's also a swimming pool. In Arcachon, trendy and charming ★★★ **Hôtel Ville D'Hiver,** 20 av. Victor Hugo (☎ 05-56-66-10-36; www.hotelvilledhiver.com; 12 units; doubles 125€–225€; MC, V), occupies a converted 19th-century factory in Winter Town. Each room, decorated in soft blues and creams, has a balcony overlooking the garden. There's an on-site wine bar, a spa, and a brasserie, which draws locals with dishes made from fresh market produce.

Inland Poitou-Charentes

Cartoon strips, Romanesque churches, and Roman vestiges are the theme for this tour, which takes you deep into a mosaic of valleys, forests, and vine-clad hillsides along the Charente River. There's wine, of course, but brandy is a regional specialty here, and at the ancient river-town of Cognac, you can taste the velveteen liquor in the great houses of Otard, Hennessey, and Martell. The area is close to both La Rochelle and Bordeaux, and this tour's destinations make ideal day trips from these cities—or you can follow this tour over 3 days.

> *Saintes's Arch of Germanicus was built for Roman emperor Tiberius and his adoptive sons, one of whom was called Germanicus.*

START Saintes is 130km (81 miles) southwest of Poitiers, 115km (71 miles) north of Bordeaux, and 70km (43 miles) from La Rochelle. **TRIP LENGTH** About 75km (47 miles).

1 Saintes. For centuries, Saintes, capital of the Saintonge region and an important stopover for pilgrims following the St-Jacques de Compostella route to Spain, provided the only bridge over the lower Charente River. A Roman edifice, now gone except for the impressive **Arch of Germanicus** (A.D. 19), once marked the city's entrance. On the same side of the river, you can visit the ★ **Abbaye aux Dames,** place de l'Abbaye (admission 2€; Apr–Sept daily 10am–12:30pm and 2–7pm, Oct–Mar daily 2–6pm; closed Christmas to New Year's Day), the region's first female-run abbey, built in the late 11th century. The abbey women, particularly an abbess known as Madame de Saintes, were powerful; they

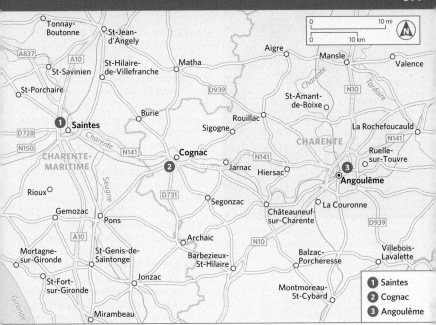

minted money, dealt directly with Rome, wore the Cross, and educated young noble girls. Across the river, on the left bank, you'll find the ★ **Roman amphitheater,** one of the largest and oldest of Roman Gaul, built in A.D. 40. The amphitheater measured 66–39m (217–128 ft.) and would have held several thousand spectators. Two doors led into the arena, the *Sanavivaria* (Door of the Living), through which the successful gladiators passed, and the *Libitinensis* (Door of the Dead), named after the goddess of funerals, through which the executed gladiators were carried off the stage. ⊕ 1 day. Saintes Tourist Office, place Bassompierre. ☎ 05-46-74-23-82. www.saintes-tourisme.fr.

From Saintes, take D24 to Chez Landarts, and join D83 to Cognac (28km/17 miles).

❷ ★★ **Cognac.** The world enjoys 100 million bottles of cognac every year, and all of them start life here in this laid-back port town on the Charente River. It's easy to identify buildings used for cognac storage: They're marked with black lichen stains from the alcohol evaporation process. The town center has its charms, namely two beautiful parks, **Parc François-1er** and **Parc de l'Hôtel-de-Ville,** as well as a 12th-century Romanesque-Gothic church, **Eglise St-Léger** (rue de Monseigneur LaCroix). But the real reason to visit is for the great cognac bottlers—Martell, Hennessy, and Otard—who offer distillery tours that end with a brandy tasting. ★★ **Otard,** 127 bd. Denfert-Rochereau (☎ 05-45-36-88-86; www.otard.com; admission 8.50€ adults, 4.50€ ages 12–18, free for children 11 and under; Apr–Oct daily 10am–noon and 2–6pm, Nov–Mar Mon–Fri 10am–noon and 2–5pm), is set in the majestic, late-medieval Château de Cognac and was the birthplace of Francois I, in 1494. Start your visit at the castle, followed by a fascinating, technical explanation of cognac production and a tasting. There are six cognacs to choose from; one of the best is the 1775 Extra, crafted from champagne *eau de vie* in its own separate cellar. It's best enjoyed neat, heated by the warmth of your hand, after which it creates a lingering taste of dried fruit, honey, and tobacco.

Where to Stay & Dine Around Poitou-Charentes

For places to stay and dine in La Rochelle, see p. 596; in Bordeaux, see p. 586.

> Cognac glasses are short, wide, and round, so that the heat from your hand can intensify the brandy's flavor.

At ★ **Hennessy,** 1 quai Hennessy (☎ 05-45-35-72-68; www.hennessy.com; tours 9€ adults, free for ages 15 and under; Mar–Dec daily; phone ahead: times vary according to language and demand), you'll be introduced to techniques such as double-distillation, before heading over the river to a state-of-the-art building where multimedia installations take you on a tour of the company's rich heritage. Once all that has whetted your appetite, it's over to the boutique for some tasting and buying. The oldest of the Cognac houses, founded in 1715, is ★★ **Martell,** place Edouard-Martell (☎ 05-45-36-33-33; www.martell.com; tours 8.50€; June–Sept daily 10am–5pm; Apr–May and Oct Mon–Fri 10am, 11am, 2:30pm, 3:45pm, and 5pm, Sat–Sun 12–5pm; winter tours by appointment only), where you'll journey deep into the musty cellars of an 18th-century mansion. The cognac ages for 6 to 8 years here, in oak demijohns; the oak's tannin gives brandy its golden hue. One of the most interesting parts of the visit is the blending room, where brandies from different origins are mixed to perfection. While in Cognac, also look out for a drink known as Pineau de Charentes, an AOC liqueur made from grape juice and brandy. It's usually enjoyed as an aperitif or dessert wine, or served inside Charentais melons as a starter. Pays Charentais wines are also good with fish and light dishes. ⏱1 day. Cognac Tourist Office, 16 rue du XIV Juillet. ☎ 05-45-82-10-71. www.tourism-cognac.com.

Leave Cognac via D945 (av. d'Angoulême), and then join N141 to Angoulême (46km/29 miles).

❸ ★ Angoulême. The quaint old town of Angoulême hugs a hilltop between the Charente and Aguienne rivers. It became the capital of paper in the Middle Ages, when dozens of mills lined the river. Today, however, it covets a more lucrative industry—comic strips. *Bandes dessinées,* as they're known in France, have long held a special place in French culture, for both adults and children. The latest adventures of characters such as Tintin, Astérix the Gaul, and Lucky Luke the cowboy not only sell faster than they roll off the presses, they decorate many of the town's buildings (ask the tourist office for a list of murals); some street names are even displayed in speech bubbles. In January, Angoulême tranforms into the site of the **Festival de la Bande Dessinée** (International Comics Festival), the centerpiece of which is the ★★ kids **Cité Internationale de la Bande Dessinée et de l'Image,** 121 rue de Bordeaux (☎ 05-45-38-65-65; www.citebd.org; admission 6€ adults, free for ages 17 and under; Sept–June Tues–Fri 10am–6pm, Sat–Sun 2–6pm; July–Aug Tues–Fri 10am–7pm, Sat–Sun 2–7pm), a museum devoted to famous cartoons and their creators. The permanent collection, on imaginary worlds, has giant, eerie cardboard decor that makes you feel as though you've been sucked into a comic strip. Apart from cartoon characters, Angoulême combines medieval buildings with elegant 18th- and 19th-century town houses built by wealthy millers. The ramparts walk is great for taking in views that stretch over the hills, flanking the Charente River almost 75m (246 ft.) below. Don't miss the ★★ **Cathédrale St-Pierre,** 4 place St-Pierre, with its intricately sculpted Romanesque-Byzantine façade, begun in 1128 and restored in the 19th century; it boasts 75 statues, each in a separate niche, representing the Last Judgment. Inside, wander under a four-domed ceiling, in and out of spots of light dancing on the floor—dapples of color from the church windows. ⏱1 day. Angoulême Tourist Office, 7 bis rue du Chat - Place des Halles. ☎ 05-45-95-16-84. www.angouleme-tourisme.com.

At Home with Cognac

Medieval Cognac was a prosperous, fortified river port involved in the salt and wine trades. Fights between the English and the French over its wealth are emblematic of the era. By the Renaissance, however, Cognac enjoyed a newfound stability and notoriety as a center of art and thought. It was during this political climate that Francois I, one of France's most important kings, was born on September 12, 1494, in the Château de Cognac, now the Otard distillery. Legend has it that on a quiet night at Château de Cognac, you can still hear the songs and laughter of the lavish banquets Francois I held during his reign. During these feasts, the king organized treasure hunts through the château. Various clues laid out in different rooms guided the guests to the banquet hall where, once everyone arrived, the feast would begin.

By the 17th and 18th centuries, many persecuted Huguenots, with family ties in England and Holland, had fled to the area, keeping the wine trade with northern Europe alive, even as the salt trade disappeared. The hitch was that wine traveled badly by sea, so merchants decided to "burn" (or

distill) the wine. All brandies are made from distilled low-alcohol wine, known as *eau-de-vie*. The cognac brandy appellation pertains only to *eau-de-vie* made in France's Cognac region. In other words, all cognacs are brandies, but not all brandies are cognacs.

The Château de Cognac is now the **Otard** distillery (☎ 05-45-36-88-88; www.otard. com/gb/index.htm; 1-hr. guided tours, by appointment only, 8.50€ adults, 4€ ages 12–18, free for ages 11 and under; call for reservation). Other cognac houses worth a detour are **Rémy-Martin,** domaine de Merpins, rte. de Pons (☎ 05-45-35-76-66; www. visitesremymartin.com; guided tours last 1½ hr. to a full day; 15€–1,000€; by reservation only), and **Camus,** 29 rue Marguerite-de-Navarre (☎ 05-45-32-28-28; www.camus. fr; tour information available upon request). If you're short on time and can't do a tour, **La Cognathèque,** 8 place Jean-Monnet (☎ 05-45-82-43-31; www.cognatheque.com), is a good retail outlet that prides itself on having the widest selection from all the distilleries, though you'll pay for the convenience of having everything under one roof.

Bordeaux

Bordeaux, capital of the Gironde, is surrounded by the vines of châteaux whose names—Margaux, Mouton-Rothschild, and Latour—are synonymous with oenological excellence (see "Bordeaux for Wine Lovers," p. 562). The city center will woo you, too, from the elegant quays of the Garonne River, whose boat-bejeweled waters glisten under the sun, to the 18th-century squares, fine museums, and Gothic churches. You could squeeze this tour into 2 days, but to allow for leisurely pit stops in cafes, which are another highlight here, spend 3 days exploring this beautiful city on foot, by futuristic tram, or on a bike.

> Cafes line the streets leading to the St-Eloi bell tower in Bordeaux.

START Bordeaux is 578km (359 miles) southwest of Paris and 549km (341 miles) west of Lyon.

1 ★ **Place des Quinconces.** After a caffeine burst in any of the nearby cafes, start your day at this monumental, tree-lined expanse. Its centerpiece is a humongous decorative fountain—a 43m-high (141-ft.) ode to the genius of liberty and a metaphoric summary of French Republican values. Tram: Quinconces.

2 ★★ **Le Grand Théâtre.** Built by architect Victor Louis from 1773 to 1780 on the site of an old Gallo-Roman temple, this theater is a stunning neoclassical affair with Corinthian-style columns topped with 12 statues of muses and goddesses. Inside, the great staircase so struck architect Charles Garnier that he used it as a model for his Paris Opéra in 1862. ⏱ 15 min. (1 hr. for the tour). Place de la Comédie. ☎ 05-56-00-85-95. www.opera-bordeaux.com. Admission 3€. Tours Wed and Sat 2pm, 3:30pm, and 5pm. Tram: Grand Théâtre.

3 **Quartier des Grands Hommes.** This area is known as the "golden triangle," thanks to three expensive, 18th-century streets—cours Georges Clemenceau, cours de l'Intendance,

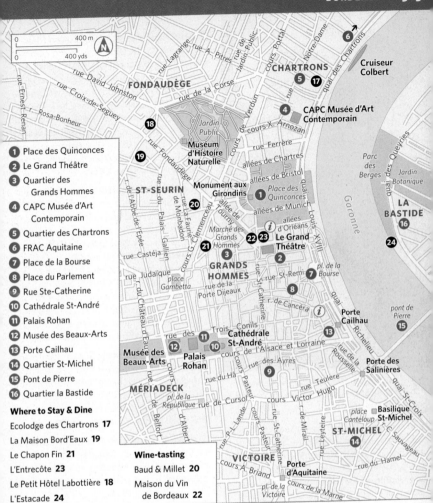

1 Place des Quinconces
2 Le Grand Théâtre
3 Quartier des Grands Hommes
4 CAPC Musée d'Art Contemporain
5 Quartier des Chartrons
6 FRAC Aquitaine
7 Place de la Bourse
8 Place du Parlement
9 Rue Ste-Catherine
10 Cathédrale St-André
11 Palais Rohan
12 Musée des Beaux-Arts
13 Porte Cailhau
14 Quartier St-Michel
15 Pont de Pierre
16 Quartier la Bastide

Where to Stay & Dine

Ecolodge des Chartrons 17
La Maison Bord'Eaux 19
Le Chapon Fin 21
L'Entrecôte 23
Le Petit Hôtel Labottière 18
L'Estacade 24

Wine-tasting

Baud & Millet 20
Maison du Vin de Bordeaux 22

and the allées de Tourny—all adorned by Bordeaux's typical flamboyant, neoclassical

Getting Around Bordeaux

The city has three easy-to-use tramlines (www.infotbc.com): A, B, and C. Tickets cost just 5.40€ (5 trips) or 10.60€ (10 trips). The city center is also easy to walk around. Or hire a bike from **Esprit Cycle Bordeaux,** 27 rue Nancel Pénard, near place Gambetta (☎ 05-56-58-78-34; www.espritcyclesbordeaux.com; from 15€/day; Mon–Fri 8:30am–7pm, Sat 10am–7pm).

facades. Just off cours de l'Intendance, **Le Passage Sarget** dates from 1878 and is wonderfully atmospheric, with old-world shops and a tearoom. Tram: Grand Théâtre.

4 ★★★ CAPC Musée d'Art Contemporain. Less conformist and somehow snappier than equivalent museums in Paris, Bordeaux's temple to contemporary art is housed in an old harbor warehouse and carries both permanent and temporary collections that run from the 1960s onward. More than 600 works by 100-plus artists are a permanent fixture here, including French painting from the 1970s and 1980s, and a myriad of audiovisual features

> *Just north of Quartier St-Michel, the medieval, bell-topped St-Eloi gate makes a pretty entrance to the old town.*

and eerie projections. The museum's buzzing roof cafe is a good spot for lunch and a coveted hangout for those wanting to see and be seen. ⏲ 2 hr. 7 rue Ferrère. ☎ 05-56-00-81-50. www.bordeaux.fr. Free admission to permanent collections; temporary collections 5€ adults, 2.50€ students. Tues and Thurs–Sun 11am–6pm; Wed 11am–8pm. Closed Mon and bank holidays. Tram: CAPC or Jardin Public.

⑤ ★★ Quartier des Chartrons. Bordeaux's old wine merchants' quarter, which has been used for wine trade since Roman times, spans quai des Chartrons to Jardin Public (pleasant public gardens prized by joggers). It was within these prestigious, often narrow streets that the city amassed its fortune. Nowadays, the area is renowned for its bohemian residents and dozens of antiques shops, especially along **rue Notre-Dame,** a paradise for treasure hunters. At no. 10, look out for the **Temple des Chartrons,** one of France's most wonderful neoclassical Protestant churches. ⏲ 1 hr. Tram: Chartrons.

⑥ FRAC Aquitaine. Bordeaux's second den of modern art takes you to the up-and-coming former docks, **Bassin à Flots.** Set in Hangar G2, the museum displays cutting-edge pieces of contemporary art by modern artists considered to have made their mark on art history. This is a perfect spot in which to start the evening in any of the Bassin's trendy bars (see "Bordeaux Nightlife," p. 587). ⏲ 1 hr. Quai Armand Lalande. ☎ 05-56-24-71-36. http://frac-aquitaine.net. Free admission. Tram: Bassin à Flots.

⑦ ★★ Place de la Bourse. On this emblematic 18th-century square, decorative masks of Bacchus and various sea gods join with filigree balconies to create riotously beautiful facades. Here you'll find the **Musée National des Douanes,** 1 place de la Bourse (☎ 05-56-48-82-82; www.musee-douanes.fr; free admission; Tues–Sun 10am–6pm), a former customs house that now contains a museum dedicated to the history of French customs officers—the only one of its kind in France and a must for French history fans. ⏲ 1 hr. Tram: Place de la Bourse.

⑧ ★★ Place du Parlement. The left-hand road from place de la Bourse leads to this postcard-perfect neoclassical square, lined with cafes. It's a fine place for coffee or lunch; from here you can watch the passing crowds in front of the pretty 1867 stone fountain. Tram: Place de la Bourse.

⑨ ★ Rue Ste-Catherine. Follow the rue du Parlement from place du Parlement to France's longest pedestrian shopping street (rue Ste-Catherine)—a full 1.5km (1 mile) of high-street shopping therapy. ⏲ 1 hr.

⑩ ★★★ Cathédrale St-André. Consecrated by Pope Urban II in 1096, this huge structure on place Pey-Berland was the scene of Eleanor of Aquitaine's marriage to the then-future King Louis VII in 1137. Separate from the rest of the church is the **★★ Tour Pey-Berland,** a jewel of flamboyant Gothic architecture topped with a gargantuan gilded copper statue of Our Lady of Aquitaine. Climb its 231 steps, and you'll be rewarded by some of the finest cityscapes in Bordeaux. ⏲ 1 hr. Place Pey-Berland. ☎ 05-56-81-26-25. http://pey-berland.monuments-nationaux. fr. Admission (tower only) 5€ adults, 3.50€ reduced. June–Sept daily 10am–1:15pm and 2–6pm; Oct–May Tues–Sun 10am–12:30pm and 2–5pm. Tram: Hôtel de Ville.

⑪ ★★ **Palais Rohan.** On the same square as the cathedral, the Palais Rohan, built in 1771, houses Bordeaux's city hall, the Hôtel de Ville. Along with the **Grand Théâtre** (② on this tour), this imposing edifice marks the introduction of neoclassicism to Bordeaux and is particularly photogenic. Tram: Hôtel de Ville.

⑫ ★★ **Musée des Beaux-Arts.** In the Hôtel de Ville's garden, Bordeaux's fine arts museum is particularly attention-grabbing thanks to an outstanding collection from the 15th to 20th centuries, with works by Perugina, Titian, Rubens, Veronese, Delacroix, and Marquet. ⊕ 1½ hr. 20 cours d'Albret, Jardin du Palais-Rohan. ☎ 05-56-10-20-56. Admission 4.50€ adults, free for students and children. Wed–Sun 11am–6pm. Tram: Hôtel de Ville.

⑬ ★★ **Porte Cailhau.** This 15th-century triumphal gate evokes Charles VIII's victory at Fornoue in Italy. It looks like something straight out of a Hans Christian Andersen novel and offers today's visitors a panoramic view over the river. ⊕ 45 min. Entrance in Place du Palais. No phone. Admission 3€. Tours June–Sept daily 2–7pm. Tram: Porte de Bourgogne.

⑭ ★★★ **Quartier St-Michel.** This predominantly medieval district is dominated by the tapered bell tower of the **Basilique St-Michel,** constructed in stages between the 14th and 16th centuries. Its north door is particularly impressive, crowned with shells, and the chapel is dedicated to St. James, with a central painting of *The Apotheosis of St. James* (1631). Just across the square (the setting for a vibrant daily food market), the **Fleche St-Michel,** erected in 1472, is the second-tallest stone tower in France (after the cathedral at Strasbourg, p. 300, ③) at 114m (374 ft.). Climb the 228 steps for sweeping cityscapes and wonderful photo opportunities. ⊕ 45 min. Place Canteloup. No phone. Admission 3€. June–Sept daily 2–7pm, Tues–Fri 10:30am–1pm. Tram: St-Michel.

⑮ ★ **Pont de Pierre.** Jutting out over the water between the St-Michel Quarter and up-and-coming Bastide (stop ⑯), this is easily one of France's prettiest bridges. Five hundred meters (1,640 ft.) long with 17 arches, it was commissioned by Napoleon in 1822 so that he could march his army across the river during his Spanish invasion campaign. Tram: Porte de Bourgogne or Stalingrad.

> *The Musée des Beaux-Arts displays a fabulous collection of paintings spanning 600 years.*

⑯ ★ **Quartier la Bastide.** For years, Bordeaux's right bank was an industrial hub, separate from the historical center. Nowadays it's one of the city's emerging districts, affording the best panoramic views over Bordeaux's riverfront from the quai des Queyries. Its banks have become a coveted spot for Sunday strolls. The **Jardin Botanique,** esplanade Linné, rue Gustave Carde (☎ 05-56-52-18-77; free admission; summer daily 8am–8pm, winter 8am–6pm), is a must for gardeners, with 10 hectares (25 acres) devoted to the conservation of local flora and biodiversity. If you can, stay in Bastide until sunset to watch Bordeaux twinkle from across the water. ⊕ 2 hr. Tram: Jardin Botanique.

Mirroir d'Eau

Hydraulic engineer Jean-Max Llorca designed the world's largest reflecting pool —literally, an inch of stagnant water pumped over a granite slab, like a melted ice-rink— opposite the place de la Bourse. The fountain first creates a mist, which, when settled, becomes an inky mirror in which the square is reflected. It's a stunning sight, especially at sunset as Bordeaux's lights begin to sparkle.

Where to Stay & Dine in Bordeaux

> *Trendy but friendly, L'Estacade restaurant offers the best views over Bordeaux, day or night.*

★★★ Ecolodge des Chartrons CHARTRONS

This antiques-filled guesthouse is typical of Bordeaux and is in a top spot for rifling through the Chartrons Quarter's antiques shops. The owners have made the place as environmentally friendly as possible, combining "green" materials such as wood fiber, cork, and wool with solar panels, water-saving faucets, and energy-efficient light bulbs. Rooms are lovely, with marshmallow mattresses and a mix of modern and classic touches. 23 rue Raze. ☎ 05-56-81-49-13. www. ecolodgedeschartrons.com. 5 units. Doubles 95€–130€. MC, V. Tram: Chartrons.

★★ La Maison Bord'Eaux JARDIN PUBLIC

Step into the cobblestone courtyard, and you're in a world where cutting-edge contemporary design and traditional 18th-century architecture create poetic harmony. Guestrooms are decorated in bold, unified colors, and a large comfy bed takes pride of place. 113 rue Dr. Albert Barraud. ☎ 05-56-44-00-45.

www.lamaisonbord-eaux.com. 6 units. Doubles 130€–200€. MC, V. Tram: Jardin Public.

★★★ Le Chapon Fin GRANDS HOMMES MODERN FRENCH

The best restaurant in town occupies an early-20th-century organic rococo monument, crafted from distressed rocks into an Art Nouveau–style grotto. The menu is just as original, with artful renditions of fresh foie gras, Pauillac lamb grilled with peppers and mushrooms, succulent crayfish and scallops braised in spices and wine, and desserts to die for. 5 rue Montesquieu. ☎ 05-56-79-10-10. Reservations required. Lunch menu 38€, dinner menu 60€–90€. MC, V. Lunch and dinner Tues–Sat. Tram: Grand Théâtre.

Travel Tip

For more places to dine, explore the quays, rue St-Rémi, and place du Parlement, all of which are filled with restaurants.

★ **L'Entrecôte** QUINCONCES *FRENCH STEAK-HOUSE* The steak here is legendary, so be prepared to wait for a table, but once the tender morsels melt on your tongue, all will be forgotten. The quality of meat isn't the only thing to write home about: The sauce, a secret recipe

Wine Tasting in Bordeaux

Nothing can beat the experience of tasting wines in the châteaux that made them (see p. 562), but you can come pretty close in the following places:

★★★ **Baud & Millet.** At this fabulous wine bar, cheeses are served with a choice of 950 wines from the vaulted cellar, and knowledgeable staff members passionately talk you through what you taste. *19 rue Huguerie.* ☎ *05-56-79-05-77. Menu 15€–30€. MC, V. Mon–Sat 10am–11pm. Tram: Quinconces.*

★★ **Maison du Vin de Bordeaux.** For simple tastings in a chic setting with white walls, modern art, and 18th-century touches, head for the **Bar à Vin,** where glasses start at 3€ (☎ 05-56-00-43-47; http://baravin.bordeaux.com; 11am–10pm). For actual wine-tasting lessons, the on-site **Ecole du Vin,** 3 cours du 30 juillet (☎ 05-56-00-22-85; http://ecole.vins-bordeaux.fr; tram: Quinconces), offers a 2-day course from 350€. Two-hour workshops, summer lessons, and evening classes are also available.

that has been handed down from mother to offspring for more than 50 years, is as tasty as can be. *4 cours du 30 juillet.* ☎ *05-56-81-76-10. www.entrecote.fr. Steak 16€, a la carte 25€. MC, V. Lunch and dinner daily. Tram: Quinconces.*

★★★ **Le Petit Hôtel Labottière** JARDIN PUBLIC Exquisitely restored to its former 18th-century glory, this city mansion's two rooms belong to a past era. The furniture and knickknacks are of museum quality. Breakfast is served in a beautiful walled garden. Don't forget to look at the painting by Pierre Lacour (1774) in the guest entrance—it's the same one as in Bordeaux's Grand Théâtre (p. 582, ❷). *14 rue Francis Martin.* ☎ *05-56-48-44-10. 2 units. Doubles 180€. MC, V. Tram: Jardin Public.*

★ **L'Estacade** BASTIDE *CONTEMPORARY FRENCH* Set across the river from the main town, this trendy restaurant, on stilts over the water, offers you a glimpse of what foreign sailors must have seen when they first cruised up the estuary into Bordeaux in the 18th century. Foodwise, expect excellent duck, steak, and seafood dishes, and wines by local producers. The lunch menu is an excellent value. *Quai de Queyries.* ☎ *05-57-54-02-50. www.lestacade. com. Lunch menu 16€, a la carte 40€. MC, V. Lunch and dinner daily. Tram: Stalingrad.*

Bordeaux Nightlife

A multitude of low-key bars congregate around **place de la Victoire** (tram: Victoire) and along the **Garonne's quays,** while **rue St-Rémi** buzzes with late-night cafes (tram: Place de la Bourse). Clever urban rehabilitation has turned the **Bassin à Flots** docks, north of the center (tram: Bassin à Flots), into a hot spot for fashionable bars and clubs. **La Dame de Shanghai,** 1 quai Armand Lalande (☎ 05-57-10-20-50; www.damedeshanghai.com), is a riverboat restaurant and nightclub dressed up like a 1930s Shanghai gentlemen's club. The dining area's authentic panache is carried on down to the dance floor on the lower deck. Just down the road, in Hangar 19, **Ice Bar,** quai de Bacalan (☎ 05-57-00-10-15; www. iceroom.fr), has, as its name suggests, a bar made entirely of ice, and serves delicious frozen cocktails.

La Rochelle

As you meander along La Rochelle's picturesque cobblestone streets, past stately mansions, fine museums, and bourgeois facades, remember this: The town has had a history of backing the wrong side. In 1628, its affiliation to the Calvinists and the English led Cardinal Richelieu (based in Brouage; see p. 555, ❼) to siege the city for 13 months—an event that saw 23,000 people starve to death within these very walls. Ironically, today La Rochelle is where most people come to overeat at the abundance of seafood restaurants around the old harbor. With 2 days here, you'll be able to dip into the town's cultural attractions and still have time to relax in shops and cafes.

> *This chic seaside town has one of the prettiest ports in France, framed by two postcard-perfect medieval towers.*

START **La Rochelle is 467km (290 miles) southwest of Paris and 183km (114 miles) north of Bordeaux.**

❶ ★★ **Le Vieux Port.** Strolling La Rochelle's old port, where boats bob in the shadow of three imposing medieval towers (stop ❷ on this tour), is akin to walking through 1,000 years of history. From a wee, 10th-century fishing village to an important port from which frigates set out to explore the New World in the 17th and 18th centuries, La Rochelle's fortified harbor has witnessed every event, including Cardinal Richelieu's murderous 1627–28 siege. Start your day with a coffee in one of the numerous cafes here, then walk along quai Valin to **rue St-Nicolas** (just behind), where arty boutiques and secondhand bookshops provide ample distraction. ⏱ 1–2 hr.

❷ ★★★ **Les Tours de La Rochelle.** At 42m (138 ft.) high, equipped with a labyrinth of stairways and corridors, the late-14th-century **Tour St-Nicolas** symbolized La Rochelle's power and fortune in its day, and originally guarded the town against surprise attacks. From its second floor you can enjoy a view of the town, the harbor, and La Rochelle's offshore islands. Just opposite, the **Tour de la Chaîne** was built in the 1300s as an anchor

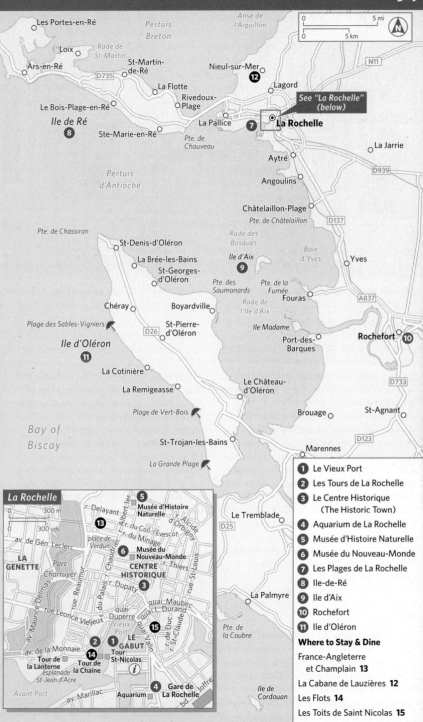

Les Portes-en-Ré
Loix
Ars-en-Ré
Rade de St-Martin
St-Martin-de-Ré
La Flotte
Le Bois-Plage-en-Ré
Rivedoux-Plage
Ile de Ré **8**
Ste-Marie-en-Ré
La Pallice
Pertuis Breton
Anse de l'Aiguillon
Nieul-sur-Mer **12**
Lagord
N11
See "La Rochelle" (below)
7 La Rochelle
La Jarrie
Aytré
D939
Pte. de Chauveau
Pertuis d'Antioche
Angoulins
Châtelaillon-Plage
D137
Pte. de Châtelaillon
Pte. de Chassiron
St-Denis-d'Oléron
La Brée-les-Bains
St-Georges-d'Oléron
Rade des Basques
Ile d'Aix **9**
Baie d'Yves
Yves
Pte. des Saumonards
Pte. de la Fumée
Fouras
A837
Chéray
Boyardville
Rade de l'Ile d'Aix
Ile Madame
Plage des Sables-Vigniers
Ile d'Oléron **11**
St-Pierre-d'Oléron
D26
Port-des-Barques
Rochefort **10**
La Cotinière
La Remigeasse
Le Château-d'Oléron
D733
Plage de Vert-Bois
Bay of Biscay
St-Trojan-les-Bains
Brouage
St-Agnant
D123
Marennes
La Grande Plage
Le Tremblade
D25
La Palmyre
Pte. de la Coubre
Ile de Cordouan

La Rochelle
r. Delayant
Musée d'Histoire Naturelle **5**
13
av. de Gén. Leclerc
place de Verdun
r. Albert-Ier
r. du Coll. l'Evescot
r. du Minage
r. d'Alcide d'Orbigny
LA GENETTE
Parc Charruyer
Musée du Nouveau-Monde **6**
CENTRE HISTORIQUE
r. Thiers
rue St-Louis
av. Maurice Delmas
rue Réaumur
r. du Palais
rue Chaudrier
r. Dupaty
3
av. Léonce Vieljeux
quai Duperré
quai Maubec
quai L. Durand
2 **1**
Vieux Port
15
rue de Duc
rue St-Claude
quai Valin
av. de la Monnaie
Tour de la Lanterne
esplanade St-Jean-d'Acre
Tour de la Chaîne
14
LE GABUT
Tour St-Nicolas
Avant Port
av. Marillac
Aquarium **4**
Gare de La Rochelle
bd. Joffre

1 Le Vieux Port
2 Les Tours de La Rochelle
3 Le Centre Historique (The Historic Town)
4 Aquarium de La Rochelle
5 Musée d'Histoire Naturelle
6 Musée du Nouveau-Monde
7 Les Plages de La Rochelle
8 Ile-de-Ré
9 Ile d'Aix
10 Rochefort
11 Ile d'Oléron

Where to Stay & Dine

France-Angleterre et Champlain **13**
La Cabane de Lauzières **12**
Les Flots **14**
Les Toits de Saint Nicolas **15**

> *Wander serendipitously through La Rochelle's historic street to find the locals' cafes, boutiques, and art galleries.*

piece for the large, forged-iron chain (hence the name) that stretched across the harbor, protecting Protestant La Rochelle from hostile Catholic warships during the French Wars of Religion. Once you've visited its eerie rooms, head up rue Sur les Murs to the ★★★ **Tour de la Lanterne,** built between 1445 and 1476. This ornate monument is named after its glazed turret, where a beacon was lit every night in order to guide ships. When it wasn't doing lighthouse duty, the tower was used as a jail, a function that would carry on into the 19th century. During your look around, spare a thought for the poor priests who were tossed from the monument's summit during the Wars of Religion, and keep your eyes peeled for the graffiti etched into the stone by the tower's former prisoners. ⏱ 2¼ hr. ☎ 05-46-41 74-13. http://la-rochelle.monuments-nationaux.fr. Admission: 8€ adults to all three towers, 6€ to each individual tower; free for ages 17 and under. Apr–Sept daily 10am–6:30pm; Oct–Mar 10am–1pm and 2:15–5:30pm.

③ **Le Centre Historique (The Historic Town).** La Rochelle's historic town beckons with bourgeois buildings, hidden churches, and arch-covered streets (look for the 200 or so gargoyles as you walk the city), which are great for shopping and strolling. The tourist office,

2 quai Georges Simenon Le Gabut (☎ 05-46-41-14-68; www.larochelle-tourisme.com), runs excellent guided tours in English with themes such as history and gastronomy. If you decide to go it alone, you'll find that the prettiest *rues,* with their old-world arcades, are **rue du Palais; rue du Temple; rue Chaudrier; and rue des Merciers,** with its half-timbered houses. Whatever you do, don't miss the **Hôtel de Ville** (City Hall), an explosion of cream-colored, flamboyant Gothic and Renaissance stonework, with busy facades and intricately carved statues. ⏱ 2 hr. City Hall, place de l'Hôtel de Ville. ☎ 05-46-51-51-51. Guided visits June and Sept and school holidays daily 3pm; July–Aug daily 4pm; Oct–May Sat-Sun 3pm. Closed some public holidays.

FrancoFolies—Music Festival

Each July, La Rochelle celebrates French music and *chanson* in a loud, colorful festival known as **FrancoFolies** (www.francofolies.fr), one of France's biggest and best popular-music celebrations. Gigs take place across town and feature all sorts of styles, from folk and rock to electronic and jazz. If you can find somewhere to stay (book very early), it's a particularly fun time to visit.

④ ★★★ kids **Aquarium de La Rochelle.** One of the best aquariums in France rises high at the water's edge in La Rochelle. It is home to an impressive array of flora and fauna from the oceans of the world: Sharks and gigantic rays are, of course, well represented. So, too, are lesser-known creatures, including bulbous frogfish, tiny spotted garden eels (which look like funny cartoon characters, sticking their snakelike heads out of the sand to catch zoo-plankton drifting on the current), and electric-blue and orange mandarin fish from the Pacific Ocean. The aquarium doubles as a marine study center and has pioneered many of the techniques used for re-creating natural habitats. The visit ends in the tropical greenhouse amid terrapins, newts, and a steamy tank of piranhas. After a quick tour of the boutique, the rooftop restaurant, **Café de l'Aquarium** (☎ 05-46-50-17-17; www.cafe-aquarium.com; 2 courses 19€, 3 courses 21€, kids menu 7.90€), ironically offers decent seafood and a fantastic panorama over the port. ⏲ 2½ hr. Quai Louis Prunier. ☎ 05-46-34-00-00. www.aquarium-larochelle.com. Admission 13€ adults, 10€ ages 3–17, free for children 2 and under. July–Aug daily 9am–11pm; Apr–June and Sept daily 9am–8pm; Oct–Mar daily 10am–8pm.

⑤ kids **Musée d'Histoire Naturelle.** In 1770, naturalist Clément Lafaille bequeathed to La Rochelle a jamboree of sculpted wooden cabinets filled with stuffed mammals, insects, and birds from his travels. Over the next 200 years, several other naturalists and ethnographers added their own collections, creating this intriguing, historical museum where more than 10,000 objects are displayed inside the 300-year-old Hôtel du Gouvernement, a stunning mansion granted to La Rochelle by Napoleon in 1808. ⏲ 1 hr. 28 rue Albert 1er. ☎ 05-46-41-18-25. www.museum-larochelle.fr. Admission 4€ adults, free for ages 17 and under. May 15–Sept Tues–Fri and 1st Sun of the month 10am–7pm, Sat–Sun and some public holidays 2–7pm, 1st Sat of the month until 9pm; Oct–May 14 Tues–Fri and 1st Sun of the month 9am–6pm, Sat–Sun and some public holidays 2–6pm, 1st Sat of the month until 9pm.

⑥ ★ **Musée du Nouveau-Monde.** Come here to learn about the history of La Rochelle and how this relatively anonymous port played a

> *Fish swim overhead in underwater corridors inside the fabulous Aquarium de La Rochelle.*

prominent role in the colonization of the New World, including North and South America and the West Indies. The 18th-century town house is rich with architectural details, and the displays trace the port's 300-year history, including LaSalle's discovery of the Mississippi Delta in 1682 and the settling of the Louisiana territory. ⏲ 1 hr. Hôtel Fleuriau, 10 rue Fleuriau. ☎ 05-46-41-46-50. Admission 4€ adults, free for ages 17 and under. Mon and Wed–Sat 10:30am–12:30pm and 1:30–6pm; Sun 3–6pm.

La Rochelle's Ports

With four ports (for fishing, trade, cruise ships, and yachts), La Rochelle is an important maritime city. Its **Port des Minimes** is the biggest yachting center on France's Atlantic coast and hosts the annual **Grand Pavois,** a vast, international nautical trade fair. The former **Bassin des Chalutiers** (now the Bassin des Grands Yachts) is also used for the **Volvo Ocean Race** (formerly the Whitbread competition).

> *The Musée d'Histoire Naturelle, with hundreds of century-old stuffed animals, is fun for budding naturalists.*

7 ★★ **Les Plages de La Rochelle.** Before you leave town, don't miss watching the sun set from one of La Rochelle's beaches. Within walking distance from the Old Port, via rue Sur les Murs and over a little bridge within La Rochelle's former fortifications, is **Plage de la Concurrence** (☎ 05-46-41-27-80), with fine sand and views onto the Tour de la Lanterne. Or head to **Plage des Minimes,** La Rochelle's biggest beach, just beyond the Minimes yachting marina (☎ 05-46-44-47-79). Amenities include restaurants, toilets, and some special-needs services. In the summer it swarms with bodies, but off-season

Day Trips from La Rochelle

From La Rochelle, the offshore islands of Ré (**8**), Aix (**9**), and Oléron (**11**) are all close enough for a day trip and provide enough sea, sand, and white-washed, cobblestone lanes to make you feel as if you're away from it all. You could even slacken the pace and stay for a couple of nights. Or stick to the mainland and head to Rochefort, La Rochelle's historic rival. Here you can wander pretty 17th-century streets, visit several quirky museums, and "fly" over the water on France's last remaining transporter bridge.

you can walk its expanses practically alone, listening to the waves break gently on the sand and watching the masts of nearby yachts poke through the horizon like a forest of totem poles.

8 ★★ **Ile de Ré.** A few kilometers off the coast of La Rochelle, this chic island—famous for its salt marshes, wildlife, bourgeois inhabitants, and fishing shacks—is ringed with 69km (43 miles) of white, sandy beaches and holds nature reserves crisscrossed with bike paths (see "Ile de Ré Bike Rental"). **St-Martin-de-Ré,** the main town, is pretty (though it can be expensive and overrun in summer), with whitewashed houses, hollyhock-lined cobblestone streets, a buzzing port, and quaint old churches. Don't miss the fortifications built by Vauban in the 1600s, 1 rue du Palais (☎ 05-46-09-58-25; Feb–Nov and Christmas holidays daily 10am–sunset, July–Aug daily 10am–11:30pm). The rickety old church bell tower offers the best vistas of the island, especially at night when everything twinkles. **Loix,** farther north, houses the island's last-standing tidal mill and a working **salt museum,** rte. de la Passe (☎ 05-46-29-06-77; www.marais-salant.com). **Ars-en-Ré** is famous for its black-and-white church tower and delectable oysters; check out the oyster farm **L'Huîtrière de Ré,** Le Martray (☎ 05-46-29-44-24;

www.huitrieredere.com). **Les Portes-en-Ré,** on the northern tip, is cherished by artists who flock here for peace and quiet. **La Couarde en Mer** is one of Ré's prettiest villages, with 5km (3 miles) of golden sands, a market, and some nifty little lanes. You could also stop at **Ste-Marie de Ré,** famous not only for its Gothic bell tower but for four unexpectedly palatable beers, served at **Bieres de Ré,** 11 ZAC des Clémorinants (☎ 05-46-43-82-63; http://bieresdere.fr). **Access** to Ile de Ré is via toll bridge (9€–17€ per car, depending on the season). Leave La Rochelle on avenue du 8 Mai 1945; then, at the Lagord island, take the second exit onto N237, then D735 (24km/15 miles).

9 ★★ **kids Ile d'Aix.** This unspoiled island, where you can move around only on foot or by bike, is where Napoleon was held before being exiled to St. Helena. Mementos of his life and military campaigns are preserved in the small but interesting **Musée Napoléon.** You can also see the camel Napoleon rode during the Egyptian campaign (along with stuffed dodos and rhinos from Africa) in the **Musée Africain** (☎ 05-46-84-66-40; www.musees-nationaux-napoleoniens.org; admission to both museums 4.50€, free 1st Sun of the month; Apr–Oct daily 9am–noon and 2–6pm; Nov–Mar Wed–Mon 9:30am–noon and 2–5pm), a curious 1930s haven of taxidermy. Aix is a center for mother of pearl, and you can learn all about the precious shell's history and admire some spectacular specimens in the

Ile de Ré Bike Rental

Cycland has 10 bicycle rental agencies on the island, with one handy address right off the toll bridge at Les Paux de Sablanceaux. Pick up some wheels here, and drop them off at any other location. Cycland also provides maps. ☎ *05-46-09-97-54. www.cycland.fr. Half-day 6.50€, full day 10€, 2 days 13€. July–Aug daily 8:45am–7pm; Sept–June daily 9:30am–12:30pm and 2–6:30pm.*

Maison de la Nacre, place de l'Eglise (☎ 05-46-84-66-17; admission 4€ adults, 1.50€ ages 9–15, free for children 8 and under; Apr–June and Sept daily 10am–12:30pm and 1–5pm, July–Aug daily 10am–6pm). To cycle around the island, **kids Cyclaix,** rue Marengo (☎ 05-46-84-58-23; www.cyclaix.com), rents a range of bikes (mountain, tandem, children's chariot), from 8.50€ a day. From La Rochelle, take N237 (toward Rochefort) and join D137/E602 (toward D937/Fouras), then D937 to Fouras (34km/21 miles); park here and catch a ferry to the Ile d'Aix (30-min. crossing from Pointe de la Fumée; ☎ 08-20-16-00-17; 0.12€/min.). Ile d'Aix Tourist Office, 6 rue Gourgaud (☎ 05-46-83-01-82; www.iledaix.fr).

10 ★★ **Rochefort.** This pretty 17th-century port, lined with the former homes of wealthy merchants, was the setting for Jacques

> *With its nature preserves laced with bike paths, Ile de Ré is popular with cyclists.*

> Car-free Ile d'Aix's rocks and beaches harbor a treasury of interesting shells.

Demy's celebrated 1967 *Les Damoiselles de Rochefort* musical, starring Gene Kelly and Catherine Deneuve. Today it's a welcoming harbor and spa town, with cafes and boutique-filled streets. Unmissable for its sheer size is the gigantic **Corderie Royale,** rue Audebert (☎ 05-46-87-81-44; www.corderie-royale. com; admission 8€; daily Apr–June and Sept 10am–7pm, July–Aug 9am–7pm, Oct–Mar 10am–12:30pm and 2–6pm; closed Dec 25 and Jan), Louis XIV's military base, built by Jean-Baptiste Colbert between 1666 and 1669 to construct the king's armada. At 374m (1,227 ft.), it was the longest military edifice of its era, mounted on a raft of oak beams to stabilize its foundations over the marshland. The length of the building reflects the space that was required to make the frigates' ropes (*cordes,* in French—hence the building's name), which were often 200m long (about 655 ft.). The Corderie was used until 1867, when the invention of metal cables rendered traditional rope obsolete. Nowadays, part of the visit includes the **Centre International de la Mer,** a marine museum and exhibition center, and the reconstruction of the kids **Hermione,** General Lafayette's frigate, which played a key role in the American War of Independence (see "The Great *Hermione,*" p. 554). While you're in Rochefort, visit France's last working transporter bridge (one of only seven in the world), the ★ kids **Pont Transbordeur de Rochefort,** rue Jacques Demy (☎ 05-46-83-30-86; www.rochefort-ocean.com; round-trip ticket 2.20€ adults, 1.20€ ages 5–11, free for children 4 and under; daily 10am–noon and 2–5pm). Until the bridge was built in 1900, the only way across the Charente River was by boat. Nowadays, it offers a 4½-minute panoramic "flight" over the water (for pedestrians or cyclists only); just turn up and ask the bridge man to

Boat Excursions

La Rochelle has great lengths of coastline for you to investigate. The tourist office (p. 590, ❸) acts as a clearinghouse for boating outfitters **Croisières Inter-Iles,** 3 promenoir des Coureauleurs, Le Gabut (☎ 08-25-13-55-00; www.inter-iles.com), and **Navipromer,** Vieux Port (☎ 06-08-31-04-62, or 05-46-34-40-20; www.navipromer.com; Apr–Sept), which run around the neighboring islands **Ile de Ré** (⑪) and **Ile d'Oléron** (p. 595), and the 19th-century offshore prison **Fort Boyard,** now used for a TV adventure game show.

Ile d'Oléron Watersports

Oléron is a top spot for watersports, from sea kayaking and body-boarding to windsurfing, diving, and jet skiing. Here's a list of outfitters to try:

DIVING

Plongée Bouteille Oléron, La Château d'Oléron. ☎ 05-46-75-08-34. www.plongeebouteilleoleron.com.

KAYAKING, JET SKIING & WINDSURFING

CNCO, 20 bd. Felix Faure, St-Trojan-les-Bains. ☎ 05-46-76-02-08. www.cnco-st-trojan.com. **Funisland,** rte. des Huitres, La Château d'Oléron. ☎ 06-68-10-55-55. **Planète Natique,** Port du Douhet, St-Georges d'Oléron. ☎ 05-46-47-96-55 or 06-17-83-94-58.

SURFING & BODYBOARDING

Moana, La Grande Plage, St-Trojan-les-Bains. ☎ 06-80-14-36-57. www.moana-surfschool.com.

take you across. The platform leaves every 10 to 15 minutes and is attached to cables suspended from the top of the bridge. From La Rochelle leave town on N237, then join D137 (toward Marennes). Exit at junction 31 (toward Marennes) and at Vergeroux join D733, which leads to Rochefort (37km/22 miles total).

11 ★★ kids **Ile d'Oléron.** France's second-biggest island has a down-to-earth seaside vibe. The southern tip is the most untamed, with sand dunes, pine forests, and decent beaches (especially at Vert Bois and Grand Plage), while the north is still mostly used for fishing, viticulture, and farming. If you're interested in *ostréiculture* (oyster farming), head to **Château d'Oléron** (off D26, then D734), watched over by Vauban's Citadel, where upon request you can visit the working ★★ **L'Oléronnaise** oyster farm (☎ 05-46-47-50-34; www.huitres-oleron.com; by appointment only). Owner Monsieur Massé's family has been braving the waves for almost a century and sells some of the best oysters in France, including juicy *fines de claires* and rare green oysters plumped up in his shallow pools. This is authentic, no-frills farming, and you'll come away with an immense admiration for the backbreaking work of oyster farmers—especially considering today's harsh economic and environmental conditions. For a more institutionalized but equally interesting visit, head north to **St-Georges d'Oléron** (along D734, then D126),

where the ★★ kids **Fort Royer** oyster farm (☎ 05-46-47-06-48; admission 4.50€ adults, 3.50€ ages 7–16, free for children 6 and under; daily July–Aug 10:30am, 3pm, and 5pm; rest of year Tues and Thurs–Sat 3pm) offers guided tours through its park and, according to the tides, can arrange walks through the marshes, along paths of crushed oyster shells, to watch workers in action. The island's other great export is salt, and **Le Grand Village Plage** in the Port des Salines pays tribute to white gold at the **Eco-Musée,** Petit Village, rue des anciennes Salines (☎ 05-46-75-82-28; admission 4€; Apr–Sept daily 9:30am–noon and 2–6pm), where tools of the trade are displayed and explained in traditional salt cabins, and workers demonstrate salt collecting. Budding seafarers can also hire a boat and set out into the lonely salt marshes to observe wild birds and learn about the local ecosystem. If you'd rather do this on foot or by bike, spend a day meandering along the grass-lined paths of the ★★★ **Marais des Bris** (Brix Marshes) in the south. These salty flats are home to a wealth of birdlife and rare orchids. Just pick up a map at the tourist office in St-Trojan-les-Bains (☎ 05-46-76-00-86; www.st-trojan-les-bains.fr). From La Rochelle, take N237 to D137 (toward Marennes); exit D137 at junction 31 (toward Marennes) and at Vergeroux join D733. Pass through Rochefort and follow signs to Ile d'Oléron (70km/40miles total).

> *Dunes are backed by pine trees along this beach on the Ile d'Oléron.*

Where to Stay & Dine in La Rochelle

> *Fronted by a heavy anchor, Les Flots seafood restaurant on La Rochelle's harbor makes a chic spot for lunch.*

★★ **France-Angleterre et Champlain** HISTORIC TOWN A 10-minute walk from the old port and La Rochelle's arcaded shops, this establishment is furnished with an endearing combination of antiques and art objects. An aromatic garden brimming with flowers makes a sweet spot for breakfast. 20 rue Rambaud. ☎ 05-46-41-23-99. www.bw-fa-champlain.com. 36 units. Doubles 75€–165€. MC, V.

★★★ **La Cabane de Lauzières** NIEUL-SUR-MER SEAFOOD This desperately charming oyster hut just outside La Rochelle looks out over the salty flats and oyster basins toward the streamline bridge to Ile de Ré. Slurp plump oysters, fresh crabs, and mussels *marinières* with home-made fries, then raise a glass of crisp white wine to the finer things in life, which come together seamlessly here—hence the tables filled with in-the-know locals. 131 rue du Port du Plomb. ☎ 09-81-87-67-01. Menus 13€–30€. Apr–June and Sept–Oct Tues–Sun, July–Aug daily noon–2:30pm and 7–10pm; closed Nov–Mar. MC, V.

★★ **Les Flots** OLD PORT CONTEMPORARY SEAFOOD Generous and iconoclastic seafood dishes by fish-wizard chef Grégory Coutanceau have made this brasserie, set at the foot of the Tour de la Chaîne, a coveted address that attracts both locals and tourists alike. Expect dishes such as roasted lobster with black truffle potato purée and king prawns in Spanish chorizo butter. Uniformed waiters make the service a chic affair. 1 rue de la Chaîne. ☎ 05-46-41-32-51. www.les-flots.com. Daily 12:15–2pm and 7:15–10pm. Menus 26€–70€. MC, V.

★★★ **Les Toits de Saint Nicolas** ST NICOLAS/OLD PORT This friendly B&B, in La Rochelle's hippest quarter, offers gorgeous soft beige and white furnishings, beds to sink into, beautifully presented soaps and towels, and a hearty breakfast delivered to your door. Two apartments also sleep three to four or five to six people (200€–300€). 1 place de la Fourche. ☎ 06-09-82-74-76 or 06-85-11-74-62. www.lestoitsdesaintnicolas.com. 3 units. Doubles 120€. MC, V (50% deposit due upon reservation).

Fast Facts

> *France's famous TGV trains can travel at around 320km (198 miles) per hour.*

Arriving & Getting Around

BY PLANE Both Bordeaux and La Rochelle have airports. The low-cost airlines **Flybe** (www.flybe.com) and **Easyjet** (www.easyjet.com) fly from the U.K. to La Rochelle (www.larochelle.aeroport.fr); **Ryanair** (www.ryanair.com) flies from Brussels, Belgium; **Aerlingus** (www.aerlingus.com) flies from Cork, Ireland. Bordeaux's Merignac airport (www.bordeaux.aeroport.fr) is served by **Air Transat** (www.airtransat.com) from Montreal and Quebec in Canada, as well as by **British Airways** (www.britishairways.com), **BMI Baby** (www.bmibaby.com), **Easyjet,** and **Ryan Air** from the U.K. **BY TRAIN** Getting to the Atlantic coast by train is easy. La Rochelle, Poitiers, and Bordeaux are all direct destinations from Paris (3 hr. from La Rochelle and Bordeaux; 1½ hr. from Poitiers), and transfers from Bordeaux leave daily for the Bassin d'Arcachon. There are even direct trains from Paris to Futuroscope (1 hr., 20 min.). A car, however, is indispensible for the Marais Poitevin and the region's smaller settlements. **BY CAR** The whole area is well serviced by highways (A10, A83, and A89) from across France, and you can rent cars at all main train stations and the historical cities. Try www.avis.com, www.hertz.com, www.citer.fr, and www.sixt.fr.

Emergency

Police ☎17; fire department and paramedics ☎18; ambulance ☎15; emergency when calling from a cell phone ☎112.

Internet

Most hotels have Wi-Fi or a communal computer with Internet access. If not, try **Cybercafé Héroique Sandwich,** 17 rue Candale, Bordeaux, near place de la Victoire (☎05-57-59-15-00), or **Cyber Corner,** 8b rue Charles Gide, Poitiers (☎05-49-41-37-06; www.cyber-corner.fr). Both are open daily until 2am.

Post Office

In La Rochelle, **La Poste,** 6 rue de l'Hôtel de Ville. Open Monday to Friday 8:30am to 6:30pm, Saturday 9am to 5pm.

Tourist Offices

Municipal tourist offices are listed at the end of the town stops in the chapter. **AQUITAINE** 23 parvis des Chartrons, Bordeaux (☎05-56-01-70-00; www.tourisme-aquitaine.fr). **BORDEAUX** 12 cours du 30 Juillet (☎05-56-00-66-00; www.bordeaux-tourisme.com). **COGNAC** 16 rue du XIV Juillet (☎05-45-82-10-71; www.tourism-cognac.com). **LA ROCHELLE** 2 quai Georges Simenon Le Gabut (☎05-46-41-14-68; www.larochelle-tourisme.com); place des Créneaux (☎05-57-55-28-28; www.saint-emilion-tourisme.com).

14
Dordogne, the Lot & Auvergne

Favorite Moments in Dordogne, the Lot & Auvergne

North of Basque Country and the Languedoc, the lush countryside of Dordogne, with its rivers, its châteaux, its golden stone, and some of the most emblematic Gallic food products—foie gras, duck, goose, and truffles—has long been a favorite destination for travelers to France. Less frequented but with charms of their own, Auvergne (to the east) has a wealth of cheese producers, volcanoes, and a rugged countryside; and the Lot (to the south) is simply a delightful getaway where the pace of life is slow, still tied to the rhythm of the vines that produce the region's gutsy Cahors red wines.

> *PREVIOUS PAGE Precarious-looking Rocamadour has clung to its perch since medieval times.*
> *THIS PAGE Enter this ultra-modern architectural crater to visit Vulcania, a fascinating volcano theme park.*

① **Eating truffles with everything in Sorges.** The **Auberge de la Truffe** makes no secret of its specialty, in a village positively obsessed with this precious fungus. See p. 618, **⑧**.

② **Admiring the mosaics at Vesunna Musée Gallo-Romain.** The Roman villa that forms the centerpiece of this Périgueux museum is all the more amazing when you consider it was buried until 1959. See p. 631, **③**.

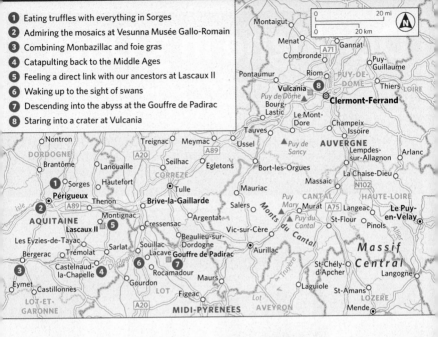

1. Eating truffles with everything in Sorges
2. Admiring the mosaics at Vesunna Musée Gallo-Romain
3. Combining Monbazillac and foie gras
4. Catapulting back to the Middle Ages
5. Feeling a direct link with our ancestors at Lascaux II
6. Waking up to the sight of swans
7. Descending into the abyss at the Gouffre de Padirac
8. Staring into a crater at Vulcania

3 Combining Monbazillac and foie gras.
How did the French figure out that grapes rotted to ambrosial sweetness would pair so perfectly with a special goose-liver pâté? Dordogne offers many chances to answer that question, not least at the Château Monbazillac. See p. 617.

4 Catapulting back to the Middle Ages.
The Château de Castelnaud's war museum demonstrates the use of a huge, working *trebuchet* catapult. See p. 621.

5 Feeling a direct link with our ancestors at Lascaux II. No photographs can prepare you for seeing prehistoric cave art in its three-dimensional state. See p. 602, 2.

6 Waking up to the sight of swans. They glide down the Dordogne River, straight out of a fairy tale, at the magical Château de la Treyne. See p. 625.

7 Descending into the abyss at the Gouffre de Padirac. A deep descent, then a ride in an underground gondola past stalactites and stalagmites, is somehow reminiscent of Dante's *Inferno*. See p. 604, 2.

> Saucisson sec (cured sausage) is the pride of the Dordogne, Lot, and Auvergne regions.

8 Staring into a crater at Vulcania.
The star of the Auvergne's science park, near the Chaîne des Puys, is a lifesize, bubbling, steaming, and spitting volcanic crater. The real though inactive crater at the top of Puy Pariou—a nearby climb—isn't bad either. See p. 627, 2.

Dordogne in 3 Days

With just 3 days in the heart of the Périgord—which is what the French prefer to call Dordogne and its surrounding region—you'll have just enough time to visit the regional capital, Périgueux; the cave paintings at Lascaux; and medieval Sarlat. En route, however, you'll pass many fine châteaux, prehistoric remains, and Roman ruins, and you'll have the opportunity to sample some of the regional delicacies that draw gastronomes in droves to this tiny pocket of southwestern France.

> *Place de la Liberté is where the action takes place on market days in Sarlat.*

START **Périgueux** is 550km (342 miles) south of Paris and 130km (81 miles) east of Bordeaux. TRIP LENGTH 65km (40 miles).

① ★★ **Périgueux.** Although it's a backwater, visitors flock to the Dordogne capital, drawn by its natural beauty, Roman remains, and culinary treats such as *foie gras* (goose liver), *oie* (goose), *canard* (duck), and *truffes* (truffles). ⏲ 1 day. For detailed information on Périgueux, see p. 630.

On Day 2, leave Périgueux via N221, join A89 east (toward Clermont-Ferrand) to exit 17, and follow signs to Montignac (55km/34 miles).

② ★★★ **Lascaux II.** Dordogne's prehistoric artwork, from around 17,000 years ago, is world-renowned as the premier example of cave painting. The volume of visitors was hastening deterioration of the images, so the originals were closed to the public and painstakingly recreated at Lascaux II. This nearby

Where to Stay & Dine

For hotels and restaurants in Périgueux, see p. 632; in Sarlat, see p. 609; elsewhere in the Dordogne, see p. 625 and 629.

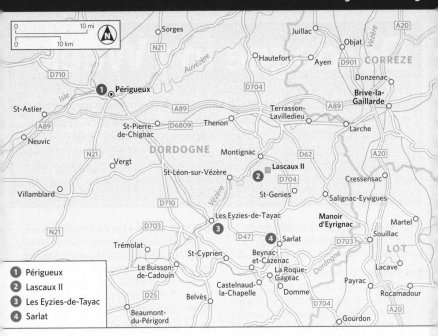

1 Périgueux
2 Lascaux II
3 Les Eyzies-de-Tayac
4 Sarlat

cave includes more than 200 paintings, in a 39m (128-ft.) display, rendered with the same level of detail as the originals. Only 2,000 visitors can enter per day, on a first-come, first-served system, so arrive early to the booking office in Montignac (or at the site itself Oct–Easter). ⏱ Tour 40 min. 2 km (1¼ miles) south of Montignac. Booking office, place du Cinéma, Montignac, near the tourist office. ☎ 05-53-05-65-65. www.lascaux.culture.fr. Admission 8.80€ adults; 5.30€ reduced; 6€ ages 6–16; free for children 5 and under. Easter–June and Sept Tues–Sun 9:15am–6pm; July–Aug daily 9am–7pm; Oct–Easter (at the Lascaux II site itself) Tues–Sun 10am–12:30pm and 2–5:30pm.

Return to Montignac, and pick up D65 and D706 southwest to Les Eyzies (21km/13 miles).

❸ **Les Eyzies-de-Tayac.** This is generally considered to be the prehistoric capital of the world. An abundance of excavations has revealed the area to have been inhabited for the last 400,000 years. It's worth visiting just to see one of the world's most respected repositories of prehistoric artifacts, the **Musée National de Préhistoire** (National Museum of Prehistory). ⏱ 1 day. See p. 607, ❺.

From Les Eyzies, take D47 east to Sarlat (20km/12 miles).

❹ ★★ **Sarlat.** Sarlat's beautifully preserved medieval town has been used as the location for so many films, it now hosts its own film festival in November (www.ville-sarlat.fr/festival). Sarlat was in fact the first town in France to benefit from the Malraux preservation order, which also saved Paris's Marais district from developers, and today 77 buildings are protected here. It's built in a dip, so park in one of the lots outside the town center and descend one of the narrow staircases to Sarlat's pedestrian-friendly streets and squares. The Carolingian **Abbaye de Sarlat** was created in the 14th century to help smother the Cathay heresy that had swept southern France. The **Cathédrale St-Sacerdos,** place du Peyrou (☎ 05-53-61-45-45; www.sarlat.fr; free admission; daily 10am–6pm), is far from the best cathedral in the country, but worth a visit to see the ornate turreted tower. **Place de la Liberté** is home to a Wednesday and Saturday morning market, one of the area's best. ⏱ 1 day. Sarlat Tourist Office, 3 rue Tourny. ☎ 05-53-31-45-45. www.sarlat.fr. See also p. 617, ❻.

Dordogne in 1 Week

With a week in Dordogne, you'll have time to explore castles, caveman art, culinary marvels, Christian sites, and beautiful green countryside (not unlike that of southern England, which may explain why the English were so keen to hold onto old Aquitaine). It's a good idea to familiarize yourself with this itinerary before you travel, because certain prehistoric sites here are lined with people regretting they hadn't planned their trips better and made reservations ahead of time.

START Sarlat is 530km (329 miles) south of Paris and 187km (116 miles) east of Bordeaux. TRIP LENGTH 365km (227 miles).

1 ★★ **Sarlat.** This famously cinematic 14th-century town is on France's Tentative List for UNESCO World Heritage nomination, thanks to its superlatively restored medieval old town, with narrow, mazelike streets full of surprises. Sarlat itself doesn't have many other sites to visit, but a concentration of attractions lie within a few miles. **Château de Beynac** (p. 620) and, just across the river, ★★★ kids **Château de Castelnaud** (p. 621), are very nearby. Or just spend a few hours in the lovely riverside village of ★★ **La Roque-Gageac,** where you can take a trip on a traditional Dordogne *gabare* boat (☎ 05-53-29-40-44; www.gabarres.com). ⏱ 1 day. See p. 603, **4**, and 617, **6**.

On Day 2, head for the Gouffre de Padirac, 66km (41 miles) southeast of Sarlat. Driving south out of Sarlat, follow signs to Souillac on D703, pick up D803 east to Martel, then drive south on D840, branching off after 4.5km (3 miles) to Veyssou and Miers. From Miers follow signs to the Gouffre de Padirac.

2 ★★ kids **Gouffre de Padirac.** The Gouffre de Padirac (Padirac Chasm) may not have any cave paintings, but staring into its abyss is a spectacular, adrenaline-pumping experience. You'll descend nearly 100m (328 ft.) through the gaping, 35m-wide (115-ft.) maw of this hole in the ground, using either the elevator or the stairs. Once down, you'll take part of the trip by gondola on the navigable subterranean river system. There are more than 40km (25 miles) of galleries here, but just 2km (1¼

> Learn all about medieval warfare at the fortified Château de Castelnaud.

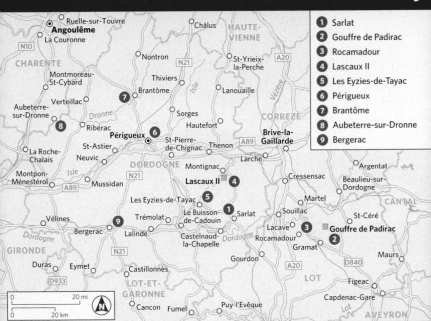

1. Sarlat
2. Gouffre de Padirac
3. Rocamadour
4. Lascaux II
5. Les Eyzies-de-Tayac
6. Périgueux
7. Brantôme
8. Aubeterre-sur-Dronne
9. Bergerac

miles) have been opened up for the 90-minute tour. The rock formations, startling river system, and atmospheric lighting make this one of the world's best caves to visit. The ticket line is usually long, so arrive early if you can. ⏲ 90 min. Rte. D90, Padirac. ☎ 05-65-33-64-56. www.gouffre-de-padirac.com. Admission 9.20€ adults, 6€ reduced. Aug daily 8:30am–6:30pm; Apr 3–July and Sept–Nov 7 times vary; closed Nov 8–Apr 2.

From Gouffre de Padirac, take D673 west to Rocamadour (10km/6¼ miles).

③ ★★★ **Rocamadour.** This collection of churches, known as the Cité Réligieuse, placed halfway up a cliff with a castle on top, is a staggering sight. Hard as it is to believe that anyone would choose to build a town in such a risky location, it's even more incredible that the settlement has withstood the ravages of nearly a millennium. Rocamadour gained fame in the 12th century, when the supposedly pristine corpse of St. Amadour (the biblical Zacchaeus) was found there, leading kings from across Western Europe to march up the 216 steps to pay tribute. During the Wars of Religion, Protestant Huguenots destroyed the saint's remains, so what you see in the

> Enter this gate in Rocamadour and prepare for a long, steep climb to the top.

> *The discovery of this prehistoric art in Lascaux forced us to reinterpret what we knew about our prehistoric ancestors.*

subterranean **Chapelle St-Amadour** is just a replica. Rocamadour is nonetheless an important staging post on the Santiago de Compostela pilgrimage route, as it has been for centuries. There are more than a few ecclesiastical buildings in the Cité Réligieuse, but the star is the Black Madonna in **Chapelle Notre-Dame,** reported to have cured sick believers. Atop the cliff is the 14th-century **Château de Rocamadour,** which was well-restored in the 19th century as the local bishops tried to revive interest in the nearly abandoned village. There's just one main street in town, lined with fine medieval houses and ornate gateways. ⏱ 3 hr. Rocamadour Tourist Office, Hôtel de Ville, rue Roland-le-Preux. ☎ 05-65-33-62-59. www.rocamadour.com. Free admission to Cité Réligieuse. Elevator to Cité Réligieuse 2€ one way, 3€ return. Feb–Apr and Oct daily 8:30am–6pm; May–June and Sept daily 8:30am–7pm;

July–Aug daily 8:30am–8pm; first 2 weeks Nov and Christmas holidays daily 9am–7pm. Closed second 2 weeks Nov and Jan.

Return to Sarlat to spend the night (55km/34 miles). On Day 3, take D704 north to Montignac and Lascaux II (27km/17 miles). GPS users beware: There's another Montignac, south of Bordeaux.

④ ★★★ **Lascaux II.** This impressive reconstruction of the world's greatest concentration of cave paintings conveys a vivid sense of the real Lascaux artwork, which had to be sealed up in order to preserve it for science. It bears repeating that an early start is essential to get tickets, as they cannot be booked in advance. ⏱ Tour 40 min. 2 km (1¼ miles) south of Montignac. Booking office, place du Cinéma, Montignac, near the tourist office. ☎ 05-53-05-65-65. www.lascaux.culture.fr. Admission

8.80€ adults; 5.30€ reduced; 6€ ages 6–16; free for children 5 and under. Easter–June and Sept Tues–Sun 9:15am–6pm; July–Aug daily 9am–7pm; Oct–Easter (at the Lascaux II site itself) Tues–Sun 10am–12:30pm and 2–5:30pm. See also p. 602, **2**.

From Montignac, take D65 and D706 southwest to Les Eyzies (21km/13 miles).

5 Les Eyzies-de-Tayac. The village is basically one street backed by protruding ridges and pockmarked cliff facades, but Les Eyzies-de-Tayac serves as the center for the abundance of prehistoric sites and painted caves throughout the Vézère Valley. It's also home to one of the world's best collections of Stone Age artifacts, the **Musée National de Préhistoire** (National Museum of Prehistory), rue du Musée (☎ 05-53-06-45-45; www.musee-prehistoire-eyzies.fr; admission 4.50€ adults, 3€reduced; July–Aug daily 9:30am–6:30pm, June and Sept Wed–Mon 9:30am–6pm, Oct–May Wed–Mon 9:30am–12:30pm and 3–5:30pm). Both the museum and the brand-new **Prehistory Welcome Center,** 30 rue du Moulin (☎ 05-53-06-06-97; www.pole-prehistoire.com), dispense literature to entice you into extending your stay and visiting other prehistoric sites in the Vézère Valley, 15 of which are UNESCO World Heritage sites. The valley also encompasses two troglodyte cities: **La Roque St-Christophe,** Peyzec-le-Moustier (☎ 05-53-50-70-45; www.roque-st-christophe.com; admission 7€ adults, 4€ ages 12–15, 3€ ages 5–11; Feb–Mar and Oct–Nov 11 10am–6pm, Apr–June and Sept 10am–6:30pm, July–Aug 10am–8pm, Nov 12–Jan 2–5pm), and **La Madeleine,** Tursac (☎ 05-53-46-36-88; www.village-la-madeleine.com; admission 5.50€ adults, 3.50€ children; July–Aug daily 9:30am–7pm, Sept–June daily 10am–6pm). Both were inhabited since prehistoric times and until very recently: La Madeleine was not deserted until the 1920s, and was last used by *Résistants* in World War II. ⏱5 hr. Les Eyzies Tourist Office, 19 av. de la Préhistoire. ☎ 05-53-06-97-05. www.leseyzies.com. See also p. 603, **3**.

From Les Eyzies on Day 4, take D47 and D710 northeast to Périgueux (45km/28 miles).

6 ★★ Périgueux. In the capital of Dordogne, you can sample some of the region's calorific specialties amid medieval streets or even

> *In summer, Périgueux's narrow, shaded streets provide welcome respite from the midday sun.*

Roman ruins. ⏱1 day. For detailed information on Périgueux, see p. 630.

From Périgueux on Day 5, take D939 north to Brantôme (26km/16 miles).

7 ★★ Brantôme. The village of Brantôme lives up to its moniker as "the Venice of Périgord." This gorgeous spot along the Dronne River, engulfed by lushly wooded hills and weeping willows, makes an ideal setting for the contemplative life. Founded in the 8th century by Charlemagne is the Benedictine **Abbaye St-Pierre de Brantôme,** place d'Abbaye (☎ 05-53-05-80-63; www.ville-brantome.fr; free admission; summer daily 10am–7pm, hours vary at other times). The abbey was nearly demolished during the Hundred Years' War, but it was rebuilt in the 15th century and went on to become one of the Aquitaine's most thriving monastic communities. The Romanesque bell tower remains, one of the oldest in France; its Gothic additions are in fine form. There are also a couple of fine-arts museums in town: the **Musée Fernand Desmoulin,** in the abbey, featuring the works of engraver Fernand Desmoulin, and the unique **Musée Reve et Miniatures** (Museum of Dreams and Miniatures), 8 rue Puyjoli (☎ 05-53-35-29-00; admission 6€ adults, 4.50€ reduced; July–Aug daily 11am–6pm, Sept–June hours vary), which showcases dolls, miniatures, and toys. The Sunday morning market and winter truffle markets in the village hall are fantastic, and on Friday nights in July and August water-jousting takes place on gondolas. All that said, you'll probably be happy enough just walking around this postcard-pretty village and lingering on its cafe terraces. Meandering around the nearby villages by car is also a pleasure; you can take in St-Jean-de-Côle, one of the Plus Beaux Villages de France, and the small Renaissance

> If you're a wine lover, stop by Bergerac's Maison du Vins, set in the former Récollets cloister (p. 616, ④).

Château de Puyguilhem (p. 623). ⏱ 1 day. Brantôme Tourist Office, bd. Charlemagne. ☎ 05-53-05-80-52. www.valdedronne.com. See also p. 618, ⑨.

On Day 6, take D78 southwest from Brantôme, passing the Château de Bourdeilles (p. 621), turn right onto D710, and continue west to Ribérac to pick up D20 west to Aubeterre-sur-Drônne (52km/33 miles).

⑧ ★ **Aubeterre-sur-Drônne.** Also on the list of Most Beautiful Villages in France, this medieval hamlet is known for its striking architecture set against white chalk cliffs; most of the houses are composed of that same white stone and have been expertly renovated. The main draw is ★ **Eglise St-Jean,** also known as the **Eglise Monolithe,** on rue St-Jean (☎ 05-45-98-65-06; www.aubeterresurdronne.com; admission 5€ adults, 2€ reduced; summer daily 10am–6pm, hours vary otherwise), which was carved out of the hillside cliff in the 5th century. It's Europe's largest subterranean church, with a 20m-high (66-ft.) nave and a Roman reliquary, unearthed in 1958, that houses more than 80 sarcophagi. **Eglise St-Jacques,** rue St-Jacques (☎ 05-45-98-50-33; June–Sept daily 9:30am–12:30pm and 2–7pm, Oct–May 9:30am–12:30 and 2–6pm), is a Romanesque 11th-century edifice, filled with sculpture and decorated with Moorish motifs. ⏱ 1 day. Aubeterre-sur-Drônne Tourist Office, 16 place Ludovic Trarieux. ☎ 05-45-98-50-33. www.aubeterresurdronne.com.

Retrace your route to Ribérac and pick up D709 south to Bergerac for the night (66km/41 miles).

⑨ **Bergerac.** Spend the morning strolling around Bergerac's old town, then have lunch and head into the vineyards for the afternoon. In the evening try another one of the many wonderful restaurants in town, and take a stroll around **Vieux Port** (Old Port), which was built in the 19th century and served as the exportation point for Bergerac's great wines. ⏱ 1 day. See p. 616, ④.

If you wish to return to Sarlat, follow the Dordogne River eastward (74km/46 miles). It's a main road that is easy to follow (but changes its number too many times to note here).

Where to Stay & Dine in Dordogne

> *The elegant Hôtel le Cro-Magnon is named after the ancestors of modern humans who lived in Les Eyzies 35,000 years ago.*

★ **Chartreuse du Bignac** BERGERAC *REGIONAL FRENCH* This four-star, 17th-century country manor 10km (6¼ miles) southeast of Bergerac is set amid fragrant prune groves with extensive views of trees and farmland. Rooms are comfortable and stylishly decorated, and the restaurant serves meals made from ingredients bought in the morning. Le Bignac, St-Nexans. ☎ 05-53-22-12-80. www.abignac.com. 12 units. Doubles 145€–300€ AE, MC, V.

★★★ **Château les Merles** BERGERAC *GASTRONOMIC* Set in an 18th-century mansion, amid forests and hills, the Château les Merles, 9km (5⅔ miles) east of Bergerac on D660, affords a peak dining and lodging experience. The service is impeccable; the gourmet restaurant, **La Bruyère Blanche,** features fine cuisine and even better wine; and there's a golf course on-site. 3 chemin des Merles, Tuilières, Mouleydier. ☎ 05-53-63-13-42. www.lesmerles.com. 15 units. Doubles 145€–255€. Main courses 25€–39€. AE, DC, MC, V. Lunch and dinner daily.

★ **Clos la Boetie** SARLAT Clos la Boetie is a four-star stunner located in an 18th-century mansion with amenities such as a spa center, a heated pool, a sauna, and much more. Rooms have four-poster beds, and the terrace has views of the garden. 95 av. de Selves. ☎ 05-53-29-44-18. www.closlaboetie-sarlat.com. 11 units. Doubles 210€–260€. AE, MC, V

Hostellerie du Passeur LES EYZIES *REGIONAL FRENCH* This old, ivy-covered manor house by the river is decorated lavishly and has a very good restaurant. Place de La Mairie. ☎ 05-53-06-97-13. www.hostellerie-du-passeur.com. 19 units. Doubles 92€–120€. Menus 32€–49€. AE, MC, V. Lunch and dinner daily.

★ **Hostellerie la Roseraie** MONTIGNAC *REGIONAL FRENCH* This romantic hotel is set in a 19th-century mansion, with hard-to-find amenities such as a 100-year-old rose garden, a waterfront terrace, and a swimming pool. Rooms

More Hotels & Restaurants

For additional hotels and restaurants in Périgueux, see p. 632; in Sarlat, see p. 609; elsewhere in the Dordogne, see p. 625 and 629.

> *Smell the roses and listen to the buzzing of the bees in Hostellerie la Roseraie's garden.*

are plush, with individualized decor in soothing pastel colors. The restaurant is a great way to sample the local fare in style. 11 place d'Armes. ☎ 05-53-50-53-92. www.laroseraie-hotel.com. 14 units. Doubles 75€–170€. Menus 25€–50€. MC, V. Lunch and dinner daily. Closed Nov–Easter.

Hôtel de Selves SARLAT
The three-star Hôtel de Selves is thoroughly modern, decorated in soft Spanish colors, and built around a lovely park. Ask for a room with a terrace, and enjoy a drink at the piano bar before (or after) walking around historic Sarlat. 93 av. de Selves. www.selves-sarlat.com. 40 units. Doubles 83€–145€. MC, V.

★ Hôtel la Couleuvrine SARLAT REGIONAL FRENCH
In the heart of Sarlat, La Couleuvrine serves as a restaurant, bistro/wine bar, and hotel. Part of the building is in the last remaining tower from the medieval town wall, and a warren of corridors lead to the 28 rooms, which feature beams, toile de Jouy, and antique desks and wardrobes. Superior room no. 22, with its view over the square, is particularly charming. The attractive restaurant has a fireplace, and the menus of Périgord specialties will not disappoint. 1 place de la Bouquerie. ☎ 05-53-59-27-80. www.la-couleuvrine.com. 28 units. Doubles 54€–72€. 3-course menus 19€–26€. AE, DC, MC, V.

Hôtel la Flambée BERGERAC
On the doorstep of the Pécharmant vineyards, this wisteria-clad hotel has an outdoor pool and a lovely garden. As suggested by its name, the restaurant serves desserts, such as *mirabelles chaud-froid,* doused in Cognac or Armagnac and set afire. Rte. de Périgueux, 49 av. Marceau-Feyry. ☎ 05-53-57-52-33. http://laflambee.com. 20 units. Doubles 62€–88€. Main courses 10€–18€; menus 17€–35€. MC, V. Lunch and dinner daily.

★ Hôtel le Cro-Magnon LES EYZIES REGIONAL FRENCH
In 1868, Cro-Magnon man was discovered on the grounds of this three-star hotel, originally built as a stagecoach inn in 1850. Rooms are comfortable, and common areas include a garden and a parlor with a huge fireplace. Some of the corridors to the rooms are hewn from surrounding bedrock. 54 av. de la Préhistoire. ☎ 05-53-06-97-06. www.hostellerie-cro-magnon.com. 15 units. Doubles 85€–90€. Menus 23€–43€. AE, MC, V. Lunch and dinner daily.

kids Hôtel le Lascaux MONTIGNAC
This modest hotel has a large garden and terrace restaurant, free parking, and a children's playground, making it ideal for families visiting the caves. 109 av. Jean Jaurès, Montignac. 11 units. Doubles 57€–67€. MC, V.

★★ **Le Grand Bleu** SARLAT *GASTRONOMIC*
For good reason, our favorite restaurant in Sarlat earned a Michelin star because of its superb food, which adapts such local products as beef, foie gras, and truffles with Szechuan spices, Japanese styles, and reworked favorites such as Périgordine sauce. The wine list is extensive, and the modern artwork is a pleasant juxtaposition with the ancient stone building and huge fireplace. 43 av. de la Gare. ☎ 05-53-31-08-48. www.legrandbleu.eu. 3-course meal 33€–90€. AE, MC, V. Lunch Thurs–Sun, dinner Tues–Sat.

★★ **Le Moulin de l'Abbaye** BRANTOME *GASTRONOMIC* Sitting on a river, in part of the town's ivy-swathed Benedictine cloister, this hotel-restaurant affords views of the town's right-angled bridge, the ancient bell tower, and the abbey. Rooms are not overly large, but they are air-conditioned and stylish. If you don't eat at the restaurant here you'll wish you had, as you spy happy guests sitting at candlelit tables on the riverside terrace. It's one of the best places to eat in a town that doesn't lack for great restaurants. 1 rte. de Bourdeilles. www.moulinabbnaye.com. ☎ 05-53-05-80-22. 19 units. Doubles from 210€. Main courses 22€, chef's menu of the day 38€. AE, DC, MC, V. Lunch and dinner daily.

Le Quatre Saisons SARLAT *REGIONAL FRENCH*
A beautiful, rustic setting complements the excellent traditional cuisine, which takes advantage of the best local seasonal ingredients. 2 côte de Toulouse. ☎ 05-53-29-48-59. www.4saisons-sarlat-perigord.com. Main courses 15€–27€. MC, V. Lunch Fri–Tues, dinner Thurs–Tues.

★ **Le Vieux Logis** TREMOLAT *FRENCH*
On a former tobacco plantation, Michelin-starred ★ **Le Vieux Logis** has been in the same family for nearly 5 centuries. (An offshoot bistro serves French food in tapas-style portions for travelers on a tighter budget.) The property also has a four-star hotel, so you can expect top service and elegant decor along with your meal. ☎ 05-53-22-80-06. www.vieux-logis.com. 6-course meal 72€. Lunch and dinner daily.

L'Imparfait BERGERAC *REGIONAL FRENCH*
This fine restaurant in the Récollets Cloisters

> *Bruyère Blanche, the restaurant at Château les Merles, near Bergerac.*

serves dishes made from the best ingredients available from the surrounding countryside. It's a great value for the money. 8 rue des Fontaines. ☎ 05-53-57-47-92. www.imparfait.com. 3-course menu 24€–29€. MC, V. Lunch and dinner daily.

Relais de Moussidière SARLAT
Just outside Sarlat, this luxury three-star hotel will transport you back more than a few centuries. The grounds are gorgeous; the rooms are full of fascinating knickknacks, many of them historic; and breakfast is included in the price. Moussidière Basse. ☎ 05-53-28-28-74. www.hotel-moussidiere.com. 35 units. Doubles 126€–176€. AE, MC, V.

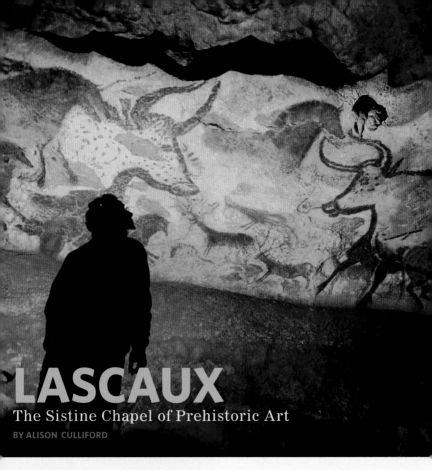

LASCAUX
The Sistine Chapel of Prehistoric Art
BY ALISON CULLIFORD

PAINTED AND ENGRAVED NEARLY 19,000 YEARS AGO, the Lascaux caves are a pantheon of prehistoric art, encompassing nearly 2,000 depictions of animals, human abstractions, and symbols, covering almost every available surface of a cave interior near Montignac in the Dordogne. The artistry, the archaeological evidence of tools used by the painters, and the philosophical questions raised by the images suggest the paintings embody the flowering of a civilization akin to the European Renaissance.

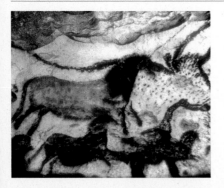

The Artists

Working by the light of their flickering tallow candles, the Lascaux painters were able to animate their subjects more dynamically than any other artists until the Renaissance. They grasped the anatomy of the beasts around them and made them seem to move—running, swimming, and necking affectionately. Most significantly, they mastered perspective and used shading to create depth. They also used natural irregularities in the stone to create sculptural effects that become clear only in candlelight. The composition of the huge animal friezes is also masterful, leading the prehistorian Henri Breuil to dub Lascaux the "Sistine Chapel of Prehistoric Art."

Interpretations

Archaeology shows that these caves were not used for human shelter but were set aside for whatever spiritual purpose the paintings served. The composition and layers of the large friezes always follow the same pattern: horses, followed by bulls, then deer, then bears. Each of these animals gives birth in a different season: spring, summer, autumn, and winter, suggesting that the paintings are an attempt to link biological with cosmic time. Prehistorian Norbert Aujoulat suggests that they're the first great book of mythologies, an early human attempt to understand the creation of the world.

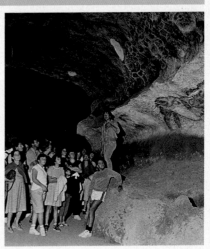

Lascaux II

Lascaux was permanently closed in 1963, because carbon dioxide exhaled by millions of visitors was deteriorating the paintings. The original cave is now a controlled environment accessible only to the scientists who monitor it. In 1983 the facsimile Lascaux II opened in a cave 200m (655 ft.) from the original. For 11 years, the artist Monique Peytral, using only the tools and techniques of the original painters, painstakingly recreated the artwork. Lascaux II contains the "Great Hall of the Bulls" and the "Painted Gallery"—the two most monumental sections of the Lascaux complex. Its nine friezes depict the black bear, the mysterious "unicorn," and the great black bull, all with other animals layered in. Running horses, ibexes, and deer overlap in perpetual movement like a stampede on an African plain. A cultural treasure in itself, Lascaux II allows you to experience the awe of the four French teenagers who, with their dog, Robot, first stumbled on this wonder of the world in 1940.

The Tools & Materials

Lascaux is one of only two caves in France adorned with prehistoric paintings, rather than with engravings and drawings. The hard, rough walls in sections of the caves made engraving difficult but were ideal for the application of color. Artists drew outlines in wood carbon and painted them with pigments, which have been found in tablet form, made from metallic oxides such as iron and manganese. Archaeologists have unearthed engraving tools made of silex and bone, suggesting that the artists crafted specific tools in order to achieve fine, precise lines. Even more impressive is the evidence of a lighting system: more than 100 clay and limestone lamps that burn animal fat. The conundrum of how the artists painted 3.5m (11½ ft.) from the ground remains unanswered.

Dordogne for Food & Wine Lovers

The southwest is widely acclaimed as the most gastronomic region of France, and the Dordogne is its epicenter, where common folk dine like royalty on local foie gras, truffles, duck, and goose—all washed down with the region's Bergerac wines or Bordeaux. Finely honed traditions and earthy origins give Périgordin cuisine its edge: Those truffles that reach the menus of the finest palace hotels in Paris come from these soils, where pigs or dogs rout them out of the ground and peasants sell them at boisterous auctions in the village hall. Start this tour south of Dordogne, in order to take in two other hallmarks of southwestern French food and drink: prunes and Armagnac.

> Prunes have been Agen's major export for centuries. You can find old tins and jars in antique shops and bars.

START Eauze is 740km (441 miles) south of Paris and 138km (86 miles) west of Toulouse. TRIP LENGTH 343km (213 miles).

1 Eauze. Situated in the Gers *département* south of Dordogne, Eauze is engaged in a protracted dispute with Condom (**2**, right) over which town is the true "Capital of Armagnac." In any case, the vineyards of Eauze are fantastic, and the myriad Armagnac wineries here

will gladly permit you a taste or three. This town of 4,000 people has a lot more rustic charm than the small city of Condom, and high season features a packed schedule of country markets, wine contests, fairs, and tasting sessions. As the center of the former province of Novempopulania, the town is rich in Gallo-Roman history. You'll find ancient treasures at the recently opened **Musée Archéologique,** place de la République (www.mairie-eauze.fr;

1	Eauze
2	Condom
3	Agen
4	Bergerac
5	Trémolat
6	Sarlat
7	Périgueux
8	Sorges
9	Brantôme

admission 4.50€ adults, 2.50€ reduced; Jan–Sept Wed–Mon 10am–noon and 2–6pm, Oct–Dec Wed–Mon 2–5pm). ⏱ Half-day. Eauze Tourist Office, place de la République. ☎ 05-62-09-83-30. www.tourisme-eauze.com.

From Eauze, drive northeast on D931 to Condom (28km/17 miles).

2 Condom. Condom is the production center for Armagnac. A close cousin to Cognac, which is made farther north near Bordeaux, Armagnac is considered a finer *digestif*. You can learn more about the distillation process, brought to life by some impressive old distilling vats, at the **Musée de l'Armagnac,** 2 rue

Jules Ferry (☎ 05-62-28-47-17; www.condom. org; admission 2.20€ adults, 1.10€ reduced; Apr–Oct Wed–Mon 10am–noon and 3–6pm, Nov–March Wed–Sun 2–5pm). ⏱ Half-day. Condom Tourist Office, 50 bd. de la Libération. ☎ 05-62-28-00-80. www.tourisme-tenareze.com.

From Condom, take D931 northeast to Agen (40km/25 miles).

Where to Stay & Dine

For hotels and restaurants in Périgueux, see p. 632; in Sarlat, see p. 609; elsewhere in Dordogne, see p. 625 and 629.

> *After prunes, Agen's claim to fame is foie gras made from the fattened livers of chaps like these.*

> *Vines surround this stone store on a Pécharmant wine estate near Bergerac.*

❸ Agen. In the Lot-et-Garonne *département* of Aquitaine, Agen is the self-proclaimed Prune Capital of France. You'll find a bowl of free prunes at the local tourist office, and in September you can attend the annual Prune Festival. Of course, *pruneaux d'Agen* are nothing like the slimy fruit that comes out of tins; semi-dried, the local prunes are firm and sticky and wonderful cooked with pork. Spend the morning checking out the **Musée de Pruneaux,** on a farm called Berino Martinet, in Granges-sur-Lot, 10km (6¼ miles) outside town (☎ 05-53-84-00-69; www.musee-du-pruneau.com; admission 3.70€, free for children 11 and under; Mon–Sat 9am–noon and 2–7pm, Sun 3–7pm). After lunch, head to **La Ferme de Souleilles** farm in Frespech (☎ 05-53-41-23-23; www.souleilles-foiegras.com; admission 4€, free for children 11 and under; Mon–Sat 10am–7pm, Sun 3pm–7pm). There Yves and Geneviève Boissière continue the 4,500-year-old tradition of making foie gras. An on-site museum explores the process and history of the practice. Anyone who finds foie gras questionable can see firsthand how it's produced and learn why it has few detractors in Périgord. At the end of the visit, you'll be rewarded with a free tasting. ⏲ 1 day. Agen Town Hall, Place Dr Esquirol. ☎ 05-53-69-47-47. www.agen.fr.

From Agen, drive north on N21 via Villeneuve-sur-Lot all the way to Bergerac (90km/56 miles).

❹ Bergerac. Cyrano de Bergerac never resided here, but the city earned the affection of big-nosed people everywhere by placing a statue of him in the city center. Few areas of the Dordogne have as many officially recognized wine appellations as Bergerac; there are more than a dozen, most of which run on the dry side. The pride of Bergerac is perhaps southwestern France's best-situated **Maison du Vin,** 1 rue des Récollets (☎ 05-53-63-57-55; www.pays-de-bergerac.com; summer 10am–7pm, closed Jan–Mar; call ahead for information). The wine rooms are in a 16th-century former Récollets cloisters built on 12th-century foundations. With gorgeous galleries and a picturesque cellar, it's a wonderful place to sample an array of wines before heading off to the vineyards of your choice. There's no obligation to buy at the Maison du Vin, but their prices are about as good as what you'll find at the vineyards.

Many visitors to Bergerac find the **Péchar-mant** red wines—produced in the vineyards that jostle the city itself on its northeastern side, and signposted from D29 as you leave toward Sarlat—are the discovery of their trip. Enjoy the afternoon touring these vineyards (you can pick up some information from Bergerac's Maison du Vin or the tourist office if you don't want to take pot luck), and perhaps visiting **Monbazillac,** too (see the box). You could also start the next day with a vineyard visit before heading east to Trémolat for lunch. ⊕ 1 day. Bergerac Tourist Office, 97 rue Neuve d'Argenson. ☎ 05-53-57-03-11. www.bergerac-tourisme.com.

From Bergerac, take D29, exiting at Cales and crossing the river to Trémolat (33km/21 miles).

⑤ Trémolat. The Dordogne River makes an extreme, horseshoe-shaped bend in this small, tobacco-growing village with fewer than 600 residents. Known as the **Cingle de Trémolat,** the bow has resulted in some of the region's best views of the river, with its charming stone bridges and the surrounding countryside. Look for signs for the **Route du Cingle** along the way. Despite its tiny size, Trémolat is a surprisingly great place to stop for lunch. There are several good restaurants in town, but the cream of the crop is Michelin-starred ★ **Le Vieux Logis** (p. 611). ⊕ 4 hr. Trémolat Tourist Office, Ilot St-Nicolas. ☎ 05-53-22-89-33. www.pays-des-bastides.com.

From Trémolat, return to D29 and continue heading east on this, D25, and D703, following the river all the way to Vézac; from there follow signs to Sarlat, via D49, D57, D46, and D704 (42km/26 miles).

⑥ ★★ Sarlat. Be sure to take advantage of Sarlat's many fine restaurants, great markets, and medieval charm. The town is in the center of a foie gras production area, so if you missed out on seeing the duck farms in Agen, you'll still have several opportunities to do so here. You'll be glad if you've arrived in Sarlat on a Tuesday or, especially, Friday, as the following mornings' markets, on the main medieval square, are among the top outdoor markets in France. You'll find produce, cheese, truffles, foie gras, meats, pastries, and countless other

Château Monbazillac

Force-fed geese and moldy grapes: This unlikely duo, in the hands of the Périgordins, has produced one of the most celebrated and ambrosial combinations in the history of food—a slice of foie gras and "its glass of Monbazillac." Three grapes—sémillon, sauvignon, and muscadelle—are allowed to go moldy on the vine, under a fungus known as "noble rot," before they are handpicked to produce this luxuriantly sweet, gorgeously colored wine. The very small AOC is centered around the village of Monbazillac, 9km (5⅔ miles) south of Bergerac. A third of the stuff is produced at the eponymous château that ferments the grapes of 60 vineyards, at the Cave de Monbazillac, rte. de Mont-de-Marsan (☎ 05-53-63-65-00; www.chateau-monbazillac.com). You can visit the cave cooperative for free, Monday through Saturday (Jan–Feb 10am-12:30pm and 2-6pm, Mar–June and Sept–Dec 10am-12:30pm and 1:30-7pm, July and Aug 9am-7pm), or pay to visit the Renaissance château-museum (admission 5.80€; Apr–May and Oct daily 10am-noon and 2-6pm, June–Sept daily 10am-7pm, Nov–Mar Tues–Sun 10am-noon and 2-5pm) for a look around, followed by a tasting.

> *You can pack an entire picnic basket with produce from Sarlat's country market—from saucisson to mushrooms and cured hams.*

delicacies, and all the while musicians and street entertainers perform. On other days and in the afternoons, the covered market on **place de la Liberté,** as well as numerous gourmet food shops, sell the region's preserved foods: jars and tins of foie gras, rillettes, *confit de canard,* jams, and liqueur wines. ◷ Half-day. Sarlat Tourist Office, 3 rue Tourny. ☎ 05-53-31-45-45. www.ot-sarlat-perigord.fr. See also p. 603, **4**.

From Sarlat, drive north on D74 to Montignac, then northwest on D67 and D6089 to Périgueux (66km/41 miles).

7 ★★ **Périgueux.** Périgueux has plenty to offer foodies. Its main contribution to French gastronomy is Périgueux sauce—a hearty brown concoction made of Madeira wine and truffles. You may see it written as *à la Périgourdine.* By any name, it's worth trying while you're here, to take advantage of the freshness of the truffles. The best streets for serious

restaurants are between cours Michel Montaigne and rue Taillefer. If you're looking for more common fare, walk along rue Salinière or rue Limogeanne. The morning markets in Périgueux are also celebrated. According to the season and the day, they take place in either place de la Claútre, **place du Coderc** or place de l'Hôtel de Ville; you'll find walnuts, foie gras, preserved duck and goose, wine, mushrooms, prunes, and many more superbly cultivated ingredients. A dedicated truffle market also takes place at certain times of the year. ◷ 1 day. For detailed information on Périgueux, see p. 630.

Sorges is 19km (12 miles) northeast of Périgueux on N21.

8 ★ **Sorges.** Funky cheeses, mushrooms, raw beef, frogs' legs, snails—hopefully by now you've tried all of these French delicacies and either deepened or developed an appreciation for them. Now it's time for diamonds—black diamonds of the kitchen, that is, otherwise known as truffles, or *truffes.* Few places are as overrun with truffles as the small village of Sorges, which has erected a museum in their honor: the ★ **Ecomusée de la Truffe** (☎ 05-53-05-90-11; www.ecomusee-truffe-sorges. com; admission 4€ adults, 2€ reduced; mid-June to late Sept daily 9:30am–12:30pm and 2:30–6:30pm). Here you can learn all about the fungus and enjoy a pleasant 3km (1¾-mile) walk that shows the truffle in its various states of production. For 100€ you can try the 5-course truffle menu at ★ **l'Auberge de la Truffe,** rte. Nationnale 21 (☎ 05-53-05-02-05; www.auberge-de-la-truffe.com; 3-course menu 28€–57€; MC, V; lunch Tues–Sun, dinner daily, but closed Sun in winter). As the name implies, it's also a hotel, which offers a week's stay with (truffle-heavy) meals included and cooking courses with the chef. ◷ 1 day. Sorges Tourist Office, Town Hall. ☎ 05-53-46-71-43.

From Sorges, cut across country west to Agonac, then northwest to Brantôme (25km/16 miles).

9 ★★ **Brantôme.** This picturesque village full of fine dining options is the perfect capper to your bacchanalian week. As a gateway to the regional park—the Parc Naturel Régional Périgord-Limousin—this spot is surrounded

Truffle Auctions

Plenty of locals make their living hunting down fungal gold and then hawking their earth-caked wares at boisterous market auctions across southwestern France. Sorges's truffle market takes place on the Sunday nearest January 20, and Brantôme holds one around that time as well. The largest auction attracts top chefs to **Lalbenque,** near Cahors in the Lot. The market takes place Tuesdays at around 2pm, from the start of December until mid-March, on Lalbenque's main street—la rue du Marché aux Truffes, naturally. The perfumelike smell of truffle permeates the air, and it's almost enough to make you forget the truffle-hunting dogs and pigs roaming about. Even if you don't have hundreds of euros to drop on a handful of truffles, you'll get a kick out of the ruckus that lasts for about half an hour after the selling begins. Truffles at these markets are a true bargain, but you'll have to start the bidding, as the sellers are doing all they can to drive up the price of this seasonal treat. If you're looking for a place to stay in Lalbenque, you won't do any better than **La Vayssade** (☎ 05-65-24-31-51; www. lavayssade.com; 5 units; doubles 64€–72€; MC, V), a *chambre d'hôte* run by Joelle and Pierre Baysse. The home is in a rustic converted stable, but the interior is all new, with lavish Arab carpets and watercolors by Joelle. You're surrounded by former truffle plantations, so you may spot a pricy mushroom or two if you stroll around the grounds. Despite the town's status as a foodie capital, there aren't many places to eat here, which makes the Baysses' home-cooking that much more appreciated.

by great natural beauty, and there are also historic monuments, castles, and churches to visit. After cruising the town center and countryside, head to ★★ **Le Moulin de l'Abbaye** (p. 611) for a fine last meal, and stay the night at the adjacent hotel. ☺ 1 day. Brantôme Tourist Office, bd. Charlemagne. ☎ 05-53-05-80-52. www.valdedronne.com.

The Best Dordogne Châteaux

Dordogne and the upper Lot are home to more châteaux than anywhere else in France. More than a thousand castles adorn the region, from feudal strongholds of the Hundred Years' War, to Renaissance follies, to 19th-century wineries—though only a fraction of them are open to the public. Base yourself in Sarlat or Brantôme to visit the clusters of châteaux around them, which is best done outside the peak summer season to avoid traffic congestion. You can also stay and dine in a château, for the full royal treatment.

> *The 12th-century Château de Beynac overlooks the Dordogne River valley.*

Château de Beynac. The site of several modern French action flicks and also the film *Chocolat*, this deservedly famous riverfront residence that looms over the hamlet of Beynac-et-Cazenac is on the official list of the Most Beautiful Villages of France. The castle was seized by Richard the Lionheart but remained in French hands during the Hundred Years' War. Dating as far back as the 12th century, when the barons of Beynac began its construction, it is a living history lesson on architectural influences: There are Romanesque influences in the keep, Renaissance remodeling in the 15th-century frescoes, and classical styling in the painted ceilings from the 17th century. It's clear you'd have a tough time toppling this fort, set high upon a limestone cliff, so it's no wonder the castle's inhabitants felt secure enough to store their stunning tapestries here, now on display for the public. Have

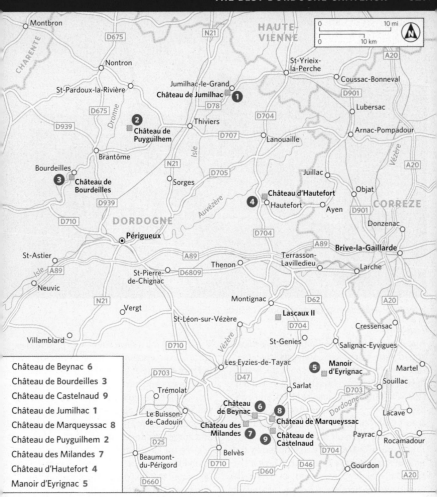

lunch in Beynac, probably in view of the next château on the list. ⏱ 2 hr. ☎ 05-53-29-50-40. www.beynac-en-perigord.com. Admission 7€ adults, 3€ children 5–11. Mar–May daily 10am–6pm; June–Sept daily 10am–6:30pm; Oct–Feb daily 10am–dusk. Beynac-et-Cazenac is 11km (6¾ miles) southwest of Sarlat: Take D57 to Vézac, then D49 for 800m (½ mile), and turn right on D703 to Beynac-et-Cazenac.

Château de Bourdeilles. Here you get two castles for the price of one: a smaller château dating from the 13th century and a larger Renaissance-era construction. They're both interesting, but the latter is the bigger draw, with its plush rooms, painted ceilings, and

famed collection of furniture, including the gilded bed of the Spanish king Charles V. The 16th-century castle is a rarity in that it was designed by a woman, Jacquette de Montbron. ⏱ 1½ hr. ☎ 05-65-27-60-60. www. bourdeilles.com. Admission 6.50€ adults, 4.50€ reduced. July–Aug 10am–5pm; Sept–May times vary. Bourdeilles is 9km (5⅔ miles) southwest of Brantôme on D78.

★★★ kids **Château de Castelnaud.** On the opposite bank of the Dordogne River this long-time English-controlled castle sat geared for battle for many years, in enmity with Beynac. It is now home to the **Musée de la Guerre au Moyen Age** (War Museum of the Middle

> *Medieval weaponry takes pride of place at Château de Castelnaud.*

Ages), with a vast collection of arms, armor, and full-size war machine replicas, such as siege catapults, a giant crossbow, the first forms of gunpowder-based artillery, and the *trebuchet* slings. They inspire shock and awe, especially in July and August when costumed actors entertain visitors with swordfighting, falconry, and catapult demonstrations. The 13th-century château was abandoned by the time of the French Revolution, but now it's splendidly restored inside and out. The castle dominates the hamlets of Beynac, Marqueyssac, and La Roque-Gageac, all pleasantly stuck in the past. ⏱ 3 hr. ☎ 05-53-31-3-00. www.castelnaud.com. Admission 7.80€ adults, 3.90€ ages 10–17; evening show 9.60€ adults, 5€ ages 10–17. Feb–Mar and Oct–Nov 11 10am–6pm; Apr–June and Sept 10am–7pm; July–Aug 9am–8pm; Nov 12–Jan 2–5pm. Castelnaud is 12km (7½ miles) southwest of Sarlat: Take D57 to Vézac, then D49 for 800m (½ mile) to D703; turn left onto D703, continue 1km (⅔ mile), and turn right on D57 to cross the river.

Château de Jumilhac. Originally dating from the 13th century, this castle was vastly modified from a feudal fortress into a luxurious Renaissance mansion during the 17th century, when it became infamous for its opulence.

The owners must have spent a fortune to create what is considered the **most romantic roof in France,** made of black, ridged tiles, filled with towers and turrets, and enhanced by ornate craftsmanship in iron and lead. There's so much to see here: parquet floors *à la Versailles,* elaborately carved fireplaces and chimneys, and gorgeous coppers in the kitchen. Underscoring the king's ransom it must have taken to build the place, a small on-site museum is dedicated to gold. You can also explore the dungeon. The château's setting in Périgord-Limousin Regional Park further enhances its beauty. ⏱ 3 hr. ☎ 05-53-52-42-97. www.jumilhac.fr. Admission 9€ adults, 8€ reduced. June–Aug daily 10am–7pm; Sept–May times vary. The château is in Jumilhac-le-Grand, 45km (28 miles) northeast of Brantôme: Take D78 to St-Jean-de-Côle, D707 to Thiviers, N21 north for 4km (2½ miles) to D78, and follow signs to Jumilhac-le-Grand.

★ kids **Château de Marqueyssac.** The greenest of castles, Mauqueyssac was built by a counselor to Louis XIV, the Sun King, at the end of the 17th century. Perhaps in homage to his patron, he created a French formal garden based on the same principles of order and symmetry that reign at the Jardins de Versailles. The hanging garden, high on a rocky promontory 130m (427 ft.) above the river, is stunning and full of surprises between the twists and turns of its boxwood scrolls. There are more than 150,000 boxwood trees carved into a vast number of shapes, including some rounded to resemble flocks of sheep or sharpened like swords. The topiary is magical when illuminated, as on Thursday nights in July and August, when the whole garden is lit by candles and animated by music. There are also scented gardens, an aviary, a rock-climbing school for children, and a wood-turning workshop. You can wander freely among the 5km (3 miles) of pathways, or take a guided tour. The château itself is closed to the public. ⏱ 2 hr. ☎ 05-53-31-36-36. www.marqueyssac. com. Admission 7.20€ adults, 3.60€ ages 10–17; joint ticket with Castelnaud 13.40€/6.70€; candlelit evenings 10€/ 5€. Feb–Mar and Oct–Nov 11 daily 10am–6pm; Apr–June and Sept daily 10am–7pm; July–Aug Fri–Wed 9am–8pm, Thurs 9am–11pm; Nov 12–Jan daily 2–5pm. The château is 11km (6¾ miles) southwest of Sarlat: Take D57 to Vézac, turn left on D57, and take the third left.

★ **Château de Puyguilhem.** Intended as a second residence and hunting lodge, this harmoniously proportioned 16th-century Renaissance structure shows us how vacationing nobles used to take it easy (perhaps from counting their money). From afar, it may not look as impressive as some others, but it's a real delight, with rococo crenellations and other interesting architectural details. It needed significant restorations after World War II, but since then the spiral staircase, interior decor, and period tapestries have returned the site to its former glory. The friendly caretaker seems to live an idyllic life in his little cottage beside it, and he may let you explore the grounds even when the château is closed. Even when it is open, it won't be crowded, so you can dream that it's yours for a spell. In the valley next door, the ruins of the Cistercian **Abbey of Boschaud** are definitely worth visiting. You'll find plenty of places to stay around nearby Brantôme, en route to the next château. ⏱ 1½ hr. ☎ 05-53-54-82-18. www. puyguilhem.monuments-nationaux.fr. Admission 5€ adults, 3.50€ reduced. July–Aug 10am–7pm; Sept–May times vary. Puyguilhem is 13km

(8 miles) northeast of Brantôme: Take D78 east to Les Roches, then D83 and D82 to Villars; the château is 1km (⅔ mile) northwest of the village.

★★★ kids **Château des Milandes.** One of the most fascinating castles in France, this graceful affair features a combination of Renaissance and Gothic styles incorporating turrets, superbly crafted gargoyles and chimeras, and stained glass. In stark contrast to the overtly violent intent of the nearby Château de Castelnaud, this castle was known as "Sleeping Beauty," due to its peaceful history as the home of French aristocrats.

Milandes's main interest is as the former home of the African-American entertainer Josephine Baker, who found a liberty and appreciation in France that she had not enjoyed in the still-segregated U.S. Showing her appreciation, she became a French citizen and joined the Resistance in World War II. Baker bought the castle in 1937 and modernized it with running water, central heating, and the first American refrigerator in the area. Having adopted a huge brood of children, she turned the castle into an amusement park, with minigolf, the largest open-air pool in the area,

> *Topiary is the star of the show in Château de Marqueyssac's gardens, but the aviary and wood-turning workshops are also intriguing.*

> *Manoir d'Eyrignac's sculpted gardens, with an abundance of box hedges and topiary, are among the most beautiful in France.*

a restaurant, and a theater—all of which led to her bankruptcy in 1968. An exhibition in the château tells her life story, and you can visit her elegant rooms and see costumes including her celebrated banana dress. Kids will also enjoy the Birds of Prey show, in which trained owls and eagles perform feats of speed and accuracy in the castle gardens. ⏱ 2 hr. ☎ 05-53-59-31-21. www.milandes.com. Admission 8.50€ adults, 5.50€ ages 5-17 (bird show included). April and Oct Mon-Fri and Sun 10am-6:15pm; May-June and Sept Mon-Fri and Sun 10am-6:30pm; July-Aug daily 9:30am-7:30pm; closed Nov-Mar. The château is 15km (9 miles) southwest of Sarlat: Take D57 to Vézac and then D49 for 800m (½ mile), turning left onto D703; continue for 1km (⅔ mile); turn right on D57 to cross the river, make another right onto D53, and hug the river for 2km (1¼ miles).

Château d'Hautefort. This hilltop castle began as a fortress in the 10th century and experienced several centuries of violence, switching from French to English hands during the Middle Ages. In the 17th century the family of the Marquis de Hautefort converted it to a castle of leisure. The Hauteforts were so popular, thanks to their generosity to the poor, that town residents actually defended both castle and family during the Revolution. That goodwill endured into the 20th century, when local residents made extensive donations in 1968 to repair the castle, which was scarred by fire. Now open to the public, this jewel of a castle features a huge English park, classic French gardens, and fully restored rooms and decor. ⏱ 2½ hr. ☎ 05-53-50-51-23. www.chateau-hautefort.com. Admission 8.50€ adults, 4€ reduced. July-Aug daily 9am-7pm; Sept-Nov 11 and Mar-May times vary. Closed Nov 12-Feb. Hautefort is midway btw. Sarlat and Brantôme, just over 50km (31 miles) from each. From Sarlat: Take D703 and D704 to Montignac, continue north (D65 and D704 again), and turn right at Temple-Laguyon. From Brantôme: Take D78 east then D68 to Sorges, continue east on D74, D705, D73, and D67; from Tortoirac D62 takes you to Hautefort.

★★ **Manoir d'Eyrignac.** Garden lovers should not miss Eyrignac, a 17th-century manor (often called a château) that has remained in the same family for more than 5 centuries. The original medieval castle was rebuilt after it burned down during the 17th-century war known as *La Fronde des Princes* (The Princes' Revolt), and in the 18th century the gardens were created in the French formal style that paid homage to the Italian Renaissance. Over successive generations they were over-planted following new fashions, but in the 1960s the owner (father of the present owner) painstakingly recreated the original gardens. Only the pavilion, the fountains, and the basins, fed from seven springs, are left from the original, but his restoration efforts led to the garden's enlistment as one of the French Ministry of Culture's Notable Gardens of France. The original trees, less than a foot high when they were first planted, are now set in Italian terracotta vases or cultivated into spiraling or buttressed forms. ⏱ 2 hr. ☎ 05-53-28-99-71. www.eyrignac.com. Admission 9.50€ adults, 6.50€ ages 14-18, 4€ ages 7-13. Apr daily 10am-7pm; May-Sept daily 9:30am-7pm; Oct daily 10am-nightfall; Nov-Mar daily 10:30am-12:30pm and 2:30pm-nightfall. The manor is 13km (8 miles) northeast of Sarlat: Heading north out of Sarlat, pick up D47 east to Ste-Nathalène; go straight through the village, continue to Guarrigues, and turn left for 1km (⅔ mile) to Manoir d'Eyrignac.

Where to Stay & Dine in a Château

Auberge de Castel Merle SERGEAC *REGIONAL FRENCH* This modest but magical country castle has been in the same family for five generations. It's simply decorated, but the stone walls speak volumes of history, and rooms have views of the woods or the courtyard. The owners cook fabulous meals, and in pleasant weather guests can dine on the terrace with a river view. The property is midway between Les Eyzies and Montignac, so it's an ideal place to stay if you're visiting the prehistoric caves (p. 606, ❹, and 607, ❺). 10km (6¼ miles) southwest of Montignac on D65. ☎ 05-53-50-70-08. www.hotelcastelmerle.com. 8 units. Doubles 45€–57€. July–Aug half-board only. Menus 19€–27€. MC, V. Lunch and dinner Tues–Sat.

Château de la Côte BRANTOME *REGIONAL FRENCH* This 15th-century, ivy-covered château near the château of Bourdeilles is surrounded by its own 6-hectare (15-acre) park with mature trees and a view over the valley. Rooms are decorated in English country-house style with flowered wallpapers and four-poster beds. The château restaurant is worthy of its setting. Biras-Bourdeilles, 3.5km (2 miles) south of Brantôme. ☎ 05-53-03-70-11. http://chateaudelacote.com. 16 units. Doubles 60€–205€. Menus 35€–59€. AE, MC, V. Lunch Sun, dinner daily.

★ **Château de la Fleunie** CONDAT-SUR-VEZERE *REGIONAL FRENCH* Dating back to the 12th century, but mainly built in the 15th, this château has it all: 33 regally appointed rooms, a swimming pool, tennis courts, driving range, billiards, a formal restaurant and more relaxed eating by the pool, and 106 hectares (262 acres) of parkland. 10km (6¼ miles) northeast of Montignac on D704. ☎ 05-53-51-32-74. www.lafleunie.com. 33 units. Doubles 75€–180€. Fixed-price menu 45€. AE, MC, V. Lunch and dinner daily.

★★★ **Château de la Treyne** LACAVE *GASTRONOMIC* Fairy-tale castles do exist, and the proof is in Château de la Treyne, with its 17th-century round tower perched on a cliff overhanging the Dordogne River. A delightful couple run

> *Stay in palatial surroundings at Château de la Treyne in Lacave, and order a kingly breakfast in bed.*

the place with a great deal of thoughtfulness and personal attention, placing sweet-smelling fresh flowers throughout, a crystal decanter with an aperitif in each room, and a walnut cake complete with the recipe on a parchment. Every room is charming, the Dordogne apartment particularly so, with a private terrace over the river where you can look down on swans gliding by. The restaurant is very fine, offering one of the top gourmet experiences in the region. ☎ 05-65-27-60-60. www.chateaudelatreyne.com. 16 units. Doubles 180€–680€. Main courses 53€–72€. AE, MC, V. Lunch and dinner daily. Closed mid-Nov to mid-Mar.

★ **Château de Monrecour** BEYNAC-ET-CADENAC This beautiful château, near that of Beynac, contains 10 rooms plus another six in the outbuildings. Here you'll enjoy an outdoor pool and take breakfast in the Salon d'Honneur hung with tapestries or on the panoramic terrace overlooking the Château des Milandes across the river. The château doesn't have its own restaurant. St-Vincent-de-Cosse, 2km (1¼ miles) east of Beynac-et-Cazenac on D703. ☎ 05-53-28-33-59. www.monrecour.com. 21 units. Doubles 75€–158€. AE, MC, V.

Volcanoes of the Auvergne

Besides the city of Clermont-Ferrand, this region is harshly rural, bordering on desolate; but its inhabitants are among the warmest in France, their food is gutsy and flavorsome, and the landscape is rich with natural wonders. The volcanoes that molded it have cooled off and grassed over, and now they make for great sightseeing and outdoor excursions. GPS is a godsend for tourists and taxi drivers here, as for all over France; still, we highly recommend you pick up lots of maps and ask even more questions than usual. The roads in Auvergne can be closed for bad weather, and small roads are often poorly signposted.

> *A fabulous destination for hikers, Puy Mary is Cantal's highest peak, almost always covered with snow in winter.*

START Clermont-Ferrand is 425km (264 miles) south of Paris. **TRIP LENGTH** 431km (268 miles); about 1 week.

① Clermont-Ferrand. Clermont-Ferrand is the thriving capital of the largely uninhabited region of Auvergne, one of the least-populated areas in Europe. Michelin, one of the largest local employers, helped unify the two cities of Clermont and Montferrand to create today's modern city, with two pleasant downtown centers and nearly half a million inhabitants. You can't miss the dark and looming ★★ **Cathédrale Notre-Dame,** place de la Victoire (☎ 04-73-98-65-00; www.notredame-clermont.cef.fr; admission (tower) 2€ adults, 1.50€ reduced; daily 9:30am–7pm), built in the 13th century from black lava stone. If you're driving, it's also worth stopping in at **kids L'Aventure Michelin,** 32 rue du Clos Four (☎ 04-73-98-60-60; www.laventuremichelin.com; admission 8€ adults, 5€ ages 17 and under; Tues–Sun 10am–6pm, July and Aug 10am–7pm), which celebrates the legacy of the Clermont-based tire manufacturer, from its maps and cars to its globally renowned food ratings and vintage advertising. ⊕ Half-day. Clermont-Ferrand Tourist Office, place de la Victoire. ☎ 04-73-98-65-00. www.clermont-fd.com.

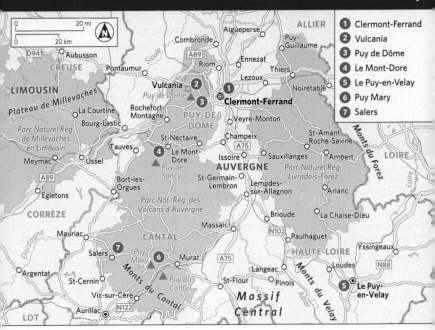

1. Clermont-Ferrand
2. Vulcania
3. Puy de Dôme
4. Le Mont-Dore
5. Le Puy-en-Velay
6. Puy Mary
7. Salers

From Clermont-Ferrand, take D941 15km (9⅓ miles) northwest to Vulcania. (Head for Orcines and you will see signs; Le Pariou is on the way.)

2 ★★★ 🄺🄸🄳🅂 **Vulcania.** This fascinating and extensive science park brings to life the forces that created the Auvergne's volcanic landscape, through room after room of exciting sound and light exhibits such as the life-size bubbling crater or the four-dimensional *Angry Earth*—a 3-D movie synchronized with the physical effects of natural disasters. Few theme parks have made their landscape such an integral part of the fun as Vulcania, with more than 23 hectares (57 acres) of informative nature trails exploring Auvergne's natural heritage. ⊕ Half-day. Rte. de Mazayes. ☎ 03-04-73-19-70-00. www.vulcania.com. Admission 21€–24€ adults, 15€ ages 6–16, free for children 5 and under. Mar 24–June and Sept–Nov 14 daily 10am–6pm (except some Mon–Tues); July 10am–7pm; Aug 10am–7:30pm; mid-July to Aug Wed until 11pm with fireworks; closed mid-Nov to mid-Mar. ⊕ 1 day.

From Clermont-Ferrand, take D941 toward Vulcania, pass the turn to Orcines, and after 2km (1¼ miles), turn right onto D68 (in the direction of Ceyssat) for 3km (1¾ miles) to the Col de Ceyssat parking area (14km/9⅓ miles).

3 ★★ **Puy de Dôme.** Rising more than 1,450m (4,750 ft.), this huge but young volcano is the star of the **Chaîne des Puys** mountain range. The formation is an abruptly steep mass of grassed-over lava created by a volcanic eruption a scant 10,000 years ago; it affords views as far as Mont Blanc, 500km (310 miles) away, on a clear day. The area is a great place for hiking, mountain biking, paragliding, and horseback riding. It also encompasses several Gallo-Roman temples dedicated to Mercury, the god of commerce and abundance, accessible via pedestrian path to the top (though you can also drive there if it's not too crowded). The climb generally takes 45 minutes each way. In 2012 an amazing, ecological year-round train will take visitors to the summit. ⊕ 1 day. Main parking area: Col de Ceyssat; ☎ 04-73-62-21-46; www.puydedome.com. Details about trekking and camping: Parc Naturel Régional des Volcans d'Auvergne, Montlosier (20km/12 miles southwest of Clermont-Ferrand); ☎ 04-73-65-64-00; www.parc-volcans-auvergne.com.

> The Puy de Dôme volcano, at more than 1,450m (4,750 ft.), is a hot spot for seasoned walkers and nature lovers.

On Day 4, the easiest way to Le Mont-Dore from Clermont-Ferrand is southwest on N89 (46km/29 miles).

4 Le Mont-Dore. Le Mont-Dore sits at the foot of **Puy de Sancy,** the tallest peak in central France, rising more than 1,886m (6,188 ft.). You may never have heard of skiing in the Massif Central, because the French have kept this secret to themselves, enjoying the comparatively low-key *après-ski* with plenty of hearty good food and pristine, uncrowded slopes. The slopes at Le Mont-Dore are on the easier side, and the length of its runs are great, going right over the mountain to the other main ski resort of Super-Besse; in contrast, Puy de Sancy is full of dangerous backcountry runs. Even in summer, the town is busy, thanks to its ancient thermal springs and more than 650km (400 miles) of moderate hiking trails around the area. Most of the trails aren't too difficult, including the 1½-hour climb to the top of Puy de Sancy. Ski lifts run year-round, for use by hikers and mountain bikers as well as skiers. ⏱ 1 day. Av. de la Libération, Le Mont-Dore. ☎ 04-73-65-20-21. www.mont-dore.com.

Take D996, D983, D2089, A75, and N102 to Le Puy-en-Velay (168km/104 miles).

5 ★★ Le Puy-en-Velay. This holy city on the Santiago de Compostela pilgrimage trail has thrived among the Christian faithful despite its remote location. It is situated in the bowl of a volcanic cone on a series of rocky outcrops and basalt pillars, three of which are crowned with a church or statue. The first sight you'll see is the 19th-century bronze statue of Mary, **Notre-Dame-de-France,** on the pinnacle of the Rocher Corneille. The 12th-century ★ **Cathédrale**

Notre-Dame, 2 rue de la Manécanterie (☎ 04-71-09-79-77; www.cathedraledupuy.org; free admission; daily 9am–7pm), is a UNESCO World Heritage site, featuring a striped facade of white sandstone and black volcanic rock. The 10th-century ★ **Chapelle St-Michel d'Aiguille,** 17 rue du Rocher (☎ 04-71-09-50-03; www.rochersaintmichel.fr; admission 3€ adults, 1.50€ reduced; summer daily 9am–6:30pm, hours vary otherwise), is set high upon a basalt rock pinnacle just north of Le Puy-en-Velay, with 12th-century frescoes and multicolored stone mosaic facade. ⏱ 1 day. Le Puy-en-Velay Tourist Office, place du Clauzel, near La Mairie. ☎ 04-71-09-38-41. www.ot-lepuyenvelay.fr.

The cross-country trip from Le Puy-en-Velay west to Murat via Langeac and St-Flour is picturesque (120km/75 miles). It's faster to take N102 up to Brioude, cut across to the autoroute, and then take N122 from Massiac to Murat.

6 ★★ kids Puy Mary. Rising 1,783m (5,850 ft.), Puy Mary is a pyramid of grassy natural beauty and a haven for nature walkers. The main footpath is at **Pas de Peyrol,** but drivers may appreciate the winding route up when it's open, from June through October, if they can put up with the traffic. A new visitor center was recently constructed, along with a new park-and-ride bus, which is highly recommended. Bike riding, horseback riding, skiing, and other outdoor activities are readily available here. ⏱ 4 hr. www.puymary.fr.

From Murat in summer you can cross the Peyrol Pass, the highest in France, reaching Salers after only 44km (27 miles). In winter it's a 95km (59-mile) round-trip via Aurillac.

7 Salers. Known for its beef and for Cantal and Salers cheeses, this stunning village of 400 has more cows than people. Salers's moniker—"the black diamond on a green carpet"—is fitting, as most of the buildings are made from gray-black volcanic rock. Salers was an administrative region of some import in the 16th century, thus the lofty architecture. You'll find plenty of mansions, such as the stunning Renaissance-style **place Tyssandier d'Escous;** the **Maison de Bargues,** with its ornate stone balcony; and the 13th-century **Maison de la Ronade.** ⏱ 1 day. Salers Tourist Office, place Tyssandier d'Escous. ☎ 04-71-40-58-08. www.salers-tourisme.fr.

Where to Stay & Dine Amid the Volcanoes

All Seasons Puy-en-Velay Centre LE PUY-EN-VELAY *BRASSERIE* In the commercial center, this three-star hotel provides the chance to shake off the dirt and grass in a modern and clean environment. The Alsatian tavern restaurant is a nice change of pace in this region but is nonetheless hardy, to fill you up after a day of rigorous activity. 47 bd. Marechal Fayolle. ☎ 04-71-09-32-36. www.accorhotels.com. 50 units. Doubles 71€–84€. Main courses 15€–20€. AE, MC, V. Lunch and dinner daily.

★★ **La Belle Meunière** CLERMONT-FERRAND *GASTRONOMIC* Just west of Clermont-Ferrand, in the suburb of Royat, this hotel-restaurant is a superb value. The creatively put-together menus feature truffles and mushrooms in season, while the rooms feature Art Nouveau stained glass, making them a real treat for the price. 25 av Vallée, Royat, 3km (1¾ miles) east of Clermont-Ferrand. ☎ 04-73-35-80-17. www.la-belle-meuniere.com. Doubles from 48€. 3-course menu 39€–69€. MC, V. Lunch Tues–Fri and Sun, dinner Tues–Sat.

★ **L'Auberge du Col de La Moréno** PUY DE DOME *REGIONAL FRENCH* After a hike up Puy de Dome, nothing is better than a filling *truffade* (a variation on potatoes au gratin made with gluey cheese and pork morsels). This local specialty is on many menus, but in this rustic inn you get the real thing, made to owner Raphael Dubernat's grandmother's recipe and served with green salad and charcuterie. The cozy dining room and bar offers a chance to get to know some locals in a relaxing atmosphere. Col de la Moréno, St-Gènes Champanelle. ☎ 04-73-87-16-46. www.aubergemoreno.com. Main courses 15€–20€. MC, V. Dinner Mon–Sat.

★ **Hôtel de Russie** MONT-DORE *REGIONAL FRENCH* With a log-cabin decor and red and white textiles, La Russie pays homage to the Russians who used to come here to take the waters. Its newly modernized and comfortable

> *A truffade at L'Auberge du Col de La Moréno.*

rooms are complemented by a cozy restaurant serving traditional *auvergnate* fare. 3 rue Favart. ☎ 04-73-65-05-97. www.lerussie.com. 33 units. Doubles 59.90€–75€. Main courses 13.50€–18.90€. MC, V. Lunch and dinner daily.

★★ **Le Baillage** SALERS *GASTRONOMIC* Salers's grandest hotel is also great fun, like its bubbly owner and decorator, Madame Gouzon. Her husband, Jean-Michel, is the award-winning chef in Le Baillage's restaurant, where guests dine on Salers beef with a *forestière* sauce, *foie gras poêlée,* and AOC cheeses in a dressed-up setting, with impeccable service. An outdoor swimming pool and beauty treatment rooms complete the picture. Rue Notre-Dame. ☎ 04-71-40-71-95. www.salers-hotel-baillage.com. 26 units. Doubles 50€–115€. Menus 26€–42€. AE, MC, V. Lunch and dinner daily.

Périgueux

On the Isle River, this town of about 30,000 is best known

for its archaeological museums; Périgueux holds its own alongside any French city in terms of its collections, from the Gallo-Roman city of Vesunna, as Périgueux was once called, to other remarkable prehistoric sites nearby. In the kink of the river are two distinct historic quarters: the Roman one, called La Cité, and the medieval one, called Le Puy St-Front, which is dominated by the cathedral. Be sure to leave plenty of time for food shopping in this gastronomic town where market day is one long feast.

> If it weren't for electricity and modern piping, parts of Périgueux's old center would look unchanged since medieval times.

START Périgueux is 550km (342 miles) south of Paris and 130km (81 miles) east of Bordeaux.

❶ ★ Cathédrale St-Front. The pride of local architecture is this 12th-century construction—the largest cathedral in southwestern France. Built on the ruins of a burned abbey, it was designed in the shape of a Greek cross, with no fewer than five impressive cupola domes and many turrets. The church is largely in the Byzantine style, but it also displays Merovingian, Carolingian, Romanesque, and Gothic elements, as it has suffered in numerous wars and been frequently updated. ⏱ 40 min. Place de la Clautre. ☎ 05-53-53-10-63. www.tourisme-perigueux.fr. Admission 2.50€ adults, 1.50€ reduced. Daily 10am–7pm.

❷ ★★ Musée d'Art et d'Archéologie du Périgord. This former Augustinian convent in the Puy St-Front quarter houses one of the top archaeological museums in France. Most impressive is the prehistory collection, including Neanderthal skeletons, bone, and antler engravings from 35,000 B.C., but the collection also includes Gallo-Roman, medieval, and Renaissance artifacts and art. ⏱ 1½ hr. 22 cours Tourny. ☎ 05-53-06-40-70. www.musee-perigord.museum.com. Admission 4.50€ adults, 2.50€ reduced, free for children 5 and under. Apr–Sept Mon and Wed–Fri 10:30am–5:30pm, Sat–Sun 1–6pm; Oct–Mar Mon and Wed–Fri 10am–5pm, Sat–Sun 1–6pm.

Périgueux's Food Markets

Périgueux's food markets are as great an attraction as its ancient ruins. The daily **Place du Coderc Market** is largest on Wednesdays and Saturdays. From mid-November until the end of March, you can also find the **Marché au Gras,** plying foie gras and other preserved regional specialties, on place St-Louis on Wednesdays and Saturdays. A summer truffle market takes place on Saturdays in July and August, on **place St-Silain.** All markets are open only in the morning.

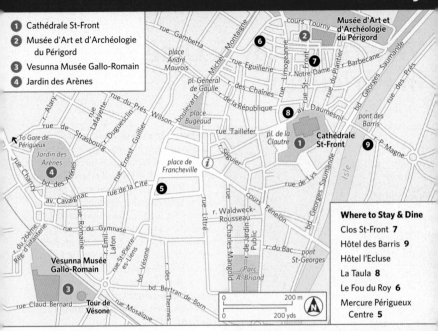

1 Cathédrale St-Front
2 Musée d'Art et d'Archéologie du Périgord
3 Vesunna Musée Gallo-Romain
4 Jardin des Arènes

3 ★★★ **Vesunna Musée Gallo-Romain.** Périgueux was once a Roman city of 20,000 inhabitants, with a forum, a basilica, baths, an amphitheater, and a 6.5km (4-mile) viaduct. The patron saint of this prosperous place was Vesunna (or "Vésone" to the French), who represented good luck and trade. The prestigious new Musée Gallo-Romain, designed by Jean Nouvel, was built on the archaeological site of the best preserved part of Roman Périgord; it is surrounded by the Jardin de Vésone, where part of the goddess's sanctuary still stands (the "Tour Vésone). An exemplary marriage of modern and ancient architecture, the museum is a trove of fascinating antiquity including stunning murals and a restored collection of quotidian objects from the 1st to the 3rd centuries. It culminates in an ancient villa, undiscovered until 1959. ⏲ 2 hr. 62 rue de Vésone. ☎ 05-53-42-91. www.vesunna. fr. Admission 6€ adults, 4€ ages 6–25, free for children 5 and under. July–Aug daily 10am–7pm; Apr–June and Sept Tues–Fri 9:30am–5:30pm, Sat and Sun 10am–12:30pm and 2:30–6pm; Oct–Mar Tues–Fri 9:30am–12:30pm and 1:30–5pm, Sat and Sun 10am–12:30pm and 2:30–6pm.

4 **Jardin des Arènes.** This circular garden in La Cité contains the remains of the Roman amphitheater. Only fragments are left, but the

> The 2,000-year-old Tour Vésone dates from the era when the surrounding area was the Gallo Roman capital of Aquitaine Gaul.

garden itself enables you to see the scale of what was one of the largest amphitheaters in ancient Gaul. Fountains and lime trees make it a pleasant place to relax for a while.

Where to Stay & Dine in Périgueux

> Guests feast on Périgord specialties at the Hôtel l'Ecluse, just outside Périgueux.

Clos St-Front *REGIONAL FRENCH*

This fine restaurant serves modern and regional cuisine. The decor includes huge fireplaces, a terrace surrounded by fragrant lime trees, and modern art. The foie gras with local strawberries is a delight. 5 rue de la Vertu. ☎ 05-53-46-78-58. www.leclossaintfront.com. 3-course menu 28€–65€. MC, V. Lunch Tues-Sun, dinner Tues-Sat.

Hôtel des Barris

This small hotel may be a budget option but an effort has been made to imbue its rooms with some charm and personality. It also offers great views of both the river and the cathedral and is just a short walk from the city center. 2 rue Pierre Magne. ☎ 05-53-53-04-05. www.hoteldesbarris.com. 14 units. Doubles 53€–59€. MC, V.

★★ Hôtel l'Ecluse *REGIONAL FRENCH*

One of the best lodging experiences to be found around Périgueux is this three-star combination of rustic and elegant located 10km (6¼ miles) west of the city. Set next to the Lisle River, it's a peaceful idyll that also offers superb value. The restaurant, which boasts a charming terrace and great views from the dining room, serves delicious Périgord specialties. Make sure to try some of the hotel's award-winning red wines. Rte. de Limoges, Antonne. ☎ 05-53-06-00-04. www.ecluse-perigord.com. 47 units. Doubles 50€–70€. Menus 20€–32€. Lunch and dinner daily. AE, MC, V.

La Taula *REGIONAL FRENCH*

This welcoming restaurant with a long dining room serves regional specialties such as stuffed duck neck. It's a good value for dishes made from impeccably fresh local ingredients. 3 rue Denfert-Rochereau. ☎ 05-53-35-40-02. 3-course menu 30€–36€. MC, V. Lunch and dinner Tues-Sun.

★ Le Fou du Roy *REGIONAL FRENCH & SEAFOOD*

With rustic furnishings, fine seafood, and themed menus, this place is a local treasure. The scallops are a treat, as is the *Burger du Roy*, which features foie gras and roasted apples. 2 rue Michel de Montaigne. ☎ 05-53-09-43-77. www.guide-du-perigord.com. 3-course lunch menu 21€, dinner menu 43€. MC, V. Lunch Mon-Fri, dinner Tues-Sat.

★ Mercure Périgueux Centre

This new Mercure really lives up to the "center" in its name, as it is right between the old town and Roman remains, facing a park. Extremely comfortable rooms in a gold and brown scheme, private parking, and free Wi-Fi make it a great base for exploring the city. 7 place Francheville. ☎ 05-53-06-65-00. www.mercure.com. 66 units. Doubles 70€–99€. AE, DC, MC, V.

Fast Facts

Arriving

BY PLANE Most people drive or take the train to Dordogne and Auvergne. However, it is possible to fly into the **Bergerac Dordogne Périgord Airport** (☎ 05-53-22-25-25; www.bergerac. aeroport.fr), which offers flights from Paris and various U.K. cities. Alternatively, Clermont-Ferrand's **Aéroport de Clermont-Aulnat** (☎ 04-73-62-71-00), about 4km (2½ miles) northwest of the town center, receives about 80 flights a day from all over France plus Italy, Switzerland, and Belgium. **Air France** (☎ 08-20-82-08-20) flies here from Paris. **BY TRAIN** Trains from Paris reach Clermont-Ferrand in 3½ hours and Périgueux in about 5 hours. Trains from small towns in Auvergne and Dordogne usually require a connection. From Périgueux, for example, there are direct trains to Les Eyzies-De-Tayac (30 min.). To reach Montignac/Lascaux, rail service runs to the neighboring hamlet of Condat-le-Lardin, 9.5km (6 miles) northeast, where taxis (☎ 05-53-51-80-46) continue to Montignac. It is also possible to travel by train from Lyon, Toulouse, Bordeaux, Marseilles, and many other regional towns. For train information, call ☎ 36-35 or 08-92-35-35-35. **BY CAR** The best way to reach and explore the Auvergne and the Dordogne is by car. To reach Périgueux from Paris, take A10 south to Orléans, and then A71 south to Vierzon; continue along A20 south to Limoges, and then pick up N21 south to Périgueux. To drive to Les Eyzies-De-Tayac from Périgueux, start along D710 southeast to Le Bugue, follow the rural road east for a short distance, and then look out for the sign pointing to Les Eyzies-de-Tayac. The easiest way to reach Montignac is to drive northeast from Les Eyzies on D706 for 19km (12 miles). Clermont-Ferrand is best approached by car from Paris or Lyon. The 4-hour drive from Paris begins along A10 south to Orléans, continuing south along A71 to Clermont-Ferrand. From Lyon, take A47 west to St-Etienne, traveling northwest on A89 to Clermont-Ferrand. If you're driving to Albi or Cordes-sur-Ciel from Toulouse, take N88 north.

> *Whenever possible drive upward, and the views in these fabulous regions will prove more rewarding.*

ATMs/Cashpoints
See p. 703, France Fast Facts.

Emergencies
See p. 704, France Fast Facts.

Internet Cafes
PERIGUEUX La Cyber Tour 9 cours Fénelon (☎ 05-53-02-51-76; www.lacybertour.fr).

Post Offices
CLERMONT-FERRAND 1 rue Maurice Busset (☎ 04-73-30-65-42). **PERIGUEUX** 1 rue du 4 Septembre (☎ 05-53-03-61-10). **SARLAT** Place du 14 Juillet (☎ 05-53-31-73-10).

Safety
The Auvergne and Dordogne regions are pretty safe. In an emergency, call 17 for the police, 18 for the fire department or paramedics, and 15 for an ambulance.

Tourist Offices
Municipal tourist offices are listed at the end of the town tour stops throughout the chapter. **AUVERGNE** ☎ 08-10-82-78-28; www. auvergne-tourisme.info. **DORDOGNE** ☎ 05-53-35-50-24; **WWW.DORDOGNE-PERIGORD-TOURISME.FR. THE LOT** 107 quai Cavaignac, Cahors (☎ 05-65-35-07-09; www.tourisme-lot.com). **PERIGUEUX** 10 av. Cavaignac (☎ 05-53-06-48-10; www.ville-perigueux.fr). **VOLCANS D'AUVERGNE REGIONAL PARK** ☎ 04-73-62-21-45; www.parc-volcans-auvergne.com.

Favorite Moments in the North & Picardie

At the crossroads between the U.K. and Belgium, the northern tip of France is EU-oriented and rich in industry. It also offers a wealth of birdlife, marshes, and beaches, plus soaring Gothic cathedrals, World War I battlefields, and world-class museums. You'll notice a distinct Flemish influence in the place names, pointy roofs, windmills, and canals, creating a landscape unlike any other in France. Here are our favorite experiences in this fascinating region.

> PREVIOUS PAGE *The view from the top of Lille's Hôtel de Ville.* THIS PAGE *Shopping in Lille.*

❶ **Walking along the wild clifftops of Cap Gris-Nez.** This stretch of coastline, between Calais and Boulogne-sur-Mer, affords some spectacular panoramas over sand dunes and past lighthouses, where ferries and heavy cargo ships dot the waves. See p. 646, ❷.

❷ **Cavorting like film stars at Le Touquet.** Le Touquet and its beaches have been a playground for the rich and famous for more than 150 years. The casino and racecourse still draw their fair share of celebrity faces today. See p. 647, ❹.

❸ **Spending, spending, spending in Lille.** Vieux Lille (the city's Old Town) is the shopping capital of the North, teeming with antiques, food shops, and designer clothes boutiques. Euralille alone has 120 boutiques. See p. 654.

1 Walking along the wild cliff tops of Cap Gris-Nez
2 Cavorting like film stars at Le Touquet
3 Spending, spending, spending in Lille
4 Exploring 21st-century art
5 Bird-watching at the Parc du Marquenterre
6 Kayaking in the Baie de Somme
7 Exploring Naours, the spooky "City Below the Earth"
8 Honoring WWI soldiers at Thiepval
9 Shopping at Amiens's Marché sur l'Eau
10 Seeing your kids' faces light up over history
11 Tucking into a meal at L'Aubergade

4 **Exploring 21st-century art.** Greater Lille's brand-new **LaM** is the first museum in the whole of northern Europe to feature the principal elements of both 20th- and 21st-century art. See p. 654, 9.

5 **Bird-watching at the Parc du Marquenterre.** Fourteen huts offer you the best chances to spot northern pintails, black-tailed godwits, and migratory species from across the globe. See p. 647, 5.

6 **Kayaking in the Baie de Somme.** The estuary is a showcase of this region's rich flora and wildlife, including one of France's biggest seal colonies. See p. 647, 5.

7 **Exploring Naours, the spooky "City Below the Earth."** Just north of Amiens, 30m (98 ft.) below the surface, a former 3rd-century quarry has become a working underground city with a church, 300 chambers, and six chimneys. The aboveground park also has windmills and a museum of Picardie life. See "Naours, an Underground Museum," p. 650.

8 **Honoring World War I soldiers at Thiepval.** The Somme battlefields are littered with war memorials such as the imposing arch at Thiepval, dedicated to the 75,085 British and South African soldiers who went missing in action between July 1915 and March 1918. It is the most important British monument in France. See p. 645, 3.

9 **Shopping at Amiens's Marché sur l'Eau.** For the entire month of June, the canal-rich St-Leu Quarter hosts a waterborne market. From stalls set up on traditional wooden barges, vendors ply local flowers, melons, blackberries, and other goods. See p. 650, 5.

10 **Seeing your kids' faces light up over history.** In Samara, France's biggest archaeological park, they'll learn about flinting stones, see reconstructions of prehistoric dwellings, visit a botanical garden, and run around burning off energy. See p. 650.

11 **Tucking into a meal at L'Aubergade.** Langoustines served with a caramelized carrot purée, or traditional stuffed cabbage with foie gras: Dining at L'Aubergade, just outside Amiens, is one deeply satisfying culinary experience. See p. 651.

The North & Picardie in 1 Week

Miles of grass-topped chalk cliffs run from the busy port of Calais to walled Boulogne-sur-Mer. Then there's the marshy Flandre Maritime area, which slows the pace along the Canal de la Basse Colme, before the cities of Lille, Arras, and Amiens quicken the pace again with their top-end museums and architecture. Flemish Lille is accessible via high-speed Eurostar trains from London and Thalys trains from Brussels; south of the city is Arras, with cobbled squares and underground wartime tunnels; and Amiens is the capital of Picardie, with the largest cathedral in France and a chocolate-box town center.

> *Lille's city hall bell tower is one of 56 Belgian and French belfries under UNESCO protection.*

START Calais is 113km (70 miles) west of Lille, and 296km (184 miles) north of Paris. **TRIP LENGTH** 280km (174 miles) on both highways and country roads.

1 Calais. The 34km (21-mile) Dover-to-Calais ferry route across the Channel between England and France draws millions of travelers to Calais every year, yet few people bother to visit the city, instead heading to the vast **Cité Europe** shopping mall just outside town (on A16 at junction 41 or 43, or take bus 1 from the city center; www.citeeurope.com). Calais is worth a visit, however. Behind its austere, post–World War II facade, the city is home to monuments such as the Flemish-Tudor–style **Hôtel de Ville,** place du Soldat Inconnu (☎ 03-21-46-62-00), with its red-brick, UNESCO-protected bell tower and **Les Bourgeois de Calais (Burghers of Calais)** statue by Auguste Rodin; the glorious neo-baroque **Théâtre** (bd. Pasteur); and the bright white **Phare de Calais,** the lighthouse on boulevard des Alliés (admission 4.50€ adults, 2.50€ ages 5–15; mid-July to Aug daily 10am–noon and 2–6:30pm; Sept to mid-July Wed and Sat 2–5:30pm, Sun 10am–noon and 2–5:30pm), with its 271 steps that lead to head-spinning views over the sea.

The North & Picardie in 3 Days

If you have only 3 days in the region, follow stops **7** to **9** on this tour: Lille, Arras, and Amiens.

1 Calais
2 Cap Blanc-Nez & the Côte d'Opale
3 Boulogne-sur-Mer
4 St-Omer
5 Cassel
6 Bergues
7 Lille
8 Arras
9 Amiens

After lunch, you can choose to skip stop ❷ of this tour and stay in Calais. Fashion fans shouldn't miss the starkly modern ★★ **Cité Internationale de la Dentelle et de la Mode** (Transatlantic City of Lace and Fashion Museum), on quai de la Gendarmerie (☎ 03-21-00-42-30; www.citedentelle.calais.fr; admission 5€ adults, 2.50€ ages 6–18; Apr–Oct Wed–Mon 10am–6pm; Nov–Mar Wed–Mon 10am–6pm; closed Jan 1–15). Exhibitions include dresses and accessories by Chanel, Dior, and Givenchy and underwear by Chantal Thomass. Calais's World War II story is movingly recounted in the **Musée de Mémoire 39-45,** in an eerie old German blockhouse at Parc St-Pierre (☎ 03 21-34-21-57; http://museeguerrecalais.free.fr; admission 6€ adults, 14€ families [2 adults, 2 children]; Feb–Apr and Oct–Nov Wed–Mon 11am–5pm; May–Sept daily 10am–6pm; closed Dec–Jan). Rodin sculptures and fine works by artists from the Dutch and Flemish schools are on display at the **Musée des Beaux Arts,** on rue Richelieu (☎ 03-21-46-48-40; admission 4€ adults, 2€ ages 18–25; Tues–Sat 10am–noon and 2–5pm; Sun 2–5pm). ⏱ Half-day, or 1 day if you skip ❷. Calais Tourist Office, 12 bd. Clemenceau. ☎ 03-21-96-62-40. www.calais-cotedopale.com.

After lunch leave Calais on D940 (toward Boulogne-sur-Mer); it's 20km (12 miles) to Cap Gris-Nez, 40km (25 miles) to Cap Blanc-Nez.

❷ ★★★ **Cap Blanc-Nez & the Côte d'Opale.** Spend the afternoon walking along the Channel's wild, windblown Côte d'Opale, where the Cap Gris-Nez and Cap Blanc-Nez headlands afford windswept views over the waves. ⏱ Half-day. See p. 646, ❷.

Continue for 34km (21 miles) along the coast on D940 to Boulogne-sur-Mer, or take A16, exiting at junction 32 (30km/19miles).

❸ ★★ **Boulogne-sur-Mer.** Rise early on Day 2 and head straight to the rampart-ringed **Haute Ville** (Upper Town) of this important fishing port. A splendid medley of 17th- and 19th-century buildings awaits, including the neoclassical **Palais de Justice** (Law Courts) and the Louis XV–style **Hôtel de Ville** (City Hall), built in 1734. The gray-stone, 12th-century *beffroi* (bell tower) is the oldest building in Boulogne, originally built as the dungeon for the city's first château. From here, follow the restaurant-lined **rue de Lille** to the **Basilique Notre-Dame** (☎ 03-21-99-75-98; Sept–Mar

> *This poster from the Musée de Mémoire 39–45, in Calais, denounces a French communist politician who became a fascist during World War II.*

This huge, impressive aquarium is home to more than 35,000 creatures, including penguins, sea lions, and sharks ⏱ 1 day. Boulogne-sur-Mer Tourist Office, Forum Jean Noël, quai de la Poste and parvis de Nausicaä. ☎ 03-21-10-88-10. www.tourisme-boulognesurmer.com.

On Day 3, leave Boulogne on the route de St-Omer, which becomes D341; at the roundabout, take N42 and follow signs to St-Omer via D942 and D928 (54km/34 miles).

④ ★ St-Omer. Relax for a spell in this stately 17th- and 18th-century town with cobblestone streets, pretty gardens, a canal, and impressive religious monuments. When it's time to move on, check out the **Musée de l'Hôtel Sandelin,** 14 rue Carnot (☎ 03-21-38-00-94; admission 4.50€; Wed-Sun 10am–noon and 2–6pm), a small decorative-arts museum filled with treasures; the **Cathédrale Notre-Dame de St-Omer,** 5 Enclos Notre Dame (☎ 03-21-38-23-86), with its superb organ and 13th-century tiles; and the **Bibliothèque Municipale,** 40 rue Gambetta (☎ 03-21-28-35-08), with fabulous manuscripts from the nearby 15th-century St-Bertin Abbey. After lunch, head 5km (3 miles) out of town to **La Coupole History and Remembrance Centre,** on rue du Mont-à-Car (D210) in Helfaut (admission 9€ adults, 5€ ages 5–16; July-Aug daily 10am–7pm; Sept-June daily 9am–6pm). The Nazis used this gigantic underground bunker from 1943 to 1944, to store and launch V2 rockets—the first missiles to reach the stratosphere, and the secret weapon Hitler hoped to use to destroy London. ⏱ 1 day. St-Omer Tourist Office, 4 rue du Lion d'Or. ☎ 03-21-98-08-51. www.tourisme-saintomer.com.

Early on Day 4, leave St-Omer for Cassel. Head toward A26 (via D942), but don't join it; instead pick up D933 after Arques (24km/15 miles).

⑤ ★★★ Cassel. Northeast of St-Omer, you'll enter the **Flandre Maritime,** a flat, Flemish-looking agricultural plain dissected by narrow waterways, marshlands, canals, and windmills. The hilltop town of Cassel features a Grand Place reminiscent of an English market town, panoramic views, and elegant houses dating from the 16th to the 18th centuries. Open since autumn 2010, the **Musée de Flandre,** in the 16th-century Hôtel

daily 10am–noon and 2–5pm; Apr-Aug daily 9am–noon and 2–6pm), whose dome, inspired by Paris's Panthéon (p. 72, ⑨), is visible for miles. The basilica was built between 1827 and 1866 to replace a cathedral destroyed during the Revolution. On rue de Bernet, don't miss the 13th-century, moated **château,** built for the counts of Boulogne (☎ 03-21-10-02-20; admission 4.50€ adults, 3€ students, free for ages 17 and under; Mon-Fri 10am–12:30pm and 2–5:30pm; Sat-Sun 10am–12:30pm and 2:30–6pm; closed Dec 25–Jan 1). The first military château built without a dungeon, it houses a remarkable collection of art from Egyptian times to the mid-20th century.

Have lunch on rue de Lille or on seafood-rich quai Gambetta (on the east bank of the Liane River); then spend the rest of the day around Boulogne's beaches and at the kids **Nausicaä** sea life center, on boulevard Ste-Beuve (☎ 03-21-30-99-99; www.nausicaa.fr; admission 17.40€ adults, 11.20€ ages 3–12, free for children 2 and under; July-Aug daily 9:30am–7:30pm; Sept to early Jan and mid-Jan to June daily 9:30am–6:30pm).

de la Noble-Cour castle, 26 Grand Place (☎ 03-59-73-45-60; http://museedeflandre. cg59.fr; admission 5€ adults, 3€ ages 18–25, free for ages 17 and under; Tues–Sat 10am–noon and 2–6pm; Sun 10am–6pm), explores the culture of Flanders through works by Flemish masters and world-renowned contemporary artists plus rare collections of religious, historical, ethnographic, and geographical works. ⏱ Half-day. Cassel Tourist Office, 20 Grand Place. ☎ 03-28-40-52-55. www.cassel-horizons.com.

In the afternoon, take D218A (left) out of Cassel and join D196 to Bergues (20km/ 12 miles).

6 Bergues. This old fortified wool town is where French director Danny Boon filmed his 2008 award-winning comedy *Bienvenue chez les Ch'tis (Welcome to Ch'ti Country),* putting Nord Pas de Calais back on the map. The town's **belfry** is impressive, as is the tower of the **Abbaye de St-Winoc** (founded in the 11th century), which looks like a witch's hat. You can see plenty of 16th- and 17th-century

Flemish works in the **Musée Municipal,** set inside a glorious 17th-century mansion (admission 1.30€; Wed–Fri 2–5pm; Sat–Sun 10am–noon and 2–5pm). East of Bergues (on D3), near the border with Belgium, is an early-12th-century windmill, **Noordmeulen,** believed to be the oldest in Europe (Apr–Sept Tues and Fri 2–5pm). ⏱ Half-day–1 day. Bergues Tourist Office, 5 place du Général de Gaulle, Hondschoote. ☎ 03-28-62-53-00. www.bergues.fr.

From Bergues on Day 5, take A25, exiting at junction 5 for Lille (64km/40 miles).

7 ★★★ Lille. If you have only a day in the capital of the North, spend some time around place du Général de Gaulle, shopping, eating, drinking beer, and soaking up the laid-back atmosphere, before visiting a museum of your choice. ⏱ 1 day. For detailed information on Lille, see p. 652.

On Day 6, leave Lille along A1, exit at junction 16, and follow signs to Arras-centre via D950 and D917 (52km/32 miles).

> Today many markets take place in Lille's Vieille Bourse (Old Stock Exchange).

> *Arcaded Flemish-style facades line Arras's main square.*

8 ★ **Arras.** The capital of the Artois region is an elegant assembly of arcaded squares; 17th-century, Flemish-style facades; and Art Deco buildings. Almost everything you see—besides the Art Deco style, which was applied to new buildings after 1919—was painstakingly reconstructed in its original style after World War I, when 80% of the city was destroyed. Relics of the Great War can still be seen in the ★★ **Carrière Wellington,** rue Delétoille (☎ 03-21-51-26-95; www.carriere-wellington.com; admission 6.60€ adults; 3€ ages 17 and under; daily 10am–12:30pm and 1:30–6pm; closed mid-Dec to mid-Jan). It was from these medieval chalk quarries that 24,000 Allied soldiers emerged to attack the invading Germans on April 9, 1917. You can still see the soldiers' graffiti, and clever lighting and sound effects plunge you into the oppressive atmosphere of the war. Also fascinating are **Les Boves,** 10th-century storage tunnels that served as a subterranean army camp for the 1917 offensive. The tunnels are accessible on guided tours from the tourist office. Aboveground, the flamboyant, Gothic-style **Hôtel de Ville** (City Hall), place des Héros, is topped by a UNESCO-protected, 15th- and 16th-century-style *beffroi* (belfry). Take the elevator 75m (246 ft.) to the top (2.70€) for a panoramic view of the countryside. Inside the Abbaye St-Vaast, 22 rue Paul Doumer, the

★ **Musée des Beaux Arts** (☎ 03-21-71-26-43; admission 4€ adults, 2€ ages 17 and under; Wed–Mon 9:30am–noon and 2–5:30pm) is worth visiting for its medieval sculpture, religious paintings, and 19th-century landscapes by Jean-Baptiste Camille Corot and other artists from the School of Arras. Arras's most recent cultural addition is ★★★ kids **Cité Nature,** 25 bd. Schuman (☎ 03-21-21-59-59; www.citena-ture.com; admission 7€ adults, 3€ ages 3–18; Tues–Fri 9am–5pm; Sat–Sun 2–6pm). Architect Jean Nouvel transformed this former Art Deco lamp factory into a cultural and scientific center devoted to food, agriculture, the environment, and health. ⏱ 1 day. **Arras Tourist Office, place des Héroes.** ☎ 03-21-51-26-95. www.ot-arras.fr. Sept–Mar Mon–Fri 10am–noon and 2–6pm, Sat 9am–noon and 2–6pm, Sun 10am–12:30pm and 2:30–6:30pm; Apr–Aug Mon–Sat 9am–6:30pm, Sun 10am–1pm and 2:30–6:30pm.

On Day 7, take D197 from Arras (toward Le Touquet); where Amiens is signposted, turn off to join N425, then pick up N25 to Amiens (74km/46 miles).

9 ★★ **Amiens.** Highlights in the adorable capital of Picardie include Jules Verne's house and Amiens's towering Gothic cathedral. ⏱ 1 day. For detailed information on Amiens, see p. 648.

Where to Stay & Dine in the North & Picardie

★★ **Ardres Bridge Cottage** PONT D'ARDRES/ CALAIS *FLANDERS CUISINE* Just 14km (8⅔ miles) from Calais, this typical northern farmhouse has two simple, comfortable rooms. At breakfast the hosts ply you with homemade jams, tarts, and baguettes. Home-cooked meals, ordered in advance, include local specialities such as *moules marinières* (mussels). 678 rue du Fort Bâtard (take A16 from Calais, exiting at junction 46). ☎ 03-21-96-63-92, 06-82-02-13-47. www.ardres-bridge-cottage.com. 2 units. Doubles 50€. Dinner 20€. No credit cards.

★★ **Enclos de l'Evêché** BOULOGNE-SUR-MER HAUTE VILLE *CONTEMPORARY FRENCH* This mid-19th-century mansion near the Boulogne basilica has large and airy rooms; some have Jacuzzis. The restaurant serves excellent lobster, foie gras, fish with seasonal vegetables, local cheeses, and *crème brûlée*. 6 rue de Pressy. ☎ 03-91-90-05-90. www. enclosdeleveche.com. 5 units. Doubles 70€– 135€. 3-course menu 20€–25€. MC, V. Lunch Tues–Sun, dinner Tues–Sat.

★ **Hotel-Restaurant L'Industrie** ST-OMER CENTER *SEAFOOD/FLANDERS CUISINE* On a pedestrian street near the cathedral, the Industrie is simple but charming, with small, modern rooms. The restaurant menu might include fresh fish, *Ch'ti* cheeses, and rack of lamb. 22 rue Louis Martel. ☎ 03-21-11-51-35. www.lindus.fr. 7 units. Doubles 69€–75€ (half-board available). 3-course menu 16€–18€. MC, V.

★★★ **La Corne d'Or** ARRAS CENTER This 18th-century family mansion is a fine, central place to stay. Rooms have lovely period touches, bold colors and fabrics, and a distinct air of grandeur. The copious breakfast is served in a 19th-century colonial-style dining

> Moules marinières *(mariners' mussels)* is one of several regional specialties on the menu at Ardres Bridge Cottage.

room. 1 place Guy Mollet. ☎ 03-21-58-85-94. www.lamaisondhotes.com. 6 units. Doubles 79€–116€ (some sleep 5). MC, V.

Arriving & Getting Around

By Train. Trains run to Amiens, Arras, Calais, Lille, Boulogne-sur-Mer, and Le Touquet (see www.voyages-sncf.com). Most visitors from the U.K. arrive either via the Channel Tunnel or the ferry from Dover to Calais, or by Eurostar from London St. Pancras to Lille. (See p. 698, Savvy Traveler, for more information on these modes of travel.)

By Car. Picardie and the North are easy to reach by car, with the A1 highway running straight from Paris past Arras to Lille; the A16 running from Paris to Amiens; and the A8 linking Lille to Brussels. From these *autoroutes,* numerous major "N" and smaller "D" roads link the minor destinations in this chapter.

By Plane. The nearest airports are in Paris (p. 140) and in Beauvais (Beauvais-Tillé Airport), 61km (38 miles) south of Amiens; Beauvais is served by Ryanair from the U.K. and Ireland.

Note

For hotels and restaurants on the coast, see p. 647; in Amiens, see p. 651; in Lille, see p. 655.

The Somme Battlefields Circuit

During World War I (1914–18), the battles in the Somme Valley (mostly in 1916) were some of the most horrific ever recorded, causing some 1.5 million casualties. Today a 40km (25-mile) circuit between Albert and Péronne takes you around the cemeteries where soldiers from some 25 nations are at rest. This selection can be visited on a day trip from Amiens. For more information, see www.somme-battlefields.com.

> *The Thiepval Memorial honors British and South African soldiers killed in the region during World War I.*

START Albert is 29km (18 miles) northeast of Amiens on D929. **TRIP LENGTH** 60–100km (about 40–60 miles), mostly on country roads.

❶ Musée Somme 1916, Albert. The Somme Trench Museum, in a former crypt below the town's basilica, offers an excellent introduction to World War I events in the Somme via scenes of trench life and collections of original uniforms and equipment, weaponry, and other materials rescued after the war from the surrounding fields and trenches. Rue Anicet Godin, Albert. ☎ 03-22-75-16-17. www.musee-somme-1916.eu. Admission 5€ adults, 3€ ages 6–18. Jun–Sept daily 9am–6pm; Oct–May daily 9am–noon and 2–6pm.

Where to Stay & Dine

For hotels and restaurants in Amiens, see p. 651.

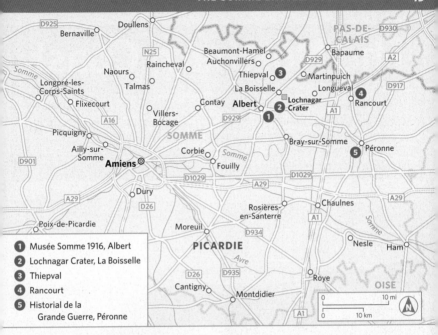

1 Musée Somme 1916, Albert
2 Lochnagar Crater, La Boisselle
3 Thiepval
4 Rancourt
5 Historial de la
   Grande Guerre, Péronne

From Albert, continue on D929 to La Boisselle (4km/2½ miles).

2 Lochnagar Crater, La Boisselle. Scars of the Great War were left not only inside the minds of surviving soldiers, but throughout the Somme countryside, which still bears the marks of battle and front lines. Nowhere is this more evident than in La Boisselle where, at the start of the 1916 battles, a huge explosion in open farmland left an impressive depression known as the Lochnagar Crater.

From La Boisselle, continue on D929, and at Pozières turn left onto D73 to Thiepval (6.5km/4 miles).

3 Thiepval. The British government erected this 45m-tall (148-ft.) memorial for the 75,085 British and South African soldiers killed here between July 1915 and 1918. Sixteen pillars form the base of the arch, onto which the names of the missing soldiers are engraved. The monument, built by Sir Edwin Lutyens in 1932, is still a pilgrimage site for many British families.

Retrace your route to Pozières and turn left onto D929. At Bapaume, join D917, and at Le Transloy, join D1017 to Rancourt (28km/17 miles total).

4 Rancourt. Rancourt's French remembrance chapel, 2 rte. nationale (☎ 03-22-85-04-47; free admission; daily 8am–6pm until 5pm Oct–Mar), is the site of an official memorial service held annually on the second Sunday of September. The chapel's burial ground is the largest French war cemetery in the Somme—the resting place of some 8,566 men, and a testimony to the violent battles in the final 3 months of the offensive, from September to November 1916.

From Rancourt, follow D1017 to Péronne (10km/6¼ miles).

5 Historial de la Grande Guerre, Péronne. Set inside old fortifications that were damaged during the fighting, the fascinating and moving Museum of the Great War displays the military and personal effects of soldiers who left their lives behind on the front lines. It also examines propaganda used during the war and illustrates the Battle of the Somme's social impact. Château de Péronne, place André Audinot, Péronne. ☎ 03-22-83-14-18. www.historial.org. Admission 7.50€ adults, 3.80€ ages 7-18. Daily 10am–6pm.

The Northern Coast

The coastline between Calais, Boulogne, and Le Touquet is dramatic, wind-swept, and thrumming with wildlife. The Baie de Somme beckons with its vast, sandy expanses, where the Somme River's fresh water mingles with the sea. The landscape here is wild and flat, reflecting the sky like a silver mirror and harboring fabulous marine life and birds.

> The Côte d'Opale's white cliffs mirror those of Dover, across the English Channel.

START Calais is 113km (70 miles) west of Lille and 296km (184 miles) north of Paris. **TRIP LENGTH** About 1 week; 180km (112 miles), mostly on coastal and country roads.

① **Calais.** Calais's austere, post–World War II buildings give way to a more charming city center. ⏲ Half-day to 1 day. See p. 638, **①**.

Drive southwest from Calais along D940 past Sangatte toward Escalles. You can reach the cliffs and beaches from Escalles, or before Escalles turn right onto Sente du Blanc-Nez to Cap Blanc-Nez (25km/16 miles total).

② ★★★ **Cap Blanc-Nez & the Côte d'Opale.** The undulating ★★★ **Cap Blanc-Nez** and ★★★ **Cap Gris-Nez** beaches and plateaus are part of the Côte d'Opale (Opal Coast), whose white cliffs are reminiscent of those in Britain, just across the straits. The cliffs are prime spots for watching seabirds. On some

beaches, you can observe sea life, see ominous World War II blockhouses, and watch boats cruising between France and England. The Cap Gris-Nez is farther south: Take D940 south to **Wissant** (where the beach is strewn with concrete vestiges of the war) past **Audinghen,** and turn right onto D191. Or continue on D940 to **Audresselles,** with its fishermen's cottages and beaches brimming with rock pools, where crabs, seaweed, and winkles hide. ⏲ 1–2 days. www.cote-dopale.com.

Follow D940 to Boulogne-sur-Mer (15km/9⅓ miles).

③ ★★ **Boulogne-sur-Mer.** The busy marina gives way to a scenic old, walled town. ⏲ 1 day. See p. 639, **③**.

From Boulogne, take A16 toward Amiens/Paris, exit at junction 26, and follow signs to Le Touquet (40km/25 miles).

> *A beach in the 19th-century seaside resort Le Touquet.*

4 ★ **kids Le Touquet.** This 19th-century seaside resort—with its golden sand, posh villas, golf courses, racecourse, casino, and pine forests—is so popular with Parisians, it's nicknamed Paris-Plage (Paris Beach). ⏱ **1 day.** Le Touquet Tourist Office, Palais des Congrès, place de l'Hermitage. ☎ 03-21-06-72-00. www. letouquet.com.

From Le Touquet, follow D940 to Le Crotoy (52km/32miles).

5 ★★★ **Baie de Somme.** Here the Somme River meets the sea, which thunders into the Baie de Somme like a locomotive each full and new moon, inundating the salty marshes where sheep usually graze; during an equinox, waves can reach 10m (30 ft.). Charming fishing towns and resorts, linked by the D940, pepper the edges of the bay. As you travel south, you'll cross first ★ **Le Crotoy,** the picturesque fishing port where Jules Verne once lived; then ★★★ **St-Valéry-sur-Somme,** with its pretty quays and lovely medieval town. On the other side of the bay, **Cayeux-sur-Mer** is a resort famed for its wooden beach huts and high tides. From St-Valéry, you can kayak along the estuary and observe the wild seals. The ★★★ **kids Club de Kayak de Mer et de Va'a**

de la Baie des Phoques (☎ 03-22-60-08-44; www.baiedesphoques.org; 40€) runs 2-hour safaris. You can watch migrating birds from huts over sand dunes and in the woods of the ★★★ **Parc du Marquenterre,** north of Le Crotoy, 25bis chemin des Garennes, St-Quentin-en-Tourmont (☎ 03-22-25-68-99; admission 9.90€ adults, 7.90€ ages 6–18, free for children 5 and under; daily 10am–6pm; closed late Dec–early Jan). ⏱ **2-3 days.** St-Valéry-sur-Somme Tourist Office, 19 place St-Martin. ☎ 03-22-60-93-50. www.saint-valery-sur-somme.fr. See also www.baiedesomme.fr.

Where to Stay & Dine

For hotels and restaurants in Calais and Boulogne-sur-Mer, see p. 643

The seafood is delicious and couldn't be fresher at ★ **Chez Mimi,** 90 rue Accary in Audresselles (☎ 03-21-32-94-00; www.resto.fr/chezmimi; lunch 16€–30€; MC, V; call for hours; closed Dec–Jan), a kitschy, old-fashioned seaside restaurant decorated with *pierrot* (mime clown) paintings and memorabilia. In Noyelles-sur-Mer, ★★★ **Château de Noyelles,** 28–30 rue du Maréchal Foch (☎ 03-22-23-68-70; www.chateaudenoyelles.com; 8 units; doubles 95€–195€; MC, V), is a sophisticated 19th-century château set amid trimmed lawns and flower beds. Rooms are lovely in whites, blues, and pale greens with period touches.

Amiens

The boldly Gothic Cathédrale Notre-Dame d'Amiens is France's largest cathedral—reason alone to visit the capital of Picardie. There's also the luxurious 19th-century Maison de Jules Verne, where the author lived for 18 years, the medieval Hortillonnages market gardens, and the treasure-filled Musée de Picardie. Amiens is also an ideal base for visiting the Somme battlefields (p. 644).

> The Musée de Picardie's painting collection includes works by Tiepolo, El Greco, Corot, Picasso, and others from the 17th to the 20th centuries.

START Amiens is 116km (72 miles) from Paris and 95km (59 miles) from Lille.

1 ★★★ **Maison de Jules Verne.** In this stately town house, Jules Verne plunged himself into his imaginary worlds, delving 20,000 leagues under the sea and traveling around the world in 80 days from his armchair every day between 5am and 11am. The museum spreads over four floors, from a winter garden to the attic, through which you relive the adventures of Verne's characters. Touching period rooms convey how the house would have looked in Verne's day, and a collection of more than 700 objects reveals the author's personality and his sources of inspiration. ⏱ 1½ hr. 2 rue Charles Dubois. ☎ 03-22-45-45-75. www. amiens.fr. Admission 7€ adults, 5€ ages 18–25; 3€ ages 8–17. Apr–Oct Mon and Wed–Fri 10am–12:30pm and 2–6:30pm; Sat–Sun 11am–6:30pm. Nov–Mar Mon and Wed–Fri 10am–12:30pm and 2–6pm; Sat–Sun 2–6pm.

Travel Tip

Park your car along boulevard Jules Verne or in the lot at place de Longueville.

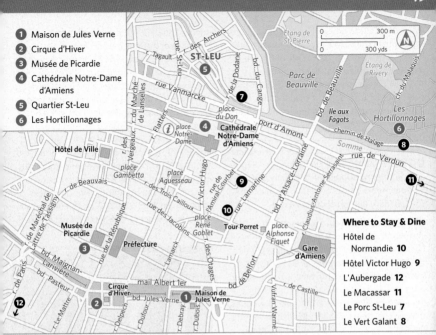

1. Maison de Jules Verne
2. Cirque d'Hiver
3. Musée de Picardie
4. Cathédrale Notre-Dame d'Amiens
5. Quartier St-Leu
6. Les Hortillonnages

Where to Stay & Dine

Hôtel de Normandie **10**
Hôtel Victor Hugo **9**
L'Aubergade **12**
Le Macassar **11**
Le Porc St-Leu **7**
Le Vert Galant **8**

② ★ **Cirque d'Hiver.** Jules Verne inaugurated this beautiful wooden winter circus, surrounded by a park, in 1889. It was designed by Emile Ricquier, pupil of Gustave Eiffel, whose famous tower was inaugurated the same year in Paris (p. 48, ⑤). Today it is used for concerts. ⏱ 15 min. Place de Longueville.

③ ★★ **Musée de Picardie.** This museum is one of the finest in France, intriguing visitors with its collection of Egyptian and Greek antiquities, and pieces from around the Picardie region. The medieval collection offers *objets d'art* and sculptures from the 12th to the 16th centuries. An amazing assembly of paintings from the 17th to the 20th centuries includes works by El Greco, Ribera, Boucher, Fragonard, Courbet, Corot, Picasso, and Bacon. ⏱ 2 hr. 48 rue de la République. ☎ 03-22-97-14-00. www.amiens.fr. Admission 5€. Tues and Fri-Sat 10am-noon and 2-6pm; Wed 10am-6pm; Thurs 10am-noon and 2-9pm; Sun 2-7pm. Closed Mon.

④ ★★★ **Cathédrale Notre-Dame d'Amiens.** There are two ways to visit Amiens's dazzling, UNESCO-protected, 13th-century cathedral: looking up 42m (138 ft.) to its medieval vaults and columns, or gazing down at its 234m-long (768-ft.) labyrinth. The cathedral was

> The Cathédrale Notre-Dame d'Amiens houses the head of John the Baptist.

started in 1220 to house the head of St. John the Baptist (still visible today), brought back from the Crusades in 1206. One of the biggest Gothic cathedrals ever constructed, it's 145m (475 ft.) tall with a girth of 200,000 cubic meters (more than 7 million cubic feet). It also wows with remarkable Gothic statuary and doors with fabulous polychromy, restored by Eugène Viollet-le-Duc in the 1850s. ⏲ 45 min. (1 hr. with guided tour). Place Notre-Dame. ☎ 03-22-71-60-50. Free admission. Apr–Sept daily 8:30am–6:30pm; Oct–Mar daily 8:30am–5:30pm. Audio-guides available. Guided tours Fri–Sun (daily during school holidays).

⑤ ★★ Quartier St-Leu. Just below the cathedral, across the water, the St-Leu Quarter, separated from the rest of Amiens by the Canal de la Somme, used to be a thriving medieval craft center, bustling with water mills. Today its narrow streets contain art galleries, bookshops, and antiques boutiques, making the area a wonderful place to wander on foot or by boat; ask at the tourist office, 40 place Notre-Dame (☎ 03-22-71-60-50; www.amiens-tourisme.com), about boat trips. During the Saturday morning *Marché sur l'Eau* (water market, which takes place throughout June), farmers from the nearby Hortillonnages marshlands (stop ⑥, below) hawk their fares from small boats floating on the waters. ⏲ 1–2 hr.

⑥ ★★ Les Hortillonnages. Cultivated since the Middle Ages by market gardeners, these bucolic "floating" gardens, enclosed by branches of the Somme and Avre rivers, extend over 300 hectares (741 acres) accessible only by boat on a guided tour. The canals that intersect the gardens are called *rieux,* navigable only on *barques a cornet* (pronounced *cornay*), Amiens's typical flat-bottomed boats, which have a raised front designed to protect the banks. This part of town is awash in bright pink, red, and yellow flora in spring and summer, and in earthy browns and greens in autumn and winter. ⏲ 2 hr. Association pour la Protection et Sauvegarde des Hortillonnages, 54 bd Beauvillé. ☎ 03-22-92-12-18. Opening hours vary; call to check, or ask at the tourist office.

Naours, an Underground Museum

Picardie's limestone plateau is a veritable Swiss cheese, having been dug out over the centuries to make refuges called *muches* ("hideouts" in the Picard language). Those in Naours (20km/12 miles north of Amiens) encompass 300 chambers, public squares, stables, wells, chimneys, and a chapel, all of which could accommodate 2,600 people plus their livestock. The British used these areas during World War I, as did the occupying German forces during World War II. **La Cité Souterraine** is a fascinating place to visit, with or without children. ⏲ 4 hr. 5 rue des Carrières, Naours. ☎ 02-33-93-71-78. www.grottesdenaours. com. Admission 10€ adults, 8€ ages 4–12, free for children 4 and under; 5€ gardens only. Feb–Apr and Sept–Dec 15 daily 10am–noon and 2–5pm; May–Aug 9:30am–6:30pm.

Side Trip for Kids

Just 18km (11 miles) west of Amiens is France's biggest archaeological park, ★★ **Samara.** This vast, rural complex of prehistoric dwellings includes workshops demonstrating how to make flint weapons, start a fire without matches, create pottery, grind corn, and weave clothes. A menhir-lined alley leads to the park, where a botanical garden introduces your wee ones to more than 600 plant varieties. *Rte. de St-Sauveur, La Chaussée-Tirancourt.* ☎ *03-22-51-82-83. www.samara.fr. Admission 9€ adults, 7.50€ ages 6–18, 25€ families (2 adults, 2 children). Mon–Fri 9:30am–5:30pm; Sat–Sun 10:30am–6pm.*

Where to Stay & Dine in Amiens

Hôtel de Normandie GARE/CENTER
Between the cathedral and the station, this hotel is an excellent value with simple, airy rooms; modern furnishings; and hearty breakfasts served in an Art Deco dining room. 1bis rue Lamartine. ☎ 03-22-91-74-99. http://hotel-normandie-80.com. 28 units. Doubles 47€–70€. MC, V.

Hôtel Victor Hugo CATHEDRAL
This friendly, family-run hotel behind the cathedral has old-fashioned but brightly colored guest rooms accessed by an old wooden staircase. The simple, comfortable rooms are a good value for the money. 2 rue de l'Oratoire. ☎ 03-22-91-57-91. www.hotel-a-amiens.com. 10 units. Doubles from 44€. MC, V.

★★ **L'Aubergade** DURY-LES-AMIENS *HAUTE CUISINE* Five minutes from Amiens's center by car, Michelin-starred chef Eric Boutté creates dreamy dishes such as rabbit roasted with prunes and mushrooms and perfect pear soufflé. 78 rte. nationale (take RN1 toward Paris, exiting at Amiens Sud). ☎ 03-22-89-51-41. www.aubergade-dury.com. 3-course menu from 39€. Main courses from 30€. MC, V. Lunch and dinner Tues–Sat. Closed 2 weeks in Aug.

★★★ **Le Macassar** CORBIE
This avant-garde hotel just outside Amiens seduces lovers of interior design with tasteful antiques and art-filled suites, each inspired by the 1920s. Prices include evening cocktails. Dinner is served upon request. *Note:* It's not suitable for children. 8 place de la République (17km/11 miles northeast of Amiens on D929/D30). ☎ 03-22-48-40-04. www.lemacassar.com. 5 units. Doubles 175€–250€. MC, V.

★ kids **Le Porc St-Leu** QUARTIER ST-LEU
ROTISSERIE On the edge of the Somme River, this diner with red banquettes specializes in hearty pork dishes—roasted, in a burger, in a sausage, cured, boiled, and casseroled. Lamb, beef, and fish are available, too. 45-47 quai Bélu. ☎ 03-22-80-00-73. http://www.picardieweb.com/restaurant-porcsaintleu. 3 courses 30€. MC, V. Lunch and dinner daily.

> *Michelin-starred L'Aubergade is just outside the center of Amiens.*

★★ **Le Vert Galant** HORTILLONNAGES *FRENCH*
In the heart of the Hortillonnages floating gardens, friendly waiters serve classic French dishes such as confit of duck and mustardy steak. 57 chemin de Halage. ☎ 03-22-92-04-27. www.le-vert-galant.com. Lunch menu 9€–18.90€; dinner menu 29€–39€. MC, V. Lunch and dinner daily.

Lille

On the Deûle River, Lille (aka Rijessel) belonged to the powerful counts of Flanders until it became French in 1667, under Louis XIV. In the 19th century, it was a center for the textile and metal industries, before falling into major decline in the 1950s. Today, the high-speed Eurostar train has made Lille *the* cultural hub of northern France—a bustling metropolis of top-notch museums and cobblestone streets sheltering quaint shops, cafes, and restaurants.

> Markets, concerts, and other events take place on place Rihour, which bustles even on a relatively quiet day.

START Lille is 220km (317 miles) north of Paris and 113km (70 miles) east of Calais.

1 ★ **Place du Général de Gaulle (Grand Place).** This square is the city's hub, lined with cafes and Flemish architecture such as the arcaded 17th-century **Vieille Bourse** (Old Stock Exchange), where markets frequently take place, and the **Grand Gard,** built in 1717 to house the king's soldiers, though it's now headquarters to the Théâtre du Nord theater company. ⊙ 30 min.

2 ★ **Place du Théâtre.** Adjacent to Grand Place, this majestic square harbors the magnificent **Opéra de Lille,** built in 1907 in the style of Paris's **Opéra Garnier** (p. 44, **8**). Towering over the square is the **Chambre de Commerce** (Chamber of Commerce), founded in 1701 by Louis XIV, with a 76m-high (249-ft.) belfry. The architect, Louis-Marie Cordonnier, used a neo-regionalist style inspired by the late-17th-century stone and brick **Beauregard Row** houses opposite. ⊙ 20 min.

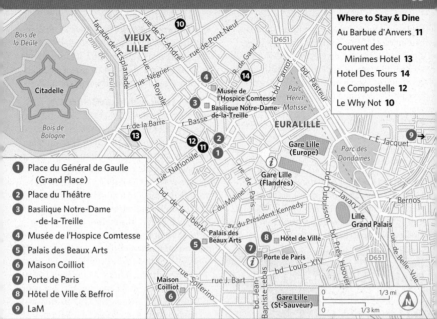

Where to Stay & Dine

Au Barbue d'Anvers **11**

Couvent des
   Minimes Hotel **13**

Hotel Des Tours **14**

Le Compostelle **12**

Le Why Not **10**

1 Place du Général de Gaulle
   (Grand Place)

2 Place du Théâtre

3 Basilique Notre-Dame
   -de-la-Treille

4 Musée de l'Hospice Comtesse

5 Palais des Beaux Arts

6 Maison Coilliot

7 Porte de Paris

8 Hôtel de Ville & Beffroi

9 LaM

3 Basilique Notre-Dame-de-la-Treille. Lille's
13th-century, Gothic-style basilica is named
after the city's medieval statue of the Virgin protected by an iron *treille* (trellis). Started in 1854,
it was completed much later, in the 1990s, by
Pierre-Louis Carlier and Peter Rice, engineer for
Centre Pompidou in Paris (p. 61, ❹). The building's central ogive is covered with 110 sheets of
white marble, just 28mm (1.1 inches) thick. ⊕ 20
min. Place Gilleson. www.cathedralelille.com. Free
admission. Mon–Sat 10am–noon and 2–6:30pm;
Sun 10am–1pm and 3–6pm.

4 Musée de l'Hospice Comtesse. Next to the
basilica, this former hospital was founded in
1237 by Countess Jeanne de Flandre and remained in service until 1939. It feels like a small,
17th-century Flemish convent, with paintings,
tapestries, wood sculptures, and porcelain from
the region. ⊕ 45 min. 32 rue de la Monnaie. ☎ 03-
28-36-84-00. Admission 3.50€ adults, 2.50€
ages 12–25, free for children 11 and under. Mon
2–6pm; Wed–Sun 10am–12:30pm and 2–6pm.
Closed 1st weekend in Sept.

5 ★★★ Palais des Beaux Arts. This gorgeous
19th-century building houses the second-
largest general-interest museum in France
(after the Louvre), featuring European
paintings by Rubens, van Dyck, and Goya;

> *The Palais des Beaux Arts is the second-
largest general-interest museum in France.*

sculptures by Carpeaux and Rodin; and key examples of 19th-century French painting, such as Courbet's *L'après-dînée à Ornans (After Dinner at Ornans)*. Don't miss the 18th-century relief maps, used by the French kings during wartime, of fortified towns in northern France and Belgium. ⏱ 1½ hr. Place de la République. ☎ 03-20-06-78-00. www.pba-lille.fr. Admission 5.50€ adults, 3.80€ ages 12–25, free for children 11 and under. Mon 2–6pm; Wed–Sun 10am–6pm. Closed 1st weekend in Sept.

6 Maison Coilliot. Art Nouveau fans shouldn't miss Maison Coilliot, designed by Hector Guimard, famed for the Art Nouveau entrances to Paris's Métro stations. 14 rue de Fleurus. Not open to the public.

Shopping in Lille

Lille is a shopping capital. On the first weekend in September, Europe's largest flea market, the **Grande Braderie de Lille,** fills the city streets with antiques, books, clothes, and kitchenware. Year-round, the Old Town is the place for luxury brands in fashion and design. An antiques market takes place every Sunday morning on place du Concert. In the pedestrianized center, you'll find department stores, and on Grand Place, **Le Furet du Nord,** one of Europe's biggest bookshops. The Jean Nouvel-designed shopping mall **Euralille,** behind the station (www.euralille.com), houses 120 shops and a hypermarket; while the multiethnic **Quartier de Wazemmes,** on rue Gambetta and place de la Nouvelle Aventure, is the realm of spice markets and discount bazaars. In south Lille, the up-and-coming **Faubourg des Modes** (around rue du Faubourg des Postes) is the new fashion quarter, filled with boutique-ateliers where young stylists sell their own collections.

7 ★★ Porte de Paris. Built between 1685 and 1692, this white triumphal arch celebrates Louis XIV's conquest of Lille in 1667. Victory sits atop trophies of arms, flags, and a crown of laurels on the Sun King's head. Place Simon Vollant.

8 ★★★ Hôtel de Ville and Beffroi. City Hall was built between 1924 and 1932, combining local traditions (triangular gables, basket-handle windows) and modernity (concrete for the structure, Art Nouveau and Art Deco decor). Fine collections of contemporary art line the walls of the interior; perhaps most original is a fresco painted by Icelandic artist Erro (born Guðmundur Guðmundsson, in 1932), which tells the history of Lille in the form of a comic strip. Back outside, you can't help but notice the UNESCO-protected *beffroi* (belfry), propped up by Lydéric and Phinaer, the giants who founded the city. Built between 1929 and 1931, it is the region's highest belfry at 104m (341 ft.). You can climb to the top on guided visits each Friday and Saturday at 10:30am and 11:30am. Reserve with the tourist office, place Rihour (☎ 08-91-56-20-04; www.lilletourism.com). ⏱ 30 min.–1hr. Place Roger Salengro. City Hall Mon–Fri 8am–5pm; Sat 8am–noon.

9 ★★★ LaM. Just outside of Lille's center, the spanking new LaM (Museum of Modern and Contemporary Art and Art Brut) houses a prestigious collection of 20th-century art and, for the first time in Europe, 21st-century art, including Art Brut (Raw Art). A total of 4,500 works—many never before displayed to the public—are exhibited, and certain sections of the museum are devoted to major temporary exhibitions. Inside, expect to see works by Georges Braque, Amadeo Modigliani, Pablo Picasso, and others, while outside, you can wander the gardens amid sculptures by Alexander Calder. ⏱ 2 hr. 1 allée du Musée, Villeneuve d'Ascq. ☎ 03-20-19-68-68. www.musee-lam.fr. Admission 7€ adults, 5€ ages 17 and under, free for everyone 1st Sun of the month. Tues–Sun 10am–6pm.

Getting Around

Leave your car at **place du Général de Gaulle** (☎ 03-20-31-83-78; 1.80€/hr) and use Lille's excellent Transpole métro, tramway, and bus system (www.transpole.fr).

Where to Stay & Dine in Lille

> At Le Compostelle, diners feast in a beautifully restored former way station on the St-Jacques-de-Compostelle pilgrimage route.

★★ Au Barbue d'Anvers GRAND PLACE *LILLOIS*
At the bottom of a courtyard within a 16th-century brick building, this traditional *Ch'ti estaminet* (pub) serves local dishes such as *la carbonnade flamande, waterzoï,* ham in beer jelly, and rabbit pâté with juniper berries. There are 45 beers to choose from, too. 1bis rue St-Etienne. ☎ 03-20-55-11-68. www.lebarbuedanvers.fr. Lunch menu 20€–24€; dinner menu 35€; 3 courses 40€. MC, V. Lunch and dinner Mon–Sat.

★ Couvent des Minimes Hotel CENTER-WEST
This converted 17th-century convent with a glass atrium/dining room provides a mix of period and contemporary features throughout. Rooms are a decent size and modern. 17 quai du Wault. ☎ 03-20-30-62-62. www.alliance-lille. com. 83 units. Doubles 215€–420€. MC, V.

Hotel Des Tours CENTER
Right by the Musée de l'Hospice Comtesse, this unremarkable hotel is an easy walk from most spots on this tour. Guest rooms are no-frills, modern, and comfortable. 27 rue des Tours. ☎ 03-59-57-47-00. www.hotel-des-tours.com. 64 units. Doubles 130€–215€. MC, V.

★★ Le Compostelle GRAND PLACE *CONTEMPO-RARY FRENCH* This 16th-century French-style restaurant is in a lovely setting littered with sculpted pillars and friezes. Inside, the decor is chic and contemporary. The menu might include turbot marinated in lemon and ginger or roasted duck with curried apricots and asparagus. Vegetarian dishes are available. 4 rue St-Etienne. ☎ 03-28-38-08-30. www. lecompostelle.fr. Lunch 18€–23€; dinner 29€–46€. MC, V. Lunch and dinner daily.

★ Le Why Not OLD TOWN *CONTEMPORARY FRENCH* Under brick arches in a modern dining room, feast on French cuisine with a fresh twist: duck roasted with ginger and polenta, snails roasted with star anise, lobster with asparagus risotto, and chocolate fondant with hazelnuts. 9 rue Maracci. ☎ 03-20-74-14-14. www.lewhynot-restaurant.fr. Lunch 21.50€–25€; dinner 28.50€–33€. MC, V. Lunch Tues–Fri, dinner Tues–Sat.

France's History & Culture

> One of the best times to see
Mont-St-Michel is at night,
when the medieval city takes
on a magical quality.

France's 10 Greatest Cultural Hits

1.
2.
4.
5.
3.

① Eiffel Tower. For the 1889 World's Fair in Paris, France celebrated the engineering prowess of the Industrial Revolution with this elegant, lattice ironwork tower. Until New York's Chrysler building was finished in 1930, the 324m (1,063-ft.) opus of engineer Gustave Eiffel was the tallest man-made structure in the world. See p. 48, ⑤.

② Lascaux. Few of the world's prehistoric cave paintings are as well preserved as those in Lascaux, in the Dordogne region: The high-antlered elk, bulls, and horses pursued by arrows look as if they were painted yesterday. The real site was closed in 1963 for the sake of research and preservation, but don't snub the fabulously recreated copies at Lascaux II. See p. 602, ②.

③ Coco Chanel. Who hasn't admired Chanel's trademark "little black dress"? Coveted by the rich and famous over the last century, the couturier's legacy lives on in wardrobes, in museums, and on catwalks worldwide. See p. 677.

④ New Wave Cinema. In the 1950s and 60s, many French filmmakers rejected classic-style cinematography in favor of their own form, coined by critics as "La Nouvelle Vague" (New Wave). Directors such as Jean-Luc Godard, François Truffaut, Eric Rohmer, and Claude Chabrol used the social and political upheavals of postwar France to feed much of their work, often studying Western classics and applying low-budget, avant-garde stylistic direction. Their films are emblematic of the movement and of art-house cinema as a whole. See p. 446.

⑤ Impressionism. Between the 1870s and 1920s, painters such as Claude Monet, Edouard Manet, and Pierre-Auguste Renoir invented this brazen alternative to the rigidity of the neoclassic and Romantic ideals lionized at the time, adopting a free, open style characterized by deceptively loose compositions; swift, visible brushwork; and, often, light colors. For subjects, they turned away from the historical depictions of previous styles and toward landscapes and scenes of daily life. See p. 672.

⑥ Victor Hugo. The 19th-century writer and statesman gave the western world two of its

most-read novels: *Les Misérables* (p. 675) and *The Hunchback of Notre-Dame.* But he was also known as France's greatest poet, with the publication of *Les Contemplations* and *Les Légendes des Siècles.*

7 Citroën 2CV. The French love to drive. No other car comes as close to the French heart than its beloved, rickety Citroën 2CV. It was designed to move the nation away from horses and carts, but it continued to seduce the utilitarian population from 1948 to the 1990s with its low operating costs.

8 Philosophy. Intellectuals (namely, writers and philosophers) are revered in France, so it is no surprise that the country should have produced some of the world's leading thinkers. After Montaigne, who established essay writing as an art form in the 16th century, came Descartes, master of logic, and Enlightenment thinker Voltaire, famed for his 1759 satire *Candide.* More recently, in the 1940s, Jean-Paul Sartre led the Existentialist movement, based on the premise that philosophical thought should focus on the conditions of individual existence and on each person's own emotions, actions, responsibilities, and thoughts.

9 Edith Piaf. The "Little Sparrow" is universally regarded as France's greatest popular singer, presenting *Chanson* to the world with *"La Vie en Rose"* and *"Non, Je ne Regrette Rien."* In 2007, actress Marion Cotillard won an Oscar for her interpretation of Piaf in Oliver Dahan's film *La Môme* (in English, *La Vie en Rose*). Piaf died at age 47 of liver cancer and rests in peace today in Paris's Père-Lachaise Cemetery. See p. 69, **12**.

10 Coq au Vin. France produces around 400 types of cheese; it is the world's leading center for wine; each region has its own cuisine; and mealtimes can last for hours. However, if one dish captures the intricacy of the art of French cuisine, it's this hearty creation, native to Burgundy, which draws on the best of the land: red wine, a well-nourished male chicken, mushrooms, and onions—and the unique skills of the chef.

A Timeline of French History

CHARLEMAGNE.

EARLY YEARS

58–51 B.C. Julius Caesar conquers Gaul (roughly, today's north-central France).

52 B.C. The Romans build Lutetia, later Paris, on an island in the Seine River.

2ND CENTURY A.D. Christianity reaches Gaul.

Under Clovis I, the ferocious Franks defeat the Roman armies and establish the Merovingian dynasty.

768 Charlemagne (768–814) (left) becomes the Frankish king and establishes the Carolingian dynasty, ruling all the land between northern Italy, Bavaria, and Paris.

1000

1066 William the Conqueror of Normandy invades England and conquers King Harold's army at the Battle of Hastings, depicted in the Bayeux Tapestry (p. 213, ❸).

1163 The first stone is laid for Notre-Dame de Paris Cathedral (left).

1270 Louis IX (St. Louis) dies, along with most of his army, in Tunis on the Eighth Crusade.

1309 Philip the Fair establishes the Avignon papacy, which lasts nearly 70 years and almost trumps Rome as the seat of Catholicism.

1347–51 The bubonic plague (Black Death) kills 33% of the population of Europe.

1400

1431 The English burn Joan of Arc at the stake in Rouen (left) for resisting their occupation of France.

1453 The Hundred Years' War ends, expelling the English Plantagenet dynasty from France.

1562–98 Catholics fight Protestants; Henri IV converts to Catholicism and issues the Edict of Nantes, granting limited rights to Protestants.

1643–1715 Louis XIV, the Sun King, develops a powerful army, but wars in Flanders and court extravagance sow the seeds of decline.

1789–94 The most famous event in French history: the French Revolution. Rioters storm the Bastille prison on July 14, 1789, and the terrible Reign of Terror begins.

1800

1799 General Napoleon (left) unites opposing factions. His victories in Italy solidify his power in Paris.

1814-15 Napoleon fails to take Russia and abdicates. The English defeat him at Waterloo and exile him to St. Helena.

1830-48 Eighteen years of monarchy with Louis-Philippe end with elected president Napoleon III (nephew of Napoleon I).

1851-71 President Napoleon names himself Emperor Napoleon III.

1870-71 Paris falls to Franco-Prussian invaders. France gives up Alsace-Lorraine but colonizes North Africa and Southeast Asia.

1900-1958

1914-18 World War I (left). French casualties exceed four million.

1934 The Great Depression begins; clashes between left- and right-wing ideologies spur a political crisis.

1936 Germans march into the demilitarized Rhineland.

1939 Germany invades Poland, and France declares war.

1940 Paris falls to Germany on June 14. General de Gaulle, exiled in London, directs French Resistance fighters.

1944 Allied invasion of Normandy (see p. 216).

1945 World War II ends with Germany's defeat.

1954-58 Algeria wins independence from France and refugees flood into France.

1958-2010

1958 De Gaulle calls for a France independent from the United States and Europe.

1968 Students riot in Paris, and de Gaulle resigns.

1981 François Mitterrand (left) becomes the first Socialist president since World War II.

1994 Old wounds are healed as the Channel Tunnel links France to England.

1995 Jacques Chirac wins the French presidency.

2000-2002 The euro is officially introduced and, 2 years later, adopted.

2007-2010 Nicolas Sarkozy is elected president in May 2007. He marries singer Carla Bruni in 2008. After several scandals—including the 2010 expulsion of the Romani—his party, the rightist UMP, preps for the 2012 elections. The Left is divided.

A Brief History of France

> Les Captives—*a scene from the conquest of the Gauls by Julius Caesar's armies.*

> Charlemagne is remembered as the greatest medieval king.

Julius Caesar & Early Gaul

In 58 B.C., the boundaries of Roman Gaul, the ancient region corresponding roughly with France and Belgium, extended deep into the forests of the Paris basin and up to the edges of the Rhine. By 52 B.C., Julius Caesar had colonized an island in the Seine (today's Ile de la Cité in Paris, founded by Celtic settlers, the Parissi), naming it Lutetia. As the Roman Empire declined, however, its armies retreated to colonies along a strip of the Mediterranean coast, including Arles and Nîmes (which retain some of the best Roman monuments in Europe today). The rising Christian church, for all its abuses, was a guardian of civilization during the centuries of anarchy following Rome's decline, even if the Christianity adopted by many chieftains was viewed as heretical by Rome.

Clovis, Catholicism & the Merovingian Dynasty

In the 5th century A.D., when Clovis (king of Gaul's Franks) converted to Catholicism, he cleverly swung the approval of the pope, the support of the archbishop of Reims, and the loyalty of many Gallic tribes who'd grown disenchanted with anarchy. In fact, one could say that Clovis's baptism was the beginning of a collusion between the Catholic church and the French monarchy that would flourish until the French Revolution in 1789.

When Clovis died in 511, his kingdom was split among his heirs, effectively founding the Merovingian dynasty. This began a period of feudalism that lasted more than 250 years, a quasi-anarchic time often referred to as the Dark Ages (compared to the enlightened colonization by the Romans).

Charlemagne & France vs. Germany

The Carolingians emerged from the wreckage of the Merovingian court. By the mid-8th century, after halting several Muslim invasions, their empire stretched from the Pyrenees deep into the German forests, encompassing much of modern France, Germany, and northern Italy. Chief among the Carolingians was Charlemagne, France's pride and joy, crowned in Rome on Christmas Day 800. Despite his magnetism and a legacy as the great uniter of Christian Europe, cultural rifts formed in his sprawling empire, and by the time of his death, most of it was divided between two of his three squabbling heirs: Charles of Aquitaine annexed the western region and Louis of Bavaria took the east. Historians credit this hugely important division with the development of modern France and Germany as separate nations, although these "new" countries were soon invaded by Vikings from the north, Muslim Saracens from the south, and Hungarians from the east.

The Middle Ages: Anglo-French Rivalry & St. Louis

In 1154 the annulment of Eleanor of Aquitaine's marriage to Louis VII of France (reigned 1137–80) and her subsequent marriage to Henry II of England (reigned 1154–89) placed the western half of France under English control—an act that would bring about centuries of Anglo-French rivalry. However, this also was a period of growth for France, both architecturally—with the construction of magnificent Gothic cathedrals—and socially, as France's population grew and its social order settled. Ruling families formed alliances through marriages, and the size of the territory controlled from Paris doubled. Philippe Auguste (Philip II, reigned 1179–1223), in particular, infiltrated more prominent families than anyone else in France, successfully marrying members of his family into the Valois, Artois, and Vermandois dynasties. He did much to advance the country. After ongoing conflicts, he reclaimed the regions of Normandy and Anjou in western France from the English. And he overhauled government, bringing financial stability to France and enriching the middle classes—something

that made him popular with ordinary folk.

Louis IX (St. Louis, reigned 1229–70) emerged as the 13th century's most memorable king. He ceded most of the military conquests of his predecessors to the English, but it was under his rule that the world received such architectural wonders as Notre-Dame and Ste-Chapelle in Paris.

> *The Black Death, which decimated a third of Europe's population, was frequently portrayed in medieval European art.*

The Black Death, the Hundred Years' War & the French Renaissance

The first half of the 14th century saw an increase in the wealth and power of the French kings and in overall prosperity. But the country was hit hard, along with the rest of Europe, when the **Black Death** (bubonic plague) took hold in 1348, killing an estimated 33% of Europe's population, decimating the population of Paris, and setting the stage for the exodus of the French monarchs to

safer climes in such places as the Loire Valley.

In the mid-14th century, the **Hundred Years' War** began (1337–1453), with the English and French (the Plantagenet and Valois houses, respectively) squabbling over power. The English managed to control almost all the north (Picardy and Normandy), Champagne, parts of the Loire Valley, and the huge region called Guyenne—until Joan of Arc, age 19, stepped in and rallied French troops, settling French Charles VII on the throne in Reims Cathedral. The English soon bit back, declaring her a heretic and burning her at the stake in 1431. Her death was not in vain: The French eventually managed to drive out the discontented English, leaving them only the Norman port of Calais.

In the late 1400s, Charles VIII married Brittany's last duchess, Anne, unifying France with its Celtic-speaking western outpost. But during this period the greatest credit goes to François I (reigned 1515–47), who strengthened the monarchy financially and politically, and husbanded the arts into a form of patronage (notably, the French Renaissance) that French monarchs would approve for centuries.

The *Grand Siècle*

In 1624, Louis XIII (reigned 1610–43) appointed Catholic Cardinal Richelieu his chief minister. Richelieu amassed enormous power, practically running the country until his

> *The Sun King Louis XIV is most remembered for his warfare and love of the arts.*

> *In many Revolutionary paintings, a pert-breasted woman, Marianne, represents the French Republic.*

death in 1642. His aim—to invest the monarchy with total power—paved the way for the eventual absolutism of Louis XIV.

Louis XIV (the Sun King, named after his emblem; reigned 1643–1715) was just 9 when he ascended to the throne, but he became the most powerful monarch Europe had seen since the Roman emperors. At this time, France's population had grown to around 20 million (in contrast to 8 million in England and 6 million in Spain); France's colonies in Canada, the West Indies, and America (Louisiana) were stronger than ever; and its ports, especially Bordeaux, also grew and prospered with its success in the West Indian slave and sugar trades. The economy and the arts flourished, as did a sense of aristocratic style that is remembered with bittersweet nostalgia today. There is perhaps no better symbol of this

universal surplus than Louis's palace at Versailles, one of France's most flamboyant monuments.

Under the Sun King's orders, however, France conducted a series of expensive wars that, coupled with high taxes and bad harvests, stirred up much discontent.

The Revolution

In the 18th century, the Enlightenment (an intellectual movement headed by great French thinkers such as Rousseau and Voltaire) was instructing the world on the struggle against absolutism, religious fanaticism, and superstition. From this era emerged the Declaration of the Rights of Man, an enlightened document published in 1789; its influence has since been cited as a model of democratic ideals. That same year, when "the people" overthrew authority by storming the Bastille prison in Paris, fate was sealed: Europe would never be the same again. On August 10, 1792, troops from Marseille, aided by a Parisian mob, threw Louis XVI and his Austrian-born queen, Marie

Antoinette, into prison. A year later they were guillotined on place de la Concorde.

In the ensuing bloodbaths and reigning terror (known in French simply as *La Terreur*), thousands of heads rolled off the guillotines, providing both the most heroic and the most horrible anecdotes in French history.

> *France's self-proclaimed emperor Napoleon was actually born off the mainland in Corsica.*

The Rise of Napoleon

A political and military genius, Napoleon Bonaparte, appeared on the landscape just when the French were becoming sickened by the anarchy following their Revolution. He promised to reunite France and bring an end to the chaos. And so in 1799, at the age of 30, he was crowned First Consul and Master of France.

Napoleon's many successful military campaigns greatly increased France's power in Europe. However, a failed invasion of Russia in 1812 (resulting in his infamous retreat from Moscow, during which 400,000 French soldiers died in Russia's harsh winter) greatly weakened his army, and in 1815 he was defeated at the Battle of Waterloo by combined armies of the English, Dutch, and Prussians. He was exiled to the British-held island of St. Helena in the South Atlantic, where he died, some say by poison, in 1821.

The Bourbons & the Second Empire

In 1814, following Napoleon's abdication, the Bourbon monarchy that was overthrown by the Revolution was re-established with Louis XVIII and, later, Charles X. A renewal of the ancient regime's oppressions, however, didn't sit well in a France that favored new, egalitarian causes.

In 1830, Charles X was removed from power after a succession of uprisings, and Louis-Philippe, duc d'Orléans, was elected king under a liberalized constitution. His reign lasted for 18 years until another revolution, in 1848, saw Napoleon III (Bonaparte's nephew) become president—and later, in 1851, emperor.

This was an era of rebirth: The clergy gained in status,

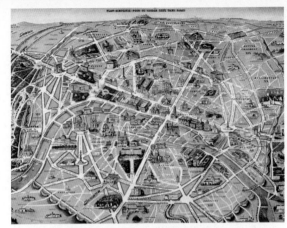

> In this 19th-century map of Paris, you can see where the city boundaries once lay—roughly today's boulevard Péripherique.

steel production began, a railway system and Indochinese colonies were established, new technologies fostered new kinds of industry, and Baron Georges-Eugène Haussmann radically altered Paris by demolishing medieval slums in favor of the grand, uniform boulevards the world knows today.

However, in 1870 the Prussians defeated Napoleon III at Sedan and held him prisoner along with 100,000 of his soldiers. The Prussians then besieged Paris, which once again brought bloodshed to the capital. When they finally withdrew, in 1871, peace and prosperity slowly returned. The Impressionists revolutionized the art world. Writers such as Flaubert and Proust redefined the French novel. The world's most famous edifice, the Eiffel Tower, was built as part of the 1889 Universal Exposition.

By 1890, a new corps of satirists (among them Emile Zola) had exposed the country's wretched living conditions and the underlying hypocrisy of late-19th-century French society. The 1894 Dreyfus Affair exposed the corruption of French army officers who had destroyed the career and reputation of a Jewish colleague (Albert Dreyfus), who was falsely and deliberately punished for treason. These ethnic tensions would lead to further divisiveness in the 20th century.

The World Wars

International rivalries, thwarted colonial ambitions, and conflicting alliances led to World War I (1914–18), which, after decisive German victories for 2 years, degenerated into the mud-slogged horror of trench warfare. Mourning between four and five million casualties, Europe suffered psychological scars that have never really healed. After the Allied victory, economic problems, plus demoralization stemming from years of fighting, encouraged the spread of socialism and communism. The French

> *Student protests in 1968 led to the resignation of Charles de Gaulle.*

> *In 1940, Hitler's armies marched through the defeated French capital from the Arc de Triomphe.*

government, led by Georges Clemenceau, demanded every centime of reparations it could from a crushed Germany.

The worldwide depression that followed had devastating repercussions in France. The crisis reached a crescendo on June 14, 1940, when Hitler's armies marched down the Champs-Elysées, as a puppet French government was established at Vichy under the authority of Marshal Pétain. The immediate collapse of the French army is viewed as one of the most significant humiliations in modern French history, and it is still difficult to broach the subject of occupation and collaboration today.

Pétain and his regime cooperated with the Nazis, deporting more than 75,000 French Jews to German extermination camps. Meanwhile, pockets of resistance fighters waged small-scale guerrilla attacks against the Nazis throughout the war, and free French forces continued to fight along with the Allies on battlegrounds such as North Africa. Charles de Gaulle, the irascible giant whose personality is forever associated with the politics of his era, established himself as the head of the French government in exile, operating first from London and then from Algiers.

One of the most documented and inspirational battles of World War II took place on June 6, 1944. The largest armada in history (mainly British and American soldiers) landed on the beaches of Normandy. Paris rose in rebellion before the Allied armies arrived, and on August 26, 1944, Charles de Gaulle entered the capital as head of the government. The Fourth Republic was declared even as Nazi snipers shot their last from scattered rooftops throughout the city.

The Postwar Years

The Fourth Republic (1946–58) witnessed the rise and fall of 22 governments and 17 *premiers* (prime ministers). Thousands of French soldiers died on foreign soil as colonies in North Africa and Indochina rebelled. After a bitter defeat in 1954, France ended the war in Indochina and freed its former colony. It also granted internal self-rule to Tunisia and, under slightly different circumstances, Morocco (both in 1956).

It was the 1958 rebellion against French rule in Algeria, however, that signaled the end of the Fourth Republic. De Gaulle was called back from retirement to initiate a new constitution, the Fifth Republic, with stronger executive controls. Yet to almost everyone's dissatisfaction, de Gaulle ended the Algerian war in 1962 by granting independence. Streams of *pieds-noirs* (French-born residents of Algeria) flooded back into metropolitan France, often settling in makeshift refugee camps in Provence and the Languedoc.

In 1968, still more social unrest came about when a violent coalition hastily formed between the nation's students and its blue-collar workers. Their fierce demonstrating led to the collapse of the government, and de Gaulle resigned. Power passed to his second-in-command, Georges Pompidou, and his successor, Valéry Giscard d'Estaing, both of whom continued de Gaulle's policies.

Modern France

When François Mitterrand took center stage in 1981, he was the first Socialist leader since World War II. He stayed for two terms, during which he spent billions of francs on his *Grands Projets,* all controversial architectural additions (such as the Louvre's pyramids, the Opéra Bastille, the Cité de la Musique, and the Grande Arche de la Défense) that have woven their way into Paris's permanent and well-loved skyline.

On May 7, 1995, after Mitterand's death, ex-mayor of Paris Jacques Chirac won the presidency. But Chirac's popularity faded in the wake of unrest caused by an 11.5% unemployment rate, a barrage of terrorist attacks by extreme Algerian Muslims, and an economy struggling to meet European Union entry requirements. A wave

> *Before becoming the French president, Nicolas Sarkozy was mayor of the Paris suburb of Neuilly-sur-Seine.*

of terrorist attacks in 1995 brought an unfamiliar wariness to the nation's capital: Six bombs killed seven people and injured 115.

Then it was France's turn to infuriate the world: Throughout 1995 and early 1996, the nation enraged everyone from Greenpeace to the governments of Australia and New Zealand by resuming the policy of exploding nuclear bombs on isolated Pacific atolls. In 2002 France kissed *au revoir* to its beloved franc and watched as the introduction of a new currency, the euro, caused prices to rise.

The year 2003 was a dark one: Attacks against Jews reached their highest level since World War II—an anti-Semitic tendency that coincided with heightened tensions in the Middle East. Washington's decision to invade Iraq drove a wedge between the United States and France. When George W. Bush arrived in Paris in June 2004, thousands of antiwar and anti-Bush protesters marched through the streets.

France Today

In May 2007, rightist Nicolas Sarkozy was elected the sixth president of the Fifth Republic. His election was followed almost immediately by a publicized romance with ex-model and singer Carla Bruni and their marriage in February 2008. The same year, opinion polls registered his popularity at an all time low (35%)—a negative image reinforced when a skirmish at the Salon de l'Agriculture saw the president utter *"Casse toi, pauve con"* ("P*ss off, stupid twat") to a man who had just insulted him.

Sarkozy's mandate is not an easy one, thwarted as it is by the worldwide financial crisis. However, he has left a trail of controversial laws and scandals, including the banning of *burqas* (the outer garment worn by some Islamic women to cover their bodies and faces in public) in public places and the expulsion of the Romani population from French territory (2010). The 2012 elections will determine whether Sarkozy receives a second mandate.

French Architecture

Roman 125 B.C.–A.D. 450
Provence was Rome's first transalpine conquest, and the legions of Julius Caesar quickly subdued the Celtic tribes across France, converting it into Roman Gaul.

Nîmes (p. 432) preserves from the 1st century B.C. a 20,000-seat amphitheater, a Corinthian temple called the "Square House," a fine archaeology museum, and the astounding **Pont du Gard,** a 47m-long (154-ft.), three-story aqueduct made of cut stones fitted without mortar.

From the Augustan era of the 1st century A.D., **Arles** (p. 397, ❹) preserves a 25,000-seat amphitheater, and the city's excellent antiquity museum shows examples of Roman and Gallo-Roman art, statuary, and architecture. The nearby **Glanum** (p. 395, ❷) excavations outside **St-Rémy-de-Provence**

Roman Features
- The load-bearing arch
- The use of concrete, brick, and stone

(p. 395, ❷) offer a complete, albeit ruined, glimpse of an entire Roman provincial town, from a few pre-Roman Gallic remnants and a 20 B.C. arch to the last structures sacked by invading Goths in A.D. 480.

Romanesque 800–1100
After the Roman Empire, during the monastic realm, when the church became increasingly influential, new styles appeared in religious architecture. Romanesque churches were large, with a wide nave and aisles to accommodate the faithful who came to hear Mass and to worship at the altars of various saints. To support the weight of all that masonry, the walls had to be thick and solid (meaning they could be pierced by only a few small windows) and had to rest on huge piers, giving churches from the Norman era a dark, somber feeling. The **Cathédrale St-Bénignes** in Dijon (p. 336, ❹) was the first French Romanesque church, but of that era only the crypt remains. The **Cathédrale St-Pierre** in Angoulême (p. 533, ❸), typical of the style, has a single large nave, a rounded apse with small radiating chapels, and a pair of transept mini-apses.

Gothic Architecture
By the 12th century, engineering developments freed architecture from the heavy, thick walls of the Romanesque era and allowed ceilings to soar, walls to thin, and windows to proliferate. Gothic was France's greatest homegrown

Romanesque Features
- Rounded arches: These load-bearing architectural devices allowed architects to open up wide naves and spaces, channeling the weight of the stone walls and ceiling across the curve of the arch and into the ground through the columns or pilasters.
- Thick walls.
- Small and infrequent windows.

architectural style, copied throughout Europe.

Instead of dark, relatively unadorned Romanesque interiors that forced the eyes of the faithful toward the altar, the Gothic interior enticed the churchgoers' gaze upward to high ceilings filled with light. The priests still conducted Mass in Latin, but now peasants could "read" the stories told in stained-glass windows and colored carvings. The squat, brooding exteriors of the Romanesque fortresses of God were replaced by graceful buttresses and soaring spires, which rose from town centers like beacons of religion. The statuary, the spire, and some 150 glorious stained-glass windows of the **Cathédrale Notre-Dame de Chartres** (p. 138) make it a must-see, while the **Cathédrale Notre-Dame de Reims** (p. 254, **1**) has more than 2,300 exterior statues and stained glass that ranges from 13th-century rose window originals to 20th-century works by Marc Chagall. **Paris's Cathédrale Notre-Dame** (p. 40, **7**) has good buttresses, along with a trio of France's best rose windows, portal carvings, a choir screen of carved reliefs, and gruesome gargoyles (many are actually 19th-century neo-Gothic). The sine qua non of stained glass, of course, is Paris's **Ste-Chapelle** (p. 46, **1**).

Renaissance 1500–1630

In architecture as in painting, the Renaissance came from Italy and was only slowly Frenchified. And as in painting, its rules stressed proportion, order, classical inspiration, and precision in order to create unified, balanced structures. The Loire Valley is home to many Renaissance châteaux. Foremost is the Loire's **Domaine National de Chambord** (p. 147, **2**), started in 1519, probably according to plans by Leonardo da Vinci. In contrast, the **Château de Chenonceau**

Gothic Features

- Pointed arches: These could carry more weight than rounded ones.

- Cross vaults: Instead of being flat, the square patch of ceiling between four columns arches up to a point in the center, creating four sail shapes, sort of like the underside of a pyramid.

- Flying buttresses: These free-standing exterior pillars, connected by graceful, thin arms of stone, help channel the weight of the building and its roof out and down into the ground.

- Stained glass: The multitude and size of Gothic windows allowed them to be filled with Bible stories and symbolism portrayed in colorful patterns of stained glass. The use of stained glass was more common in the later Gothic periods.

- Spires: These pinnacles of masonry seem to defy gravity and reach toward heaven.

- Gargoyles: Sculptures in the form of often hideous faces or chimeras adorn the exterior to chase away evil spirits.

Renaissance Features

- A sense of proportion.

- A reliance on symmetry

- The use of classical orders: This specifies three types of column capitals—Doric, Ionic, and Corinthian.

- Steeply pitched roofs: They often feature dormer windows (upright windows projecting from a sloping roof).

(p. 149, **4**), home to many a French king's wife or mistress, is a fanciful fairy-tale castle built in the middle of a river. The **Pierre Lescot** wing of the Louvre (p. 50, **1**) is another fine example of Renaissance architecture.

Beyond the Renaissance 1630–1800

During the reign of Louis XIV, art and architecture were subservient to political ends. Buildings were grandiose and severely ordered on the Versailles model. Opulence was

Classical Features

- Highly symmetrical, rectangular structures based on the classical orders.

- Projecting central sections topped by triangular pediments.

- Mansard roof: A defining feature and true French trademark, developed by François Mansart, a mansard roof has a double slope—the lower is longer and steeper than the upper.

- Dormer windows.

- *Oeil-de-bouef:* These "ox-eyes" are small, round windows that poke out of the roof's slope.

saved for interior decoration, which increasingly became detailed and self-indulgent **rococo** (especially from 1715–50, after the death of Louis XIV). Externally, rococo was noticeable only in a greater elegance and delicacy. In Paris, seek out Delamair's Marais town house, the **Hôtel de Soubise** (1706–12), and the prime minister's residence, the **Hôtel Matignon** (1721), by Courtonne. For rococo decor, check out the **Clock Room** in Versailles.

Rococo tastes didn't last long, however, and soon a **neoclassical** movement was raising structures, such as Paris's **Pantheon** (1758), that were even more strictly based on ancient models than the earlier classicist designs had been.

Louis Le Vau (1612–70) was the chief architect of the Louvre, from 1650 to 1670, a project that put him and his collaborators—including **François Mansart** (1598–1666), interior decorator **Charles Le Brun** (1619–90), and unparalleled landscape gardener **André Le Nôtre** (1613–1700)—on Louis XIV's radar and landed them the commission to rebuild **Versailles** (1669–85) as Europe's grandest palace.

19th-Century

The 19th century saw several distinct styles, starting with the **First Empire** (1804–14) under Napoleon Bonaparte, distinguished by elegant neoclassical furnishings, and strong lines often accented with a simple curve. The ultimate paean to the classical style was the **Arc de Triomphe** (1836; p. 48, **6**), Napoleon's imitation of a Roman triumphal arch.

Under the **Second Empire,** during Napoleon III's reign,

> Initially built as a temporary structure, the Eiffel Tower is now inseparable from Paris.

classicism was reinterpreted in a dramatic mode—especially by Baron Haussmann (1809–91), who cut broad boulevards through the city's tangled medieval neighborhoods to restructure Paris. The **Place de l'Etoile,** anchored by the Arc de Triomphe, from where long boulevards such as the Champs-Elysées stretch outward, is a Haussmann classic.

The **Third Republic** (or early industrial era) saw the advent of World Fairs (*Expositions Universelles),* when Paris took center stage. The fairs of 1878, 1889, and 1900 were catalysts for constructing huge glass-and-steel structures that showed off modern techniques and the engineering prowess of the Industrial Revolution. Such Parisian monuments as the **Eiffel Tower** (p. 48, **5**) and **Basilique du Sacré-Coeur** (p. 90, **10**) were produced.

Soon architects and decorators rebelled against the

mass production dictated by the Third Republic and stressed the uniqueness of craft in a movement that became known as **Art Nouveau.** They created asymmetrical, curvaceous designs based on organic inspiration (plants and flowers) in such mediums as wrought iron, stained glass, tile, and wallpaper (see *"L'Art Nouveau,"* p. 293). The style was less an architectural mode than a decorative one, though you can still find some of the original Paris Métro entrances designed by **Hector Guimard** (1867–1942), notably at the Abbesses and Porte Dauphine stations on line 2.

Modern Architecture

France commissioned some ambitious architectural projects in the 20th century, most of them the *Grand Projets* (*Grand Travaux,* or "Great Works") of the late François Mitterrand. Many were considered controversial, outrageous, or even offensive. Besides a concerted effort to break convention and look stunningly modern, nothing unifies the look of this architecture—except the fact that non-French architects designed much of it. Britain's **Richard Rogers** and Italy's **Renzo Piano** turned architecture inside out—literally—to craft the eye-popping **Centre Pompidou** (1977), Paris's modern art museum. Exposed pipes, steel supports, and plastic-tube escalators wrap around the exterior. Chinese-American maestro **I. M. Pei** was called in to cap the Louvre's new entrance with **glass pyramids** (1989), placed smack in the center of the palace's 17th-century courtyard. Also in 1989, Paris's

> *The main structure of Metz's daring, new Centre Pompidou building is made of wood.*

opera company moved into the curvaceous, dark glass space of the **Opéra Bastille** (p. 133), designed by Canadian **Carlos Ott.** (Unfortunately, the acoustics have been lambasted.)

A legacy from Jacques Chirac's reign is the predominantly red and black, cubic **Quai Branly Museum** (p. 53, ⑥)—a showcase for non-European Arts, opened in 2006. Designed by Frenchman Jean Nouvel, it has added a contemporary edge to the cityscape along the river by the Eiffel Tower. One of

France's latest architectural editions is the **Centre Pompidou-Metz** (p. 275, ⑩), the Paris museum's sister establishment designed by Franco-Japanese architect duo Jean de Gastines and Shigeru Ban, which opened in 2010 in Metz. It's an enormous structure (reportedly inspired by a Chinese hat that Ban found in Paris) with a translucent fiberglass roof covered in Teflon and a 77m-high (253-ft.) metal spire—a nod to the 1977 opening of the Centre Pompidou in Paris.

Tomorrow's Paris

Over the years, Paris, as the seat of power, has of course seen its fair share of architectural legacies, from the kings of France to Fifth Republic presidents. So it comes as no surprise that the capital's skyline is set to change again, under the impetus of Nicolas Sarkozy's government: In a bid to make Paris a convenient, livable, and environmentally sustainable city of the future, the propositions of 10 architecture agencies (including Ateliers Jean Nouvel, of Quai Branly fame, and Atelier Christian de Portzamparc, the brains behind Parc de la Villette) are being studied for the new "Grand Paris." Projects range from highly conceptual towers and futuristic train stations to a "floating" Métro system over the *peripherique* (Paris's circular highway). See www.legrandparis.culture.gouv.fr.

French Art History

> The Bayeux Tapestry illustrates William and Harold's struggle for the English throne.

Romanesque Art

Wall paintings and frescoes were key elements of Romanesque art. You'll find excellent examples at **Cathédrale Notre-Dame** in **Le-Puy-en-Velay** (p. 628, **5**). The most notable example of Romanesque artistry is the **Bayeux Tapestry** (dating to 1066–77)—69m (226 ft.) of embroidered linen telling the story of William the Conqueror's defeat of the English (p. 213, **3**).

Renaissance Art

Renaissance art developed in Italy in the late 1400s, but arrived and flourished in France from the 1500s to the mid-17th century, especially under François I (reigned 1515–47), who took Leonardo da Vinci under his wing in Amboise (p. 148, **3**). The spread of humanism, trade (and war) with Italy, the exploration of the so-called New World, and

the developments of new techniques and art forms (notably in printing, the sciences, and literature) created new social codes and etiquette. All these elements were reflected in art—from music and painting to sculpture. Two of France's most important Renaissance painters were **Jean Clouet** (1480–1541) and his son **François Clouet** (1520–72). You can see the younger Clouet's *Le Bain de Diane* (featuring Diane de Poitiers, Henri II's beloved mistress) in Rouen's **Musée des Beaux-Arts** (p. 226, **5**). Other French artists of talent in this period include painter **Jean Fouquet of Tours** (1420–81), considered the inventor of portrait miniature, and sculptors **Jean Goujon** (1510–72), who sculpted the statues on Pierre Lescot's wing of the Louvre (the *Cour Carrée,* or Square Courtyard), and **Germain Pilon** (1537–90), the hand behind great works such as the *Résurrection du Christ (Resurrection of Christ)* and the monument containing Henri II's heart, both on display at the Louvre (p. 50, **1**).

Impressionism

By far the best-known French art movement is Impressionism. Formal, rigid neoclassicism and idealized Romanticism rankled some late-19th-century artists interested in painting directly from nature. They portrayed light in ways hitherto unseen, by applying loose strokes or dabs to suggest (rather than define) the light's reflections. It was with **Claude Monet** (1840–1926)

> Monet's Impressions, Sunrise was what spurred the term Impressionism.

that the Impressionist movement began, with an 1874 exhibition in which Monet showed his loose, J. M. W. Turner–inspired *Impression, Sunrise* (1874). One critic focused on it to lambaste the whole exhibition, deriding it all as "Impressionist." Far from being insulted, the show's artists adopted the word for their movement. Monet's *Water Lilies* hangs in the basement of Paris's **Musée de l'Orangerie.** You can visit his studio and gardens at **Giverny,** north of Paris (p. 137). Another great Impressionist was **Pierre-Auguste Renoir** (1841–1919), famed for his figures' ivory skin and chubby pink cheeks—a throwback from the artist's beginnings as a porcelain painter. The greatest sculptor of the Impressionist era was undoubtedly **Auguste Rodin** (1840–1917), who crafted remarkably expressive bronzes, refusing to idealize the human figure as had his neoclassical predecessors. The **Musée Rodin** (p. 52, ❹), his former Paris studio, contains, among other works, his *Burghers of Calais* (1886), *The Kiss* (1886–98), and *The Thinker* (1880). Paris's **Musée d'Orsay** (p. 51, ❷) displays many works by the aforementioned artists.

> *Matisse's* Grand Intérior Rouge *(on show in the Pompidou Centre) was painted in 1948.*

Post-Impressionism

After Impressionism came post-Impressionism—a term coined in 1910 to describe those artists who rejected the limitations of Impressionism by choosing vivid, often unnatural colors, applying thick layers of paint, and emphasizing geometric forms. The long list of post-Impressionist painters includes **Paul Cézanne** (1839–1906), who adopted the short brush strokes, landscapes, and light color palette of his Impressionist friends, but sought to give more of a sense of monumentality and permanence; and **Paul Gauguin** (1848–1903), who developed synthetism (black outlines around solid colors) while hopping around the South Pacific, where he was inspired by local styles and colors, as in *Femmes de Tahiti sur la Plage* (1891). **Henri de Toulouse-Lautrec** (1864–1901) is most famous for his depictions of bohemian life in Paris (dance halls, cafes, and top-hatted patrons at fancy parties), as in the barely sketched *La Danse Mauresque* (1895). **Vincent van Gogh** (1853–90), a Dutchman who adopted France as his home, combined divisionism, synthetism, and a touch of Japanese influence, painting with thick, short strokes (*Sunflowers* series, 1887). **Henri Matisse** (1869–1954) took a hint from synthetism and added wild colors and strong patterns to create fauvism (a critic described those who used the style as *fauves,* meaning "wild beasts"), as seen in his *Grand Intérior Rouge* and *Goldfish Bowl* (1914). Several of Matisse's works are on display in the **Musée Matisse** in Nice (p. 469, ❹). His masterpiece, the **Chapelle du Rosaire** (1949–51), a chapel he designed and decorated, is near Vence (p. 450, ❹).

Cubism

French-born **Georges Braque** (1882–1963) and Spanish-born **Pablo Picasso** (1881–1973) painted objects from all points of view at once, rather than using tricks like perspective to

> *This Fernand Léger–style window was added to the Musée Fernand Léger in Biot in 1990.*

fool viewers into seeing three dimensions. The result, called "cubism," was expanded upon by the likes of **Fernand Léger** (1881–1955) in his work *Wedding, 1911.*

Hasidic Jewish artist **Marc Chagall** (1889–1985) is hard to pin down. He traveled widely in Europe, the United States, Mexico, and Israel; his painting started from cubism and picked up inspiration everywhere to fuel a brightly colored, allegorical, often whimsical style. You'll find a museum devoted to Chagall in Nice (p. 470, ❺), several of his stained-glass windows in the **Cathédrale Notre-Dame** in Reims (p. 254, ❶), and his painted ceiling in Paris's **Opéra Garnier** (p. 44, ❽).

Contemporary Art

For an introduction to French art today, see "Best Modern & Contemporary Art" in chapter 3 (p. 60).

French High & Popular Culture

> Born in 1810, Romantic pianist and composer Frédéric Chopin died of tuberculosis at the age of 39.

Classical Music

As in all European countries, music has been an integral part of French society for well over a millennium. During France's medieval period, Gregorian chants in Latin were predominant. So were the songs of troubadours, who set poems to music, recounting the epic adventures of knights and maidens—medieval dramas that were, in many ways, the ancestors of opera. Poetry also inspired France's Renaissance composers, who flourished under the reign of François I. It was under Louis XIV, however, that the names of one of France's most famous composers came to light: **Jean-Baptiste Lully** (1632–87) was a favorite of the Sun King's; in fact, the king danced in many of the ballets composed by Lully during the 1650s and 1660s.

When Romanticism arrived in France in the late 18th and early 19th centuries, it exploded classical musical conventions. Orchestras became larger, and new instruments, such as the bass clarinet and the contrabassoon, were added. French Romantic composer **Hector Berlioz** (1803–69) is considered the father of modern orchestration; and Franco-Polish pianist **Frédéric Chopin** (1810–49) is still revered for his intricate piano compositions in the Romantic style. The nationalistic sentiment left behind by the Franco-Prussian war in 1870 spurred some remarkable symphonies, particularly by **César Franck** (1822–90) and **Ernest Chausson** (1855–90). But by the early 20th century, Romanticism no longer corresponded to the unsettled climate of pre- and postwar France and Europe, and Expressionism and neoclassicism took center stage, notably with composers **Claude Débussy** (1862–1918) and **Maurice Ravel** (1875–1937).

La Chanson Française & Beyond

From **Mistinguette** (1920s–30s) and **Edith Piaf** (France's most famous torch singer and icon of 1940s Paris) to **Jacques Brel** and **Georges Brassens** (political "poets" of the 1950s), French music has always put an emphasis on "good text"—often at the cost of the music accompanying it. One artist who understood the importance of both good music and good text was **Serge Gainsbourg** (1928–91), who started out singing "ye-ye" pop (light French pop music) in the 60s but branched out to produce some of the most influential concept albums to have come out of France. Current French artists bent on resuscitating *chanson* à la Gainsbourg are **Benjamin Biolay** (www.benjaminbiolay.com), **Charlotte Gainsbourg** (Serge's actor-daughter with British actress Jane Birkin; www.charlottegainsbourg.com), and **Vincent Delerm** (www.vincentdelerm.com), to name but a few. Often thought of as the French Elvis Presley, **Johnny Halladay** has remained one of the country's top performers since the 1960s. He's probably best known outside of France for his recent film role in Johnnie To's 2009 thriller, *Vengence*.

Today, France's biggest exports are electro-pop bands, such as **Daft Punk** (www.daftpunk.com), who hit Hollywood in 2010 with the soundtrack to Disney's 3-D movie *Tron;* **Phoenix** (www.wearephoenix.com), who have recently written music for Sofia Coppola's film, *Somewhere;* and **Air** (http://en.aircheology.com), who wrote music for Sofia Coppola's cult movie *The Virgin Suicides* (1999); plus French rap, which has come a long way since the 1980s, when **MC Solaar** ruled the charts. Current bands like **NTM** (www.supreme-ntm.com) boast uncompromisingly sharp rhymes and tight beats. But a marked trend for Anglo-Saxon–style electro-rock is also producing a stream of promising French bands, such as the immensely talented Strokes-esque **Neimo** (www.myspace.com/neimo), who sing in the Queen's finest English, and **Pony Pony Run Run** (www.myspace.com/ponyponyrunrun). Also check out up-and-coming electro-pop act **Monkey Anna** (www.myspace.com/musicmonkeyanna).

French Literature

Literature holds a special place in French hearts—probably because they're so good at writing it: The Nobel

> *Nicolas Godin is one half of the group Air (the other member is Jean-Benoît Dunckel).*

prize in literature has been awarded to more French authors than to those from any other country. The first great French writer was undoubtedly the 16th-century doctor **Rabelais,** remembered for his sharp satires featuring epic characters such as Gargantua the giant, supposedly fabricated as remedies for his patients.

The 19th century was the golden age of French novels (especially humanist). A few of the era's masterpieces include the following: *Madame Bovary* by **Gustave Flaubert,** in which carefully wrought characters, setting, and plot present the tragedy of Emma Bovary; *Les Misérables*, by **Victor Hugo,** a classic tale of social oppression and human courage set in the era of Napoleon I; selected works by the master of short stories, **Guy de Maupassant;** *The Devil's Pool,* by **George Sand,** which depicts French peasant life; the very long *À la recherche du temps perdu* (typically translated as *Remembrance of Things Past*), by **Marcel Proust;** and *La Comédie Humaine*, by **Honoré de Balzac.**

The Creator of Operetta

During the Second Empire, German-born French composer (and cellist) of the Romantic era **Jacques Offenbach** (1819–80) wrote amusing, popular, and often satirical musical shows that became known as *operettas* (light opera). These witty, musical parodies set a precedent for the Broadway and West End musicals of the 20th and 21st centuries, and his works are still popular today— especially *La Belle Hélène, The Tales of Hoffmann,* and *Orpheus in the Underworld.*

> *The moon in Georges Méliès's 1902 film* A Trip to the Moon *has become a symbol of early cinema.*

In the 21st century, France's most celebrated and controversial author is **Michel Houellebecq,** known in particular for his novels *Les Particules Elémentaires* (1998) and *Platforme* (2001). With his cruel but humorous descriptions of the sexual inadequacies of men in the 1990s and 2000s, many consider him a literary pioneer—an upholder of the literary provocation of the Marquis de Sade. But to his critics, he's a peddler of sleaze.

For an American's take on the City of Lights, try *The Ambassadors* and *The American,* by Henry James. Representing a very different era are *A Moveable Feast,* by **Ernest Hemingway,** his recollections of Paris during the 1920s; and *The Autobiography of Alice B. Toklas,* by **Gertrude Stein,** her account of 30 years in Paris. Also from this era is *Tropic of Cancer,* by **Henry Miller**, the semi-autobiographical story of his years in Paris.

For a more contemporary (and lighter) read, try *Me Talk Pretty One Day,* by **David Sedaris,** a summing up of French culture told in a remarkably hilarious way from the viewpoint of an American tourist. Or read Stephen Clarke's light-hearted and clichéd **A Year in the Merde,** which tells the funny tale of Paul West, an English businessman who is given a year's contract by a French entrepreneur.

French Cinema

French brothers **Auguste** and **Louis Lumière** (known as the *Frères Lumière*) invented the moving picture between 1882 and 1885 by piercing holes into photo film to advance it through a camera known as the *cinematograph.* The brothers screened the world's first public movie in 1895 in the Grand Café in Paris's Grands Boulevards quarter—a projection of ten films, including their first ever recording, *Sortie des Usines Lumière* (Workers Leaving the Lumière Factory), from Lyon. Next came **Georges Méliès** (1861–1938), the inventor of several technical and narrative cinematographic developments—especially special effects, which earned him the title of "Cinemagician." His most famous film is the black-and-white 1902 *A Trip to the Moon* (featuring the moon as a human face with a spaceship that has landed in its eye), inspired by novels by H. G. Wells and Jules Verne.

The golden era of French

Jules Verne

French writer Jules Verne (1828–1905) is known as the founder of modern science fiction. Many of his stories, such as *Twenty Thousand Leagues Under the Sea, Voyage to the Center of the Earth,* and *The Mysterious Island,* have become classics, and he is the second most translated author in the world after Agatha Christie. Verne wrote about space, air travel, and underwater exploration long before the technology had been invented, proving immense qualities of foresight. You can visit the genius's former home in Amiens (p. 648, ❶) and a museum in his honor in Nantes (p. 181, ❾), where Verne lived until age 14.

> *The late Algerian-born French designer Yves Saint Laurent in 1960.*

cinema, however, was undoubtedly the *Nouvelle Vague* (New Wave; see p. 446), when directors such as **François Truffaut** and **Jean-Luc Godard** created wonderful, atmospheric, and realistic scenes of daily life in the 1950s and 1960s.

More recent French hits include *Amélie* (by **Jean-Pierre Jeunet**), a modern-day fairy-tale story shot in the picturesque cobblestone streets of Paris's Montmartre district; and *Le Placard,* or *The Closet* (by **Francis Veber**), with Gérard Depardieu, Daniel Auteuil, and Thierry Lhermitte—a funny 2001 movie that deals with the issue of homosexuality in French society. Hard-hitting *La Haine* (English title: *Hate,* by **Mathieu Kassovitch,** starring the then relatively unknown Vincent Cassel) was made in 1995 but foreshadows the 2005 riots in the Parisian ghettos.

France, of course, has been the setting for many a film

by American directors. Clichés of French romance and comedy abound in such films as *French Kiss* (by **Lawrence Kasdan**), *Before Sunrise* (by **Richard Linklater**), and *A Good Year* (by **Ridley Scott**), in which an English trader (Russell Crowe) learns the value of love (and wine) in sun-drenched Provence. If suspense is more your genre, check out 1998's *Ronin* (by **John Frankenheimer**), an action movie with thrilling car chase scenes throughout the streets of Paris.

Fashion

Twice a year Paris bursts at the seams (quite literally) with fashion weeks, during which International and French haute couture houses (such as Dior, Jean-Paul Gaultier, Chanel, and Givenchy) show off the next season's wares to thousands of journalists and eager onlookers. France's supremacy in the domain of designer fashion was established over a

100-year period between the 1860s and 1960s, when some of the world's greatest fashion houses were founded. Seamstress and hat maker **Coco Chanel** started one of them (in 1925)—an act that would bring the world the LBD (Little Black Dress), coveted for its simple, timeless elegance and versatility. In postwar France, **Christian Dior** greatly influenced fashion with his "New Look" in 1947—a collection of dresses with narrow waists, full skirts, and bodices. Another important house of this period was **Hubert de Givenchy,** which opened in 1952.

In the 1960s France's youth criticized haute couture and looked to London for more casual styles. It was at this time (in 1966) that **Yves Saint Laurent** launched a brand-new concept: *prêt-à-porter,* turning to mass manufacturing to produce styles "ready to wear" off the coat hanger. With more focus on marketing and manufacturing, the 1970s to 1990s saw a string of fashion houses arrive, notably **Christian Lacroix** and **Jean-Paul Gaultier.** This soon was accompanied by the conglomeration of many French couture houses under luxury multinationals like LVMH.

Nowadays many foreign designers run French houses: German designer **Karl Lagerfeld** heads Chanel for instance, and Brit **John Galliano** is the creative brain behind today's Dior. Nevertheless, the image remains distinctively French: elegant and wearable, with a dose of *ooh la la.*

French Food

> *France produces more than 400 cheeses.*

> Moules-frites *is one of France's best-loved dishes.*

For the French, food is much more than sustenance; it is a link to heaven. Mealtimes take pride of place (even if the country has not been spared the advent of TV dinners or too-short lunch breaks), often lasting several hours, with a starter (*entrée*), a meat or fish main course (*plat*), and dessert. Sometimes *fromage* (cheese) is served before the dessert, too.

Traditional foods and wines often benefit from strict controls and aging processes, and there can be no substitution for the real thing, crafted according to centuries-old methods—be it goat cheese from the Loire, *jambon de Bayonne,* or a fine Bordeaux wine.

An AOC label (*Appellation d'Origine Contrôlée*) indicates that a food is made according to established, traditional standards.

Universal Favorites in France
For this nation still very much attached to its *terroir* (the land, and the fruits it produces), regional cuisine dominates in kitchens from the North (Nord Pas de Calais) to Provence. It would be impossible to list each region's most famous dishes here; however, some dishes have transcended regional frontiers to become national staples and can be found in restaurants across the country. Here are a few dishes to look out for:

BOEUF BOURGUIGNON
As its name suggests, this beef stew, simmered in red wine with bacon, baby onions, and mushrooms, comes from Burgundy, but it is loved nationwide.

COQ AU VIN
This Burgundy dish, made with a male chicken that is flambéed in brandy and then stewed in red wine with mushrooms and onions, is unbeatable on a cold day.

CREME BRULEE
Vanilla cream topped with caramelized sugar is probably the most famous dessert in France. It is easy to make but difficult to perfect; you can often judge a chef's capacities by his *crème brûlée.*

CREPES
From traditional Brittany *crêperies* to fast-food stalls across major cities, the ham-and-cheese pancake is ubiquitous.

> *Coffee is usually served short, and often with a free chocolate.*

> *When hunger strikes, you can't beat a ham, cheese, and egg crepe.*

ESCARGOTS
Snails are not just a cliché; many restaurants serve them in melted garlic butter infused with parsley.

FROMAGE
From runny, ripe Camembert to crumbly *crottin* (goat cheese, sometimes rolled in ash) to creamy, tangy Roquefort, France produces around 400 varieties of cheese. In the top restaurants, before dessert a cheese trolley is presented, with the best of local produce.

GRATIN DAUPHINOIS
Thinly sliced potatoes are layered with cream, nutmeg, and Gruyère cheese and baked slowly until soft on the inside and crispy on the outside.

MOULES MARINIERES
Mussels steamed with white wine, onion, lemon, and parsley.

SALADE DE CHEVRE
Goat cheese melted onto toast, served on crisp lettuce.

STEAK-FRITES
Steak served with hand-cut fries is a nationwide specialty.

French Breakfast

The French don't usually eat eggs, meat, or cereal for breakfast. Most hotels catering to a foreign clientele have adapted to demand, but local establishments offer instead a fresh baguette (a stick of bread with a golden, crispy outer shell and a soft, fluffy middle), buttery *croissants*, *pain au chocolat* (a square-shaped croissant with a *baton* of melted chocolate in the middle), and *brioche* (a sweet bread made with milk). Coffee *(café)* is the preferred morning pick-me-up—especially *café au lait* (or *café crème*, as it is called in some areas), an espresso mixed with warm milk.

French Wine

> Bottles of Bordeaux from St-Emilion.

France's love of the vine goes back to a time way before the Romans spread the lore and practice of winemaking throughout the country. Over the centuries, the French have learned to domesticate the vine in ways unrivaled elsewhere in the world, selecting the best varieties and crossing them with others to create new ones. Today there are thousands of different grape varieties (*cépages*), yet only a few dozen have the qualities required for fine winemaking. There are 10 principal wine-growing regions in France: The most famous are

For information on champagne, see "Dom Pérignon: The Monk & His Bubbly," p. 248.

Bordeaux, Burgundy, Champagne, Alsace, and the Loire, but you'll also find great *vin* in Provence and Corsica, the Jura and Savoie, the Southwest, Languedoc-Roussillon, and the Rhône. While you are traveling in France, here are the main grape varieties you'll find:

Reds

Red wines are made from red grapes. The juice of red grapes is colorless; color appears when the grapes are crushed, thus transferring the pigment from the flesh, skin, and pits to the liquid.

CABERNET FRANC This *cépage* is similar to cabernet sauvignon and has grown on land around Bordeaux since the 15th century. It also likes the soils along the Loire Valley,

producing some excellent fruity wines that can be drunk young.

CABERNET SAUVIGNON The most famous grape in the world is actually a cross between sauvignon blanc and cabernet franc grapes. They are mainly used in wines from Bordeaux and the Médoc, and they tend to create excellent, full-bodied, spicy wines that should be stocked for a good few years in a cellar to bring out the celebrated flavors.

GAMAY The principle grape for Beaujolais wines, it is also known for its acidity and low tannin content, often producing fruity, floral reds. Gamay grapes are mostly cultivated along the Loire.

GRENACHE This *cépage* originated in Spain and came to France in the 14th century. Grenache grapes make wines that are high on alcohol and low on acidity; more often than not, they are mixed with other grape varieties, such as syrah.

MERLOT These famous Bordelais grapes thrive in the chalky-clay soils of the right bank of the Garonne River, St-Emilion, and Pomerol. They produce subtle, fruity wines with undertones of black currant and plum.

PINOT This very old variety is rumored to come from Burgundy. You could say it is genetically unstable, as it has fathered many different *cépages* (pinot noir, meunier, gris, and blanc, to name but a few). This varietal is also highly affected by growing conditions. In Burgundy for instance, it can produce a totally different wine every 500 meters (1,640 ft.). Pinot grapes are also used in Champagne and Alsace.

SYRAH Wines made with syrah grapes are usually dark in color, with strong legs and peppery or violet undertones. Many wines on the Mediterranean use this varietal.

Whites

Most white wines are produced from the juice of white grapes; when pressurized under the right conditions, however, some red grapes can produce white wine. Champagne, for instance, is often made from red pinot noir and pinot meunier grape varieties.

CHARDONNAY This most famous grape variety actually resulted from crossing the medieval gouais blanc variety (from the Jura and Franche Comté) with the pinot noir. What a fusion! Chardonnay is known for its aromas such as *brioche,* fresh butter, nuts, grilled bread, pineapple, and exotic fruits, and is hardy enough to adapt to climatic and soil changes.

CHENIN This *cépage* is best at home in the Loire, but has exported well to South Africa where it is called "steen." It is a versatile grape that produces standard table wines as well as fizzy Crémant and the occasional vintage.

GEWURZTRAMINER This is the ultimate aromatic grape, used in Alsace since 1870. It is a branch of the sauvignon blanc family, whose grapes are pink in color. Wines are velvety in texture but sweet, exotic, and spicy in flavor. Some of the most expensive gewürztraminer wines come from late harvests called *vendanges tardives,* where the grape is picked just before it rots, giving extra body and sweetness to the final liquor.

MUSCAT These grapes form a huge family that probably originated in Asia. Many wines in Alsace are made from a variety of this *cépage,* the most common being *le Muscat d'Alexandrie.* Its wines tend to be very dry and aromatic.

RIESLING This variety began life in Germany, but some experts argue that the Romans brought it to France. Nevertheless, you'll find it nowadays only in vineyards in Alsace, where it produces excellent dry, elegant, lemony whites that rival Chardonnay.

SAUVIGNON This limestone-loving *cépage* has been around the Loire and Bordeaux regions for centuries. It makes crisp, dry wines best enjoyed young. Sauvignon grapes are used exclusively to make Sancerre and Pouilly wines in the Loire, as well as the occasional white from Bordeaux, but otherwise they are mixed with sémillon varieties.

SEMILLON This southwestern grape is rarely used alone, but it adds body and texture when mixed with other grape-types. Sauterne wines in particular use sémillon grapes.

Popping the Cork

How you open a bottle of wine in France is as important as how you drink it. Here's how the French experts do it:

- Using a knife, cut around the foil covering the cork, just below the ring of the bottle.
- Remove the upper part of the foil you have just cut, to prevent the wine from coming into contact with the metal.
- Rub the neck of the bottle with a cloth. Don't be put off if there's mold on the bottle; it simply proves that it was stocked in a cellar.
- Push the corkscrew right into the middle of the cork, taking care not to pierce the cork at the bottom end.
- Take out the cork and listen to the pop.
- Once the cork is removed, squeeze it to check elasticity—the older the cork, the harder it is to press. Then smell the cork, which should have absorbed some of the odor from the wine. This is the best way to tell whether the wine is drinkable or has been "corked" (gone off). A wine that has gone off will leave a vinegar-like smell on the cork.

The Best Special Interest Trips

> PREVIOUS PAGE *Each year, the greatest bike race in the world—La Tour de France—whizzes through the French capital.* THIS PAGE *Learning to cook at Petits Farcis in Nice: Chef Rosa Jackson invites you into her lovely home.*

Culinary Travel

Food & Wine Tours

For many people, a trip to France is all about gastronomy. France's range of excellent cuisine and wine is unrivaled in the world, making the country the perfect choice for an epicurean holiday. If your idea of a perfect vacation is eating and drinking your way around the country, you can do just that, thanks to the following outfitters:

Michelin (☎ 877/304-2051 in the U.S.; www.michelinfoodandtravel.com), the famous award body that grants those sought-after Michelin stars, offers customized food and travel itineraries to suit your tastes. Either call or fill in a form online to explain what you're looking for, your time frame, and your budget. With this information, they'll concoct a trip that explores one or several regions, taking you everywhere from the quaintest of French cafes to 3-star Michelin restaurants. On a smaller, more personal scale, **Edible Paris** (www.edible-paris.com) and **Petits Farcis** (www.petitsfarcis.com) in Nice, both run by Francophile food writer Rosa Jackson (☎ 06-81-67-41-22), offer cooking classes and guided food itineraries around Paris and Nice, respectively. With Petits Farcis, you can tour Nice's cours Saleya market to learn about Provençal ingredients, before taking a cooking class with Rosa in her charming home in the old

town. Edible Paris offers personalized itineraries (half-day to 3 days) and the chance to discover Paris with a food guru—English-speaking restaurant critics, food writers, and professional cooks who spend their spare time sniffing out the very best food shops and restaurants to share with you during your Paris break. Prices average at 200€ a day.

If you've ever fancied truffle hunting, try the 4-day winter course offered by **Greedy Goose Cooking Holidays** (Le Bourg, Ambeyrac; ☎ 05-65-81-54-01; www.greedygoose.net; annedyson@wanadoo.fr), between December and the end of January in Dordogne's Lot Valley. Two gorgeous truffle-hunting Dalmatians and their knowledgeable owners take you deep into the forest, before guiding you home to sample the black diamonds you've found. Anne Dyson, owner of Greedy Goose and author of several books, with more than 30 years of cooking experience, also runs 1- to 6-day cooking courses in her beautiful home. A 1-day cooking class is 150€ a day; a truffle-hunting holiday starts from 600€; and a 6-day cooking course costs from 1,300€.

If you're looking to learn about wine tasting and wine growing while seeing some astoundingly gorgeous countryside, try **Wine Tour in France,** which organizes tours led by wine experts around Bordeaux, Cognac, Burgundy, and Champagne (www.winetourinfrance. com; Bordeaux: bordeaux@winetourinfrance. com, ☎ 05-56-44-27-68; Cognac: cognac@ winetourinfrance.com, ☎ 03-80-34-16-65; Burgundy: bourgogne@winetourinfrance.com, ☎ 03-80-34-16-65; Champagne: champagne@ winetourinfrance.com, ☎ 03-26-83-91-04). **French Wine Explorers** is a U.S.-based company that organizes customized and prepackaged private wine tours across France (☎ 877/261-1500 in the U.S.; www.wine-tours-france.com). **Decanter Wine Tours** (☎ 888/ 672-7167 in the U.S.; 06-08-25-00-54 (in France); decantertours.com) offers customized wine tours that include meals in the wineries and tastings in the most prestigious wine regions of France (especially Burgundy and Bordeaux).

Cooking Classes

For those looking to improve both their French language and their cooking, **Ecole des Trois Points** (☎ 04-77-71-53-00 in France, or

0871/717-4226 in the U.K.; www.3ponts.edu) in the Loire Valley offers week- and month-long French lessons and cookery courses. Although it's a learning holiday, only the mornings are actually spent in the classroom studying grammar. After lunch it's all about relaxation, before you and the school's professional chef cook everybody a three-course meal. Only French is used throughout your stay, which can be hard—but after a week your French-speaking confidence and ability will undoubtedly improve. Prices start at 1,440€.

The infamous Georges-Auguste Escoffier (1846–1935) taught the Edwardians how to eat. Today the **Hôtel Ritz** maintains the **Ritz-Escoffier Ecole de Gastronomie Française,** 38 rue Cambon, Paris 75001 (☎ 01-43-16-30-50; www.ritzparis.com), which offers demonstration classes of the master's techniques. A 1-hour lesson costs just 55€, or you can opt for half-day lessons, which start at 140€. Courses, taught in French and English, start at 1,100€ for 1 week and up to 11,400€ for 6 weeks.

Le Cordon Bleu, 8 rue Léon-Delhomme, Paris (☎ 800/457-2433 in the U.S., or 01-53-68-22-50 in France; www.cordonbleu.edu), established in 1895, is the most famous French cooking school. It's where Julia Child learned to perfect her *pâté brisée* and *mousse au chocolat.* The best-known courses last 10 weeks, after which you are awarded a certificate. Many enthusiasts prefer a less intense immersion and opt for a 4-day workshop or a 2-hour demonstration class. Enrollment in either one is first-come, first-served; prices start at 50€ for a demonstration and start at 925€ for the 4-day workshop. Classes are in English.

Language Classes & Other Learning Trips

French Instruction

The Alliance Française, 101 bd. Raspail, Paris (☎ 01-42-84-90-00; www.alliancefr.org), a nonprofit organization with a network of 1,100 establishments in 138 countries, offers French-language courses to some 350,000 students. The school in Paris is open all year; month-long courses range from 400€ to 900€, depending on the number of hours per day. Request information and an

> *The Alliance Française in Paris.*

application at least 1 month in advance. In North America, the largest branch is the Alliance Française in Chicago (☎ 800/6-FRANCE 637-2623; www.afusa.org). A clearinghouse for information on French-language schools is **Lingua Service Worldwide,** in Connecticut (☎ 800/394-LEARN 5327 or 203/263-6294; www.linguaserviceworldwide.com). Its programs are available in many cities throughout France. They cost $1,043 to $2,940 for 2 weeks, depending on the city, the school, and the accommodations.

Music

At **French Music Holidays** in Poitou-Charentes, you can learn jazz, ensemble music, and choir singing in an idyllic setting. Basic musical skills are a must (music reading and good knowledge of your instrument). As well as gaining new musical skills and honing existing ones, it's a fine opportunity to meet new people. Courses take place in the summer, last for 6 days, and include all food and beverages

> *Fancy a bird's-eye view of France? Learn to fly with Limousin-based Nearly Heaven.*

throughout your stay. Multi-occupancy rooms start at 12€ a night (course costs 430€; ☎ 05-49-87-45-48 or 06-10-73-33-97; www. frenchmusicholidays.com).

If you'd rather listen to music than make it, one outfit that coordinates hotel stays in Paris with major musical events, usually in at least one (and often both) of the city's opera houses, is **Dailey-Thorp Travel,** in Wyoming (☎ 800/998-4677 or 307/673-1555 in the U.S.; www.daileythorp.com). Sojourns tend to last 3 to 7 days and, in many cases, tie in with performances in other cities (usually London, Berlin, or Milan). Expect accommodations in deluxe hotels such as the Hôtel du Louvre or the Hôtel Scribe, and a staff that has made arrangements for all the nuts and bolts of your arrival in, and artistic exposure to, Paris.

Photography
France's beauty inspires photography; whether you're an enthusiastic beginner or you want to finesse your technique, award-winning professional photographer Roger Stowell offers photography vacations at **Camera Hols,** 40km (25 miles) inland from La Rochelle on the west coast (www.camerahols. com or info@camerahols.com; 3 nights 700€; 5 nights 900€). These residential courses, for

a maximum of four people, include lunches in local restaurants and 4-course evening meals, lovingly cooked by Roger's wife.

Piloting
If you've ever dreamed of soaring like a bird, you can learn to fly a two-seater plane with **Nearly Heaven** (based in the Limousin)—even if you don't speak French: Owner Sue Virr is the only qualified English-speaking, registered flying teacher in France. You can opt for a few introductory hours in the air or take a 4-week course that can lead to a private pilot's license. Either way, you're in for some breathtaking scenery. Sue also offers *gîte* accommodation (☎ 05-55-48-17-50; info@nearlyheaven.com or www.nearlyheaven.com). Prices vary, so contact Sue for more details.

Writing, Poetry & Crafts
For anyone who has ever fancied themselves a crime book writer, or who would like to find inspiration for poetry in a new setting, **Les Soeurs Anglaises** (☎ 05-53-91-38-40; ☎ 0797/369-9892 in the U.K.; www. lessoeursanglaises.com) in the Dordogne region runs a variety of workshops in English. If writing isn't for you, you can learn to knit and sew, make picture frames or toys, or learn all sorts of other crafts. The setting is dreamy: a

> *France offers cyclists a range of scenery, from mountainous slopes to flat seaside roads such as this one.*

lovingly restored country house in a gorgeous landscaped garden with a heated pool. Home-cooked food and local wines make mealtimes special, too. At least 5% of participants' fees go to **The Cambodian Children's Fund.** Prices start at 375€ for 3 days and 4 nights.

If you've ever fancied learning to paint, you can free your inner artist and use France's famous light (the inspiration behind many an art movement; see p. 672) to concoct your own tableaux at **Le Moulin Annepont** (☎ 05-46-94-48-82; www.moulinannepont.com; prices start at 35€ a day), in Charente-Maritime between La Rochelle, Saintes, and Cognac. The farmhouse, the waterfall, and a cascade in the back garden provide endless inspiration, as professional painters start you with still lifes and then move you on to landscapes. Beginners are welcome. Drawing workshops are also offered by **Ateliers Artichaut** in Brittany (2 hours from 10€; full-day including lunch 45€; ☎ 02-98-99-06-91 or 06-78-98-87-03 mobile; tim.bates@orange.fr or www.artichautateliers.com), which offers a range of activities, from pottery or print making for adults to courses for children. Courses last either a day or 2 hours and can therefore be mixed in with the rest of your holiday.

Outdoor Activities A to Z

Barge Cruises
Before the advent of the railways, many crops, building supplies, raw materials, and finished products were barged through France on a series of rivers, canals, and estuaries. Many of these waterways retain their old-fashioned locks and pumps, allowing shallow-draft barges easy access through the idyllic countryside. Massachusetts-based **French Country Waterways, Ltd.** (☎ 800/222-1236 or 781/934-2454; www.fcwl.com) leads 1-week tours through Burgundy and Champagne. For double occupancy, the price ranges from $6,995 to $8,195. **Le Boat,** in Florida (☎ 800/992-0291 or 800/734-5491; fax 727/530-9747; www.leboat.com), focuses on regions of France not covered by many other operators. The company's luxury crafts fit through the narrow canals and locks of Camargue, Languedoc, and Provence. Each 6-night tour has 10 passengers in five cabins outfitted with mahogany and brass, plus meals prepared by a Cordon Bleu chef. Prices vary widely. **Go Barging** (☎ 800/394-8630; www.gobarging.com) operates Great Island Voyages, featuring river cruise ships. Fares start at $4,590 per person (double occupancy) for a 6-night cruise, including room, breakfast, and dinner. Bicycles are carried on board for sightseeing trips. This company also offers cruises in the Loire Valley and the south of France.

Cycling Tours
Some of the best cycling tours of France are offered by Vermont-based **VBT** (☎ 800/245-3868; www.vbt.com), which offers trips in five of the most scenic parts of France, from

> *Fasten your saddle and giddyup, whether you choose a fully fledged riding vacation or a few hours of pony trekking.*

Burgundy, to the Loire Valley, Provence, and sometimes the Normandy coast. Packages start at $3,295 per person for a 10-day trip (2 days of which are spent traveling), including airfare. **Classic Adventures,** in New York (☎ 800/777-8090; fax 585/964-7297; www.classicadventures.com), sponsors 6- to 10-day spring and fall tours of the Loire Valley and the Dordogne. Accommodations are upscale, and tours are van-supported and escorted. The 6-day tour of the Loire Valley, including room, breakfast, and dinner, is $3,449 per person. **Euro-Bike & Walking Tours,** in Illinois (☎ 800/321-6060 or 406/655-4591; www.eurobike.com), offers 10-day tours in the Dordogne ($4,298 per person), 11-day tours in Provence ($4,498 per person), and 8-day

tours of the Loire Valley ($3,498 per person). All are escorted and include room, breakfast, and dinner. **Go-today.com,** a division of Europe Express based in Washington state (☎ 800/227-3235; www.go-today.com), has biking and walking tours of Bordeaux, Burgundy, the Dordogne, the Loire Valley, and Provence. An 8-day, self-guided bike tour is $1,750 per person, double occupancy. All tours include overnight accommodations and most meals. Guided tours include van support and a guide; on nonguided tours, you'll always have the name of an English-speaking local contact. **Bike Tours France** is also an excellent outfitter, offering tours in Burgundy, the Loire, Alsace, Provence, and Bordeaux. Some tours can even be worked in with the Tour de France, so you can watch the competition one day, then cover a nearby part of the Alps the next (www.biketoursfrance.com; ☎ 888/396-5383). Prices start at $3,995 for 6 days.

You could also try the **Discover France** website (www.discoverfrance.com), which offers self-guided walking and cycling tours. It works in the same way as guided tours (the route and accommodations are prepared, and you don't have to transfer your luggage between stops), but you have the liberty of following the routes at your own pace, without a guide. For more details, call ☎ 800/960-2221 or e-mail contact@discoverfrance.com.

Concoct Your Own Itineraries

A handy website to have up your sleeves is **www.france-voyage.com,** which lets you put together your own customized vacation itinerary. Click on the "Create your itinerary" icon, then choose between interests (culture, architecture, well-being, nature, and leisure activities). Choose the desired pace of your trip, and indicate your starting and ending points, and it will churn out an itinerary that includes a map and GPS coordinates.

GOLF

France Golf Tours, 32 rue Nungesser et Coli, 75016 Paris (☎ 01-41-22-00-81; www.france-golf-tours.com or info@francegolftours.com) is for the epicurean golfer looking to combine a workout on the green with gourmet French cuisine and wine, château visits, and a trip to Paris. Some trips even include a barge cruise in Provence.

Horseback Riding

Whether you're an experienced rider looking to work on dressage techniques, or you just want the thrill of cantering around the countryside, **Harris Horses Holidays,** in the Gironde (run by ex-professional show-jumper Johnny Harris and his instructor wife, Jackie), cater to riders of any level, from beginners to experts. If you own your own pony, you can even bring your steed along to compete in a local tournament. Riding mostly takes place in the morning so that you can spend the afternoon visiting the region. The Harrises' eldest son, Michael, is available for tennis coaching if you want to get really active after your rides. Prices start at 920€ per week with half-board, 145€ a day/night (☎ 05-57-49-19-37; jackieharris2005@aol.com or www.harrishorses.com).

Hot-Air Ballooning

The world's largest hot-air balloon operator is Florida-based **Buddy Bombard's Private Europe** (☎ 800/862-8537 or 561/837-6610; www.buddybombard.com). It maintains about three dozen hot-air balloons, some in the Loire Valley and Burgundy. The 5-day tours, costing $9,834 per person (double occupancy), incorporate food and wine tasting and all meals, lodging in Relais & Châteaux hotels, sightseeing, rail transfers to and from Paris, and a daily balloon ride over vineyards and fields. **Bonaventura Balloon Co.,** in California (☎ 800/FLY-NAPA 359-6272] or 707/944-2822; www.bonaventuraballoons.com), meets you in Paris and takes you on the high-speed train to Burgundy, where your balloon tour begins, carrying you over the scenic parts of the region. Guests stay in a 14th-century mill, now an inn owned by a three-star chef.

Tennis Tours

Die-hard fans around the world set their calendars by the French Open, held at Paris's

> *The Loire Valley is one of the best regions in France for a hot-air balloon ride.*

Roland-Garros stadium. You can book your hotel and tickets to the event on your own, but if you're unsure about scheduling, consider getting help from a California-based company, **Advantage Tennis Tours** (☎ 800/341-8687 or 949/661-7331; www.advantagetennistours.com). It typically books packages including 5 or 6 nights of hotel accommodations in Paris, 2 or 3 days on Center Court, and the skills of a bilingual hostess; rates per person, without airfare, begin at $3,455, double occupancy, depending on your choice of hotel and the duration of your visit.

18
The Savvy
Traveler

> Paris's iconic Métro opened in 1900 and has been an integral part of city life ever since.

Before You Go

Government Tourist Offices

IN THE U.S. Information line only (☎ 514/288-1904; info.us@franceguide.com or http://us.franceguide.com).

IN CANADA 1800 Ave. McGill College, Ste. 1010, Montreal, Quebec, H3A 3J6 (☎ 514/288-2026; canada@franceguide.com or http://ca-en.franceguide.com).

IN THE U.K. Lincoln House, 300 High Holborn, WC1V 7JH (☎ 090/6824-4123, 0.60€/min. at all times; info.uk@franceguide.com or http://uk.franceguide.com).

IN IRELAND Information line only (☎ 15-60-235-235, 0.95 €/min.; info.ie@franceguide.com or http://ie.franceguide.com).

IN AUSTRALIA Level 13, 25 Bligh St., 2000 Sydney (☎ 61-02/9231-5244; info.au@franceguide.com or http://au.franceguide.com).

Best Times to Go

April to June and late September to October are the best times for traveling in France; temperatures are usually mild, and the crowds aren't as intense as they are between mid-June and August, when the summer rush arrives. Much of the country goes on vacation from late July to August 15, so certain restaurants and shops are closed (except at the spas, beaches, and islands where the French escape to). This is especially true in Paris, when tourists pretty much have the city to themselves. From late October to Easter, most attractions operate on shorter winter hours. Many hotels and restaurants take a 2-week break over Christmas and the New Year, or in January.

Festivals & Special Events

For an exhaustive list of events beyond those listed here, check http://events.frommers.com, where you'll find a searchable, up-to-the-minute roster of what's happening in cities all over the world.

JANUARY

Le Rallye de Monte Carlo (Monte Carlo Motor Rally). The world's most venerable car race. Contact the Monaco Tourist Office (☎ 03-77-92-16-61-16; www.acm.mc). Usually mid-January.

FEBRUARY

Carnival de Nice. Parades, boat races, music, balls, and fireworks are all part of this celebration. The climax is the 114-year tradition of burning King Carnival in effigy, after Les Batailles des Fleurs (Battles of the Flowers), when teams pelt each other with blooms. Contact the Nice Convention and Visitors Bureau (☎ 08-92-70-74-07 [0.34€/min.]; www.nicecarnaval.com). Late February to early March.

La Route du Mimosa (The Mimosa Trail), French Riviera. In winter the 130km (80-mile) stretch between the pretty perched village Bormes-les-Mimosas and perfume capital Grasse comes alive with forests of bright yellow mimosa flowers. Mimosa parades take place in Mandelieu and St-Raphael, and the tourist offices organize walks through mimosa forests and visits to mimosa farms. Visit bormes@laroutedumimosa.fr or www.bormeslesmimosas.com. January to March.

Salon de l'Agriculture (Agricultural Fair), Place de la Porte de Versailles 75015, Paris. Paris's Porte de Versailles exhibition center becomes a giant farmyard with displays of prize-winning animals from across the country. Winegrowers, chefs, cheese makers, and other artisans flaunt their wares, too, making it a hot spot for foodies. Visit www.salon-agriculture.com or contact the Paris Tourist Office (www.parisinfo.com). Mid- to late February.

Fête du Citron (Lemon Festival), Menton. Near the Italian border on the Riviera, France's lemon-growing capital celebrates its yellow fruits with colorful parades and sculptures made from lemons. Contact the Menton Tourist Office (☎ 04-92-41-76-76; www.tourisme-menton.fr). Mid-February to March.

MARCH

Foire du Trône, Reuilly Lawn, Bois de Vincennes, 75012, Paris. This mammoth amusement park operates daily from 2pm to midnight. Call ☎ 01-46-27-52-29, or visit www.foiredutrone.com. End of March to end of May.

APRIL

International Marathon of Paris. Runners from around the world compete. Call ☎ 01-41-33-14-00, or visit www.parismarathon.com. Early April.

Les 24 Heures du Mans. This motorcycle race is on a grueling 4km (2½-mile) circuit,

4.5km (2¾ miles) south of Le Mans. Contact l'Automobile Club de l'Ouest (☎ 02-43-40-24-24) or the Le Mans Ticket Office (☎ 04-73-91-85-75; www.lemans.org). Mid-April.

MAY

Festival International du Film (Cannes Film Festival). Movie madness transforms this city into a media circus. Admission to films in the competition is by invitation only. Other films play 24 hours a day. Contact the Festival International du Film, 3 rue Amélie, 75007 Paris (☎ 01-53-59-61-00; www.festival-cannes.org). Mid-May.

Grand Prix de Formule 1 de Monaco (Monaco Grand Prix). Hundreds of cars race through the narrow streets and winding roads in a blend of high-tech machinery and medieval architecture. Call ☎ 03-77-93-15-26-00 or 03-77-92-16-61-16, or visit www.acm.mc or www.grand-prix-monaco.com. Mid-May.

French Open Tennis Championship, Stade Roland-Garros, 75116, Paris (Métro: Porte d'Auteuil). The open features 10 days of men's, women's, and doubles tennis on the hot, red, dusty courts. Call ☎ 01-47-43-48-00, or visit www.fft.fr. Late May to early June.

JUNE

Paris Jazz Festival. Paris's Parc Floral opens its green, flowery expanses to jazz concerts by top French and international musicians. Pack a picnic and let the rhythm fill your ears. Call ☎ 01-48-72-32-97, or visit www.parisjazzfestival.fr. June to early August.

Cinéscénie de Puy du Fou (sound-and-light show), Château du Puy du Fou, Les Epesses (La Vendée), Brittany. A cast of 2,500 actors and dozens of horses celebrate the achievements of the Middle Ages, complete with music, a laser show, and other lighting effects. Call ☎ 08-29-09-10-10 (0.18€/min), or visit www.puydufou.com. Early June to early September.

Paris Air Show. France's military-industrial complex shows off its high-tech hardware. Fans, competitors, and industrial spies mob Le Bourget Airport. Call ☎ 01-53-23-33-33, or visit www.paris-air-show.com. Mid-June in alternate years; next is mid-June 2013.

Gay Pride Parade. A France-wide stream of parties, exhibitions, and parades patterned after those in New York and San Francisco.

Most main cities take part in raising awareness against homosexual discrimination. Paris's event is the biggest, loudest, and most colorful. Contact Lesbian and Gay Pride Ile de France, 3 rue Perrée, Box 8, Paris 75003 (☎ 01-72-70-39-22; www.inter-lgbt.org). Late June.

JULY

Festival d'Aix-en-Provence. A musical event par excellence, with everything from Gregorian chant and opera to melodies composed on synthesizers. Performances are held in the city's theaters and monuments. Call ☎ 04-34-08-02-17, or visit www.festival-aix.com). Throughout July.

Colmar International Festival, Colmar. Classical concerts are held in public buildings of one of the most folkloric towns in Alsace. Call ☎ 03-89-20-68-97, or visit www.festival-colmar.com. First 2 weeks of July.

Festival de Chopin, Paris. Everything you've ever wanted to hear by the Polish exile who lived most of his life in Paris. Piano recitals take place in the Orangerie du Parc de Bagatelle, 75116. Call ☎ 01-45-00-22-19, or visit www.frederic-chopin.com. Early July.

Tour de France. Europe's most hotly contested bicycle race sends crews of wind tunnel–tested athletes along an itinerary that detours deep into the Massif Central and ranges across the Alps. The finish line is on the Champs-Elysées. Call ☎ 01-41-33-14-00, or visit www.letour.fr. First 3 weeks of July.

Festival d'Avignon. This world-class festival has a reputation for exposing new talent to critical scrutiny and acclaim. The focus is usually on avant-garde works in theater, dance, and music. Many of the dance and theater performances take place in either the 14th-century courtyard of the Palais des Pâpes or the medieval Cloître des Carmes (Carmes Cloister). Call ☎ 04-90-14-14-60, or visit www.festival-avignon.com. Book way in advance for accommodations. Last 3 weeks of July.

Bastille Day. Celebrating the birth of modern-day France, the nation's festivities reach their peak with street fairs, pageants, fireworks, and feasts. In Paris, the day begins with a parade down the Champs-Elysées and ends with fireworks over the Eiffel Tower. July 14.

Paris Quartier d'Eté. For 4 weeks, music, dance, theater, and artistic installations rule the whole of Paris and the Ile de France. Expect performances in the city's museums and streets, and at monuments such as the **Arènes de Lutèce** and the **Cour d'Honneur** at the Sorbonne, both in the Quartier Latin. Call ☎ 01-44-94-98-00, or visit www.quartierdete.com. Mid-July to mid-August.

Nice Jazz Festival. The most prestigious jazz festival in Europe. Concerts begin in the afternoon and go on until late at night (sometimes all night) on the Arènes de Cimiez, a hill above the city. Contact the Nice Tourist Office (☎ 08-92-70-75-07; www.nicejazzfestival.fr). Mid-July.

FrancoFolies de La Rochelle. A celebration of modern French music, with a heavy accent on today's young generation of *chansonniers,* who mix traditional *chanson* with rock and pop. A great way to come to grips with modern French music. Call ☎ 05-46-28-28-28, or visit www.francofolies.fr. Mid-July.

AUGUST

Festival InterCeltique de Lorient, Brittany. Celtic verse and lore are celebrated in the Celtic heart of France. The 150 concerts include classical and folkloric musicians, dancers, singers, and painters. Traditional Breton *pardons* (religious processions) take place in the once-independent maritime duchy. Call ☎ 02-97-21-24-29, or visit www.festival-interceltique.com. Early August.

Rock en Seine, Paris. France's hippest music festival attracts big names of the rock world to Paris's Parc St-Cloud. A friendly, Woodstock-like atmosphere reigns. There are even "Mini Rock" concerts for families with young children. Visit contact@rockenseine.com or www.rockenseine.com. End of August.

Jazz en Paese, Corsica. Jazz music has had a presence in Corsica since World War II, when the Americans chose Ghisonaccia as their Mediterranean base. The Jazz in Paese festival, held across Le Fiumorbo Valley, pays tribute to this history with international jazz acts hot off the plane. Concerts are held over 4 nights, each in a different village, and toward the end of the festival, you can partake in an anachronistic concert held at an altitude of 2,000m (6,560 ft.) along the mountainous, G20 hiking route. Call ☎ 06-87-74-81-79 (mobile), e-mail costantini.pm@wanadoo.fr, or visit www.jazzinpaese.com. Early to mid-August.

SEPTEMBER

Grande Braderie de Lille. During the first weekend of September, Lille's center turns into one huge party zone with antique fairs, secondhand sales, food stands, and all-night entertainment. Restaurants sell buckets of *moules-frites* (mussels and fries), competing to build the biggest mountain of empty shells in front of their restaurant. Contact the Lille Tourist Office for details (☎ 03-59-57-94-00; www.lilletourism.com). First week of September.

Beaujolais Nouveau. Each year the new Beaujolais wines are sold across the country in restaurants, bars, and markets. Look out for signs that say, "Beaujolais Nouveau." In Paris many restaurants participate, and a festive ambiance prevails. Third week of November.

La Villette Jazz Festival. Paris's northeastern Parc de la Villette swings to the rhythm of international jazz artists, centered on the Cité de la Musique concert hall and music museum. Past festivals have included Herbie Hancock, Shirley Horn, and other international biggies. Call ☎ 01-40-03-75-75, or visit www.citedelamusique.fr. Early to mid-September.

Festival d'Automne, Paris. One of France's most famous festivals is one of its most eclectic, focusing mainly on modern music, ballet, theater, and art. Call ☎ 01-53-45-17-00, or visit www.festival-automne.com. Mid-September to late December.

OCTOBER

Paris Auto Show, Porte de Versailles Expo, 75015. This is the showcase for European car design, complete with glistening metal, glitzy attendees, lots of hype, and the latest models. Call ☎ 01-56-88-22-40, or visit www.mondial-automobile.com. Two weeks in October (dates vary).

Perpignan Jazz Festival. Musicians from everywhere jam during what many consider to be Languedoc's most appealing season. Call ☎ 04-68-35-37-46, or visit www.jazzebre.com. Throughout October.

Prix de l'Arc de Triomphe, Hippodrome de Longchamp, 75116, Paris. France's answer to England's Ascot is the country's most prestigious horse race, concluding the equine season in Europe. Call ☎ 01-49-10-20-30, or visit www.france-galop.com. Early October.

FRANCE'S AVERAGE DAYTIME TEMPERATURE & RAINFALL

	JAN	FEB	MAR	APR	MAY	JUNE	JULY	AUG	SEPT	OCT	NOV	DEC
TEMP °F	43	45	52	59	64	68	73	72	66	59	45	40
TEMP °C	6	7	11	15	18	20	23	22	19	15	7	4
RAINFALL (IN.)	3.2	2.9	2.4	2.7	3.2	3.5	3.3	3.7	3.3	3.0	3.5	3.1

NOVEMBER

Annecy Wine & Food Festival, Annecy. Just south of Annecy in Sevrier, along the lake, the annual Annecy Wine & Food Festival is a place to free your inner epicurean. Around 100 exhibitors offer tastings of wines and the region's finest produce. Call ☎ 04-50-45-00-33, or visit www.salondesvins.org. Early November.

Les Trois Glorieuses, Clos-de-Vougeot, Beaune, and Meursault. Three Burgundian towns stage the country's most important wine festival. Though you may not be able to gain access to many of the gatherings, the tastings and other amusements will keep you occupied. Reserve early, or visit on day trips from nearby villages. Contact the Beaune Tourist Office (☎ 03-80-26-21-30; via www.ot-beaune.fr). Third week in November.

DECEMBER

Christmas Fairs, Alsace (especially Strasbourg). More than 60 villages celebrate a traditional Christmas. The events in Strasbourg have continued for some 430 years. Other towns with celebrations are Münster, Sélestat, Riquewihr, Kaysersberg, Wissembourg, and Thann. Call ☎ 03-89-24-73-50, or visit www.tourisme-alsace.com. Late November to December 24.

Fête des Lumières, Lyon. In honor of the Virgin Mary, lights are placed in windows throughout the city. Call ☎ 04-72-10-30-30, or visit www.lumieres.lyon.fr. Early December through early January.

Fête de St-Sylvestre (New Year's Eve). Though it takes place nationwide, in Paris this holiday is most boisterously celebrated in the Quartier Latin. At midnight, the city explodes. Strangers kiss, and boulevard St-Michel and the Champs-Elysées become virtual pedestrian malls. December 31.

Weather

France's weather varies from region to region and even from town to town. Despite its latitude, Paris never gets very cold, and snow is rare. May tends to be the driest month across the country. The hands-down winner for wetness is Brittany. Brest receives a staggering amount of rain between October and December. The Mediterranean coast in the south has the driest climate; most rain falls during spring and autumn, and summers are comfortably dry—beneficial to humans but deadly to vegetation, which often dries and burns up in the parched months. All of Provence dreads *le mistral,* an unrelenting local wind that most often blows in the winter for a few days but can last up to 2 weeks.

Cellphones

To use your cellphone in France, you must have a GSM (Global System for Mobiles) phone; this allows you to make calls anywhere in the world, though it can be expensive. If you're planning to make lots of calls, it may be less expensive to rent a cellphone from a French provider (**Orange,** www.orange.com or **SFR,** www.sfr.fr) or to purchase a prepaid phone chip to use in your phone. GSM phones function with a removable plastic SIM card, encoded with your phone number and account information. In France, you can purchase a phone and SIM card for about 100€, and buy prepaid minutes. To rent in advance of your trip a phone outfitted for use in France, check www.roadpost.com, www.intouchglobal.com, or Cellhire (www.cellhire.com). U.K. mobiles all work in France; call your service provider before departing your home country to ensure that the international call bar has been switched off and to check on call charges, which can be extremely high. Remember that you are also charged for calls you *receive* on a U.K. mobile used abroad.

Getting There & Around

By Plane

FROM NORTH AMERICA

All major airlines fly to Paris from the U.S. cities listed below. Once you fly into **Orly** or **Charles de Gaulle, Air France** (☎ 800/237-2747 in the U.S.; www.airfrance.com) can fly you to other airports in France (see www.aeroport.fr for a list of airports). **American Airlines** (☎ 800/433-7300; www.aa.com) offers daily flights to Paris from Dallas–Fort Worth, Chicago, Miami, Boston, and New York. **Delta Airlines** (☎ 800/241-4141; www.delta.com) flies nonstop to Paris from Atlanta, Cincinnati, and New York. **United Airlines** (☎ 800/538-2929; www.united.com) flies nonstop to Paris from Newark and several times a week, depending on the season, from Houston. **US Airways** (☎ 800/428-4322; www.usairways.com) offers daily service from Philadelphia to Paris.

Air France (☎ 800/237-2747 in the U.S.; www.airfrance.com) offers a daily nonstop flight between New York and Nice, and also offers regular flights between Paris and such North American cities as Newark, Washington D.C., Miami, Atlanta, Boston, Cincinnati, Chicago, New York, Houston, San Francisco, Los Angeles, Montreal, Toronto, and Mexico City.

Canadians usually choose **Air Canada** (☎ 888/247-2262 in the U.S. and Canada; www.aircanada.com) flights to Paris from Toronto and Montreal. Two of Air Canada's daily flights from Toronto are shared with Air France and feature Air France aircraft.

FROM AUSTRALIA

Getting to Paris from Australia always involves a stopover, because **Air France** (☎ 36-54; 0.34€/min telephone sales in France; ☎ 1300 390 190 in Australia; www.airfrance.fr) has discontinued direct flights. **Qantas** flies from Sydney to Singapore and other locations with service to Paris (www.qantas.com.au). Consequently, on virtually any route, you have to change planes at least once and sometimes twice. **British Airways** (☎ 1300-767-177 in Australia; www.britishairways.com) flies daily from Sydney and Melbourne to London, where you can catch one of several connecting flights to Paris. **Qantas** (☎ 612/13-13-13 in Australia; www.qantas.com.au) can route passengers from Australia into London, where you make connections for the hop across the Channel. Qantas also flies from Auckland, New Zealand, to Sydney and on to London.

FROM THE U.K.

From London, **Air France** (☎ 0870/142-4343 in the U.K.; www.airfrance.com) and **British Airways** (☎ 0844/493-0787 in the U.K.;

Ecotourism

Interest in *agrotourisme* and *oenotourisme*, in which guests stay on farms, vineyards, and other agricultural properties, is increasing. Guests enjoy the rural setting, sometimes partake in farming activities, and enjoy food and wine produced on the properties. If you're interested in **wine tourism,** find ideas on www.tourisme-oenotourisme.com. To stay on a working farm, try **Un Lit au Pré** (www.unlitaupre.fr). For general ecotourism information, **Responsible Travel** (www.responsibletravel.com) is a great source of sustainable travel ideas from a spokesperson for responsible tourism in the travel industry. Another organization that promotes responsible tourism practices is **Sustainable Travel International** (www.sustainabletravelinternational.org). You can find **The International Ecotourism Society**'s ecofriendly travel tips, statistics, and touring companies and associations—listed by destination under "Your Travel Choice"—at the TIES website, www.ecotourism.org. In the U.K., the **Association of Independent Tour Operators** (AITO; www.aito.co.uk) is a group of interesting specialist operators leading the field in making holidays sustainable.

If you read French, check out the site **Voyageons Autremement** (www.voyageons-autrement.com), which is full of resources on French ecotourism. The national website for the French railway system (www.voyages-sncf.com) also offers CO_2 comparison tools and awards responsible tourist outfitters (from hotel chains to vineyards) with an annual trophy.

Europe-Wide Rail Passes

Many North American travelers to Europe take advantage of the excellent **Eurail Global Pass,** which allows you unlimited travel over a select period of time (from 15 days to 3 months) in 21 Eurail affiliated countries. Unless you'll be traveling through Europe extensively before arriving in France, however, it's not particularly cost-effective. Prices for first-class adult travel range from $687 for 15 days to $1,926 for 3 months. Children 4 to 11 pay half fare; those 3 and under travel for free. Additional global pass options include the **Eurail Global Pass Saver,** which offers a special deal for two or more people traveling together; and the **Eurail Global Youth Pass,** for travelers ages 12 to 25, which allows second-class travel for between $446 for 15 days and $1,255 for 3 months. A better bet for those limiting their travel to France and the surrounding territory is the **Eurail Select Pass,** which offers unlimited travel on the national rail networks of any three, four, or five bordering countries out of the 21 Eurail nations linked by train or ship. A sample fare: For 6 days in 2 months, you pay $481 for three countries. **Eurail Select Pass Youth** for travelers under 26 allows second-class travel within the same guidelines as Eurail Selectpass, with fees starting at $315. **Eurail Select Pass Saver** offers discounts for two or more people traveling together (first-class travel) within the same guidelines as Eurail Select Pass, with fees starting at $410 per person.

BUYING A PASS

In North America, contact **Rail Europe** (☎ 800/622-8600 in the U.S., ☎ 800/361-RAIL in Canada; www.raileurope.com). Rail Europe can also provide information on rail/drive versions of the passes. No matter what

everyone tells you, you can buy Eurail Passes in Europe as well as in America (at the major train stations), but they're more expensive. You can also buy these passes from travel agents or rail agents in major cities such as New York, Montreal, and Los Angeles. For details on the rail passes available in the United Kingdom, visit or call **NationalRail Inquiries,** Victoria Station, London SW1V 1JZ (☎ 08705/848-848), whose staff can help you find the best option for your trip. Some of the popular options are the Inter-Rail and Under 26 passes, entitling you to unlimited second-class travel in 26 European countries.

EUROSTAR

For those traveling from the U.K. to France, the **Eurostar** is a good option—especially if your first stop in France is Calais, Lille, or Paris. Trains run from London St. Pancras, Ashford, and Ebbsfleet in the U.K. to Paris, Disneyland Resort® Paris, Calais, and Lille. London to Lille takes under 2 hours, and from here you can bypass Paris to continue southeast to Lyon, the Rhone Valley, and Provence; westward to Brittany, Poitou Charentes, and the Loire; or southwest toward Languedoc-Roussillon, Bordeaux, and neighboring regions. Paris's Gare du Nord station is now under 2½ hours from London; from the French capital's six main train stations, you can reach thousands of destinations across the country. You can also pick up a **Thalys train** (www.thalys.com) from the Gare du Nord, serving Brussels in just 1 hour, as well as other northern European cities such as Amsterdam and Cologne. For more information on Eurostar and its routes throughout the continent, see www.eurostar.com or call ☎ 08432/186-186 (in the U.K.).

www.britishairways.com) fly frequently to Paris; the trip takes 1 hour. These airlines operate up to 17 flights daily from Heathrow. Many travelers also fly out of the London City Airport in the Docklands.

Direct flights to Paris operate from many other U.K. cities such as Manchester, Liverpool, Leeds-Bradford, Edinburgh, and Birmingham. Contact **Air France, British Airways,** or

British Midland (☎ 0870/607-0555 in the U.K.; www.flybmi.com). Also check the low-cost airlines **Ryan Air** (☎ 0871/246-0000; www.ryanair.com), **BMI Baby** (☎ 0905/828-2828; www.bmibaby.com), **Jet2** (☎ 0871/226-1737; www.jet2.com), **Flybe** (☎ 0871/700-2000; www.flybe.com), and **Easyjet** (☎ 08-99-65-00-11 in France, 0905/821-0905 in the U.K.; www.easyjet.com).

Daily papers often carry ads for cheap flights. Highly recommended **Trailfinders** (☎ 0845/058-5858; www.trailfinders.com) sells discount fares.

FROM IRELAND
Check **Aer Lingus** (☎ 0818/365000; www. aerlingus.com) and **Ryan Air** (see p. 697).

INSIDE FRANCE
Once you're inside the country, Air France assures internal flights, including those to Corsica. Corsica is also served by **Air Corsica** (www.aircorsica.com; ☎ 04-95-29-05-09), landing in Bastia, Calvi, and Ajaccio from such cities as Paris, Lyon, Marseille, and Nice.

By Train

The world's fastest trains link some 50 French cities, allowing you to get from Paris to just about anywhere else in the country within hours. With 39,000km (24,233 miles) of track and about 3,000 stations, **SNCF** (French National Railroads; www.voyages-sncf.com) is fabled for its on-time performance. You can travel in first or second class by day and in couchette by night. Most trains have dining facilities. Visit www.tgv-europe.com for information in English.

If you plan to travel a lot on European railroads, get the latest copy of the *Thomas Cook European Train Timetable.* This 500-plus-page book documents all of Europe's main passenger rail services with detail and accuracy. It's available for sale online at www.thomascookpublishing.com.

By Ferry from England

Ferries and hovercrafts operate day and night, with the exception of last-minute cancellations during storms. The major routes include at least 12 trips a day between Dover or Folkestone and Calais or Boulogne. Hovercrafts and hydrofoils make the trip from Dover to Calais, the shortest distance across the Channel, in just 40 minutes during good weather. The ferries may take several hours, depending on the weather and tides. If you're bringing a car, it's important to make reservations—space below decks is usually crowded. Timetables can vary, depending on weather conditions and many other factors.

The leading operator of ferries across the channel is **P&O Ferries** (☎ 0871/664-5645 in the U.K.; www.poferries.com). It operates car and passenger ferries between Portsmouth, England, and Cherbourg, France (three departures a day; 4 hr. 15 min. each way during daylight hours; 7 hr. each way at night); and between Portsmouth and Le Havre, France (three departures a day; 5½ hr. each way). Most popular is the route between Dover, England, and Calais, France (25 sailings a day; 75 min. each way).

By Channel Tunnel (Chunnel) from England

The Chunnel accommodates not only trains but also cars, buses, taxis, and motorcycles. **Eurotunnel,** a train carrying vehicles under the Channel (☎ 0870/535-3535 in the U.K.; www.eurotunnel.com), connects Calais, France, with Folkestone, England. It operates 365 days a year, running every 15 minutes during peak travel times. Before boarding Eurotunnel, you pay or show your ticket at a tollbooth, then pass through Immigration for both countries at one time. You travel in air-conditioned carriages, remaining in your car or stepping outside to stretch your legs, and an hour later, you simply drive off.

Once in France, motorists who don't wish to drive long distances can travel by train with their car via a service called **Auto Train,** run by the SNCF. Visit http://autotrain.voyages-sncf. com for more information.

By Car

The major highways are A1 from the north (Great Britain and Benelux); A13 from Rouen, Normandy, and northwest France; A10 from Bordeaux, the Pyrenees, the Southwest, and Spain; A6 from Lyon, the French Alps, the Riviera, and Italy; and A4 from Metz, Nancy, and Strasbourg in the east. Paris is signposted along most major highways.

An excellent series of highways links France to continental Europe. Getting there by car from the U.K., however, requires you to take the ferry or Channel Tunnel.

Package Tours

One good source of package deals is the airlines themselves. Most major airlines offer air/hotel packages to France. Several big online travel agencies—Expedia, Travelocity, Orbitz, Site59, and Lastminute. com—also do a brisk business in packages.

RENTALS

To rent a car, you'll need to present a passport, a driver's license, and a credit card. You'll also have to meet the minimum-age requirement of the company (usually 21 or 25 years old). It usually isn't obligatory within France, but certain companies have at times asked for the presentation of an International Driver's License, even though this is becoming increasingly superfluous in Western Europe. For most, rental cars can be picked up in one French city and dropped off in another, but there are additional charges. Here is a list of car rental companies to try: **Budget** (www. budget.com), **Hertz** (www.hertz.com), **Avis** (www.avis.com), and Europcar (**National** in the U.S.; www.europcar.com).

Two United States–based agencies that don't have offices in France but act as booking agents for France-based agencies are **Kemwel Drive Group** (☎ 877/820-0668 or ☎ 207/842-2285; www.kemwel.com) and **Auto Europe** (☎ 888/223-5555; www.autoeurope. com). These can make bookings in the United States only, so call before your trip.

DRIVING RULES

Everyone in the car, in both the front and the back seats, must wear a seatbelt. Children under 12 must ride in the back seat. Drivers are supposed to yield to the car on their right, except where signs indicate otherwise, as at traffic circles. Speed limits are about 110kmph (70 mph) on expressways, and about 90kmph (55 mph) on major national highways and country roads. In towns, don't exceed 50 kmph (30 mph). If you violate the speed limit, expect a big fine.

BREAKDOWNS & ASSISTANCE

A breakdown is called *une panne* in France. Call the police at ☎ 17 anywhere in France to be put in touch with the nearest garage. If the breakdown occurs on an expressway, find the nearest roadside emergency phone box, pick up the phone, and put a call through. You'll be connected to the nearest breakdown service facility.

RECOMMENDED MAPS & ATLASES

For France as a whole, most motorists opt for Michelin map 989. For regions, Michelin publishes a series of yellow maps that are quite good. Big travel-book stores in North America carry these maps, but they're commonly available in France at lower prices. In this age of congested traffic, one useful feature of the Michelin map is its designations of alternative *routes de dégagement,* which let you skirt big cities and avoid traffic-clogged highways. They also highlight, in green, routes recommended for tourists. Another recommended option is *Frommer's Road Atlas Europe.* Handy websites to consult are www.viamichelin.fr and www.mappy.com.

PARKING

Good luck. Parking is often problematic in France, especially in big cities. You will find underground parking, often run by **Vinci** (www.vincipark.com), in most large settlements. You can expect to pay about 2€ or more an hour, and up to 25€ for overnight parking. Parking lots are usually well posted with a large white letter P on a blue background. Otherwise, look out for parking meters for street parking. When parking on the street, you have to display your ticket in your car window. It is advisable to have some loose change for parking meters, as not all take credit cards. Car break-ins are rare, but they do happen. Leave no valuables in your car, and, if possible, hide the radio. Use a supervised lot when your car is loaded with your luggage and other valuables.

Gasoline

Known in France as *essence,* gas is expensive for those accustomed to North American prices. Depending on your car, you'll need either leaded (*avec plomb*) or unleaded (*sans plomb*). **Note:** Sometimes you can drive for miles in rural France without encountering a gas station, so don't let your tank get dangerously low. Stations are easy to use. You usually fill the tank yourself, then either pay with a credit card in the machine or enter the shop to pay a cashier.

Accommodations

The French government rates hotels on a one-to-five-star system. One-star hotels are budget accommodations, two-star lodgings are quality tourist hotels, three stars go to first-class hotels, four stars are reserved for deluxe accommodations, and five-stars are for palace hotel service. In some of the lower categories, the rooms may not have private bathrooms; instead, many have what the French call a *cabinet de toilette* (hot and cold running water and maybe a bidet) in the room, while toilet and showering facilities are shared.

Overall, accommodations in France meet a good standard. More and more hoteliers are installing air conditioning, along with Internet services—either as Wi-Fi, in-room dial-up, or with a public computer for guest use in the lobby.

As elsewhere in Europe, standard rooms in France—especially in cities—tend to be rather small by American standards. Many hotels include breakfast in the room price. If they don't, remember that if you're in a city like Paris or Lyon, it may be cheaper to buy a croissant and a coffee in a nearby cafe. Also bear in mind that many hotels offer special Internet booking rates, which can offer considerable discounts.

In France it is advisable to book all your accommodations in advance. The country is one of the most visited places in the world, and hotels, B&Bs, *gîtes,* and apartments can fill up fast—especially during trade fairs or in peak holiday season.

Types of Lodging

France is known for its exceptionally charming, atmospheric accommodations. These range from historic, grand hotels set in former royal châteaux, to countryside family-run hotels (often with a restaurant attached), to old stone farmhouses that you can rent for the duration of your vacation (*gîtes),* to apartments you can rent in city centers. As a hot spot for fashion and good living, France has also seen the emergence of some seriously chic design hotels, especially in Paris, Bordeaux, and Avignon. And since environmental issues have come to a head, the country's hoteliers increasingly are offering innovative and quirky eco-lodgings that range from treehouses to Mongolian-style *yourtes* (tents); see p. 696 for ecotourism information.

Then, of course, there are France's famous *chambres d'hôtes*—B&Bs in privately owned inns or houses. They are often the best way to see the country: in direct contact with the people who live there. In addition to breakfast, many *chambres d'hôtes* offer *tables d'hôtes*—home-cooked evening meals.

International chains are omnipresent in France, especially in large cities. While the Four Seasons and some others offer atmospheric and distinctively luxurious surroundings, other middle-of-the-road chains rely on the predictability of their offerings, and you will usually find more character in locally owned and managed properties. One chain that manages to balance charm (sometimes lots of it) with midrange prices is **Best Western** (www.bestwestern.com), which has properties all over the country.

Gîtes & Apartment Rentals

For apartment, farmhouse, or cottage stays of 2 weeks or more, **Idyll Untours** (☎ 888/868-6871 in the U.S.; www.untours.com) provides exceptional vacation rentals for a reasonable price, which includes air/ground transportation, cooking facilities, and on-call support from a local resident. Best of all: Untours donates most profits to provide low-interest loans to underprivileged entrepreneurs around the world (see their website for details). **Gîtes de France** (www.gites-de-france.com) is an extremely reliable, French-based association for locating and booking farmhouses to rent in rural France. The U.K.-based **Alastair Sawdays** (www.sawdays.co.uk) also offers an excellent collection of the most charming *gîtes* and tourist apartments in France.

In the U.S., **At Home Abroad, Inc.**, 163 Third Ave., Box 319, New York, NY 10003 (☎ 212/421-9165; fax 212/228-4860; www.athomeabroadinc.com), specializes in villas on the French Riviera and in the Dordogne as well as places in the Provençal hill towns. Rentals are usually for 2 weeks. You'll receive photographs of the properties and a newsletter. **New York Habitat** (☎ 212/255-8018; fax

212/627-1416; www.nyhabitat.com) rents furnished apartments and vacation accommodations in Paris and the south of France. Bookings should be done at least 3 months in advance (even further out for the south of France) and can be arranged online or over the phone. Prices in Paris range from 300€ to 6,000€ per week, depending on the size of the apartment; in the south of France, 55€ to 1,350€ per night.

If you want to rent an apartment in Paris, the **Barclay International Group,** 6800 Jericho Turnpike, Syosset, NY 11791 (☎ 800/845-6636 or 516/364-0064; fax 516/364-4468; www.barclayweb.com), can give you access to about 3,000 apartments and villas throughout Paris (and 39 other cities in France), ranging from modest modern units to the most stylish lodgings. Units rent for 1 night to 6 months; all have TVs and kitchenettes, and many have concierge staffs and lobby-level security. The least expensive cost around $170 per night, double occupancy. Discounts are given for a stay of 1 week or longer. Rentals must be prepaid in U.S. dollars or with a U.S. credit or charge card.

Hometours International, Inc., 1108 Scottie Lane, Knoxville, TN 37919 (☎ 865/690-8484; hometours@aol.com), offers more than 400 moderately priced apartments, apartment hotels, and villas in Paris. On the Riviera, you can rent villas, with pools, at reasonable rates.

Drawbridge to Europe, Inc., 98 Granite St., Ashland, OR 97520 (☎ 888/268-1148; www.drawbridgetoeurope.com), offers everything from Paris apartments to villas scattered throughout France, including Provence. Rentals are selected for their location, interiors, and (at times) historical character.

The aptly named **Home Away,** 45 St. Clair Ave. W., Ste. 1100, Toronto, Ontario, Canada M4V 1K9 (☎ 800/374-6637; http://homeaway.com), provides private vacation villas throughout France, including apartments in Paris. Rentals lie in the most tourist-rich provinces of France, including Burgundy, the French Riviera, Provence, and the Dordogne.

Interhome, Inc., 2860 State Rd. 84, Ste. 116 PMB 241, Fort Lauderdale, FL 33312 (☎ 800/882-6864; www.interhomeusa.com), offers some 30,000 rental properties in 21 countries, including France. Take your choice:

apartment or villa. The agency is especially noted for its villas in Provence and on the Riviera.

Other agencies include **Villanet** (☎ 800/964-1891 or 206/417-3444 in the U.S.; www.rentavilla.com), which in France specializes in rentals in Provence and the Riviera. **Villas & Apartments Abroad** operates out of 183 Madison Ave., Ste. 201, New York, NY 10016 (☎ 800/433-3020 or 212/213-6436; www.vaanyc.com), and has been satisfying villa seekers for more than 30 years. It seems to have a very personalized service that hooks up customers with the right rental.

Absolu Living, 236 rue Saint Martin, 75003 Paris (☎ 01-44-54-97-17; www.absoluliving.com), is the leader in furnished apartment rentals serving the gay community. Long- or short-term apartment rentals are arranged throughout France. By renting an apartment instead of a hotel, costing from 72€ per night for two persons, you gain more space and freedom—at a lower price.

Châteaux

Now known worldwide, **Relais & Châteaux** (www.relaischateaux.com)—an organization of deluxe and first-class hostelries—began in France for visitors seeking the ultimate in hotel living and dining in a traditional atmosphere. Relais & Châteaux establishments (there are about 150 in France) are former castles, abbeys, manor houses, and town houses converted into hostelries or inns and elegant hotels. All have a limited number of rooms, so reservations are imperative. Sometimes these owner-run establishments have pools and tennis courts. The Relais part of the organization refers to inns called *relais,* meaning "post house." These tend to be less luxurious than the châteaux, but are often charming. Top-quality restaurants are *relais gourmands*.

For the ultimate in luxury, **Grand Etapes Françaises** (☎ 01-40-02-99-99; www.grandesetapes.fr), can book you into 10 châteaux or luxury hotels throughout the country. Each hotel or château is unique, and most of them lie only a 1-hour drive from Paris. For example, Le Château d'Esclimont in the Ile de France between Versailles and Chartres (see p. 139), outside the village of St-Symphorien le Château, is like a fairy-tale castle.

Bed & Breakfasts (*Chambres d'Hôtes*)

These may be one or several bedrooms on a farm or in a village or city home. Many offer one main meal a day (lunch or dinner). For B&Bs in Paris, three excellent, reliable sites are **Hôtes Qualité Paris** (www.hqp.fr), **Alcove & Agapes** (www.bed-and-breakfast-in-paris.com), and **Good Morning Paris** (www.goodmorningparis.fr). **Les Gîtes de France** also lists B&Bs (59 rue St-Lazare, Paris 75439; ☎ 01-49-70-75-75; www.gites-de-france.fr); and sometimes they're not as simple as you may think: Instead of a bare-bones farm, you may be in a mansion in the countryside. Other useful websites to check out are **www.chambres-hotes-france.org,** which lists more than 6,000 B&Bs across the country, and **www.chambres-en-france.com.**

Hotel Chains

One good, moderately priced choice is the **Mercure** chain, an organization of simple, modern hotels throughout France. Even at the peak of the tourist season, a room at a Mercure hotel in Paris rents for as little as 99€ per night (a true rarity). For more information on Mercure hotels and the chain's 100-page directory, call ☎ 800/221-4542 (in the U.S.) or visit www.mercure.com.

Formule 1 (www.hotelformule1.com) hotels are basic but safe, offering rooms for up to three people for around 40€ per night. Built from prefabricated units, these air-conditioned, soundproof hotels are shipped to a site and assembled, often on the outskirts of cities such as Paris (there are 27 in the suburbs). There are 150 of these throughout the rest of France. Like Mercure, Formule 1 is owned by the French hotel giant Accor, parent of Motel 6, which Formule 1 resembles. Formule 1's low cost makes it unprofitable for the chain to allow customers to reserve rooms from the United States, so you'll have to reserve upon arrival. For a directory, write to Formule 1/ETAP Hotels, c/o Sishe Hotel, 6–8 rue du Bois-Briard, Evry Cedex 91021 France (☎ 08-92-68-56-85; www.hotelformule1.com).

Other worthwhile economy bets, sometimes with a bit more charm, are the hotels and restaurants of the **Fédération Nationale des Logis de France,** 83 av. d'Italie, Paris 75013 (☎ 01-45-84-83-84; www.logis-de-france.fr). This is an association of 3,000 hotels, usually country inns convenient for motorists, most with one- or two-star ratings. The association publishes an annual directory.

House Swapping & Couch Surfing

For open-minded travelers, an excellent way to save money is to house swap: You stay in someone's flat or house, while they stay in yours. Several websites, including www.homeexchange.com, organize swaps. Alternatively, **Couch Surfing** (www.couchsurfing.org) is an ever-growing worldwide network whereby you get to stay on someone's couch or in a spare room for free, and in return you let travelers stay free of charge in your home.

Youth Hostels

You will generally find at least one youth hostel in French cities (several in Paris). A reliable source is **Hostelling International,** which lists hostels across the world, including France (☎ 01707/324-170 in the U.K.; www.hihostels.com).

Dining

Mealtimes are an important time of day for the French. Most cafes offer breakfast—usually a croissant or a *tartine* (baguette sliced in half with butter and jam), coffee, and orange juice. Lunchtime ranges from a sandwich on the go (normally bought in a *boulangerie*), to a *croque-monsieur* (cheese and ham toasty) and salad in a cafe or a full-fledged 3-course meal with wine in a restaurant. If you fancy a quiet bite at lunchtime, opt for a cafe. Evening meals are traditionally the most important moments of the day—a time to wind down, relax, and chatter over gourmet delights that range from hearty regional fare to intricate *gastronomique* dishes. For that iconic "waiters in bow ties and black jackets" experience, look for a *brasserie*—particularly in Paris. Typical fare ranges from unbeatable *steak-frites* (steak and fries) and French onion soup, to creamy veal *blaquette* and desserts such as rum baba and *île flottante* (egg whites whipped with sugar served in a vanilla sauce).

France's cuisine is also influenced by its immigrants. You're bound to come across appetizing Moroccan restaurants serving hot tagines, as well as Thai, Indian, and Chinese restaurants.

For an all-out wine experience, opt for a *bar à vins,* where French wines are served by the glass or bottle. Here you can usually order plates of finger food like dry *saucisson* (sausage) and *fromage* (cheese). Relaxed and full of ambience and good wine, these are great spots for educating your palate and recharging your batteries.

Generally speaking, in touristy cities, avoid restaurants advertising menus in English, as these are often tourist traps with mediocre fare.

Many restaurants offer *prix fixe* (fixed price) lunch and dinner menus. Lunch menus are always cheaper than evening menus, so you'll nearly always get more for your money at lunchtime; bear this in mind if you are looking to splurge in an expensive restaurant. Tips are usually already included in the bill, so only tip for good service, in which case 1€ or 2€ is adequate. **Note:** Many restaurants in France close for business on Sunday and Monday. If you have your heart set on a particular restaurant, call in advance, and whenever possible make a reservation.

Vegetarians have traditionally had trouble eating in France, although progress has been made; if you explain either when you reserve a table or when you arrive, the chef will usually be happy to concoct a dish, and in big cities quality vegetarian and even vegan restaurants are increasingly common. As a rule of thumb, pizzerias, *crêperies,* and Indian restaurants often offer meatless and fish-free dishes.

France Fast Facts

ATMs/Cashpoints

Most French settlements have at least one ATM that accepts Visa or MasterCard (American Express is not systematically accepted), so withdrawing cash is usually very easy. The machines usually detect foreign cards, too, offering a choice of languages so that you can follow the instructions. All work in the usual way, with PIN numbers.

Business Hours

Hours in France are erratic. Most banks are open Monday to Friday from 9:30am to 4:30pm, and Saturdays from 9am to noon. Many, particularly in smaller towns or villages, take a lunch break (at varying times). Hours are usually posted on the door. Most museums close 1 day a week (often Tues), and they're also generally closed on national holidays. Usual hours are from 9:30am to 5pm. Some museums, particularly the smaller ones, close for lunch from noon to 2pm. Again, refer to the individual museum listings. Generally, shops are open Monday to Friday from 9am to 5pm, with a break for lunch. In larger cities, stores are open from 9am or 9:30am (or often 10am) to 6pm or 7pm, without a break for lunch. In some small stores, the lunch break can last 2 hours, beginning at 1pm. Thursdays usually mean longer hours (until 8pm) in large cities.

Customs

Customs restrictions for visitors entering France differ for citizens of the European Union and for citizens of non-E.U. countries.

FOR U.S. CITIZENS For specifics on what you can bring back from your trip to France, download the invaluable free pamphlet *Know Before You Go* online at www.cbp.gov, or contact U.S. Customs Border Protection (CBP), 1300 Pennsylvania Ave. NW, Washington, DC 20229 (☎ 877/CBP-5511, or 703/526-4200 from abroad).

FOR CANADIAN CITIZENS For a clear summary of Canadian rules, call for the booklet *I Declare,* issued by the Canada Customs and Revenue Agency (☎ 800/461-9999 in Canada, or 204/983-3500 from outside Canada; www.cbsa-asfc.gc.ca).

FOR U.K. CITIZENS For information, contact **HM Revenue & Customs** at ☎ 0845/010-9000, or +44/(0)2920/501-261 from outside the U.K., or consult the website www.hmrc.gov.uk.

FOR AUSTRALIAN CITIZENS A helpful brochure available from Australian consulates or Customs offices is *Know Before You Go.* For more information, call the **Australian Customs Service** at ☎ 1300/363-263 (+61-2/6275-6666 from outside Australia) or log on to www.customs.gov.au.

FOR NEW ZEALAND CITIZENS Request the free pamphlet *New Zealand Customs Guide for*

Travelers, Notice no. 4, from New Zealand Customs Service, The Customhouse, 17–21 Whitmore St., Box 2218, Wellington (☎ 0800/428-786; or +64-9/300-5399 from overseas: www.customs.govt.nz).

Electricity

Like most of continental Europe, France uses the 220-volt system (two-round prongs), so in general, expect 220 volts, 50 cycles—and bring an adapter.

Embassies & Consulates

All embassies are in Paris. EMBASSY AND CONSULATE OF THE UNITED STATES 2 av. Gabriel; ☎ 01-43-12-22-22; Métro: Concorde. EMBASSY OF CANADA 35 av. Montaigne; ☎ 01-44-43-29-00; Métro: Franklin D. Roosevelt. EMBASSY OF THE UNITED KINGDOM 35 rue du Faubourg St-Honoré; ☎ 01-44-51-31-00; Métro: Concorde; open Monday through Friday from 9:30am to 1pm and 2:30 to 5pm. CONSULATE OF THE UNITED KINGDOM 18 bis rue d'Anjou; ☎ 01-44-51-31-02; Métro: Concorde; open Monday through Friday from 9am to noon and 2 to 5pm.

The United States also maintains a consular "Presence Post" in several French cities: BORDEAUX 89 quai des Chartrons 33300 (☎ 05-56-48-63-85). LYON 1 quai Jules Courmont 69002 Lyon (☎ 04-78-38-36-88 or 04-78-38-33-03 consular information and appointments). MARSEILLE place Varian Fry, 13286 (☎ 04-91-54-92-00). NICE ☎ 04-93-88-89-55. RENNES 30 quai Duguay-Trouin 35000 (☎ 02-23-44-09-60). STRASBOURG 15 av. d'Alsace 67000 (☎ 03-88-35-31-04). TOULOUSE 25 allées Jean Jaurès 31000 (☎ 05-34-41-36-50).

Emergencies

While at a hotel, contact the front desk to summon an ambulance or to do whatever is necessary (or call the ambulance directly and inform the staff); however, for something like a stolen wallet, go to the police station in person. Elsewhere, you can get help anywhere in France by calling ☎ 17 for the police; ☎ 18 for the fire department *(pompiers),* whose members double as paramedics (and sometimes reply faster than an ambulance); and ☎ 15 for an ambulance. The all-encompassing European emergency call number is ☎ 112.

Etiquette & Customs

Shoulders should be covered when entering most churches. It is polite to say *"bonjour"* (hello), *"merci"* (thank you), and *"au revoir"* (good-bye) when you enter or leave a shop or restaurant. Even if you don't speak French, memorize these three expressions; using them is looked upon favorably and can help in many ways.

Event Listings

To keep abreast of France's temporary art exhibitions and events check out the **What's On When** website (www.whatsonwhen.com), which lists the main events for the whole of France month by month. Government tourist offices and local tourist offices are also excellent sources for information on local events.

Family Travel

Most French hoteliers let children 12 and under stay in a room with their parents for free (it's best to negotiate when booking), and nearly all will provide cots. A good resource for traveling with young children is the U.K.-based **Tots to Travel** website (www.totstotravel.co.uk), which lists family-friendly accommodations and destinations across France. Many restaurants offer children's menus or will at the very least offer a kid-size portion. For European Union kids 17 and under, admission is free to most state-run museums (sometimes for ages 25 and under, too).

Gay & Lesbian Travel

France is one of the world's most tolerant countries toward gays and lesbians. "Gay Paree" boasts a large gay population, with many clubs, restaurants, organizations, and services. Lesbian or bisexual women can also pick up a copy of *Lesbia.* This publication and others are available at Paris's largest, best-stocked gay bookstore, **Les Mots à la Bouche,** 6 rue Ste-Croix-de-la-Bretonnerie, 4e (☎ 01-42-78-88-30; www.motsbouche.com; Métro: Hôtel-de-Ville), which carries publications in both French and English.

Health

In general, France is a safe destination. You don't need shots, food is safe, and the water is potable. It is easy to get a prescription filled, and hospitals in nearly all destinations have English-speaking doctors and well-trained staffs.

Contact the **International Association for Medical Assistance to Travelers** (IAMAT; ☎ 716/754-4883 in the U.S., or 416/652-0137 in Canada; www.iamat.org) for tips on travel and health concerns in the countries you're visiting, and for lists of local English-speaking doctors. The **United States Centers for Disease Control and Prevention** (☎ 800/311-3435 or 888/232-6348 in the U.S.; www.cdc.gov) provides up-to-date information on health hazards by region or country and offers tips on food safety. **Travel Health Online** (www.tripprep.com), sponsored by a consortium of travel medicine practitioners, may also offer helpful advice on traveling abroad. You can find listings of reliable medical clinics overseas at the **International Society of Travel Medicine** (www.istm.org).

The following government websites offer up-to-date, health-related travel advice:

- Australia: www.smartraveller.gov.au
- Canada: www.hc-sc.gc.ca
- U.K.: www.nathnac.org
- U.S.: www.cdc.gov/travel

Holidays

Many offices and shops and some museums in France are closed on the following national holidays:

- January 1, New Year's Day
- Easter Sunday and Monday
- May 1, Labor Day
- May 8, Victory Day
- June 2, Ascension Day
- June 12, Pentecost
- July 14, Bastille Day
- August 15, Assumption of the Virgin
- November 1, All Saints' Day
- November 11, Armistice Day
- December 25, Christmas

Insurance

In addition to specific insurers mentioned below, you might want to browse the insurance products of these U.S.-based companies: **Travel Insured International** (☎ 800/243-3174; www. travelinsured.com) and **Travelex**

Insurance Services (☎ 800/228-9792, or 603/328-1965 outside the U.S. or Canada; www.travelex-insurance.com). In the U.K., contact **Endsleigh** (☎ 0800/028-3517; www.endsleigh.co.uk); in Australia, contact the **Australian Federation of Travel Agents** (AFTA) (☎ 1300/363-416; www.afta.com.au).

The cost of travel insurance varies widely, depending on the destination, the cost and length of your trip, your age and health, and the type of trip you're taking. Insist on seeing any policy and reading the fine print before buying. In the U.S., you can get estimates from various providers through **InsureMyTrip.com.** Enter your trip cost and dates, your age, and other information, for prices from more than a dozen companies, or call 800/487-4722. In the U.K., try **Columbus Direct** (☎ 0870/033-9988; www.columbusdirect.net).

What to Do If You Get Sick Away from Home

U.S. CITIZENS

For travel abroad, you may have to pay all medical costs upfront and be reimbursed later. Medicare and Medicaid do not provide coverage for medical costs outside the U.S. Before leaving home, find out what medical services your health insurance covers. To protect yourself, consider buying travel medical insurance.

U.K. CITIZENS

U.K. nationals will need a European Health Insurance Card (EHIC; ☎ 0845/605-0707 in the U.K.; www.ehic.org.uk) to receive free or reduced-cost health benefits during a visit to a European Economic Area (EEA) country (European Union countries plus Iceland, Liechtenstein, and Norway) or Switzerland.

For emergency numbers, see p. 704. If you suffer from a chronic illness, consult your doctor before your departure. Pack prescription medications in your carry-on luggage, and carry them in their original containers, with pharmacy labels—otherwise they won't make it through airport security. Carry with you the generic name of prescription medicines, in case a local pharmacist is unfamiliar with the brand name.

Trip cancellation insurance will help retrieve your money if you have to back out of a trip or depart early, or if your travel supplier goes bankrupt. Trip cancellation traditionally covers such events as sickness and natural disasters. The latest news in trip cancellation insurance is the availability of "any reason" cancellation coverage—which costs more but covers cancellations made for any reason. You won't get back 100% of your prepaid trip cost, but you'll be refunded a substantial portion. **TravelSafe** (☎ 888/885-7233 in the U.S.; www.travelsafe. com) offers both types of coverage. **Expedia** also offers any-reason cancellation coverage for its air-hotel packages.

If your credit card or other insurance doesn't cover lost luggage, consider purchasing baggage insurance as part of your comprehensive travel-insurance package. If your luggage is lost, immediately file a lost-luggage claim at the airport, detailing the luggage contents. Most airlines require that you report delayed, damaged, or lost baggage within 4 hours of arrival. The airlines are required to deliver luggage, once found, directly to your house or destination free of charge.

For travel overseas, most U.S. health plans (including Medicare and Medicaid) do not provide coverage, and the ones that do often reimburse you only after you return home. As a safety net, you may want to buy travel medical insurance. If you require additional medical insurance, try **MEDEX Assistance** (☎ 410/453-6300; www.medexassist.com) or **Travel Assistance International** (☎ 800/821- 2828; www. travelassistance.com); for general information on services, call the company's **Worldwide Assistance Services, Inc.** (☎ 800/777-8710).

U.K. nationals will need a European Health Insurance Card (EHIC) to receive free or reduced-cost health benefits during a visit to France. The European Health Insurance Card replaces the E111 form, which is no longer valid. For advice, ask at your local post office or see www.dh.gov.uk/travellers.

Internet Access

Wi-Fi has become a common amenity in most hotels throughout France, especially in business-oriented hotels. Many hotels that do not have Wi-Fi or other in-room Internet connections provide access through a public computer.

Internet cafes are not as common in France as they might be, although most towns have at least one. Don't be surprised, however, if you have to share the room with online game players. Fees are usually around 5€/hour. For a partial list of cybercafes in France, check www.cybercafe.com. Many French cities now have public Wi-Fi, however, and numerous cafes offer free Wi-Fi while you drink a coffee.

Legal Aid

The French government advises foreigners to consult their embassy or consulate (see p. 704) in case of an arrest or similar problem. The staff can generally offer advice on how you can obtain help locally and can furnish you with a list of local attorneys. If you are arrested for illegal possession of drugs, your country's embassy and consular officials may not be able to interfere with the French judicial system. A consulate can advise you only of your rights.

Lost & Found

Make a photocopy of the first few pages of your passport and write down your credit card numbers (and the serial numbers of your traveler's checks, if you're using them). Leave this information with someone at home—to be faxed to you in an emergency—and swap it with your traveling companion. This can speed the process of replacing your personal documents if they're lost or stolen. Be sure to tell all your credit card companies the minute you discover that your wallet has been lost or stolen, and file a report at the nearest police station. Your credit card company or insurer may require a police report number or record of the loss.

Use the following numbers in France to report your lost or stolen credit card: **American Express** (☎ 336/393-1111 collect; www. americanexpress.com); **MasterCard** (☎ 08-00-90-13-87; www.mastercard.com); **Visa** (☎ 08-00-90-11-79; www.visaeurope.com). Your credit card company may be able to wire you a cash advance immediately or deliver an emergency card in a day or two.

Mail & Postage

Larger packages should be sent from the national post office, *La Poste*. You can also buy postcard stamps at *tabacs* (tobacco stores) in all towns.

Money

France's currency is the euro, whose banknotes come in denominations of 5€, 10€, 20€, 100€, 200€, and 500€, and in coins of .02€, .05€, .10€, .20€, .50€, 1€, and 2€. For the most up-to-date currency conversion information, go to www.xe.com.

The best way to get cash in France is at ATMs or Cashpoints (see "ATMs/Cashpoints," above). While credit cards are accepted at almost all shops, restaurants, and hotels, some places won't take them (and banks often levy a 2 to 3% conversion fee above the 1% the credit card company takes in order to convert purchases made in a foreign currency). Always have some cash on hand for incidentals and sightseeing admissions. Avoid exchanging money at commercial exchange bureaus and hotels, which often have the highest transaction fees. Also, be sure you have a valid PIN number for your bank card or credit card (five- and six-digit numbers won't work in France).

Passports

Allow plenty of time before your trip in order to apply for a passport; processing normally takes 3 weeks but can take much longer during busy periods (especially spring). Keep in mind that if you need a passport in a hurry, you'll pay a higher processing fee.

FOR RESIDENTS OF AUSTRALIA Contact the **Australian Passport Information Service** at 131-232, or visit the government website at www.passports.gov.au.

FOR RESIDENTS OF CANADA Contact the central **Passport Office,** Department of Foreign Affairs and International Trade, Ottawa, ON K1A 0G3 (☎ 800/567-6868; www.ppt.gc.ca).

FOR RESIDENTS OF IRELAND Contact the **Passport Office,** Setanta Centre, Molesworth Street, Dublin 2 (☎ 01/671-1633; www.irlgov.ie/iveagh).

FOR RESIDENTS OF NEW ZEALAND Contact the **Passports Office** (☎ 0800/225-050 in New Zealand; www.passports.govt.nz).

FOR RESIDENTS OF THE UNITED KINGDOM Visit your nearest passport office, major post office, or travel agency, or contact the **United Kingdom Passport Service** (☎ 0870/521-0410; www.ukpa.gov.uk).

FOR RESIDENTS OF THE UNITED STATES To find your regional passport office, either check the U.S. State Department website or call the **National Passport Information Center** toll-free number (☎ 877/487-2778) for automated information. Note that to obtain a passport for a child in the U.S., the child must be present, in person, with both parents at the place of issuance; or a notarized statement from the parents is required.

Pharmacies

In France this is called *la pharmacie*. Pharmacies take turns staying open at night and on Sunday; the local Commissariat de Police should be able tell you the location of the nearest one. Or, if a pharmacy is closed, look for a sign on the window indicating where the nearest open drugstore can be found. Bear in mind that French pharmacies give advice on medication for a range of discomforts, so if your health problem is not an emergency, try the pharmacy before dipping into your health insurance with a doctor's appointment.

Safety

The most common menace, especially in large cities—particularly Paris and Marseille—is the plague of pickpockets and petty criminals. Never leave valuables in a car, and never travel with your car unlocked. Much of the country, particularly central France, the Northeast, Normandy, and Brittany, remains relatively safe, although no place in the world is crime-free. Wherever possible, check your baggage into a hotel and then go sightseeing, instead of leaving it unguarded in the trunk of a car, which is easy to break into.

Senior Travelers

Many discounts are available to seniors—men and women of the *trosième age* (third age) as the French call their seniors. **Air France** offers seniors a 10% reduction on its regular nonexcursion fares within France. Some restrictions apply. Discounts of around 10% are offered to passengers ages 62 and older on select Air France international flights. Be sure to ask for the discount when booking. Members of **AARP**, 601 E St. NW, Washington, DC 20049 (☎ 888/687-2277; www.aarp.org), get discounts on hotels, airfares, and car rentals. AARP offers members a wide range of benefits, including *AARP The Magazine* and a monthly newsletter. Anyone over 50 can join. Many reliable agencies and organizations target the 50-plus market. **Elderhostel** (☎ 800/454-5768 in the U.S.; www.elderhostel.org) arranges worldwide study programs for travelers ages 55 and over.

Recommended publications offering travel resources and discounts for seniors include the quarterly magazine *Travel 50 & Beyond* (www.travel50andbeyond.com) and the best-selling paperback *Unbelievably Good Deals and Great Adventures That You Absolutely Can't Get Unless You're Over 50* (McGraw-Hill), by Joann Rattner Heilman. **Frommers.com** offers more information and resources on travel for seniors.

Generally speaking, seniors over age 60 are usually entitled to discounted admission to museums and other sights throughout France. Discounts may also extend to theater and transport.

Smoking

Smoking is banned in all public places indoors, so cafe terraces are still often awash in smoke.

Telephone Calls
To call France:

1. Dial the international access code: 011 from the U.S.; 00 from the U.K., Ireland, or New Zealand; or 0011 from Australia.

2. Dial the country code: 33.

3. Dial the city code, which is always two digits, beginning with a zero—but drop that first zero (it should be used only from within France).

4. Dial the eight-digit number.

To call an international number while you are in France:

1. Dial 00 and then the country code (1 for U.S. or Canada, 44 for the U.K., 353 for Ireland, 61 for Australia, 64 for New Zealand).

2. Dial the area code (dropping the first "0") and number. For example, if you wanted to call the British Embassy in Washington DC, you would dial ☎ 00-1-202-588-7800.

For **international directory assistance** (in English): Dial ☎ 118 700. For **operator assistance** in calling your home country, dial the toll-free number ☎ 08-00-99-00, plus

the digits of your country code (for example, ☎ 08-00-99-00-1 for the U.S. and Canada). **Toll-free numbers** begin with 08 and are followed by 00. But be careful: Numbers that begin with 08 followed by 36 carry a 0.35€/minute surcharge.

Time Zone

France is 6 hours ahead of Eastern Standard Time (EST) in the United States; it's 1 hour ahead of London and 9 hours behind Sydney. Daylight Saving Time goes into effect in France each year from the end of March through the end of October.

Tipping

Tipping is far less important in France than in other countries, particularly the U.S. The rule of thumb is this: Tip if you're happy with the service. In taxis this can mean rounding up the fare to the next whole euro. In hotels, you can tip the chambermaid or concierge. In restaurants, service is always included (although you might not see it marked on the bill), so tip only for extra-good service; 1 to 2 euros is a respectable amount for a meal, or .50€ in cafes.

Toilets

The French are renowned for dirty public toilets. Unfortunately, it's a stereotype that is too often true, although they are getting better. The Turkish loo (literally, a hole in the floor) is gradually disappearing even in highway rest stop toilets. The more chic the establishment, the better the toilet. Public toilets are designated as WC (water closet), or as *Femme* (women) and *Homme* (men), or just by the initials *F* and *H*. It's a good idea to carry some tissues (and wipes) in your pocket or purse—they often come in handy.

Travelers with Disabilities

Most disabilities shouldn't stop anyone from traveling. There are more options and resources out there than ever before. Facilities for travelers in France, and nearly all modern hotels, provide accessible rooms. Older hotels (unless they've been renovated) may not provide elevators, special toilet facilities, or wheelchair ramps. The TGVs (high-speed trains) are wheelchair accessible; older trains have compartments for wheelchair boarding. On the Paris Métro, passengers with disabilities are able to sit in wider seats. Guide dogs ride free. However, some stations don't have escalators or elevators.

Knowing which hotels, restaurants, and attractions are accessible can save you a lot of frustration. **Association des Paralysés de France,** 17 bd. Auguste-Blanqui, Paris 75013 (☎ 01-40-78-69-66; www.apf.asso.fr), provides documentation, moral support, and travel ideas for individuals who use wheelchairs. In addition to the Paris office, it maintains an office in each of the 90 *départements* (the "ministates" into which France is divided) and can help with hotels, transportation, sightseeing, house rentals, and (in some cases) companionship for paralyzed or partially paralyzed travelers. It's not, however, a travel agency.

Organizations that offer a vast range of resources and assistance to travelers with disabilities include **MossRehab** (☎ 800/CALL-MOSS 225-5667; www.mossresourcenet. org), the **American Foundation for the Blind** (AFB; ☎ 800/232-5463; www.afb.org), and **Society for Accessible Travel & Hospitality** (SATH; ☎ 212/447-7284; www.sath.org). **AirAmbulanceCard.com** (☎ 877/424-7633) is now partnered with SATH and allows you to preselect top-notch hospitals in case of an emergency.

Access-Able Travel Source (www.access-able.com) offers a comprehensive database on travel agents from around the world with experience in accessible travel; destination-specific access information; and links to such resources as service animals, equipment rentals, and access guides. Many travel agencies offer customized tours and itineraries for travelers with disabilities, among them **Flying Wheels Travel** (☎ 507/451-5005; www.flyingwheelstravel.com) and **Accessible Journeys** (☎ 800/846-4537 or 610/521-0339; www.disabilitytravel.com).

Flying with Disability (www.flying-with-disability.org) is a comprehensive information source on airplane travel. The "Accessible Travel" link at Mobility-Advisor.com (www.mobility-advisor.com) offers a variety of travel resources to persons with disabilities. Also check out the quarterly magazine ***Emerging Horizons*** (www.emerginghorizons.com), available by subscription.

British travelers should contact **Tourism for All** (☎ 0845-124-9971 in the U.K. only; www.tourismforall.org.uk) to access a wide range of travel information and resources for elderly people and those with disabilities.

For organizations that offer resources to travelers with disabilities, go to Frommers.com.

Useful Phrases & Menu Terms

Basics

ENGLISH	FRENCH	PRONUNCIATION
yes/no	oui/non	wee/nohn
okay	d'accord	dah-core
please	s'il vous plaît	seel voo play
thank you	merci	mair-see
you're welcome	de rien	duh ree-ehn
hello (during daylight hours)	bonjour	bohn-jhoor
good evening	bonsoir	bohn-swahr
goodbye	au revoir	o ruh-vwahr
What's your name?	Comment vous appellez-vous?	ko-mahn voo za-pell-ay-voo?
My name is . . .	Je m'appelle . . .	jhe ma-pell . . .
Happy to meet you	Enchanté(e)	ohn-shahn-tay
Miss	Mademoiselle	mad-mwa-zel
Mr.	Monsieur	muh-syuh
Mrs.	Madame	ma-dam
How are you?	Comment allez-vous?	kuh-mahn tahl-ay-voo?
Fine, thank you, and you?	Très bien, merci, et vous?	tray bee-ehn, mair-see, ay voo?
Very well, thank you	Très bien, merci	tray bee-ehn, mair-see
So-so	Comme ci, comme ça	kum-see, kum-sah
I'm sorry/Excuse me	Pardon	pahr-dohn
I'm so very sorry	Désolé(e)	day-zoh-lay
That's all right	Il n'y a pas de quoi	eel nee ah pah duh kwah

Getting Around/Street Smarts

ENGLISH	FRENCH	PRONUNCIATION
Do you speak English?	Parlez-vous anglais?	par-lay-voo ahn-glay?
I don't speak French	Je ne parle pas français	jhuh ne parl pah frahn-say
I don't understand	Je ne comprends pas	jhuh ne kohm-prahn pas
Could you speak more loudly/more slowly?	Pouvez-vous parler un peu plus plus fort/plus lentement?	poo-vay-voo par-lay un puh ploo for/ploo lan-te-ment?
Could you repeat that?	Répetez, s'il vous plaît?	ray-pay-tay, seel voo play
What is it?	Qu'est-ce que c'est?	kess kuh say?
What time is it?	Qu'elle heure est-il?	kel uhr eh-teel?
What?	Quoi?	kwah?
How?/What did you say?	Comment?	ko-mahn?
When?	Quand?	kahn?
Where is . . . ?	Où est . . . ?	ooh eh . . . ?
Who?	Qui?	kee?
Why?	Pourquoi?	poor-kwah?
here/there	ici/là	ee-see/lah

left/right	à gauche/à droite	a goash/a drwaht
straight ahead	tout droit	too drwah
I'm American/Canadian/British	Je suis américain(e)/canadien(e)/anglais(e)	jhe sweez a-may-ree-*kehn*/can-ah-dee-*en*/ahn-glay (*glaise*)
Fill the tank of a car], please	Le plein, s'il vous plaît	luh plan, seel voo *play*
I'm going to . . .	Je vais à . . .	jhe vay ah . . .
I want to get off at . . .	Je voudrais descendre à . . .	jhe voo-*dray* day-son-drah ah
I'm sick	Je suis malade	jhe swee mal-*ahd*
airport	l'aéroport	lair-o-*por*
bank	la banque	lah bahnk
bridge	le pont	luh pohn
bus station	la gare routière	lah gar roo-tee-*air*
bus stop	l'arrêt de bus	lah-*ray* duh boohss
by bicycle	en vélo/par bicyclette	ahn *vay*-low/par bee-see-*clet*
by car	en voiture	ahn vwa-*toor*
cashier	la caisse	lah *kess*
cathedral	la cathédral	lah ka-tay-*dral*
church	l'église	lay-*gleez*
dead end	une impasse	ewn am-*pass*
driver's license	le permis de conduire	luh per-mee duh con-*dweer*
elevator	l'ascenseur	lah-sahn-*seuhr*
stairs	l'escalier	les-kal-*yay*
entrance (to a building or a city)	une porte	ewn port
exit (from a building or a freeway)	une sortie	ewn sor-*tee*
fortified castle/palace	le château	luh sha-*tow*
garden	le jardin	luh jhar-dehn
gasoline	du pétrol/de l'essence	dew pay-*trol*/de lay-*sahns*
ground floor	rez-de-chausée	ray-de-show-*say*
highway to . . .	la route pour	lah root por
hospital	l'hôpital	low-pee-*tahl*
insurance	les assurances	lez ah-sur-*ahns*
luggage storage	la consigne	lah kohn-*seen*-yuh
museum	le musée	luh mew-*zay*
no entry	sens interdit	sehns ahn-ter-*dee*
no smoking	défense de fumer	day-*fahns* de fu-may
on foot	à pied	ah pee-*ay*
1-day pass	le ticket journalier	luh tee-*kay* jhoor-nall-ee-*ay*
one-way ticket	l'aller simple	lah-*lay* sam-pluh
police	la police	lah po-*lees*
rented car	la voiture de location	lah vwa-*toor* de low-ka-see-on
round-trip ticket	l'aller-retour	lah-*lay*-re-*toor*
second floor	le premier étage	luh prem-ee-*ehr* ay-*taj*

slow down	ralentir	rah-lahn-*teer*
store	le magasin	luh ma-ga-*zehn*
street	la rue	lah roo
suburb	banlieu/environs	bahn-*liew*/en-veer-*ohns*
subway	le Métro	luh *may*-tro
telephone	le téléphone	luh tay-lay-*phone*
ticket	un billet	uh *bee*-yay
ticket office	la vente de billets	lah vahnt duh bee-*yay*
toilets	les toilettes/les WC	lay twa-*lets*/les vay-*say*
tower	le tour	luh toor

Necessities

ENGLISH	FRENCH	PRONUNCIATION
I'd like . . .	Je voudrais . . .	jhe voo-*dray* . . .
a room	une chambre	ewn *shahm*-bruh
the key	la clé (la clef)	la *clay*
I'd like to buy . . .	Je voudrais acheter . . .	jhe voo-dray ahsh-*tay* . . .
aspirin	des aspirines/des aspros	deyz ahs-peer-*eens*/deyz ahs-*prohs*
cigarettes	des cigarettes	day see-ga-*ret*
condoms	des préservatifs	day pray-ser-va-*teefs*
a dictionary	un dictionnaire	uh deek-see-oh-*nare*
a dress	une robe	ewn robe
envelopes	des envelopes	deyz ahn-veh-*lope*
a gift (for someone)	un cadeau	uh kah-*doe*
a handbag	un sac	uh sahk
a hat	un chapeau	uh shah-*poh*
a magazine	une revue	ewn reh-*vu*
a map of the city	un plan de ville	uh plahn de *veel*
matches	des allumettes	deyz a-loo-*met*
a necktie	une cravate	ewn cra-*vaht*
a newspaper	un journal	uh zhoor-*nahl*
a phone card	une carte téléphonique	ewn cart tay-lay-fone-*eek*
a postcard	une carte postale	ewn carte pos-*tahl*
a road map	une carte routière	ewn cart roo-tee-*air*
a shirt	une chemise	ewn che-*meez*
shoes	des chaussures	day show-*suhr*
a skirt	une jupe	ewn jhoop
soap	du savon	dew sah-*vohn*
socks	des chaussettes	day show-*set*
a stamp	un timbre	uh *tam*-bruh
trousers	un pantalon	uh pan-tah-*lohn*
writing paper	du papier à lettres	dew pap-pee-*ay a let*-ruh

How much does it cost?	C'est combien? /	say comb-bee-*ehn*?/
	Ça coûte combien?	sah coot comb-bee-*ehn*?
That's expensive	C'est cher/chère	say share
That's inexpensive	C'est raisonnable/	say ray-son-*ahb*-bluh/
	C'est bon marché	say bohn mar-*shay*
Do you take credit cards?	Est-ce que vous acceptez	es-kuh voo zaksep-*tay* lay kart
	les cartes de credit?	duh creh-*dee*?

In Your Hotel

ENGLISH	FRENCH	PRONUNCIATION
Are taxes included?	Est-ce que les taxes	ess-keh lay taks son com-*preez*?
	sont comprises?	
balcony	un balcon	uh bahl-cohn
bathtub	une baignoire	ewn bayn-*nwar*
bedroom	une chambre	ewn *shawm*-bruh
for two occupants	pour deux personnes	poor duh pair-sunn
hot and cold water	l'eau chaude et froide	low showed ay fwad
Is breakfast included?	Petit déjeuner inclus?	puh-*tee* day-jheun-*ay* ehn-*klu*?
room	une chambre	ewn *shawm*-bruh
shower	une douche	ewn dooch
sink	un lavabo	uh la-va-*bow*
suite	une suite	ewn sweet
We're staying for . . . days with	On reste pour . . . jours avec	ohn rest poor . . . jhoor ah-*vek*
with air-conditioning	avec climatisation	ah-*vek* clee-mah-tee-zah-sion
without	sans	sahn
youth hostel	une auberge de jeunesse	oon oh-bayrge-duh-jhe-ness

In the Restaurant

ENGLISH	FRENCH	PRONUNCIATION
I would like . . .	Je voudrais	jhe voo-*dray*
to eat	manger	mahn-*jhay*
to order	commander	ko-mahn-*day*
Please give me . . .	Donnez-moi, s'il vous plaît . . .	doe-nay-*mwah,* seel voo play . . .
a bottle of . . .	une bouteille de . . .	ewn boo-*tay* duh . . .
a cup of . . .	une tasse de . . .	ewn tass duh . . .
a glass of . . .	un verre de . . .	uh vair duh . . .
a plate of . . .	une assiette de . . .	ewn ass-ee-*et* duh . . .
an ashtray	un cendrier	uh sahn-dree-*ay*
bread	du pain	dew pan
breakfast	le petit déjeuner	luh puh-*tee* day-zhuh-*nay*
butter	du beurre	dew burr
the check/bill	l'addition/la note	la-dee-see-*ohn*/la noat
Cheers! (To your health!)	A votre santé	*ah* vo-truh sahn-*tay*

Can I buy you . . .	Puis-je vous payer . . .	*pwee*-jhe voo pay-*ay*
a drink?	un verre?	uh *vaihr*?
cocktail	un apéritif	uh ah-pay-ree-*teef*
dinner	le dîner	luh dee-*nay*
fixed-price menu	un menu	uh may-new
fork	une fourchette	ewn four-*shet*
Is the tip/service included?	Est-ce que le service est compris?	ess-ke luh ser-vees eh com-*pree*?
knife	un couteau	uh koo-*toe*
napkin	une serviette	ewn sair-vee-*et*
pepper	du poivre	dew *pwah*-vruh
platter of the day	un plat du jour	uh plah dew jhoor
salt	du sel	dew sell
soup	une soupe/un potage	ewn soop/uh poh-*tahj*
spoon	une cuillère	ewn kwee-*air*
sugar	du sucre	dew *sook*-ruh
tea	un thé	uh tay
Waiter!/Waitress!	Monsieur!/Mademoiselle!	mun-*syuh*/mad-mwa-*zel*
wine list	une carte des vins	ewn cart day *van*
appetizer	une entrée	ewn en-*tray*
main course	un plat principal	uh plah pran-see-*pahl*
tip included	service compris	sehr-*vees* cohm-*pree*
drinks not included	boissons non comprises	bwa-*sons* no com-*preez*
cheese tray	le plâteau de fromage	luh plah-*tow* duh fro-*mahj*

Shopping

ENGLISH	FRENCH	PRONUNCIATION
antiques store	un magasin d'antiquités	uh maga-*zan* don-tee kee-*tay*
bakery	une boulangerie	ewn boo-lon-zhur-*ree*
bank	une banque	ewn bonk
bookstore	une librairie	ewn lee-brehr-*ree*
butcher	une boucherie	ewn boo-shehr-*ree*
cheese shop	une fromagerie	ewn fro-mazh-*ree*
dairy shop	une crémerie	ewn krem-*ree*
delicatessen	une charcuterie	ewn shar-koot-*ree*
department store	un grand magasin	uh grah maga-*zan*
drugstore	une pharmacie	ewn far-mah-*see*
fishmonger shop	une poissonerie	ewn pwas-son-*ree*
gift shop	un magasin de cadeaux	uh maga-*zan* duh ka-*doh*
greengrocer	un marchand de légumes	uh mar-*shon* duh lay-*goom*
hairdresser	un coiffeur	uh kwa-*fuhr*
market	un marché	uh mar-*shay*
pastry shop	une pâtisserie	ewn pa-tee-*sree*

supermarket	un supermarché	uh soo-pehr-mar-*shay*
tobacconist	un tabac	uh ta-*bah*
travel agency	une agence de voyages	ewn azh-ahns duh vwa-*yazh*

Colors, Shapes, Sizes, Attributes

ENGLISH	FRENCH	PRONUNCIATION
black	noir	nwahr
blue	bleu	bleuh
brown	marron/brun	mar-*rohn*/bruhn
green	vert	vaihr
orange	orange	o-*rahnj*
pink	rose	rose
purple	violet	vee-o-*lay*
red	rouge	rooj
white	blanc	blahnk
yellow	jaune	jhone
bad	mauvais(e)	moh-*veh/vaise*
big	grand(e)	gron/gronde
closed	fermé(e)	fer-*meh*
down	en bas	ahn *bah*
early	de bonne heure	duh bon *urr*
enough	assez	as-*say*
far	loin	lwan
free/unoccupied	libre	*lee*-bruh
free/without charge	gratuit(e)	grah-*twee*/grah-*tweet*
good	bon/bonne	bon/bun
hot	chaud(e)	show/shoad
near	près	preh
open (as in "museum")	ouvert(e)	oo-*ver*/oo-*vert*
small	petit(e)	puh-*tee*/puh-*teet*
up	en haut	ahn *oh*
well	bien	byehn

Numbers & Ordinals

ENGLISH	FRENCH	PRONUNCIATION
zero	zéro	zare-*oh*
one	un	uh
two	deux	duh
three	trois	twah
four	quatre	*kaht*-ruh
five	cinq	sank
six	six	seess
seven	sept	set

eight	huit	wheat
nine	neuf	nuf
ten	dix	deess
eleven	onze	ohnz
twelve	douze	dooz
thirteen	treize	trehz
fourteen	quatorze	kah-*torz*
fifteen	quinze	kanz
sixteen	seize	sez
seventeen	dix-sept	deez-*set*
eighteen	dix-huit	deez-*wheat*
nineteen	dix-neuf	deez-*nuf*
twenty	vingt	vehn
twenty-one	vingt-et-un	vehnt-ay-*uh*
twenty-two	vingt-deux	vehnt-*duh*
thirty	trente	trahnt
forty	quarante	ka-*rahnt*
fifty	cinquante	sang-*kahnt*
sixty	soixante	swa-*sahnt*
sixty-one	soixante-et-un	swa-*sahnt*-et-*uh*
seventy	soixante-dix	swa-sahnt-*deess*
seventy-one	soixante-et-onze	swa-sahnt-et-*ohnze*
eighty	quatre-vingts	kaht-ruh-*vehn*
eighty-one	quatre-vingt-un	kaht-ruh-vehn-*uh*
ninety	quatre-vingt-dix	kaht-ruh-venh-*deess*
one hundred	cent	sahn
one thousand	mille	meel
one hundred thousand	cent mille	sahn meel
first	premier	*preh*-mee-ay
second	deuxième	*duhz*-zee-em
third	troisième	*twa*-zee-em
tenth	dixième	*dees*-ee-em
twentieth	vingtième	*vehnt*-ee-em
thirtieth	trentième	*trahnt*-ee-em
one-hundredth	centième	*sant*-ee-em

The Calendar

ENGLISH	FRENCH	PRONUNCIATION
January	janvier	*jhan*-vee-ay
February	février	*feh*-vree-ay
March	mars	marce
April	avril	a-*vreel*
May	mai	meh
June	juin	jhwehn
July	juillet	*jhwee*-ay
August	août	oot
September	septembre	sep-*tahm*-bruh
October	octobre	ok-*toh*-bruh
November	novembre	no-*vahm*-bruh
December	décembre	day-*sahm*-bruh
Sunday	dimanche	dee-*mahnsh*
Monday	lundi	*luhn*-dee
Tuesday	mardi	*mahr*-dee
Wednesday	mercredi	*mair*-kruh-dee
Thursday	jeudi	*jheu*-dee
Friday	vendredi	*vawn*-druh-dee
Saturday	samedi	*sahm*-dee
yesterday	hier	ee-*air*
today	aujourd'hui	o-jhord-*dwee*
this morning/this afternoon	ce matin/cet après-midi	suh ma-*tan*/set ah-preh-mee-*dee*
tonight	ce soir	suh *swahr*
tomorrow	demain	de-*man*

Index

Photo Credits

Note: l= left; r= right; t= top; b= bottom; c= center